An incisive critique of Mormon claims from the perspective of historic Christian faith. This is a much-needed book that gives the Christian answer to Mormonism!

This book gives penetrating answers to key Mormon truth claims, but with fairness, accuracy, insight and sensitivity. It will engender many fruitful conversations between Latter-day Saints and evangelicals. Beckwith, Mosser, and Owen have wisely perceived a gaping hole in evangelical scholarship: the response to Mormon scholarly apologetics. This volume is much needed.

The New Mormon Challenge is a wake-up call that Mormon scholarship and apologetics are striving, with success, to reach new heights. The book is itself a new level of scholarly engagement with Mormonism on an array of crucial and unexplored issues. Neither the wake-up call nor the book can be ignored.

This intriguing book raises a host of questions that stimulate thought about the relationship between not only Mormons, but also similar new religious movements, and orthodox Christianity. It represents a new wave of evangelical reactions to groups like the Mormons who sit on the uneasy frontier between traditional Christianity and other religious traditions, and it deserves to be read by all who are concerned to defend and promote historic Christianity.

In terms of both content and tone, *The New Mormon Challenge* establishes a new and higher standard for dialogue between evangelical Christians and the LDS. Interacting respectfully with the best of Mormon scholarship, this book capably addresses central issues such as the nature of God, materialism, and the credibility of the Book of Mormon. It deserves a wide and careful reading.

ROBERT A. PYNE
PROFESSOR OF SYSTEMATIC THEOLOGY
DALLAS THEOLOGICAL SEMINARY

THE
NEWMORMON CHALLENGE

FRANCIS J. BECKWITH . CARL MOSSER . PAUL OWEN
general editors

THE
NEWMORMON
CHALLENGE

Responding to the Latest Defenses
of a Fast-Growing Movement

ZONDERVAN™

GRAND RAPIDS, MICHIGAN 49530

ZONDERVAN™

The New Mormon Challenge
Copyright © 2002 by Francis J. Beckwith, Carl Mosser, Paul Owen

Requests for information should be addressed to:
Zondervan, *Grand Rapids, Michigan 49530*

Library of Congress Cataloging-in-Publication Data

The new Mormon challenge : responding to the latest defenses of a fast-growing movement /
   Francis J. Beckwith, Carl Mosser, and Paul Owen, general editors.
       p. cm.
   Includes bibliographical references and index.
   ISBN 0-310-23194-9 (Hardcover)
   1. Church of Jesus Christ of Latter-day Saints—Apologetic works.   2. Church of Jesus
Christ of Latter-day Saints—Doctrines.   I. Beckwith, Francis.   II. Mosser, Carl, 1972–
III. Owen, Paul, 1970–
   BX8635.5.N49   2002
   289.3—dc21   2001006899
                                                                                                              CIP

This edition printed on acid-free paper.

All Scripture quotations, except in chapter 4 and unless otherwise indicated, are taken from the
Holy Bible: New International Version®. NIV®. Copyright © 1973, 1978, 1984 by International
Bible Society. Used by permission of Zondervan. All rights reserved. The translation of Scriptures
in chapter 4 is the author's own. Italics in Scripture quotations have been added for emphasis.

Interior design by Beth Shagene

Printed in the United States of America

02 03 04 05 06 07 08 /❖ DC/ 10 9 8 7 6 5 4 3 2

The defense of the faith should be of a scholarly kind. Mere denunciation does not constitute an argument; and before a man can refute successfully an argument of an opponent he must understand the argument that he is endeavoring to refute. Personalities, in such debate, should be kept in the background; and analysis of the motives of one's opponents has little place.

—J. GRESHAM MACHEN

One of the grand fundamental principles of "Mormonism" is to receive truth, let it come from whence it may.

—JOSEPH SMITH JR.

CONTENTS

Part I: Mormonism's Appeal, Growth, and Challenges

Part II: The Mormon Worldview

FOREWORD

The publication of this book is an important event both for Protestant evangelicals and for Mormons. Until very recently the exchanges between evangelicals and members of the Church of Jesus Christ of Latter-day Saints (LDS) have been of a very poor quality. At their worst, they amounted to little more than the trading of insults. At their best, the two groups talked past each other, with both sides regularly setting forth over-simplified and distorted accounts of what the other group believed. In contrast, the essays in this book provide a respectful and sustained exploration of some key differences between some of the basic beliefs of classic Christianity and those of Mormonism. Written by a group of evangelical scholars representing several fields of philosophical and theological expertise, the respectful tone and responsible scholarship in these essays are relatively new phenomena in evangelical works on Mormonism and represent a welcome change.

I will not speak for the LDS folks here, but as an evangelical I must confess that I am ashamed of our record in relating to the Mormon community. To be sure, there are deep differences between our worldviews. I strongly disagree with what I understand to be traditional Mormon teachings about God, about human nature, and about what it takes for a sinner to get right with God—matters on which the Latter-day Saints differ not only from standard Protestant teachings but from the Roman Catholic and Orthodox traditions as well. But none of those disagreements give me or any other evangelical the license to propagate distorted accounts of what Mormons believe. By bearing false witness against our LDS neighbors, we evangelicals have often sinned not just against Mormons but against the God who calls us to be truth-tellers.

The respectful tone of these essays, then, is a laudable attempt to set the record straight—not by coating over real disagreements, but by inviting our Mormon friends to engage in a mutual exploration of some of the most fundamental issues that bear on the human condition. This invitation is based on the conviction, stated explicitly in these pages, that these essays are not meant to be the last word spoken on any of the subjects covered. The conversation that takes place in this book is a sustained one—and it is offered with the expectation that what is said in these pages is only a first step in a discussion that needs to keep going. I hope the Mormon community—especially LDS leaders and Mormon intellectuals—will accept this invitation in the spirit in which it is offered.

The authors of these essays are obviously convinced that there are new opportunities these days for this sort of mutual exploration. Throughout its history, Mormonism has shown itself to be remarkably fluid in its theological perspective, and we have seen new signs of that fluidity in recent decades. The assumptions that allow for LDS theological fluidity—especially the strong emphasis on continuing revelation—are troublesome for evangelicals. But those assumptions also allow for significant theological revision.

Much of the revising by Latter-day Saints, of course, takes the form of a change of emphasis rather than substance. But substantial revision is not out of the question. Nor are the signs of recent change limited to the areas directly addressed by the official LDS leadership. Many "ordinary" Mormons are listening to Christian radio and watching evangelical TV programs. Some of them subscribe to evangelical magazines. New forms of cooperative local activism have emerged in North America as Latter-day Saints, evangelicals, and Roman Catholics work together to counter destructive trends in the larger culture. And on occasion, as they get to know each other better, they are even praying and studying the Bible together!

The phenomenon that is most relevant to the present discussion, however, is the emergence over the past several decades of a community of gifted Mormon intellectuals who have earned the right to be taken seriously in the larger academic community. Not only has Brigham Young University proved itself to be an important center of intellectual activity, but LDS scholars can be found throughout the ranks of the North American academy. This fact by itself should dictate that evangelicals treat Mormonism differently than the other groups that we have typically—and misleadingly—lumped together as "the cults." Christian Science has had almost no influence in the academy. And we are not being flippant in saying that the term "Jehovah's Witness scholar" has the feel of an oxymoron. But the existence of a highly intellectual Mormon subculture—where LDS scholars engage in serious exploration of other perspectives and debate these matters openly among themselves—suggests that we would do well to treat the Mormon worldview as a serious intellectual perspective.

CONTRIBUTORS

Jim W. Adams (Ph.D. candidate, Fuller Theological Seminary), Assistant Professor of Biblical Studies, LIFE Bible College, and Adjunct Professor of Biblical Studies, Azusa Pacific University.

Francis J. Beckwith (Ph.D., Fordham University), Associate Professor of Philosophy, Culture, and Law, Trinity International University.

Craig L. Blomberg (Ph.D., University of Aberdeen), Professor of New Testament, Denver Seminary.

Paul Copan (Ph.D., Marquette University), Ministry Associate, Ravi Zacharias International Ministries, and Visiting Associate Professor of Philosophy of Religion and Systematic Theology, Trinity International University.

William Lane Craig (Ph.D., University of Birmingham, England; D.Theol., University of Munich, Germany), Research Professor of Philosophy, Talbot School of Theology, Biola University.

Thomas J. Finley (Ph.D., University of California, Los Angeles), Professor and Chair of the Department of Old Testament and Semitics, Talbot School of Theology, Biola University.

Craig J. Hazen (Ph.D., University of California, Santa Barbara), Associate Professor of Comparative Religion and Apologetics, Director of the Graduate Program in Christian Apologetics, Biola University.

J. P. Moreland (Ph.D., University of Southern California), Distinguished Professor of Philosophy, Talbot School of Theology, Biola University.

Carl Mosser (Ph.D. Candidate, University of St. Andrews).

Paul Owen (Ph.D., University of Edinburgh), Assistant Professor of Bible and Religion, Montreat College.

Stephen E. Parrish (Ph.D., Wayne State University), Librarian and Assistant Professor of Philosophy, Concordia University (Ann Arbor, Michigan).

David J. Shepherd (Ph.D., University of Edinburgh), Associate Professor of Old Testament, Briercrest Biblical Seminary.

ABBREVIATIONS

Latter-day Saint Abbreviations:

BoM   Book of Mormon

BYU   Brigham Young University

CHC   B. H. Roberts, *A Comprehensive History of the Church of Jesus Christ of Latter-day Saints*. Salt Lake City: Corporation of the President, 1957.

CWHN   *Collected Works of Hugh Nibley*

D&C   Doctrine and Covenants

Dialogue *Dialogue: A Journal of Mormon Thought*

EOM   *Encyclopedia of Mormonism*. Edited by Daniel H. Ludlow, 5 vols. New York: Macmillan, 1992.

FARMS Foundation for Ancient Research and Mormon Studies at Brigham Young University

HC   Joseph Smith, *History of the Church of Jesus Christ of Latter-day Saints*. Edited by B. H. Roberts, 2d ed., rev. Salt Lake City: Deseret, 1878.

JD   *Journal of Discourses*

KFD   Joseph Smith, "King Follett Discourse" (an important funerary sermon by Joseph Smith)

LDS   Latter-day Saint, synonymous with "Mormon." An adjective referring to a member, doctrine, or practice of the Church of Jesus Christ of Latter-day Saints, headquartered in Salt Lake City, Utah

TPJS   Joseph Smith, *Teachings of the Prophet Joseph Smith*. Compiled and edited by Joseph Fielding Smith. Salt Lake City: Deseret, 1976.

Components of the LDS Standard Works:

The Book of Mormon:

1 Nephi
2 Nephi
Jacob
Enos
Jarom
Omni
Words of Mormon
Mosiah
Alma
Helaman
3 Nephi
4 Nephi
Mormon
Ether
Moroni

Doctrine and Covenants:

Sections 1–138
Official Declaration 1
Official Declaration 2

Pearl of Great Price:

Moses
Abraham
Joseph Smith—Matthew
Joseph Smith—History
Articles of Faith

Bible Translations:

ASV	American Standard Version
AV	Authorized Version (also known as the King James Version)
LBP	Living Bible Paraphrased
KJV	King James Version (also known as the Authorized Version)
NAB	New American Bible
NASB	New American Standard Bible
NASB[95]	New American Standard Bible, 1995 update
NIV	New International Version
NJB	New Jerusalem Bible
NKJV	New King James Version
NRSV	New Revised Standard Version
RSV	Revised Standard Version

Scholarly Abbreviations:

AB	Anchor Bible
ABD	*Anchor Bible Dictionary.* Edited by D. N. Freedman. 6 vols. New York: Doubleday, 1992.
AEL	*Ancient Egyptian Literature.* M. Lichtheim. 3 vols. Berkeley: University of California Press, 1971–80.
AnBib	Analecta biblica
ANET	*Ancient Near Eastern Texts Relating to the Old Testament.* Edited by J. B. Pritchard. 3d ed. Princeton: Princeton University Press, 1969.
AOS	American Oriental Series
AUSS	*Andrews University Seminary Studies*
BA	*Biblical Archeologist*
BAR	*Biblical Archeology Review*
BASOR	*Bulletin of the American Schools of Oriental Research*
BDB	F. Brown, S. R. Driver, C. A. Briggs, *Hebrew and English Lexicon of the Old Testament.* Oxford: Clarendon, 1907.
Bib	*Biblica*
BSac	*Bibliotheca Sacra*
CBQ	*Catholic Biblical Quarterly*
CBQMS	Catholic Biblical Quarterly Monograph Series
DDD	*Dictionary of Deities and Demons in the Bible.* Edited by K. van der Toon, B. Becking, and P. W. van der Horst. Leiden: Brill, 1995.
EvQ	*Evangelical Quarterly*
HAR	*Hebrew Annual Review*
HAT	Handbuch zum Alten Testament
HBT	*Horizons in Biblical Theology*
HSM	Harvard Semitic Monographs
HSS	Harvard Semitic Studies
HUCA	Hebrew Union College Annual
IDB	*The Interpreter's Dictionary of the Bible.* Edited by G. A. Buttrick. 4 vols. Nashville: Abingdon, 1962–77.

IDBSup   *Interpreter's Dictionary of the Bible: Supplementary Volume.* Edited by
         K. Crim. Nashville: Abingdon, 1976.
JANES   *Journal of the Ancient Near Eastern Society*
JAOS   *Journal of the American Oriental Society*
JBL   *Journal of Biblical Literature*
JJS   *Journal of Jewish Studies*
JNES   *Journal of Near Eastern Studies*
JPSTC   Jewish Publication Society Torah Commentary
JQR   *Jewish Quarterly Review*
JSOT   *Journal for the Study of the Old Testament*
JSOTSup Journal for the Study of the Old Testament: Supplement Series
JTS   *Journal of Theological Studies*
KBL   L. Koehler and W. Baumgartner, *Lexicon in Veteris Testamenti libros.* 2d
         ed. Leiden: Brill, 1958.
LXX   The ancient Greek translation of the Old Testament known as the
         Septuagint
MT   Masoretic Text of the Hebrew Old Testament
NIBCOT   New International Biblical Commentary on the Old Testament
NIDOTTE *New International Dictionary of Old Testament Theology and Exegesis.*
         Edited by W. A. VanGemeren. 5 vols. Grand Rapids: Zondervan, 1997.
OBT   Overtures to Biblical Theology
OEAE   *The Oxford Encyclopedia of Ancient Egypt.* Edited by Donald B. Redford.
         3 vols. Oxford: Oxford University Press, 2001.
Or   *Orientalia*
OTL   Old Testament Library
OTS   Old Testament Studies
SBLMS   Society of Biblical Literature Monograph Series
SBLWAW   Society of Biblical Literature Writings from the Ancient World
SBT   Studies in Biblical Theology
ST   *Studia theologica*
ThTo   *Theology Today*
TDOT   *Theological Dictionary of the Old Testament.* Edited by G. J. Botterweck
         and H. Ringgren. Translated by J. T. Willis, G. W. Bromiley, and D. E.
         Green. 11 vols. Grand Rapids: Eerdmans, 1974–.
UF   Ugarit-Forschungen
VT   *Vetus Testamentum*
VTSup   Supplements to Vetus Testamentum
WBC   Word Biblical Commentary
ZAW   *Zeitschrift für die alttestamentliche Wissenschaft*

INTRODUCTION:
A Much-needed and Challenging Book

FRANCIS J. BECKWITH,
CARL MOSSER,
AND PAUL OWEN

It has been rightly said that of the making of books there is no end (Eccl 12:12), but the making of books that are worth reading is rare. The saying can be adapted to the subject of this book: of the making of books on Mormonism there is no end, and the making of books worth reading is rare. We believe that the book in your hands, *The New Mormon Challenge,* is a rare book that is worth reading. Directed primarily to evangelicals and Latter-day Saints, this book really ought to be read by anyone with an interest in the truth claims of Mormonism, regardless of religious background or reason for interest. We think we can safely say, without presumption, that *The New Mormon Challenge* is a truly groundbreaking and epoch-marking book.

A few years ago two of us wrote an article calling attention to the fact that LDS scholars were producing a wealth of material defending Mormon truth claims but that evangelical critiques of Mormonism were not keeping pace. (Some of the ways in which LDS scholars are creatively defending their faith are described in chapter 2.) The title of our article vividly described the state of affairs as we saw it: "Mormon Scholarship, Apologetics and Evangelical Neglect: Losing the Battle and Not Knowing It?" (*Trinity Journal* n.s. 19 [Fall 1998]: 179–205). That article proved to be controversial in some circles, and there were some on both sides of the divide who misunderstood its intent and misrepresented its contents. Be that as it may, most people who read the article seem to have come around to seeing that the basic claims of it were entirely correct. The main point of the article was not to laud LDS apologetic scholarship or to highlight evangelical shortcomings. Rather, the main point was the call issued in the conclusion for evangelical scholars to make themselves aware of the work of their LDS counterparts and to thoughtfully engage the new LDS scholarly apologetics.

The three of us have assembled a team of respected Christian scholars to produce an initial answer to the call made in that article. *The New Mormon Challenge* is the first installment of what we hope will be several books and articles by us as well as others, remedying the neglect. In this volume we have focused on four areas. In Part I, two chapters describe Mormonism's appeal and its challenges to historic Christian faith. These chapters are primarily descriptive in nature, laying some groundwork for properly understanding the background and rise of the new Mormon challenge. Neither, however, gives an introductory overview of LDS history, culture, and belief. For that we heartily recommend another book that will serve as an excellent companion to this one: Richard and Joan Ostling's *Mormon America: The Power and the Promise* (HarperSanFrancisco, 1999).

In Part II, five chapters focus on evaluating various aspects of the Mormon and Christian worldviews. Such topics as the doctrine of creation, the nature of God, the nature of humanity, the source of moral values, and the problem of evil are discussed. Part III consists of two chapters. The first addresses issues related to LDS claims about whether the early Christians were monotheists. The second tackles the controversial issue of Mormonism's relationship with the Christian faith and whether it should be considered a Christian denomination. Part IV consists of two chapters evaluating two important questions about Mormonism's "keystone scripture," the Book of Mormon: Does the Book of Mormon evidence having an ancient Near Eastern background? and Is the Book of Mormon a translated text?

Clearly, this book is primarily a response to some of the new challenges Mormonism presents to orthodox Christian faith. But the book itself will chal-

lenge Christians. It will challenge certain stereotypes and misinformed caricatures Christians commonly, but regrettably, have about the Mormon faith; it
will challenge the Christian community to approach the tasks of "countercult" apologetics and the evangelization of Mormonism differently; it will challenge pastors, missionaries, and denominational leaders to think more deeply
about their ministry philosophies; it will challenge Christians at all levels to be
more open to working with Latter-day Saints in areas of common social concern. This book will challenge the Christian community—from the person
in the pew, to the pastor in the pulpit, to the scholar teaching in the seminary—to recognize and effectively respond to the new Mormon challenge. To
this end, we hope this book will be an invaluable resource that accomplishes
many things other books on Mormonism do not attempt.

Latter-day Saint readers will soon notice several things about this work
that mark it out from all others. Perhaps most noticeable, this is not one more
book on Mormonism by evangelicals *for* evangelicals; it was written for and
to Latter-day Saints as well as for and to evangelical and other orthodox
Christians. In fact, in several of the chapters the authors have included sections in which they speak specifically to the members of the LDS community
(and not simply *at* them). In marked distinction from many evangelical works
on Mormonism, LDS readers will find that the authors are respectful, charitable, and courteous throughout. They have worked hard to accurately understand Mormon positions before attempting to critique them. Great effort was
taken to ensure that the misconceptions and caricatures that so often plague
works on this subject are avoided. Rather than attacking easy targets and
propped-up straw men, the authors of *The New Mormon Challenge* have
engaged the thought of the most knowledgeable and articulate LDS scholars.
They have interacted with Mormonism's best and brightest in order to critique Mormonism at its strongest, for such a noble people deserve nothing
less, and the high calling of the Christian scholar demands it.

A Note About Mormon Doctrine

Many Christian books on Mormonism suffer from two significant failures. The
first is the failure to properly appreciate the diversity of views that have historically been held within Mormonism. Second is the failure to keep abreast of
developments in contemporary LDS theology. Too often Mormon theology has
been presented as monolithic and homogenous. Many writers have a tendency
to classify any teaching by Joseph Smith, Brigham Young, or other LDS prophets

and apostles as "official Mormon doctrine." Latter-day Saints, however, do not view the teachings of their apostles and prophets in that manner. Nor, indeed, have LDS apostles and prophets, who have regularly had differences of opinion between themselves as to what constitutes church doctrine.

To use distinctions that go back at least to the LDS theologian and General Authority B. H. Roberts, one does well to distinguish between doctrinally binding Mormon theology, traditional Mormon theology, common Mormon beliefs, and that which is permissible as Mormon theology. When one studies LDS theology with these distinctions in mind, it becomes apparent that the body of doctrinally binding LDS theology is surprisingly small. A fairly stable and large body of traditional LDS theology can easily be identified, but one soon realizes that Mormon theology is not static. During the last thirty years, and especially the last ten to fifteen years, other LDS theologies have gained in popularity, perhaps even becoming dominant. The traditional LDS theology described in many books on Mormonism is, on many points, increasingly unrepresentative of what Latter-day Saints actually believe. Rather than focus exclusively on "official Mormon doctrine" or traditional Mormon doctrine, the authors of *The New Mormon Challenge* have tried to focus on doctrines that are either: (1) widespread and historically held positions; (2) widespread contemporary views; or (3) minority views permitted within contemporary Mormonism that seem to be the most plausible and defensible of LDS options.

Because of the fluid nature of Mormon theology, it is all too easy for outsiders to misjudge what views are most commonly held among the majority of Latter-day Saints. The authors of this book have tried to represent fairly the current state of Mormon theology both at the popular level and among representative LDS intellectuals (excluding liberal Mormon views that have been censured by the LDS hierarchy). But the authors have not always come to the same conclusions. Indeed, even the three editors have some differences of opinion among themselves. In itself, this lack of complete consensus testifies to the plurality of views and shifting of currents one finds in contemporary Mormonism. To adapt a colorful phrase one of the editors once heard: trying to figure out just what constitutes Mormon theology is like trying to nail Jell-O dipped in olive oil to the wall. If at some point Mormon theology has not been represented with 100 percent accuracy, it is not for lack of trying.

A Note About the Nature and Structure of This Book

As a work responding to LDS scholarship, the discussions in this book are necessarily of a scholarly nature. We have tried, however, to make this work accessible to as many people as possible. Technical language has been kept to a minimum, and issues that are of importance primarily to scholars but not to the general reader have been confined to the notes. A certain amount of technical language is unavoidable in a work like this. Moreover, because of the interdisciplinary nature of the work, even those who have some training in biblical studies, theology, or philosophy may find themselves unfamiliar with some terminology used in some chapters. To help the reader follow the discussion in those sections where technicality cannot be avoided, we have done three things. First, we have given each of the four parts of the book its own introduction in which we introduce the chapters in a manner that we hope will allow readers to understand the whole of the chapters even if some of the details elude them. Second, where it has been necessary to make reference to the biblical texts in their original Hebrew, Aramaic, or Greek, the texts have been transliterated (i.e., put into Roman characters). Third, we have compiled a glossary of terms appended to the end of the volume. It is not exhaustive, but it should nonetheless prove beneficial. It also includes entries on terms distinctive to Mormonism that some non-Latter-day Saints may be unfamiliar with.

Since we have provided introductions for each of the four main parts of the book, we will not summarize the chapters here. But three chapters deserve special mention because of their length and because of the significance of their subject matter. The more one studies the differences between LDS and orthodox Christian theologies, the more apparent it becomes that the chief differences from which most others stem is this: while the orthodox Christian traditions all affirm that there is but one God who is the absolute Creator of all other reality, Mormonism has historically denied the absolute creation of the world and has affirmed a plurality of deities. The chief point of theological dispute between Christians and Latter-day Saints, then, is whether there is one unique God who is a true Creator or not. Latter-day Saint scholars, often appealing to the work of non-LDS specialists, have argued that the ancient Jews and earliest Christians were not strict monotheists and did not affirm the absolute creation of the world. In contrast, we contend that the belief in a unique Creator God is at the heart of biblical faith, that it is true, and that it has been tenaciously held by Jews and Christians from the earliest times. We also maintain that Mormonism's chief foundational error is its forsaking of this most fundamental doctrine. For these reasons, we have allowed the chapters on the doctrine of creation and the chapter on monotheism to be significantly longer than the others. They are, however, divided into easily digestible sections and can be read in two or three sittings if one does not have the stamina to read them all at once.

A Note About the Contributors

The contributing authors to *The New Mormon Challenge* were not chosen because they are experts on Mormonism. To the contrary, most of them were chosen primarily because of their expertise in some other area. No doubt some will see this as a shortcoming. We obviously see this as a benefit, and it was intended from the outset. The kind of response we felt was needed was one in which individual scholars studied some aspect of Mormonism or some apologetic claim made by LDS scholars related to an area in which they already possessed a measure of expertise. Thus, for example, David Shepherd was asked to evaluate, from the position of expertise he has gained studying ancient Semitic translations and translation theory in general, whether the Book of Mormon is a translated text. J. P. Moreland was asked to evaluate Orson Pratt's defense of a Mormon materialist understanding of human persons because of his knowledge of physicalist ontologies and his expertise on the mind-body problem. Paul Copan and William Lane Craig were asked to combine their expertise on different aspects of the doctrine of creation to examine the LDS doctrine of creation and to defend the orthodox Christian view of *creatio ex nihilo* against charges made by LDS and other scholars. And so it goes for most of the chapters. In short, we asked the authors to lend us their expertise in some area in order to tackle this or that aspect of LDS theology.

It is worth noting that the contributors and editors of this book represent a broad spectrum of the evangelical movement. They come from a variety of denominational backgrounds, including Presbyterian, Evangelical Free, General Baptist, Foursquare Gospel (i.e., Pentecostal), Anglican, Lutheran (Missouri Synod), Free Methodist, and the evangelical wing of the Society of Friends. They include both laymen and ordained or licensed ministers. Some have been pastors, youth pastors, church planters, or missionaries. Several have participated in extensive evangelism and apologetics ministries on college and university campuses. All are engaged, at some level, in the training of Christian men and women for various kinds of ministries. Each contributor is someone who has one foot in the academy and one foot in the work of the local church.

Though the authors are all evangelical Protestants, they are representative of a much broader constituency. The positions they defend in this book are not provincial evangelical positions or even specifically Protestant positions. They are, rather, doctrinal beliefs that C. S. Lewis so famously identified with "mere Christianity." There is very little in this book that could not have been written by any Orthodox, Catholic, or Protestant who affirms the ecumenical creeds of the early church. The authors have written as evangelicals, knowing that one of the two major parts of their primary audience will be other evangelicals. But most of the comments they make to or about their fellow evangelicals apply equally to all orthodox Christians. The important point here is this: this book is not about the differences between evangelicalism and Mormonism. The issues discussed are deeper than that.

A Note to Evangelical Readers

Augustine once said that the bishop is the servant of the servants of God. In like manner, the contributors to this book are scholars who seek to put their skills to use in the service of God's people. One of our intentions is for the chapters of this book to serve as resources for Christians who have been confronted with LDS criticisms of orthodox Christian belief but who are not sure how to respond. We have also sought to evaluate Mormon theology in fresh ways and in areas that are rarely, if ever, discussed in other books on Mormonism. Evangelicals are encouraged to use the material in this book in defending and commending their faith. It is our sincere hope that this book will make a genuine difference and that many more people will embrace the divine truth than if it had not been written.

The New Mormon Challenge is not just a resource; it is also intended as a model for those involved in apologetics and those engaging in interreligious dialogue with their LDS family, friends, and coworkers. Too often theological discussions between Christians and Mormons lapse into conflicts of personality, accusations of dishonesty or insincerity, and even into competitions in which the participants seek to out-demean and out-insult one another. We place the greater responsibility for these shortcomings on the members of our own faith community. Our encouragement is to follow the example of the authors of this book, who provide their answers with gentleness and respect (cf. 1 Pet 3:15). Furthermore, if the LDS views discussed in this book are shown to be mistaken, Latter-day Saints should not be forced to defend them. Often, for some inexplicable reason, Christians have insisted that Mormons cannot change their theological positions unless the entire package of LDS theology is given up at once. This seems to us misguided. Rather, Christians should encourage their LDS acquaintances to "use their agency" and adopt better theological positions when their old ones have been shown to be inadequate. Incremental change is still change and can lead to more substantive transformation.

A Note to LDS Readers

We have mentioned that *The New Mormon Challenge* is a response to some of Mormonism's challenges and itself poses several challenges (in a different sense) to the Christian community. Additionally, and perhaps more significantly, this book challenges Latter-day Saints to reevaluate some of their beliefs. The authors and editors of this book are not interested in doctrinal dispute for the sake of dispute. We are not interested in attacking and tearing down the beliefs of others like some sort of bellicose theological terrorists. But neither are we willing to avoid confrontation, as if the competing truth claims of Christianity and Mormonism are merely insignificant disputes about mere opinion. We are theological realists who believe that doctrine matters. We are firmly convinced that we are called to defend and proclaim the faith that God revealed to the prophets of Israel and in the unique person of his Son (Heb 1:1–4). That faith was once and for all time delivered to the people of God as a sacred trust (Jude 3). We take that trust seriously and consider it our duty to answer those LDS arguments that promote positions we find incompatible with true biblical faith. With the biblical writers, we recognize, unlike so many people today, that what one believes matters in very important ways and that false beliefs can be fatal to one's spiritual well-being (cf. 1 Tim 4:16).

It is out of a genuine concern and care for our LDS neighbors that we have invested much time and energy in this project. We hope and often pray that the Latter-day Saints will have the ears to listen and the courage to respond. For we believe that God is calling them at this time to reconsider some of Mormonism's traditional truth claims. We invite our LDS friends to consider afresh for themselves the claims of the historic Christian faith. In both our tone and our approach, we have endeavored to present Christian orthodoxy as attractively as possible, so that the Living God might use our labors as a means of bringing biblical light and life into the arena of interreligious dialogue between our respective communities—and perhaps do even more.

PART I

Mormonism's Appeal, Growth,
and Challenges

Introductory Essay

All too often Christians have tended to view Latter-day Saints as belonging to one of only three possible categories: those who are sincere but unintelligent; those who may be sincere and intelligent but simply are uninformed about the facts of the Bible, Christian history, and Mormonism; and those who are intelligent and informed but are dishonest and insincere. It has been thought that if the "facts" are simply presented, sincere and intelligent Latter-day Saints will necessarily see that Mormonism is false and Christianity true. If a Mormon does not see this after she has been presented with the facts, then she must either be unintelligent or dishonest. Of course, those who end up dealing with Latter-day Saints as if they can fall into only one of these categories probably do so without having thought about whether there could be more categories. If one simply reflects on the matter and applies a little common sense, it should be clear that not only *could* there be more categories, there *should* be. In particular, there should be room to admit that some Latter-day Saints are intelligent, knowledgeable, and sincere, and yet feel that there are good reasons for believing that Mormonism is true even if they recognize that there are some problematic areas.

To consider all Mormons as either unintelligent, uninformed, or dishonest can only have a distorting effect on one's understanding of Mormonism and the Mormon people. Presupposing such an overly narrow classification system has led many to view certain LDS beliefs as so bizarre and obviously false as to find it very difficult to understand how any rational person could believe them. In turn, it has often been assumed that the earliest Mormons, especially, must have been unintelligent, gullible rubes to have been deceived by Joseph Smith. In chapter 1, Craig Hazen shows that this was not at all the case. To the contrary, early Mormonism actually held considerable intellectual appeal to the knowledgeable nineteenth-century person. It presented a view of the universe that seemed to accord with current scientific theories. It also seemed to answer effectively many of the Enlightenment criticisms of Christianity and the Bible that had trickled down to the villages of frontier America. Joseph Smith's Mormonism, especially in the hands of capable promoters like the brother-apostles Orson and Parley Pratt, was in many ways an attempt to create a scientific Christianity impervious to the criticisms that seemed to be fatal to traditional Christianity. Mormonism was birthed, in part, as a radical exercise in Christian apologetics. Although Smith and his followers developed a movement that held intellectual appeal to potential converts in the nineteenth century, they did not, in the process, restore a pristine Christianity immune to all of "apostate" Christianity's shortcomings. Rather, they so changed the contents of Christianity as to create a new religious movement, one that, as subsequent chapters will show, faces very serious intellectual problems of its own.

Hazen notes that many of the aspects of LDS doctrine that resonated with nineteenth-century scientific speculations and skeptical attacks on Christianity do not have the same appeal they once had. Mormonism has continued to be attractive to potential converts, though usually for reasons other than intellectual ones. Today people are more often attracted to Mormonism's high moral values and its stress on the importance of families. In fact, the Church of Jesus Christ of Latter-day Saints attracts hundreds of thousands of converts each year through the efforts of its truly massive missionary program, and it is predicted to become the first world religion to arise since Islam. Within this fast-growing movement a cadre of LDS intellectuals has arisen who intelligently defend their faith and continue the tradition of promoting the strengths of the LDS position vis-à-vis orthodox Christianity.

In chapter 2 Carl Mosser discusses the challenge that Mormonism's rapid growth presents to the task of world missions and the challenge that the new LDS scholarly apologetic presents to Christian apologetics and evangelism. He challenges Christian theologians and apologists to keep up with trends in contemporary LDS theology rather than relying on outdated and inaccurate portraits of Mormon doctrine. Mosser begins by evaluating widely cited predictions about Mormonism's future growth and ascendancy to the status of a world religion. Arguing that the predictions are sound and should not be dismissed as some evangelical leaders have done, he notes that the particular way in which the Church of Jesus Christ of the Latter-day

Saints grows should be of particular concern to missionaries, pastors, and denominational leaders.

In the second part of his essay, Mosser describes how, in recent years, a community of well-trained LDS scholars has arisen who are defending their faith in rigorous ways. The vigor of this movement shows that Mormonism has not lost its intellectual appeal entirely and still seems defensible to intelligent, well-informed persons. Mosser describes the work of the LDS scholars and the challenge this presents to the task of Christian apologetics. Lastly, Mosser describes recent trends in LDS theology, some of them encouraging. He invites Christian theologians to study contemporary LDS theology, both in order to evaluate it and as an opportunity to do theology in the kind of apologetic context that has led to the most fruitful theological insights in every age of church history.

The chapters by Hazen and Mosser are largely descriptive in nature and serve as backdrop to the chapters that follow. Most readers should carefully attend to these chapters before reading the others in the book, for before critiquing a position, one should first have some understanding of it. Hazen and Mosser's essays do much to shatter certain inaccurate stereotypes about the Latter-day Saints that have for too long been uncritically accepted by the Christian community. These stereotypes have had a detrimental effect on Christian-LDS relations and, we believe, on evangelism. Subsequent chapters will be appreciated much more once those inaccurate stereotypes have been exposed.

THE APOLOGETIC IMPULSE IN EARLY MORMONISM
The Historical Roots of the New Mormon Challenge

CRAIG J. HAZEN

Craig J. Hazen is Associate Professor of Comparative Religion and Christian Apologetics at Biola University and Director of the Graduate Program in Christian Apologetics. He earned a B.A. from California State University, Fullerton; studied law and theology at the International Institute for Law and Theology in Strasbourg, France; and earned an M.A. and Ph.D. in religious studies from the University of California at Santa Barbara. Dr. Hazen is the author of *The Village Enlightenment in America: Popular Religion and Science in the Nineteenth Century* (University of Illinois Press) and editor of the philosophy journal *Philosophia Christi*. His academic work has received multiple awards for excellence from the American Association for the Advancement of Science and the American Academy of Religion. His articles have appeared in *Journal of the American Scientific Affiliation, Journal of Christian Apologetics,* and the *Proceedings of the International Congress of the History of Science,* among others.

The flamboyant governor of Minnesota, former theatrical wrestler and Navy SEAL Jesse "the body" Ventura said in a highly publicized and provocative interview that he considered religious people to be inherently "weak-minded" folk. By doing so he was parroting a popular notion of armchair agnostics that people who embrace religion are gullible and needy; they are people willing to give up all or a certain amount of rationality in order to have their emotional needs met by some type of spirituality or superstition.

A furor ensued in his state, and his popularity rating plunged, but to some extent the governor's remark had some basis in reality. Many get the same impression very quickly by talking to the rank-and-file devotees in most religious movements. The average believer generally does not have the training or the interest in articulating or defending a coherent, systematic worldview that captures and makes sense of his or her faith. This is certainly true with regard to the movements that are addressed in this essay, evangelical Christianity and Mormonism. Both movements have been characterized as anti-intellectual, and detractors have not been slow with insults to both groups along those lines. What both Christians and Mormons in North America know, though, is that those who characterize and insult the groups in this way are themselves not particularly well informed.[1] In both modern American evangelicalism and Mormonism there are significant pockets of believers who are scholars and thinkers, people who are committed to making a vigorous defense of their respective faiths based on reason and on the very best evidence. Whether the case these thinking believers make is sound and persuasive is another question, but the fact that there *are* LDS and evangelical Christian scholars who would very much like to show that their belief systems are eminently reasonable is not up for dispute.

The accusation of anti-intellectualism and gullibility on the part of believers was especially rife in the early years of the Church of Jesus Christ of Latter-day Saints. As religious historian Jan Shipps put it, outsiders saw Mormonism pandering "to the superstitious, the gullible, and the fearful." They would accuse "Mormonism of 'blinding' its adherents so effectively that when they heard Smith's report of his visions and his explanation of the origins of the Book of Mormon, they could not distinguish truth from falsehood."[2] Just a month after the publication of the Book of Mormon, newspaper editors like Abner Cole of the Palmyra, New York, *Reflector* began the lampooning and discrediting of the new "Gold Bible," Joseph Smith (1805–44), and his followers. Mormon historian Richard L. Bushman correctly noted that early on there was simply an assumption that "they had to be dull because it was axiomatic that superstition flourished in ignorance."[3]

That there were undiscerning converts to Joseph Smith's new religion in the nineteenth century is a given. That they were all, or even mostly such, is a myth. Clearly, there was an advantage to early opponents of the Mormon movement's slapping a pejorative label on those who chose to join. It made the overall task of response and refutation much easier and perhaps more effective. Some adversaries at the time went so far as to claim that Joseph Smith was adept at the power of "animal magnetism" or "fascination" and hence could wield undue influence over the minds of potential converts.[4] These kinds of characterizations held on for years. Esteemed Mormon historian Leonard J. Arrington tried to gauge popular views of the movement in the nineteenth century by examining fiction that involved the Latter-day Saints in the plot line. He discovered that almost every one of the fifty novels that described Mormon life saw the people as incurably ignorant if not also lecherous and depraved.[5]

One can not make full sense of the initial rise of Mormonism without recognizing that there were strong elements in it that resonated with thoughtful people on the frontier. I do not mean by this that the "rational" element was the only factor, perhaps it was not even the primary or secondary factor to which one can attribute the success of the early LDS movement. But for many at the time there was undoubtedly a logic to it and certainly enough cultural resonance of a rational sort in the message of the Mormon "restoration" of Christianity to attract intelligent, reflective people. Of course, I am not talking here about professors, academics, or trained scholars—there were none in the early LDS Church.[6] But here I would make the same point that social anthropologist Stanley Jeyaraja Tambiah and historian of Mormonism D. Michael Quinn both make: that we should be sure to carve out a "distinction between the academic and the folk, not between intelligent and unintelligent."[7] We are discussing here very bright but not highly educated people on the frontier who were unwilling to join a religious movement without what they thought were good reasons.[8]

Arrington, as well as sociologist and observer of Mormonism Thomas O'Dea, saw an emergent intellectual tradition in the early years of the church where others had overlooked it. Indeed, Arrington saw the LDS intellectual tradition emerging in four stages of development with the earliest "formative stage" (1830–44) dominated by four very bright men: Joseph Smith himself, First Counselor Sidney Rigdon, and the brother-apostles Orson and Parley P. Pratt.[9] O'Dea saw the "intellectuality" in the Book of Mormon itself because of "its recognition of currents of thought other than and antagonistic to its own point of view, and especially in its awareness of current skepticism and rationalism"; and he thought it clearly offered a message that could be considered a "reasonable answer to problems of existence and salvation."[10] Ironically, in an article explicating the anti-intellectualism in Mormon history, Davis Bitton noted that in the early years the Mormon faith seemed overall *less* hostile to the intellect than it might have in later years. The new doctrines being promulgated appeared to some to be "more satisfying, more readily understandable, and more 'logical' to the average person." He wrote that "although such a congeries of beliefs made the Mormon religion thoroughly unpalatable to Catholicism and the main branches of Protestantism, it was Mormonism which, in the context of the time, was easily more rationalistic."[11] Even toward the end of Arrington's "formative stage," one could occasionally find neutral observers on the frontier being surprised and impressed by the LDS missionary efforts: "If a thorough knowledge of the scriptures, talent, tact, sound reasoning, and powerful argument are qualifications, then Elder Maginn is fully qualified for the duties of his office.... His reasoning was plain, logical and conclusive to the mind of every candid hearer."[12]

Mormon historian Steven C. Harper recently published an illuminating study along these lines. He examined the writings of average new converts to the LDS faith, as opposed to the writings of established authorities and missionaries of the church, in order to better measure what exactly it was that attracted Americans to the new movement in the young republic. Harper began by looking at one of the last great statements on the side of the "ignorance and gullibility" interpretation of Mormon conversions that was set forth by David Brion Davis in his influential essay "The New England Origins of Mormonism." In his essay, Davis asserted that "Mormonism can be seen as the extreme result of the evils of literal-mindedness" and that the growth of the Latter-day Saints represented an outburst of "extreme mysticism" and superstition. However, in the same essay, Davis hinted at the fact that this interpretation did not tell the whole story about the launching of the church. He was willing to admit that although their missionaries drew converts from the areas of enthusiastic revivals, the LDS approach to doctrine was "always by argument rather than emotional oratory."[13] Harper's review of the literature revealed that since Davis's study, "time and scholarship have shown early Mormonism to be more than 'the inconsequential product of ignorance.'" For the average believers who chose to follow Smith, Harper concluded, one cannot escape the fact that "one finds [the word] 'reasonable' and its relatives used frequently by writers trying to describe what it was in Mormon theology that caused conversion in them." Harper is careful to point out, however, that this does not diminish the fact that Joseph Smith and others were part of a "visionary culture" and that many nonrational factors and currents came into play. But the idea that there was nothing intellectually satisfying in the early LDS message for those that encountered it should be abandoned.[14]

Indeed, I would take these observations about the popular intellectual attraction of the early Mormon message one step further. I think it is safe to say that the Mormon Restoration of "true" Christianity was itself a movement with an apologetic message at its center. Joseph Smith and the other leaders of the new church were in agreement that something was terribly wrong with the state of the Christian faith in their day and that no tinkering with a doctrine here or a ritual there was going to correct it. Enlightenment thinking had taken a dramatic toll on a range of sacred ideas, and the various churches themselves were finishing the job via revival campaigns against one another. In many ways, I believe, Mormonism represents Joseph Smith's attempt to save Christianity by reinventing it (what the Latter-day Saints would call "restoring" it) and then outdoing rival forms in the religious marketplace of his day on the basis of superior authority, rationality, and relevance.[15] Ironically, in the course of "restoring" Christianity, the Latter-day Saints eventually made it unrecognizable and less relevant for later generations not steeped in popular nineteenth-century categories of thought.

Nevertheless, in the face of the resurgence of LDS apologetics in our own day, it can be enlightening to see how this movement captured the hearts—but more importantly, in this case, the minds—of religious seers in its first generation and how the popular apologetic trajectory was set in the early years. In order to gather clues as to what attracted people to this radical new movement, I will take my cue from Arrington, Harper, and other historians of Mormonism and look to the converts who chose the Latter-day Saints over other vigorously competing religious options confronting them.[16]

A More Biblical Faith

People who encountered early LDS teaching were impressed with the Book of Mormon and how it and the Bible "mutually and reciprocally corroborate each other."[17] The language and themes appeared to early converts to have a seamless flow. Harper noted that one nearly universal commonality was that the new Saints were contemplative Bible readers. A perceived harmony between the original and the latter-day revelations was essential for their acceptance of the Mormon message. Of course, it was not long before Smith himself admitted by his actions that the Bible was a less than perfect guide—or, as Philip L. Barlow put it, "an inadequate religious compass"—because soon after completing the Book of Mormon, he began adjusting the biblical text by producing an "inspired translation" of portions of Genesis and Matthew.[18] But even his retranslations had the resonant language and themes necessary to give the impression of harmony in the context of the Restoration.[19]

The biblical messages preached by LDS missionaries and leaders seemed to have a common sense and a plainness about them for which potential converts longed. As has been observed by a number of scholars, Mormon teachers were able to achieve this primarily because they were both *literal* and *selective* in their approach to the Bible. By focusing primarily on biblical passages that served Restoration purposes, such as the nature of the primitive church, the belief in apostasy and later restoration, millennialism, and so on, they could use the Bible more strategically as a pointer to the latter-day activities and avoid the complexities that faced Protestant biblicists in harmonizing texts and doctrines throughout all sixty-six books. This was a decided advantage over competitors, but it was more of a strategic dodge than a long-term solution to problems in the text of the Bible. Careful selection of texts to promote and careful selection of texts to neglect was one of the ways that Joseph Smith "'out-Bibled' the traditional biblicists who surrounded him."[20] In fact, the selection of texts was so clear-cut that Arrington and Bitton noticed that it would not be difficult to compile a special "Mormon Bible including only Mormon proof texts" that would be the size of a small book. Like the followers of other sects of their day, agreed Arrington and Bitton, "the Mormons utilized 'selective emphasis.'"[21] In his extensive study of the place of the Bible in LDS thought, *Mormons and the Bible*, Barlow concluded that early Mormon "scriptural literalism is not absolute; it is in fact highly selective."[22] This selective emphasis, consistent linguistic ring, and thematic commonality helped convince "convert after convert" to embrace Mormonism because "it satisfied their yearnings for a truly biblical Christianity."[23]

A More Direct Connection to Christ

Religious seekers also seemed to be impressed by Mormonism's authentic Christian "primitivism," that is, their attempt to be faithful to the unadulterated and unmediated teachings of Christ and his apostles. After all, it was eminently reasonable to seek out the Christianity that was lived and spoken by the Lord Jesus himself. The first name for the body of new Mormon believers founded on April 6, 1830, was the "Church of Christ," and Mormon converts were calling themselves "The True Followers of Christ."[24] The simplicity of the name spoke volumes about one of the most important original aims: to return to the fullness of the pure ancient gospel.

The Mormons, of course, were not the only ones reasoning in this way. The notion of primitivism, also called restorationism or restitutionism by historians, was one of the most compelling religious forces of the day.[25] American religious historian Nathan O. Hatch called it the "quest for the ancient order of things"; all of the varieties of Christianity that were springing up in the early republic seemed to have at root a "common conception that Christian tradition since the time of the apostles was a tale of sordid corruption in which kingcraft and priestcraft wielded orthodoxy to enslave the minds of the people" and that pure Christianity could only be encountered if one could get back to its uncorrupted form.[26] This restorationist impulse was especially strong for indigenous American Christian movements. Established denominations that had deep Old World roots felt the impact of the primitivist movement only in an occasional fringe faction. Popular religious leaders such as Elias Smith, Lorenzo Dow, Alexander Campbell, Francis Asbury, Barton Stone, and William Miller all preceded Joseph Smith with a robust call to return to the pristine era of the New Testament church.

It is well known that Joseph Smith and his family had significant contact with this primitive-gospel thinking.[27] His grandfathers, his uncle, and his parents all held this view; and his mother, Lucy Mack Smith, lamented the difficulty in trying to choose a church because "they are all unlike the church of Christ as it existed in former days!"[28] According to Smith's mother, her husband, Joseph Sr., likewise would not join any "system of faith" that was not of the "ancient order, as established by our Lord and Savior Jesus Christ, and his apostles."[29]

If Christian restorationism was utterly sensible to thinking seekers, and if more is better, then Mormons had a distinct advantage due to the *depth* of the apostasy and the *glory* of the restoration that they envisioned. According to more mainstream primitivists such as Asbury, Campbell, Stone, and others, there was a falling away from the original apostolic teaching and order in the Dark Ages that culminated in the near extinction of the true church. But for them a remnant always remained. The Reformation heralded a valiant attempt to return to New Testament teaching, but it had failed to cast off many of the creeds and traditions of men that still stood in the way of a full relationship with the Christ of the New Testament. In their view the situation was grave, and few worshipped in ultimate purity, but surely the "gates of hell" had not prevailed against God's remnant.

By contrast, in the Mormon view the darkness of apostasy that fell on the original church was earlier and more complete than imagined by their competitors of the time. The extent of the "falling away" for the Mormons was captured in what was perhaps the most religiously divisive statement penned during this period. Joseph Smith, in an account that is still at the very heart of the LDS movement today, claimed that no less than the Father and the Son themselves made a universal pronouncement personally to him about the religious systems of his day. Smith recalled the divine personages saying unequivocally that he "must join none of them, for they were *all* wrong . . . *all* their creeds were an abomination in his sight; that those professors were *all* corrupt; that: 'they draw near to me with their lips, but their hearts are far from me, they teach for doctrines the commandments of men, having a form of godliness, but they deny the power thereof.'"[30] This was the concept of primitivism par excellence, wiping the slate clean from the death of the last apostle of New Testament times to the reinstatement of the prophetic and apostolic order under Smith himself. And it was not just the teachings that were corrupt and an abomination, but the teachers themselves—their *hearts* were not of God. It was a clean sweep of the religious hearts and minds for 1,800 years.[31] Smith's "first vision" constituted not only a simple trumping of competing denominations of his period, but also a trumping of competing primitivist ideologies as well.[32] One does not have to wonder why the "Disciples of Christ" founder Alexander Campbell became one of the most focused early critics of the LDS movement—the core of his spiritual raison d'être was being surpassed by the LDS vision of the Restoration, and the Mormon version was also making a mockery of the primitivist program in general. One of the most educated men in the early

LDS Church, though, found this new ultraprimitivism utterly compelling. Former Baptist minister Orson Spencer, once having "cursed 'Mormonism' in my heart," found the LDS version of the "ancient gospel" irresistible and without parallel. "What could I do," he asked. "Truth had taken possession of my mind—plain, simple Bible truth."[33]

For some early converts the persuasiveness of the LDS Restoration was not just manifest in new revelation and apostolic and prophetic offices. Many believed because the New Testament was coming alive in reports around the frontier—biblical miracles were being performed at the hands of the Saints. Barlow noted that "biblical episodes did not seem 'once upon a time' to them, for they experienced such miracles—relived such episodes—in their own lives."[34] The Book of Mormon first raised the issue of latter-day miracles—an issue that would become a hyper-primitivist feature with the power to set the Latter-day Saints apart from the Protestant pack. Moroni asked the very question that was being asked of the religious leaders of Smith's time: "And if there were miracles wrought then, why has God ceased to be a God of miracles and yet be an unchangeable Being? And behold, I say unto you he changeth not; if so he would cease to be God; and he ceaseth not to be God, and is a God of miracles."[35] Yale historian Jon Butler has noticed that some at the time observed this to be one of Mormonism's most "salient features."[36]

The first reported miracle was an exorcism performed by Smith on Newel Knight at Knight's father's home in Colesville, New York, in June of 1830, which garnered significant notoriety. In June of 1831 "the most dramatic and well-attested" example of an exorcism was performed on several people at one meeting. The news of this occurrence quickly spread via newspaper to states such as Vermont and even Missouri.[37] Other types of dramatic biblical fare, such as raising the dead, walking on water, and multiplying loaves and fishes, were not, however, in the offing—perhaps because in a July 1830 revelation Smith and Oliver Cowdrey were warned against seeking after miracles.[38] Healings and exorcisms, however, were allowable exceptions. Just as the quickly spreading reports of the exorcisms seemed to magnify the attention beyond their actual numbers, reports of physical healings were also magnified. Newspapers in western New York and Ohio reported alleged healings and "divers miracles" in 1830–31, but they also reported failures. "These newly commissioned disciples [Oliver Cowdrey, Peter Whitmer, Parley P. Pratt, and Ziba Peterson] have totally failed thus far in their attempts to heal."[39] One of Smith's own failures to heal—

Warren Doty, who ended up dead "in spite of all efforts and promises to the contrary"—was reported in a paper as far away as New England in the *Independent Chronicle & Boston Patriot.*[40]

On occasion, an immediate healing at the hands of Mormon elders was given direct credit by a convert as the reason for joining the church. Steven C. Harper relates the account of Bible-believer Esaias Edwards, who appeared to be drawn to some aspects of the Mormon teaching but needed some type of threshold evidence to be finally persuaded:

> By "a close examination of the scriptures," Edwards concluded that "the Latter-day Saints was [*sic*] the only people that believed and practiced them in full." He determined that the saints could prove that beyond reasonable doubt by healing his sick wife, upon which he "covenanted" that he would be baptized. Edwards invited Alexander Williams, a Mormon elder, to "administer to my wife that she might be healed of her sickness." The two men prayed, and Williams "layed [*sic*] his hands upon her head and rebuked the disease in the name of Jesus Christ. Her pains immediately left her, and she was filled with the spirit of God." The couple became life-long converts.[41]

Edwards's testimony of a miraculous healing drawing him to the faith, however, was by no means the usual pattern. Indeed, the Saints actually taught against using miraculous signs as "proofs" for people coming to faith, but rather taught converts to use them simply as a "great benefit" to their fellow human beings as outlined in Mosiah 8:18. Sidney Rigdon argued this way when Oliver Cowdrey failed at his wonder working on an important early missionary journey, reportedly saying that the faith "was not intended to be confirmed in that way."[42] After reading through scores of early missionary accounts, Steven C. Harper concluded that miracles and spirit manifestations "came usually in small groups of believers or among those on the brink of baptism."[43] There were no reports of stupendous public miracles as signs of the Restoration, just individual healings, infrequent exorcisms, and reports of "speaking in tongues."[44]

The *reports* of the healings were far more important than the actual mended bodies because the reports provided precious attention and a way to transcend publicly the claims of competing "sects." Most important, whether actual supernatural events occurred or not, was the fact that the Mormons were *open* to miracles such as healing, exorcism, and latter-day revelation. This openness yet again set the LDS primitivism over and above the other primitivisms, which generally taught that divine messages and miraculous works had passed with the end of the apostolic age. Given the fact that the New Testament paints a picture of Jesus and the apostles awash in healings and miracles, reasonable people looking for "the one true Church" vis-à-vis the New Testament would have been imprudent not to give the Mormon message, with its openness to such divine actions in their own day, careful attention.

There was one other important "rational" factor in the Mormon variety of primitivism that was influential in persuading thinking seekers of the primacy of the LDS Restoration as opposed to other types. Just as Joseph Smith had an unimpeded connection to God as a latter-day prophet, so the LDS Church had an unimpeded connection with Jesus and the apostolic church—a connection that was, in LDS thinking, impossible for other restorationists to achieve. In June of 1844, just nine days before his death in the Carthage jail in Illinois, Smith himself summed up the type of hyper-primitivist argument that had been successful against the Protestant competitors on the mission field:

> The old Catholic church traditions are worth more than all you have said. Here is a principle of logic that most men have no more sense than to adopt. I will illustrate it by an old apple tree. Here jumps off a branch and says, I am the true tree, and you are corrupt. If the whole tree is corrupt, are not its branches corrupt? If the Catholic religion is a false religion, how can any true religion come out of it? If the Catholic church is bad, how can any good thing come out of it? The character of the old churches have always been slandered by all apostates since the world began. . . . Did I build on any other man's foundation? I have got all the truth the Christian world possessed, and an independent revelation in the bargain, and God will bear me off triumphant. . . . I would still go on, and show you proof upon proofs; all the Bible is equal in support of this doctrine, one part as another.[45]

Anti-Roman Catholic rhetoric was a large part of the currency of the restoration economy, and the Mormons used it very effectively against their primitivist counterparts. The "principle of logic" that Smith pointed out is one by which Mormons were able to hoist the "sectarians" on their own petard. After all, the Protestants were by definition an offshoot of the very church they pilloried. Because of the common vitriolic rhetoric, the Mormons had a point that could be persuasive: it was absurd to think that something good could have been spun off or been birthed by such a corrupt and demonic system as Roman Catholicism. Early convert Joel Johnson listed this as the number one reason to embrace Mormonism rather than the competing sects: "Firstly, that as all Protestant sects had sprung from the Church of Rome, they have no more authority ... than the Church of Rome, and if she was the mother of harlots, they must consequently be her daughters; therefore none of them could be called the Church of Christ."[46]

The sources of the anti-Catholic sentiments and their ubiquity in the colonies and the young republic are well known.[47] Likewise well known is the fact that the anti-papal expressions could be used to support a wide range of causes. But what better cause than that of the Protestant restorationists seeking to throw off the shackles of corrupt human tradition bequeathed it by the "whore of Babylon" herself? Although some in the "burned-over district" (so-called because it was a hotbed of religious fervor and revival movements) and beyond may never have had contact with a Roman Catholic, they were certainly familiar with periodicals such as *The Protestant, Priestcraft Exposed and Primitive Religion Defended,* and *The Anti-Romanist* that painted the picture of nefarious apostates "covering their hypocrisy with the cloak of *religion,* and with more than serpent's guile, worming themselves into the confidence and affections of their unsuspecting victims."[48] Even a more mainstream newspaper like the *Rochester Observer* used language such as "the Beast" and the "mother of abominations" to describe the Roman Church.

Mormons were certainly not opposed to using the nativist rhetoric themselves, for it served their restorationist ideals well. Indeed, Fawn M. Brodie has pointed out that early in the writing of the Book of Mormon, Smith vigorously attacked the Catholic Church. She pointed out that 1 Nephi 13 and 14 refer (prophetically, of course) to "that great and abominable church, which is the mother of abominations, whose founder is the devil."[49] Apostles and other missionaries of the early LDS Church not infrequently joined the founder in these types of expressions.[50] The Mormons saw their own use of nativist speech and writing as thoroughly legitimate, but for the Protestants of their day, it was a sign of the greatest myopia and hypocrisy. Even though restoration-minded preachers like Alexander Campbell called for the complete "casting off human creeds and traditions, Catholic and Protestant," the Mormons argued that try as they might, they would not be able to do it, because it was from those traditions that they derived their "authority and priesthood."[51]

The distinct advantage for the early LDS in the rivalry of the primitivist environment was having a fresh encounter with the Father, the Son, John the

Baptist, and the apostles in modern times that allowed them conceptually to make a cleaner break from the past than their restorationist competitors. The "authority" granted to them from the true holders of the "keys," allowed them to present their movement as having leapfrogged the long historical trail of religious apostasy and corruption. Indeed, as Jan Shipps noted, "the very first Mormons did not merely have a past that differed from the past of other nineteenth-century Americans; they had no recent past at all. . . . The 'Great Apostasy' . . . left the Saints with an enormous 1,400- to 1,800-year lacuna in their religious history." Due to this huge hiatus, the parallels they saw between their experiences and biblical characters made much more sense to them.[52] The Mormons stood on no one's shoulders but those of the New Testament figures themselves.

More Reasonable Beliefs

Another important factor that early converts declared to be influential was that the LDS preachers seemed to be clearing up intractable doctrinal conflicts and controversies that appeared ever-present on the religious landscape of the new republic—especially in revival regions such as western New York. Joseph Smith's several statements in the canonical account of his "first vision" present this at the outset as a key problem to be solved by any restoration of the true faith. Smith recalled that his mind was

> at times greatly excited, the cry and the tumult were so greatly incessant. The Presbyterians were most decided against the Baptists and Methodists, and used all their powers of both reason and sophistry to prove their errors, or, at least to make people think they were in error. On the other hand, the Baptists and Methodists in their turn were equally zealous in endeavoring to establish their own tenets and disprove all others. In the midst of this tumult of opinions, I often said to myself: What is to be done? Who of all these parties are right; or, are they all wrong together?[53]

Although there is much to doubt about Smith's rendition of his encounter with the divine "personages" in the woods of Palmyra, no one doubts that the apparent religious tumult of his day was a real and signifi-cant driving force for him in devoting his life to a breakaway religious cause. To the interested observer at the time, the Christian denominations—that in retrospect had tremendous commonality of belief—seemed to be as dif-ferent as Muslims and Buddhists might seem to us today. The inter- and intra-denominational battles were noteworthy for their rancor.[54] Hence for those truly concerned about the states of their souls, this was a situation of grave concern. There was also a sense that the "priests" and "professors" of traditional Christianity had led the faithful astray on a number of doctrines that simply did not concur with the way the world looked in the more enlightened and democratic age of the early 1800s. Authoritative alternatives to traditional stances on these problems in theology were therefore alluring to thoughtful seekers.

For instance, the LDS notion of a universal atonement of Christ was especially attractive. In a reaction to the "Calvinist-Baptist" doctrine that seemed to be offering a range of "unreasonable" ideas like a capricious God, no human freedom, original sin, and salvation only for the predestined, the idea that one could rescue God and man from such apparent injustices was utterly intriguing. Also attractive was the throwing out of the idea of salvation as a passive religious experience and replacing it with "salvation imminently accessible and immediately available." Nathan O. Hatch has observed that the populist religious movements of the day seemed to many to be offering a more reasonable approach to some of the difficult issues, and that the Mormons were no different. "The argument against Calvinism pitted enlightened common sense against scholastic metaphysics of the educated elite," Hatch wrote. "As people became more insistent on thinking theologically for themselves, the carefully wrought dogmas of Calvin, Edwards, and Hopkins were dismissed as 'the senseless jargon of election and reprobation.'"[55] Hatch cited several confused seekers of the era who were relieved to hear the "Methodist gospel" over against the Calvinist teaching that left so many questions unanswered. Said one Billy Hibbard of a Methodist preacher he encountered, "I heard for the first time, a doctrine that I could understand. There was no contradiction, but he could prove his doctrine from scripture and reason."[56] Humorous barbs from frontier preachers about Calvinist orthodoxy became standard fare, setting the stage well before Smith began his ministry. Popular songs with lyrics such as the following circulated:

If this be the way,
As some preachers say,
That all things were order'd by fate;
I'll not spend my pence,
To pay for nonsense,
If nothing will alter my state.[57]

The Mormons joined in this chorus, but as in other areas of popular religious thought at the time, they went several steps further than many of the competing primitivists in the denouncement of strict Calvinist theology. Smith seemed to have a tremendous sense for the populist religious "marketplace," and he put his prophetic stamp of approval on a collection of doctrines and methods of delivery that hit the mark with religious seekers—at least enough to get his movement off the ground.[58] For instance, in addition to doing away with predestination and reinstating a commonsense notion of human freedom to respond to the gospel—something with which other restorationists were in line—he also included certain aspects of universalism likely gleaned from his father, Joseph Smith Sr., and his grandfather, Asael Smith, that were unusually attractive in his part of the country.[59] The notion of universal salvation could take on different details depending on which group was proffering it, but all of them worked toward banishing the notion of eternal conscious punishment in a place of unfathomable torment.[60] Universalism was one of the strongest points of intersection between the Enlightenment and Protestant theology and was an important component in what I have elsewhere called the "village Enlightenment"—the way in which religious people in rural areas and on the frontier co-opted and modified concepts from the elite Enlightenment to serve their own needs.[61]

If one were clever enough to make a biblical case for some type of universalism (no easy task, but many thought they had achieved it[62]), one would have a powerful tool to solve a number of problems that troubled thinking people. The LDS conception of the afterlife was just such a tool. The only humans that would ultimately be lost were a handful of "cognizant apostates" who "suffered themselves through the power of the devil to be overcome," or in other words, "the sons of perdition who deny the Son after the Father has revealed him."[63] "*All others*," wrote modern LDS apostle Bruce R. McConkie, "are saved from death, hell, the devil, and endless torment."[64] This was obviously not a pure universalism in that some—the very few most diabolical and recalcitrant, who simply would not turn no matter what light was given them—would be lost. Ironically, although Mormonism has traditionally embraced a modified universalism, the Book of Mormon itself contains what must be read as anti-universalist rhetoric. On closer examination, though, one could argue that its main focus seems to be against those who believe in *no punishment at all* after death for the wicked—a notion that some groups of universalists were also against because of its apparent injustice toward the truly wicked.[65] Either way, early convert Zerah Pulsipher found in Mormonism just what he had been looking for—a spiritually vital religion that for the most part excluded "souls left in Hell fire to all eternity." He had heard about "an ancient record or Golden Bible" and thought "it might be something that would give light to my mind upon principles that I had been thinking of for years." Pulsipher "read it through twice and gave it a thorough investigation and believed it was true."[66]

Although the Book of Mormon seemed to have a mixed message on universalism, Joseph Smith and Sidney Rigdon removed any lingering ambiguity concerning the LDS position on the final destination of the dead in an 1832 revelation on the topic (D&C 76) that helped set the course for the Mormon view to the present day.[67] Everyone in the next life (except for the small handful of "sons of perdition") would ultimately enter (perhaps after a limited time in a purgatorial setting) one of the "three degrees of glory" of which even the lowest level (the telestial) has a glory that "surpasses all understanding" (D&C 76:89). Given the options offered by religious competitors, Smith and Rigdon may have revealed the most attractive formula on the frontier. They seemed to include the best aspects of all the afterlife scenarios available: postmortem opportunities for salvation, limited punishment for those who really deserve it, and eventual paradise for everyone except (as a popular sense of justice demanded) the devil, his demons, and their intractable followers. Whether it was intentional or not, this "degrees of glory" revelation, which included the "Celestial kingdom" as the highest level and the "Terrestrial kingdom" in the middle,[68] provided the answer to another important question that was probably being asked by early seekers: Why must I join the church if in the end all are going to be saved anyway? Answer: to have a shot at the highest state of glory.[69]

The universal nature of the atonement taught in the early LDS movement offered answers to other troubling questions—especially about the eternal destiny of several classes of people. What was the final fate of innocent children? Those not able to respond? Those who had never heard the gospel? Getting a definitive answer to these questions from the Bible, and traditional Christian theology seemed unlikely—especially in the chaotic environment of the burned-over district. The Bible simply did not address the questions directly, and the answers different Protestant church leaders derived by inference from the text contained elements of doubt by scriptural necessity. Not so in the LDS system.[70] Perhaps one of the greatest comforts that the average person found in the Book of Mormon in a day when childhood mortality was many times higher than it is today was a definitive answer to the first question. The death of young children was a ubiquitous source of pain and grief for people of the time; hence, the authority of the reported words of Christ himself in Moroni 8 must have been a profound comfort. The text taught that "little children are whole" and "alive in Christ," for they are "not capable of committing sin"; and it reassured parents that if they only "repent and be baptized, and humble themselves" they will be "saved with their little children."[71]

A similar message answered the perennial question about the ultimate fate of the unevangelized, that is, those who had never had the proper opportunity to hear and respond to the LDS gospel. As Smith and Rigdon prophesied in 1832 and again in 1836, "All who have died without a knowledge of this Gospel, who would have received it if they had been permitted to tarry, shall be heirs of the celestial kingdom."[72] In Smith's thinking, though, an official LDS baptismal rite could not be waived even for those departed before the Restoration. Hence, in a revelation that seemed to tie up the loose ends of the LDS system—and that certainly went further than any religious competitor on the scene—Smith instituted baptism for the dead, which opened the door to all generations past to have their encounter with the Mormon message of salvation. In an 1840 letter and an 1841 revelation, Smith provided a means by which living saints could be baptized on behalf of departed relatives (and several decades later, on behalf of just about anyone) to ensure their full opportunity to be saved. "You will undoubtedly see its consistency and reasonableness," Smith wrote after preaching on it for the first time in a heartfelt response to a woman who had lost an unbaptized son, for "it presents the Gospel of Christ in probably a more enlarged scale than some have imagined it"—an assertion that would certainly have been a dramatic understatement to Smith's non-LDS contemporaries.[73] The expanse of the salvation opportunities enchanted early converts like Benjamin Brown, who found the LDS position on the afterlife far more compelling than the other options such as "the Universalist system," which before his introduction to Mormonism he considered "the most reasonable of the various denominations."[74]

The apologetic power of the LDS claim to have solved many of the problems at the root of the Christian infighting simply cannot be minimized. In 1837 Apostle Parley Pratt capitalized on this power in his little book, *A Voice of Warning*, perhaps the most important early noncanonical Mormon book, in which he included a chapter entitled "A Contrast Between the Doctrine of Christ and the False Doctrines of the Nineteenth Century." In juxtaposed columns, Pratt set forth the "Doctrine of Men" on one side and the LDS answer called the "Doctrine of Christ" on the other—an arrangement that he thought provided an apologetic rout of apostate Christianity. This book circulated widely and, as LDS document scholars Peter Crawley and Chad Flake maintained, "erected a standard for all future Mormon pamphleteers . . . which would be used by others for the next hundred years."[75] Missionaries like Pratt "competed directly and intensely for converts, confident that their message could stand up well in head-to-head encounters with other proselyters."[76]

The persuasive power of popular doctrinal repackaging may have had a greater affect on potential converts than other aspects of the early Mormon faith. Indeed, Steven C. Harper reiterated an important point made by historian of Mormonism, Klaus Hansen, twenty years earlier. Based on the words of early converts, it was not the supernatural origins of the Book of Mormon, the modern prophet, and priesthood authority that seemed to help most people to embrace the extraordinary doctrines held by the Latter-day Saints. Rather, it was the reverse. The extraordinary doctrines and the popular problems that they seemed to solve helped many along the road to the acceptance of all the rest.[77] The offering of ostensible solutions to age-old theological conundrums was one of the strongest points of resonance within the popular Enlightenment culture and was heralded by the LDS evangelists of the time. These proffered solutions played the role of a stepladder for many to get over the implausibility of Smith's visions, his prophethood, and the fantastic story of his discovery and translation of the Book of Mormon.

A New Cloud of Witnesses

In response to the Enlightenment skepticism in Europe and North America, apologists for the traditional view of the Christian faith had established several lines of argument to defend the authenticity of the Bible, the biblical miracles, and the work and words of Christ. Every line of argument they had that pointed back to the historicity of Christ and the supernatural feats surrounding him at some point included the testimony of the apostolic witnesses of Jesus and his resurrection.[78] Authentic and reliable witnesses and testimony of the ancients and their texts had become the backbone of the defense of Christianity against the enlightened deists, rationalists, and skeptics who were still making their case in Smith's day. Indeed, Robert N. Hullinger has envisioned the real impetus behind Smith's religious activities, especially the writing of the Book of Mormon, to be his "intention to defend

God" in the face of deism and Enlightenment skepticism.[79] In my view, Hullinger's focus was too narrow in that there was much more to Smith's program than just his response to Christianity's Enlightenment foes.[80] But I do believe that Hullinger's thesis was one important aspect of Smith's program—especially with regard to reestablishing a strong set of latter-day witnesses and testimonies to help in the restoration of Christianity in the face of such challenges. If the modern foes of Christianity could be repelled by the testimony of witnesses from ancient times, how much more so by the witnesses of God's supernatural intervention in their own day.[81]

Everyone who opened the Book of Mormon encountered these new witnesses—in this case the signed testimony of eleven witnesses who were alive in their own day.[82] Eight of the witnesses testified to seeing the engraved plates of gold with "the appearance of ancient work and of curious workmanship."[83] Three others testified to seeing the plates, to seeing an angel that accompanied them, and to hearing the voice of God. This was not unlike the biblical witness of the Apostle John, who also expressed his testimony in resolute empirical language: that "which we have heard, which we have seen with our eyes, which we have looked at and our hands have touched—this we proclaim concerning the Word of life" (1 John 1:1). Like jurors hearing testimony in a trial, converts like Eli Gilbert were won over by this evidence. "I read it again and again with close attention and prayer. I examined the proof; the witnesses, and all other testimony," he reported. And he decided that the rules of the game were the same for both the Bible and the Book of Mormon; the witnesses confirmed them both. "If I let go the book of Mormon," he reasoned, "the bible might also go down by the same rule."[84]

Not only did the Book of Mormon contain the statements of living witnesses, but the very fact that it existed was itself a powerful and tangible witness for the first generation of the Restoration era. As Leonard Arrington and Katherine Hanson Shirts confirmed, "The Book of Mormon *itself* was conceived as another piece of evidence 'to the convincing of the Jew and Gentile that Jesus is the Christ, the Eternal God.'" Unlike doctrines, creeds, and other ideas that could be more easily ignored or passed off, the tangible nature of a published text claiming to be on par with the Holy Bible "had to be accounted for in some specific way." The very fact that it was there and seemed credible to some was a real leg up on the competition. But the fact that it also invited investigation and seemed to be in fact something testable—whether or not it could pass any such tests—was in and of itself persuasive. Add to that the notion that the text contained features that "within the frame of reference at the time" would have excited "a modern marketing expert," and you had a tangible product that, properly presented, had the ability to propel the movement to the front of the primitivist pack. Such was the Book of Mormon as witness.[85]

Of course, there were other aspects of the LDS schema that "witnessed" to the truth of the Restoration. The very existence of latter-day prophets, apostles, priests, and other biblical accoutrements helped to give the impression that ancient times had dawned anew. There were also abundant personal testimonies of LDS converts about their own experience of the Holy Spirit's witness to their hearts. I will not cover that aspect because at that point the Mormons competed on a level playing field. Almost all of the frontier preachers and their converts could and did claim parallel experiences. However, I must point out that although I am not addressing personal experience here, some type of internal "witness" was the most commonly mentioned factor in LDS conversion.[86] After all, not everyone, perhaps not even most, needed external substantiation. On the other hand, the reports are also clear that it was not at all uncommon for a variety of external evidences to lead a seeker to the point of conversion. Some thoughtful people on the frontier, looking for a blend of the "revelatory and the empirical," found what they were looking for in the LDS movement.

A Tailor-made Restoration

Although some of the issues and evidence that attracted early converts may not be particularly persuasive today, early Mormonism seemed to provide a view of the world that had a special resonance for the popular nineteenth-century American mind. Indeed, it appeared almost tailor-made. I agree with Klaus J. Hansen that given what the people of this time were looking for, "if Mormonism had not already existed, it would have had to be invented."[87] I also agree with Fawn M. Brodie that the best explanation points, not to Smith's ignorance or delusions, but to "his responsiveness to the provincial opinions of his time.... His mind was open to all intellectual influences, from whatever province they might blow."[88] Gordon Wood's influential essay, "Evangelical America and Early Mormonism," was especially persuasive on this point. Wood showed that the complex questions raised during the Reformation and the Enlightenment, usually only seriously entertained by the educated elite, had by Joseph Smith's generation penetrated every aspect of American popular culture.[89]

To be sure, given the Enlightenment currents swirling about at the popular level, traditional Christians at the time had their hands full reconciling their faith with these new ways of looking at the world. Add to this mix the democratic ideals of the young republic and the individualism of the frontier—both of which affected popular religious thought at the time—and you had a situation that was going to take a generation or two for Christian theologians and laypersons to sort out in an intellectually satisfying way. In this milieu, the advent of the prophet, the Book of Mormon, and the restored church was in many respects a truncation of the more conventional path to a coherent view of their world. From this standpoint, Joseph Smith was himself an apologist for Christianity—a man with one foot in the Scriptures and another in the controversies of his day. But his method of reconciliation was dramatically to reenvision Christianity to the point of creating, in Jan Shipps' words, "a new religious tradition."[90]

The "Keys" to a Global Apologetic Vision

The experiences of early converts have helped to confirm the apologetic nature of Joseph Smith's mission and the way in which the LDS message seemed to answer nagging questions being asked about religion by thinking people of his day. But if this observation is accurate, one might expect the apologetic tone set in the first generation to carry on to the next. Not only did this aspect of the faith carry over, but it was magnified many times in some of the most prominent figures. Perhaps the best example of this is found in the lives and work of two of the original twelve apostles, the brothers Orson (1811–81) and Parley P. Pratt (1807–57). The Pratts were the most influential writers and the closest the young church would come to having bona fide intellectuals in their midst.[91] Writing at the LDS Church centennial in 1930, John Henry Evans wrote that there simply was "no leader of the intellectual stature of Orson Pratt" in "the first hundred years of 'Mormonism.'"[92] His brother Parley has been called by historians "the father of Mormon intellectuals" and "one of the seminal intellectual figures in [LDS] Church history."[93] They were also the two most vibrant and prolific apologists for LDS doctrines and the new Mormon view of the world. Both had enough contact with Smith from the start to have captured the apologetic ethos of the founder, and both lived long enough and wrote enough focused material of an apologetic nature to set the course for an enduring tradition.

Perhaps due to their extensive missionary travels, which included visits to intellectual centers in the United States and abroad, the Pratts saw better than most that the utterances of the prophet contained key elements for an intellectual revolution and not just an extended religious revival. Both of them believed that due to this unique source of revelational data, they were able to solve serious intellectual problems that bedeviled the rest of humankind—they believed they could see fully where others saw only in part. Hence, of special interest to the Pratts were Smith's teachings that had obvious implications for philosophy and science in their day: the ultimate material essence and eternality of the cosmos, the corporeality and plurality of the gods, the nature of the will and intelligence, the premortal existence of humans, and so on. From these building blocks of thought, they constructed what they believed was an unassailable worldview that answered questions that had stumped generation after generation of the world's most profound thinkers and scholars.[94] Parley Pratt's magnum opus, the *Key to the Science of Theology*, was a good example of this LDS frame of mind. Finished two years before his murder in Arkansas in 1857, his book captured the remarkable optimism, enthusiasm, and certitude that characterized the intellectual activities on behalf of the church in this new age:

> It should be a matter of serious thought and investigation, without respect to party, sect, or creed, whether there should not, in the very nature of circumstances and future Millennial hopes, be an entire remodeling, or reorganization of religious society, upon the broad basis of revealed knowledge, tangible fact, and philosophical, scientific and spiritual Truth, a universal "standard" of immutable Truth, instead of numberless systems founded on uncertainty, opinion, mere human impression, or conjecture.[95]

For Parley Pratt, the competitive religious marketplace was still very much alive a quarter-century after the founding of the church. Indeed, for him the market had expanded dramatically. He was no longer competing against primitivist opponents in backwoods villages and towns. He was prepared to take on "systems" of thought worldwide. As a foundation for this global apologetic vision, he offered his treatise, the *Key*, which laid out the plan (à la Joseph Smith) for proper thinking on nearly every popularly debated issue of the mid-nineteenth century.

Perhaps it was because he lived several decades longer, but Orson Pratt thought that the springboard of Mormon revelation could propel him even further.[96] Orson wrote what I think is the most philosophically literate LDS treatise of his day. In the *Absurdities of Immaterialism*, Pratt argued valiantly, but by no means flawlessly, for an LDS version of materialism in response to an exposé against "mormo-materialism" by a British minister.[97] (See J. P. Moreland's essay in this volume for a modern philosophical perspective on their debate.) Later Orson, an avid amateur scientist and mathematician, tried his hand at no less than reworking and hence "saving" several of the scientific theories of the great Enlightenment icon Sir Isaac Newton. Pratt saw Newton as a great hero, but he also saw that important correctives were needed in light of the prophetic revelation that "there is no such thing as immaterial matter" (or substance).[98] Newton's law of gravity postulated *immaterial* forces acting between all particles or bodies with mass in the universe, but the very notion of immateriality was contradicted by LDS revelation. The apostle therefore reformulated Newton's law into the "Self-moving Theory" in which particles intelligently willed to "approach" one another instead of being passively "attracted" by immaterial (read *nonexistent* by Pratt) forces. The same mathematical law for gravitation applied, but in Pratt's view the particles *knew* the law and followed it *willfully* with a force "which varies inversely with the square of the distance."[99] In even grander fashion, Pratt produced a work entitled the *Key to the Universe,* in which he presented a "new theory" of celestial mechanics built on the Mormon materialist metaphysic. He eliminated Newton's proposed nonmaterial universal ether and replaced it with a material (or "ponderable") version that helped to strike a perfect balance between gravitational attraction and the oceans of "resisting ethereal medium."[100]

Although he had been thinking about this theory for decades, the *Key to the Universe* (1879) was Orson Pratt's last published work. Orson's *Key,* like his brother Parley's, represented the pinnacle of LDS apologetics in the nineteenth century—especially with Orson's definitive correctives to the greatest figure of the Enlightenment, Lord Verulam himself.[101] In a way, Pratt reprised the sacred story of the initial visitation to young Joseph when "An angel from on high, / The long, long silence broke." Orson, too, humbly sought answers to the great cultural questions of his day after generations of the most learned priests and professors had tried. In the midst of the intellectual confusion, he too sought wisdom from God; and in response, long-hidden scientific laws were revealed and restored through him.[102] Pratt looked like a real apostle going about his business.

You Can't Go Home Again

Aside from the Pratts and other midcentury missionaries, the prominence of the LDS apologetic tradition did wane somewhat in the era that followed the death of the founder in 1844 for two primary reasons. First, the next prophet-leader, Brigham Young, did not give his attention to it the way Joseph Smith had. Young focused his mental energies more on the logistical and political issues involved in the emigration and establishment of the church in the Great Basin of the Western United States. Second, as the church moved to the far reaches of the frontier, the competition for religious seekers that birthed and fueled the apologetic endeavors of the earlier years was simply not an issue in such isolation. Nevertheless, those on the mission field, like the brothers Pratt, especially in parts of North America and Europe, found the continued promulgation and defense of the Mormon view of the world essential to their efforts.

Not until the turn of the century did other LDS luminaries begin taking on the daunting task of explaining and defending the faith. The well-educated scientists James E. Talmage (1862–1933) and John A. Widtsoe (1872–1952) wrote important works on science and doctrinal issues, many of which are still read today.[103] Their contemporary, B. H. Roberts (1857–1933), set the intellectual bar to new heights for the LDS, being twice voted by modern Mormon scholars as the top intellectual in their history.[104] Roberts wrote in the areas of scripture studies, LDS Church history, and theology; but he "was not a theologian of the first order, as he was not a major historian. He was simply the best theologian and historian that Mormonism had in its first century" or, as another Mormon scholar concluded, the pioneer Utah equivalent of a "Renaissance Man."[105] Ironically, although he was the greatest defender of the LDS faith in the twentieth century, he also wrote one of the most challenging (and, I believe, devastating) books ever written on the difficulties and problems with the Book of Mormon as an authentic ancient text from the Americas.[106]

Mormon philosopher and intellectual leader in his own right Sterling McMurrin, writing in the mid–1980s, lamented, and I believe accurately, that

> Since Roberts's death half a century ago, the Church has suffered a steady decline in matters pertaining to religious thought, a decline accompanied by a growth of irrationalism and anti-intellectualism from which there is no clear indication of recovery in the foreseeable future. Some important sociological studies of Mormonism have been made and an entire generation of competent historians have produced careful and reliable studies of the Church's history. But comparatively little has been done in leadership

circles in matters pertaining to morals, religion, and philosophy, except, of course to enjoin Church members to accept the established doctrine and live lives of virtue. Notwithstanding a brief respite in the 1960s and 1970s, the Church has discouraged its best historians, and it has consistently resisted serious and competent thought in religion and philosophy. Perhaps a resurgence of interest in Roberts's work will point to a more productive future.[107]

I am not sure that Professor McMurrin would view the growth of Mormon apologetic activity in the 1980s and 1990s as "a more productive future"; nevertheless, in response to popular and scholarly challenges from evangelical Christians—and perhaps more importantly, from disaffected Mormon intellectuals—a new generation of LDS scholars has arisen to try to clarify and defend the faith that was—to paraphrase Jude 3—"once *restored* to the Saints." The prolific scripture scholar Hugh W. Nibley inspired the new movement; and the think tank known as "FARMS" (the Foundation for Ancient Research and Mormon Studies), now officially associated with Brigham Young University, has put legs to it by sponsoring the publication of hundreds of pages each year toward the understanding of the LDS scriptures and responding to critics of all stripes.

Although the "apologetic impulse" for most Mormons today will likely never be as intense as it was in the early days when Joseph Smith and his fledgling church saw competition in the religious marketplace of the frontier as their lifeblood, the tradition is still alive among a small coterie of LDS scholars in our own generation.[108] In many ways the current generation of apologists has a much more difficult job facing them. The resonance that many of the LDS theological, philosophical, and scientific statements had with the popular nineteenth-century mind has passed; hence, new ways of packaging and presenting the Mormon message have been necessary. Indeed, this is why historians are often taken aback by the conceptual gulf that separates the vision of the current generation from that of the founders.[109]

Also separating the LDS generations is the enthusiasm the founders had that they would rebuild global temples of thought on the foundations of latter-day revelation—revelation that would be proven objectively true in all of the arts and sciences.[110] The current generation, however, still awaits a piece of direct "threshold" evidence like the discovery of the "reformed Egyptian" language,[111] or an ancient pillar somewhere in the Western Hemisphere with an inscription confirming the existence of Nephite or

Jaredite civilizations (not unlike the kinds of confirmatory discoveries made for the Bible in our century).[112] In lieu of a major objective confirmation for the world to see, modern LDS apologists and scholars regularly conclude with a common call for a spiritual affirmation of key factual claims, so that those "who desire a fully satisfying resolution of these questions will do best to accept Moroni's invitation to find their own spiritual witness of the [Book of Mormon's] truth through personal study and prayer."[113]

Nineteenth-century America was fertile ground for a number of new religious movements with astonishingly similar theological commitments.[114] I believe the evidence is utterly compelling that Joseph Smith acquired most of his ideas from the same environment that spawned some of the exact same thinking—without divine visitations—in leaders such as spiritualist Andrew Jackson Davis, mind-cure founder Phineas Parkhurst Quimby, and phrenologist Orson S. Fowler.[115] But the popular intellectual atmosphere that supported such movements has itself moved on, and those in our day who wish to defend the LDS Restoration cannot recapture the advantage their forebears enjoyed.

Conclusion

Like its early nineteenth-century counterpart, the modern LDS Church has to live with certain factual—and in some cases testable—claims about specific historical events surrounding its origin as well as claims about ancient history in the Western Hemisphere. These kinds of claims guarantee that the "apologetic impulse" in one form or another will continue, for there will always be some in the church who believe that LDS faith and history should never be compartmentalized. A faithful few will always try valiantly to reconcile LDS teachings with the historical record in the most sophisticated way possible. If Orson or Parley Pratt were alive today, I believe they would be first in line to join the revitalized effort to defend the LDS faith in this manner.

Evangelical Christians who work in the area of Mormon studies for missionary purposes would do well to notice this longstanding apologetic impulse. Empty charges of deception, gullibility, and ignorance did not do well in the early years of Mormonism and will do even less well today. There are many Latter-day Saints who take their faith very seriously on an intellectual level and have dedicated their careers to reconciling the conflicts and problems found in Mormon history, doctrine, and scripture—often earning doctorates in key disciplines to equip themselves for the task. Successful

Christian missionaries to the Latter-day Saints will be the ones who understand the depth and breadth of the new Mormon apologetic endeavor and the historical context from which their apologetic emerges.

In my opinion, the new Mormon apologists have a very long way to go to produce a convincing case for the truth of the Restoration through Joseph Smith Jr. I do not envy their task, because so many of the raw materials for a robust defense are missing. Mormon scholars have inherited a less-than-coherent metaphysic, a continued mistrust of the Bible, some difficult theological conundrums, and a devastating drought of "threshold" evidence that does not allow the broader scholarly community to take seriously the claims made in and about LDS sacred texts. The LDS movement that once resonated with popular nineteenth-century thinking is struggling to find new chords to strike at the beginning of the twenty-first century. In many respects, evangelical Christians in America are rediscovering their intellectual heritage at the same time. Hence, the time is ripe for a new type of dialogue between evangelicals and the Latter-day Saints. I am therefore grateful to the editors and contributors of this volume for setting a new tone for the dialogue and for caring enough about the Mormon people in our own day to address "the new Mormon challenge" at the highest levels and to do so with "gentleness and reverence" (1 Pet 3:15).

2

AND THE SAINTS
GO MARCHING ON
The New Mormon Challenge
for World Missions, Apologetics,
and Theology

CARL MOSSER

Carl Mosser is a Ph.D. candidate in New Testament studies
at the University of St. Andrews, Scotland. Mosser earned
a B.A. in biblical languages from LIFE Bible College; an
M.A. in theology, an M.A. in New Testament, and an M.A.
in philosophy of religion and ethics from Talbot School of
Theology; and a Th.M. in philosophy of religion/apologet-
ics from Fuller Theological Seminary. He has published significant articles on Mormonism in *Trinity Journal* and the
FARMS Review of Books (an LDS publication).

O f all the "alternative religious movements" birthed in the last 250 years,
Mormonism is by far the most successful. It has achieved a high degree
of social acceptability, and its members have an influence in the realms of
politics and corporate business that is disproportionate to their numbers.

The Church of Jesus Christ of Latter-day Saints, many of its leaders having been successful businessmen prior to accepting church callings, has, over the years, shrewdly built up impressive financial holdings to support its religious goals. But two things, perhaps, mark Mormonism's success more than anything else: the LDS Church's growth from 6 members at its founding in 1830 to over 11 million today, and the massive missionary force it fields around the world, making Mormonism continually visible to outsiders.

Evangelicals have often underestimated the challenge Mormonism's success poses to evangelism and world missions, if they have considered it at all. This problem is exacerbated by the fact that as a community, evangelicals tend to be poorly informed about advances in LDS apologetics and theology. Latter-day Saints, unlike the members of most other New Religious Movements or "cults,"[1] have begun to enter the academy and produce genuine works of scholarship that have apologetic significance for Mormon truth claims. They have also begun to develop their theology in ways that render many traditional portraits and, in turn, the critiques based on those portraits, inaccurate and outdated. Some of the developments in LDS theology are encouraging; it is important to keep track of all of them if evangelicals are to formulate more effective responses to those LDS teachings that are incompatible with true Christian faith.

It is the purpose of this chapter to discuss some of the challenges as well as some of the opportunities that Mormonism presents to evangelicals in the areas of world missions, apologetics, and theology. Along with the previous chapter, this one is largely descriptive in nature and seeks to provide some background for understanding the context and development of the LDS scholarship to which subsequent chapters respond. Unlike the other chapters in this book, this one is addressed primarily to evangelicals in, or preparing for, positions of leadership in denominational, parachurch, academic, and local church settings rather than to a general evangelical and LDS audience. Of course, I expect others to "eavesdrop," and I will occasionally direct comments to other readers.

The chapter will be divided into four main parts. The first will focus on Mormonism's rapid growth in recent years, on its missionary program, and on predictions that it will soon attain the status of a world religion. I will argue that though it may not be accurate to say that Mormonism will soon become a world religion, the predictions of phenomenal growth nonetheless appear sound and should not be shrugged off as some have attempted to do. The specific way in which Mormon growth occurs should be of particular concern to missiologists, missionaries, and pastors. In the second part I will discuss the increasing presence of LDS scholars in the academy and how this translates into an apologetic challenge that requires the response of evangelical Bible scholars, historians, and philosophers. The subsequent essays in this book are an initial response to this challenge, but it will be evident that the skills of other evangelical scholars could be profitably put to use in service of the people of God and the evangelization of Mormonism.[2] In the third part I will discuss some important trends in contemporary Mormon theology and the opportunity this presents to evangelical theologians. The final part of the chapter will make some suggestions about how the evangelical community can effectively meet Mormonism's challenges.

Mormonism's Challenge for World Missions

The Next World Religion?

In 1969 Jack W. Carlson boldly predicted that by the year 2000 the Mormon population of the world would rise from 2.6 million of the world's 3 billion inhabitants to 8.5 million of a projected 5 billion inhabitants.[3] Carlson was mistaken. The world's population and LDS Church membership both exceeded his predictions, but not equally. World population grew approximately 20 percent higher than predicted; LDS membership exceeded the prediction by 29 percent. In the year 2000, world population reached 6.1 billion persons, and LDS Church membership surpassed 11 million members (with slightly more than half living outside the United States).

In 1984 Rodney Stark, the eminent sociologist of religion and professor at the University of Washington, wrote an important article in which he made an even bolder prediction. He claimed that with Mormonism we are witnessing the rise of a new world faith. In that article he attempted to demonstrate "that the Church of Jesus Christ of Latter-day Saints, the Mormons, will soon achieve a worldwide following comparable to that of Islam, Buddhism, Christianity, Hinduism, and the other dominant world faiths." He stated: "Indeed, today they stand on the threshold of becoming the first major faith to appear on earth since the Prophet Mohammed rode out of the desert."[4]

Stark went on to examine the patterns of growth in the then–150 years of Mormonism's existence. He considered various factors that are known to slow the growth of other religious movements and found that Mormonism has historically grown even when those factors were present. This is due largely to the fact that Mormonism is unsurpassed in its missionary efforts and has many social benefits to offer converts. These and other factors favor a continued rate of rapid growth.

Stark initially projected that if Mormonism continues to grow at a somewhat *slower* average rate than it did in the 1960s, 70s, and 80s, it will have a membership of more than 265 million people within a hundred years.[5] In a 1996 update of his original study, comparing his projections with fifteen years of actual growth,[6] Stark found that actual growth *exceeded* his most optimistic prediction by nearly a million persons. If one recalculates from 1997 membership figures with the same rate of growth Stark used in his initial study, Mormonism will have a membership of over 580 million by the end of the century.[7]

One might be skeptical of Stark's projections; many social scientists initially were. Stark reports that after publishing his predictions, he received considerable resistance from peers.[8] Some had assumed that Mormonism's tremendous rate of growth was largely the result of higher-than-average birth rates and that sooner or later those rates would level off. In response, Stark pointed out that most Mormon growth was from converts, not natural increase. He buttressed the point by showing that in 1991 there were 3.97 converts for every child baptized. The ratio has since increased: according to recent data, there are now 4.23 converts for every child baptized.[9] As Stark says, this allows us to see something of immense significance about Mormonism: *at any given moment, the majority of Latter-day Saints are first-generation converts.*[10]

Other colleagues argued that the pool of potential converts was rapidly drying up and would soon be "fished out" and that LDS growth rates would then plummet. Behind this thinking was the view that the worldwide trend toward modernization would inevitably result in the secularization of society. As scientific knowledge increases, religious beliefs will be increasingly viewed as superstitious and implausible; thus, there will be fewer viable converts over which the religions will have to compete for survival. Stark responds by showing that the modernization thesis, widely touted as it has been for 150 years, simply does not correspond to reality and is built on faulty observations. Data suggests that Mormonism, like many conservative religions, including evangelical Christianity, actually tends to thrive amidst the pressures of modernization and secularization.[11] Other studies have confirmed that Mormonism has the capability to respond to modernization and secularization by adaptation without giving up its theological and social con-

2. And the Saints Go Marching On

servatism.[12] Contrary to trends found in other religious denominations, higher education does not tend to have a significant secularizing influence on the membership of the LDS Church.[13] Mormonism also experiences great growth when high numbers of non-LDS people move into traditional LDS strongholds. Despite several decades of "Gentile" influx, the LDS percentage of the population of Utah is higher today than it has been in more than a century. The reason, again, is not larger average family sizes as much as it is conversions. According to Rick Phillips, two of the LDS Church's missions in Utah obtain more converts than any other mission in the United States or Canada.[14]

In a follow-up to his 1984 article, Stark responded to those who criticized him for making a straight-line prediction. He went back to 1880 membership figures and projected Mormon growth between 1880 and 1980 post facto, using the same methods as his original study. He additionally considered several environmental factors that might have slowed Mormon growth during this time: the polygamy crisis of 1890, World War I, the Great Depression, and World War II. His study confirmed that major environmental disruptions like these have historically slowed LDS growth. But it also showed that their overall impact was quite limited. For the entire hundred-year period, despite forty years of wars and depression, his projection was off by only 0.2 percent. With the joy of vindication Stark wrote: "The fact is that straight-line projections will be accurate unless or until something basic changes in the process involved. That is, unless there is a really dramatic shift in the basis on which current Mormon growth rests, the past does reveal the future."[15]

One difficulty with the self-reported membership figures of any religious denomination is knowing how accurate those figures are. Some denominations have been known to deliberately inflate their numbers, and others use faulty means of data collection that result in inflation. In case one should think that the LDS Church has deliberately inflated her official membership figures, as is sometimes suggested, one should note Stark's comments about them: "One of the great scholarly advantages in studying the Mormons," he writes, "is the extraordinary detail and high quality of their records and their recognition that statistics are at least as vital as names and dates."[16] "It is worth noting," he further states, "that Mormon statistics are extremely reliable (is there another denomination that actually sends out auditors to check local figures?).... [T]he research efforts of other denominations shrink to insignificance when compared with the quality, scope, and sophistication of the work of the Mormon social research department. . . . [T]he right data are being collected in the right way."[17]

The membership figures reported by the LDS Church, as with all denominations, do not represent actual church attendance and commitment. As with other groups, the LDS Church has names on its roles of many members who are inactive and people who no longer consider themselves adherents to the faith. But to the degree that any denomination's membership figures indicate anything, the LDS figures are indicative of tremendous growth during the last few decades and the potential for even greater growth in the decades ahead. Thus, I agree with Stark that if there is no change in the process, LDS growth rates will remain close to what they have been during the last three decades, and the Church of Jesus Christ of Latter-day Saints will become one of the world's largest religious organizations within the lifetimes of our children and grandchildren. I do not, however, agree that if LDS membership fully meets or even exceeds Stark's highest projections, this would constitute Mormonism as a world religion. It is worth commenting on this, since predictions about Mormonism's ascendancy to the status of a world religion are sometimes used in propaganda for and against the movement.

Defining precisely what constitutes a world religion is not a simple task, and I will not attempt to do so here. But one thing that should be clear on reflection is that all of the religions commonly classified as world religions have many more characteristics in common than having a large number of adherents. As Douglas Davies rightly points out, approaching the question of a group's potential status as a world religion "is not answered merely by citing membership figures: size of membership needs complementing with the more crucial elements of the power of belief and practice as they extend through a variety of cultural bases."[18] The "cultural bases" Davies lists include such things as distinctive attitudes toward death, ethics, and beliefs about the origin and destiny of the self that are central to cultural presuppositions.[19] It should also be observed that world religions make large contributions to the structures around which much of life is organized in a society—the weekly pattern of work, rest, and worship; holidays and calendars; marriage, sexual norms and customs, and so forth. In short, world religions contribute to cultures in important foundational ways that other religions do not.

According to Davies, "Mormonism seems to possess the basic features required in a world religion but does not manifest all of them to a sufficient degree to make it self-evident that it already possesses that status."[20] In the main, I agree with this. However, when some of the other cultural contributions of the world religions are considered, I think it is more accurate to say that Mormonism possesses many, but not all, of the basic features required of a world religion. When it comes to the important cultural distinctives, a world religion contributes to a society. Here Mormonism is simply not very distinctive; for the most part it simply follows the cultural patterns it has inherited from the Christian society in which it was birthed.

For example, Latter-day Saints worship on Sundays, celebrate Christian holidays like Christmas and Easter, and do not celebrate any distinctively Mormon religious holidays.[21] Even in those areas of the world where Mormonism is the dominant religion—some of the islands in the South Pacific and the "Mormon Corridor" of the Western United States[22]—there is no indication that a distinctively Mormon culture is emerging. To the contrary, Mormonism has developed a distinct subculture, in several respects similar to the evangelical subculture (if you browse in an LDS bookstore, the similarities will be apparent to you). The LDS subculture is clearly a part of the larger "Christian" (i.e., Western) culture and does not appear to be on the road to supplanting it. In non-Christian cultures such as are found in the Middle East, Asia, and parts of Africa, Mormons relate to those cultures in much the same way that Protestants and Catholics do. In the early years of Mormonism's exile in Utah, it looked like a distinctively Mormon culture might indeed arise. Such things as the United Order (a system of communal cooperatives run on LDS principles) and the introduction of the "Deseret Alphabet" would have surely done much to set LDS society apart if they had succeeded. But they failed; and from the early twentieth century to the present, Latter-day Saints have consistently rejected any attempts to segregate Mormon culture from the culture at large. They have, in fact, worked to assimilate Mormonism. The current emphasis on insisting that Mormonism is a Christian faith only further fortifies this trend. Thus, one should conclude that Mormonism is not a world religion. Nor does it appear likely that it will ever become one.[23] Even if it fulfills the highest growth predictions discussed earlier, which appear to be sound, Mormonism lacks some very important cultural elements that would allow for it to ever be classified as a world religion. But this should not lessen evangelical concerns about LDS growth in the least.

How Ought Evangelicals to View This Growth?

How should evangelicals respond to predictions of portentous growth for the LDS Church? Perhaps evangelicals should rejoice. After all, the Church of Jesus Christ of Latter-day Saints claims to be a Christian faith. With respect to many of the battles being fought in the so-called culture wars, evangelicals and Latter-day Saints are allies. Both profess strong commitments to "traditional family values." Both are disturbed by the moral, social, and psychological damage that results from gambling, pornography, drugs, and alcohol. Both resist the pressures to accept extramarital cohabitation, homosexuality, and sexual promiscuity as acceptable "alternative lifestyles." Both are concerned with the increasingly hostile stance public institutions and agencies take toward religion in policy decisions. And the LDS Church has vast financial resources that increase with its membership and that can be used to fight the political battles that must be won in order to reverse the tide of the culture wars.[24] Large financial contributions from the corporate LDS Church and additional giving encouraged by church leaders from its members were significant factors in the outcome of recent political battles over homosexual marriage in Hawaii, Alaska, and California. So too was the activism, talent, and voluntarism of numerous individual Mormons.

It is right for evangelicals, as fellow concerned citizens, to partner with Latter-day Saints in our common causes. We can rejoice that the LDS Church is willing to take unpopular stands similar to our own that are increasingly viewed as politically incorrect and "intolerant." We can also be thankful that the LDS Church liberally commits its financial resources and that LDS members liberally commit their time and talents to these causes. To the degree that these are benefits of LDS Church growth, we can, in a sense, see this growth as a good thing. But given the theological commitments of Mormonism and our fundamental theological commitments as evangelicals, I do not think that we can in good theological conscience view LDS Church growth and predictions of Mormonism ascending to the status of a world religion (even if only in the sense of a very large worldwide religion) as a good thing. The primary reason that we cannot comes from the fact that many Mormon teachings depart radically from biblical and historical Christian faith. Even if Christianity is defined so broadly as to include numerous heterodox movements,[25] I do not believe that at this time Mormonism can be categorized as Christian in any very useful or theologically significant sense—as much as we might hate to see such a noble people outside the faith. This, of course, is a controversial claim and one that Latter-day Saints are often offended by.[26] I will not defend it here since my primary audience for this chapter will already agree and space will simply not permit me to do so (however, see Craig Blomberg's chapter in this volume).[27]

Can We Afford to Shrug Off the Predictions?

Some evangelicals are not bothered by predictions of Mormonism's growth, given the growth rate among evangelical denominations worldwide. In a letter to the editor responding to an article on predictions about Mormonism's growth, Jim Montgomery, president of Dawn Ministries, notes that evangelicalism around the world is growing at a rate of 6 to 7 percent a year.[28] Even if that rate were to drop to 5 percent annually, the current 600 million evangelicals would become more than 30 billion by the time Mormons reach 267 million. "So what's the big deal about 267 million Mormons by AD 2080?" he asks. Several things can be said in reply.

First, Montgomery apparently fails to consider the source of most of Mormonism's convert growth. Almost all converts to Mormonism come from a nominally Christian background. I know of no scientific studies that have determined the precise makeup of the religious background of LDS converts, but according to several "eyeball" estimates I have seen or heard reported, 75–80 percent of Mormon converts come from specifically Protestant backgrounds. (It should be noted, however, that the proportion of converts from Catholic backgrounds is rapidly growing.) A well-known saying within LDS circles, based on the average size of a Baptist church in America, is "We baptize a Baptist church every week." Whatever the actual figures are, the fact is that far more people convert to Mormonism from evangelical churches than vice versa. Second, given the current levels of biblical and theological literacy in evangelical churches and the kinds of converts produced by certain segments of the church growth movement, I am skeptical that evangelicalism is growing in the right kind of way to stave off groups like the Mormons. An increasingly theologically illiterate laity and an entertainment-focused pastoral ministry opens wide the doors of opportunity for Mormonism and other heterodox movements to attract converts from our churches.

Paul Carden observes that "few Christians in the field of missions seem to recognize the multi-faceted threat of the cults around the globe, consistently underestimating their resources, their determination, and the long-term impact they make on evangelism and church-planting."[29] With respect to Mormonism specifically, it must be pointed out that neither the Book of Mormon nor the message of LDS missionaries can make much sense to someone who lacks at least some basic knowledge of the Bible or Christian belief. Latter-day Saints translate the Book of Mormon into many languages; to my knowledge they do not engage in Bible translation, nor are LDS missionaries sent into lands where the Bible has not yet been translated. Mormonism's spread into new cultures is literally dependent on the success of Bible translation organizations like SIL/Wycliffe Bible Translators. Neither does Mormonism's primary message of the restoration of the "fullness of the gospel" make much sense unless there are Christian churches already established that lack this "fullness." Thus, Mormon growth largely depends on the prior success of Protestant and Catholic missionaries. This provides a third important reason why evangelicals cannot afford to shrug off predictions of Mormon growth: Mormon missionaries don't evangelize, they proselytize. Mormonism is religion that gets its life mostly from preexisting forms of Christianity. The predictions of incredible growth for the LDS Church are also predictions of loss for Protestant, Catholic, and to a lesser extent, Orthodox churches—with Protestantism sustaining the greatest losses (though that could easily change).

Fourth, at present the LDS Church has approximately 60,000 missionaries on the field engaged in full-time proselytizing, with an additional 6,000 more engaged in various service assignments (e.g., healthcare workers, craftsmen, and educators). These numbers make the LDS Church the single largest missionary-sending organization in the world.[30] These missionaries convert well over 310,000 people annually. If the size of the LDS missionary force continues to increase proportionate to the growth of the LDS Church, in *fifteen years* there will be 110,000 full time LDS missionaries on the field.[31] These missionaries will be converting more than 672,000 persons annually.[32] Nothing indicates that the growth of the LDS Church or its missionary force will slow down between now and then. In fact, the General Authorities of the LDS Church are actively trying to increase the percentage of eligible men and women who serve missions for the church. Within the next fifty years the LDS Church could easily have a full-time missionary force of 400,000 converting more than 2.5 million people annually. As things now stand it is very possible that the LDS Church's already immense missionary program will, in the not-too-distant future, be larger than all Protestant and Catholic missionary efforts combined.

Montgomery may be optimistic about there being 30 billion evangelicals by the time there are 267 million Mormons. I am not. If evangelicals shrug off predictions of tremendous growth for a religion like Mormonism, they do so at risk to the health of evangelicalism. Most importantly, however, the "big deal" is that in 2080 there will be 267 million (or more) souls mistakenly assuming that they are part of the one true Christian church. Between now and then, hundreds of millions more will have died making this assumption. If we believe that the message of traditional Mormonism is not the same saving message that we find in the New Testament, then we have a moral responsibility to our fellow human beings, including Latter-day Saints and those they would proselytize, to make a big deal of the predictions of LDS growth.

It is clear to me that the current evangelical response to Mormonism (and to New Religious Movements generally) does not significantly retard the spread and growth of the LDS faith (and other NRMs) at the expense of the orthodox Christianity. We must somehow bring about what Stark calls "a change in the process" if we want to prevent Mormonism from becoming one of the largest worldwide faiths at our expense. Something will have to shift the basis on which its current growth rests. I am convinced that a major factor contributing to Mormon growth is the widespread biblical and theological illiteracy among the laity of Protestant and Catholic churches. People in our churches need to be grounded better in basic biblical doctrine. We should also investigate other factors that contribute to LDS growth and redress those that are due to failing within the Christian community. This cannot be accomplished by leaving the task solely up to the numerous small and financially strapped apologetics ministries. Nor are the vast majority of those engaged in such ministry equipped to do all that needs to be done, even if finances and personnel were not so limited. A proper response to Mormonism (and othe NRMs) will require the entire evangelical community.

The World's Fastest Growing Religion?

Before moving on to the next area of challenge, I would like to direct a few comments to LDS readers who may be eavesdropping on the conversation. I have often heard Latter-day Saints make assertions such as this: "Mormonism is the world's fastest growing religion. Do you know why? Because it's the one true church." Others tell me that they regularly hear similar claims. A casual Internet search led me to Web sites using this kind of argument to defend and promote not only Mormonism but also Islam, Buddhism, Scientology, and Baha'i. The idea that being the fastest growing religion is indicative of divine favor seems to be widespread. Though this is not an argument that I have seen LDS scholars make, because it is so widespread at the popular level it is worth noting some of its deep problems.

Of the many claimants to the title, is Mormonism actually "the world's fastest growing religion"? A major problem is that it is simply not possible to determine in any meaningful way which religion is the world's fastest growing. First of all, there simply is not enough reliable data on all the world's religions to make such a determination. Second, what sort of people should be counted as members of a religion? Should these include inactive and merely cultural adherents whose names are on the rolls, or only active participants? And how, exactly, should we distinguish between cultural, active, and inactive members? Third, should we look at percentage growth, sheer numerical growth, or some other index of growth? As far as percentages go, Mormonism is far from being the world's fastest growing religion, since many small religious movements easily beat it. For example, any movement growing from 200 members to 600 members in a year would have an annual growth rate of 300 percent, while Mormonism's rate, as we have pointed out, is around 4.1 percent. If one counts sheer numbers, then the title probably goes to Islam, simply because of the rapid population increases in Muslim societies around the world. Furthermore, how do we determine what counts as a religion for comparative purposes? Should we compare Mormon growth with the growth of the world religions (Christianity, Islam, Judaism, Hinduism, and Buddhism)? Or should it be broken down into major segments of each (e.g., Protestantism, Catholicism, Orthodoxy, Sunni Islam, Shi'a Islam)? Or do we simply compare individual religious organizations? This is the problem of figuring out the best way to compare "apples with apples" rather than "apples with oranges."

It should be clear that all claims to being the world's fastest growing religion are fraught with grave difficulties. Any argument of this type is predicated on an unproven and probably unprovable premise. As Latter-day Saints use this argument, they are usually presupposing the LDS doctrine that there is only one organization on earth that is "the true church" of Jesus Christ. I think what they mean to claim is that the LDS Church is the fastest growing religious organization *that claims to be a Christian church,* not the fastest growing religion per se. But this is really not very helpful. In some parts of the Christian tradition, there are many organizations that consider one another to be part of the same religion, even when "religion" is defined more narrowly than the level of world religions, or even Protestantism, Catholicism, or Orthodoxy. More accurate comparisons might be made with confederated families of denominations, such as the worldwide fellowships of Anglican/Episcopal churches, Lutheran churches, and Reformed churches. Even more helpful would be comparison with identifiable multidenominational movements such as evangelicalism or, more narrowly, Pentecostalism. We have already seen in passing that evangelicalism has a higher worldwide growth rate than Mormonism.

These many problems aside, even when one compares Mormonism with individual organizations within the evangelical Christian tradition, it is clear that the LDS Church is not the fastest growing. Even when confining the comparison to young movements, it is easy to find organizations that are experiencing greater growth both in terms of percentage and in terms of sheer numbers. For example, the Assemblies of God denomination, founded in 1914, eighty-four years after the founding of Mormonism, has approximately 35 million members worldwide—24 million more than the Church of Jesus Christ of the Latter-day Saints. The Assemblies of God hope to reach 100 million members by 2014.[33] There are other deep difficulties with the kind of claim discussed in this subsection, but I think it should be clear enough from the difficulties that have been mentioned that Latter-day Saints should not want to interpret Mormonism's growth as evidence in itself of divine favor. Nor should anyone else interpret numerical growth or size as in itself evidence of divine favor or disfavor.

Mormonism's Challenge for Apologetics

Mormonism and the Academy

Mormonism stands out from other New Religious Movements in its attitude toward higher education and scholarship. The largest private university and the second largest two-year college in the nation are both LDS Church-owned: Brigham Young University in Provo, Utah, and Ricks College in Rexburg, Idaho (soon to become a four-year institution renamed Brigham Young University-Idaho). In addition, the LDS Church operates the LDS Business College, Brigham Young University-Hawaii and the BYU Jerusalem Center for Near Eastern Studies in Israel. The LDS Church's two current four-year schools are both nationally ranked in the annual *U.S. News & World Report* annual survey of colleges and universities.[34] In Virginia, Mormons have established Southern Virginia College as the first independent Mormon college on a model similar to the Christian college movement.[35] As LDS Church-owned schools increasingly turn away students because they have reached full capacity, there is talk of starting more private LDS institutions in the future. At present an approximate 42,000 students attend Mormon colleges and universities. Perhaps more significant, a little more than 265,000 students attend LDS Institutes of Religion adjacent to or near some 1,400 college and university campuses across the United States and Canada where they receive religious instruction at both the undergraduate and graduate level. To assist missionaries from Third World countries to get a college or university education, LDS leaders recently announced the creation of the Perpetual Education Fund. This fund is intended to have the success in education that was experienced by the Perpetual Immigration Fund (which enabled tens of thousands of Latter-day Saints living abroad to move to Utah in the second half of the nineteenth century). It appears that LDS leaders are intent on having a highly educated and thoroughly indoctrinated membership.

If the modernist controversy of the early part of the twentieth century and the current postmodern phenomenon teach us nothing else, it is that the important battles vying for the minds of men and women are won or lost in the halls of academia. What goes on in the so-called real world is largely a by-product of those battles and their outcomes. The saying is true: "If you want to influence the world, influence the world of ideas." It seems that a growing number of Latter-day Saints have learned that lesson.

Traditionally, Mormons have tended to study the hard sciences, law, and business. However, because of their relevance to LDS truth claims, Latter-day Saints have increasingly entered the humanities in recent years. The blossoming of historical and sociological scholarship on Mormonism and the important LDS contribution to this is expected and well known, so I will not discuss it here.[36] More important for the purposes of this essay is the entrance of Latter-day Saints into other fields of scholarship that have apologetic significance to LDS truth claims. Currently some are being encouraged by the granting of fellowships to pursue graduate degrees in New Testament, Christian Origins, Hebrew, Ancient Near Eastern Studies, Egyptology, Mesoamerican archeology, philosophy, and other relevant disciplines. The schools where these degrees are pursued are equally significant: Oxford, Yale, Claremont, Harvard, Duke, Graduate Theological Union/U.C. Berkley, UCLA, Notre Dame, Catholic University, University of Toronto, Hebrew University, and the University of North Carolina-Chapel Hill among others.[37] Some of these fellowship recipients are now beginning to secure teaching positions.[38] One of the fruits of such investments will be an increasing voice in the academy and the world of ideas in years to come.

But already Latter-day Saints have a voice. It is worth mentioning that there are many Mormons who are professors at non-LDS colleges and universities. Most teach in the hard sciences, business, and literature departments. However, a few teach in departments of theology, archeology, history, and other fields related to Christian-Mormon debates.[39] Some even hold endowed chairs, and others are university or college presidents.[40] No other

New Religious Movement is nearly so well represented among college and university faculties.

Another mark of Mormonism's increasing success in the academy is LDS participation in relevant professional societies and publication in mainstream academic venues. There are devout Latter-day Saints who participate and at times have held regional positions of leadership in the Society of Christian Philosophers, the American Schools of Oriental Research, the American Academy of Religion (AAR), and the Society of Biblical Literature (SBL). In recent years this presence has become more noticeable as the Foundation for Ancient Research and Mormon Studies at BYU (FARMS) has sponsored a large booth at the annual meeting of the AAR/SBL.

In recent years LDS scholars have published in important series such as the SBL Dissertation Series,[41] the Harvard Semitic Monographs,[42] Studia Pohl[43] and Discoveries in the Judean Desert.[44] Their work has appeared in numerous influential journals, including *Revue de Qumran, Journal for the Study of the Pseudepigrapha, Journal for the Study of Judaism, Jewish Quarterly Review, Harvard Theological Review, Vigiliae Christianae, Church History, Faith and Philosophy, Religious Studies, Journal of Speculative Philosophy,* and the *International Journal for the Philosophy of Religion.*[45]

Increasingly, LDS scholars participate in joint projects of the larger academic world. Four Latter-day Saints are on the International Dead Sea Scrolls Editing Team.[46] Latter-day Saints have contributed to such standard reference works as the *Anchor Bible Dictionary, Oxford Companion to the Bible, Oxford Encyclopedia of Archeology in the Near East, Encyclopedia of the Dead Sea Scrolls, Old Testament Pseudepigrapha,* and the *Cambridge Companion to Philosophy.*[47] Finally, the presence of Latter-day Saints in the academy is reflected by the contribution of essays to *Festschriften* and other multiauthor scholarly books.[48] One such book, published by an evangelical publishing house, was edited by a Latter-day Saint and included three LDS essays with those of prominent evangelical contributors.[49]

The LDS scholars who participate in the activities of the broader academy have not failed to catch the attention, if not of evangelicals, at least of some of their Catholic, Jewish, mainline Protestant, and secular peers. For instance, one of the fathers of contemporary LDS apologetic scholarship, Hugh Nibley, has received praise from prominent scholars such as Jacob Neusner, James Charlesworth, Cyrus Gordon, Raphael Patai, and Jacob Milgrom.[50] The late dean of the Harvard Divinity School, George MacRae, once lamented, while hearing Nibley lecture, "It is obscene for a man to know that much!"[51] Nibley and his LDS colleagues have not worked in a cloister, but many evangelical scholars are unaware of their work.

It should be clear that already Mormons have achieved a place in the academy unparalleled by any other group commonly classified as a New Religious Movement. If Mormon growth continues at a rate anywhere near its current one, and if Mormons continue encouraging their students to pursue graduate degrees in the fields listed above, one can only presume that the LDS presence in the academy will continue to grow and that this will be used to the furtherance of LDS truth claims. As it is, the majority of LDS scholarship, including that published in non-LDS venues, supports a cumulative argument for LDS truth claims in some way or other (often as pieces to a larger puzzle that has yet to be fully assembled).

Scholarly Arguments for Mormon Truth Claims

As might be expected, Latter-day Saints produce scholarly works to respond to common criticisms against Mormon truth claims. For example, John Sorenson has attempted in a monograph to show that the geographic and material cultural references in the Book of Mormon can be plausibly understood in a manner consistent with Mesoamerican geography and archeology.[52] Latter-day Saint scholars with training in Egyptology have produced studies trying to give reasons to believe that the Book of Abraham is an ancient scriptural document despite the universally acknowledged fact that its contents can by no means be described as a translation, in the usual sense of the word, of any of the extant Joseph Smith Papyri.[53] A Mormon with a background in linguistics has attempted to show that Native American languages show Semitic influences, evidence of cultural contact between the ancient Americas and the Ancient Near East.[54]

I have no background in Mesoamerican studies, Egyptology, or Native American languages, so I cannot authoritatively evaluate whether these studies are sound. But one should observe what these examples of LDS scholarship accomplish, even if they are sound. The third example attempts to establish something that one would expect to be the case if LDS claims about the historicity of the Book of Mormon are true. If one could not at least argue that Native American languages show Semitic influence, then that would count against the idea that there were large cultures in the Americas descended from Semitic immigrants as the Book of Mormon purports.[55] The first two examples are attempts to produce necessary "defeater-defeaters"; that is, they provide answers to criticisms that could defeat fundamental Mormon truth claims in order to allow Mormons to continue rationally affirming their faith. None of these three examples of defensive scholarship, however, provide much in the way of positive evidence for Mormonism or the Book of Mormon. A common mistake made by lay Mormon apologists, assuming that this scholarship is sound, is their construing successful defeater-defeaters as positive evidence. But LDS scholars also produce apologetic scholarship that attempts to do more than establish necessary conditions or produce defeater-defeaters.

It is a foundational belief of Mormonism that the church Christ founded in the first century apostatized but was restored through the work of Joseph Smith in 1830. It is claimed that Joseph Smith reintroduced to the world a pristine Christianity replete with truths and insights that had been lost in the "Great Apostasy." According to the apostasy thesis, the process of Hellenization and the influence of pagan Greek philosophy corrupted Christianity. Precious truths were forgotten, the transmission of the Bible was interfered with, inspired books were lost, and the canon was inappropriately deemed closed. The lenses of Hellenistic thinking caused and continue to cause traditional Christianity to misread and misunderstand the Bible. The Christian tradition of theological absolutism and ontological Trinitarianism is unbiblical, and creedal orthodoxy has much to do with Athens but little to do with Jerusalem. As evidence of Joseph Smith's restoration of Christianity and the soon return of Christ, God allowed Smith to miraculously restore ancient texts and doctrines that had been lost for nearly two millennia.

Mormon scholars have undertaken the task of demonstrating these claims. They begin with the claim that the Book of Mormon is an ancient text written by people of Israelite lineage who established civilizations in the Americas. Much effort is being spent to show that the Book of Mormon reflects a genuinely ancient Near Eastern background, evidences the marks of translation from Semitic languages, contains subtle Hebrew poetic and literary devices, and evidences the hand of multiple authors redacted by a later scribe. In order to establish such claims, LDS scholars have employed the tools of redaction criticism, comparative philology, background studies, linguistics, and form criticism. It is claimed that though the Book of Mormon may reflect some aspects of the nineteenth century due to the way in which Joseph Smith translated the gold plates, there are features of the text that are too authentic, too subtle, and too complex to be the product of any nineteenth-century author and that cannot be attributed to mere mimicking of the Old Testament. One LDS scholar makes the following challenge to the scholarly world:

> It claims to be an ancient book, and it must be examined and criticized in terms of its claim. . . . Since nobody could feasibly invent a work the length of the Book of Mormon which represented ancient Near Eastern society accurately. . . , subjecting the book to the test of historical integrity would be a rather easy task for any specialist to undertake. . . . It is precisely this dimension of historical criticism, however, which has been almost totally neglected in attempts to establish the book as a fraud.[56]

In addition to the alleged ancient features of the Book of Mormon, LDS scholars try to show that distinctive doctrines of the LDS Church have no precedent in the nineteenth century or in any of the centuries preceding it back to ancient times. But, it is claimed, these distinctive beliefs *do* have parallels among the ancient Jews and earliest Christians. In this regard, Mormons have taken a keen interest in the Dead Sea Scrolls, the Pseudepigrapha, the Nag Hammadi codices, and the writings of the Church Fathers. They have, on occasion, discovered some striking parallels, to say the least. Even the world's foremost authority on the Pseudepigrapha, James Charlesworth, acknowledges parallels between the Pseudepigrapha and the Book of Mormon that he describes as "important parallels. . . that deserve careful examination."[57] Since many of the texts in which such parallels are found were not even discovered until the twentieth century, Mormons challenge the world to explain them apart from Smith's claim to divine revelation. They in effect ask: "Is it really rational to believe that a New York farm boy recreated so many elements of the ancient world all by himself? Could *anyone* in the nineteenth century have pulled this off?"

In addition to discovering parallels with the ancient world, LDS scholars are attempting to free the Bible from what they perceive to be naturalistic and unbelieving scholarship on the one hand, and, on the other, a believing scholarship whose vision has been blinded by an inheritance of Hellenistic philosophy. This is a part of the argument that is still largely undeveloped, but the apparent goal is to examine the primary data of the historical and cultural contexts in which the Bible was written and to build the contextual superstructure necessary for a historico-grammatical interpretation that is both historically and culturally justified *and* at odds with orthodox Christian theology.

Finally, in the discipline of the philosophy of religion Latter-day Saints are presenting arguments for their unique understanding of God as an embodied being, literally an exalted man.[58] They are trying to exploit the advantages of their finite theism to account for the problem of evil, Hume's argument against design in the universe, and the conceptual and logical difficulties that attend absolutist and Trinitarian conceptions of God.[59] In so doing, they are both doing original work and drawing off of the work of process theologians; proponents of the "Open View of God"; social Trinitarians; and historic finite theists like John Stuart Mill, William James, and Edgar Sheffield Brightman.[60] In addition, their materialistic ontology and optimistic religious humanism are presented as attractive alternatives for the modern person living in a scientific age.

In response to an earlier article on LDS scholarship and apologetic that I coauthored with Paul Owen (one of the coeditors of this volume), one LDS scholar commented: "I wish we really were doing as well as you guys said we were." I don't think his point was that we had overstated the accomplishments of LDS scholarship. Rather, when these accomplishments are described in a dense summary that does not point out weaknesses, as I have given above, this can create the illusion that the community of LDS scholars is larger than it is or that it has accomplished more than it has. The fact is that the community of LDS scholars is not yet a large one, and there are many weaknesses that one could cite of LDS scholarship generally. But it is also a fact that the number and quality of LDS scholars producing apologetically relevant works is growing. The Foundation for Ancient Research and Mormon Studies (FARMS) provides both funding and venues for publishing explicitly apologetic works through its imprints and journals.[61]

In light of the history of evangelical scholarship in the twentieth century, it should be evident that Mormonism is in the early stages of developing a scholarly community with the potential to accomplish much more than it has thus far. The defenses of Mormon beliefs and history can only become more sophisticated and sound more credible as time goes by. Even if there is some risk that my discussion gives a slightly overstated impression of the current state of LDS scholarship, the point of my discussion should not be mitigated: it is important that evangelical critiques of Mormonism keep pace with its defenses.

The Challenge for Theology

The Rise of Mormon "Neo-orthodoxy"

As early as 1967, Mormon sociologist O. Kendall White detected a movement within Mormon theology away from the traditional synthesis forged in the late nineteenth and early twentieth centuries by B. H. Roberts, James Talmage, and John Widtsoe that came to be identified with Mormonism. In a masters thesis, several journal articles, and an important 1987 book, White convincingly showed that there was indeed a noticeable trend within Mormon theology away from the traditional synthesis. He also noticed that this development within Mormon theology in some ways paralleled the neo-orthodox reaction against Protestant liberalism. Thus, he labeled the trend "Mormon Neo-orthodoxy."[62]

White argued that optimistic humanism, finite theism, and emphasis on human merit in attaining salvation characterize traditional Mormon theology. It is a thoroughly anthropocentric (human-centered) theology. Mormon neo-orthodoxy, on the other hand, stresses the omnipotence and sovereignty of God, human sinfulness and inability to merit salvation, and the necessity of salvation by grace.[63] It is a theocentric (God-centered) theology. Mormon neo-orthodox theology moved away from the traditional synthesis in much the same way that Protestant neo-orthodoxy repudiated classical liberalism.

This kind of nontraditional Mormon thinking is not without precedent within LDS history. "The explosion of historical scholarship in Mormon studies during the past two decades," White tells us, "has disclosed the essential Protestant flavor of earliest Mormon beliefs and has provided an authentic foundation for Mormon neo-orthodox theology."[64] In White's estimation, "Mormon neo-orthodoxy may be closer to Protestant fundamentalism and neo-orthodoxy than to what I and others esteem to be traditional Mormon thought."[65] White is convinced that "Mormon neo-orthodoxy is similar to Mormon theology of 1830–35" and "may be conceived as a return to the earliest 'Mormon' beliefs and, consequently, as an authentic expression of Mormon theology."[66] Though Kendall White admits that Mormon neo-orthodoxy can be viewed as an authentic expression of Mormon theology, he is not favorable to it. He feels that Mormonism's success is in large part due to its traditional theological synthesis. In his opinion, Mormon neo-orthodoxy's challenge to that traditional synthesis represents an ominous threat to Mormonism's future.[67]

Robert L. Millet, a professor of ancient scripture and for many years the Dean of Religious Education at Brigham Young University, responded to White's book in the university's flagship journal.[68] These are Millet's concluding remarks:

Kendall White is correct in detecting a movement afloat in Mormonism in the latter part of the twentieth century. It is a movement toward a more thoroughly redemptive base to our theology, but a movement that is in harmony with the teachings of the Book of Mormon and one that may be long overdue. These recent developments may represent more of a retrenchment and a refinement than a revision. I believe that 'few things portend a more ominous future' for us than to fail to take seriously the Book of Mormon and the redemptive theology set forth therein; the only real 'crisis' to fear would be attempts to build Mormonism upon any other foundation.[69]

Since Kendall White's initial studies of Mormon neo-orthodoxy of the late 1960s and his 1987 update, a new generation of LDS theologians has arisen. Their work continues the trend away from the traditional synthesis of Roberts, Talmage, and Widtsoe. Similar to the Mormon neo-orthodox theology White describes, these contemporary LDS theologians emphasize God's sovereignty and tend to describe God in absolutist terms. They speak of human sinfulness and inability, stress the substitutionary nature of Christ's atonement, describe justification as a forensic act of God, and insist that only Christ's work on our behalf can merit salvation or even exaltation. They promote an understanding of the relationship between works and grace that is openly modeled after noted evangelical pastor John MacArthur's expositions of "Lordship salvation."

Some of these contemporary LDS theologians hesitate to say that there are Gods above God the Father. A few go so far as to openly call Mormonism's traditional infinite regress of Gods a mistake and deny that Mormonism's affirmation that the Father is an exalted man entails that there was ever a time at which he was not God. While still affirming that humans are of the same species of being as God, they do not believe that the LDS belief in exaltation to godhood implies that we will become equal to God or even Gods—we will always be gods with a lowercase *g*.

The primary theological tool employed by these contemporary LDS theologians is exegesis of the Bible and the Book of Mormon. As anyone who has read the Book of Mormon knows, its theology is largely orthodox in nature. It is also common knowledge that distinctive doctrines of traditional Mormonism come, not from the Book of Mormon, but from Joseph Smith's later teachings as represented by the later sections of the Doctrine and Covenants, the Pearl of Great Price, and the King Follett Discourse. So it should not come as a surprise if a Mormon theology grounded in the exegesis of the Bible and Book of Mormon moves toward Christian orthodoxy in some respects.

For several reasons I hesitate to label this contemporary movement neo-orthodox. The characteristics Kendall White associated with neo-orthodoxy— God's sovereignty, human depravity, and salvation by grace—are not the first ones that the word *neo-orthodox* conveys to many people's minds, at least among evangelicals. Second, I am not fully convinced that this movement is primarily a reaction to the crisis of secularization as White claims Mormon neo-orthodoxy is. Rather, it seems to be a natural by-product of the LDS Church's emphasis of the last twenty-five years on the Book of Mormon and its teachings. If it is a reaction to anything, it is to the charge that Mormon theology does not come from the Book of Mormon. Third, there are some noticeable and important theological differences between the contemporary LDS theologians and some that White characterized as neo-orthodox. Finally, a hallmark of the contemporary Mormon theologians is their minimalistic, almost *sola scriptura* approach to what they consider authoritative LDS teachings (albeit with the larger LDS canon).[70]

Keeping Up with Contemporary Mormon Theology

Judging from the reaction of many evangelicals to Stephen Robinson's contribution to the book he coauthored with evangelical scholar Craig Blomberg, *How Wide the Divide? A Mormon and an Evangelical in Conversation,*[71] the theological trends I have been describing caught a lot of people by surprise. Many accused Robinson of being dishonest in describing what Mormons believe. His contribution was labeled as a public relations scheme to beguile unwary Christians who don't know what Mormonism "really teaches." Some were a bit more charitable and granted that perhaps Robinson was honestly reporting his personal beliefs. But, they insisted, Robinson did not officially represent the LDS Church, so his personal beliefs were merely the idiosyncratic views of a BYU professor and not characteristic of what is taught within Mormonism. Therefore, Robinson's theology does not need to be taken seriously.

Had Robinson's evangelical critics kept abreast in their reading of current LDS literature, they would have known that what Robinson said in *How Wide the Divide?* was very much the same thing he and other popular LDS thinkers have been saying to LDS audiences for years. They would have known too that Robinson's views were hardly idiosyncratic. In fact, the brand of Mormon theology Robinson presented counts several LDS General Authorities among its adherents.

When I have discussed these theological trends with other evangelicals, some have been very resistant to the notion that there has been any theological development within contemporary Mormonism. They have insisted, a priori, that what Robinson and others like him teach is really no different than traditional Mormonism; it only appears closer to orthodoxy because it has been given a veneer of orthodox-sounding terminology.[72] I have been told that this literature ought to be ignored and that we should focus our critiques on "real" Mormonism, that is, the traditional synthesis. This kind of reply reminds me of a comment philosopher John Bishop makes while reproving atheists who refuse to criticize anything except traditional concepts of God: "They jealously guard the kind of God they don't believe in!"[73] Likewise, some evangelical apologists jealously guard the kind of Mormonism they don't believe in.

There are still many Latter-day Saints like Kendall White whose theology is quite traditional and who do not like the direction in which writers like Robinson are leading LDS theology. Eugene England, for example, makes several telling critical comments of Robinson's views in his review of *How Wide the Divide?*[74] His comments make it clear that traditional-minded Latter-day Saints do not see Robinson's theology as merely traditional Mormonism with an orthodox-sounding veneer. For example, *How Wide the Divide?* confirmed England's feeling that "the grace in [Robinson's famous] bicycle parable is more Protestant than Mormon." In general, "Robinson's formulations about salvation and judgment, as well as other crucial concepts, seem more Evangelical than Mormon." England speaks of "Robinson's rather complete capitulation" on the issue of "scriptural literalism" (i.e., biblical inerrancy) and complains that Robinson "seems to want to define the resources for Mormon theology much too narrowly." Significantly, England admits that "Robinson and others may indeed be shifting the balance of Mormon theology," and he countenances that this may be a useful correction "to a popular Mormon overemphasis on salvation by works or God's finitude." However, he fears that it will lead to theological intolerance on the part of Mormons who follow this path. In the end, England somewhat half-heartedly says that he trusts "Mormons will cling to doctrines of modern revelation."[75]

England's hope, however, seems to be unwarranted. "Neo-orthodox" or "minimalist" writers like Stephen Robinson, Robert Millet, and Gerald Lund are extremely popular among LDS readers and are popular as Fireside speakers. Through their writing and speaking, they are greatly influencing the thought of the general LDS populace. It should also be pointed out that LDS traditionalists like England are increasingly being pushed to the borders of LDS orthodoxy. England himself resigned his long-standing teaching position at BYU in order to take a position down the road (literally) at Utah Valley State College shortly before his recent death. Those in position to influence the direction Mormonism heads in the twenty-first century are mostly non-traditionalists. Millet recently completed some ten years serving as Dean of Religious Education at BYU and continues as a professor. Robinson recently completed two terms as the chair of the Department of Ancient Scripture and also continues as a professor. For several years future LDS leaders have been sitting and continue to sit under the instruction of teachers like Millet, Robinson, and the faculties they have shaped. There can be no doubt that these students will echo their teachers' instruction as they climb the ranks within the Mormon hierarchy. The current neo-orthodox and minimalist trends in LDS theology are gaining ascendancy in popular LDS theological discourse and will continue to do so in the future. Interestingly, one can already detect the influence of minimalist scholars in the teachings of some important LDS General Authorities.[76]

For some time I have advocated that evangelicals focus their critiques of Mormon theology on its contemporary versions. A common objection to this is the insistence that we should only critique "official" LDS theology. While there is much I could say in response to this objection, let me make just a few points. First, the Book of Mormon is an official work of LDS theology. It is said to be their "keystone scripture." To the degree that contemporary trends in Mormon theology reflect the teachings of the Book of Mormon, they have all the official sanction they need.

Second, if we ignore contemporary LDS theologians because their views do not *yet* have official church sanction, then many Latter-day Saints will find our critiques largely irrelevant because they do not interact with the views they themselves hold.[77] It is only common sense that our critiques of Mormon thought ought to be critiques of what Mormons are actually thinking. After all, are not actually held beliefs the ones that will hinder or facilitate true knowledge of God? Besides, when we insist that Mormons "really believe" the traditional synthesis when many do not, our credibility is called into question. If we describe Mormonism without even mentioning the important nontraditional trend, we end up presenting a caricature and thereby bear false witness against our neighbor.

Because contemporary Mormon theology is in some ways closer to Christian orthodoxy (note well: I am not saying that it *is* orthodox), its errors are less glaring. The lay person is less likely to notice them. It is important that evangelical theologians produce expositions and charitable but firm critiques of this brand of Mormonism. This is important to do in order to have an accurate understanding of the dynamics of contemporary Mormonism (for its own sake). It is also important to do in order to make available to our laity accurate resources that will both protect them from error and equip them for witnessing to their LDS acquaintances.

The contemporary LDS theologians I have been describing are far more theologically articulate in expressing and defending their beliefs than the LDS General Authorities, and they present a more plausible version of Mormonism than their traditionalist colleagues do. There is, therefore, a very good strategic reason for focusing our critiques of Mormonism primarily on contemporary neo-orthodox or minimalist versions. If we can successfully criticize a very minimal version of Mormonism, then our arguments will probably apply to more pronounced versions a fortiori. The reverse does not hold true.

Changing Our Approach and Our Attitudes to Meet Mormonism's Challenges

The rapid growth of Mormonism alone warrants reexamination of evangelical approaches to the Church of Jesus Christ of Latter-day Saints. But there are those who resist change. Two developments within Mormonism—the rise of a genuine scholarly community and the development of minimalist theologies—will not allow us to keep doing things according to the model we inherited. It will become increasingly important for evangelical leaders in various capacities and at all levels to familiarize themselves with contemporary Mormonism as it continues to grow and evolve into a major religious movement.

The missionary force of the LDS Church is immense and poses a serious challenge to evangelical missionary work around the world. Missiologists and missionaries need to develop strategies for effectively meeting the challenge. The nature of LDS growth also presents challenges to pastors, Christian education directors, denominational leaders, and those involved in theological education. For Mormonism is not growing only out on the "mission field" but also in the fields of the missionary sending nations. It is important that the various elements of the evangelical community work together to develop strategies for meeting the Mormon challenge at home. It will require that parts of our community move away from those approaches to local church ministry that avoid apologetic and theological engagement in favor of coddling a cultural Christianity or that prefer to be so "seeker-sensitive" that they can only be described as entertainment driven.[78] An important part of any effective strategy (but not the only part) will be a renewed emphasis on expository and doctrinal preaching in our churches. Perhaps too, the ancient notion of catechism should be revived and adapted for contemporary church life. These are *in addition to* the current emphases in many churches on worship, discipleship, and fostering community. In short, we need to *do* our Christianity better.

The LDS apologetic has increased considerably in its sophistication and use of scholarly tools. When evangelical writers refuse to interact with Mormonism's most articulate literature, this gives Latter-day Saints and others the impression that we are not interested in truth or in trying to genuinely understand the beliefs of our neighbors. It gives the impression that we are only interested in one set of data, the one that supports our case, and are stubbornly unwilling to consider any other evidence. This, in turn, leads to the feeling that we evangelicals are interested only in tearing down the beliefs of others, by whatever means necessary, rather than in presenting principled and well-reasoned critiques.

Evangelical biblical scholars, historians, and philosophers need to evaluate and respond to the apologetic claims of LDS scholars. Some need to make Mormonism an area of academic specialization. Mormonism has produced a few fine scholars and a larger number that are genuinely competent in their respective disciplines. The community of LDS scholarship is still comparatively small, and no Latter-day Saints have yet distinguished themselves as world-class biblical scholars, philosophers, or theologians (as several evangelicals have).[79] But the fact is that Mormonism has developed a nascent community of genuine scholars whose work must be given serious consideration by their evangelical counterparts. If it is not already clear, the subsequent chapters in this book should show that some of the new LDS apologetic is sophisticated enough that effectively demonstrating its errors requires specialized training in certain disciplines. Moreover, organizations like the Foundation for Ancient Research and Mormon Studies (FARMS) are doing much to ensure that in years to come the community of LDS scholars producing apologetically significant works continues to grow in number and quality. Lest some of the mistakes of the modernist controversy be repeated, it is imperative that qualified evangelicals engage the new Mormon apologetic at this stage, as the authors of *The New Mormon Challenge* have done on a few topics.

The common insistence on interacting only with "official" LDS literature rather than with scholarly and theological literature needs to be laid aside; as a simple matter of genre, theological critiques ought to be done on theological literature (rather than to the kind of devotional literature the General Authorities usually write). But there are other reasons to engage this literature as well. Contemporary Mormon theology does not merely present evangelical theologians with a challenge; it also provides opportunities. Perhaps most noteworthy is the opportunity to do theology in a way that is potentially very fruitful. Let me briefly explain.

When one surveys the history of Christian theology, it quickly becomes evident that many of the greatest theological insights occur in the course of responding to heterodox doctrines. The Judaizers who followed the Apostle Paul around the Mediterranean provided a foil for Paul and opportunities to develop his grand doctrine of justification by faith. The Arian controversy forced the church to think hard and deep about what the Bible says about the Father, Son, and Spirit and how they relate to one another. The result—the blessing of the heresy, one might say—was a more accurate and profound understanding of the nature of the God of our salvation. Augustine's debate with Pelagius and similar arguments during the Reformation led to important insights about our own human nature and the extent of God's saving grace. Indeed, in every age the fruit of the toil of rigorously engaging heterodoxy is deepened insight into God's revelation. Mormonism's heresies are legion; they are also very interesting and often unique in the history of heresy. Responding to them requires the theologian to examine issues and texts from new perspectives, to respond to new questions and objections, and to formulate theology more precisely in certain areas. In short, Mormonism provides the evangelical theologian with a mine of opportunities to explore God's truths against the backdrop of a unique foil.

Contemporary LDS theology also provides another type of opportunity for evangelical theologians and leaders. Though Mormonism is still far from Christian orthodoxy, it must be admitted that some of the trends in contemporary LDS theology are encouraging—and can be encouraged further. Moreover, several LDS scholars indicate their being open, even desirous, to engage in theological dialogue with knowledgeable evangelicals. The ecumenical movement of the last 150 years has done much to make both evangelicals and Latter-day Saints skittish about interreligious and even intrareligious dialogue.[80] Many ecumenical "dialogues" are not so much open dialogues as they are meetings in which people of different and mutually exclusive religious backgrounds meet to invent common ground and write off historical differences as the misunderstandings of less enlightened predecessors. This type of "dialogue" is something neither evangelicals nor Mormons can engage in with integrity.[81] But in principle, there is no reason why evangelicals and Latter-day Saints cannot engage in a fruitful theological dialogue of a very different nature, one in which deep theological differences are openly, frankly, and charitably discussed. Indeed, given the many charges of misunderstanding and caricature made by both sides against the other, it is important for this to occur. Such a principled dialogue need not and should not be viewed as a replacement for proclaiming and defending our respective faiths. Apologetics and evangelism must continue, but that need not preclude genuine interreligious dialogue from occurring.

Conclusion

Mormonism's challenges are real and can be dismissed only at a cost evangelicals should be unwilling to pay. But they are by no means insurmountable. In this chapter I have described in condensed form the predictions of incredible future growth for Mormonism, the development of sophisticated scholarly defenses of Mormon truth claims, and important trends in LDS theology that are in some ways closer to Christian orthodoxy than traditional Mormonism has been. In a discussion like this, however, there is the danger that some readers might misinterpret my comments. So in conclusion, I would like to make an attempt at preempting misunderstanding by directing some comments both to Latter-day Saints and to evangelicals.

To Latter-day Saints I want to state very clearly that I do not believe that Mormonism's challenges are anything more than challenges. I have no fear about Mormonism growing so much at the expense of evangelicalism that it actually cripples the evangelical movement. Indeed, while I have many criticisms about things that I observe in my own community, it is also clear to me that the Holy Spirit is moving mightily in many segments of it. I am optimistic and see within the movement strengths and virtues that I believe will ensure its continued health and growth. Nor do I believe that LDS scholars can actually pull off their task of rationally defending LDS truth claims. I could be wrong about this, of course. But, having put much time and energy into reading LDS scholarly writings—reading them very charitably, mind you—and conducting research in light of the claims these writings make, I am convinced that the task of LDS apologetics is ultimately doomed to failure. My concern about LDS apologetics is not that Mormonism will be proven true, but that the arguments of LDS scholars will either wrongly convince or shake the faith of those who do not have the skills to properly investigate the issues.

With respect to contemporary trends in LDS theology, to the chagrin of some of my evangelical acquaintances, I admit that I find some of them encouraging, and I pray that they will continue. I think LDS writers like Stephen Robinson, Robert Millet, and Blake Ostler have, in different ways, taken some important steps in the right direction—not nearly enough steps that I can in good conscience consider Mormonism a legitimately Christian faith, but nonetheless steps in the direction that I hope the LDS Church as a whole follows. I am encouraged by the fact that the LDS Church is increasingly emphasizing its commitment to the centrality of Jesus Christ in its doctrine, and I do not believe this is merely a public relations ploy. As I see things, this emphasis is sometimes largely verbal in nature, but not always. There are signs that it is deeper in some quarters. I am optimistic that this emphasis on Christ could result in greater attention being paid to the Christological issues that the early Christian community struggled through. Perhaps it could even lead Mormonism to affirm what I believe is a biblically faithful understanding of Christ as the second person of the Trinity, fully God and fully human—the only kind of Christ that can save us from our sins. Though I do not believe that the Book of Mormon is scripture and that it is historical or entirely accurate in its theology, I am even gladdened, in an odd way, to see Latter-day Saints increasingly endeavoring to adopt its largely orthodox theology while they downplay teachings like those found in the King Follett Discourse.[82] I hope that openly stating these things will not result in a retrenching reaction by traditional elements of the LDS community.

To evangelicals I would like to point out that as a community, with respect to Mormonism and other New Religious Movements, we have often succumbed to the sinful habits of caricaturing and demonizing the enemy, recycling arguments that have long been answered, refusing to admit genuine mistakes, and being generally uncharitable. The Golden Rule should be applied in the realm of apologetics just as in every other area of life. Combating error should never be used by Christ's ambassadors as an excuse to display un-Christlike behavior. If we want to effectively meet Mormonism's new challenges, as I believe the Lord is calling us to do, it will require that we adopt new attitudes and new approaches. If we listen to the Spirit's voice in this area and pay close attention to what he is doing, the opportunity lies before us to see a true marvelous work and a wonder. May it be so—to the everlasting praise of the Father, the glory of the Son, and honor of the Spirit, the one true and living God.

PART II

The Mormon Worldview

Introductory Essay

One of the few uncontroversial statements one can make about Mormonism and Christianity is that traditional Mormonism and historic Christianity reflect two very different worldviews. That is, they offer different and conflicting views of God, humanity, and the nature of reality that impinge upon how we should live in the world.[1] At the heart of every worldview is its understanding of God and the universe. From this understanding flow most of the other key components of a worldview. For nearly two millennia Christians have confessed in all their creeds that God is the "Maker of heaven and earth." The Nicene Creed specifies that this includes "all things visible and invisible." At the heart of the Christian worldview is the idea that God is the creator of all other reality; there is a fundamental distinction between Creator and creation. Mormonism, however, has historically taught that God is not the creator of all other reality.

The creedal affirmations of Christians are but reaffirmations of the first verse of the Bible, which majestically proclaims: "In the beginning God created the heavens and the earth." Thomas V. Morris points out that the biblical doctrine of creation is the key to a distinctively theistic perspective on reality. He writes, "This one statement captures the heart of a theistic worldview. We live in a created universe. For centuries, theists have held that the single most important truth about our world is that it is a created world. And it is no exaggeration to add that it is one of the most important truths about God that he is the creator of this world."[2] It was, in fact, the doctrine of creation out of nothing (*ex nihilo*) that most fundamentally distinguished the Judeo-Christian view of God and the world from the various religions of the ancient Near East and philosophical systems of Classical Greece—all of which assumed that the world had been formed out of eternally preexisting chaotic matter.

The doctrine of creation impinges on every other aspect of our understanding of reality. According to Christian teaching, it is God's absolute creation and continuing conservation of the universe that accounts for its existence, order, rationality, goodness, and beauty. It is because God created the universe *ex nihilo* and proclaimed it good that we can be assured that evil is not somehow part of the fabric of the universe but a parasite that will one day be overcome. Furthermore, according to many historians of science, the Christian doctrine of creation played a significant role in the rise and development of modern science by providing many of its basic presuppositions. It has been shown that the doctrine of *creatio ex nihilo* was one of the reasons the scientific revolution occurred in Christian Western Europe rather than in the ancient world or some other culture.[3] It could even be argued that, apart from the presuppositions supplied by the Christian doctrine of creation, modern science (realistically understood) would be impossible and that divorcing science from the ground of these presuppositions makes it irrational.[4]

In distinction from Christian teaching, a fundamental component of the traditional LDS worldview is the rejection of creation *ex nihilo*. Instead, as was so common in the pagan religions and philosophies of antiquity, according to the Mormon doctrine of "creation," God formed the world out of eternally preexisting chaotic matter. Mormon scholars claim that this doctrine of creation out of matter is taught in the Bible. They further claim that it was the original teaching found in the earliest Christian churches and changed only later when Christianity capitulated to the ideals of Greek philosophy in its battle with Gnosticism.

In chapter 3, the first chapter of this section, Paul Copan and William Lane Craig team up to answer these charges and to defend the traditional doctrine of creation *ex nihilo*. In the first part Copan and Craig describe the LDS doctrine of creation. In the second part they demonstrate that creation *ex nihilo* accurately describes the view of creation presupposed and affirmed in the Old and New Testaments. They show that rather than being an invention of the early church, this view of creation was affirmed by the ancient Jews and inherited by the earliest Christians. Lastly, they present two philosophical and two scientific arguments that point to the orthodox Christian view. On the basis of the biblical, theological, philosophical, and scientific evidence, Copan and Craig encourage Latter-day Saints to reconsider their traditional views of creation out of eternally preexisting matter.

In chapter 4, Jim W. Adams writes from the perspective of an Old Testament scholar on some related themes. Latter-day Saints have claimed that their view of God, creation, and humanity is biblical and enjoys particularly strong support from the Old Testament. Adams sets out to describe the Old Testament view of God, creation, and humanity and compare it with the LDS view. He begins by discussing the religious beliefs of Israel's ancient Near Eastern neighbors. These pagan religions serve as a backdrop against which the nature of Old Testament religion can be clearly seen. Adams discusses the Old Testament evidence and shows that in several important respects Old Testament religion was markedly and intentionally different from its Near Eastern counterparts. This is followed by a sketch of what Latter-day Saints have typically taught about the nature of God, creation, and humanity. Adams compares this with the Old Testament material and concludes that traditional LDS views do not accord well with the Old Testament. Rather, in some important respects they more closely resemble the beliefs that the Old Testament writers repudiated.

One test of the viability of any worldview is how well its God concept (or lack of God concept) can help answer various ultimate questions about the world in which we live. The presumption here is that a true view of ultimate reality will have greater explanatory power than competing views. In chapter 5, philosopher Stephen E. Parrish compares the classical Christian concept with what he terms the "monarchotheistic" Mormon concept of God. He evaluates how well each concept can answer such questions as: Why does God exist? Why does anything else exist and stay in existence? Why are there moral laws? He shows that the classical Christian concept of God can provide powerful answers to such questions, while the Mormon concept of God cannot. Complementing Parrish's discussion, Carl Mosser has added to his chapter a discussion of the Mormon solution to the problem of evil. The problem of evil is the chief philosophical problem that LDS scholars have said their God concept can solve better than can the classical Christian concept of God. In particular, LDS philosophers have claimed that classical Christianity's commitment to creation *ex nihilo* exacerbates the problem. Mosser argues, to the contrary, that it is the LDS view that exacerbates the problem—so much so that a solution to the practical problem of evil is impossible. He also maintains that only belief in a God who created all things *ex nihilo* can guarantee the eschatological confidence of evil's ultimate and permanent demise that is so central to a truly Christian view of the world.

In chapter 6, Francis J. Beckwith picks up on a problem briefly discussed earlier by Parrish. Beckwith commends the Latter-day Saints for their commitment to the objectivity of moral values and praises them for their work on moral issues in the public sphere. He shows, however, that the existence of the kinds of objective moral values that Latter-day Saints and evangelicals are alike committed to do not appear able to be grounded in the LDS worldview. Beckwith discusses the nature of moral values and how they seem to point to the existence of an immaterial, transcendent Creator of the universe. The LDS view of God denies all three of these attributes. Furthermore, Beckwith shows how the LDS God is a contingent being and thus cannot ground moral values, which are necessary; whereas the necessary God of classical Christianity can. Beckwith considers whether Latter-day Saints might be able to account for the existence of objective moral values by appealing to some sort of Platonism, Aristotelian final causes, social contract theory, or the supervenience of moral values on matter. None of the options appears to be viable, and Latter-day Saints are encouraged to allow their correct views of morality to inform their view of God's nature.

One of the distinctive commitments of Mormonism has been its traditional affirmation of a materialist or physicalist ontology. That is, LDS doctrine has historically taught that the only sorts of things that exist are material in composition. That commitment, as Beckwith shows, is one reason why objective moral values seem not to be at home with the other components of the LDS worldview. In chapter 7, J. P. Moreland goes in a different direction and discusses Mormonism's unique understanding of the nature of human persons as composed of a physical body and a spirit that is a "more refined" form of matter. In the nineteenth century, LDS apostle Orson Pratt wrote an essay entitled "The Absurdities of Immaterialism." Pratt argued that the traditional Christian view of human persons as being composed of a physical body and an immaterial soul was philosophically absurd and that the LDS version of materialism was superior. Moreland responds to Pratt's long-unanswered essay.

Though Pratt has proven to be one of the brightest thinkers Mormonism has ever produced, Moreland shows that Pratt had an inadequate theory of existence, that his understanding of substance was mistaken, and that he confused properties with events. Having a right understanding of such notions as these, however, is crucial in properly assessing the composite nature of human persons; and misunderstanding them will skew one's analysis, as it did Pratt's. Apart from these shortcomings, Moreland raises a serious difficulty with Pratt's view and with physicalist views generally: the problem of personal identity and the unity of consciousness. Moreland closes by first encouraging Latter-day Saints to reconsider their physicalist understanding of human persons, and then directing some comments of advice to Christians who have in recent years adopted the physicalist views so popular in the secular academy.

CRAFTSMAN OR CREATOR?
An Examination of the Mormon Doctrine of Creation and a Defense of *Creatio ex nihilo*

PAUL COPAN AND
WILLIAM LANE CRAIG

Paul Copan is a ministry associate at Ravi Zacharias International Ministries and Visiting Associate Professor of Philosophy of Religion and Systematic Theology at Trinity International University. He earned a B.A. from Columbia International University, an M.A. in philosophy of religion and an M.Div. from Trinity Evangelical Divinity School, and a Ph.D. in philosophy from Marquette University. Dr. Copan is the author of *True for You, But Not for Me* (Bethany House) and *That's Just Your Interpretation* (Baker). He is the editor of *Will the Real Jesus Please Stand Up?* (Baker) and coeditor of *Jesus' Resurrection: Fact or Figment?* (IVP) and *Who Was Jesus? A Jewish-Christian Dialogue* (Westminster/John Knox). His articles have appeared in *Philosophia Christi, Journal of the Evangelical Theological Society,* and *Trinity Journal.*

William Lane Craig is Research Professor of Philosophy at Talbot School of Theology, Biola University. He earned a

B.A. from Wheaton College; an M.A. in philosophy of religion and an M.A. in church history from Trinity Evangelical Divinity School; a Ph.D. in philosophy from the University of Birmingham, England; and the D.Theol. in systematic theology from the University of Munich, Germany. A Christian philosopher of international repute, Dr. Craig is the author of *The Kalam Cosmological Argument* (Macmillan/Barnes & Noble), *The Only Wise God* (Baker), and *Reasonable Faith* (Crossway), and coauthor of *Theism, Atheism, and Big Bang Cosmology* (Clarendon). His articles have appeared in numerous journals, including *Astrophysics and Space Science, Australasian Journal of Philosophy, British Journal for the Philosophy of Science, International Studies in the Philosophy of Science, Modern Theology, New Testament Studies, Origins and Design, Philosophia Christi,* and *Religious Studies.*

Others take the view expressed by Plato, that giant among the Greeks. He said that God had made all things out of pre-existent and uncreated matter. . . . How could God be called Maker and Artificer if His ability depended on some other cause, namely on matter itself? If He only worked on existing matter and did not Himself bring matter into being, He would be not the Creator but only a craftsman.

—*ATHANASIUS*, DE INCARNATIONE, *2.3–4*

The first verse of the Bible begins by declaring one of the most fundamental things we can know about God and the world we live in: God created the heavens and earth. This affirmation has been proclaimed by Christians in all centuries and has almost always been understood to mean that God created all things out of nothing (*ex nihilo*). That is, God did not work with uncreated, preexisting materials but created literally everything by divine fiat. In contrast, Mormonism has traditionally taught that matter is eternal and that God is (roughly speaking) an Artificer or Shaper or Organizer of eternal matter (or perhaps some semisubstantial *Urstoff* that is neither being nor nonbeing).¹ *This,* Latter-day Saints have claimed, is what "creation" is—not creation out of nothing.

It is not unusual to hear Mormons charge that the Christian doctrine of creation *ex nihilo* is an example of imposing unwarranted philosophical or theological grids upon Scripture. B. H. Roberts, an important LDS theologian who was also a member of the First Council of Seventy, declared that "Christians converted into dogma the false notion of the creation of the universe out of 'nothing,' assuming God's transcendence of the universe. They accepted the idea that 'creation' meant absolutely bringing from non-existence into existence, and ultimately pronounced anathema upon those who might attempt to teach otherwise."² Mormons have typically attributed the reason for this alleged conversion of doctrine to the undue influence of Greek philosophy on the early church fathers. Mormon scholars claim that their doctrine represents the biblical view free from "theological add-ons,"³ especially the influence of Greek philosophy.⁴

Furthermore, according to Stephen E. Robinson, the Mormon view of creation does not contradict contemporary science: "The Big Bang theorists don't conclude that the universe was created out of nothing, only that everything as it now exists was created out of something else, i.e., the singularity. And the singularity is not non-existence. I am not a physicist, but my understanding is that LDS doctrine argues for the laws of conservation of matter and energy, rather than being contradicted by them."⁵

This essay consists of three main parts.⁶ In Part I we lay out the relevant LDS scriptures pertaining to creation and what various Mormon authorities and scholars have maintained regarding this doctrine, briefly contrasting this with the Christian view. In Part II we put forward a biblical and theological case for the Christian doctrine of *creatio ex nihilo* in response to the claims of LDS scholars. We argue that Mormon exegetes have failed to prove that the biblical authors conceived of creation as a mere fashioning of previously existing materials; indeed, the Mormon position itself is a "theological add-on." We show that the doctrine of *creatio ex nihilo* captures the intent of the biblical authors. Then we argue that *creatio ex nihilo,* contrary to Mormon claims, was not the invention of early Christian theologians who had imbibed too much Greek philosophy. Rather, Jews and Christians alike believed it long before it was formalized as a doctrine.

In Part III we discuss the philosophical and scientific support for *creatio ex nihilo.* We present—contra Mormonism—various deductive/philosophical arguments against the possibility of an infinite past: (1) from the impossibility of an actual infinite, and (2) from the impossibility of the successive formation of an actual infinite. It will be demonstrated that LDS arguments for an infinite past are seriously flawed and misguided. In the last segment, we examine inductive/scientific arguments that undermine LDS cosmology and strongly support the Christian doctrine of *creatio ex nihilo*. In light of the well-established Standard Big Bang cosmological model and the attendant scientific facts of the universe's expansion and the thermodynamic properties of the universe, other cosmological models (steady state, oscillating, vacuum fluctuation, chaotic inflationary, quantum gravity) to which LDS thinkers might appeal in support of their doctrine either fail to avert the absolute beginning predicted by the Standard Model or are scientifically less plausible than the Standard Model. The scientific evidence points to creation out of nothing. We close on a positive note with some reflections on how the biblical, philosophical, and scientific evidence for *creatio ex nihilo* might best be accommodated within the scope of Mormon theology.

Section I: The Doctrine of Creation in Mormonism and in Christianity

In this section, we will sketch out a range of views of creation held by Mormons and follow with a brief description of the orthodox Christian doctrine of creation. Our ensuing criticisms will apply to the array of LDS positions. As we mentioned earlier, the LDS view of creation has usually been understood by Mormons and non-Mormons alike to be an organization (or reorganization) of eternally preexistent, uncreated matter. Even if there is variation among Latter-day Saints on the exact nature of this eternal "stuff," all reject the doctrine of creation out of nothing. But do they have to? Increasingly, Latter-day Saints insist that only the Standard Works of their church and the voice of the living prophet (i.e., the president of the LDS Church) are doctrinally binding. As far as we know, the current prophet has made no pronouncement on the doctrine of creation. The Standard Works have quite a lot to say on the subject, and we will examine what they say. What will be most striking, however, is what they do not say.

Creation in the Extrabiblical LDS Standard Works

In the Book of Mormon we are told that "there is a God, and he hath created all things, both the heavens and the earth, and all things that in them are" (2 Nephi 2:14). We are encouraged to "Believe in God; believe that he is, and that he created all things, both in heaven and in earth" (Mosiah 4:9). For if there were no God, "there could have been no creation" and we would not exist (2 Nephi 11:7). We are also told that Jesus Christ is "the Son of God, the Father of heaven and of earth, the Creator of all things from the beginning" and that we should "believe on his name" (Helaman 14:12; cf. 3 Nephi 9:15). Similar orthodox thoughts on creation are also found in the early sections of the Doctrine and Covenants (e.g., D&C 14:9 [1829] and 45:1 [1831]). In The Pearl of Great Price a portion of Joseph Smith's "translation" of the Bible has been canonized as the Book of Moses (part of Smith's translation of Genesis). Written in 1830, the section on creation closely follows the Authorized (or King James) Version of the Bible when it states: "And the earth was without form, and void; and I caused darkness to come up upon the face of the deep; and my Spirit moved upon the face of the water; for I am God" (Moses 2:2). The first noticeable divergence from typical Christian views of creation is the Book of Moses' claim that God created all things, including every human being, "spiritually" before they were created physically (Moses 3:5, 7). Significantly, however, there are no hints that God created out of preexisting matter in these passages from the Book of Mormon, the earliest sections of the Doctrine and Covenants, or the early "translation" of Genesis canonized as the Book of Moses. One could even argue that some of these early passages imply *creatio ex nihilo*.

Sections of the Doctrine and Covenants written just a few years after Mormonism's official founding appear to mitigate considerably the earlier emphasis on God or Christ having created all things when we learn that there are many things that do not seem to have been created at all. This is most noticeable in a section written in 1833, Doctrine and Covenants 93.[7] The idea that God created all things is still affirmed (D&C 93:10), but it soon becomes clear that "to create all things" is not to be taken strictly. There are some things that were neither created nor made: "Man was also in the beginning with God. Intelligence, or the light of truth, was not created or made, neither indeed can be" (D&C 93:29). In contrast with 2 Nephi 11:7's equating our very existence with being created, the next verse seems to equate existence with the autonomy of being uncreated: "All truth is independent in that sphere in which God has placed it, to act for itself, as all intelligence also; otherwise there is no existence" (D&C 93:30). A few verses later the same revelation adds: "For man is spirit. The elements are eternal, and spirit and element, inseparably connected, receive a fulness of joy" (D&C 93:33).

It is in the Book of Abraham, published in 1842, that the idea that God created from preexisting materials is first clearly stated. Abraham 3:18 discusses creation in relation to the eternal preexistence of spirits. One of these spirits, who "was like unto God," said, "We will go down, for there is space there, and we will take of these materials, and we will make an earth whereon these [others] may dwell" (Abraham 3:24). A few verses later this idea is incorporated into a reworking of the Genesis creation narrative:

And then the Lord said: Let us go down. And they went down at the beginning, and they, that is the Gods, organized and formed the heavens and the earth. And the earth, after it was formed, was empty and desolate, because they had not formed anything but the earth; and darkness reigned upon the face of the deep, and the Spirit of the Gods was brooding upon the face of the waters. And they (the Gods) said: Let there be light; and there was light. (Abraham 4:1–3)

It is interesting to observe that none of the passages we have looked at in the LDS Standard Works explicitly denies that God created the universe *ex nihilo*. The Book of Abraham creation narrative implies that *the earth* was created from preexisting materials, but it does not preclude the possibility that God created this matter *ex nihilo* at some point prior to the earth's formation. Doctrine and Covenants 93 does say that "intelligence, or the light of truth" was not created or made, that "man was in the beginning with God" and the elements are "eternal." However, all parties agree that there is some equivocation on the meaning of the word *intelligence* in the LDS scriptures; so it need not be taken as a reference to the primal part of a human being. In fact, the epexegetical equation of "intelligence" with "light of truth" indicates that "intelligence" here probably refers to what Doctrine and Covenants 88 calls the "light of Christ," which is "in all things, which giveth life to all things, which is the law by which all things are governed, even the power of God who sitteth upon his throne" (D&C 88:13). Understood in this way, uncreated intelligence/light of truth can be viewed as part of God's eternal being.

The affirmation that "man was in the beginning with God" and that the elements are eternal can be understood in a relative sense and need not imply that they are literally uncreated. The reason why comes from the Book of Moses, where God tells Moses: "And worlds without number have I created. . . . But only an account of *this earth, and the inhabitants thereof,* give I unto you. For behold, there have been many worlds that have passed away by the word of my power" (Moses 1:33, 35; emphasis added). If Doctrine and Covenants 93 also applies only to this earth and its inhabitants, then it need only imply that human beings and the elements already existed at the beginning of *this* world, not that they have literally existed forever. The difficulty of locating the absolute creation of human beings and the elements before the beginning of this earth is easily solved by appeal to the Book of Moses' claim that all things, including humans, were created spiritually before they were created physically (Moses 3:5, 7).[8] This way of reading the text also has the advantage of removing the tension between Doctrine and Covenants 93 and 2 Nephi 11:7.

If Latter-day Saints really are bound only by their Standard Works and the revelations of the current prophet, then it seems to us that the way is open to them to affirm *creatio ex nihilo*. To be sure, as we will see next, this has not been the position affirmed in traditional or contemporary Mormon theology. But, in principle there is no reason to think that present-day LDS president Gordon Hinckley could not reject traditional Mormon beliefs about preexisting matter or chaos reorganized by God and embrace beliefs more in keeping with traditional, creedal Christianity. We will argue in Parts II and III that there are very good biblical, philosophical, and scientific reasons why Latter-day Saints should affirm *creatio ex nihilo* rather than what has traditionally been affirmed. Barring some canonical reason that we have overlooked or some official pronouncement against it, there does not appear to be any reason why they cannot.

Joseph Smith and Other Early Mormon Leaders on Creation

Whether Mormonism would be able to affirm *creatio ex nihilo* will hinge on just how Joseph Smith's prophethood is understood and what authority, if any, his extracanonical statements have. At present there does not appear to be any consensus on this within the LDS community. Stephen E. Robinson insists that *nothing* outside the LDS Standard Works is doctrinally binding except official statements of the First Presidency and/or Quorum of the Twelve Apostles. Nineteenth-century sermons by LDS leaders are in particular cited as bearing no doctrinal authority.[9] In contrast, Max Nolan declares: "Joseph Smith . . . described himself as more than a mere commentator on the scriptures—he claimed to be in prophetic communication with God, a transmitting medium for new scripture."[10]

If the idea that *creatio ex nihilo* is false is not explicitly found in the LDS Standard Works, it is represented throughout the LDS tradition. Near the end of his life (1844), in his most famous sermon, Mormonism's founder openly denounced *creatio ex nihilo*. In a claim to be biblical, Joseph Smith declared that the world was not created out of nothing as traditional Christian doctrine has held:

> You ask the learned doctors why they say the world was made out of nothing, and they will answer, "Doesn't the Bible say he *created* the world?" They infer, from the word *create*, that it must have been made out of nothing. Now, the word *create* came from the word *baurau* [*sic*], which does not mean to create out of nothing; it means . . . to organize the world out of

chaos—chaotic matter, which is element, and in which dwells all the glory. Element had an existence from the time he [God] had. The pure principles of element which can never be destroyed; they may be organized and reorganized, but not destroyed. They had no beginning, and can have no end.[11]

Ironically, this interpretation of Genesis 1:1 does not appear in Smith's translation of the Bible.

Brigham Young, Smith's immediate successor, taught similarly in his sermons. According to Young, God created from an "eternity of matter," and "when He speaks, He is obeyed, and matter comes together and is organized."[12] Young expressed strong disagreement with creation *ex nihilo*: "To assert that the Lord made this earth out of nothing is preposterous and impossible. God never made something out of nothing."[13] Furthermore, God creates according to eternally "fixed laws and regulations"[14] or "natural principles."[15] So, technically, there is no such thing as a miracle. If we know the chemical process of how, say, water is turned to wine, we mortals can actually perform this deed.[16] God is, after all, "the greatest chemist there is."[17] Parley Pratt, one of Mormonism's first converts and apostles, declared that "there exists [*sic*] all the varieties of elements, properties, or things" that are "eternal, uncreated, self-existing." He adds: "Not one particle can be added to them by creative power. Neither can one particle be diminished or annihilated."[18] Parley Pratt's brother and fellow apostle Orson Pratt asserted in 1876 that what Mormons mean by "creation" is merely "organization" and that the materials of which the earth is composed are "eternal." God did not create out of nothing, and, according to Pratt, *no* "Scripture" (i.e., the Bible and LDS Standard Works) "intimates such a thing."[19] Pratt says that he drew this conclusion when he "began to study the Hebrew language" and "learned that the material of which this earth was made always did exist, and that it was only an organization or formation which took place."[20]

Creation in Traditional Mormon Theology

Joseph Smith's views on creation were formalized by James E. Talmage in *A Study of the Articles of Faith*.[21] Talmage declares that God is "the Creator of all things."[22] But God the Creator is not the only eternally existent entity. According to Talmage, "something must have existed always, for had there been a time of no existence, a period of nothingness, existence could never have begun, for from nothing, nothing can be derived. The eternal existence of something, then, is a fact beyond dispute. . . . [W]hat is that eternal something—that existence which is without beginning and without end? Matter and energy are eternal realities."[23] Of course, matter requires something to activate it. God is the Organizer and Activator of matter. If we are to speak of a "beginning," we can only speak of it in relative terms—namely, the beginning of "every phase of existence" or "each stage of organization."[24] Later Talmage adds, "By [God] matter has been organized and energy directed. He is therefore the Creator of all things that are created."[25]

In 1910, B. H. Roberts wrote that God is constrained in exercising his power by certain "external existences": "Not even God may place himself beyond the boundary of space. . . . Nor is it conceivable to human thought [that] he can create space or annihilate matter. These are things that limit even God's omnipotence."[26] He added that "even [God] may not act out of harmony with the other external existences [such as duration, space, matter, truth, justice] which condition or limit him."[27] Mormon theologian John Widtsoe maintains that belief in creation out of nothing does nothing but cause confusion: "Much inconsistency of thought has come from the notion that things may be derived from an immaterial state, that is, from nothingness."[28] In addition to this assertion, Widtsoe asserts that God cannot create matter [out of nothing] nor can he destroy it: "God, possessing the supreme intelligence of the universe, can cause energy in accomplishing his ends, but create it, or destroy it, he cannot."[29] The sum of matter and energy, whatever their form, always remains the same.

Creation in Contemporary Mormon Theology

Similar statements about creation from the authors quoted above and other influential traditional Mormon theologians could be multiplied many times over. Contemporary Mormon scholarship affirms this view as well. For example, the recent *Encyclopedia of Mormonism* asserts that creation is "organization of preexisting materials."[30] In an article entitled "A Mormon View on Life," Lowell Bennion states: "Latter-Day Saints reject the *ex nihilo* theory of creation. Intelligence and the elements have always existed, co-eternal with God. He is tremendously creative and powerful, but he works with materials not of his own making."[31] (Notice that, as with Roberts above, Bennion recognizes that the denial of *creatio ex nihilo* necessarily limits God's power.)

Mormon philosopher Blake Ostler writes that "Mormons have rejected the Creator/creature dichotomy of Patristic theology and its logical correlaries [*sic*], *creatio ex nihilo* and the idea of God as a single infinite Absolute."[32] Elsewhere Ostler expounds on the Mormon view of creation as reorganization:

> The Mormon God did not bring into being the ultimate constituents of the cosmos—neither its fundamental matter nor the space/time matrix which defines it. Hence, unlike the Necessary Being of classical theology who alone could not *not* exist and on which all else is contingent for existence, the personal God of Mormonism confronts uncreated realities which exist of metaphysical necessity. Such realities include inherently self-directing selves (intelligences), primordial elements (mass/energy), the natural laws which structure reality, and moral principles grounded in the intrinsic value of selves and the requirements for growth and happiness.[33]

Stephen E. Robinson's views on creation illustrate that a diverse range of views on creation is possible within contemporary Mormon theology. By his own admission, diverging from the traditional view, he writes: "I would not be comfortable with saying that God cannot bring eternal matter into being nor destroy it." Rather, Robinson would say that "God creates matter out of chaos and can return it to chaos, and that chaos is not matter as we know it, but a level of existence that human beings cannot comprehend. For me chaos is not matter, but neither is it non-existence."[34] As he understands things, God created matter out of chaos and then created the world out of this matter. We cite him at length:

> The one thing about the LDS view that most writers have missed (including some LDS writers) is that while matter is eternal, it is eternal only in an unorganized state. All matter as we know it is already "organized." It already obeys laws imposed upon it by God. What is eternal is chaos, matter that obeys no principles or laws, in which the atomic structures do not exist, nor are the elemental forces of nature (God's power) yet present, i.e., the strong force, weak force, gravity, electromagnetic force.
>
> My understanding of creation is . . . that [God] takes primordial chaos (the LDS term is "matter unorganized") and creates or "organizes" the elements as we know them. Then he builds a universe out of the matter he has created.
>
> All matter as human beings experience it is already "organized," having been permeated by the light of Christ, the creative principle of the universe. Chaos or "matter unorganized" is beyond human experience or comprehension. Thus for the LDS the essential components of matter, like

the essential components of spirit, are eternal. But their existence as matter or as spirits is dependent upon the creative power of God. The difference between the orthodox and the LDS view, then, would be that the orthodox say God created matter out of nothing, while I would say that God created matter out of chaos or matter unorganized.[35]

The view Robinson expresses here is in some ways an improvement on the traditional Mormon view of creation. For in this view, the universe seems to be dependent on God in some sense more significant than merely being an Organizer or Craftsman, and Robinson does not seem to believe that this applies only to "this world." However, we do not think that Robinson's position or the traditional Mormon view can account for the full range of evidence we will discuss in the sections that follow.

Creation in Christian Theology

In contrast to LDS views, the traditional Christian doctrine maintains that God is the ultimate Originator of the material universe and all *other* reality. For instance, the Fourth Lateran Council of 1215 formally declared: "We firmly believe and simply confess that there is only one true God ... who by his almighty power brought every creature into being from nothing [*de nihilo condidit*]." There are two main features to the doctrine of creation out of nothing: (1) all things are *ontologically dependent* upon God for their very being; and (2) the universe and all other reality apart from God *began* and have not always existed.[36]

O. Kendall White asserts that the "typical" Mormon criticism of *ex nihilo* creation as absurd misses the point of *ex nihilo* creation, which is that everything that exists is totally dependent on God for its being.[37] It is undeniable that some Christian theologians believe creation is nothing more than ontological dependence (i.e., God's providential sustenance of all existent things, preventing them from lapsing into nonbeing).[38] These thinkers see temporal origination as irrelevant—or nearly so.[39] We shall argue, though, that this view of creation does not capture the thrust of this key Christian doctrine, which declares that God is distinct from all other reality, *which he not only sustains but also has brought into being a finite time ago.*

Augustine captures the Christian doctrine nicely when he argues that since God alone is Being, he willed to exist what formerly did not exist or had no being. God is not a mere shaper of formless and eternal primordial matter. He adds, "You did not work as a human craftsman does, making one thing out of something else as his mind directs. . . . Your Word alone created [heaven and earth]."[40] For Christians, creation *ex nihilo* more properly refers to both the temporal origination and ontological dependence of the material world on God's decree.[41] This, we will argue, is the view best supported by the biblical, theological, philosophical, and scientific evidence.

So Creator (2) and sustainer (1)

Section II: Biblical and Theological Support for *Creatio ex nihilo*

The Claims of Mormon Scholars and Their Allies

According to Stephen Robinson, there is "no evidence for *creatio ex nihilo* in Judaism before the Hellenistic period, nor in early Christianity before the late second Century."[42] What, then, does the biblical evidence set forth? According to Stephen Robinson, "the Hebrew word *bara* is insufficient evidence to establish a doctrine of creation *ex nihilo*. *Bara* means create, build, sculpt—but not 'bring into being out of nothing.' If, in fact, *bara* meant 'create out of nothing' it would have been unnecessary for post-biblical writers to clarify by adding the *ex nihilo!*"[43] Similarly, according to B. H. Roberts, "there is nothing in the word [*create*] itself . . . that demands any such interpretation [i.e., an *ex nihilo* one] of its use in Holy Scripture."[44] And again, "there is nothing in the word 'create' itself that requires its interpretation to mean 'create out of nothing.'"[45]

One tack some Mormons have used is the appeal to a word's etymology to grasp its meaning. B. H. Roberts does so in the instance of the word *create*, which is indeed a precarious route to take. He admits what the *Jewish Encyclopedia* indicates—namely, that "most of the Jewish philosophers find in Gen. 1:1 that 'creation' meant 'creation out of nothing.'"[46] This fact is quite telling and, of course, supports the traditional understanding of creation as opposed to the LDS view. But then Roberts commits the exegetical fallacy of appealing to etymology to support the LDS interpretation of the text: "*The Jewish Encyclopedia* says that the etymological meaning of the verb ("create") is 'to cut out and [to] put into shape' [fashion], and thus presupposes the use of material."[47] He then extrapolates the theological point that God's creation involved a fashioning "out of pre-existent material."[48] He adds later: "The etymology of the verb 'create' implies creation from pre-existing materials."[49]

Modern linguists and exegetes have repeatedly shown that using etymology to establish word meaning is misguided. For example, the English word *nice* has apparently been derived from the Latin *nescius,* which means 'ignorant.'[50] But we do not therefore imply that a "nice" person is an ignoramus! In most cases, the synchronic[51] usage of a word rarely means what it originally meant (i.e., etymologically). As biblical scholar Moisés Silva emphatically states: "Modern studies compel us to reject this attitude [i.e., appealing to etymology as giving us the 'basic' or 'real' meaning of a word] and distrust a word's history."[52] Similarly, James Barr asserts: "The main point is that the etymology of a word is not a statement about its meaning but about its history."[53]

Now it is well known that *bârâ'* (create) is used for, say, God's creation of the people of Israel (e.g., Isa 43:15) or his creation of a clean heart (Ps 51:12), but obviously this should not be understood as being *ex nihilo*. More to the point: when we look at specific texts related to God's creation of the universe, which viewpoint is (best) supported by Scripture—the LDS understanding or the Christian one? And if, at worst, the Bible is neutral about which of these two positions (relative or absolute creation) is true, then Mormon scholars have still failed to prove their claim that the Bible endorses their view.

Some LDS scholars and apologists try to buttress their position by appealing to the work of Gerhard May, Professor of Theology at the Johannes Gutenberg Universität in Mainz, Germany.[54] In his book *Creatio ex nihilo: The Doctrine of "Creation Out of Nothing" in Early Christian Thought*, May expresses the commonly held LDS view that the text of the Bible does not demand belief in creation *ex nihilo*.[55] Unfortunately, May—along with Mormon scholars in general—does little to defend this claim. While he makes passing reference to certain biblical passages that seem to hint at the doctrine of *creatio ex nihilo*, he does not seriously interact with them, seeming to pass them off lightly. He focuses on patristic study (as his subtitle indicates) rather than on biblical exegesis. When Mormon scholars refer to May or cite works that depend on May's analysis, this really does not strengthen their case but rather ends up weakening their argument, for these sources tend to pass over the exegesis of biblical texts (as May does) and move immediately into the theological discussion of rabbis and theologians.[56] Mormon scholarship itself is remarkably silent on biblical exegesis regarding creation.

May's own silence on scriptural analysis ends up weakening his position because, if properly done, sound biblical exegesis refutes the notion that creation out of nothing is a mere theological invention. For instance, Romans 4:17 (where God is said to call into being things that are not) and Hebrews 11:3 (where the visible world is not created from anything observable) are passages that May simply writes off as fitting in with other statements of Hellenistic Judaism—statements that *seem* to affirm absolute creation out of nothing but are actually only asserting belief in world-formation out of pre-existent material.

One wonders if that is all there is to the matter. It seems that such assertions, given without any arguments whatsoever, can be rather misleading. Indeed, May gives the false impression that *creatio ex nihilo* was nothing more than the invention of well-meaning Christian theologians who were trying to defend what they believed to be the biblical notions of God's absolute sovereignty, freedom, and omnipotence in the face of heretical gnostic doctrines.[57] We believe that examining the relevant biblical passages more extensively will adequately show that the traditional teaching of *creatio ex nihilo* has strong biblical grounds as opposed to the notion of creation from eternally preexistent matter.

Biblical Support for *Creatio ex nihilo*

Old Testament

It has become popular in some scholarly circles to insist that the Old Testament's view of creation must be similar to the views of Israel's ancient pagan neighbors, all of whom held to some version of creation out of preexisting matter. This is not established on the basis of Old Testament passages as much as demanded by some scholarly reconstructions of the evolutionary development of Israel's history. Many scholars, however, remain firmly convinced that the Old Testament writers' understanding of creation was quite different from the pagan views. This is a point that they (and we) believe can be established from the text of the Old Testament itself, both from individual passages and from the general outlook of the Old Testament as a whole.

For example, Walther Eichrodt expresses the implicit assumption that the Old Testament makes regarding absolute creation: "The idea of the absolute beginning of the created world thus proves to be a logical expression of the total outlook of the priestly narrator."[58] According to Eichrodt, Isaiah 40:21, which refers back to Genesis 1:1 but uses the parallel expression "from the foundation of the earth," is "a clear reference to an absolute beginning," and this is not an "arbitrary judgment."[59] He considers the doctrine of *creatio ex nihilo* "incontestable"[60]—especially in light of the author's strict monotheism as well as his radical distinction between ancient cosmogonies, in which the gods emerged out of preexisting matter, and his own. Eichrodt argues that "the ultimate aim of the [creation] narrative is the same as that of our formula of creation *ex nihilo*."[61] Although this formula does not occur in the Old Testament, the object of God's creative activity is "heaven and earth and all that is in them"; so God's creation cannot be restricted to "the stars and things on earth" but must include "the entire cosmos."[62] The fact that "heaven and earth" is a merism signifying "the totality of cosmic phenomena" points us toward an absolute beginning of the universe—including matter.[63] In fact, there is "no single word in the Hebrew language" to express totality; thus this phrase is used.[64] Claus Westermann agrees: Genesis 1:1 does not refer to "the beginning of something, but simply The Beginning. *Everything* began with God."[65]

Another Old Testament scholar, R. K. Harrison, asserts that while *creatio ex nihilo* was "too abstract for the [Hebrew] mind to entertain" and is not stated explicitly in Genesis 1, "it is certainly implicit in the narrative."[66] The reader is meant to understand that "the worlds were not fashioned from any pre-existing material, but out of nothing"; "prior" to God's creative activity, "there was thus no other kind of phenomenological existence."[67] Similarly, even Edwin Hatch admits that while Greek Platonic language helped give "philosophical form" to the developed Christian doctrine of creation, the belief that God was "not merely the Architect of the universe, but its Source" had "probably been for a long time the unreasoned belief of Hebrew monotheism."[68] That is, metaphysical language and systematization would later flesh out what was indicated by the Old Testament creation texts.

We noted earlier what Joseph Smith said the Hebrew word for *create*— *bârâ'* (or, as he puts it, *baurau*) actually means. However much one loads this word with theological significance, *bârâ'* does not by itself entail creation out of nothing—or reorganization, for that matter. Shalom M. Paul, an Assyriologist cited by LDS scholar Stephen D. Ricks,[69] points out that *bârâ'* by itself does not imply creation *ex nihilo* (although Paul admits that 2 Maccabees 7:28 does).[70] However, the significance about *bârâ'* is not that it implies creation *ex nihilo* by itself, but that *God* is always the subject of this verb.[71] A related Hebrew word *'asah* ('make') is different in that anyone could *make* something—that is, from preexisting materials. Moreover, when *bârâ'* is used, there is never any mention of preexisting materials that God used. The product is always mentioned—never any material.[72] Thus, *bârâ'* is a word best suited to express the concept of creation out of nothing. In fact, no other Hebrew term would do. Furthermore, the idea of *creatio ex nihilo* is implied in Genesis 1:1, since no "beginning" for God is mentioned.[73]

Because God is always the *subject* of *bârâ'*, interpreters regularly recognize that the word *create* inescapably refers to *divine* activity.[74] German theologian Jürgen Moltmann captures this well: "To say that God 'created' the world indicates God's self-distinction from that world, and emphasizes that God desired it. . . . It is the specific outcome of his decision of will. Since they are the result of God's creative activity, heaven and earth are . . . contingent."[75] In light of this, Joseph Smith's understanding of the Hebrew word *create* is mistaken since he was applying *reorganization* to *bârâ'* when it should properly have been applied to *asah*.

In contrast to ancient cosmogonies, in which there was no absolute beginning, Genesis distinguishes itself by positing an absolute beginning. *Elohim* was not limited by chaos when creating (as the gods were in the Babylonian cosmogony, for instance) but is sovereign over the elements. Genesis 1 stands as an independent assertion, claiming that God created the entire cosmos. In fact, the very structure of Genesis 1:1 argues for creation out of nothing. Grammatically and contextually, a very good case can be made for seeing Genesis 1:1 as referring to absolute creation.[76] John Sailhamer remarks, "Biblical scholars have long believed the idea of 'creation from nothing' can be found in the opening phrase of Genesis 1. . . . There is little else the text *could* mean other than 'creation out of nothing.' The simple notion that the world has a 'beginning' would itself seem to necessitate that it was created 'from nothing.'"[77]

Moltmann comments on *bârâ'*, which is used "exclusively as a term for the divine bringing forth."[78] He points out that the verb *bârâ'* never has an object (i.e., never takes an accusative) mentioning a material out of which something has been made. This, he says, reveals that "the divine creativity has no conditions or premises. Creation is something absolutely new. It is neither potentially inherent nor present in anything else."[79] As Werner Foerster has written, creation in Genesis 1 "arises out of nothing by the Word of God."[80] Consequently, Genesis should not be translated, "In the beginning, *when* God created the heavens and the earth, the earth was a formless wasteland," as the New American Bible does.[81] Even Bernhard Anderson, who sees Genesis 1:2 as referring to creation out of chaos, concedes that "stylistic studies" favor Genesis 1:1 as being an "absolute declarative sentence."[82] This absolute understanding of Genesis 1:1 and its status as an independent clause is borne out by the Septuagint's rendering[83] as well as in "all the ancient versions."[84]

Commentators Keil and Delitzsch declare that "in the beginning" (*berêshît*) "is used absolutely," and a translation such as "In the beginning, when . . ." simply "cannot" be a reasonable treatment of the text.[85] In their estimation, "the context" indicates "the very first beginning."[86] Thus, the eternity of the world or the existence of any "primeval material" is ruled out by language such as the absolute phrase "in the beginning" or the totalistic merism "the heaven[s] and the earth," which was, again, the very best the Hebrews could do to express entirety.[87] Bruce Waltke notes the unanimity in "both the Jewish and Christian tradition" about the first word in the Bible being in an "absolute state" and that the first verse is "an independent clause." He then comments: "Moses could not have used any other construction to denote the first word as in the absolute state, but he could have opted for a different construction to indicate clearly the construct state."[88]

Old Testament scholar Thomas McComiskey concurs that the word *bârâ'* emphasizes the *initiation* of the object, the bringing about of something new.[89] Further support is garnered from Edward P. Arbez and John P. Weisengoff, who show that besides there being nothing in the text of Genesis to affirm that chaotic matter existed before God's action,[90] the use of the verb *bârâ'* in the context of Genesis 1 makes the best sense if it is understood as creation *ex nihilo*. For instance, God's activity (expressed by *bârâ'*) brings about the universe ("heavens and earth") "in the beginning" (i.e., the universe had a beginning through the action of God). Nor is there any mention of anything preexistent that God used. 'To create' is more fitting a translation than is 'to fashion' or 'to shape' or the like.[91] These scholars conclude quite forcefully that "the whole of Gen. 1 is permeated with the idea of the absolute transcendence of God and of the utter dependence of all being on God for its existence. The idea of a 'creatio ex nihilo' seems to be so logically bound up with the author's view of God that one can hardly refuse to see it in his opening statement."[92] Kenneth Mathews's analysis of Genesis 1 leads him to conclude: "The idea of *creatio ex nihilo* is a proper theological inference derived from the whole fabric of the chapter."[93]

We must also clear away the confusion that comes with the Septuagint's rendering of Genesis 1:2: *hê de gê ên aoratos kai akataskeuastos* (And/now the earth was unseen/invisible and unformed). This Greek translation clearly reflects a Hellenistic influence,[94] and English versions such as the AV and RSV Hellenistically render the Hebrew phrase *tôhû wabôhû* as "without form and void." Translating it thus has actually contributed to a somewhat Greek outlook in the thinking of some Christians. According to this reading, the earth is some kind of amorphous mass. But the wording of this phrase, when taking into consideration later biblical usage (some of which harks back to Genesis 1:2), leads to the better (and less-Hellenized) rendering of the land as being desolate and uninhabitable: "a desert and a wasteland," as Victor

Hamilton translates it.[95] Medieval Jewish interpreters who were not influenced by the Septuagint took this perspective as well.[96] Further reinforcing the point is the fact that later Greek versions of the Septuagint *departed from* a Platonic view of creation to a more biblical one: (Aquila: "empty and nothing"; Symmachus: "fallow and undistinct").[97] Furthermore, our earliest Semitic Targumim (interpretive renderings of the Hebrew Bible) have "no trace of the concepts" found in the Septuagint.[98] For example, Targum Neophiti I (which is no later than the third century A.D. and is possibly pre-Christian) renders Genesis 1:2 as "desolate without human beings or beast and void of all cultivation of plants and of trees," which captures the Hebrew usage. Ironically, it is the LDS cosmology that appears more similar to Greek thought than Mormons realize!

So there is no need to see Genesis 1:2 as referring to eternally preexistent matter. As Keil and Delitzsch offer: "*and the earth was without form and void,*' not before, but when, or after God created it."[99] Rather, "there is nothing belonging to the composition of the universe, either in material or in form, which had an existence out of God prior to this divine act in the beginning."[100] Although LDS scholars appear to assign exegetical priority to Genesis 1:2, this is misguided. As Foerster indicates: "Gn 1:1 is placed before the account as a title, and it thus controls v. 2 as well."[101]

Lending further support to *creatio ex nihilo* in Scripture is that God (or Christ) is said to be the Creator or the ultimate Source of the totality of existing things. Although Gerhard May leads one to believe that the biblical evidence for creation out of nothing is ambiguous, it is hard to improve on the totalism of biblical language: "from him ... are all things" (Rom 11:36); "through [Christ] are all things" (1 Cor 8:6 NRSV); "God, who created all things" (Eph 3:9); "by him all things were created" (Col 1:16; cp. 20); "you created all things, and by your will they existed and were created" (Rev 4:11 NRSV). The clear implication of Yahweh's title "the first and ... the last" (Isa 44:6) or "the Alpha and the Omega" (Rev 1:8) is that he is the ultimate originator and only eternal being. Proverbs 8:22–26 (NRSV) states that before the depths were brought forth (i.e., most likely the "deep" of Gen 1:2), Wisdom was creating with God. Nothing else besides the Creator existed—and this would preclude any preexistent matter. As Derek Kidner notes, "Wisdom is both older than the universe, and fundamental to it. Not a speck of matter (26b), not a trace of order (29), came into existence but by Wisdom."[102]

In addition, the notion of *creatio ex nihilo* is reinforced when Scripture declares the eternality and self-sufficiency of God in contrast to the finite created order (Ps 102:25–27; cp. Heb 1:10–12). The God "who called forth creation out of nothing has power also to reduce it to nothing again."[103] Implicit throughout Isaiah 40–48 is the supreme sovereignty and utter uniqueness of Yahweh in creation, beside whom there was no other god— or anything else—when he created: "I am the first and . . . the last" (44:6; cp. 48:12); "I am the LORD, who has made all things" (44:24); "I am the LORD, and there is no other" (45:18; cf. 46:9). As Wolfhart Pannenberg comments, "[Old Testament] statements about creation in (e.g., Pss. 104:14–30; 139:13; 147:8f.) refuse to limit the creative power of God by linking it with preexistent matter. Like the thought of creation by the Word in Gen. 1, they imply the unrestricted freedom of God's creative action that the phrase 'creation out of nothing' would later express."[104]

Moreover, the doctrine of creation assumes that God's word *alone* is what brings the universe about—not simply God's word acting on previously existing matter. Psalm 33 declares that it was simply "by the word of the Lord [*tô logô tou kyriou*]" and "the breath of his mouth" that "the heavens were made"; he "spoke" or "commanded," and it was "created/established [*ektisthêsen*]" (6, 9).[105] There are simply no preexisting conditions to which God is subject; it is God's commanding word that brings creation into being.[106] As Bruce Waltke states, the Old Testament does not present an "eternal dualism" of God and primordial matter. Rather, various Scriptures "clearly states that only God is eternal—he made everything (e.g., Neh. 9:6; Job 41:11; Ps. 102:25; Heb. 11:3; Rev. 1:8)."[107]

Thomas McComiskey summarizes nicely the thrust of the Old Testament understanding of *creation*: "The limitation of this word to divine activity indicates that the area of meaning delineated by the root [of *bârâ*] falls outside the sphere of human ability. Since the word never occurs with the object of the material, and since the primary emphasis of the word is on the newness of the created object, the word lends itself well to the concept of creation *ex nihilo*, although that concept is not necessarily inherent within the meaning of the word."[108]

New Testament

Regarding the New Testament, a passage that deserves significant attention is Hebrews 11:3: "By faith we understand that the universe was formed at God's command, so that *what is seen* [*to blepomenon*] was not *made* [*katêrtisthai*] out of what was visible [*mê ek phainomenôn*]." This text declares that the visible universe "was not made out of equally visible [preexistent] raw material; it was called into being by divine power."[109] Jaroslav Pelikan states that this passage, along with Romans 4:17, "explicitly" teaches creation out of nothing.[110]

The word order of the phrase in Hebrews 11:3 (*mê ek phainomenôn*) is common in Classical Greek and should be rendered "from things unseen."[111] The philosophical sense of *ta phainomena* referred to sense experience.[112] The physical worlds (*tous aiônas*) are described as being that which is seen (*to blepomenon*) in contrast with that which is invisible—namely, the word of God.[113] Paul Ellingworth argues that the phrase in Hebrews 11:3 *rhêmati theou*—"the word/command of God" (which reflects the thinking of Psalm 33:6)—would "conflict" with any idea that the visible world was made out of materials in the invisible world. It is much more satisfactory to understand *tois aiônas* as referring to the visible world and thus as synonymous with *to blepomenon*.[114]

In Hebrews 11:3, C. F. D. Moule states, "the reference seems to be to creation *ex nihilo*, the *visible* having come into being out of the *invisible*."[115] Commentator William Lane remarks that although Hebrews 11:3 does not state *creatio ex nihilo* in positive terms, negatively, "it denies that the creative universe originated from primal material or anything observable."[116] Lane goes on to assert that the writer's insistence that the universe was not brought into being from anything observable "would seem to exclude any influence from Platonic or Philonic cosmology. It may, in fact, have been the writer's intention to correct a widespread tendency in hellenistic Judaism to read Gen 1 in the light of Plato's doctrine in the *Timaeus*."[117] What is *invisible* out of which the *visible* came into being? Commentator Craig Koester observes that the context and structure of the verse make the "most viable" referent the power of God's word, not some transcendent realm: "What cannot be seen is the Word of God. . . . God's Word brought into being a universe that is seen."[118] So, contrary to May's assertion, Hebrews 11:3 states something that is quite distinct from Classical Greek concepts of creation.

A second important passage is Romans 4:17, which speaks of "the God who gives life to the dead and calls [forth] things that are not as though they were." Latter-day Saint scholar Keith Norman cites Foerster in his comments on Romans 4:17, claiming that Foerster says that "one can call forth only that which already exists" rather than out of nothing, which is a "logical impossibility."[119] Ironically, Foerster actually gives a powerful defense of the biblical doctrine of creation out of nothing. In the preceding paragraph he said that creation "arises out of nothing by the Word of God."[120] The comment quoted by Norman continues: "*But God* calls forth what does not yet exist," and we must not try to take "the *mê onta* [things which do not (yet) exist] as though in some sense they were *onta* [existing things]."[121] Furthermore, Foerster cites 2 Corinthians 4:6 (echoing Gen 1:3), where God calls the light out of darkness, as another reference to creation out of nothing by God's word.[122]

It is clear that in Romans 4:17 the Apostle Paul is not expounding a theory of creation. Rather, he is making a theological point that presupposes a certain view of creation, creation out of nothing. New Testament scholar James Dunn admirably explains the relationship between Paul's understanding of creation and how Paul relates it to his point about redemption in Romans 4:17. Dunn's comments are worth quoting at length, since they also have application to other aspects of LDS theology:

> Paul calls on this theological axiom not simply because it is a formula few if any of his readers would dispute, but because it clearly implies also the relationship which must pertain between this creator and his creation. As creator he creates without any precondition: he makes alive where there was only death, and *he calls into existence where there was nothing at all.* Consequently that which has been created, made alive in this way, must be totally dependent on the creator, the life-giver, for its very existence and life. Expressed in such terms the statement provides the governing principle by which all God's relationship with humankind must be understood, including salvation and redemption. Unless God is inconsistent, the same principle will govern God's dealings as savior: he redeems as he creates, and he reckons righteous in the same way in which he makes alive. That is to say, his saving work depends on nothing in that which is saved; redemption, righteous-reckoning, is not contingent on any precondition on the part of the recipient; the dead cannot make terms, that which does not exist cannot place God under any obligation—which is to say that the individual or nation is dependent on the unconditional grace of God as much for covenant life as for created life. It was this total dependence on God for very existence itself which man forgot, his rejection of that dependence which lies at the root of his malaise ([Rom] 1:18–28).[123]

In addition to the clear affirmations in Hebrews 11:3 and Romans 4:17, other New Testament texts also support creation *ex nihilo*. Referring to creation, John 1:3 unambiguously states that all things—that is, "the material world"—came into being through the Word.[124] The implication is that all things (which would include preexistent matter, if that were applicable to the creative process) exist through God's agent, who is the originator of everything.[125] This is borne out by the fact that though the Word *was* (*ēn*), the creation *came to be* (*egeneto*).[126] Raymond Brown comments: "Thus the material world has been created by God and is good."[127] So when Scripture speaks of God's creation, there is an all-embracing nature to it. Despite their lack of precise formulation of a doctrine of *creatio ex nihilo*, writes Walther Eichrodt, the biblical writers have "a natural habit of speaking as comprehensively as possible about Yahweh's creative power."[128]

Colossians 1:16–17 speaks comprehensively when it declares that *all things* were created *in* and *through* Christ (NRSV). The totalistic merism in Genesis 1:1 ("the heavens and the earth") is expressed in the phrase "all things." The mention that he has created things "in heaven and on earth"— which corresponds to or parallels[129] "things visible and invisible" (*ta orata kai ta aorata*)—indicates that these expressions "embrace everything for there are no exceptions."[130] N. T. Wright declares that "all things" could be translated "the totality."[131] Not only this, but Christ is *before* all things. The implication is that there was a state of being in which Christ existed and the universe did not. As F. F. Bruce notes, "The words ['before all things'] not only declare His temporal priority to the universe, but also suggest his primacy over it."[132] The text of Colossians 1:16–17 suggests two affirmations:[133] (1) Christ's creating (bringing all things into being), and (2) his sustaining them in being. The fact that in him "all things hold together" (1:17) emphasizes his sustaining "what He has brought into being."[134] Without such an activity, "all would disintegrate."[135] These various New Testament texts seem to warrant the conclusion, in agreement with Foerster, that "creation out of nothing by the Word explicitly or implicitly underlies the NT statements [regarding creation]."[136]

In light of the above discussion, it is a serious distortion to portray the doctrine of creation out of nothing as a purely postbiblical phenomenon, as some Mormon apologists have done. *Where in the relevant scholarly references to which LDS scholars point is there rigorous exegetical treatment of the relevant biblical passages on creation?* The silence is deafening. Yet the biblical data indicate that God was in some way prior to all that is (i.e., there was a state of affairs in which God existed and nothing else), which is the basis for the doctrine of *creatio ex nihilo*. The doctrine of creation out of nothing is biblical even if it was not stated in precisely those words until later. So the doctrinal formulation of creation out of nothing is, as Moltmann puts it, "unquestionably an apt paraphrase of what the Bible means by 'creation.'"[137]

One wonders what LDS scholars would take as unambiguous evidence for creation out of nothing in Scripture (or even extrabiblical sources). It seems that they would not be satisfied with any formulation in a given text other than "creation out of absolutely nothing" or the like before admitting to the possibility of finding clear evidence of the doctrine of *creatio ex nihilo*. Apart from the strong case just made for the biblical doctrine of creation out of nothing, we must note that even if the biblical evidence *were* ambiguous and the biblical writers took no position on this issue, the LDS view would not win by default. For we are not dealing with an either/or situation (*either* the Bible explicitly teaches creation out of nothing, *or* the LDS view is true by default). Rather, the LDS position has its own burden of proof that must be shouldered. On the one hand, Mormons have neglected to interact with biblical scholarship on this subject; on the other, they have put forth no significant positive exegetical evidence for their own position. We would challenge LDS scholars to interact more intentionally with the biblical text and with biblical scholarship.

Creatio ex nihilo: Extrabiblical Evidence

The noted philosopher of science Ian Barbour has boldly declared, *"Creation 'out of nothing' is not a biblical concept."*[138] Rather, it was merely a postbiblical development to defend God's goodness and absolute sovereignty over the world against "Gnostic ideas regarding matter as evil or as the product of an inferior deity."[139] Furthermore, according to Barbour's thinking (as well as that of Mormons), the Bible is not simply ambiguous about the nature of God's relationship to creation but actually asserts that God created from preexistent materials: "Genesis portrays the creation of order from chaos, and . . . the *ex nihilo* doctrine was formulated later by the church fathers to defend theism against an ultimate dualism or a monistic pantheism. We still need to defend theism against alternative philosophies, but we can do so without reference to an absolute beginning."[140] Thus, the doctrine of *creatio ex nihilo* is not theologically necessary: "This is not the main concern expressed in the religious notion of creation."[141]

In the last section we pointed out—and gave reasons for rejecting—Gerhard May's statement that the doctrine of creation out of nothing is "not demanded by the text of the Bible."[142] May offers no substantiation for this claim. Indeed, we have seen that the *opposite* is the case. The substance of May's (and Barbour's) argument is that Christian thinkers in the second century tried to formulate a doctrine of creation in response to Gnosticism (with its emphasis on emanations) and Middle Platonic thought (with its emphasis on eternally preexistent matter), resulting in their formulation of the doctrine of *creatio ex nihilo*.[143] Up until this point, there had been no explicit formulation of precisely how God created the world.

This is just the line of reasoning that some Mormons take. Latter-day Saint scholar Hugh Nibley says that it is not until we get to the "Doctors of the Church" that we hear of creation *ex nihilo*.[144] Prior to this time, we have "the creation everywhere being conceived of as the act of organizing 'matter unorganized' (*amorphos hylê*), bringing order from disorder."[145] Stephen Robinson makes a similar point: "There is no evidence for *creatio ex nihilo* in Judaism before the Hellenistic period, nor in early Christianity before the late second century."[146] The doctrine of creation out of nothing is thus a theological add-on to Scripture, and Robinson points to a particular article by B. W. Anderson on creation (as do Mormon scholars Daniel C. Peterson and Stephen D. Ricks).[147]

However, Robinson's own assertion is not quite accurate either. The *fuller* context of Anderson's point makes plain that the *Old Testament*—not the New Testament or the early church fathers—is in view: "In later theological reflection upon the meaning of creation, the sovereignty of the Creator was further emphasized by the doctrine that the world was created out of nothing (II Macc. 7:28; cf. Rom. 4:17; Heb. 11:3). It is doubtful, however, whether this teaching is explicitly in Gen. 1 or anywhere else in the OT."[148]

We have already dealt with matters biblical on the subject of creation. But what about the claim that this doctrine was a theological innovation or invention? We shall argue that this, too, is false.

Scholars agree that with Irenaeus, the doctrine of *creatio ex nihilo* was well established. Irenaeus also argued that the world was not coeternal with God:

> But the things established are distinct from Him who has established them, and what [things] have been made from Him who has made them. For He is Himself uncreated, both without beginning and end, and lacking nothing. He is Himself sufficient for this very thing, existence; but the things which have been made by Him have received a beginning. . . . He indeed who made all things can alone, together with His Word, properly

be termed God and Lord; but the things which have been made cannot have this term applied to them, neither should they justly assume that appellation which belongs to the Creator.[149]

Later, Augustine himself simply declared that God "created heaven and earth out of nothing."[150]

Some early Christian writers (not to mention Philo of Alexandria) who were influenced by Middle Platonist thought, such as Justin Martyr, Athenagoras, and Clement of Alexandria, seem to have maintained that matter had existed before the creation of the world. It has been argued that some of these men actually believed that preexistent matter had itself been created *ex nihilo* at some point.[151] Less debatable is the fact that they all appear to have viewed matter as being in some sense contingent and dependent on God.[152] N. Joseph Torchia, discussing the views of the earliest of these writers, notes that in them "we find a well-defined ontological distinction between God and matter," and that for each, "God is the unbegotten, ultimate causal principle for everything which exists."[153] Thus, in a very important respect, even the clearly Hellenistically influenced views of these early Christians disagree with the common belief of Platonism and Mormonism that matter has eternally existed and is ontologically independent of God.

Despite the undeniable influence of Middle Platonism on some early Christian thinkers, we must be cautious about attributing ambiguity to the biblical text about creation out of nothing simply because the overlapping of certain concepts common to both Middle Platonism and Scripture may blur one's perspective somewhat. F. F. Bruce reminds us that "the idea of imposing form on pre-existent matter is Greek rather than Hebrew in origin."[154] It must be remembered that Jewish thought was preoccupied with the God of the cosmos rather than with the cosmos itself,[155] with the *creatio* rather than the *ex nihilo*.[156] The Old Testament's writers viewed natural phenomena primarily as pointers to God, who created them and whose glory was revealed through them (e.g., Ps 104).

We can go further by asserting that the *Umwelt* of Old Testament Judaism (and, by implication, that of early Christianity) furnished an appropriate context for belief in creation out of nothing. Such a belief would not have been foreign to the Hebrew (and early Christian) mentality. To give support to this claim, we will note a variety of relevant extrabiblical Jewish and Christian passages that attest to the fact that *creatio ex nihilo* was not alien to biblically influenced thinking.

Many have suggested that the intertestamental book of 2 Maccabees states clearly the traditional doctrine of *creatio ex nihilo*. There a mother pleads with her son to willingly accept torture rather than recant his beliefs: "I beg you, child, look at the sky and the earth; see all that is in them and realize that God made them out of nothing [*hoti ouk ex onton epoiēsen auta ho theos*], and that man comes into being in the same way" (2 Macc 7:28). Bernhard Anderson sees the doctrine of *creatio ex nihilo* set forth in this passage,[157] and Gerhard von Rad maintains that "the conceptional formulation *creatio ex nihilo* is first found" in this passage.[158] The Jewish understanding of creation was that "the world as a whole can only be understood in the context of its coming into being,"[159] according to Claus Westermann. It is, then, not a large step from this assumption to state that 2 Maccabees 7:28 indeed speaks of creation out of nothing.[160]

According to Dead Sea Scrolls scholar Craig Evens, it is "highly probable that the men of Qumran believed in creation *ex nihilo*." The reason for this judgment can be seen in how the Qumran writings describe creation.[161] For example, we see reference to creation out of nothing in "The Rule of the Community":

> From the God of knowledge stems all there is and all there shall be. Before they existed he made all their plans, and when they came into being, they will execute all their works in compliance with his instructions, according to his glorious design without altering anything. (1QS III.15–16)[162]

Another quotation from the same scroll echoes this same idea of God's absolute creation:

> By his knowledge everything shall come into being,
> and all that does exist
> he establishes with his calculations
> and nothing is done outside of him. (1QS XI.11)

The Qumran writings notably stress God's absolute sovereignty: God creates for his own glory, and the very being of the universe originates from him. "[Without you] nothing is done, and nothing is known without your will" (1QH IX.8). Another segment reinforces these themes:

> And in the wisdom of your knowledge
> you have determined their [i.e., humans'] course
> before they came to exist.

multiple references to C.Ex. NiL.
in apocryphal & other early writings
3. Craftsman or Creator?

And with [your approval] everything occurs
And without you nothing occurs. (1QH IX.19–20)

God's creative action takes place by his wisdom (and power)—not pre-existing materials. Reading the "Hymn to the Creator in Psalms" (11Q5 XXVI.9–15), we see that God "established the dawn with the knowledge of his heart"; he "made the earth with his strength" and established "the world with his wisdom." "With his knowledge he spread out the heavens."[163] Again, we are pointed toward creation *ex nihilo* rather than away from it.

The noted first-century rabbi Gamaliel seems to have reflected this concept of creation in his thinking. A philosopher challenged him: "Your God was indeed a great artist, but he had good materials [unformed space/void, darkness, water, wind, and the deep] to help him." Gamaliel, wishing that this philosopher's spirit would burst (or "give up the ghost"),[164] declared, "All of them are explicitly described as having been created by him [and not as preexistent]."[165]

In the *Shepherd of Hermas,* the first command is to believe that God brought all things "into existence out of nonexistence."[166] In light of this reference, Denis Carroll comments that this is the first allusion to *creatio ex nihilo* in Christian literature.[167]

The Jewish pseudepigraphal book *Joseph and Aseneth,* whose date ranges from as early as the second century B.C. through the second century A.D., contains a passage that also seems to imply *creatio ex nihilo.* Aseneth, having thrown her idols out of the window and put on sackcloth for a week, addresses the God of Joseph:

> Lord God of the ages,
> who created all (things) and gave life (to them),
> who gave breath of life to your whole creation,
> who brought the invisible (things) out into the light,
> who made the (things that) are and the (ones that) have an
> appearance from the non-appearing and non-being,
> who lifted up the heaven
> and founded it on a firmament upon the back of the winds. . . .
> For you, Lord, spoke and they were brought to life,
> because your word, Lord, is life for all your creatures. (12:1–3)

Second Enoch, which was written in the late first century A.D., also reflects the doctrine of creation out of nothing: "I commanded . . . that visible things should come down from invisible" (25:1ff.); "Let one of the invisible things come out solid and visible" (26:1; cf. 24:2; 33:4).

Composed around 100 A.D., the *Odes of Solomon* (written originally, most probably, in Syriac)[168] indicate creation out of nothing:

> And there is nothing outside of the Lord,
> because he was before anything came to be.
> And the worlds are by his word,
> And by the thought of his heart. (16:18–19)

In the early second century the author of *Second Baruch* penned these words: "O thou . . . that hast fixed the firmament by the word, . . . that hast called from the beginning of the world that which did not yet exist" (21:4). In his dissertation on 2 Baruch, Frank James Murphy comments that *creatio ex nihilo* is being expressed here, indicating that the present visible world is not eternal. It had a beginning.[169]

A final example is taken from the *Apostolic Constitutions*, which was written perhaps as early as the mid-second century A.D. and which reflects a belief in creation out of nothing. The "one who is truly God" is "the one who is before things that have been made . . . the only one without origin, and without a beginning." The eternal God is the one through whom "all things" have been made. He is "first by nature and only one in being."[170]

One final point: Mormon scholars[171] will periodically cite a source such as Jonathan Goldstein, who says that "medieval Jewish thinkers still held that the account of creation in Genesis could be interpreted to mean that God created from pre-existing formless matter."[172] This is simply not true and is a misreading of these exegetes. Rather, all the medieval Jewish exegetes (Ibn Ezra, Rashbam, Rambam, etc.) uniformly follow Rashi in *presupposing* creation out of nothing. How so? They assume, for example, that because water already exists in Genesis 1:2, this could not be absolute creation (i.e., out of nothing). That is, the creation described in 1:1 is not the first thing God creates. Interestingly, Rashi was the first, so far as we know, to read *berêshît* ("in the beginning") as construct ("in beginning") rather than absolute ("in the very beginning").[173] Absolute creation took place before, and here God is working with his own created materials to create further. It was not *grammatical* grounds that led Rashi to formulate *berêshît* as a construct, but rather the subject matter. Ibn Ezra, who followed Rashi in the "construct" view, believed that God had *previously* created the water, which he then later used to create within selective aspects of the universe. Old Testament scholar John Sailhamer summarizes:

> Neither Rashi nor Ibn Ezra appears to have rejected the traditional view [of *berêshît* as absolute] on grammatical grounds, thinking the construct reading was the better reading. Rather they believed it was the only reading that would solve the apparent difficulty of the "water" in v.2 not being accounted for in v.1. In fact, Ibn Ezra warned his readers not to be "astonished" at the suggestion of a construct before a verb, which suggests that he himself felt some difficulty in reading *berêshît* before a finite verb as a construct and that he anticipated the same reaction in his readers.
>
> Both Rashi and Ibn Ezra produced examples to show that a finite verb after a construct noun was permissible. Both the fact and the nature of their defense of their reading in 1:1 betrays their own uneasiness with such a reading.[174]

Thus, these medieval Jewish exegetes did not believe that God created out of eternally preexisting material. Rather, according to their thinking, God was the originator of *any* finite materials he may have used to create in Genesis 1. As Foerster comments, "In later Judaism, both in Rabb[inic] and pseudepigr[aphal] writings, it is clearly stated that God alone created the world by His Word, i.e., that He called it into existence from nothing."[175] He goes so far as to say that "the idea of a pre-existence of matter" was "alien" to rabbinic literature.[176] Ramban, commenting on Genesis 1:1, even declared: "This is the root of faith, and he who does not believe in this and thinks the world was eternal denies the essential principle of the [Judaic] religion and has no Torah at all."[177]

In the end we see a remarkable continuity amongst those who penned 2 Maccabees, the Dead Sea Scrolls, Jewish translations of the Old Testament into Greek, the Semitic Targumim, and various medieval Jewish commentaries. Hence, the conviction that God created absolutely everything is taken for granted by a good number of pertinent independent sources. The Mormon view of creation, which is perhaps most compatible with process theology,[178] cannot be sustained.

Despite the commonly heard assertion that there was "wholesale adoption of Greek philosophical metaphysics,"[179] it is clearly the Christian doctrine that is *not* influenced by Greek thought at this juncture. Ironically, it is the LDS conception of creation that is obviously in line with Greek thought—a variation of neo-Platonic thinking, to be exact. It is the Latter-day Saints who follow Plato's character Timaeus through whom he asserted:

> This is in the truest sense the origin of creation and of the world. . . .
> Wherefore also finding the whole visible sphere not at rest, but moving in
> an irregular and disorderly fashion, out of disorder [God] brought order,
> considering that this was in every way better than the other.[180]

To sum up thus far: We have tried to show that the LDS belief that God created the world out of eternally preexisting, unorganized material or chaos does not square with the biblical text and that the literature cited by LDS scholars consistently fails to grapple with it. To the contrary, in the Bible we find the doctrine of creation *ex nihilo* clearly set forth. It is, in truth, extremely difficult to imagine how an un-Hellenized Hebrew would conclude from the biblical text that God and some unorganized matter (or chaos) coexisted from eternity. Moreover, there is good warrant for asserting that the doctrine of creation out of nothing was not itself constructed *ex nihilo* by second-century Christian theologians, for this view was held by Jewish and Christian writers alike before this time. It is rather the LDS view that is found to be incompatible with Scripture.

Section III: Philosophical and Scientific Support for *Creatio ex nihilo*

Their commitment to the biblical doctrine of *creatio ex nihilo* brought the church fathers into head-on collision with the Greek conception of the eternity of matter. For both Plato and Aristotle, the greatest of the Greek thinkers, creation consists, not in God's bringing the world into being out of nothing, but in his imposition of form upon formless prime matter, thereby fashioning a cosmos out of chaos.[181] As we have seen, despite the tremendous pressure exerted by Greek philosophical thought, the church fathers with few exceptions refused to relinquish a Hebraic understanding of creation for this Greek conception. Because Aristotle had not merely asserted but had *argued* for the eternity of world, Christian theologians could not rest content with citing biblical proof-texts for the Judeo-Christian view but engaged Greek thinkers in philosophical discussion of their competing paradigms. The last great champion of *creatio ex nihilo* before the advent of Islam was John Philoponus (d. 580?), an Aristotelian commentator from Alexandria, who in his works *Against Aristotle* and *On the Eternity of the World Against Proclus* initiated a tradition of argumentation for *creatio ex nihilo* based on the impossibility of an infinite past, a tradition subsequently enriched by medieval Muslim and Jewish theologians and then transmitted back again into Christian scholastic theology.[182] Any person who rejects the doctrine of *creatio ex nihilo* cannot responsibly ignore this tradition but must respond substantively to such thinkers as al-Ghazali, Saadia ben Gaon, Bonaventure, and their modern counterparts.

The argument for the doctrine of *creatio ex nihilo* may be formulated on the basis of the following premises:

1. The temporal series of past physical events either had a beginning or is beginningless.
2. If the temporal series of past physical events had a beginning, the beginning was either created or uncreated.
3. The temporal series of past physical events is not beginningless.
4. The beginning was not uncreated.

The argument has two stages: the first demonstrates the *ex nihilo* aspect of the doctrine, and the second stage demonstrates the *creatio*. For from (1) and (3), it follows logically that

5. The temporal series of past physical events had a beginning.

This is a beginning before which there are no temporal physical events and therefore represents an absolute beginning. From (2) and (5) it follows logically that

6. The beginning was either created or uncreated.

Finally, (4) and (6) logically imply

7. The beginning was created.

The argument is obviously logically valid, so the question of its soundness devolves to the truth of its four premises. Now premises (1) and (2) are necessarily true, since they have the form of the Law of Excluded Middle: *p* or not-*p*. Premise (4) will not be contested by Mormon theologians, since they do not reject *creatio* but only *ex nihilo*. They deny that the temporal series of past physical events ever had a beginning. But if it did, they would agree that it was created, since, to quote James Talmage again, "from nothing, nothing can be derived."[183] So the dispute focuses on premise (3).

In order to assess the truth of (3), it will be helpful to define some terms. By a "physical event," we mean any change occurring within the space-time universe. Since any change takes time, there are no instantaneous events. Neither could there be an infinitely slow event, since such an "event" would in reality be a changeless state. Therefore, any event will have a finite, nonzero duration. In order that all the events comprising the temporal series of past events be of equal duration, we arbitrarily stipulate some event as our standard and, taking as our point of departure the present standard event, we consider any series of such standard events ordered according to the relation *earlier than*. The question is whether this series of events had a beginning or not. By a "beginning," one means a first standard event. It is therefore not relevant whether the temporal series had a beginning *point* (a first temporal instant). The question is whether there was in the past an event occupying a nonzero, finite temporal interval that was absolutely first, that is, not preceded by any equal interval.

In what follows, we shall present two independent deductive arguments and two independent inductive arguments on behalf of premise (3) and consider Mormon responses to these arguments. We shall leave it to Mormon theologians to present whatever arguments they can for their own position, namely,

3'. The temporal series of past physical events is beginningless.

We know of no good arguments, deductive or inductive, for (3'), nor are we aware of any arguments for (3') offered by Mormon theologians. But whatever they may think of our arguments for (3), Mormon thinkers must shoulder the burden of proof for their own position, just as we have tried to do for ours.

Deductive Arguments

Argument from the Impossibility of an Actual Infinite

The first argument we shall consider is the argument based on *the impossibility of the existence of an actual infinite*. While potential infinites can exist, no actual infinite can exist, for such a real existence would entail absurdities. Because an actually infinite number of things cannot exist, the series of past events must be finite in number, and hence, the temporal series of past physical events is not beginningless. We may formulate the argument as follows:

1. An actual infinite cannot exist.
2. An infinite temporal regress of events is an actual infinite.
3. Therefore an infinite temporal regress of events cannot exist.

With regard to the first premise, it is important to understand that by "exist" we mean "have extra-mental existence," or "be instantiated in the real world." We are contending, then, that an actual infinite cannot exist in the real world. It is usually alleged that this sort of argument has been invalidated by Georg Cantor's work on the actual infinite and by subsequent developments in set theory. But this allegation seriously misconstrues the nature of both Cantor's system and modern set theory, for the argument does not contradict a single tenet of either. The reason is this: Cantor's system and set theory are simply a universe of discourse, a mathematical system based on certain adopted axioms and conventions, whereas our argument concerns the real world. What we shall argue is that while the actual infinite may be a fruitful and consistent concept within a postulated universe of discourse, it cannot be transposed into the real world, for this would involve counterintuitive absurdities.

Hence, we have no intention whatsoever of trying to drive mathematicians from their Cantorian paradise. Our strategy is that of Wittgenstein, when he remarked: "I would say, 'I wouldn't dream of trying to drive anyone from this paradise.' I would do something quite different: I would try to show you that it is not a paradise—so that you'll leave of your own accord. I would say, 'You're welcome to this; just look about you.'"[184] While the

Cantorian theory may be perfectly consistent, given its axioms and conventions, we think that it is intuitively obvious that such a system could not possibly exist in reality. The best way to show this is by way of concrete examples that illustrate the various absurdities that would result if an actual infinite were to be instantiated in the real world.

Let us use one of our favorites, Hilbert's Hotel, a product of the mind of the great German mathematician David Hilbert.[185] Let us imagine a hotel with a finite number of rooms. Suppose, furthermore, that all the rooms are full. When a new guest arrives asking for a room, the proprietor apologizes, "Sorry, all the rooms are full." But now let us imagine a hotel with an infinite number of rooms and suppose once more that *all the rooms are full.* There is not a single vacant room throughout the entire infinite hotel. Now suppose a new guest shows up, asking for a room. "But of course!" says the proprietor, and he immediately shifts the person in room #1 into room #2, the person in room #2 into room #3, the person in room #3 into room #4, and so on, out to infinity. As a result of these room changes, room #1 now becomes vacant, and the new guest gratefully checks in. But remember, before he arrived, all the rooms were full! Equally curious, according to the mathematicians, there are now no more persons in the hotel than there were before: the number is just infinite. But how can this be? The proprietor just added the new guest's name to the register and gave him his keys—how can there not be one more person in the hotel than before?

But the situation becomes even stranger. For suppose an infinity of new guests show up at the desk, asking for a room. "Of course, of course!" says the proprietor, and he proceeds to shift the person in room #1 into room #2, the person in room #2 into room #4, the person in room #3 into room #6, and so on out to infinity, always putting each former occupant into the room number twice his own. Because any natural number multiplied by two always equals an even number, all the guests wind up in even-numbered rooms. As a result, all the odd-numbered rooms become vacant, and the infinity of new guests is easily accommodated. And yet, before they came, all the rooms were full! And again, strangely enough, the number of guests in the hotel is the same after the infinity of new guests check in as before, even though there were as many new guests as old guests. In fact, the proprietor could repeat this process *infinitely many times* and yet there would never be one single person more in the hotel than before.

But Hilbert's Hotel is even stranger than the German mathematician made it out to be. For suppose some of the guests start to check out. Suppose the guest in room #1 departs. Is there not now one person fewer in the hotel? Not according to the mathematicians! Suppose the guests in rooms #1, 3, 5 . . . check out. In this case an infinite number of people have left the hotel, but according to the mathematicians, there are no fewer people in the hotel! In fact, we could have every other guest check out of the hotel and repeat this process infinitely many times, and yet there would never be any fewer people in the hotel.

Now suppose the proprietor does not like having a half-empty hotel (it looks bad for business). No matter! By shifting occupants as before, but in reverse order, he transforms his half-vacant hotel into one that is jammed to the gills. One might think that by these maneuvers the proprietor could always keep this strange hotel fully occupied. But one would be wrong. For suppose the persons in rooms #4, 5, 6 . . . checked out. At a single stroke the hotel would be virtually emptied, the guest register would be reduced to three names, and the infinite would be converted to finitude. And yet it would remain true that the *same* number of guests checked out this time as when the guests in rooms #1, 3, 5 . . . checked out! Can anyone believe that such a hotel could exist in reality?

Hilbert's Hotel is absurd. Since nothing hangs on the illustration's involving a hotel, the above sorts of absurdities show in general that it is impossible for an actually infinite number of things to exist.[186] There is simply no way to avoid these absurdities once we admit the possibility of the existence of an actual infinite. Laymen sometimes react to such absurdities as Hilbert's Hotel by saying that since we really do not understand the nature of infinity, these absurdities result. But this attitude is simply mistaken. Infinite set theory is a highly developed and well-understood branch of mathematics, so these absurdities can be seen to result precisely because we *do* understand the notion of a collection with an actually infinite number of members.

Again, we underline the fact that what we have said in no way attempts to undermine the theoretical system bequeathed by Cantor to modern mathematics. Indeed, some of the most eager enthusiasts of the system of transfinite mathematics are only too ready to agree that these theories have no relation to the real world. Thus, Hilbert, who exuberantly extolled Cantor's greatness, nevertheless held that the Cantorian paradise exists only in the ideal world invented by the mathematician. He concludes that

the infinite is nowhere to be found in reality. It neither exists in nature nor provides a legitimate basis for rational thought—a remarkable harmony between being and thought. . . . The role that remains for the infinite to play is solely that of an idea—if one means by an idea, in Kant's terminology, a concept of reason which transcends all experience and which completes the concrete as a totality—that of an idea which we may unhesitatingly trust within the framework erected by our theory.[187]

Our case against the existence of the actual infinite says nothing about the use of the idea of the infinite in conceptual mathematical systems.

The second premise of this argument states that *an infinite temporal regress of events is an actual infinite.* The second premise asserts that if the series or sequence of changes in time is infinite, then these events considered collectively constitute an actual infinite. The point seems obvious enough, for if there has been a sequence composed of an infinite number of events stretching back into the past, then an actually infinite number of events have occurred. Because the series of past events is an actual infinite, all the absurdities attending the real existence of an actual infinite apply to it.

To recapitulate: since an actual infinite cannot exist and an infinite temporal regress of events is an actual infinite, we can conclude that an infinite temporal regress of events cannot exist; that is to say, the temporal regress of events is finite. Since the temporal regress of events is finite, the temporal series of past physical events is not beginningless. And this is the second premise of the original syllogism that we set out to prove.

The few Mormon philosophers there are have taken almost no cognizance of this argument. Blake Ostler, a determined critic of *creatio ex nihilo,* is one who has done so. Granting that "if this argument or any of its related variants is sound, then . . . certain formulations of Latter-day Saint theism [are] incoherent," Ostler tries to discount the argument because it "has been accepted by very few philosophers and in fact has been refuted, decisively in my view, by a number of modern philosophers."[188] Actually, until Cantor's work in the late nineteenth century, the view that actual mathematical infinites do not exist was universally held, and, as we have seen, even the aura of legitimacy won by Cantor for the mathematical concept of the actual infinite says nothing about its ontological status. In any case, such appeals to authority cut no philosophical mustard once we have inquired concerning the *arguments* supporting the respective positions.

So what arguments of the philosophers cited by Ostler does he mean to endorse? This is far from clear. His claim that "Thomas Aquinas and William of Ockham both rejected infinity arguments based on logic" is simply false, for both Aquinas and Ockham held that an actually infinite multitude is impossible. Aquinas thought to evade the implications of this position for the finitude of the past by asserting that the temporal series of past events is merely potentially, but not actually, infinite. But this claim is plainly false, for in order to be potentially infinite, the past would have to be finite but growing in a backward direction, which is absurd. Moreover, Ostler overlooks the fact, pointed out by Kretzmann, whom he cites, that Aquinas did in fact accept these arguments as probability arguments for the finitude of the past, even if he thought they fell short of absolute proof.[189]

Ostler's assertion that Kant considered the question of the past's (in)finitude to lead to an antinomy masks the fact that Kant thought the argument based on the impossibility of the successive formation of an actual infinite (to be discussed below) sound and, indeed, rationally compelling. Will Ostler, then, defend Kant's argument for the antithesis of his first antinomy, an argument that, as one of us has elsewhere argued,[190] is not sound? The objections of Oppy, Grünbaum, Swinburne, Sorabji, and Mackie, cited without comment by Ostler, have all been answered in the philosophical literature;[191] so which of their arguments does Ostler mean to endorse, and how will he answer the published replies? Mormon scholars cannot rest content with merely citing authorities but must be willing to get their hands dirty by grappling with the arguments.

Fortunately, in response to an argument by Beckwith and Parrish, Ostler does have something more to say. With respect to the present argument, he asserts:

> The fallacy is that, as the mathematician Cantor has elegantly shown, not all infinite sets must be equal. Cantor bids us to consider two infinite but unequal sets, the set of all ordinal numbers and the set of all even numbers. The coherence of infinite sets that are unequal can be demonstrated by pairing members of each set into a one-to-one correspondence. Even though both sets are infinite, the set of even numbers is only half as large as the set of ordinal numbers.[192]

This analysis is seriously mistaken.[193] It is true that once one takes into account nondenumerable sets, there are in Cantorian set theory infinite sets of different sizes; but infinite sets that are denumerable are all the same size. Thus, the set of even numbers and the set of ordinal numbers both have the same cardinality, $\aleph_0$; that is to say, they both have the same number of members or are the same size, even though the set $\{1, 2, 3, \ldots\}$ has all the members which {2, 4, 6, . . .} has, plus an infinite number besides. In erroneously asserting that the latter set is "only half as large" (itself a notion inapplicable to infinity!) as the former, Ostler himself bears witness to the paradoxical nature of the actual infinite. Hence, when Ostler says that if we have an infinite number of baseball cards and we give away 100,000, we have fewer cards left, though still an infinite number,[194] he is flatly wrong, for both collections can be put into a one-to-one correspondence with the set of natural numbers. In order to avoid the contradictions involved in subtraction of infinite quantities, transfinite arithmetic simply prohibits such inverse operations by fiat—but if actual infinites can really exist, we cannot prevent our baseball fan from giving away some of his cards!

Ostler also protests that if the mathematical theory of infinite sets is logically coherent, then actual infinites must be really possible: "If the notion is logically coherent, then there is a possible world in which it can obtain."[195] But as one of us explains in a reply to Oppy, this objection conflates strict logical possibility with broad logical possibility. The proponent of the argument need not deny that, granted its axioms and conventions, Cantorian set theory is internally consistent; but that says nothing about whether actual infinites are metaphysically possible, that is to say, whether there is a possible world containing actual infinites. The latter question is a metaphysical question that cannot be answered merely on the basis of a system's freedom from strict logical inconsistency.

Apart from these misconceived objections, we are unaware of any Mormon response to this first argument for the finitude of the past. Thus, we have good reason to think that the temporal series of past physical events is not beginningless.

Argument from the Impossibility of the Successive Formation of an Actual Infinite

The second argument that we shall consider is the argument based on *the impossibility of forming an actual infinite by successive addition*. If an actual infinite cannot be formed by successive addition, then the series of past events must be finite, since that series is formed by successive addition of one event after another in time.[196]

The argument may be formulated as follows:

1. The temporal series of events is a collection formed by successive addition.

2. A collection formed by successive addition cannot be an actual infinite.

3. Therefore, the temporal series of events cannot be an actual infinite.

Here we do not assume that an actual infinite cannot exist. Even if an actual infinite can exist, the temporal series of events cannot be such, since an actual infinite cannot be formed by successive addition, as the temporal series of events is.

The first premise seems obvious enough. The collection of all past events prior to any given point is not a collection whose members all coexist. Rather, it is a collection that is instantiated sequentially or successively in time, one event following on the heels of another. The series of past events is not a tenselessly existing continuum, all of whose members are equally real. Rather, the temporal series of events is a collection formed by successive addition.

The second premise asserts that a collection formed by successive addition cannot be an actual infinite. Sometimes this is described as the impossibility of traversing the infinite. In order for us to have "arrived" at today, existence has, so to speak, traversed an infinite number of prior events.[197] But before the present event could arrive, the event immediately prior to it would have to arrive; and before that event could arrive, the event immediately prior to it would have to arrive; and so on *ad infinitum*. No event could ever arrive, since before it could elapse there would always be one more event that had to have happened first. Thus, if the series of past events were beginningless, the present event could not have arrived, which is absurd! The only way in which an actual infinite could come to exist in the real world would be to be instantiated in reality all at once, simply given in a moment. As Russell states: "Classes which are infinite are given all at once by the defining properties of their members, so that there is no question of 'completion' or of 'successive synthesis.'"[198]

To suggest that the past could be infinite is to assert that a person could have completed a countdown of the negative numbers, ending at zero, a task which seems impossible. It might be said that in an infinite amount of past time, such a task is not impossible, since to every number there corresponds a moment of time at which to count it. But that only pushes the problem back a notch: how could an infinite series of moments elapse sequentially? If the past is actually infinite, then why did the person not finish his countdown of the negative numbers yesterday or the day before, since by then an infinite series of moments had already elapsed? No matter how far along the series of past moments one regresses, he would have already completed his countdown. Therefore, at no point in the infinite series of past moments could he be finishing the countdown. For at any point an actually infinite sequence of moments would have transpired and the countdown would have already been completed. Thus, at no time in eternity will we find the person counting, which is absurd, since we supposed him to be counting from eternity. And at no point will he finish the countdown, which is equally absurd, because for the countdown to be completed, he must at some point have finished. What this scenario really tells us is that an actually infinite temporal regress is absurd.[199]

Hence, we may conclude that a collection formed by successive addition cannot be an actual infinite. Since the temporal series of events is a collection formed by successive addition, we conclude: Therefore, the temporal series of events cannot be an actual infinite. This means, of course, that the temporal series of past physical events is not beginningless. This is, again, the third premise in our original argument.

In his review of Beckwith and Parrish's book, Ostler indicts this argument as "a slight-of-hand trick like Zeno's paradoxes, for even though a baseball must pass through an infinite number of halfway points to reach the catcher's mitt, somehow the baseball actually makes it to the mitt."[200] He thereby fails to note two crucial disanalogies of an infinite past to Zeno's paradoxes: whereas in Zeno's thought experiments the intervals traversed are *potential* and *unequal,* in the case of an infinite past the intervals are *actual* and *equal.* Ostler's claim that the baseball must pass through an infinite number of halfway points to the mitt is question-begging, for it already assumes that the whole interval is a composition of an infinite number of points, whereas Zeno's opponents, like Aristotle, take the line as a whole to be conceptually prior to any divisions we might make in it. Moreover, Zeno's intervals, being unequal, sum to a merely finite distance, whereas the intervals in an infinite past sum to an infinite distance. Thus, it remains mysterious how we could have traversed an infinite number of equal, actual intervals to arrive at our present location.

Ostler also charges that the argument is "a disaster in reasoning," for it commits the fallacy of composition by inferring that because the number of past events is infinite, there must be an "infinitieth" event somewhere in the past. By contrast, "one who believes that the universe is infinitely old does not assert that one of those days was the infinitieth day which occurred an infinite number of days ago."[201] It should be evident from our exposition of the argument, however, that Ostler's charge is groundless. None of the versions of this argument reasons by composition. Moreover, most versions of this argument presuppose that every particular event in an infinite past would lie at a finite temporal distance from the present so that there can be no talk of an infinitieth event. In response to Beckwith and Parrish's observation that this argument in no wise presupposes an infinitieth day in the past, Ostler retorts, "Now this is a remarkable response indeed, for the authors claim their argument is even stronger if the premises are false!" But it is evident that there is no premise in the argument that states or entails that there existed an infinitieth event in the past.

Finally, Ostler offers a positive argument for the possibility of an infinitely old universe:

> It seems that no matter how far back in time one goes to any particular past moment, it is logically possible that the world existed at that moment. But how large is the series or collection of moments at which it is possible that the world existed? The number certainly appears to be unlimited or infinite. But if the collection of times at which it is possible that the world exists is infinite, it follows that it is coherent to assert that the world is infinitely old.[202]

The idea here seems to be that we regress in time to some point t_n in the finite past and ask, could there have been an earlier moment t_{n-1} at which the universe existed? The answer is that at every moment t_n we can conceive of a possible world having a moment t_{n-1} at which the universe existed. So far so good; but how does it follow that there is a possible world in which t_n is preceded by an infinite number of moments? Ostler thinks that because the number of possible worlds with longer and longer finite pasts is unlimited, there is a possible world having an infinite past. This is as logically fallacious as reasoning that because one can count higher and higher finite numbers without limit, therefore there must be an infinitieth number. Ostler has, ironically, fallen prey to the very fallacy that he charged against the present argument. In his own words: "It is like saying that there cannot be an infinite number of integers unless one of them is the 'infinitieth' integer—which is clearly wrong-headed."[203] Thus, his positive argument for the possibility of an infinite past is unavailing.

This completes the philosophical case in support of premise (3):

3. The temporal series of past physical events is not beginningless.

We have argued that the impossibility of the existence of an actual infinite implies that the temporal series of past physical events is not beginningless and that even if an actual infinite could exist, the impossibility of forming an actual infinite by successive addition implies that the temporal series of past physical events is not beginningless. We may now turn to the empirical confirmation of this argument.

Inductive Arguments

The Expansion of the Universe

In 1917, Albert Einstein made a cosmological application of his newly discovered gravitational theory, the General Theory of Relativity (GTR).[204] In so doing he assumed that the universe is homogeneous and isotropic and that it exists in a steady state, with a constant mean mass density and a constant curvature of space. To his chagrin, however, he found that GTR would not permit such a model of the universe unless he introduced into his gravitational field equations a certain "fudge factor" Λ in order to counterbalance the gravitational effect of matter and so ensure a static universe. Unfortunately, Einstein's static universe was balanced on a razor's edge, and the least perturbation would cause the universe either to implode or to expand. By taking this feature of Einstein's model seriously, in the 1920s the Russian mathematician Alexander Friedman and the Belgian astronomer Georges Lemaître independently were able to formulate solutions to the field equations which predicted an expanding universe.[205]

The monumental significance of the Friedman-Lemaître model lay in its historicization of the universe. As one commentator has remarked, up to this time the idea of the expansion of the universe "was absolutely beyond comprehension. Throughout all of human history the universe was regarded as fixed and immutable and the idea that it might actually be changing was inconceivable."[206] But if the Friedman-Lemaître model were correct, the universe could no longer be adequately treated as a static entity existing, in effect, timelessly. Rather, the universe has a history, and time will not be a matter of indifference for our investigation of the cosmos.

In 1929 the astronomer Edwin Hubble showed that the red-shift in the optical spectra of light from distant galaxies was a common feature of all measured galaxies and was proportional to their distance from us.[207] This red-shift, first observed by Vesto Slipher in 1926, was taken to be a Doppler effect indicative of the recessional motion of the light source in the line of sight. Incredibly, what Hubble had discovered was the isotropic expansion of the universe pre-dicted by Friedman and Lemaître on the basis of Einstein's GTR. It was a ver-itable turning point in the history of science. "Of all the great predictions that science has ever made over the centuries," exclaims John Wheeler, "was there ever one greater than this, to predict, and predict correctly, and predict against all expectation a phenomenon so fantastic as the expansion of the universe?"[208]

According to the Friedman-Lemaître model, as time proceeds, the dis-tances separating galactic "particles" become greater. It is important to understand that as a General Relativity-based theory, the model does not describe the expansion of the material content of the universe into a preex-isting, empty Newtonian space, but rather the expansion of space itself. The ideal particles of the cosmological fluid constituted by the matter and energy of the universe are conceived to be at rest with respect to space but to recede progressively from one another as space itself expands or stretches, just as buttons glued to the surface of a balloon would recede from one another as the balloon inflates. As the universe expands, it becomes less and less dense. This has the astonishing implication that as one reverses the expansion and extrapolates back in time, the universe becomes progressively denser until one arrives at a state of "infinite density"[209] at some point in the finite past. This state represents a singularity at which space-time curvature, along with temperature, pressure, and density, becomes infinite. It therefore constitutes an edge or boundary to space-time itself. P. C. W. Davies comments:

> If we extrapolate this prediction to its extreme, we reach a point when all distances in the universe have shrunk to zero. An initial cosmological sin-gularity therefore forms a past temporal extremity to the universe. We can-not continue physical reasoning, or even the concept of spacetime, through such an extremity. For this reason most cosmologists think of the initial singularity as the beginning of the universe. On this view the big bang rep-resents the creation event; the creation not only of all the matter and energy in the universe, but also of spacetime itself.[210]

The term "Big Bang," originally a derisive expression coined by Fred Hoyle to characterize the beginning of the universe predicted by the Friedman-Lemaître model, is thus potentially misleading, since the expansion cannot be visualized from the outside (there being no "outside," just as there is no "before" with respect to the Big Bang).

The standard Big Bang model, as the Friedman-Lemaître model came to be called, thus describes a universe that is not eternal in the past but that came into being a finite time ago. Moreover—and this deserves underscoring—the origin it posits is an absolute origin *ex nihilo.* For not only all matter and energy, but space and time themselves come into being at the initial cosmological singularity. As Barrow and Tipler emphasize, "At this singularity, space and time came into existence; literally nothing existed before the singularity, so, if the Universe originated at such a singularity, we would truly have a creation *ex nihilo.*"[211] On such a model, the universe originates *ex nihilo* in the sense that at the initial singularity it is true that *There is no earlier space-time point* or it is false that *Something existed prior to the singularity.*

Now such a conclusion is profoundly disturbing for anyone who ponders it. For the question cannot be suppressed: *Why does the universe exist rather than nothing?* There can be no natural, physical cause of the Big Bang event since, in Quentin Smith's words, "it belongs analytically to the concept of the cosmological singularity that it is not the effect of prior physical events. The definition of a singularity . . . entails that it is *impossible to extend the spacetime manifold beyond the singularity. . . .* This rules out the idea that the singularity is an effect of some prior natural process."[212] Sir Arthur Eddington, contemplating the beginning of the universe, opined that the expansion of the universe was so preposterous and incredible that "I feel almost an indignation that anyone should believe in it—except myself."[213] He finally felt forced to conclude, "The beginning seems to present insuperable difficulties unless we agree to look on it as frankly supernatural."[214]

Standard Big Bang cosmogony thus presents what Mormon theologian Keith Norman has called "a serious challenge to the Mormon version of the universe."[215] Observing that the Standard Model sounds remarkably like "the orthodox doctrine of creation *ex nihilo,*" he observes that "both the theoretical physicist and the Christian philosopher give the same answer to the question of what preceded the universe: 'Nothing.' . . . 'Prior to the beginning' has no meaning in the absence of space and time. The universe, therefore, was created 'out of literally nothing.'"[216] Given Mormon commitment to the eternity of matter and a spatiotemporal deity who does not transcend the laws of nature, Norman confesses that, "In contrast to the apparent harmony between modern physics and traditional Christianity on the subject of creation and the substantiality of material being, Mormon doctrine now seems to be a relic of the nineteenth century."[217]

Mormon theologians therefore have a vested interest in finding some alternative theory to the Standard Model. The difficulty is that those alternatives which have been proposed turn out, on closer examination, either to be untenable or not to avoid the absolute beginning predicted in the Standard Model.[218] The devil is in the details, and once you get down to specifics you find that there is no mathematically consistent model that has been so successful in its predictions or as corroborated by the evidence as the traditional Big Bang theory. For example, some theories, like the Oscillating Universe (which expands and recontracts forever) or the Chaotic Inflationary Universe (which continually spawns new universes), do have a potentially infinite future but turn out to have only a finite past.[219] Vacuum Fluctuation Universe theories (which postulate an eternal vacuum out of which our universe is born) cannot explain why, if the vacuum was eternal, we do not observe an infinitely old universe.[220] The Quantum Gravity Universe theory propounded by the famous physicist Stephen Hawking, if interpreted realistically, still involves an absolute origin of the universe even if the universe does not begin in a so-called singularity, as it does in the standard Big Bang theory.[221] In sum, according to Hawking, "Almost everyone now believes that the universe, and *time itself*, had a beginning at the Big Bang."[222]

With each successive failure of alternative cosmogonic theories to avoid the absolute beginning of the universe predicted by the Standard Model, that prediction has been corroborated. Of course, in view of the metaphysical issues raised by the prospect of a beginning of the universe, we may be confident that the quest to avert such a beginning will continue unabated.[223] Such efforts are to be encouraged, and we have no reason to think that such attempts at falsification will result in anything other than further corroboration of the prediction of a beginning. In the meantime, the beginning of the universe *ex nihilo* cannot be wished away.

Thermodynamic Properties of the Universe

If this were not enough, there is a second inductive argument for the beginning of the universe based on the evidence of thermodynamics. According to the Second Law of Thermodynamics, processes taking place in a closed system always tend toward a state of equilibrium. For example, if we had a bottle containing a sealed vacuum, and we introduced into it some molecules of gas, the gas would spread itself out evenly throughout the bottle. It would be virtually impossible for the molecules to retreat, for example, into one corner of the bottle and remain. This is why when we walk into a room, the air in the room never separates suddenly into oxygen at one end and nitrogen at the other. It is also why, when we step into the bath, we may be confident that it will be an even temperature instead of frozen solid at one end and boiling at the other. It is clear that life would not be possible in a world in which the Second Law of Thermodynamics did not operate.

Now our interest in this law is with what happens when it is applied to the universe as a whole. The universe is, on a naturalistic view, a gigantic closed system, since it is everything there is and there is nothing outside it. What this seems to imply is that, given enough time, the universe and all its processes will run down, and the entire universe will come to equilibrium. This is known as the heat death of the universe. Once the universe reaches this state, no further change is possible. The universe is dead.

There are two possible types of heat death for the universe. If the universe will eventually recontract, it will die a "hot" death. Beatrice Tinsley describes such a state: "If the average density of matter in the universe is great enough, the mutual gravitational attraction between bodies will eventually slow the expansion to a halt. The universe will then contract and collapse into a hot fireball. There is no known physical mechanism that could reverse a catastrophic big crunch. Apparently, if the universe becomes dense enough, it is in for a hot death."[224] If the universe is fated to recontraction, then as it contracts the stars gain energy, causing them to burn more rapidly so that they finally explode or evaporate. As everything in the universe grows closer together, the black holes begin to gobble up everything around them, and eventually begin themselves to coalesce. In time, "All the black holes finally coalesce into one large black hole that is coextensive with the universe,"[225] from which the universe will never remerge.

But suppose, as is more likely, that the universe will expand forever. Tinsley describes the fate of this universe: "If the universe has a low density, its death will be cold. It will expand forever at a slower and slower rate. Galaxies will turn all of their gas into stars, and the stars will burn out. Our own sun will become a cold, dead remnant, floating among the corpses of other stars in an increasingly isolated Milky Way."[226] At 10^{30} years the universe will consist of 90 percent dead stars, 9 percent supermassive black holes formed by the collapse of galaxies, and 1 percent atomic matter, mainly hydrogen. Elementary particle physics suggests that thereafter protons will decay into electrons and positrons so that space will be filled with a rarefied gas so thin that the distance between an electron and a positron will be about the present size of our galaxy. At 10^{100} years, some scientists believe that the black holes themselves will dissipate by a strange effect predicted by quantum mechanics. The mass and energy associated with a black hole so warp space that they are said to create a "tunnel" or "worm-hole" through which the mass and energy are ejected into another region of space. As the mass of a black hole decreases, its energy loss accelerates, so that it is eventually dissipated into radiation and elementary particles. Eventually all black holes will completely evaporate, and all the matter in the ever-expanding universe will be reduced to a thin gas of elementary particles and radiation. Equilibrium will prevail throughout, and the entire universe will be in its final state, from which no change will occur.

Now the question that needs to be asked is this: If given enough time the universe will reach heat death, then why is it not in a state of heat death now, if it has existed forever, from eternity? If the universe did not begin to exist, then it should now be in a state of equilibrium. Like a ticking clock, it should by now have run down. Since it has not yet run down, this implies, in the words of one baffled scientist, "In some way the universe must have been *wound up.*"[227]

Some people have tried to escape this conclusion by adopting an oscillating model of the universe that never reaches a final state of equilibrium. We have already noted that such a model of the universe is physically and observationally challenged. But suppose we waive those considerations. The fact is that the thermodynamic properties of this model imply the very beginning of the universe that its proponents seek to avoid. For entropy increases from cycle to cycle in such a model, which has the effect of generating larger and longer oscillations with each successive cycle. Thus, as one traces the oscillations back in time, they become progressively smaller until one reaches a first and smallest oscillation. One scientific team explains, "The effect of entropy production will be to enlarge the cosmic scale, from cycle to cycle. . . . Thus, looking back in time, each cycle generated less entropy, had a smaller cycle time, and had a smaller cycle expansion factor then [*sic*] the cycle that followed it."[228] Zeldovich and Novikov conclude, "The multicycle model has an infinite future, but only a finite past."[229] In fact, astronomer Joseph Silk estimates, on the basis of current entropy levels, that the universe cannot have gone through more than a hundred previous oscillations.[230]

Even if this difficulty were avoided,[231] a universe oscillating from eternity past would require an infinitely precise tuning of initial conditions in order to endure through an infinite number of successive bounces. A universe rebounding from a single infinitely long contraction is, if entropy increases during the contracting phase, thermodynamically untenable and incompatible with the initial low entropy condition of our expanding phase. Postulating an entropy decrease during the contracting phase in order to escape this problem would require us to postulate inexplicably special low entropy conditions at the time of the bounce in the life of an infinitely evolving universe. Such a low entropy condition at the beginning of the expansion is more plausibly accounted for by the presence of a singularity or some sort of quantum creation event.

Indeed, thermodynamics may provide good reasons for affirming the reality of the singular origin of space-time postulated by the Standard Model. Penrose states, "I have gradually come around to the view that it is actually misguided to ask that the space-time singularities of classical relativity should disappear when standard techniques of quantum (field) theory are applied to them."[232] For if the initial cosmological singularity is removed, then "we should have lost what seems to me to be the best chance we have of explaining the mystery of the second law of thermodynamics."[233] What Penrose has in mind is the remarkable fact that as one goes back in time, the entropy of the universe steadily decreases. Just how unusual this is can be demonstrated by means of the Bekenstein-Hawking formula for the entropy of a stationary black hole. The total observed entropy of the universe is 10^{88}. Since there are around 10^{80} baryons in the universe, the observed entropy per baryon must be regarded as extremely small. By contrast, in a collapsing universe the entropy would be 10^{123} near the end. Comparison of these two numbers reveals how absurdly small 10^{88} is compared to what it might have been. Thus, the structure of the Big Bang must have been severely constrained in order that thermodynamics as we know it should have arisen. So how is this special initial condition to be explained?

According to Penrose, we need the initial cosmological singularity, conjoined with the Weyl Curvature Hypothesis, according to which initial singularities (as opposed to final singularities) must have vanishing Weyl curvature.[234] In standard models, the Big Bang does possess vanishing Weyl curvature. The geometrical constraints on the initial geometry have the effect of producing a state of very low entropy. So the entropy in the gravitational field starts at zero at the Big Bang and gradually increases through gravitational clumping. The Weyl Curvature Hypothesis thus has the time asymmetric character necessary to explain the second law. By contrast, the Hartle-Hawking model "is very far from being an explanation of the fact that past singularities have small Weyl curvature whereas future singularities have large Weyl curvature."[235] On Hawking's time symmetrical theory, we should have white holes spewing out material, in contradiction to the Weyl Curvature Hypothesis, the Second Law of Thermodynamics, and probably also observation.[236] If we remove the initial cosmological singularity, we render the Weyl Curvature Hypothesis irrelevant and "we should be back where we were in our attempts to understand the origin of the second law."[237]

Could the special initial geometry have arisen by sheer chance in the absence of a cosmic singularity? Penrose's answer is decisive: "Had there not been any constraining principles (such as the Weyl curvature hypothesis) the Bekenstein-Hawking formula would tell as that the probability of such a 'special' geometry arising by chance is at least as small as about one part in $10^{1000B(3/2)}$ where B is the present baryon number of the universe [~10^{80}]."[238] Thus, Penrose calculates that, aiming at a phase space whose regions represent the likelihood of various possible configurations of the universe, "the accuracy of the Creator's aim" would have to have been one part in $10^{10(123)}$ in order for our universe to exist.[239] He comments, "I cannot even recall seeing anything else in physics whose accuracy is known to approach, even remotely, a figure like one part in $10^{10\,(123)}$."[240] Thus, the initial cosmological singularity may be a virtual thermodynamic necessity.

So whether one adopts a recontracting model, an ever-expanding model, or an oscillating model, thermodynamics implies that the universe had a beginning. According to P. C. W. Davies, the universe must have been created a finite time ago and is in the process of winding down. Prior to the creation, says Davies, the universe simply did not exist. Therefore, he concludes, even though we may not like it, we must say that the universe's energy was somehow simply "put in" at the creation as an initial condition.[241]

The Alternatives Before Us

The advances in physical cosmology during the past century have put Mormon scientists, who take such empirical evidence seriously, in an extraordinarily difficult position. For if we postulate some causal agency responsible for the origin of the universe in order to explain the origin of the universe *ex nihilo*, such an ultramundane being, as the cause of space and time, must transcend space and time and therefore exist atemporally and nonspatially, at least sans the universe. This transcendent cause must therefore be changeless and immaterial, since timelessness entails changelessness, and changelessness implies immateriality. Such a cause must be beginningless and uncaused, at least in the sense of lacking any antecedent causal conditions.

This entity must be unimaginably powerful, since it created the universe out of nothing. All of this, while consonant with traditional theism, stands in stark contradiction to the usual Mormon conception of God.

David Bailey, a Mormon NASA scientist, acknowledges that the Big Bang theory "is now generally accepted as the correct description of the origin of the universe" and adds, "The weight of evidence supporting the theory has increased to the point that it must be taken seriously by anyone attempting to form a scientifically tenable theology."[242] As an LDS scientist, Bailey wants a theology that is scientifically tenable; but the Mormon concept of God as a finite, physical product of a beginningless progression flies in the face of Big Bang cosmogony. According to Bailey, "The LDS concept of God . . . posits that God is a real, tangible being who co-exists with natural laws in the universe. Probably the most extreme Latter-day Saint 'heresy' in the minds of other Christian sects is the law of eternal progression ('as man is, God once was, and as God is, man may become'). This doctrine, first enunciated by Joseph Smith and later elaborated by other LDS presidents, is now a fundamental tenet of the faith."[243] However, he admits,

> The notion that everything in our universe originated in a big bang approximately 15 billion years ago creates some problems for Mormon theology. A God who exists in space and time should reside within the observable universe. In that case, God is not eternal in a literal and absolute sense but instead came into being after the big bang. . . .
>
> The traditional LDS concept of eternal elements (D&C 93:33) runs into a similar difficulty if it is literally interpreted to mean that matter has always existed and cannot be created or destroyed. The conversion of mass to energy and the transmutation of matter . . . are well established physical phenomena. Furthermore, all matter originated in the big bang.[244]

The Big Bang represents the origin of all matter and energy, even of physical space and time themselves, as we have seen. Therefore, to hold that matter/energy are eternal or that God is the physical product of a beginningless progression is irreconcilable with the theory. The problem posed by the Big Bang for Mormon theology is especially severe, not merely because the Big Bang theory supports creation *ex nihilo,* but because the Mormon concept of God as an extended material object existing in the universe requires, in connection with Big Bang cosmogony, that God himself (or his progenitors) came into being *ex nihilo.* Thus, Big Bang cosmogony is a veritable dagger at the throat of Mormon theology.

In fact, even if the universe did not have a singular beginning point, the Mormon concept of God seems hopelessly irreconcilable with contemporary cosmogony. For Mormon theologians construe God as a physical entity wholly immanent in the universe. A time-reversed extrapolation of the expansion of the universe constitutes a process of universal, gravitational self-collapse governed by the same Hawking-Penrose singularity theorems that determine the behavior of a black hole. Almost any textbook on astrophysics will contain a vivid description of what happens to the unfortunate space traveler who happens to cross the boundary of a black hole. As he is pulled irresistibly into the maelstrom, tidal forces will tear his body to shreds before he is finally collapsed into an indistinguishable thread. The same fate awaits the Mormon God as we extrapolate backward toward the Big Bang. The idea that there has been an infinite progression of humanoid deities consorting with one another from eternity is worse than scientific poppycock—it is a fairy tale of Olympian proportions.

The thermodynamic evidence for the beginning of the universe has also put Mormon scientists in an awkward position. On the one hand, they recognize the implication of the present thermodynamic disequilibrium for the finitude of the past and will sometimes even employ the argument as part of a natural theology. Henry Eyring, professor of chemistry at the University of Utah, for example, after explaining the inevitable heat death of the universe, asks, "How did the universe get wound up?" and ascribes the initial input of energy to the Creator.[245] But while such a conclusion accords well with the orthodox Christian concept of God as a nonphysical, transcendent being who creates the universe *ex nihilo,* it is irreconcilable with the traditional Mormon understanding of God as a temporal, material being immanent in the universe. Not only must God, on the Mormon conception, have a beginning, but he must also come to an end, either being swallowed up and crushed into oblivion in the Big Crunch or else literally disintegrated into the cold, dark recesses of outer space—a pitiable deity, indeed!

In order to avoid this theologically unacceptable conclusion, some Mormon thinkers take the obvious route of denying that God is physically immanent in the universe. Thus, Harrison asks, "What happens to God in this recollapse? Hopefully [*sic*] he stands outside the universe and is not caught in the crunch!"[246] Eyring explains that there is a "sixth world" beyond the universe: "This is the world that existed before the 'big bang.' It is the world of the Creator, who provided the energy to wind up the watch . . . this sixth world is without beginning and end of space and time. Presiding over all is the Creator."[247] But given the Mormon concept of God as a finite, physical, spatiotemporal being, the Creator must exist in some discrete space-time manifold, in which case, as we shall see, it becomes unintelligible how he can be causally related to our world.[248] Eyring himself lapses back into thinking of God as immanent, for he confesses, "I worship the wisest being in the universe."[249] That this statement is meant literally is evident by his progressive comparison with the wisest person in the room, in the city, in the state, in the country, in the world, in the universe. But if the Mormon God is in the universe in this sense, he cannot escape the implications of the Second Law of Thermodynamics.

It might be thought that God, even if a physical object wholly immanent in the universe, might be able to miraculously escape the implications of natural laws. But an intriguing feature of Mormon theology is that most Mormon thinkers follow B. H. Roberts in his claim that God, as a finite, physical entity located wholly in space and time, does *not* transcend the laws of nature. According to Erich Paul, "The 'authorized' Mormon position" is that the laws of nature and the laws of God are identical, so that there is no room for the supernatural.[250] Therefore, in Bailey's words, "there is no such thing as a miracle."[251] God's being is therefore governed by the same laws of gravitation and thermodynamics that govern any physical object in space-time.

Given the fluidity of Mormon doctrine, perhaps Mormon theologians would do well to repudiate the tradition that limits God's power to the naturally possible and to maintain that he transcends the limits of natural law. But such a revisionist view would, however, leave our problem unsolved, for the existence of such a God (or his progenitors) would still be irreconcilable with Big Bang cosmogony, since the physical deities, like marbles in a batch of rising dough, would preclude the time-reversed expansion from collapsing past the point at which it has squeezed all the deities shoulder to shoulder into as tight a fellowship as possible, thereby violating the singularity theorems. This is so absurd, not only scientifically but also theologically, as to be unentertainable.

Some Mormon thinkers have tried to preserve God's eternal existence by denying that God does exist in our space-time manifold originating in the Big Bang. For example, Harrison asserts, "If we truly believe that our entire universe was created by God, then one naturally assumes that he existed prior to that creation, outside our perceived universe, implying that his time is different from our time."[252] God is thus able to create not only our universe via the Big Bang but other universes as well. But while this suggestion works well on an orthodox Christian concept of God, it is untenable on the Mormon concept of God as an extended, physical entity. Such a God would have to be a material object existing in a distinct space-time manifold; but, as Bailey explains, "current theories of fundamental physics and cosmology forbid any communication with or intervention by inhabitants of universes beyond the one created in the big bang."[253] It is impossible for the Big Bang singularity to have a physical cause, since it is the termination of all past-directed space-time trajectories. Thus, it cannot be linked to a discrete space-time manifold or any object existing therein. Thus, Bailey actually understates the case when he says that the present suggestion leads to "a mere deist concept of God,"[254] for the deist God was at least the Creator of the universe, which cannot be said of a deity existing in another space-time.

Norman appeals to eleven-dimensional superstring theory in an attempt to justify the idea that God may exist in dimensions other than those of our four-dimensional space-time manifold.[255] But this suggestion is simply a misappropriation of science.[256] In the first place, the additional dimensions postulated in such theories are part of our space-time manifold. The idea is not that other manifolds exist, but rather that our manifold is not, as we have always thought, four-dimensional, but is eleven-dimensional. Since these are all dimensions of the same manifold, they all come to exist through the Big Bang; moreover, any object that exists in one dimension of the manifold exists in them all. Secondly, these additional dimensions are compactified, that is, rolled up so tightly that they are subatomic in proportion. That is precisely why they are not perceived by us. But then it is impossible to think that they could be inhabited by humanoid deities. Thirdly, these additional dimensions are all of them *spatial* dimensions; there is no additional temporal dimension. But that entails that all of them evolve together in the one dimension of time that we know and ultimately have a common origin. It is simply science fiction to imagine these dimensions as separate spatiotemporal worlds in which transcendent deities live and move.

Other Mormon thinkers have sought to escape these difficulties by rejecting the Standard Model and availing themselves of alternative cosmogonic theories. Such attempts have about them something of an air of grasping at straws, however, since the alternative theories are never examined in detail, nor is any attempt made to show that the models they offer are better explanations of the data than the Standard Model. For example, Bart Kovallis appeals to Linde's Chaotic Inflationary Model to justify Mormon belief in multiple "worlds,"[257] but he fails to show how such a model can preserve God's eternal existence, given its past geodesic incompleteness. And Kent Harrison appears to endorse Vacuum Fluctuation Models when he says with respect to the Big Bang, "This 'nothing,' the vacuum, seems to be remarkably active in modern physics, because particles, maybe even universes, can come into or out of existence from the vacuum."[258] But he is silent when it comes to the difficulties such models face with respect to the infinitude of the past, not to speak of why we ought to adopt them rather than the Standard Model. Norman appeals vaguely to the suggestion that "black holes... may constitute passageways or singularities into alternate dimensions or universes. The matter that disappears from our universe into a black hole could then explode into existence in another one.... [O]ur universe may have been an enormous black hole in a different universe."[259] But it is not clear what theory Norman means to endorse here. If black holes represent space-time singularities, then, as we have seen, it is physically impossible that they constitute passageways to other space-time domains. If he means to suggest merely that wormholes to other regions of space-time or even other manifolds exist, that does nothing in itself to explain how the past could be beginningless. In any case, not only is there simply no evidence of such so-called "white holes" spewing out energy, in contradiction to the Second Law of Thermodynamics, into our universe, but the Big Bang itself is not a white hole, since it is a low-entropy event, as we have seen. And even if there were such wormholes, no physical object, such as a Mormon deity, could pass through one to another universe but would, instead, be crushed to extinction. If Mormon scientists mean to offer or endorse alternative cosmogonic models, then they must get serious about examining the implications of such models for the past's finitude and showing us why such models constitute better explanations of the evidence than the Standard Model.

What to Do?

So what to do? As if embarrassed by his own speculative suggestions, Norman finally confesses,

> Rather than trying to explain away or simply ignore the implications of a Big Bang cosmology, perhaps Mormons should recognize the need to update their theology. It is unreasonable, on both practical and theoretical grounds, to expect Joseph Smith to have given us an account of creation based on late twentieth-century physics.

... If we are to persist in the claim that our theology encompasses natural and not just mythical truth, then we are obliged to come to terms with a science devoted to material reality. It is no longer possible to pretend there is no conflict. Given the dynamic nature of Mormon theology, and the mechanism of progressive revelation in accordance with our capacity to receive, such a reconciliation is by no means far-fetched.[260]

How might such a reconciliation look? Bailey, desirous of having a scientifically tenable theology, advocates a reinterpretation of Mormon scriptures.[261] Referring to Doctrine and Covenants 93:33, he says, "A more tenable interpretation of this scripture is that it is intended to rebut the notion of the *ex nihilo* creation of the earth."[262] This reinterpretation of Mormon doctrine would be a development welcomed by any orthodox Christian. One can only second Bailey's conclusion that "one positive aspect of Mormon theology from a scientific viewpoint is its unequivocal rejection of the doctrine of the creation of the earth *ex nihilo*. Primitive Christians also rejected such a notion.... The question of whether or not the entire universe was 'created out of nothing,' however, is a different matter."[263] Indeed. And on Bailey's view, Mormons may embrace *creatio ex nihilo* with respect to the universe.

But then what does this retrenchment imply for the doctrine of eternal progression and the Mormon concept of God? Again, Bailey advocates reinterpretation of the relevant Scriptures: "A straightforward solution to this dilemma is to abandon a strict interpretation of the word *eternal*, as is suggested in Doctrine and Covenants 19:6–12. After all, 15 billion years may not be forever, but it is so far beyond our comprehension as to be eternal for all practical purposes."[264] Again, the orthodox Christian can only rejoice at such a solution, for then the world is affirmed to be finite in its past temporal duration and to have had a beginning.

But what, then, of the Mormon concept of God? Bailey's answer is stunning: "In that case God is not the being who crafted the universe at the big bang. If there is such a being, it is a deity beyond him."[265] In this breathtaking affirmation, Bailey states that God—that is, the typical Mormon God (Elohim) described by Joseph Smith and worshipped by millions of Mormons—*is not truly God*. Rather, the true God is beyond him; the true God is the Creator of the universe *ex nihilo*. Bailey hastens to add that "Mormon theology, of course, allows the possibility of a hierarchy of deities (D&C 121:28)."[266] But such an attempted mollification of Bailey's revisionary view cannot conceal its radical implications. As we have seen, no physical, spatiotemporal entity can be the Creator of the Big Bang. If there is a Supreme God who is the Creator of the universe (and any "deities" therein), he must be an immaterial, nonphysical, non-spatiotemporal being with the power to create the world out of nothing. This is the classical concept of God, the Lord God *pantokrator. Soli Deo gloria!*

Bailey is, of course, merely a Mormon scientist, not a theologian. We harbor no illusion that many LDS theologians will adopt his solution. But Mormon theology in the past has shown itself to be remarkably fluid. Ostler remarks that "many Mormons, and possibly most non-Mormons, have failed to grasp the wide latitude of possible beliefs which can be tolerated within the tradition of Mormon thought."[267] These range, he says, all the way from an absolutist view of God as omnipotent and omniscient to a finitist view of God. Since the 1960s a movement known as "Mormon neo-orthodoxy" has arisen within the LDS organization, emphasizing such themes as God's absoluteness and complete otherness, along with man's contingency and temporal creation.[268] Is it impossible that within the fold of such a movement Mormon thinkers might blend finitism's doctrine of eternal personalism with absolutism's emphasis on the complete otherness of God by means of the doctrine of *creatio ex nihilo*? This is devoutly to be hoped.[269] As was suggested earlier, the LDS Standard Works do not seem to provide any reason why this cannot happen. So long as a reconciliation such as Bailey's proffered solution is not officially repudiated by the LDS Church, Mormons should feel free to affirm the doctrine of *creatio ex nihilo* and with it the orthodox concept of God as the immaterial, transcendent, almighty Creator of the universe.

4

THE GOD OF ABRAHAM, ISAAC, AND JOSEPH SMITH?
God, Creation, and Humanity in the Old Testament and Mormonism

JIM W. ADAMS

Jim W. Adams is Assistant Professor of Biblical Studies at LIFE Bible College and Adjunct Professor of Biblical Studies at Azusa Pacific University. He earned a B.A. in biblical languages from LIFE Bible College and an M.A. in biblical studies from the C. P. Haggard School of Theology, Azusa Pacific University, and is a Ph.D. candidate in Old Testament studies at Fuller Theological Seminary.

Judaism and Christianity have historically affirmed and insisted that there is but one true and living God. He is not embodied, he is not a material being, and he transcends the cosmos. He is the unique creator of the universe, and nothing exists apart from his creative will. It is in his image and likeness that humans were made to serve as his representatives on earth. Jews and Christians claim to root this basic understanding of God and creation in the revelations received by the patriarchs and prophets of ancient Israel.[1]

Latter-day Saints disagree with this understanding of God and creation. In its place they have historically affirmed that God is an embodied being, literally an exalted man. He does not transcend the universe, nor did he create its fundamental components. Rather, matter eternally preexisted in a chaotic state, and God created by imposing order upon it. The most fundamental part of the human person has eternally existed. When the spirits of Adam and Eve entered this world, bodies were fashioned for them that looked like God's own body. Latter-day Saints have claimed that the classical understanding of God shared by Jews and Christians is the product of Greek philosophy and that it is the LDS concept that is found in the Old Testament. For example, LDS scholar Stephen E. Robinson writes: "The real objection to the LDS belief in an anthropomorphic Father comes, not from the Hebraic world of the first Christians, nor from Jesus and his Jewish disciples, nor from their Judeo-Christian writings. The real objections are rooted in the God of the philosophers, in the Hellenistic conception of God as an absolute being abstract, ultimate, and transcendent. *The LDS God is the God of the Hebrew Bible,* but he is not the God of the philosophers."[2]

Clearly, the differences between these two understandings of God and creation are more than academic; they differ at the most fundamental level. It is a curious phenomenon that Jews, Christians, and Latter-day Saints could all appeal to the Old Testament and yet come up with two views so radically different from one another. In light of this curious discrepancy, with the claims of the Latter-day Saints in mind, in this essay I will examine the Old Testament view of God, creation, and humanity. This will be done by contrasting the Old Testament view with the views of Israel's ancient Near Eastern neighbors. After discussing the Near Eastern and Old Testament views, I will look at the traditional LDS understanding of God, creation, and humanity. In the final section of the essay, I will make some comparisons between the ancient Near Eastern, Old Testament, and traditional LDS views.

I. The Ancient Near Eastern Backdrop of the Old Testament

The ancient Israelites did not live in a cultural vacuum isolated from their neighbors. To the contrary, the pages of the Old Testament are clearly saturated in Israel's cultural environment (e.g., laws, literary genres, etc.). Nor were the writers of the Old Testament completely unaware of the pagan views of God and the world that were commonly held in the ancient Near

East. Israel's prophets regularly had to rebuke the people and their leaders for adopting syncretistic and compromising views. When one understands the views of Israel's cultural neighbors, one gains a much greater appreciation of the significance of many Old Testament texts that oppose those views. This section will explore how the ancient Near Eastern peoples generally understood the origins of their world (cosmogony), the origin of their gods (theogony), and the nature of their gods and humanity.[3]

Canaanite culture is obviously an important part of the backdrop to the Old Testament. However, it is debated among scholars whether Canaanite literature in fact contains any actual cosmogony.[4] Far more useful for the purposes of this essay are the religious literatures of Egypt[5] and Mesopotamia.[6] Both contain extensive and elaborate creation myths that reflected the people's view of their gods and the gods' relationship to the universe. They are also exceptional representatives of the typical worldview of the ancient Near East. By examining the basic tenets of these two cosmogonies under topical categories, we will be able to see some of the general characteristics displayed by all pagan religions.[7] (Please note, the use of *pagan* is this chapter is simply shorthand for ancient non-Israelite cultures and their religious beliefs.)

Egyptian and Mesopotamian Cosmology

Egyptian civilization flourished for nearly three millennia and produced a varied, complex, and continually evolving religion. This religion had a mythology that was formulated and reformulated while continually adding myths in an attempt to assimilate and integrate each and every aspect of Egyptian belief.[8] But many of the basic features of Egyptian belief remained fairly constant. For the ancient Egyptian, cosmic order (*ma'at*) was established at "the first time" of creation.[9] The four principle elements of the universe were earth, primeval waters, sky, and air, each of which were also considered gods. The earth god Geb floated on the primeval waters of Nun. The sky god Nut was above, and between the earth and sky was Shu, the air god.[10] The two central sources of life for the ancient Egyptian were the sun, predominantly identified as the creator god Rê, and the Nile, both having cycles of birth and death.[11]

Mesopotamia is the plain between the Tigris and Euphrates Rivers (roughly modern Iraq). Beginning in the third millennium, Mesopotamians developed and recorded their understandings of the origins of the universe in the Sumerian language.[12] Although the Sumerian texts exhibit cosmogonical ideas, to date no myth has been found that is concerned primarily with the origins of the universe.[13] The most comprehensive cosmogony produced by the Mesopotamians is entitled *Enûma Elish* ("When above"), written on seven tablets in Akkadian and typically designated as the standard Mesopotamian cosmogony.[14] This myth will be the primary focus of our examination, supplemented by reference to other texts.

Mesopotamian cosmology essentially depicted the universe as formed of superimposed cosmic levels. In general, the earth is in the middle, the stars and heaven are above, and the cosmic water and the underworld are below.[15] The Mesopotamians believed that there was nothing inanimate in the universe but that all phenomena were alive, with each entity having a personality and a will.[16] The universe was considered a cosmic society or state that functioned as a primitive democracy with a hierarchy of power. The highest authority in the universe and sole possessor of power was the "assembly of the gods," whose members were ranked according to the god's inherent natural force and wisdom in the art of magic. The four highest-ranking officers were first, Anu, "sky"; second, Enlil, "storm"; third, Ninhursaga, "earth"; and fourth, Ea/Enki, "water."[17] These gods, along with the rest of the assembly, deliberated, determined, and carried out the course of all things and the destiny of all beings in the universe.[18]

General Characteristics of the Egyptian and Mesopotamian Cosmogonies

As will be seen below, the myths of Israel's ancient Near Eastern neighbors are often strange and sometimes strike the modern reader as being rather coarse in their details. But underlying or presupposed by the myths are identifiable elements of a basic worldview. The great Jewish biblical scholar Yehezkel Kaufmann lists the basic characteristics pagan cosmogonies have in common as "a primordial realm which harbors the seeds of all being; a theogony telling of the birth of gods who are sexually differentiated and who procreate; the creation of the cosmos out of the primordial stuff—the same out of which the gods emerged, or from some 'divine' substance. Also prevalent is the idea of several divine acts of creation, i.e., creation is not a single act, it has several divine 'roots.'"[19] When Egyptian and Mesopotamian cosmologies are examined in more detail we find that they conform to this pattern. I will illustrate this under several subheadings.

Primordial Waters and Matter

Egyptian mythology presumes that before creation there was a preexistent realm identified as "nonexistence," which is the realm of chaos with its constituent elements being the limitless primeval waters of Nun and total darkness.[20] Pyramid Text, Utterance 486 speaks of the king coming from the primordial waters of Nun:

> Hail, O waters brought by Shu,
> Which the twin springs raised,
> In which Geb has bathed his limbs,
> So that hearts lost fear, hearts lost dread.
> Pepi was born in Nun
> Before there was sky,
> Before there was earth,
> Before there were mountains,
> Before there was strife,
> Before fear came about through the Horus Eye.[21]

Chaos → Order theme

According to the Hermopolis cosmogony, there were thought to be eight pre-creation gods, the Ogdoad, who represented formless chaos.[22]

In a similar manner, the Mesopotamian *Enûma Elish* describes the beginnings of the universe as an undefined chaotic mass:

> When on high the heaven had not been named,
> Firm ground below had not been called by name;
> Naught but primordial Apsu, their begetter,
> (And) Mummu[23]-Tiamat, she who bore them all,
> Their waters commingling as a single body;
> No reed hut had been matted, no marsh land had appeared,
> When no gods whatever had been brought into being,
> Uncalled by name, their destinies undetermined—
> Then it was that the gods were formed within them. (Tablet I:1–9)[24]

Prior to creation, there is only the primeval waters personified by Apsu and Tiamat. Nothing else exists, not even the gods.[25] From this undifferentiated mass all existence finds its origin.[26]

Theogony

In each of the Egyptian cosmogonic myths there is a single primordial creator god, who is understood as creating all existence.[27] In general, the creator god self-generates from within the chaotic nonexistence, comes "into being by himself,"[28] or an egg is produced bearing the creator god and marks the beginning of creation.[29] While the creator god is alone in Nun and has nowhere to stand,[30] a primeval hillock emerges from these waters.[31] The creator god then appears upon the small mound and/or is equated with it and brings order and light. From the hill he begins to create the gods and human beings, and he fashions the cosmos. The most significant of the early creation myths is the Heliopolis Cosmogony. Pyramid Text, Utterance 600 reads:

> Atum Kheprer, you have come to be high on the hill, you have arisen on the Benben stone in the mansion of the Benben in Heliopolis, you spat out Shu, you expectorated Tefnut, and you put your two arms around them as the arms of a *ka* symbol, so that your *ka* (personality) might be in them. . . . O great Ennead which is in Heliopolis—Atum, Shu, Tefnut, Geb, Nut, Osiris, Isis, Seth, Nephthys—children of Atum, extend his heart (goodwill) to his child (the king) in your name of Nine Bows.[32]

Atum creates the Ennead, the nine great gods,[33] beginning with Shu and Tefnut (goddess of moisture), who subsequently procreate Geb and Nut. These two in turn give birth to two more couples, Osiris (who embodies order) and his sister-wife Isis, and Seth (who represents disorder) and his sister-wife Nephthys.[34] The Pyramid Texts also present Atum creating through masturbation while alone on the primeval hill, thereby bringing forth Shu and Tefnut by himself.[35] According to the Coffin Text, Spell 76, Atum created Shu and Tefnut by spitting.[36]

In Enûma Elish the gods are engendered as the primordial waters Apsu and Tiamat mix together. Tablet I:10–20 reads:

> Lahmu and Lahamu were brought forth, by name they were called.
> Before they had grown in age and stature.
> Anshar and Kishar were formed, surpassing the others.
> They prolonged the days, added on the years.
> Anu was their heir, of his fathers the rival;
> Yea, Anshar's firstborn, Anu, was his equal.
> Anu begot in his image, Nudimmud.
> This Nudimmud was of his fathers the master;
> Of broad wisdom, understanding, mighty in strength,
> Mightier by far than his grandfather, Anshar.
> He had no rival among the gods, his brothers.

In this theogony Apsu and Tiamat procreate Lahmu and Lahamu,[37] who in turn engender Anshar and Kishar (the two horizons), who some years later give birth to Anu. The sky god then begets in his likeness Nudimmud (= Ea).[38]

All Existence Finds Its Origin in the Primordial Realm

In Egyptian mythology all existence, including that of the gods, finds its origin in the primeval waters of Nun, who is thus often identified as "the father of the gods."[39] As mentioned above, Nun along with darkness, make up the dark boundless realm of nonexistence that never becomes part of existence and is a domain that transcends and limits the gods.[40] Spell 17 of the Book of the Dead, a text from the Late Period, presents the creator god Rê-Atum self-generating in Nun and rising onto the primeval hill. From the mound, Rê-Atum creates the Ennead by naming eight parts, or four pairs, of his body, and with each utterance a new god comes into existence. According to the Memphite theology found on the so-called Shabaka Stone (no. 498 in the British Museum), Ptah is identified as the creator god. Ptah was a god from the early period associated with the earth. Here Ptah is explicitly equated with Nun and Naunet, the primeval waters of the Ogdoad, along with the primeval hill Tatenen, and is said to have produced the creator god Atum, the rest of the Ennead, and all existence.[41]

The Mesopotamian Enûma Elish presents the defeat of preexistent chaos and the establishment of cosmic order in two separate stages, by two different gods.[42] Essentially, the conflict between order and disorder arises because the engendered gods are those who actively pursue order, whereas the chaos pair, Apsu and Tiamat, prefer to rest and remain inactive, thus producing disorder. The initial part of the story tells of Ea's defeat of Apsu (Tablet I:11–77), while the majority of the epic tells of Marduk's defeat of Tiamat and the subsequent creation of the cosmos. Regarding the latter, Marduk is said to have been born to Ea and Damkina and is identified as "the wisest of gods." Following Ea's and Anu's failure to conquer Tiamat, Anshar turns to Marduk for help. Marduk agrees to go against Tiamat, but only with the condition that the gods confer upon him supreme authority over them and the universe.[43] After the discussion of the Assembly, the gods agree and confer upon Marduk the authority of kingship.[44] In order to determine whether Marduk has acquired the magical powers given to him, the gods present a test for him. The efficacy of Marduk's command is thereafter proven, and the gods confirm his superiority.[45]

Commissioned by the gods and armed with various weapons and magic, Marduk approaches for war as a thunderstorm. Kingu and his army enter into a state of confusion, leaving only an undaunted Tiamat. Marduk and Tiamat face off, and all of Tiamat's reciting of her charms and casting of her spells are of no avail. Marduk thus conquers chaos:

Then joined issue Tiamat and Marduk, wisest of gods.
They strove in single combat, locked in battle.
The lord spread out his net to enfold her,
The Evil Wind, which followed behind, he let loose in her face.
When Tiamat opened her mouth to consume him,
He drove in the Evil Wind that she close not her lips.
As the fierce winds charged her belly,
Her body was distended and her mouth was wide open.
He released the arrow, it tore her belly,
It cut through her insides, splitting the heart.
Having thus subdued her, he extinguished her life. (Tablet IV:93–103)

Following his victory, Marduk organizes the cosmos with the body of Tiamat. He first splits Tiamat's body in two. He lifts up one half to form the sky, and with the remaining half he fashions the earth.[46]

Magic

For the Egyptian, the power of the universe was found in the art of magic, which was employed by both the gods and humanity. Magic is a force that is implemented through utterance and deed.[47] According to the Instruction for Merikare, the creator god made for all human beings "magic to be weapons to ward off what may happen."[48] At the same time, magic is understood as existing before all the gods and other existent realities, and without magic creation would have been impossible.[49] It is by magic that the creator god self-generates.[50] The god Hike, who is one of the three powers that provide for creation to take place, personifies "magic"; and it is Hike that ensures the realization of the utterance of the creator god.[51] In fact, "magic" protects the sun god so that it can reappear daily on the horizon unopposed.[52] Moreover, maintenance of the cosmic order is through magic. As seen above, the realm of chaos remains an antagonistic force that the gods (along with the Pharaoh) continue to battle, and magic is the weapon of warfare.[53]

Magic in Mesopotamia had essentially the same uses and characteristics as in Egypt.[54] As seen above in Enûma Elish, Marduk is endowed with magic and is considered the king of the gods because of his wisdom in the art of magic. Along with force, it is with the use of magic that he subdues Tiamat. This is also true of Ea's earlier defeat of the primeval waters of chaos by devising a magical scheme:

Ea, the all wise, saw through their scheme.
A master design against it he devised and set up,

Made artful his spell against it, surpassing and holy.
He recited it and made it subsist in the deep,
As he poured sleep upon him. Sound asleep he lay.
When Apsu he had made prone, drenched with sleep,
Mummu, the adviser, was powerless to stir.
He loosened his band, tore off his tiara,
Removed his halo (and) put it on himself.
Having fettered Apsu, he slew him.
Mummu he bound and left behind lock. (Tablet I:60–70)

Humanity

There is no specific or separate account of the creation of humankind in the Egyptian cosmogonies, only brief fragments depicting its origin.[55] What is clear, however, is that creation was depicted on a continuum beginning with the gods down to human beings. For the Egyptian there was no real line of distinction between the gods and humanity; the difference between them was one of degree, not kind. Wilson remarks: "Between god and man there was no point at which one could erect a boundary line and state that here substance changed from divine, superhuman, immortal, to mundane, human, mortal.... With relation to gods and men the Egyptians were monophysites: many men and many gods, but all ultimately of one nature."[56] This can be seen especially in the parallel structure of certain texts. In the Coffin Text, Spell 1130, the creator god states: "I created the gods from my sweat, and mankind from the tears of my eye."[57] In the Hymn to Ptah, the creator god is exalted as the "Eldest god of the primeval time, who shaped mankind and formed the gods."[58] In fact, human beings are the "images of god." According to the Instruction for Merikare, humankind is "the cattle of god" and "they are likenesses of him which issued from his flesh."[59] All of humanity are images of the gods and are the equals of the gods as proved by their actions.[60]

According to Enûma Elish, humankind was created in order to relieve the gods of their manual labors.[61] Summoning the gods to the Assembly, Marduk inquires of the gods who initiated the rebellion. The gods identify Kingu as the rebel, and they bring him before Ea, kill him, and from his blood humanity is formed:

> They [the gods] bound him [Kingu], holding him before Ea. They imposed on him his guilt and severed his blood (vessels). Out of his blood

they fashioned mankind. He imposed the service and let free the gods. (Tablet VI:34–36)

Another Akkadian text describing the creation of humankind is found in the *Atrahasis Epic* (I: 192–248). As in Enûma Elish, humankind is created in order to relieve the gods of their laborious work and establish their freedom forever. Humanity is created by the birth goddess Mami (= Nintu) out of clay mixed with the blood and flesh of a slain god.[62] Thus, as with Egypt, there is no real line of demarcation between the gods and humankind.

Summary

From the cosmogonies of these two ancient cultures, several important conclusions can be drawn that are important for this essay. First, the people of both Egypt and Mesopotamia were polytheistic (accepted many gods).[63] Although at times each religion acknowledged a superior or high god such as Marduk or Amun-Rê,[64] that did not constitute the dismissal of other gods from their respective pantheons.[65] Second, each cosmogony contains a theogony that presents the origin and genealogy of the gods with the primary purpose of specifying the hierarchical role of each god in their respective pantheon.[66] In fact, any god in the pantheon could be proclaimed supreme over the others when that god was addressed or called upon for help. Third, the gods are constituent with the matter of the universe, and in fact the gods are typically depicted as a personification of a particular natural phenomenon (e.g., sun, sky, water). Hence, the gods do not transcend the material world and are limited to the power of the phenomena they personify. Fourth, the gods are engendered beings and are often depicted as creating other gods by begetting them.

Fifth, fundamental to each of the cosmogonies is a preexisting primordial realm represented by the primeval waters of chaos wherefrom the gods, humanity, and nature find their ultimate origin. Sixth, this primordial realm transcends the gods. It limits their power, and its fundamental laws of operation are laws to which the gods are subject. Kaufmann describes these last two features as the distinguishing mark or "fundamental idea" of paganism. He describes it as:

> the idea that there exists a realm of being prior to the gods and above them, upon which the gods depend, and whose decrees they must obey. Deity belongs to, and is derived from, a primordial realm. This realm is conceived of variously—as darkness, water, spirit, earth, sky, and so forth—but always

as the womb in which the seeds of all being are contained. Alternatively, this idea appears as a belief in a primordial realm beside the gods, as independent and primary as the gods themselves. Not being subject to the gods, it necessarily limits them. The first conception, however, is the fundamental one. This is to say that in the pagan view, the gods are not the source of all that is, nor do they transcend the universe. They are, rather, part of a realm precedent to and independent of them. They are rooted in this realm, are bound by its nature, are subservient to its laws. To be sure, paganism has personal gods who create and govern the world of men. But a divine will, sovereign and absolute, which governs all and is the cause of all being—such a conception is unknown. There are heads of pantheons, there are creators and maintainers of the cosmos; but transcending them is the primordial realm, with its pre-existent, autonomous forces.[67]

In such a worldview the supreme power within the universe is magic—the gods need it, employ it, and are vulnerable to it. Concerning magic in the pagan world, Kaufmann writes:

> Corresponding to the mythological conception of deity is the magical character of the pagan cultus. Magic is an art whose purpose is to move occult powers to act in a desired manner. It utilizes means which are automatically efficient, irrespective of the will of the gods.... The power of magic transcends the gods: they themselves employ it, for they too are in need of this almighty instrument which is independent of them and their will. The gods are great magicians, and there are even skilled specialists in this art among them.[68]

Lastly, there is no strict demarcation between the gods and humankind. Divine nature and human nature are not different in kind but only in degree. This monophysite ("one nature") view allows for humans (such as the Pharaoh) to be exalted to the status of a god. Kaufmann observes: "The continuity of the divine and human realm is the basis of the pagan belief in apotheosis, in the possibility of man's attaining godhood. The idea manifests itself in various forms: in the cult as the worship of deified men; in eschatology as the promise of ultimate immortality, of joining the gods, or even rising above them."[69]

II. The Old Testament View of God and Creation

In the Old Testament there are numerous texts from a number of different genres that present Israel's understanding of creation and its relationship with God and humanity.[70] Because Israel did not arise in a cultural vacuum, it is important to look at these texts in light of the beliefs common in the ancient Near East. Knowledge of the cultures surrounding ancient Israel can lead to important insights that help us properly understand the Old Testament in its historical-cultural context.

Some scholars have approached the comparative study of Old Testament and ancient Near Eastern texts with the operative assumption that the views expressed in each must be roughly the same and that differences between them must be mostly superficial. As a result, priority is given to Egyptian and Mesopotamian texts, and Old Testament passages are interpreted on the assumption of similarity. This seems to me a methodologically flawed approach to understanding the Old Testament. Following such an approach will lead to differences being minimized or suppressed and texts being forced to fit the theory rather than the theory being modified to conform to the texts. It must be kept in mind that one reason to read the Old Testament against the backdrop of the literature produced by Israel's cultural neighbors is to discover the points of discontinuity that made Israelite culture and Old Testament religion distinctive.

When freed from assumptions about how ancient Near Eastern and Old Testament views must necessarily be continuous, one finds that in several important respects the views expressed by the Old Testament writers stand in stark contrast to those of Israel's cultural neighbors. This is not to suggest that the Israelites had nothing in common with their neighbors. There were many commonalties, even with regard to creation. In fact, on occasion the Old Testament writers even employed some of the same imagery found in Egyptian, Mesopotamian, and Canaanite texts. But, if one pays close attention, it becomes clear that even when similar imagery is used, often it was used in different ways. More often than not the imagery was employed in polemical fashion against typical Near Eastern views.

In direct contradistinction to the specific pagan views described above, in the Old Testament we find the following: God alone is the maker of heaven and earth, God instituted and is not subject to the laws of his creation, God is transcendent over and distinct from his creation, God has neither a theogony nor a pantheon, God created humanity as a distinct race of beings which bears his image, and God is God alone. In this section I will briefly discuss each of these distinctive characteristics of Old Testament theology.

God Is the Maker of Heaven and Earth

In the Old Testament one finds that a main concern of the biblical writers was how to live in light of the fact that Yahweh is a true Creator. In contrast to the gods of the nations, Yahweh transcends the created order. He existed prior to the world's temporal beginning, and the world exists solely because of his creative activity. His creative activity does not rely on preexisting matter, natural laws, or magic. Yahweh did not create through cosmic battle with other gods or through any kind of sexual activity; Yahweh created by simple divine decree. Nowhere in the Old Testament is it explicitly and precisely stated that God created the heavens and the earth "out of nothing" (*ex nihilo*). But the concept expressed by the phrase *creatio ex nihilo* seems to accurately capture what was assumed by the Old Testament writers when they spoke of Yahweh as the creator of the heavens and the earth.

In the creation account of Genesis 1 we are told that "the earth was formless and empty, darkness was over the surface of the deep" (1:2).[71] Taking the Genesis account in isolation from the rest of the Old Testament and assuming that it must reflect common ancient Near Eastern views, some have presumed that it must be referring to some kind of preexistent matter or primordial realm when it speaks of a formless and empty earth (an understanding fostered by some translations' rendering it "formless void") and "the deep." But when one looks at other Old Testament passages, it becomes clear that this is not how the ancient Israelites understood it. Two texts that illustrate this well are Psalm 104 and Proverbs 8.[72] In Psalm 104:5–9 the psalmist declares:

> You are the one who set the earth on its foundations,
>   it cannot move for ever and ever.
> The deep covered it like a garment,
>   the waters stood above the mountains.
> From your rebuke they fled;
>   from your loud thunder they ran way.
> They rose up to the mountains, ran down into the valleys
>   to the place that you set for them.
> You established a boundary they cannot pass,
>   they will never return to cover the earth.

In this text we see that God initially set the earth upon its immovable foundations (v. 5), and *then* the mountains are covered over with "the deep" (v. 6). Clearly, "the deep" is not some primordial realm or preexistent reality out of which God created. The earth and the mountains are described as already having been created by God before "the deep." Furthermore, we see that God has complete control over "the deep": he rebukes it, sets boundaries for it, and decrees what it can and cannot do (vv. 7–9).[73]

Proverbs 8:22–31 discusses how God created the world in wisdom. For this essay, what is important to notice in this passage is: (1) the temporal sequence between the begetting of Wisdom and God's creating the world; (2) the totalistic description of every aspect of reality having been created with a temporal beginning; (3) the fact that there was a time when the deep did not exist; and (4) Yahweh's transcendence and complete mastery over the deep. Wisdom proclaims about herself:

> Yahweh begot me at the beginning of his ways,
> > the first of his works of old.
> Ages ago I was set up,
> > at the start, before the beginning of the earth.
> When there were no deeps I was brought forth,
> > when there were no springs abounding with water.
> Before the mountains were settled,
> > before the hills, I was brought forth.
> When he had not yet made the earth and fields,
> > nor the first clods of the world's soil.
> When he put the heavens in place, I was there,
> > when he marked out the horizon on the face of the deep,
> When he made firm the skies above,
> > when he strengthened the sources of the deep,
> When he fixed the sea its limit
> > so that the waters would not transgress his command,
> > when he marked out the foundations of the earth,
> There I was beside him—the master workman,[74]
> > and I was delight day after day,
> > playing before him all the time,
> Playing on the surface of his earth,
> > and my delight is in human beings.

It is clear from this passage that Yahweh existed prior to creation. Wisdom declares that Yahweh is the creator of the world and is accomplished in wisdom (see also Prov 3:19–20), not magic, matter, or law. Thus, it seems fair to say that the author assumes creation *ex nihilo*.

Genesis 1:1–2:4a is considered the primary creation text in the Old Testament. It has already been noted that it has often been used to support the idea that God did not, in fact, create *ex nihilo*. It is true that God's creative activity in Genesis 1:2 begins with darkness, earth, and the deep already present. However, in light of Psalm 104 and Proverbs 8, it should be clear that the ancient Israelites would not have understood this along the lines of typical Near Eastern creation accounts. In fact, though the primary purpose of the Genesis account is not to specify precisely how God created the world, scholars have long recognized that it is polemical in nature.[75] Unlike many pagan accounts, there is no conflict or cosmic battle involved in the creation process. God does not employ magic but simply issues his decree. As shown earlier, both the Egyptian and Mesopotamian cosmogonies begin with preexistent darkness, waters, and matter out of which the gods arise or self-create.[76] In part, the author of Genesis is confronting these ancient cultures' mythological ideas and declaring who the true creator and master of the universe is—God, not some preexistent reality. As Hartley rightly states, the focus in Genesis 1:1–2:4a "is on God's sovereignty over the dynamic movement between cosmos and chaos, so as to discount pagan cosmogonies as a valid way of understanding the world's origin. As a result, the theme of creation out of nothing was not addressed because it was not an issue. Nevertheless, the wording of this account does not conflict with the idea of creation *ex nihilo*, which is taught in other Scriptures" (e.g., Prov 8:22–31).[77] In addition, Genesis 1:1 functions as a heading for the whole account, signifying that the creation of the world is the work of God.[78] In addressing the question "Is it *creatio ex nihilo* or not?" in Genesis 1, Claus Westermann remarks that the question "is not relevant to the text"; however, "had the question been put to him [the author] he must certainly have decided in favor of *creatio ex nihilo*."[79] In Psalm 104 and Proverbs 8 we see the authors go behind the Genesis account and more clearly state ideas that assume *creatio ex nihilo*.[80]

Over and over again the Old Testament boldly affirms that God is the creator of the universe. It declares that Yahweh is "Maker of heaven and earth," often doing so in the midst of jubilant expressions of praise and worship (e.g., Pss 115:15; 121:2; 124:8; 134:3; 146:6; Neh 9:6; Jer 32:17; Jon 1:9).[81] For example, in a manner similar to Genesis 1:1–2:4a, in Psalm 33 the psalmist declares:

> By the word of Yahweh the heavens were made
> and by the breath of his mouth all their host.
> He gathers together the waters of the sea like a heap
> and puts the deeps in storehouses.
> Let all the earth fear Yahweh;
> let all the inhabitants of the world be in awe of him.
> For he spoke and it came to be;
> he commanded and it stood forth. (cf. Ps 148:4–6)

In sum, the Old Testament presents a view of God and creation that is radically different from the cosmogonies of the ancient Near East. In Israel's understanding, God existed prior to creation and created the heavens and the earth *ex nihilo*. One can only agree with the first article of the Apostles' Creed: "I believe in God the Father Almighty, Maker of heaven and earth."

God Instituted and Is Not Subject to the Laws of Creation

Whereas in the ancient Near Eastern cosmogonies prior to creation a primordial realm of matter exists, already governed by inherent natural laws or magic, in Genesis 1:1–2:4a the narrative presents God as creating the world and establishing the laws that govern the universe. God creates light and then divides the light from the darkness (v. 4). God then names the two elements, an act that establishes the particular role of each element and displays God's dominion over it (see Gen 2:20; 2 Kgs 23:34; 24:17).[82] In the same manner, God makes an expanse that separates the floodwaters and thereby fixes an upper and lower region of waters, and he names the expanse "heavens" (vv. 6–8). God then divides the lower waters from the land and fixes the boundaries of the waters (see also Job 38:8–11) and names each (vv. 9–10). God commands the earth to produce vegetation and fruit and provides the various plants with the ability to reproduce (vv. 11–12). God creates the luminaries and fixes their course in the heavens in order to determine days, years, and seasons; to provide light; to rule the day and night; and to separate light from darkness (vv. 14–18).[83]

God creates all the creatures in the water, sky, and earth and grants to them the ability to reproduce after their kind (vv. 20–25). Finally, God creates humankind and blesses it. He gives humans the ability to procreate and commands them to do so. The Genesis account further informs us that humanity was created and commanded to rule over the creatures of the earth (vv. 26–28). According to Genesis 1, God created the heavens and the earth and the totality of its inhabitants, and God decreed the functions and boundaries of the universe.

Elsewhere in the Old Testament we see that God actively controls the workings of the cosmos through laws he has instituted (see Job 38:22–38). Yet, at the same time, he continually supplies the needs of the earth and its inhabitants (Pss 65:9–10; 145:14–16; Jer 5:24; 10:13). In fact, all life is utterly dependent on God's sustenance (Ps 104:27–30). As creator, God is the owner of the earth:

> The earth is Yahweh's and all that is in it,
>> The world and all those who dwell in it.
> For he has founded it upon the seas,
>> And established it upon the rivers.
>> (Ps 24:1–2; see also Deut 10:14; Ps 89:11)

As creator and owner of the earth, God has absolute sovereign domin-ion over the world and is thus King (Pss 24:7–10; 93:1–5; 1 Chr 29:11). Since Yahweh is both Creator and King, Isaiah proclaims: "Yahweh of hosts, God of Israel, who is enthroned on the cherubim, you are the God, you alone, over all the kingdoms of the earth; You yourself made the heavens and the earth" (37:16).[84] Hence, because God is the creator of heaven and earth, he has universal rule over all the nations.[85]

We see in the Old Testament that, unlike human beings, God is not subject to the laws of creation since he is the creator and owner of the uni-verse. A prime example of this is the account of the plagues before Israel's exodus from Egypt (Ex 7:8–12:32). The plagues were brought about by Yahweh in order to degrade the Egyptian gods, and they demonstrated his unrivaled superiority (Ex 9:14–16; 12:12; 18:11; Num 33:4).[86] The plagues were specifically directed against the Pharaoh (who was considered a god), and the Egyptians and Israelites were to acknowledge the uniqueness and supremacy of Yahweh since there is nothing that can be compared to him in all the earth (Ex 7:17; 8:10, 22; cf. 9:14–16). At the same time, the plagues demonstrated that "the earth is Yahweh's" (Ex 9:29; see also 19:5).

From early times the Pharaoh was often identified as the "son of Rê," the "image of Rê," or even "Rê," along with other divine epithets.[87] Upon his accession and coronation, the Pharaoh became divine;[88] and, like the creator god, his primary responsibility was to maintain *ma'at*, cosmic order.[89] With the death of his predecessor, the coronation of the new king involved an empowering with magic for this very purpose.[90] In the Exodus account, the Pharaoh is shown to have no such ability to control nature and is proved to be no match for Yahweh.[91] Hence, the plagues have a dual function: (1) they expose the Egyptian king's incapability to maintain order; and (2) they display Yahweh's supremacy over all other gods as the one who alone owns the earth and controls the forces of nature.[92] Each plague demonstrates God's sole ability to manipulate a particular aspect of cre-ation from its original created mode of being and then subsequently restore it to his created intended order.[93]

God Is Transcendent Over and Distinct from His Creation

Unlike the gods of Egypt and Mesopotamia, the God of the Old Testament is never described as coming out of, or being derived from, any primordial stuff, but is explicitly shown as transcendent *over* the created material. This can be specifically seen in Genesis 1:2: "And the earth was a desert waste and darkness was over the deep and the Spirit of God was hovering *over* the waters."[94] God is not presented as self-generated as in the Egyptian cosmogonies or engendered as in Enûma Elish. Moreover, God does not exist as a part of the material realm; he is the creator of it! God is not the sun, moon, or stars; he is their creator. Matter is not considered divine; rather creation testifies of one greater, its creator (e.g., Ps 19:1–3). Thus, as Hartley states, "the Creator God exists independently from and transcends all matter."[95] Furthermore, created matter is perishable, not eternal, whereas Yahweh endures forever. In the words of Psalm 102:

> Long ago you laid the foundation of the earth,
>   and the heavens are your handiwork.
> They may perish, but you remain,
>   while they all wear out as clothing.
> You can change them like garments and they are put away,
>   but you are the same and your years do not end.

Here we see that matter is clearly considered transient, whereas God endures forever. Consequently, God is completely free from and is transcendent over creation. God is not restricted by anything; he does in and with creation as he wishes.

God Has No Theogony or Pantheon

Nowhere does the Old Testament present a myth of the origin of God or the begetting of other gods. Unlike the gods of the nations, the God of the Old Testament has no nativity, no parents, and no offspring; he has no genealogy, and he does not die. The Old Testament assumes from beginning to end that God has always existed and has always existed as God. This is expressed clearly in Psalm 90:2: "Before the mountains were born, and (before) you gave birth to the earth and the world, even from everlasting to everlasting, you are God!"

In light of the Near Eastern cultural context in which ancient Israel arose, it is truly striking that within the entire Old Testament there is absolutely no trace of a theogony. God is never described as being another god's "son," nor is God ever called "father of the gods."[96] Yahweh is never presented as participating in sexual or procreative activity. Furthermore, Yahweh is never spoken of having a consort with whom he might procreate.[97] As Kaufmann observes, in the Old Testament "creation is not depicted as a sexual process, nor does it proceed from the seed of the god, his blood, spittle, tears, or the like" as was so common in the pagan religions.[98] In addition, nowhere is God spoken of as being threatened with being killed or dying.

It is also significant that the Old Testament gives no indication that God is merely the high god of a pantheon as was so common in the ancient Near Eastern religions. The Old Testament does present Yahweh as having a council whose members offer advice and are delegated certain responsibilities (e.g., Job 1:6–12; 2:1–6; Isa 6:1–13; Zech 3:1–7). Israel's prophets were also participants in the council and were messengers of Yahweh (cf. 1 Kgs 22:19–23; Jer 23:16–22).[99] Yet in contrast to Ugaritic and Mesopotamian mythology, those assembled around God are always depicted as nameless heavenly beings without personality or profile. They do not possess any autonomy or independence apart from Yahweh and his word; they are completely subordinate and inferior to him (cf. Ps 89:5–7).[100] The members of Yahweh's council are understood as heavenly beings but are rarely, if ever, identified as *'elohim,* "gods" (and in the few places where one might argue that they are, it is clear that the members of the council are different in kind from Yahweh).[101]

God Created Humankind in His Image

Yahweh proclaims through Isaiah: "I myself made the earth and I created humanity upon it" (45:12a). Genesis 1:26–27 presents God's creation of humankind:

> Then God said: "Let us make humankind (*'adam*) in our image (*tselem*), according to our likeness (*dᵉmut*), and let them rule over the fish in the sea and over the birds in the heavens and over the cattle and over all the earth, and over all the creeping things that creep on the earth." So God created (*bara*) humankind in his image, in the image of God he created it, as male and female he created them.[102]

From the perspective of the whole narrative, these verses present the creation of human beings as the pinnacle of God's creation. God has created the world in such a way that it is "good" for human habitation. What is significant for this essay is that human beings are created and thereby have a beginning. The repetition of the verb *bara'* emphasizes who created and what was created. Humankind is not described as existing prior to God's creation. As with the rest of what God created, there is no indication that God created human beings from any eternal, independently preexisting materials. Genesis 2:7 makes clear that humanity is made from the created matter of the universe. The man (*ha'adam*) was formed from the dust of the ground (*ha'adamah*),[103] and as material, humankind will return to the earth (Gen 3:19; Pss 104:29; 146:4). God formed or shaped (*yatsar*) human beings (see also Job 10:8; Ps 119:73; Isa 29:16) as he shaped the animals (Gen 2:19). But formed matter in and of itself is not alive. Thus, God gives the inanimate man life by breathing into his nostrils, suggesting that humans are composed of more than mere matter. As the life-giver, God is also the one who takes life away (Ps 90:3). Hence, God alone has the power of life and death. Yahweh can thereby proclaim about himself:

> See now that I, even I, am he,
>   and there is no other God besides me;
> I myself put to death and I make alive
>   I wound and I myself heal;
>   And no one can deliver from my hand. (Deut. 32:39; see also
> 1 Sam. 2:6; 2 Kings 5:7)

Humanity is distinguished from all other creatures by the fact that it is created in the image (*tselem*) and in the likeness (*demut*) of God (Gen 1:26). What exactly the term *tselem* means in relation to humanity has been the source of scholarly debate.[104] But careful analysis of the various occurrences of the noun throughout the Old Testament leads to the conclusion that a *tselem* "represents" something.[105] Hence, the most natural understanding of humankind created in the image of God is that human beings are God's image or representative on earth. This is confirmed by God's command for humanity to rule over God's creation on his behalf (v. 28; see also Ps 8:5–8).

According to David Clines, humankind is God's representative on earth and thus "is itself the image of God."[106] Clines's conclusion is based on several factors. First, "when Yahweh is seen in vision, some 'appearance' (*mar'eh*) is described, yet there is no real (*demut*) 'likeness, configuration' that can be described, nor any *tselem* 'image, shape.'"[107] There are instances when Yahweh appears in human form (e.g., Gen 18), yet this is only a form that he has assumed for the sake of a temporary manifestation.[108] Furthermore, making images representing God is forbidden, one reason being that it is impossible to do so because God is formless. This is chiefly seen in Deuteronomy 4:15–18: "Watch yourselves carefully since you saw no form (t*munah) at all on the day Yahweh spoke to you at Horeb out of the midst of the fire; beware lest you act corruptly by making any graven image for yourselves in the form (t*munah) of any figure, the likeness of male and female, the likeness of any beast. . . any winged bird. . . anything that creeps on the ground. . . any fish."

Second, Clines analyzes the meaning of *image* in the ancient Near East. According to Clines, the primary function of worshiped images was to be the dwelling place of spirit or fluid that derived from the being whose image it was. Human beings could also be the dwelling place of a deity. More importantly, the king in Mesopotamia and Egypt was regarded as the lifelong incarnation of a god. The visible and tangible body of the king is only the covering for the god or the dwelling of the god. "The king as image of the god is his representative. The king has been created by the god to be his image."[109] From this examination, Clines concludes that humanity is the image of God that represents God on earth in every way.[110]

The term *tselem,* however, also indicates that to some degree human beings are like God and resemble him. This is enhanced by the use of the similar noun *d*mut* (Gen 1:26a; 5:1), which tends to convey the idea of two objects corresponding to one another (see, e.g., 2 Chr 4:3; Ps 58:4).[111] Still, the text never indicates *how* humankind is like God. An obvious correspondence between God and humankind would include that both speak, hear, see, and feel.[112] However, what is certain is that humanity does not resemble God in nature or in bodily form, for in the Old Testament God is never presented as an embodied being or even a physical being. Furthermore, the Old Testament assumes throughout that human beings do not have the divine nature of God: God creates, but human beings cannot create in the same sense; God is the sole Creator, but humans are creatures; humans die, but God is immortal.[113]

God Is God Alone

In the ancient Near Eastern religions the divine nature was shared by many gods. It has been pointed out that it was even shared by human beings since there really was no clear demarcation between divine and human nature. In the Old Testament, however, we find that God is a completely unique and incomparable being; he is God absolutely.[114] The Old Testament speaks of God's incomparability, and to demonstrate his uniqueness God is often contrasted with humankind.[115] In Numbers 23:19 Balaam asserts: "God (*'el*) is not man (*'ish*), that he should lie, nor a son of man (*ben 'adam*) that he should change his mind." Samuel exclaims to Saul about Yahweh's nature: "And also the Glory of Israel does not lie nor change his mind; for he is not a man (*'adam*) who changes his mind" (1 Sam 15:29). Isaiah contrasts humanity, along with material beings, with God: "The Egyptians are mortal (*'adam*) and not God (*'el*), and their horses are flesh (*basar*) and not spirit (*ruah*)" (Isa 31:3a). Ezekiel confronts the king of Tyre, who has asserted his personal equality with God but is exposed as a mere mortal. The king claims, "I am a god (*'el*), I sit in the seat of gods (*'elohim*)." However, when Yahweh brings judgment through another nation, the king will be denounced as a mere mortal because he is "a man (*'adam*) and not God (*'el*)" (Ezek 28:2; see also v. 9).[116] Unlike the pagan religions of the ancient Near East, the Old Testament makes a clear distinction between the divine and human. God is clearly not a human being, but divine; humans are created beings, not divine. The categories are mutually exclusive.

Yahweh, through the prophet Hosea, extends this distinction even further by declaring: "I am God (*'el*) and not man (*'ish*), the Holy One in your midst" (11:9). God is not only distinct from humankind, but he is totally distinct in holiness. Holiness is not an attribute of Yahweh but is "the quintessential nature of Yahweh as God."[117] Being holy (*qadosh*), God is wholly *other than,* incomparable to all in his created order.[118] In certain instances even what God does can be considered unique and so can be qualified as "strange" or "alien" (Isa 28:21). Holiness indicates God's unapproachableness, and a vision of the holy God is simultaneously awe-inspiring and frighteningly terrible (e.g., Lev 9:23–24).[119] God is so completely holy that a human being cannot see him and live (Gen 16:13; Ex 33:20; Judg 13:22). In addition, "God's holiness implies his absolute power over the world."[120] The great theophany at Sinai depicts the violent reaction of creation when the holy God descends upon the mountain. Despite the wondrous spectacle, the people are warned not to approach too close lest they die (Ex 19:18–25).[121] Similarly, Micah describes the coming forth of Yahweh, and, as at Sinai, the appearing of the holy God in creation causes violent upheavals:

For behold, Yahweh is coming forth out of his place,
And will come down and tread on the high places of the earth.
And the mountains will melt under him
And the valleys will burst apart,

like wax before the fire,
like waters poured down a steep place.
(Mic 1:3–4; see also Judg 5:4–5)

Although members of Yahweh's council are different in nature as compared to humanity, God is also distinct in nature from heavenly beings. This is explicitly evident in Psalm 89:

And the heavens have praised your wondrous work, O Yahweh;
and also your faithfulness among the assembly of the holy ones.
For who among the clouds is equal to Yahweh?
Who is like Yahweh among the sons of God?
God, greatly feared in the council of the holy ones,
and awesome above all around him!
O Yahweh God of hosts.
Who is like you, O Mighty Yahweh?
and your faithfulness around you?

Here Yahweh is distinguished from heavenly beings by his wondrous power and might. No supernatural being can be compared to Yahweh. Even more impressive, Yahweh is greatly feared and worshiped by these beings.

God is also incomparable in his *otherness* to all other gods worshiped in pagan religions. The psalmist proclaims, "There is no one like you among the gods, my Lord, and there are no works to compare with yours" (86:8). The psalmist also rhetorically asks, "Who is God except Yahweh?" (Ps 18:31a; see 2 Sam 22:32a) with the obvious answer: no one! In Elijah's direct challenge between Yahweh and the Canaanite god Baal, the proof of *divinity* is on trial, asking the question "Who is really God?" (1 Kgs 18:20–40).[122] Following Elijah's prayer, Yahweh answers with fire, and the people respond: "Yahweh, he is the God, Yahweh, he is the God" (v. 39).[123] In comparison to Yahweh, all other so-called gods are in fact "no gods" (see Deut 32:15–21; 2 Kgs 5:15; Jer 2:11, 27–28; 5:7; Hos 8:6). As the psalmist declares:

For great is Yahweh, and greatly to be praised;
He is to be feared above all gods.
For all the gods of the peoples are worthless things,
but Yahweh made the heavens. (Ps 96:4–5)

Yahweh's incomparability is a major theme in the book of Isaiah. For Isaiah there is no god equal to the Holy One. "To whom will you compare me as an equal?" Yahweh rhetorically asks (Isa 40:25; see also 46:5). Yahweh is incomparable because there is no other god who existed before him and there will be none following (43:10b). Throughout chapters 40–55 Yahweh challenges the Babylonian gods to prove their divinity by announcing a future event and producing that declaration (cf. 41:21–29). However, the gods are incapable of fulfilling such a challenge, for they are mere idols manufactured by human beings (40:18–20; 44:9–20). In fact, they are incapable of doing good or evil (41:23b), and they are less than nothing, while their action is nonexistent (41:24). These gods must be carried from place to place (46:7a); they cannot speak, hear, or deliver anyone from trouble (7b).

In direct contrast, Yahweh can and does announce and fulfill future events and is thereby divine. Therefore, Yahweh declares of himself: "I am the first and I am the last! And except for me, there is no God!" (44:6b). Yahweh is the sole deity because he is the creator of the universe who is the incomparable master over all. He has no peer, for he alone can weigh the world and its inhabitants effortlessly (40:12–26). As creator and master of creation, Yahweh is the Lord of history. Yahweh alone has the power to control history; he is "the one who forms light and creates darkness, makes peace and creates disaster" (45:7). In comparison to Babylon's idol gods, Yahweh has no equal. Hence, Yahweh asks, "To whom will you liken me or equate, or compare me that we should be alike?" (46:5; see also 40:18a; 40:25; 44:7). Yahweh then answers, "For I am God and there is no other God! And there is none like me!" (46:9b). According to Isaiah, there is no other God besides Yahweh, for any other so-called gods do not even exist! (cf. 45:21b–22; 46:9b).

In a similar fashion, Psalm 82 presents a picture of the death of the gods and proclaims the God of Israel as the one true God of the universe.[124] This unique psalm polemically employs mythological language imagery portraying the common worldview of the ancient Near East, which understands the cosmos as ruled by the decisions of a divine assembly.[125] As seen above in Enûma Elish, the gods would assemble together, typically with one high god presiding, to deliberate over political or judicial issues, military action, and the decreeing of history. However, there is nothing that requires the assembly in Psalm 82 to be Yahweh's council.[126] Here God opposes this divine assembly as he pronounces judgment on the "the council of El" (ba'adat 'el) or "divine assembly" (v. 1).[127] God's condemnation of those who think they are gods rests on the gods' failure to provide order for humanity on earth (vv. 1–4). In fact, these self-proclaimed gods are incapable of executing justice, for they lack the necessary qualities of being divine and thus have no knowledge and walk in darkness (v. 5a). Consequently, order in the cosmos is being threatened (v. 5b).[128] Thus, the gods "inability to carry out their function proved them to be lacking the power necessary to be 'gods.'"[129] Although those in the assembly are identified as gods (*'elohim*) and sons of Elyon (v. 6), God sentences them to death (v. 7). Hence, God condemns all other gods to mortality and thereby has sole claim to deity.[130] The psalm announces the death of the gods, leaving the only one who can be identified as God.[131] The God of the Old Testament alone has universal authority and is thereby the only one who possesses the power of life and death.[132] The psalm ends with the God of Israel being implored to judge the earth. He can do so because he is the only true God, and he alone possesses all the nations (v. 8). As Isaiah exposes the gods as nonexistent and nothing, so Psalm 82 unmasks the pagan gods for who they really are—no gods.

Throughout the Old Testament, Yahweh is displayed and proclaimed as unique and incomparable to all other beings. This uniqueness and incomparability is demonstrated in the Exodus event. Following Israel's deliverance through the sea, the peerless Yahweh is praised:

Who is like you among the gods, Yahweh?
Who is like you, magnificent in holiness,
    awesome in praiseworthy deeds, doing the miraculous? (Ex 15:11)

These rhetorical questions clearly assert that Yahweh is holy and thereby possesses supreme power and that he is incomparable to all other gods. Thus, in the Exodus the Israelites discovered the uniqueness of their God and that the Egyptian 'gods' could do nothing to stop Yahweh's people from leaving Egypt.[133]

Yahweh's uniqueness and incomparability is also expressed in Israel's central theological confession identified as the *Shema,* literally translated: "Hear, O Israel, Yahweh our God Yahweh one" (Deut 6:4).[134] The Shema is a positive affirmation of the first commandment that definitively forbids the worship of another god (Deut 5:7; Ex 20:3). The first part of the confession, "Yahweh our God," presents Israel's declaration that Yahweh is Israel's God and that there is no other god whom it is proper to worship. The second part, "Yahweh one," declares Yahweh's *uniqueness* that stems primarily from the surrounding context of the Shema. No other god can be compared to Yahweh (3:24), and there is no other God except Yahweh (4:35, 39; 32:39).

Yahweh alone is Israel's God, and Israel is to recognize Yahweh as God exclusively (6:5).[135] Along with Yahweh's incomparability, the second part simultaneously confesses the *unity* of Yahweh.[136] Yahweh is not divided in his nature, manifestations, or purpose.[137] Yahweh is not the brand name of a cosmic corporation; he is one God, whose name is Yahweh.[138] There is no manifestation of divinity that is not Yahweh. Moreover, Yahweh is not the chief god of a pantheon as Amun-Rê in Egypt or Marduk in Babylon; Yahweh is the sole manifestation of divinity—he is one, not many. In addition, Yahweh is not divided in his purpose and will. Yahweh is one: faithful, consistent, not divided, but true within.[139] God is thus one both in being and in purpose.

With the above analysis, the Shema is a monotheistic confession that Yahweh alone is God ("one God"). Patrick Miller summarizes the theological implications of the passage: "The monotheism that arises out of this Deuteronomic center claims that there is only one ultimate or absolute—the power that undergirds all reality is one and not multiple, faithful and not capricious, a whole and not divided, and therefore capable of purpose and power because this one is not controlled and limited by other forces."[140]

The monotheism confessed by the Shema is explicitly seen in Zechariah's eschatological use of the text: "Yahweh will be king over all the whole earth. On that day Yahweh will be one and his name will be one" (14:9). Here Zechariah is declaring that a time is coming when the sovereignty, uniqueness, and the unity of Yahweh will be acknowledged by all of humanity.[141] All idol gods will be erased and will be forgotten forever (Zech 13:2).

The idea of monotheism has been a hotly debated topic among scholars and has only intensified in its discussion.[142] The discovery of Hebrew inscriptions and idolatrous figurines have further fueled the argument that the religion of Israel was, in fact, not monotheistic but polytheistic for much or even all of its history.[143] However, the Old Testament is clear and consistent throughout that worship of any other god is absolutely forbidden and condemned. The Old Testament repeatedly bears witness to the fact that among the populace there were numerous periods of time during which Israel was syncretistic and was practicing a heterodox or "popular" religion.[144] Thus, one should not at all be surprised to find syncretistic inscriptions, figurines, and cultic objects that associate Yahweh with pagan thought.[145] Yet Israel's failure does not nullify the fact that the Old Testament writers present Yahweh as the one and only true God. The Old Testament throughout is monotheistic; Yahweh alone is God and is to be exclusively recognized as such. During much of Israel's existence its religious practice was syncretistic, but the religion sanctioned by the inspired writers of the Old Testament is clearly monotheistic in its orientation.[146]

Summary

To summarize, matter is not preexistent, and Yahweh is truly the maker of heaven and earth as he created the world *ex nihilo*. Being creator, God established the laws of the universe; and as owner of the world, he is not subject to those laws. God is transcendent over, and distinct from, creation. God has no beginning or end, since there is no myth of God's origin or demise in the Old Testament. Human beings, though, are created by God and are constituent with created matter. There are no other beings that can be classified or identified as God, but only Yahweh. God is holy and is thus wholly *other than*, and incomparable to, any other being; he has no peer whatever. Yahweh is the one and only God.

III. The Traditional Mormon View of God and Creation[147]

Thus far we have discussed the views of God, creation, and humanity common in the ancient Near East and those of the Old Testament. We have found that on several key points there is a stark contrast between the views of the Old Testament writers and those of Israel's pagan neighbors. We are now in a position to briefly describe traditional LDS views about God, creation, and humanity and to then offer some comparative analyses in the final section of this essay. In my description I do not intend to make any determination about what constitutes normative LDS doctrine. Rather, I only intend to give a few brief descriptions that fairly represent what many Latter-day Saints have historically taught, with some deference being given to the teachings of Joseph Smith.

The World Was Created out of Preexistent Matter

In a "quasi-official" sermon, the King Follett Discourse, Joseph Smith taught that God did not create the world *ex nihilo* but from eternally preexisting, chaotic matter.[148] Smith stated: "God had materials to organize the world out of chaos—chaotic matter, which is element, and in which dwells all the glory. Element had an existence from the time he had. The pure principles of element are principles which can never be destroyed; and they may be organized and reorganized, but not destroyed. They had no beginning, and can have no end."[149]

In the previous chapter Paul Copan and William Lane Craig show that Smith's denial of *creatio ex nihilo* may not necessarily be demanded by the LDS Standard Works, but it has received widespread endorsement in traditional and contemporary Mormonism. For my purposes it will suffice to note that within traditional Mormon theology the material of which the world is constituted was not created by God, at least not in any absolute sense. Instead, on the Mormon view, "the elements are eternal" (D&C 93:33) and exist independently of God's will. God "created" the world by organizing, shaping, or forming preexistent matter and was limited in what he could create by matter's inherent nature.

The World Was Created After a Precreation Conflict

In the Book of Abraham, a part of the Pearl of Great Price, we find the most distinctive creation account within the LDS Standard Works. In Abraham 3:1–10 we see that before the creation of this world there already exists "a structured cosmos, with many stars, one above another, with their different periods and orders of government."[150] There is some kind of social order in which preexistent spirits exist and are differentiated in status by their intelligence, with God "more intelligent than they all" (3:19) dwelling "in the midst of them all" (3:21). There appears to be some kind of assembly of Gods who meet together, and one "like unto God" (3:24) stands among the members of the assembly and suggests that they go down to a place where there is room and "take of these materials, and we will make an earth whereon these [souls] may dwell" (3:24). The Lord asks whom he should send, and one "like the Son of Man" and "another" volunteer to go, but "the second was angry and kept not his first estate; and, at that day, many followed after him" (3:27–28).

This incident is somewhat elaborated upon in another creation account found in the Book of Moses, also a part of the Pearl of Great Price. The cause of the dispute between the two volunteers stems from their different plans to redeem humanity once it has been created. Because the second volunteer, Satan, "rebelled against me [the Lord God], and sought to destroy the agency of man . . . by the power of mine Only Begotten, I caused that he should be cast down" (Moses 4:3). Within LDS theology it is understood that when Satan rebelled, a third of the spirits in heaven joined in his rebellion, and there was a great war in heaven.

After the war in heaven and the casting down of Satan and his followers, the divine assembly follows through with its plan to create. We are told:

"And then the Lord said: Let us go down. And they went down at the beginning, and they, that is the Gods, organized and formed the heavens and the earth" (Abraham 4:1). The account then follows the general pattern of the account in Genesis 1, but throughout it is "the Gods" of the assembly who are involved in the creative activity. The significance of this account for the purposes of this chapter is not merely that there was a heavenly conflict prior to creation, but that the conflict had to do with creation itself. The conflict was over the sort of world the Gods should fashion, and what determined that was who won in the conflict.

All Things Find Their Origin in a Primordial Realm

We have already seen that in Mormon theology matter has eternally existed with God. Additional uncreated realities include the "intelligence" or primal part of every person (whether human, angelic, or divine) and the fundamental laws and principles that govern reality. For example, Mormonism's founding prophet stated in his King Follett Discourse:

> We say that God himself is a self-existent being. . . . It is correct enough; but how did it get into your heads? Who told you that man did not exist in like manner on the same principles? Man does exist upon the same principles. . . . The mind or intelligence which man possesses is co-equal [i.e., co-eternal] with God himself. . . . There never was a time when there were not spirits; for they are co-equal [co-eternal] with our Father in heaven. . . . Intelligence is eternal and exists upon a self-existent principle. It is a spirit from age to age, and there is no creation about it. . . . The first principles of man are self-existent with God.[151]

Elsewhere, Smith affirmed that "the spirits of men are eternal."[152] He made reference to "laws of eternal and self-existent principles"[153] and "the laws that govern the body and spirit of man."[154] These laws are clearly on ontological par with God, matter, and intelligences as uncreated and coeternal realities for, according to Smith, "any principle which is not eternal is of the devil. . . . The first steps in [the] salvation of man is the laws of eternal and self-existent principles."[155]

Latter-day Saint philosopher Truman Madsen summarizes these elements of the Mormon worldview by stating, "God is forever surrounded by us, by co-eternal intelligences, and by the self-existent elements and principles of reality. These are as unoriginated as He is."[156] According to another LDS philosopher, David Paulsen, "God has always acted within a physical environment of uncreated mass-energy, a social environment of other selves, and within a framework of eternal laws and principles. These aspects of the world which are co-eternal with Him condition and limit Him."[157] More recently, Paulsen has expressed it this way: "Contrary to classical Christian thought, Joseph explicitly affirmed that there are entities and structures which are coeternal with God himself (D&C 93:23, 29). In my reading of Joseph's discourse, these eternal entities include chaotic matter, intelligences (or what I will call primal persons), and law-like structures and principles."[158] In sum, it is clear that in traditional LDS thought God, all other persons, and the fundamental matter and laws of nature find their origins in a primordial realm that eternally preexisted the creation of the world.

God Is Immanent Within the Universe and Subject to Eternal Laws

As we have just seen, the God of Mormonism has eternally existed within the uncreated environment of a preexisting universe. It appears, then, that on the traditional LDS view, God is fully immanent within the universe and does not transcend it. Furthermore, it is well known that in Mormon thought God is understood to be a physically embodied being: "The Father has a body of flesh and bones as tangible as man's" (D&C 130:22a). Even his spirit must be material in nature since in Doctrine and Covenants 131:7–8 we are given the axiomatic principle that "there is no such thing as immaterial matter [i.e., immaterial substance]. All spirit is matter, but it is more fine or pure, and can only be discerned by purer eyes. We cannot see it, but when our bodies are purified we shall see that it is all matter."

From the fact that God consists entirely of matter follows an important implication. As was seen above, Joseph Smith believed that matter—and even spirits (and thus "spirit matter")—are governed by self-existent laws and principles. It follows from this that God is subject to, and limited by, the uncreated laws that govern reality at the most fundamental level. He is also limited by the inherent nature and capacities of matter and spirit matter. It would seem, too, that even if God's spirit could somehow pervade the rest of the material universe, he could not really transcend the universe.[159]

An early associate and friend of Joseph Smith's, the Apostle Parley Pratt, recognized this implication when he wrote: "Each of these Gods, including Jesus Christ and His Father, being in possession of not merely an organized spirit, but a glorious immortal body of flesh and bones, is subject to the laws which govern, of necessity, even the most refined order of physical existence. All physical element, however embodied, quickened or refined, is subject to the general laws necessary to all existence."[160] Furthermore, according to Pratt, "These laws are absolute and unchangeable in their nature, and apply to all intelligent agencies which do or can exist." Therefore, they "apply with equal force to the great, supreme, Eternal Father of the heavens and of the earth, and to His meanest subjects."[161]

God Creates and Acts Through the Use of Eternal Law

God is not considered the Creator or Sustainer of the universe, he does not transcend material existence since he is himself composed fully of matter, and he is subject to the same fundamental laws of reality that govern everything else. It follows from this that God must *work through* or *use* natural law to accomplish his goals; he cannot act from "outside" the realm of nature. Joseph Fielding Smith wrote, "The Lord works in accordance with natural law."[162] The more recent LDS apostle Bruce R. McConkie, in his book *Mormon Doctrine,* states that "[God] himself governs and is governed by law."[163] Philosopher David Paulsen also recognizes this when he writes, "In the total context of Mormon revelation, it is clear that God's power is not correctly described as absolute power to suspend the operations of all natural laws, but rather *the power to maximally utilize natural laws to bring about His purposes.*"[164]

Writing in the *Encyclopedia of Mormonism,* Carl Hawkins and Douglas Parker state that "Latter-day scriptures and other sources do not explicitly state that eternal law exists independently or coeternally with God." This is highly questionable in light of the quotations listed above. But even if it is not explicit, Hawkins and Parker say that "this characteristic of eternal law is sometimes inferred, however, from two concepts that do have support in scripture and other LDS sources." These two concepts are: (1) God is governed (bound) by law (cf. Alma 42:13, where it says that God would cease to be God if justice were violated); and (2) Intelligence and truth were not created but are coeternal with God (D&C 93:29–30). They go on to say that "consistent with the eternal laws, God fashions and decrees laws that operate in the worlds he created and that set standards of behavior that must be observed in order to obtain the blessing promised upon obedience to that law."[165]

Though at least one contemporary LDS writer has rejected the notion of eternal law,[166] it seems accurate to say that the classic Mormon position is that eternal law is the self-existent, unauthored law that God himself honors and administers as a condition of perfection and godhood. It is because of his great intelligence that he is able to use this law to accomplish his ends. This being the case, in classic LDS theology "a miracle is defined as a divine interference with the operation of nature by the employment of other natural laws."[167] Concurring, the late Mormon apostle and theologian James Talmage wrote:

> Miracles are commonly regarded as occurrences in opposition to the laws of nature. Such a conception is plainly erroneous, for the laws of nature are inviolable. However, as human understanding of these laws is at best but imperfect, events strictly in accordance with these laws may appear contrary thereto. The entire constitution of nature is founded on system and order; the laws of nature, however, are graded as are the laws of man. This operation of higher law in any particular case does not destroy the actuality of an inferior one. . . . All miracles are accomplished through the operation of the laws of nature.[168]

God and Humans Are of the Same Species of Being

In one of his boldest theological statements, Joseph Smith declared: *"God himself was once as we are now, and is an exalted man, and sits enthroned in yonder heavens! . . . I say, if you were to see him today, you would see him like a man in form—like yourselves in all the person, image, and very form as a man. . . . He was once a man like us."*[169] Stephen E. Robinson states: "We [Latter-day Saints] believe that *God and humans are the same species of being* and that all men and women were his spiritual offspring in a premortal existence."[170] It is important to note that traditionally Latter-day Saints have acknowledged that this claim is not derived from the Bible but from Joseph Smith's recounting of his first vision: "I saw two Personages, whose brightness and glory defy all description, standing above me in the air" (Joseph Smith—History 1:17).[171] With this presupposition, Stephen Robinson states: "Latter-day Saints believe that humankind is created in the image of God (Gen 1:26–28). We take this quite literally to mean that God has a physical image and that humanity is created *in it*."[172] Such an understanding is explicitly stated in the Book of Mormon:

> And never have I [the Lord] showed myself unto man whom I have created, for never has man believed in me as thou hast. Seest thou that ye are created after mine own image? Yea, even all men were created in the beginning after mine own image. Behold, this body, which ye now behold, is the

body of my spirit; and man have I created after the body of my spirit; and even as I appear unto thee to be in the spirit will I appear unto my people in the flesh. (Ether 3:15–16)

Theogony and Apotheosis

A very significant characteristic of the traditional Mormon view of God is illustrated by the fact that the *Encyclopedia of Mormonism* includes an entry specifically titled "Theogony." The author, Charles R. Harrell, correctly observes: "Theogony refers to the origin of God and has been a subject of religious inquiry throughout the ages. Ancient peoples, notably Sumerians, Egyptians, Greeks, and Romans, developed elaborate genealogies for their various gods, rationalizing and mythologizing the birth and characteristic of each. This is in contrast to the monotheistic, Judeo-Christian view that God is eternal, uncaused, and without origin."[173] Harrell goes on to note that the LDS theogonic view differs from others because it is far more inclusive. Whereas the ancient theogonies were concerned almost exclusively with the gods of the pantheons, the LDS view is also applicable to human beings. Harrell states, the LDS view "is based on a doctrine of eternal existence (see D&C 93:13–14). By embracing truth and light, uncreated intelligence is capable of growing in knowledge, power, and organization until it arrives at the glorified state of Godhood, being one with God."[174] Thus, Bruce McConkie could state that it was because of Joseph Smith's teaching of how "God came to be God" and the potential for human beings to likewise become Gods that "the term *theogony* takes on a meaning for the Latter-day Saints which is far beyond anything that the world has supposed."[175]

Though some contemporary LDS writers have expressed agnosticism about whether there was ever a time in which God was not a God, or have even rejected the idea, the traditional LDS position clearly affirms that the being we know as God himself went through this process to become a God. In the words of David Paulsen, "The being who is God has not always been God—i.e., he has not always qualified for the honorific title 'God'—a distinction earned through a process of growth and development toward God-liness."[176] There is little specific detail about this theogony beyond the fact that it parallels the process by which we can become gods. Again, Paulsen: "At some distant point in an infinite past, He earned the right to be 'God' through a process which men, as his children, are now repeating."[177] Joseph Smith appears to describe the beginning of the LDS theogonic story when he informs us that: "God himself, *finding he was in the midst of spirits and glory,* because he was more intelligent, saw proper to institute laws whereby the rest could have a privilege to advance like himself."[178]

One of the distinctive characteristics of the LDS theogony is that the process by which God became God in some sense parallels our own experiences in progressing toward the same goal. Human beings have the potential of becoming what God has already become. In the words of the famous Lorenzo Snow couplet, "As man now is, God once was; / As God now is, man may become." What makes such a radical human potential possible is the belief that humanity and deity represent one species of being. Stephen E. Robinson recognizes this when he writes, "The soil from which the LDS doctrine of deification grows is the belief that humans are of the divine species and that the scriptural language of divine paternity is not merely figurative."[179] Thus, Mormons are thoroughgoing monophysites, not just with regard to the nature of Christ, but with regard to divine and human nature period. It is from this monophysite view that the LDS doctrine of exaltation to Godhood stems.

Summary

With what has been discussed, particular conclusions can be deduced about the nature of the God of Mormonism and his relationship with creation. First, all forms of matter are eternal and self-existent, including intelligences. Second, the "primal part" of God and humans is "intelligence," and they are of the same species of being. Third, God and humanity constitute what is divine or potentially divine in the universe. Fourth, God is an exalted man, but he is a more developed intelligence and thereby has the honorific title "God," which other human beings can potentially attain. Fifth, God is presently God, but he has not always been God. Sixth, because God is a being composed entirely of the eternal matter of the universe, he is subject to and limited by the inherent nature of that matter and the eternal natural laws that govern it. Finally, it is through the manipulation of uncreated eternal laws and principles that God brings about his purposes.

IV. A Brief Comparative Analysis

Based on the above three sections, the reader should already have made various comparisons in his or her mind. I will briefly compare and contrast the views of cosmogony, the nature of God/gods, and the nature of humanity in the ancient Near East, the Old Testament, and classic Mormon theology.

Because of space constraints I will not be able to mention all of the significant similarities and dissimilarities one could cite. Instead, I will simply point out a few of them.

In regard to the material universe, the typical pagan view describes a primordial realm wherefrom the gods and the rest of creation are derived. The God of traditional Mormonism "finds himself" in such a primordial realm in which is also found chaotic matter, eternal laws and principles and other intelligences. Moreover, Mormons hold, God did not create the universe in any absolute sense; he merely organized the primordial matter. In contrast, the Old Testament depicts no preexistent material or realm from which God emerged or created. The only preexistent thing or being is God himself.[180] God created the universe *ex nihilo* and established the laws that govern the workings of the world.

In pagan thought there is a primordial realm that transcends the gods, and they must follow its laws and decrees. In Mormon thought eternal matter and eternal principles are also transcendent over God, and he too is subject to the eternal laws of a reality he did not create. In distinction, the Old Testament does not describe anything whatever as being transcendent above or beyond God. Yahweh himself is the transcendent one, and because he is the creator of the universe, he is not subject to, or limited by, anyone or any other phenomena. As shown above, the pagan gods are not the source of all being, nor can they transcend the universe. The gods are constituent with a primordial realm that is precedent to and independent of them. The gods find their origin in this realm and are subservient to its laws. Whereas the historic LDS view of God resembles the pagan idea of deity, the God of the Old Testament is radically different, and the Old Testament writers repudiate any such notions.

In pagan religions, in order for the cosmos to exist and to survive in the world, the gods, along with human beings, learn and engage in the art of magic. According to historic LDS theology, God found himself more intelligent than the other intelligences and thus organized the cosmos and set up ways for other intelligences to reach divinity. Although traditional Mormon theology does not speak of magic per se, by his intelligence God uses the eternal laws of the universe in a functionally equivalent manner to achieve his purposes. The God of the Old Testament, however, does not acquire wisdom or need magic to create or to perform a miracle; he is the sole source of wisdom and the creator and owner of the universe. Yahweh does as he wills with and within creation.

Pagan religions are typically polytheistic and have theogonic myths about the coming to be of their gods. This is especially true in the pagan religions of the ancient Near East. As seen above, the gods find their ultimate origin in the primordial realm, but they are also conceived through procreation. There are multiple divine beings with, at times, a high god presiding over a hierarchically arranged pantheon. The pagan cosmogonies also blur the distinction between the natures of the gods and human beings. There is no real demarcation between humanity and the divine, and this allows for *apotheosis,* the belief that humans can be exalted to the level and status of the gods. Within Mormonism we find very similar concepts. In historic Mormon thought, God was a premortal intelligence among many uncreated intelligences. Somehow he evolved to become a God (possibly having himself been procreated by a God above him). Going a step beyond pagan thought, human beings and God are not merely of the same species, but all G/gods are exalted men, including the high God of this world. All human beings are by nature the same being or class as God, although in an embryonic stage of development.

Daniel Peterson, a contemporary Mormon scholar, claims that the divine council of God in the Old Testament consists of premortal human beings and that Abraham 3:22–23 is a textbook instance of this assembly (see above).[181] Hence, God is the high god over a divine assembly whose members are deified human beings. Peterson derives this conclusion from a conflation of biblical data and Canaanite literature centering on Psalm 82 and Jesus' quotation of verse 6 in John 10:33. Peterson's central argument is founded on an assimilation of biblical and Ugaritic references to the council of El.[182] Because the messengers of the council of El were gods and the messengers of Yahweh's council were human prophets, "in the biblical and other references of the council of El," there is "a blurring of distinction between mortal human beings and angels, between mortal human beings and gods."[183] Despite serious methodological problems with such an approach, from a biblical standpoint the Old Testament never even alludes to the fact that a prophet was considered divine or a "god." In his examination of the participants in Yahweh's council, Cooke discusses the role of the prophets:

> The prophet is nowhere explicitly identified as one of the "sons of (the) God(s)," "holy ones," "divine council," or accorded membership in the divine council; the true prophet, however, has access to the heavenly assem-

bly's deliberations, acts as messenger and bearer of the divine counsel to the people, and is a representative of Yahweh who exhibits a kind of psychic identity with Yahweh. The prophet remains mortal. He is not "divinized," except in the highly qualified sense that he becomes the bearer of the divine will and purpose and—to some extent—power.[184]

Thus, if Peterson is correct about the similarity between the divine assembly in LDS literature and the divine council in Ugaritic literature, then we see another instance in which the LDS position is unlike the Old Testament position.

In contrast to the pagan and Mormon view of the divine and human natures, the Old Testament presents a completely distinct view. There is no theogony presented in the Old Testament, nor does it speak of God's origin. Yahweh was God before creation and is God without creation. Unlike God, human beings are created and have a beginning. God is absolutely distinct from humankind and all other supernatural beings (e.g., angels, demons). God has no bodily form and is a spiritual being. It is true that God made human beings a little less than himself (Ps 8:5), but human beings are not, nor do they possess, nor will they possess, the potential of becoming a god in the same sense that God is God. In fact, in the Old Testament any attempt by human beings to close the gap between the human and divine realm brings judgment from the one and only God, Yahweh (cf. Gen 2:4b–3:24). Thus, there are no other beings that can be classified as God—with an uppercase 'G.' Yahweh alone is God, and even if other beings can sometimes be referred to as "gods," this in no way compromises his uniqueness as the one absolute, transcendent, sovereign creator of all other reality.

In the final analysis, the view of God, creation, and humanity found in traditional Mormonism has very little to do with the God presented in the Old Testament. Instead, in some important respects the God conceived by Mormonism resembles the gods of pagan thought (see chart below). There are important differences between Mormon and pagan views, to be sure, and they should not be brushed aside. (It would, therefore, be a serious mistake to say that Mormonism is a form of neopaganism.) But when contrasted with the God of the Old Testament and the "gods" of the Near East, the God of the classical LDS tradition should be classified as a "god" (lowercase 'g'), despite his great power, intelligence, and moral virtue (the latter an attribute few of the pagan gods possess). This is further confirmed by the fact that LDS writers have on occasion openly stated that in LDS theology

"God" is merely an honorific title and does not refer to a unique being. In contrast, according to the Old Testament Yahweh is the one and only God by the very nature of his being. He is distinct from all other reality and in a class by himself because he is the Creator of absolutely all things; and humans are created beings who represent God on the earth.

Theological Categories	Pagan Thought	Traditional Mormon	Old Testament
Preexistent	Primordial realm	Primordial matter	God
Transcendent	Primordial realm	Primordial matter	God
Power	Wisdom–magic	Intelligence–laws	God
Nature of gods/ God	Material	Material	Spirit/ Non-matter
Divinity	Polytheistic	Quasi-polytheistic	Monotheistic
Human/divine	Blurred	Identical	Distinct

Conclusion

At the beginning of this chapter it was observed that Jews, Christians, and Latter-day Saints claim that their most basic understandings of God, creation, and humanity are rooted in the texts of the Old Testament. Yet curiously, the traditional LDS view is radically different than the view held in common by Jews and Christians. What is to explain this discrepancy? Jews and Christians debate among themselves and with each other about many doctrines and over the proper interpretation of many biblical passages, yet there is little dissent when it comes to most of the fundamental issues about the nature of God and the created status of the cosmos and humanity. The great majority of Jews and Christians find themselves in basic agreement about what the Hebrew Bible says on these issues. It would be absurd, then, to attribute the discrepancy to ambiguity in the biblical texts.

Stephen E. Robinson states, on behalf of the Latter-day Saints: "We accept the Bible (the LDS use the King James Version) as the inspired word of God—every book, every chapter, every verse of it—as revealed to the apostles and prophets who wrote it." So far so good. But then Robinson adds: "We also hold the Book of Mormon, the Doctrine and Covenants, and the Pearl of Great Price to be the word of God."[185] Therein, I believe, lies the source of the discrepancy. These other books that the LDS consider as the word of God, along with their interpretations and midrashic expansions of the biblical texts, at many points contradict the view of God, creation, and humanity found in the Old Testament. Even more contradictory are the later teachings of Mormonism's founding prophet, Joseph Smith. In some significant ways the traditional LDS positions hark back to the pagan views of ancient Israel's Near Eastern neighbors—views that the Old Testament patriarchs, prophets, and psalmists intentionally rejected in light of the revelation they received from the one true and living God. This is an unfortunate conclusion to reach, and one that Latter-day Sants will surely be uncomfortable with. However, it seems unavoidable in light of the evidence. It is hoped that LDS theology will develop further in the direction of the biblical revelation and that one day such a conclusion will not have to be drawn.

A TALE OF TWO THEISMS
The Philosophical Usefulness of the Classical Christian and Mormon Concepts of God

STEPHEN E. PARRISH

(WITH CARL MOSSER)

Stephen E. Parrish is Librarian and Assistant Professor of Philosophy at Concordia University in Ann Arbor, Michigan. He earned a B.S. from Eastern Michigan University, an A.M.L.S. from the University of Michigan, and an M.A. and Ph.D. in philosophy from Wayne State University. Dr. Parrish is the author of *God and Necessity: A Defense of Classical Theism* (University Press of America) and coauthor of *See the Gods Fall: Four Rivals To Christianity* (College Press) and *The Mormon Concept of God: A Philosophical Analysis* (Edwin Mellen). His articles have appeared in *Criswell Theological Review*, *Philosophia Christi*, and *Trinity Journal*.

O f what use is the concept of God? From the philosopher's point of view, a concept of God is useful if it can explain certain things. These include things like why anything exists rather than nothing, why the universe is orderly, why there are ethical truths, and other matters of ultimate importance. Throughout history different philosophers, theologians, and even scientists have proposed that God is the final explanation for one or more of these issues. However, there is more than one concept of God on the market. Some concepts are so radically different from one another that it has been said that one person's theism is another person's atheism. It is also the case that some God concepts have a greater ability than others to explain these ultimate issues. The ability of a God concept (or an atheistic system) to explain the ultimate questions about the world we live in is one important indicator of its truth or falsity.

A concept of God is basically a system of ideas of what God is like and how he is related to the world. It is an overall, though not necessarily comprehensive, view of God. Different God concepts explain issues differently. How one's ideas about God explain questions of ultimate importance will have very practical implications for the rest of one's religious views. As Gordon H. Clark has written, "The source of all contrasts between paganism and Christianity is the difference in their concept of God. In any system the ultimate principle determines the form of the whole."[1] How we view the nature of God will also play an important role in how we view ourselves, the world around us, the purpose of life, and how we should live. Unlike some philosophical or scientific concepts, in this case the theoretical is immensely practical. It is well to spend time thinking seriously about the concept of God, for finally, God is more than a concept. He is, at least according to Christian theism, the ultimate reality with whom we have to do.

Many Latter-day Saints (informally known as Mormons) have claimed that Joseph Smith's revelations settle many questions about the nature of God and that Smith's insights provide explanations to ultimate questions that are more persuasive than those of other God concepts. The fact is, however, that there are differences of opinion among Mormons about the nature of God. There is so much flux in what Mormons believe about God that it is very difficult to determine just what Mormonism is committed to: what is merely traditional, which statements by LDS General Authorities are representative of common LDS beliefs, and which are merely speculative private opinions. This can make things rather frustrating for the student of Mormonism (whether critical or friendly), who, after attempting to establish a position by quoting Mormon authorities, including past prophets of the church, is then told that the position presented does not represent what Latter-day Saints now believe.

This tremendous flux about what Mormons believe ultimately stems, I believe, from the fact that Smith's teachings did not actually bring greater precision to our understanding of God. Rather, his many conflicting statements introduce more questions and problems than they solve. Another contributing factor is the structure of Mormon authority, which is centered on a living prophet who may give new revelations and interpretations at any time—even if they conflict with previous revelations and interpretations by earlier prophets. According to LDS philosopher James E. Faulconer, "One of the spin-offs of a belief in continuing revelation is an implicit refusal to allow theology to be set once and for all."[2] Despite these difficulties in defining the Mormon concept of God, as Faulconer admits, there are some unchanging core doctrines common to most LDS theologies.[3]

In the first part of this chapter I briefly describe two different God concepts. The first is classical Trinitarian monotheism. This is the concept of God that has been held by the vast majority of Christians through the centuries. The second is a version of the Mormon concept of God that I will term "Mormon monarchotheism." *Monarchotheism* is the theory that there is more than one God, but one God is clearly preeminent among the gods; in effect, he is the monarch or ruler of all the gods.[4] I choose this form of Mormon theism because it is, in my opinion, the most plausible concept of God that has to date been put forward by any significant number of Latter-day Saints. It will be shown that, contrary to what many people assume, Mormon views of God stand in stark contrast to the classical Christian concept of God.

In the second part of this chapter, I discuss why classical Trinitarian monotheism is philosophically superior to Mormon monarchotheism. This will be done by looking at how well each view can provide answers to several important questions: Why does God exist? Why does anything else exist and continue in existence? Why is the universe orderly and governed by law? Why is there objective moral law? I will argue that Trinitarian monotheism gives coherent and satisfying explanations for these questions, whereas Mormon monarchotheism does not. In a supplementary section, one of the editors will similarly address the question: Can the problem of evil be solved? I will conclude with some brief reflections on the practical implications of one's view of God and some suggestions to Latter-day Saints.

Sketches of Two God Concepts

Classical Trinitarian Monotheism

Classical Monotheism

What is the classical monotheistic conception of God? In a nutshell, it may be thought of as that of God as the Greatest Possible Being.[5] God, on this conception, is that being who cannot be surpassed, even by himself. It is logically impossible that one could even conceive of a being greater than God. But what does it mean to be the Greatest Possible Being? It means, among other things, that God is personal and immaterial, the sovereign creator and sustainer of all other being, omnipotent, omniscient, omnipresent, immutable and eternal, all good and the source of moral value, necessary and unique, infinite and transcendent. What each of these attributes means will now be briefly shown.

Personal and Immaterial. God is personal. He is self-conscious and has reason, feeling, and will. He can communicate using language. He is not some vague, impersonal principle as in pantheism. Indeed, as we will see, on the Christian conception, he is three persons in one being. In effect then, on the Christian view what is really ultimate is persons, the persons who are God. To say that the classical God is immaterial is to say that he is not composed of matter or constrained by the limitations all material entities are faced with. He does not occupy space and is not governed by the laws of physics.

Sovereign Creator and Sustainer of All Other Being. God is the cause or source of everything else that exists or could exist. In classical theism, God created and sustains all other concrete being: matter, spirit, space, and time. Abstract objects like numbers eternally exist in God's mind. As the true creator of all things, God has complete power over everything. What exactly this means is somewhat different in different theologies. The basic idea is that any lesser being possesses the power it has because God grants it to that being.

Necessary and Self-Existent. There has been a good deal of controversy about this attribute of God. What I shall take it to mean is that God could not *not* exist. That is to say, he has to exist. Another way of putting it is that God exists in every possible world. The term "possible world" refers to "reality as it could have been." No matter what else was the case, God would exist. He could not fail to exist anymore than 2 + 2 could fail to equal 4. God's necessary existence implies that God is self-existent; he does not depend on the existence of anything else for his own existence. (Sometimes self-existence has also been called "necessary existence," but using the same term for distinct properties like this only breeds confusion.)

Unique. In classical theism there is only one God—and could only be one God—because there can only be one Greatest Possible Being. God is in a class by himself, and no other being could possibly approach him.

Omniscient. This is the attribute of knowing "all things." This does not mean that God knows things such as what it is like to sin or how to learn new skills. What is meant is that God knows the truth of every proposition. There is, in this sense, nothing he does not know. Traditionally this has included full knowledge of the future, though this idea has been recently challenged by some.[6]

Omnipotent. This is the attribute of being "all powerful." This does not mean that God has the power to do absurd things, such as making square circles or rocks so large that he cannot lift them. To be omnipotent is to have maximal power. God has as much power as it is possible for anything to have. As the Greatest Possible Being, he has the greatest possible power. The only "limitations" on his power are the laws of logic, and even the laws of logic are ultimately grounded in God's being.

Omnipresent and Immanent. This is the attribute of "being everywhere." This does not mean that God is literally everywhere, like some cosmic gas; he is immaterial. God is omnipresent in the sense that he knows what happens everywhere, is active everywhere, and keeps everything in existence at every moment. In practical terms, it means that God is immediately available to the entirety of his creation, and there is no place one can go to escape from his providential presence.

Transcendent. God's transcendence is the flip side of his immanence. It means that in his essential being, he is external to our universe of space, time, and matter.

Infinite. The classical God is infinite. This does not mean, contrary to pantheism, that God *is* everything. Nor does it mean that he has simply existed for an infinite amount of time. God's infinity in classical theism is shorthand for the various "omni" attributes we have just discussed. God is infinite in that he is omniscient, omnipotent, omnipresent, and so forth.[7]

Immutable and Eternal. On a weaker reading of this doctrine, God does not change in any of his essential attributes. On a stronger reading, God does not change at all, because he is not in time. On either reading, God always exists; he never came into existence, nor can he pass out of existence. Moreover, he has always existed *as God,* with all of the divine attributes.

All Good and the Source of Moral Value. God as classically conceived is all good. Ethically, he is the perfect being. Furthermore, he is the transcendent source and sanction of all good. The metaphysical foundation of ethics is in God the Creator. Because of God's immutability and necessity, we can also say that God is necessarily good. That is, he could not have been evil, nor could he ever fail morally.

It should be evident that the different properties of the classical God logically fit together. For example, God being sovereign coheres with his being omnipotent and also his being necessary, unique, and the source of all other things. This does not mean that there are no questions or problems that the classical theist must face. But it does seem to be the case that the attributes fit together very well and often seem to imply each other.[8] If there are good grounds for believing that any of these attributes correctly describes God, there will likely be good grounds for saying that all of them do.

Orthodox Trinitarianism

What has been described so far is the basic concept of classical theism. People of many different religious backgrounds might agree with it. Most Christians, Jews, some Muslims, and even some Hindus affirm this view of God. However, the specifically Trinitarian version of classical monotheism is unique to Christianity. The Trinitarian concept of God, put simply, is that the Father, Son, and Holy Spirit are the personal, unique, infinite, Creator God.[9] They are not three beings or three Gods, because Trinitarianism firmly embraces monotheism—the belief that there is only one true God. Nor are they impersonal aspects, modes, or masks of God. According to orthodox Trinitarianism, there are three distinct persons who together are one being—God.

By "one being" what is meant is that God is one thing or one entity. The persons of the Godhead are distinct persons, each a center of consciousness, but they are not separate beings from the others, nor could they conceivably exist apart from the others. The one entity that is God subsists in three persons, each of whom necessarily exists with and is dependent upon the other two. The persons of the Father, Son, and Spirit are also "in" one another, sharing the same divine love and life as well as the same divine being. Their persons "co-inhere" or interpenetrate one another. On this view, God is purely personal, and therefore ultimate reality is personal. God is also love and life being shared by a community of persons, and therefore love and community are also ultimate to reality.

Related to this is the Christian doctrine of the Incarnation. Christ, the second person of the Trinity, took on himself a human nature, both soul and body, in order to redeem the fallen human race. Orthodox Christian doctrine is that Christ is fully God and fully human. He has always been the second person of the Trinity, and since his incarnation he is also fully a human being. The doctrines of the Trinity and the Incarnation do not stem from the undue influence of Greek philosophy, as some LDS scholars and others have claimed. They stem, ultimately, from the New Testament authors' conviction that it was none other than God himself who came to redeem his creation and reconcile it to himself. (For a partial discussion of the biblical basis for Trinitarian monotheism, see Paul Owen's chapter in this book.)

The Mormon Concept of God

The Concept of God in the LDS Standard Works

We are increasingly told by some Latter-day Saints that Mormon theology should be defined strictly in terms of what is taught in the Standard Works of the LDS Church. It is worth noting that when one does examine the Standard Works, especially the Book of Mormon and earlier portions of the Doctrine and Covenants and the Pearl of Great Price, and reads them in a straightforward manner, the view of God one finds looks a lot like the classical Christian view of God. Sounding like the refrain of Handel's *Messiah,* in the Book of Mormon God is called "Lord God Omnipotent" (Mosiah 3:5, 17–18, 21; 5:2, 15). In the Doctrine and Covenants, he is referred to as "him who has all power" (D&C 61:1). The infinite goodness of God is affirmed (2 Nephi 1:10; Mosiah 5:3; Helaman 12:1; Moroni 8:3) as is his infinite mercy (Mosiah 28:4). God (or at least the Godhead) is described as "infinite and eternal, from everlasting to everlasting the same unchangeable God" (D&C 20:17, cf. v. 28), and the Son of God is likewise described as infinite and eternal (Alma 34:14, cf. vv. 10, 12). Other passages indicate or imply that God knows all things, including the future (e.g., 2 Nephi 27:10; Alma 40:8; Ether 3:25–26; D&C 130:7). In the *Lectures on Faith,* at one time printed with the Doctrine and Covenants, God is described as "the only supreme governor and independent being in whom all fulness and perfection dwell. He is omnipotent, omnipresent, and omniscient, without beginning of days or end of life."[10] All of this sounds quite typical of classical Christian orthodoxy, and no distinction between these ascriptions and orthodox ones are found in any of these passages.

Contrary to the "Standard Works alone" approach, other LDS scholars tell us that these seemingly orthodox passages should not be interpreted as such. Instead, they should be interpreted in light of later revelations and statements by Joseph Smith and other common LDS doctrines. When they are so interpreted, a very different view of God emerges. We can no longer take the ascriptions of God's omnipotence, omniscience, and infinity to mean what they do to most Christians. Rather, they are redefined in such a way as to present a very different view of God from the classical Christian view. It is hard to believe that the later teachings of Joseph Smith, especially those found in his influential King Follett Discourse, merely clarify, illuminate, or expand upon earlier teachings. Even on a very charitable reading, they appear to be simply incompatible with the kind of God concept that one finds in a straightforward reading of the LDS Standard Works, particularly those produced in Mormonism's first few years.[11]

Mormon Monarchotheism

It was noted above that there are different conceptions of God among the Latter-day Saints, but there is a good deal of overlap among the various conceptions.[12] One thing they all have in common is that they are very different from the classical Christian concept of God sketched above. I will show this by describing what I believe is the most plausible version of the Mormon concept of God, Mormon monarchotheism. There is enough overlap between this view and most other LDS positions that my comments in the second part of this chapter can be applied, with only minor modification, to all of them.

What is Mormon monarchotheism? In essence, it is a trend within contemporary Mormon theology that tends to view God, not merely as the God of this world, as in some other Mormon theologies, but as the ruler of the entire universe.[13] It does not deny that there are other gods of the same kind as God, but it maintains that God is not subordinate to any of these gods. He is the "Eternal God of all other gods" (D&C 121:32) and rules over them. Mormon monarchotheism is my term for this trend to distinguish it from other (and usually earlier) trends in Mormon thinking about God. Several LDS thinkers have expressed their understanding of God along the broad lines I will sketch below, and it seems to be widely held in popular LDS thought. Because of the great variety of views within Mormonism, however, it should not be assumed that individual Latter-day Saints would necessarily affirm everything in my description. What I present below is merely a rough sketch that I believe fairly represents what a great many Latter-day Saints who have thought about these things believe about God.

Personal and Embodied. Like the classical God, the Mormon God is personal. He is self-conscious and has reason, feeling, and will. He can communicate using language. Unlike the classical God, he is *essentially* embodied as God. According to Joseph Smith, "There is no other God in heaven but that God who has flesh and bones."[14] He is an entirely physical being and is, therefore, subject to the laws that govern and limit matter.

Organizer of the World. Mormons believe that the material universe has existed forever, without an external cause. Without God the universe would exist, but it would be in a state of chaos. The matter of the universe, being uncreated, has certain innate properties and dispositions that God cannot change and that he must work around. But on the monarchotheistic view, it seems that God does make some of the laws that govern the universe. In this way he imposes order on the preexisting chaos. It is important to note that on the LDS view, reality seems to be ultimately a chaotic mix of impersonal matter and finite personalities, but not ultimately personal as in classical theism.

Contingent and Dependent. For something to be *contingent* is for it to be able to either exist or not exist. For reasons that will become clear below, I think that the Mormon God must be contingent; he might not have existed at all.[15] Furthermore, not only does the God of Mormonism need not exist, he does not need to exist as God; he could exist and not be God. Related to this, Mormons have sometimes said that their God is necessary. But what they mean by this appears to be that he does not depend on anything else for his existence; he self-exists. This seems to me to be a misleading way to use the term *necessary.* Be that as it may, given the logic of the LDS system, it is not at all clear that the Mormon God can even be self-existent. For the Mormon God is necessarily embodied and thus depends on matter to exist. If matter had not existed, God would not have existed. This makes matter more ultimate than God. He is, furthermore, dependent on the existence of laws of nature and eternal principles in order to exist and rule.

One of Many Gods. As was mentioned above, the LDS God is one of many Gods. On the monarchotheistic view, God is the "Head God," with many other gods of the same kind subordinate to him. In strong contradistinction to the classical view, on the Mormon view humans, angels, gods, and God are all of one species. They have always existed in some form, at first as "primal intelligences."[16] Intelligences can be begotten as spirit beings in a "first estate" and then as human beings on earth. If we are successful in this "second estate," we can become gods ourselves. Those who are not entirely successful will become angels, and a few recalcitrant persons will be condemned to outer darkness. Those who become gods do so because God instituted laws to help others achieve exaltation to godhood.

An Exalted Man. In his most famous sermon, Joseph Smith taught that "God himself was once as we are now, and is an exalted man. . . . I say, if you were to see him today, you would see him like a man in form."[17] Traditionally, this has been understood to mean that there was a time when God was not God; he began as an "intelligence" and progressed to godhood. On this view, God is not merely embodied but is literally an exalted human being. More recently a few LDS thinkers have suggested that talk of God the Father being an exalted man should be understood in a manner analogous to the incarnation of Jesus; he has always been God, but at some point he incarnated himself and became a man who was exalted after resurrection.

Omniscient. Latter-day Saints have taken a variety of positions on the extent of God's knowledge. Some have taught that God knows everything, including the future, just as in classical theism. Others have believed that there are many things God does not know and that he continues to progress in his knowledge of the world, discovering new laws and principles. On this view, God's knowledge is far beyond ours, and he may even be the most knowledgeable being in the universe. Between these two positions, other Mormons have affirmed that God knows everything that can be known, but there are things that cannot be known even by God (e.g., the future free choices of human beings). Though it is confusing to do so, adherents of all three views describe God as omniscient. The first of these views is probably the most common among the average member of the LDS Church. The last view, that God knows all that can be known except things like the future, seems to be dominant among contemporary LDS philosophers.

Omnipotent. At the popular level, many Latter-day Saints appear to view God as omnipotent in much the same way that classical theists do. Others, including most LDS philosophers and theologians, affirm that God can be called omnipotent but only in a more limited sense than classical monotheists have traditionally held. This is because the God of Mormonism is literally embodied in a space-time universe. He did not create some of the basic laws governing it, and he is thus in subjection to them.[18] He is also limited in his power over other intelligences and by the inherent properties of matter. Nonetheless, Mormons believe that their God has all of the power that anyone could possibly have, given the constraints of the LDS worldview. In this sense they say that he is omnipotent.

Both Finite and Infinite. In different senses the Mormon God is both finite and infinite. He is finite because he is a physical being who occupies a limited amount of space. Also, as was shown above, many Mormons think he is limited to some degree in his knowledge and power. On the other hand, he is infinite in that he has always existed and will always exist. Moreover, his knowledge and power extend through the infinite reaches of space.[19] Latter-day Saints like Stephen Robinson object to describing God as finite.[20] However, as some LDS philosophers have pointed out, this is the technically precise description, even if it is not a very useful one religiously.[21]

Immanent but not Transcendent. In LDS thought, God is a material being who exists entirely within the space-time universe.[22] His spirit or "the light of Christ" proceeds from his presence "to fill the immensity of space" (D&C 88:12), seemingly like some impersonal cosmic gas. But God does not in any way transcend the universe. The material universe is all there is, and there is no "outside" or "beyond" it, even for God.

All Good and Subject to Principles External to Himself. In agreement with classical theists, Latter-day Saints believe that their God is all good. However, LDS thinkers do not believe that God is the basis of ethical values. This would seem to be a necessary conclusion to draw for traditional Mormonism, which teaches that God became God by obeying ethical laws and principles. Even LDS thinkers who do not believe there was ever a time when God did not exist as God deny that he is the basis of ethical values. Since the vast majority of Mormons strongly uphold the objectivity of ethical values, it follows that something else must be that basis. What that is we have not been told.

The Mormon Godhead

It should now be clear that Mormon monarchotheism represents a radically different view of God than classical Christian monotheism. It should come as no surprise that LDS notions of the Trinity and the Incarnation are also very different. In monarchotheistic Mormonism there are many gods but one ruling *Godhead.* The Godhead is comprised of three separate "personages": the Father, Son, and Holy Spirit. Among these three, God the Father is the head. Latter-day Saints use the term *personage* to indicate that the Father, Son, and Holy Spirit are not only distinct persons (which orthodox Trinitarianism emphatically affirms) but separate beings. The LDS "Trinity" is a form of tritheism: there are three gods—the Father, Son, and Holy Spirit—who are one Godhead in virtue of their shared purpose, power, and knowledge. The LDS doctrine of the Incarnation states that one of these gods, Jesus, took on a body and then, after his death, was resurrected. Unlike the path to godhood that Latter-day Saints are supposed to follow, Jesus never sinned and was somehow already a God before he came to earth.

To summarize, we have before us two radically different conceptions of God. In Mormon monarchotheism, God is a being who lives within the space-time universe. Furthermore, he is the same kind of being as we are, only much further advanced. The God of Mormonism illustrates the full achievement of human potential. In the words of Lorenzo Snow's famous couplet, "As man is, God once was; / As God is, man may become." On classical Christian monotheism, on the other hand, God is the necessary, transcendent creator of everything. Though sharing some characteristics with human beings, he is radically different than everything else that exists. As I will now show, the many differences between these two concepts of God significantly affect how well they are able to explain various important philosophical problems.

Questioning the Two God Concepts

Why Does God Exist?

To this question, classical monotheism has a ready answer, although fully explaining it is not easy. God exists because he is a necessary being and therefore cannot fail to exist. He cannot *not* exist any more than 2 + 2 can equal 5. To the further question as to why God is necessary, the best answer is that God is the Greatest Possible Being. He is omnipotent, omniscient, all good, and sovereign. And he is these things in all possible worlds. This being the case, God, not chance, is ultimate. It is he who decides what else will exist.

Things are quite different with the Mormon God. It is impossible that he be a necessary being. There are several reasons for this. One reason is that the LDS God is a material being. Latter-day Saints emphasize that God is literally an exalted man with a physical body of flesh and bone. All material objects are formed of parts. In the case of human beings, our bodies are made up of arms, legs, head, and so forth. At a more fundamental level, bodies are made of atoms, which are composed of subatomic particles. These particles act in certain regular ways, so that we say that their behavior is lawful.[23] In other words, the universe is governed by a set of natural laws. This would include the body of the Mormon God. Without these laws the Mormon God would not exist, for if matter did not behave in a lawful manner, it would not display any unity or order. So the laws of nature are necessary for the existence of the LDS God. He then cannot be the cause of the laws, for if he were, he would cause himself to exist, which is impossible.[24] So God cannot be the cause of the laws of nature.

This brings us back to the question of why the Mormon God should exist at all. He cannot necessarily exist in the sense that the God of classical theism does. As we have seen, he is dependent for his existence on external factors like the laws of nature and the existence of matter. His existence is contingent; he might not have been. Why then does he exist? There seems to be no good explanation.

This problem is exacerbated for more traditional Mormon theology. On that reading of Mormonism, God is not the original God. Joseph Smith taught that "God the Father of Jesus Christ had a Father" and that we may "suppose that He had a Father also. Where was there ever a son without a father? And where was there ever a father without first being a son?"[25] In agreement with this view, Orson Pratt wrote that "the person of our Father in Heaven was begotten on a previous heavenly world by His Father; and again, He was begotten by a still more ancient Father; and so on, from generation to generation, from one heavenly world to another still more ancient, until our minds are wearied and lost in the multiplicity of generations and successive worlds."[26] Since Mormons believe that the universe never had a beginning in time, this view implies that there are an infinite number of Gods, each of whom had another God as his father. The particular God who is the God of our earth is just one link in an infinite chain of gods.

The notion of an infinite regress of Gods is fraught with difficulties.[27] Briefly, these include the apparent scientific fact that the universe had a beginning in time and that an actual infinite regress is impossible (this is argued for in the chapter by Paul Copan and William Lane Craig in this volume). Furthermore, the idea is not taught in the Bible and does not seem to be explicitly taught in any of the other LDS Standard Works. However, given some other things that Latter-day Saints believe, it is easy to see why some Mormons derived it. Mormons believe that men and gods are of the same species and that men may become gods. Also, Joseph Smith once said that the God of this world is an exalted man who once dwelt on another earth like ours.[28] It follows that since we need our God's help in order for the earth to exist and for us to attain godhood, it seems logical that our God needed his God if he is the same species that we are. The same analysis holds for the God who helped our God, and the God who helped him, and so on.

Monarchotheistic Mormons either openly reject or are skeptically agnostic about the concept of the infinite chain of gods and of there being any gods superior to the God of our world. They think that the God of this world is in fact the head God, superior to all others, and therefore unmade by any others. This removes some of the problems with an infinite chain of Gods, but has others of its own. For one thing, it removes the explanation that the traditional LDS view gives of how "God came to be God." It also raises serious questions about the internal consistency of the Mormon worldview. All Latter-day Saints affirm that persons have always existed, or to be more precise, preexisted as spirit children and intelligences. Did the LDS God work his way from being a primal intelligence to godhood on his own? This seems absurd, especially since it seems to be impossible for us to do so on our own. On the other hand, if one thinks that he was always a God, then this seems to conflict with Smith's statement about how God *came* to be God and with the idea that we can follow the same path of eternal progression that God followed.

At another level there is a deeper problem. Even if the LDS God has always existed as God, we may still ask why the universe itself, with its purely immanent God, exists. Since Mormons think that there is no God who transcends the universe, they can give no answer other than that the universe itself is somehow self-existent. This brings us to the next question.

Why Does Anything Else Exist and Continue to Exist?

On the classical Christian view, everything that exists, other than God, is the creation of God. He brought all things into existence out of nothing and sustains them in their existence. Without God's continuous activity all other things would cease to exist. God can do all of these things because he is omniscient, omnipotent, and in sovereign control of everything.

It is otherwise with the LDS God. He is not the creator of the universe but merely its organizer. This means that the universe exists apart from anything God has done, but without God's activity it would be chaotic. Mormons are therefore committed to believing that the existence of the universe, as opposed to its order, is beyond God's control. Why then does it exist? If the universe does not exist because of a reason external to itself, such as being caused by a transcendent God, it must exist either for a reason internal to itself (Necessary Universe theory), or else for no reason at all (Brute Fact theory). I will argue that both are impossible.[29]

First, what does the Necessary Universe theory mean?[30] In it, the universe exists for reasons internal to itself. What this means is that there is a reason why the universe exists in the manner that it does, but that instead of being caused by something else (like a transcendent God), the reason is somehow in the universe itself. And since on this conception the universe, as part of its very nature, has the reason for its existence internal to itself, the universe thus exists necessarily. In the universe, on this theory, everything that happens does so because to fail to do so would entail a contradiction. Thus, the ultimate reason that an electron repels another electron is that it would be contradictory for it not to do so, in the same sense that it is contradictory that 2 + 2 = 5 is contradictory.[31]

Although many different thinkers have suggested this about the universe, it is impossible. For by the very nature of necessity, if something is necessary, then its denial must entail a contradiction. But no contradiction is obtained by denying the existence of the universe or by saying that it could have existed in some other manner than it does. For example, there is nothing contradictory about the electron mentioned above not repelling the other electron. This being the case, it does not seem impossible that the universe might have existed differently than it does, or that it might even have failed to exist at all. If either of these is possible, then the universe does not exist out of its own inner necessity.   *ontological Argument*

It might be asked, then, how the God of classical theism could necessarily exist. What contradiction is involved in his not existing? The answer to this is that by definition the God of classical theism is the Greatest Possible Being, who by definition must exist in all possible worlds (since to exist is greater than not to exist). On such a definition, to say that this God might not exist is to entail a contradiction. Either the Greatest Possible Being exists necessarily, or he cannot exist at all. Thus, there is an important disanalogy with the universe.

Since the Necessary Universe theory is false, only Brute Fact theory remains for Mormonism, which rejects a transcendent God.[32] On this theory, the universe exists, and exists in the manner that it does, ultimately for no reason at all. There may be secondary reasons why things happen (e.g., a ball falls to the ground because of gravity). But why there are such things as material objects like balls or rubber to make them from, or why the law of gravity exists, is ultimately a matter of chance: they exist for no reason.

This has disastrous implications. Let us say that a cat exists at 3:00. In everyday experience if the cat exists at 3:00, it will also exist at 3:01. According to all our observations, if things exist, they continue in existence. Of course, the cat may die or be blown up between 3:00 and 3:01. But even in these cases the matter that made up the cat's body will continue to exist, even were it trans-muted into energy. What this indicates is that there seems to be a law that objects continue in existence over time. Indeed, not only does this accord with everyday common sense, there is a law of physics that maintains it: matter and energy may change their form, but they cannot be created or destroyed. But this is a law of physics, not metaphysics. Christians believe that God created the universe, sustains it in existence, and could cause it to cease to exist if he wanted.

Let's assume for the sake of argument that Brute Fact theory is true. The laws of physics are contingent; it is logically possible that they be different than they are. Remember that on Brute Fact theory things exist ultimately for no reason. Why then should there be a law that things continue in existence over time? If the account we must give as to why our cat exists at 3:00 is that there is no reason, why should it continue to exist at 3:01, 3:02, and so on? That it exists at all times that it exists is just a brute fact, a fact for which there is no reason or cause. This being the case, there is no reason why it should continue to exist at the next moment, let alone for an indefinite period of time. And this analysis may be made of all that exists, including, it must be said, the LDS God.

Some people have trouble grasping this, so let me explain further. It may seem that everything that exists could exist for no reason, but that nonetheless there could be some law that if something exists it continues in existence. But on Brute Fact theory, laws are at most descriptions of how things act, not some sort of force that makes them act in a certain prescribed manner. This includes the laws of physics, which are contingent and thus might have been otherwise or not at all. For every object that exists, on Brute Fact theory, it is a brute fact that for every time t_1, it exists; and it is another brute fact that at time t_2, it continues to exist, and so on.[33]

We all think that if something exists, it stays in existence, or at least the matter that makes it up does. But the reason we think this is simply because that is how we regularly experience the universe. It is this regularity that cries out for an explanation. Brute Fact theory cannot explain it. On Brute Fact theory no account can be given as to why anything stays in existence.

Having denied the existence of a transcendent Creator of the universe, Brute Fact and Necessary Universe theories are the only options open to Mormonism. But we have seen that neither of these theories can give an account as to why the universe exists and stays in existence; therefore, neither can Mormonism. The classical theist can appeal to his or her transcendent, omnipotent God to explain why things go on existing. The Latter-day Saint cannot.

Why Is the Universe Orderly and Governed by Law?

Laws of Nature. The laws of nature are contingent; they could have been other than they are. For example, the speed of light is about 186,282 miles per second. There seems to be nothing logically necessary about this speed. One can easily conceive, without contradiction, that the speed could be 200,000 miles per second. This being the case, why is the speed of light always that speed rather than some other, or why does it not vary at different times and places? Indeed, one may well ask why there are any natural laws at all. If the universe is to be accounted for on the basis of Brute Fact theory, then why do the objects in the universe behave in a consistent manner?[34]

With the classical concept of God, there is not a problem. God transcends the universe and therefore is not subject to its laws. Being infinite in power and knowledge, he can control all the physical objects that he has created. In a real though nonspatial sense, the universe exists "in" God; it draws its very being from him. Thus, the classical God can explain why the universe is contingent, rational, and law-governed. It is contingent because he might have created something else or nothing at all. It is rational because its Creator is rational. It is governed by law because its Creator has decreed that it should operate in certain regular ways. Things are otherwise with the LDS God. He is a finite object in the universe. The argument given in the section above regarding the sheer existence of things also applies to their law-like behavior, so I will not repeat the details.

The Order of the Universe. We have seen that Mormonism denies that God is the cause of the existence of the universe. However, it teaches that he is the cause of the *order* in the universe. There are several reasons why it is extremely implausible that both of these be true. First, there is the matter of the LDS God having the power to control the universe. Remember that he is a finite physical object the size of a human being. Mormonism teaches that God has a spirit as well as a body. But in Mormonism spirit is defined as a refined form of matter (D&C 131:7–8). I think one may well ask how a material object the size of man can control the rest of the entire physical universe, especially if, as Mormons seem to think, the universe is infinite in extent. Even if the LDS God were only in charge of our galaxy, one of about 100 billion or so in the observable universe, the problem still seems overwhelming. Simply put, there seems to be no way that an object with a mass about the size of a human being could control objects with the mass of the entire galaxy, with its 100 or so billion stars and countless other objects. This is a simple point, but I have not seen any LDS thinker address this objection.

Second, there is the problem of why the Mormon God should have the power to do all the things he is supposed to be able to do. As we have seen, the LDS God is contingent; he might not have existed at all. If, as was shown above, the Mormon universe is ultimately a Brute Fact universe, then everything that exists in it, including the Mormon God, exists in the manner it does at every moment of its existence for no reason. Why, then, should there be a being with all the powers that the Mormon God is supposed to have? It seems improbable at best that a contingent, near-omnipotent being should exist for no reason.[35]

Third, there is the problem of the matter of the universe being amenable to God's control. Mormons believe that God did not create the matter; he merely organized it. This eternal matter has its own inherent nature, properties, and potentiality. But why should uncreated matter be inherently controllable by God (even if not absolutely controllable)? There seems to be no reason why the Mormon God should be able to organize such a vast and intricately complex material cosmos. Furthermore, for the Mormon system to work there needs to be some set of laws that govern the universe such that one object within the universe, the Mormon God, can control everything else. And these laws must hold, for no reason, over the entire universe at every moment of its existence.

Fourth, the affirmation that God is the organizer but not the creator of the material universe raises another problem about the internal consistency of the Mormon worldview. Most Mormon thinkers appeal to the intractableness of eternally existing matter as part of their answer to the problem of evil. That is, they believe that one reason that evils occur is that the material universe is not totally amenable to God's control. Yet if God has so much power over the universe that its orderliness can be attributed to his organization, then it is difficult to see how it is that he could not be in complete control of matter. This point is well illustrated by the final problem I will discuss on this point.

This problem comes from what is known as the Anthropic Principle.[36] According to many scientists, the universe seems to be "fine-tuned" so that life may exist. There are many laws (such as gravity) and cosmological constants (such as the mass of the electron) that are such that, if they had been even slightly different than they are, life would have been impossible. There are countless ways that the laws and constants could have been so that life would have been impossible and comparatively very few ways in which life could exist. In short, if these laws and constants had been established by chance, it seems vastly more likely that they would be such that there would be no life. This being the case, why are the laws and constants apparently fine-tuned?

We see again that the classical concept of God has no difficulty providing a plausible answer to the problem. As a true Creator, God can create an orderly, law-governed universe that has been purposely fine-tuned for life to exist and flourish. It is otherwise with the LDS God. He is an object within the universe dependent for his existence upon an uncreated set of laws and constants that happen to be such that he can exist. According to the Anthropic Principle, it is extremely improbable that this should just happen to be so. I maintain that the whole LDS model is, again, wildly implausible.

Why Are There Objective Moral Laws?

Latter-day Saints tend to believe in objective moral or ethical laws and truths. They are not moral relativists or subjectivists; they think there are moral laws that are necessarily binding on everyone. This position seems correct, but the question is, how can this be true in an LDS universe?

There are at least three important truths about objective ethics. First, they are necessarily person-related. That is, moral laws have only to do with persons (humans and angels are persons, as would be Klingons if they existed). It is silly to say that nonpersonal things can act morally or immorally (e.g., no one would seriously propose that a rock is acting immorally if it falls on someone's head). Second, ethical laws are necessary. That is, they could not have been otherwise. It is not the case that it just *happens* to be wrong to torture innocent people for fun but that it might have been the case that it was right. Objective ethical laws are necessary laws. Third, moral laws are transcendent. That is, they are true in every time and place in the universe.

The classical God by his very nature is an ideal candidate to be the basis of such laws. For, as we noted earlier, he exists necessarily as a person and transcends the universe. Indeed, in Trinitarianism, God necessarily exists as three persons, and the interrelation of these persons, I believe, is the basis for ethics.[37] He made us and sustains us, and we are totally obligated to him.

It is otherwise with the Mormon God. As a finite, purely immanent, and contingent being, it does not seem that he can be the foundation of necessary ethics. How then do Latter-day Saints justify their belief in objective moral values? Judging by the paucity of literature on the subject, this seems to be an issue that very few of them have given much thought to. One who has briefly written on the subject is Kim McCall.[38] He argues what seems to be basically the position of Immanuel Kant: moral laws are what one would will to be universal laws of nature. That is to say, when one decides to act morally, one must consider whether everyone who is in the same situation should do the same thing.[39]

I think that McCall's quasi-Kantian view is severely flawed, but I will not sidetrack the discussion by listing the reasons why. It will suffice to say that whatever else may be said about this ethical theory, it is independent of God. One could be an atheist and hold to this theory of ethics. By developing this view, McCall implicitly shows that the Mormon God is useless as a foundation for ethics. Once again we see that the LDS concept of God is unable to provide satisfying explanations to important philosophical issues, whereas the classical concept of God can. Of course, Mormons could try to develop other theories of the foundation of ethics. But the burden lies on them to show how the Mormon God can serve as the basis of moral law or even how there can be independent objective moral law in a Mormon universe. (For some of the difficulties facing the Mormon in this regard, see Francis J. Beckwith's chapter in this book.)

Can the Real Problem of Evil Be Solved?[40]

The problem of evil, as usually defined, is the philosophical problem created by contemplating how both God and evil can exist if God is the all-good, omnipotent, omniscient Creator of the world.[41] We have seen that Mormonism denies that God is omnipotent (in the sense that the classical God is) and that he is a Creator. It should come as no surprise, then, that the problem of evil is the one philosophical problem that LDS philosophers have argued that their concept of God can answer, whereas classical theism cannot.[42] According to Sterling McMurrin, "It is in the explanation of moral and natural evil... that Mormon theology exhibits its chief theoretic strength."[43] More recently, David Paulsen has claimed that the insights of Mormonism's founding prophet address the problem of evil in its broadest terms and that the worldview built on these insights *dissolves* the logical and soteriological problems of evil.[44] A full critique of LDS answers to the problem of evil would require at least a chapter of its own, but a few useful remarks can be made in the brief space available here.

The first thing to note is that the "how" of this problem can be read in two different ways. It can be read as indicative of a puzzle to be solved that may well be solvable; that is, it can be read with the assumption that all these propositions are true and the problem is to figure out how it is that they are true. The "how" of the argument can also be read skeptically to generate an argument from evil against the existence of God. Arguments from evil come in two versions. The logical version says these affirmations about God and evil are logically contradictory. If they are, then since we know that evil exists, it would follow that a God like the one described by classical theists cannot. The probabilistic or evidential version says it is extremely unlikely that a God like the God of classical theism could exist, given the extent and types of evil in the world. Either of these versions can come in specially adapted forms, such as the soteriological problem of evil (i.e., some people will go to hell and God is an all-good, omnipotent, omniscient Creator who seeks to save humanity).

Secondly, it should be noted that today it is generally conceded by atheistic and theistic philosophers alike that there really is no logical problem of evil.[45] There simply is no contradiction in saying that both evil and an all-good, omnipotent, omniscient Creator God exist. In order to make a contradiction, some further proposition essential to theism must be added to the set to generate a logical contradiction; however, no such proposition has been found. Inevitably, when the atheist concludes that evil and the existence of God are logically incompatible, it is because the atheist has made some assumption about the nature of God or evil that the theist is free to reject.

The evidential argument continues to be employed by many atheists, sometimes in very sophisticated forms.[46] But it is doubtful whether this version of the atheistic argument from evil can be any more successful than the logical version. Consider the judgment of Alvin Plantinga, the philosopher most widely credited with striking the death knell to the logical argument from evil.[47] In his recent and important work, *Warranted Christian Belief*, Plantinga notes that in recent years there have been several ingenious and even revealing attempts to mount a successful evidential argument from evil against the existence of God (or at least against the rationality of belief in God). He argues, however, "that they are no more successful than the older argument for inconsistency. Indeed, what is most surprising, here, is the *weakness* of these arguments."[48] After closely examining two of the most sophisticated of the new arguments from evil, Plantinga concludes that "they fail, and fail resoundingly. They fail to provide a defeater for theistic belief and, indeed, give the person on the fence little if any reason to prefer atheism to theism."[49] In fact, Plantinga claims, "There is no cogent argument for the conclusion that the existence of evil is incompatible with the existence of God; there is also no serious evidential or probabilistic argument from evil."[50]

Be this as it may, LDS philosophers tend to side with atheistic philosophers who continue to raise arguments from evil against the existence of God (that is, the God of classical theism). Latter-day Saint philosophers argue that the classical God does not exist but that the God of Mormon theism exists and escapes from the arguments from evil. The heart of LDS solutions to the problem of evil can be summarized as follows:[51] God is limited in his power and possibly in his knowledge (at least of the future actions of free beings). He is further constrained by the inviolability of the freewill ("free agency" in LDS parlance) of other beings, the uncreated laws of nature, and the intractableness of eternal matter. For various reasons related to these limitations, some evils occur that God is simply powerless to prevent. Additionally, though we cannot remember doing so, in a premortal state we agreed to enter into a world with evil and suffering in order that we might have the opportunity to be exalted to godhood as God was exalted. The experience of evil and suffering are necessary to our perfection and exaltation so that we will be able to know and appreciate good. Finally, it is said that there must necessarily be "an opposition in all things" (2 Nephi 2:11, 15); that is, evil and good necessarily coexist or neither can exist. Evil, therefore, as much as good, is a constituent part of the universe.

Key to Mormon theodicies is the denial of creation *ex nihilo*. It is argued that if God had created the world "out of nothing" rather than being constrained by what already existed, then he could have created any world he wanted—including a world in which there is no (or at least less) evil and suffering than this one. And if God is omnipotent in the sense that a God who creates *ex nihilo* is, then he could have created us already morally perfect. We would not need to go through the experience of a fallen world, and he could have ensured that none would have ever been lost. These claims about the implications of creation *ex nihilo* are quite controversial and have been argued against by Christian philosophers. Nonetheless, David Paulsen finds them persuasive and goes so far as to assert that the doctrine of creation *ex nihilo* exacerbates the problem of evil by making God an accessory before the fact.[52] There is much that could be said about LDS solutions to the problem of evil.

I (Carl Mosser) will make just a few critical comments and then raise some issues related to creation *ex nihilo* and the practical problem of evil.

First, to have true evil, and thus a real problem of evil (whether read as a puzzle or skeptically), requires that there be objective moral values.[53] Yet, as we saw in the section above, the Mormon worldview does not adequately ground such a notion. Second, the idea that there must be "an opposition in all things" is simply unfounded. As John Kekes points out, "whatever is true of phenomena requiring contrasting aspects, it is not true of good and evil. It is absurd to suppose that there can be kindness only if there is cruelty, or freedom only if there is tyranny."[54] Third, it remains the case that the amount of evil that exists in the world is problematic for Mormon theism just as it is for classical theism. Even if the Mormon God is not all-powerful or all-knowing in the classical sense, he must still be very, very powerful and very, very knowledgeable to be accounted a god. It would not have taken an omnipotent or omniscient being to have seen, for example, that Hitler and his cronies were up to no good and to eliminate them, thereby preventing and removing horrendous evil. If Latter-day Saints reply by saying that their God has good reasons for allowing certain evils that he could prevent or remove, then they are using a strategy for answering the problem of evil long employed by classical theists, and it is difficult to see the advantage of Mormon finitism.[55]

While one might argue that appeal to a doctrine of creation out of chaotic matter can solve the intellectual problem of how evil can coexist with a good and powerful God, it does so at two high costs. First of all, the Mormon view of creation naturalizes evil and implies that some of our deepest intuitions about the fundamental goodness of the world and the alien nature of evil are mistaken. Second, the problem of evil is not merely an intellectual problem; it is most fundamentally a practical problem in need of a practical solution: the final and permanent eradication of evil. It is my contention that it is the idea of creation out of preexisting chaotic matter that exacerbates the problem of evil by denying that the practical problem of evil can ever be solved. In contrast, the belief that God created the universe *ex nihilo* guarantees that the problem of evil, in the sense that matters most, can be solved. Let me briefly elaborate.

The Mormon solution naturalizes evil. If there is "an opposition in all things" and evil is an eternal constituent of the universe—a universe God did not create—then evil is simply a part of nature. If evil is just natural, then it must be asked: Why do we feel outrage and indignation when evil has been done? Our own response to evil seems to indicate that evil is not "natural"— evil testifies that something is not the way things are supposed to be. We have an intuitive sense that there is a way that things are supposed to be, a good that should prevail. We also sense that evil is a parasite on this; it is something that perverts, twists, and soils the good. This intuitive sense about the priority of good to evil is best accounted for by the intentions of a wholly good and transcendent Creator. But if evil is simply a constituent part of an uncreated universe—a part of nature—then our outrage and indignation, as well as our sense that evil does not belong, are simply irrational.

The Mormon solution implies cosmological dualism. It has often been observed that evil is associated with chaos. Evil is the breakdown of proper arrangement, authority, and morality. Evil is "things coming apart" or "breaking down"; it is destruction by reducing things to chaos.[56] If the original state of the world is chaos, then it would seem that it is evil, not good, that is most fundamental to reality. The early church fathers recognized this point when they rejected the Greek philosophical views of creation that Mormonism has resurrected.[57] For if all things were created originally and fundamentally good, as Genesis 1 and 2 indicate, then Christian theology could never be reconciled with the Platonic view of creation by a finite deity out of preexisting chaotic matter.[58] Such dualistic views mean that the world is not most fundamentally good; it is at best both fundamentally good and evil. But throughout its pages, the Bible testifies that God created the world as good, that evil is an alien intruder, and that one day it will be overcome once and for all, never to reappear.

The Mormon solution makes a real solution impossible. In Mormon theodicies, some evil is attributed to the intractableness of matter: because matter is uncreated, God is limited by its inherent nature and potentialities; he cannot do whatever he pleases with it and as a result is powerless to prevent some evils from occurring. If this is so, then a simple but significant point follows: *God will never be able to overcome evil.* In the Mormon worldview God did not create matter, he cannot destroy it, and he cannot change its nature. If evil is in part due to the inherent nature of matter, then God simply cannot overcome it. The problem of evil, in the practical sense, becomes an eternal problem. The same point can also be drawn from the idea that "an opposition in all things" is *necessary.*

Many Latter-day Saints, though, seem to have eschatological expectations about the ultimate and permanent demise of evil similar to those of orthodox Christians. But these expectations must be ruled out if God is not the Creator of the world and all therein, including matter. The Mormon God, perhaps by cooperating with other intelligences such as ourselves, might be able to develop coping strategies that limit evil or overcome it in a local sense. But bringing it to a final end is simply impossible. Frederick Sontag has noted that "to remove God from direct responsibility for evil only to find that he is incapable of overcoming it, due to lack of control over it, is a questionable advantage."[59] Indeed.

Only an omnipotent Creator can solve the problem of evil. It should be clear that once again the classical God has an immense advantage over the Mormon God: he is an omnipotent Creator who can eliminate evil. The Mormon concept of God can provide an apparently quick and easy solution to the intellectual problem of evil by denying God's omnipotence and that he is a Creator, but it does so at the expense of there ever being a solution to the real-life problem of evil. In fact, it exacerbates the problem because it rules out all hope of evil being ultimately overcome. What we can look forward to, if the Mormon concept of God and creation is true, is an eternity of struggling with evil. This is not the Christian hope of the Bible.

The biblical hope of evil's eradication is founded on the conviction that God is the transcendent Creator of the universe upon whom all things depend for their existence. Consider the following remarks that New Testament scholar Richard Bauckham makes on the book of Revelation's conviction that God the Creator will overcome evil:

> The understanding of God as Creator was not only integral to Jewish and Christian monotheism; it was also essential to the development of Jewish and Christian eschatology. If God was the transcendent source of all things, he could also be the source of quite new possibilities for his creation in the future. Creation is not confined forever to its own immanent possibilities. It is open to the fresh creative possibilities of its Creator.... Reducing the real transcendence of the Creator reduces the openness of his creation to the eschatologically new. A God who is not the transcendent origin of all things... cannot be the ground of ultimate hope for the future of creation. Where faith in God as Creator wanes, [so does hope for]... the new creation of all things. It is the God who is the Alpha who will also be the Omega.... In new creation God makes his creation eternally secure from any threat of destructive evil.... [T]he divine transcendence guarantees the coming of the kingdom.... The divine transcendence does not prevent but makes possible the eschatological destiny of creation to exist in immediate relation to God, his immanent presence, its glory and its eternal life.[60]

To be sure, the intellectual problem of evil is an important philosophical problem for classical Christian theists to face. But it should not be tackled as a threat to our faith in God or in his ability to overcome evil. Rather, it should be tackled as a puzzle whose workings we are doing our best to understand. If it should turn out that we cannot fully understand the puzzle, we can still be confident of one very important thing: the omnipotent, loving Creator of the universe has told us that he will one day overcome evil; we know that he has the power to make his promise good. It is not at all clear that the Latter-day Saint has any basis for similar hope; only an omnipotent Creator can solve the real problem of evil.

Conclusion

I (Stephen Parrish) have argued that Classical theism possesses tremendous explanatory power: given the classical God, one can explain why God and the universe exist, why the universe is orderly yet contingent, and why there are objective ethical values. Mormon theism, on the other hand, cannot explain any of these. Indeed, I can go further: from the arguments given above, it can be seen that LDS theism is improbable to the point of being impossible. Not only do Latter-day Saints get no help from their doctrine of God, but they also have some difficult questions to answer. Latter-day Saint philosopher James Faulconer remarks of his own faith community: "Often we seem not to recognize that our own view, while dispelling several misconceptions and solving several puzzles, creates it own engaging philosophical problems."[61] I find myself skeptical about how many puzzles Mormon theism can really solve, but I agree that it does create its own problems. In general, I would venture to say that Mormons have not yet done enough philosophical work to make their view a viable position.

No theology should be countenanced as possibly true, much less considered true, if it cannot account for what we know about the world we live in. For in nature God reveals himself (see Romans 1). This is in addition to what we know about God as he has revealed himself in Scripture. Furthermore, if the Standard Works of the LDS Church really are all that is doctrinally binding on Latter-day Saints, then it seems that they should be able to affirm a view of God similar to the classical concept sketched above. As we saw earlier, a straightforward reading of the Book of Mormon and the earlier parts of the other Standard Works presents a classical view, not one at all similar to traditional or monarchotheistic Mormonism. The failures of these concepts to provide adequate solutions to the philosophical problems we have looked at should provide impetus to Mormons to reexamine their own scriptures in an effort to develop a more adequate concept of God.

6

MORAL LAW, THE MORMON UNIVERSE, AND THE NATURE OF THE RIGHT WE OUGHT TO CHOOSE

Francis J. Beckwith

Francis J. Beckwith is Associate Professor of Philosophy, Culture, and Law at Trinity International University, and a Fellow of the Center for the Renewal of Science and Culture, the Discovery Institute (Seattle). He earned a B.A. in philosophy from the University of Nevada at Las Vegas, an M.A. in apologetics from Simon Greenleaf University, an M.A. and Ph.D. in philosophy from Fordham University, and an M.J.S. from Washington University School of Law (St. Louis). Dr. Beckwith is the author or editor of several books, including *Do the Right Thing: Readings in Applied Ethics and Social Philosophy* (Wadsworth) and *Politically Correct Death: Answering the Arguments for Abortion Rights* (Baker). He is the coauthor of *See the Gods Fall: Four Rivals to Christianity* (College Press) and *The Mormon Concept Of God: A Philosophical Analysis* (Edwin Mellen). He has published articles in several disciplines in journals such as *Journal of the Evangelical Theological Society; International*

Philosophical Quarterly; Journal of Law, Medicine, and Ethics; Journal of Church and State; Journal of Social Philosophy; Nevada Law Journal; Public Affairs Quarterly; Social Theory and Practice; and *Trinity Journal.*

When it comes to ethical and social issues, there is widespread agreement between classical Christians and Latter-day Saints. Stephen E. Robinson, a professor of ancient scripture at Brigham Young University, correctly notes that "Evangelicals and Latter-day Saints share the same moral standards, the same family values, the same old-fashioned standards of personal conduct."[1] Furthermore, both groups recognize that personal morality is of fundamental importance to a society's corporate character. In the words of Joseph F. Smith, sixth president of the LDS Church, "The character of a community or a nation is the sum of the individual qualities of its component members."[2] Thus, on such issues as same-sex marriage and abortion, Latter-day Saints have worked with both evangelicals and Roman Catholics in defending conservative positions on these matters in both the public square and the legal arena.[3] There is no doubt that the LDS Church encourages its people to love what is good, true, and beautiful. In the words of a popular LDS youth saying, it teaches them from an early age to "Choose the Right."

At the more fundamental level, Mormons and classical Christians agree that moral relativism is a mistaken view. Moral relativism is the view that when it comes to questions of morality, there is no absolute or objective right and wrong; moral laws are merely personal preferences and/or the result of one's culture or society. Both groups believe that their largely shared moral values are objective, that they are based on a moral law that exists apart from what people or their society may prefer or think, and that these standards are the ones against which the standards of every person and society should be evaluated.

I applaud and welcome the LDS Church's opposition to moral relativism as well as its support on social and ethical issues. I also admire the way LDS scholars tenaciously and intelligently defend their moral perspective in the public arena. However, I do not believe that the Mormon worldview adequately grounds the moral laws that the LDS Church correctly embraces. It does not provide a sufficient ontological basis for "the Right" that LDS youths are so admirably encouraged to choose. In order to show this, I will discuss three primary topics: Mormonism and the nature of moral law; God and the source of moral law; and possible alternatives Latter-day Saints might attempt to appropriate in order to provide an objective basis for their moral values. In a manner somewhat reminiscent of the way C.S. Lewis argued in his book *Mere Christianity,* I will also suggest that this kind of reflection on the nature of morality tells us some important things about the nature of the universe we live in and the God who created it.[4]

Moral Law and the Mormon Worldview

Mormonism and the Nature of Moral Law

Although LDS writings say little specifically about the nature of moral law, they do say much about the nature of laws and principles that apparently include moral laws. The founding Mormon prophet, Joseph Smith Jr., maintained that laws and principles are eternal and unchanging: "Every principle proceeding from God is eternal and any principle which is not eternal is of the devil. . . . The first step in the salvation of man is the laws of eternal and self-existent principles."[5] In the Doctrine and Covenants, Smith states that "there is a law, irrevocably decreed in heaven before the foundations of this world, upon which all blessings are predicated—And when we obtain any blessing from God, it is by obedience to that law upon which it is predicated" (D&C 130:20, 21). According to LDS philosopher Kent Robson, "LDS thought is uncommon in the Christian world in its affirmation that intelligence, truth, the 'principles of element,' priesthood, law, covenants, and ordinances are eternal."[6] Philosopher of Mormonism Sterling McMurrin writes that Mormon metaphysics is marked by *value universals* and that "in the matter of values, particularly moral values, Mormon philosophy assumes an absolutistic character. . . . Truth and goodness in the Mormon view are fixed eternally in the universe and their reality and status do not depend on what men actually think or do."[7] Joseph Smith seems to affirm a view of government that is in the natural law tradition, that is, that the purpose of government is to promote the good as well as to protect those rights that are grounded in unchanging moral laws:

> We believe that governments were instituted of God for the benefit of man. . . . We believe that all governments necessarily require civil officers and magistrates to enforce the laws of the same; and that such as will

administer the law in equity and justice should be sought for and upheld by the voice of the people of a republic, or the will of the sovereign. . . . We believe that all men are bound to sustain and uphold their respective governments in which they reside, while protected in their inherent and inalienable rights by the laws of such governments . . . and that all governments have a right to enact such laws as their own judgments have best calculated to secure the public interest. (D&C 134:1, 3, 5)

So for LDS theology the moral law is eternal and unchanging; it can be known by human beings and applied to practical matters such as the formation of just governments and just laws. To use the language of jurisprudence, there is an eternal law from which human beings may derive natural law, which ought to be employed to assess whether the positive law is truly just. Although such natural law language seems to fit well within the metaphysics of classical Christianity,[8] how does the moral law square with the Mormon worldview and its doctrine of deity? In order to answer this question, we have to take an excursion into Mormon metaphysics and the place of God in it, covering only those aspects of the Mormon worldview and deity that I believe are germane to this discussion.[9]

An Excursus on the Metaphysics of Mormonism

According to a prominent stream of LDS theology, God the Father is a resurrected, "exalted" man named Elohim, who was at one time *not* God.[10] He was once a mortal man on another planet who, through obedience to the precepts of *his* God, eventually attained exaltation, or godhood, through "eternal progression." The Mormon God, located in time and space, has a body of flesh and bone (D&C 130:22) and thus is neither spirit nor omnipresent as understood in their traditional meanings. Joseph Smith Jr. asserts:

God himself was once as we are now, and is an exalted man, and sits enthroned in yonder heavens! . . . I am going to tell you how God came to be God. *We have imagined and supposed that God was God from all eternity. I will refute this idea*, and take away the veil, so that you may see. . . . It is the first principle of the gospel to know for a certainty the character of God, and to know that we may converse with him as one man converses with another, and that He was once a man like us; yea, that God himself, the Father of us all, dwelt on an earth, the same as Jesus Christ himself did; and I will show it from the Bible. . . .

> Here, then, is eternal life—to know the only wise and true God; and you have got to learn how to be gods yourselves, and be kings and priests to God, *the same as all gods have done before you,* namely, by going from one small degree to another, and from a small capacity to a great one; from grace to grace, from exaltation to exaltation, until you attain to the resurrection of the dead, and are able to dwell in everlasting burnings, and sit in glory, as do those who sit enthroned in everlasting power.[11]

The late Mormon president Lorenzo Snow explains: "As man now is, God once was; / As God now is, man may become."[12] Tenth president of the LDS Church Joseph Fielding Smith writes:

> Some people are troubled over the statements of the prophet Joseph Smith.... The matter that seems such a mystery is the statement that *our Father in heaven at one time passed through a life and death and is an exalted man.* This is one of the mysteries.... The Prophet taught that *our Father had a Father and so on.* Is not this a reasonable thought, especially when we remember that the promises are made to us that we may become like him?[13]

A member of the LDS First Council of the Seventy, Milton R. Hunter, writes: "Mormon prophets have continuously taught the sublime truth that *God the Eternal Father was once a mortal man* who passed through a school of earth life similar to that through which we are now passing. *He became God*—an exalted being—through obedience to the same eternal Gospel principles that we are given opportunity to obey today."[14]

Once Elohim attained godhood, he then created this present world by "organizing" both eternally preexistent, inorganic matter and the preexistent primal intelligences from which human spirits are made (Book of Abraham 3:22). Mormon writer Hyrum L. Andrus explains: "Though man's spirit is organized from a pure and fine substance which possesses certain properties of life, Joseph Smith seems to have taught that within each individual spirit there is a central primal intelligence (a central directing principle of life), and that man's central primal intelligence is a personal entity possessing some degree of life and certain rudimentary cognitive powers before the time the human spirit was organized."[15] For this reason, Joseph Smith wrote that "man was also in the beginning with God. Intelligence, or the light of truth, was not created or made, neither indeed can be."[16] In other words, *the basic essence or primal intelligence of each human person is as eternal as God's is.*

The Mormon God, by organizing this world out of preexistent matter, has granted these organized spirits the opportunity to receive physical bodies, pass through mortality, and eventually progress to godhood—just as this opportunity was given him by his Father God. Consequently, if human persons on earth faithfully obey the precepts of Mormonism, they too can attain godhood like Elohim before them. And the purpose of attaining godhood is so that "we would become heavenly parents and have spirit children just as [Elohim] does."[17] Mormon philosopher David Paulsen writes: "He [the Mormon God] is perfectly just, loving, kind, compassionate, veracious, no respecter of persons, etc. But his perfections are not eternal, but were acquired by means of developmental process."[18]

Based on the statements of Mormon authorities, some LDS scholars contend that the way a premortal spirit is "organized" by God the Father is through "spiritual begetting." In this process, human spirits are somehow organized by Elohim and his wife, whereby they are conceived and born as spirit children *prior* to entering the mortal realm (although all human persons prior to spirit birth existed as intelligences in some primal state of cognitive personal existence).[19] Since God the Father of Mormonism was himself organized (or spirit-birthed) by his God, who himself is the offspring of yet another God, and so on ad infinitum, Mormon theology therefore implies that the God over this world is a contingent being in an infinite lineage of gods.[20] This is why Joseph Smith asserts that he will "preach the plurality of Gods.... I wish to declare I have always and in all congregations when I have preached on the subject of the Deity, it has been the plurality of Gods."[21]

Comparing the Mormon concept of God with the God of classical Christianity, LDS philosopher Blake Ostler writes that in contrast to the self-sufficient God who creates the universe *ex nihilo* (out of nothing),

> the Mormon God did not bring into being the ultimate constituents of the cosmos—neither its fundamental matter nor the space/time matrix which defines it. Hence, unlike the Necessary Being of classical theology who alone could not *not* exist and on which all else is contingent for existence, the personal God of Mormonism confronts uncreated realities which exist of metaphysical necessity. Such realities include inherently self-directing selves (intelligences), primordial elements (mass/energy), the natural laws which structure reality, and moral principles grounded in the intrinsic value of selves and the requirements for growth and happiness.[22]

Concurring, Mormon theologian B. H. Roberts, a member of the First Council of Seventy, writes:

> Not even God may place himself beyond the boundary of space: nor on the outside of duration. Nor is it conceivable to human thought he can create space, or annihilate matter. These are things that limit even God's omnipotence. What then, is meant by the ascription of the attribute of Omnipotence to God? Simply that all that may or can be done by power conditioned by other eternal existences—duration, space, matter, truth, justice—God can do. But even he may not act out of harmony with the other eternal existences which condition or limit him.[23]

Therefore, on this traditional view, Mormonism teaches that certain basic realities have always existed and are indestructible, even by God. In LDS theology God, like each human being, is a finite person within the universe (though always more powerful and intelligent than us). In the Mormon universe, God is not responsible for creating or sustaining (strictly speaking) matter, energy, natural laws, personhood, moral principles, or the process of exaltation. Instead of the universe being subject to him (as in classical Christianity), the Mormon God is subject to the universe (which is not to say that he does not have great power within the universe). In the words of McMurrin, "God is not the totality of original being and he is not the ultimate source or the creator of all being. This is a radical departure from the position of traditional theism, whether Christian, Jewish, or Islamic." He continues by noting that "the failure to recognize the far-reaching implications of this idea is a failure to come to grips with the somewhat distinctive quality of Mormon theology, its essentially non-absolutistic character."[24] Some thinkers, including LDS scholars, have noticed strong conceptual similarities between Mormon theism and other finite theisms and philosophical positions such as nominalism, classical materialism, and process philosophy.[25]

Moreover, Mormonism, it appears, is "committed to a thoroughgoing metaphysical materialism." Because the LDS worldview, as we have seen, "affirms the independence and self-subsistence of material element (mass-energy)," it is therefore "committed to a position of physical realism."[26] But, as Paulsen points out, Mormonism's "physicalistic commitment is even more thoroughgoing than this," for LDS scripture "explicitly repudiates the existence of any non-material substances."[27] In the words of Joseph Smith Jr., "There is no such thing as immaterial matter. All spirit is matter, but is more fine or pure, and can only be discerned by purer eyes."[28] A passage attributed to Elder Parley Pratt reads: "Nothing exists which is not material. The elementary principles of the material universe are eternal; they never originated from nonentity, and they never can be annihilated. Immateriality is but another name for nonentity—it is the negative of all things, and beings—of all existence."[29]

In sum, we first learned that the LDS Church teaches that there is an unchanging moral law that all human beings are obligated to obey. So far so good. This is something with which classical Christians (and others) agree. But then we learned in our excursion into the LDS worldview that the Mormon deity is in the same position as we are in relation to the unchanging and eternal moral law. Just as our wills, desires, and interests are independent of the existence of the moral law, so are God's will and decrees. That is, if God's decrees and acts are good, they are only good because they are consistent with an unchanging moral law that exists apart from him. God's decrees and acts are not good merely because they are God's. For God himself was once a man who, through obedience to certain eternal principles and laws, eventually became God. As Joseph Smith Jr. said:

> The first principles of man are self-existent with God. God himself, finding he was in the midst of spirits and glory, because he was more intelligent, saw proper to institute laws whereby the rest could have a privilege to advance like himself. The relationship we have with God places us in a situation to advance in knowledge. He has power to institute laws to instruct weaker intelligences, that they may be exalted with Himself, so that they might have one glory upon another, and all that knowledge, power, glory, and intelligence, which is requisite in order to save them in the world of spirits.[30]

Thus, if the Mormon God had failed to become a God, the moral law would have still been the moral law. Nevertheless, both Mormonism and classical Christianity affirm the existence of an objective, unchanging, and universal moral law. There are other aspects of the LDS worldview that are important and worth studying, but what we have covered so far, I believe, is adequate for our present purposes. It should be clear that Mormon theism is a radical departure from classical Christianity. It will soon be seen that the implications of this for moral law are significant.

God and the Source of Moral Law

The Nature of Moral Laws and the Mormon Worldview

Given the existence of moral laws, there are some observations we can make about them. First, they are known. If they were not known, then we would have to be moral skeptics. But moral skepticism is not an option for either classical Christians or Mormons. It seems, then, that both classical Christians and Mormons are committed to some form of moral realism, holding that moral laws are real objects of knowledge rather than social or philosophical constructs resulting from, and subject to, either the changes of human culture, individual preferences and desires, or the deliverances of reason or state-of-nature scenarios.

Second, moral laws are a form of communication, an activity by which one mind through statements conveys meaning to another mind. For moral laws are found explicitly in imperatives (e.g., "One ought to keep one's promises") and commands (e.g., "Keep your promises") and, implicitly, in descriptions (e.g., "Keeping promises is good").

Third, there is an incumbency to moral laws. As Gregory Koukl puts it, moral laws "have a force we can actually feel *prior* to any behavior. This is called the incumbency, the 'oughtness' of morality. . . . It appeals to our will, compelling us to act in a certain way, though we may disregard its force and choose not to obey."[31]

Fourth, when we break a significant and clear moral rule, it is usually accompanied by feelings of painful guilt and sometimes shame. For we are cognizant of our moral failure and realize that we deserve to be punished. Only sociopaths succeed in overcoming their conscience completely.

Fifth, moral laws are not material. They have no physical properties, for they have no extension, weight, or height, and they do not consist of chemicals, particles, or other parts that can be measured by scientific instruments. We do not discover them by using our sense organs, but rather, we encounter them through introspection, reflection, and/or revelation.

So moral laws are known nonmaterial realities that are a form of communication for which we have a sense of incumbency and feel painful guilt when we violate them. Given these characteristics, which metaphysical perspective best explains the existence of the moral law—classical Christianity or Mormonism? In order to answer this question, I will make four points and respond to two objections.

Mormonism's Materialist Ontology. Because the Mormon worldview is materialist, it is unclear where the moral law fits in if it is a nonmaterial reality. Now the Latter-day Saints may want to deny that the moral law is real in any ontological sense (that is, they may deny moral realism), but such a denial would be inconsistent with the Mormon claim that the moral law is an integral part of the order and nature of things, and that one's obedience to it is essential for eternal progression toward godhood. That is, if the only reality is matter, the very principles and laws that undergird the entire deity-producing superstructure would be ultimately unreal. Moreover, progression toward godhood entails real moral progress toward moral perfection, the real increase of virtue and personal goodness by the prospective deity. But to coherently claim that one is acquiring more of X, X must have some ontological reality. That is, to claim that one may acquire, nurture, and increase moral properties in one's person, it would seem that such nonmaterial and irreducible entities must exist. But if moral properties are real and are irreducibly nonmaterial, then the presence of moral properties in a material universe, in the words of atheist philosopher J. L. Mackie, "constitute[s] such an odd cluster of properties and relations that they are most unlikely to have arisen in the ordinary course of events without an all-powerful god to create them."[32]

Such an all-powerful God would not be the LDS God, for as we have seen, he is not the source of the moral law. Although the moral law is different than moral properties (i.e., "Do not murder" is different than "Life is good" and "GI Joe is more virtuous, having saved people's lives"), a moral point of view that connects moral law with personal virtue, such as Mormonism or classical Christianity, cannot have one without the other. Since the metaphysics of classical Christianity includes the existence of numerous nonmaterial things—for example, souls, God, angels—moral properties and moral law are not out of place. They fit in rather nicely.

Mormonism's Book Without an Author. Because moral laws are a form of communication, an activity by which one mind through statements conveys meaning to another mind, it is not clear how the LDS worldview can explain or justify the moral law. For there is no mind or authority behind the moral law in the LDS universe. It is simply there. But this does not seem adequate. Consider this analogy. Moral laws are like statutes; they are rules that one is obligated to obey. This obligation arises when the statutes are the result of the deliberation of a legitimate sovereign. That is, the sovereign has the moral authority to instruct its citizens to obey its statutes (assuming, of course, that the statutes do not violate some moral law). Suppose, however, that these statutes did not result from any sovereign whatsoever but were conveyed to the jurisdiction's citizens by a chief executive officer (CEO), who claims to be in charge of enforcing the statutes but who is himself not the sovereign. What if we were to ask the CEO why we should obey the statutes? He can appeal either to (a) his own authority over us, (b) a sovereign above the CEO who has the authority to both issue statutes and choose a CEO to enforce them, or (c) the authority of a book of statutes that has always existed but for which, the CEO claims, there is no author.

Suppose the CEO selects (a), and simply claims that he has authority over us. We can then ask him: Why do you have authority over us? He can either say he has always had authority over us, or he can claim to have received his authority from a sovereign above him. The first is not an option in this case, since the CEO is no sovereign and was once an ordinary citizen and thus was at one time not in a position of enforcing statutes. So he had to have received his authority from a sovereign. This leads us to option (b): there is a sovereign who issues statutes and chooses a CEO to enforce them. This only works if that sovereign was never an ordinary citizen. For if he was, then we can ask him how he received *his* authority. If he appeals to a sovereign above him, then there is either a sovereign above whom there is no sovereign, or there is an infinite regress of sovereigns. The latter is no option, for an infinite regress of sovereigns would mean that no sovereign in the series would ever be the sufficient condition for the authority passed on to the sovereign who follows him.[33] The former is an option, but if this illustration is truly a parallel to the Mormon worldview, it is no option for the Latter-day Saints. For according to the LDS worldview, every sovereign (i.e., God) was once an ordinary citizen (i.e., mortal) and thus cannot be the source of the moral law. So if there exists an eternally existing sovereign who is the source of the moral law and who has the authority to issue moral commands based on that law, the LDS worldview would be falsified.

Thus, we are left with option (c): the CEO claims that the statutes are from an authorless book that has always existed. Even though this option is analogous to the relationship between the LDS God and the moral law, it is inadequate for at least two reasons. First, why should we believe or trust what the CEO says about the moral law? After all, he admits to receiving his authority from a sovereign who did not issue the statutes that the CEO is requiring us to obey. Also, the sovereign to whose authority the CEO is appealing does not have a sufficient condition for his authority as a sovereign (i.e., the infinite regress objection). Second, statutes and laws, including moral laws, seem to be prima facie the sorts of things that are dependent on a mind for their existence and authority.

Mormon Platonism? Of course, logically it is possible that moral laws are free-floating, Platonic-like forms that are in no mind whatsoever. At least one twentieth-century philosopher of Mormonism seems to think that the LDS worldview implies some form of moral Platonism.[34] However, such Platonic forms would be immaterial and thus inconsistent with the dominant physicalist construal of the LDS worldview. In addition, philosopher Paul Copan suggests four reasons why the Platonist view of morality fails generally. Three of his reasons are relevant to our present study:[35]

First, it is inadequate in explaining the guilt and shame one feels when one violates the moral law. For it is persons, not rules or principles, that elicit in us feelings of guilt and shame.

Second, our experience indicates that moral obligation, though resting on abstract principles, is deeply connected to our obligations *toward* other persons. For example, "One ought not to take another person's life without justification" is as much a moral principle as "One ought to do what is morally right for its own sake even when no human person will ever know and no human person will ever be harmed if one would disobey." For both LDS and classical Christians, the second moral principle is a second-order principle that serves as the basis by which we should obey the first moral principle and other first-order principles. It is obvious to whom we owe our moral obligation with the first principle (i.e., other human beings), but to whom do we owe our moral obligation with the second principle? Clearly, not to other human beings, for they will not know and will not be harmed if we disobey. Perhaps to oneself? But if that were the case, one would not be doing the moral act *for its own sake* but for oneself. Perhaps we are obligated to act consistently with the second principle because of the commands of a higher finite intelligence like the Mormon God. But that will not do, because one would, again, not be doing the moral act *for its own sake*. There seems to be really only one option: our obligation to obey the second principle is bound up with a person, but only the sort of person whose nature is such that he is the source of moral principles that are to be obeyed for their own sake. That is, he is both a person and the Good. That is why we feel shame and guilt for disobeying what ought to have been done for its own sake. We have let *him* down, for we have transgressed the Good. This person is more like the God of classical theism than the God of Mormonism.

Third, Platonism implies that moral values (or principles) that have no purposing agent or mind behind them can in some purposeful way anticipate the existence of agents (in Mormonism both Gods and human beings) who can apprehend, appropriate, and employ these principles. It seems easier, however, to believe that the self-existent Creator of all that is, the God of classical theism, is the source of moral principles than some variation on Platonism.

Although the LDS case for an independently existing moral law with no mind behind it may be ultima facie justified, no Latter-day Saint has made a case for it that is consistent with LDS materialist metaphysics and moral realism (both of which seem to be central to the Mormon worldview) as well with as our moral intuitions.[36] So, prima facie, we have a reason to reject the LDS explanation of the moral law.

Divine Commands. This analysis so far seems to lead to the belief that there is a self-existent divine sovereign who is the ground of the moral law, as classical Christians believe. However, this leads to the question: Is the moral law *merely* the commands of God? Some say "yes." They are defenders of what is called Divine Command Theory (DCT). That is, moral rules ought to be obeyed because they are God's commands and God is the omnipotent Creator of the universe. In reply to DCT, some philosophers argue that it falls prey to a variation of a dilemma raised by Socrates in a question found in Plato's dialogue *Euthyphro*:[37] Is something good because God loves it, or does God love it because it is good?[38] This is called the Euthyphro Dilemma, because it seems that whichever option of the two one chooses, one chooses an undesirable answer. For if one answers the question by saying that something is good because God loves it, then "goodness" is merely the result of God's power and will and is thus arbitrary. In other words, if God says that child torture is right, it's right; but if God says that child torture is wrong, it's wrong. On the other hand, if one embraces the second horn of the dilemma—God loves it because it is good—then there is a standard of goodness outside of God to which even he is subject. But this would mean that God's commands are not the foundation of morality.

A moderate version of DCT, defended by philosopher Robert Adams, suggests one answer to this dilemma. He argues that God's command is a necessary, though not a sufficient condition, to obey God. (Just as being "female" is a necessary condition for being a "sister," it is not sufficient if the other necessary condition, "sibling," is missing.) According to Adams, God's command must be consistent with a loving character, which Adams believes

God has. Although he concedes that it is logically possible that God would command what is wrong, "it is unthinkable that God should do so."[39] An analysis of whether or not Adams's or another version of DCT can withstand the critique of the Euthyphro Dilemma is outside the scope of this chapter. Nevertheless, the point is that DCT is alive and well, despite the criticisms leveled against it.[40]

But even if DCT is an option for classical Christians, it cannot be so for Mormons. For the LDS God is not the Creator of the universe on whom all reality depends. The LDS God is in precisely the same position as the gods whose moral authority Socrates thought problematic; and the Latter-day Saints are in precisely the same position as their God was once in his life—dependent on the commands of a being, his God, who received his goodness from yet another. The Mormon God is not the being in whom morality ultimately rests, for the moral law is something that he had to obey in order to achieve his divine status. The Latter-day Saints may obey the commands of their God because they believe he is more powerful than they are, but it is not clear how this appeal to power establishes the moral conclusion that the LDS God is *justified* in issuing his commands. As political philosopher Hadley Arkes has pointed out, "The young boy who loses his first fight understands instantly that the success of his opponents cannot itself establish that they were 'right' or 'justified' in beating him up." That is, "power cannot be the source of its own justification: the fact that some men may have been successful in seizing and holding power over others cannot itself establish that they were *justified* in imposing their rule."[41]

Like many classical Christians, I do not find DCT (or its modified version defended by Adams) to be an adequate justification for the moral law.[42] But that does not mean that God is not the ground of the moral law. It simply means that it is not his commanding that gives the moral law its authority. In other words, the moral law *does* depend on God, but not because God issues moral commands and is the all-powerful Creator of the universe. Rather, it is because God's nature (or character) is such that it is eternally and perfectly good. That is, God's commands are good, not because God commands them, but because God *is good*. Thus, God is not subject to a moral order outside of himself, and neither are God's moral commands arbitrary. God's commands are issued by a perfect being who is the source of all goodness.

God's Necessary Goodness

Blake Ostler has raised two objections to this viewpoint: (1) If God is perfectly good by nature, then God's goodness is arbitrary, because he is stuck with a nature that dictates to him what is moral; and (2) If God is perfectly good by nature, then he is not really a moral agent, for a being who cannot help but do the good is not really free, and one must be free in order to be a moral agent.

Concerning the first objection, Ostler concludes that my view "entails that good and evil are arbitrary."[43] He bases this conclusion on the following reasoning:

> [Beckwith and Parrish locate] the source of moral values not in God's will, but in God's nature. Since God's will is subject to his essentially good nature, they claim that God can never will anything evil. Moreover, they argue that moral values are not arbitrary because God's nature is the same in every possible world. However, if God's nature is logically prior to God's will, then God is stuck with whatever his nature happens to dictate—and in this sense moral values are clearly arbitrary. God is not morally free on such a view because he cannot will that his nature be different.[44]

It is not clear what Ostler is claiming here and why it should count against the moral law being grounded in the nature of the God of classical Christianity. Frankly, I do not know what it means to be "stuck with" a perfect nature in every possible world. Perhaps it is like having the misfortune of being stuck with personal charm and good looks in every possible world. Nevertheless, Ostler seems to be saying that God's nature is distinct from his will, that God's nature is a sort of impersonal, undirected force to which his will is subject. Thus, if God commands, "Don't torture babies for fun," because he wills that in every possible world "torturing babies for fun is wrong," and that principle is the result of his good nature, then God's command is "arbitrary" because he has no control over the nature that apparently directs his will.

This argument does not help the LDS worldview. According to the Mormon worldview, moral law exists, and it is something outside of God to which he, like each of us, is subject. This moral law does not have its source in a mind, nor is it under the direction of any being. It simply exists. Now suppose Ostler tells us that the LDS God issues a command, "Don't torture babies for fun," that is based on the moral principle that "torturing babies for fun is wrong." Query: Could the LDS God have issued a different command based on a different moral principle, such as "torturing babies for fun is right sometimes"? And could one say that *that* principle violates the moral law? It seems that on the LDS worldview, one would have to answer yes. For if the LDS God's commands are to be considered truly moral, they must be consistent with the moral law.

But to paraphrase Ostler's critique of my view, if the moral law is logically prior to God's will, then God is stuck with whatever the moral law happens to dictate—and in this sense, moral values are clearly arbitrary. God is not morally free on such a view, because he cannot will that the moral law be different. But Ostler would clearly reject this. He would deny that an unchanging moral law that is true in every possible world is arbitrary. I would agree. However, where that moral law is located—in God's nature (the view of classical Christianity) or outside it (the LDS view)—does not seem relevant. Thus, Ostler's first objection fails.

But perhaps Ostler's second objection is more to the point: if God is necessarily perfect, as in classical Christianity, God's will is constrained by his nature, and thus he cannot be virtuous in a truly noble sense. Ostler explains:

> In my view the doctrine of God's essential goodness is a hard pill to swallow. The upshot of the doctrine is that God is not a *moral agent* because it is not possible for God to make any morally wrong decisions. It is certainly no great moral defect to be so virtuous that one does not make morally wrong decisions; it is quite another problem if the reason no wrong decisions are made is that it is *logically impossible to make a wrong decision*. . . . I prefer the Mormon view that God is a person who is worthy of praise and worship precisely because he could go wrong, but in the excellence of his personal character has freely decided to do what is good.[45]

There are several criticisms one may raise against this argument, but two will suffice for our present purposes.[46] First, though Ostler may find the idea of a God who is necessarily good a hard pill to swallow, most people, I suspect, would find the notion of a God who could go wrong far more difficult. Frankly, it is hard to see how anyone could really view the possibility of God going wrong an advantage of their concept of God. For it is a belief whose implications serve to undermine our faith in God's absolute trustworthiness. Consider the following dilemma Katherin Rogers poses for views like Ostler's:

> Some contemporary philosophers of religion insist that if God is good "by nature" then He is not good in an ethical sense. But they go on to argue that God is absolutely trustworthy because given His character and disposition doing evil is totally repugnant to Him. It is unthinkable that He do evil. This analysis is puzzling. If God's choices simply flow from his

character and disposition, if there is something about Him that forecloses evil as a really viable option, how is there choice and hence morally significant freedom involved? If it is possible for God to be tempted by evil and choose against His character, then it is not unthinkable that He would do so. I take it that ascribing morally significant freedom to God entails allowing that He really might (or really has) chosen evil.[47]

Secondly, Ostler seems to be employing the Mormon worldview to judge the classical Christian concept of God as inadequate and thus is begging the question. Let me explain. In the Mormon worldview God, like us, has duties. He is, like us, under an obligation to obey a moral law for which he is not the source. Because we and God have the same ontological status, we have the same duties in respect to the moral law. Consequently, if we and God share the same nature, then whatever is true of our achievement of virtue must also be (or have been) true of God. But it is not clear why the classical Christian must accept LDS categories on this matter. Classical Christianity is a well-developed philosophical and theological project with its own categories and resources that have long been employed to answer just the sort of objection raised by Ostler. For Ostler, a Mormon, to say that he prefers the Mormon view of God over the classical Christian view of God because the former happens to account for God's goodness in a way consistent with LDS metaphysics is not an argument against the possibility that God is the source of the moral law because he is necessarily good. It is merely an argument that the God of classical Christianity is not the God of Mormonism.

Having said that, how should Christians think about their morally good God, who is logically incapable of doing evil? First, since God and humans do not share the same nature, our relationship to the moral law is different from God's relationship to it. As finite beings who are not necessarily good, we have a duty to obey the moral law. However, because God is necessarily good, and because to have a duty to do something implies that one has the ability *not* to do it, God, strictly speaking, does not have a duty to obey the moral law. In the words of Thomas V. Morris,

> God acts in accordance with those principles which would express duties for a moral agent in his relevant circumstances. And he does so necessarily. So although God does not literally have any duties on this construal of the duty model, we can still have well-grounded expectations concerning divine conduct by knowing those principles which would govern the conduct of a perfect, duty-bound moral agent who acted as in fact God does. We

understand and anticipate God's activity by analogy with the behavior of a completely good moral agent.[48]

Second, the classical Christian view of God requires "that God has the greatest possible array of *compossible* great-making properties, not that he have all great-making properties."[49] This means that God is the being who has the best collection of great-making properties that any being can possibly have, not that he has every possible great-making property one may think of. For example, choosing good over evil is a great-making property, but being necessarily good is also a great-making property. Yet no being can both have the ability to choose good over evil and necessarily always choose good (i.e., not have the ability to choose good over evil). Thus, these are not compossible great-making properties—for no being can have both of them together. Consequently, the fact that God "lacks" the ability to do evil does not count against his moral character.

Third, even though God is necessarily good, it does not follow that he is not a *free* moral agent. Granted, his actions must be consistent with true moral principles, but he is free to choose what actions to engage in, including actions that are not necessitated by his goodness. For example, the Bible speaks of God's grace and mercy. When God is gracious and merciful, he is no doubt acting consistently with true moral principles, but he could refrain from being gracious and merciful in particular instances without violating those moral principles. He cannot, however, cease to be necessarily good. That is, because he is necessarily good, he is not free to do evil; but since he is a necessarily good *moral agent,* he is able to exercise his will and choose among any number of good or supererogatory actions.

Possible Alternatives

In light of the above arguments, Latter-day Saints may opt for other possible avenues to ground moral law in addition to the Platonist option discussed above. Given the LDS worldview, three options seem to be the most viable alternatives: social contract theory, Aristotelian final causes, and emergent moral properties. Let me briefly explain and respond to each.

Social Contract Theory

There have been many social contract theories in the history of political and moral philosophy, most notably those proposed by Thomas Hobbes,

John Locke, and John Rawls. Rawls's view seems most amenable to LDS thought, for Hobbes's view is too pessimistic and Locke's relies on the classical God to ground natural rights.

According to Rawls, a state (or government) is just if it is the result of principles people would have arrived at if they knew nothing about what they are or what they will become (i.e., whether they are rich or poor, black or white, homosexual or heterosexual, short or tall, male or female, etc.).[50] To employ Rawls's terminology, the principles of justice are those agreed to by parties in "the original position" (an imaginary time and place where there is no government) behind "a veil of ignorance" (an imaginary situation in which nobody has any personal knowledge of themselves or their futures). In other words, the principles of justice are those arrived at by means of a social contract that all the "unbiased" parties would agree on so that they can receive full political and social freedom and a minimum standard of financial entitlement just in case it turns out one is, for example, not well-off, not naturally gifted, or holds unpopular political and/or religious opinions. This means that Rawls's principles of justice have little or nothing to do with the good, the true, or the beautiful. They are principles for ensuring economic entitlement as well as for preventing conflict between individuals pursuing their own subjective preferences. They are rules for protecting one's interests as well as refereeing the conflicts that result from individuals exercising their autonomy.[51]

There are several reasons why this is not a viable option for the Latter-day Saints: (1) it denies moral realism, something that seems essential to the LDS worldview; (2) it does not explain how nonreal moral principles, derived from a hypothetical contract, have the power (or ontological wherewithal) to interact with the structures of the universe to produce Mormon Gods; and (3) contractual agreements are neither necessary nor sufficient conditions for the rightness of a moral perspective. For example, you and I can agree to a mutual suicide pact if our favorite television show is cancelled. Suppose that the show is cancelled and we go ahead and kill each other. Clearly, such an act is not morally right simply because we agreed to it. That is, we can judge the morality of that contract, or even Rawls's hypothetical contract, by appealing to preexisting principles that do not depend on a hypothetical or actual agreement for their validity. In other words, once we become aware of an agreement, hypothetical or actual, we can always ask the question, "Is it fair and is it just?" That question cannot be answered by appealing to a more primitive contract, for we can simply ask the question again. In the end, principles of morality are the means by which we assess the moral justification of contracts; they are not derived from contracts.[52]

Aristotelian Final Causes

The view that all living organisms have intrinsic purposes has its origins in Aristotle's writings. Human beings, for example, have a certain end or purpose, and if human beings live consistently with that end, such practice results in virtue and goodness. A human being that lives well becomes more personally virtuous. Moreover, human beings are social beings who participate in families, communities, villages, and cities. These entities are natural, for they are the result of human nature and its flourishing. And in turn, these entities, if they are functioning well, enhance the likelihood of increasing personal virtue, for the opportunity for virtue increases when one finds support for such practice by the communities in which one resides. Thus, human beings and their social structures have a symbiotic relationship.

Given the Mormon emphasis on family and community, the Aristotelian perspective is no doubt very attractive. However, Aristotle's ethics cannot be divorced from his metaphysics. For Aristotle the reason living organisms have final causes is because there was a First Cause that made them that way. That is, Aristotle understood that the notion of "purpose" is incoherent without a Purposer.[53] But in the LDS worldview, the universe has no Purposer, no Mind behind it. In fact, Thomas Aquinas amended Aristotle's view and with it developed an argument for the existence of the God of classical theism.[54] Thus, if the Latter-day Saints were to embrace the Aristotelian option, they would be hard pressed to maintain their traditional doctrine of God.

Emergent Moral Properties

A final alternative that might be attractive to Mormons, given their proclivity toward materialism, is the view that moral properties emerge and supervene natural (or material) entities. This is embraced by some philosophical naturalists who believe that all that exists, including emergent properties and the apparent design of the universe, are the result of the collisions of unguided matter. But this would be an odd view for the Latter-day Saints to embrace, for if there is one thing we can truly say about the LDS worldview, it is that it pictures the universe as a highly complex interaction of *purposeful* entities, principles, and laws teeming with design. So if moral properties emerge at all in the LDS universe, they do so because they are supposed to do so, not because matter collided in a way that accidentally resulted in moral properties. But such a designed universe, as design theorists point out (see note 53), demands an Intelligence to explain it. If that is the case, then the grounding and existence of such a universe, including its moral properties, must be in a Being who looks very much like the God of classical theism.

The well-known atheist philosopher J. L. Mackie understood this, and that is why he rejected the view that moral properties are emergent supervenient properties:

> If we adopted moral objectivism, we should have to regard the relations of supervenience which connect values and obligations with the natural grounds as synthetic; they would then be in principle something that a god might conceivably create; and since they would otherwise be a very odd sort of thing, the admitting of them would be an inductive ground for admitting also a god to create them. *There would be something here in need of explanation, and a being with the power to create what lies outside the bounds of natural plausibility or even possibility might well be the explanation we require.* Moral values, their objectivity and their supervenience, would be a continuing miracle. . . *a constant intrusion into the natural world.* [55]

Mormons, of course, believe in God. But they do not believe in the type of God Mackie specifically had in mind that could adequately account for morality (the God of classical theism). So the Latter-day Saints are in exactly the same position as the philosophical naturalist, except that they are committed to a type of objective morality and do not have the luxury, like the naturalist has, of abandoning this moral view and embracing some form of relativistic, subjectivist, or evolutionary ethics.

The above options seem to be the most viable alternatives to classical Christian theism that Mormons could appeal to, but they all fail. Of course, there are other philosophical options that have been put forth by philosophical naturalists to ground objective morality in a worldview that, like Mormonism, lacks the resources of classical Christian theism. Mormons could try to latch on to some of these attempts, but it is unlikely that they will succeed in grounding the kind of morality Mormon discourse presupposes, for many of these alternatives have been shown to reduce to some version or other of relativism, arbitrariness, or incoherence. Many also redefine, sometimes radically, what is moral or immoral or what it means to say that we have moral obligations.[56] Since Mormons have not, to date, advocated any of these, there is no need to address them here.

Conclusion

The purpose of this essay was to explore the question of whether the LDS worldview, in comparison to the classical Christian worldview, can adequately ground the moral law. The LDS God is one who has duties to obey an immaterial and perfect moral law that is issued from no mind but serves as the basis for the progress of a material universe that, ironically, has no metaphysical place for the moral law. The classical Christian God is a being who is necessarily good, and because he has the authority to do so, issues moral commands based on the moral law grounded in his nature.

Ironically, the Book of Mormon seems to point us in the same direction, a direction inconsistent with the mainstream of LDS theology. For example, 2 Nephi 2:13 reads:

> And if ye shall say there is no law, ye shall also say there is no sin. If ye shall say there is no sin, ye shall also say there is no righteousness. And if there be no righteousness there be no happiness. And if there be no righteousness nor happiness there be no punishment nor misery. And if these things are not there is no God. And if there is no God we are not, neither the earth; for there could have been no creation of things.

It seems, then, that the source of morality could not be a contingent being, one whose existence and moral authority are dependent on something outside itself. For in order to be *the ground* of morality, a being must not receive its existence and moral authority from another, for that other being, if it is not contingent, would then be the ground of morality. That is, a being capable of ceasing to exist or of not being good could not be the ground of morality. Second, the source of morality must be the sort of being who has the moral authority to enforce universal moral norms. Thus, if moral laws are known nonmaterial realities that are a form of communication for which we have a sense of incumbency and feel painful guilt when we violate them, it seems that the moral law must have a personal, eternal, transcendent, and perfect source. Such a being looks much like the God of classical Christianity and not much like the God of traditional Mormon thought.

At the beginning of the groundbreaking work he coauthored with Craig Blomberg, *How Wide the Divide?* Stephen Robinson relates the following story:

> I was a graduate student at Duke University when our LDS bishop, along with other local ministers, received an invitation to attend a meeting of a

citizens' committee combating the growth of adult bookstores and movie houses in our area. However, when LDS representatives actually showed up at the meeting, they were asked to leave because some of the Evangelical ministers threatened to walk out if Mormons were involved. So we withdrew, but the lesson was not lost on us—some Evangelicals oppose Mormons more vehemently than they oppose pornography.[57]

As an evangelical and a licensed minister, I am appalled by such behavior by my fellow evangelicals. Working with people from diverse religious backgrounds as citizens on issues of common moral concern is not the same as conceding theological ground to them.[58] In fact, as we have seen in this essay, common moral concern may work as a catalyst for deeper moral and theological reflection, reflection that classical Christians like C.S. Lewis have argued leads to the God of classical Christianity. My encouragement to the evangelical community is that they be willing to work with Latter-day Saints and others with whom we disagree theologically, as "co-belligerents" (to use Francis Shaeffer's term) in tackling the moral issues confronting our society in the twenty-first century. My encouragement to the LDS community is that they allow their correct beliefs about the reality of objective moral values to lead them to embrace a view of God that can adequately ground those values, a view like the God of the classical Christian tradition.[59]

THE ABSURDITIES
OF MORMON MATERIALISM
A Reply to the Neglected Orson Pratt

J. P. MORELAND

J. P. Moreland is Distinguished Professor of Philosophy at Talbot School of Theology, Biola University. Moreland earned a B.S. in chemistry from the University of Missouri, a Th.M. in theology from Dallas Theological Seminary, an M.A. in philosophy from the University of California at Riverside, and a Ph.D. in philosophy from the University of Southern California. Dr. Moreland is the author of several books, including *Christianity and the Nature of Science* (Baker), *Love Your God with All Your Mind* (NavPress), *Scaling the Secular City* (Baker), and (with Scott Rae) *Body and Soul: Human Nature and the Crisis in Ethics* (InterVarsity). He is the editor of *The Creation Hypothesis* (InterVarsity) and coeditor of *Christian Perspectives on Being Human: A Multidisciplinary Approach* (Baker), *Naturalism: A Critical Analysis* (Routledge), and *Three Views on Creation and Evolution* (Zondervan). He has published in numerous academic journals, including *American*

Philosophical Quarterly, Australasian Journal of Philosophy, Faith and Philosophy, International Philosophical Quarterly, Philosophy and Phenomenological Research, Philosophia Christi, Process Studies, Religious Studies, and *Southern Journal of Philosophy.*

The great theistic religions of historic Christianity, Judaism, and Islam differ on many things, but one thing they share in common is a rejection of a physicalist ontology. These theistic religions all agree in affirming that God is a spirit and not a physical object. Moreover, while there has been a recent emergence of Christian physicalism regarding the constitution of human persons, nevertheless, the vast majority of Christian thinkers in the history of the church have held to a dualistic anthropology in at least this sense: a human being is a unity of two distinct entities—a physical body and immaterial soul. The immaterial human soul, while not by nature immortal, is nevertheless capable of entering an intermediate disembodied state upon death, however incomplete and unnatural this state may be, and of eventually being reunited with a resurrected body.[1] Thus, theologian H. D. Lewis was correct when he observed: "Throughout the centuries Christians have believed that each human person consists in a soul and body; that the soul survived the death of the body; and that its future life will be immortal."[2]

Mormon theology is at odds with this immaterial metaphysic with regard to both God and human persons. Thus, Mormon thinker Sterling M. McMurrin asserts that Joseph Smith's general conception of reality is "essentially pluralistic and materialistic."[3] And he notes that on the Mormon view, "there is no immaterial substance and . . . spiritual entities are not less material than physical objects."[4] Finally, in Doctrine and Covenants 131:7–8 we read: "There is no such thing as immaterial matter [i.e., immaterial substance].[5] All spirit is matter, but it is more fine or pure, and can only be discerned by purer eyes. We cannot see it, but when our bodies are purified we shall see that it is all matter."

In the earliest days of Mormonism, Orson Pratt (1811–81) was among the most prolific and influential of the LDS apologists and apostles. Pratt, one of the original twelve apostles of the LDS Church, was so influential in Mormon thinking that he has been called the "Paul of Mormonism" and is acknowledged as having unrivaled intellectual stature in the first one hundred years of Mormonism.[6] To be sure, Pratt's writings are not theologically normative for Mormon thought, and indeed, some of his views are considered heretical. One of Pratt's writings, *The Holy Spirit,* published in 1856, caused considerable controversy within Mormonism and was condemned by Brigham Young as heretical speculation. Moreover, current Mormon thinkers set aside or modify certain elements in Pratt's ideology when they judge this to be necessary, even in areas of general agreement. For example, speaking of Pratt's ideas about materialism, McMurrin flatly asserts that "Pratt's ideas, published around 1850, are severely conditioned by the now outmoded Newtonian concepts of absolute space and time and by the early pre-Rutherford concept of atoms."[7]

Nevertheless, it still remains the case that Pratt's defense of Mormon materialism and his critique of immaterialism, especially with regard to the ontology of human persons, is among the most developed of any LDS thinker on this topic. As Mormon writer Max Nolan put it, Pratt's materialism was in stark contrast to the classic Newtonian view of matter as inert and purely mechanical, and on this point, Nolan acknowledges, Pratt accurately represents certain important texts in Doctrine and Covenants.[8] Nolan points out that Pratt's attempt to philosophically explicate the Mormon physicalist ontology remains among the most sustained attempts available and provides a continuing challenge to Mormon thinkers to develop a distinctively Mormon physicalist religious system.[9]

With this in mind, my main purpose is to analyze and critique Orson Pratt's defense of Mormon materialism regarding human persons. Secondarily, I address, albeit quite briefly, attempts to develop anthropological materialism in the current intellectual setting and offer some advice to evangelical Christians who are advocating forms of Christian physicalism. In addressing Pratt's materialism, I concentrate my efforts on his 1849 publication *The Absurdities of Immaterialism.* Written in part as a response to a critique of Mormon physicalism by British minister T. W. P. Taylder,[10] *The Absurdities of Immaterialism* is, in the words of contemporary Mormon scholar David J. Whittaker, "considered his [Pratt's] most important philosophical treatise."[11]

Before turning to Pratt's case for materialism, it may be useful to state one lesson to be derived from our study before we delve into the details. For those of us who serve as Christian teachers, ministers, evangelists, apologists, or lay leaders, it is not enough in dispatching our duties simply to cite, exposit, or in some other way present the words of Holy Scripture. Throughout its history, the great leaders in the church, beginning with the Apostle

Paul himself, have always combined Scripture and Right Reason, as it used to be called. As John Wesley put it, "Ought not a Minister to have, First, a good understanding, a clear apprehension, a sound judgment, and a capacity of reasoning with some closeness?"[12] Among other things, this has meant that a Christian leader needs to familiarize him- or herself with carefully crafted ideas from sources outside Scripture in order to serve adequately. More specifically, the Christian leader needs to have at least some knowledge of philosophy. To his credit, Orson Pratt sought to integrate science and philosophy into his exposition and defense of Mormon theology. In an age of anti-intellectualism, evangelical teachers and leaders need to be reminded that they should do no less.

An Exposition of Pratt's Materialism

Pratt's General Ontology

Four aspects of Pratt's general ontology are central for understanding his theological/philosophical anthropology: his views of existence; of space, time, and matter; of substance; and of property.[13] According to Pratt, *to exist* is to be located in absolute space and time (10). More specifically, it is to be spatially extended, to have temporal location, and to be divisible into separable parts (11). Elsewhere, Pratt claims that solidity is either existence itself or at least something associated with existence (16). Solidity is the essence and only essence in existence, and all substances have this as their essence (16). By "solidity," Pratt means completely filling a certain amount of space. Solidity is not a property added to something; rather, it is the very essence of the thing itself.[14] All other properties belong to solidity (16–17). Thus, love and joy are different states of solidity (17). Nothingness is that which has no relationship to space and time (11). An unextended individual with no separable parts cannot exist. Thus, Pratt argues that since immaterial substances/spirits (allegedly) have no spatial location, then they have no magnitude, and therefore they amount to mere unextended points, which for him is the same thing as not existing at all. Moreover, since an immaterial spirit is unextended, then it is without parts and is not divisible, and therefore it is nothing at all (10).

Pratt's views of *space, time,* and *matter* are clearly Newtonian. For him, space is boundless and time is endless, and each is absolute in Newton's sense (1). Space is essential to all existence and is just extension itself. As such, space is divisible. Similarly, time is essential to the existence of substances

(10). Pratt's views of matter will become clearer when we look at his notion of spirit matter below. But for now it should be pointed out that for Pratt all matter has bulk (i.e., is extended) and solidity (6). Material objects are composed of corpuscles of matter, and there are ultimate particles of matter incapable of further division (6). Gross matter (ordinary matter that makes up the tangible cosmos) consists of tiny corpuscles that cannot be created or destroyed, that have existed infinitely long, and that are characterized by primary qualities like extension, location, being in motion or at rest, resistance to inertial change, and capability of division (6, 8, 10, 13). Particles of gross matter are unintelligent substances whose behavior is mechanistic and deterministic and which can be organized into different aggregates to compose various macro-objects (7–8).

According to Pratt's atomistic ontology, in the most genuine sense, a *substance* is an ultimate corpuscle of matter as described above; but in a derived sense, other substances are aggregates composed of material substances (6). All substances have the same essence (solidity), all substances are material, and spirit is a certain type of matter (29).

Finally, Pratt believes in the existence of properties or attributes such as solidity, love, and so forth (5, 19, 20). Moreover, Pratt advocates an Aristotelian view of properties according to which properties can exist only if they belong to a substance (28). Thus, if there were no red objects, redness itself would not exist. Moreover, Pratt denies the existence of emergent properties. On his view, wholes do not have properties that are not in each part of those wholes (6, 19). So if an aggregate of material substances is intelligent, that can only be because each part of the aggregate has the property of intelligence (6–7). Lastly, Pratt seems to think that all properties are capable of quantification (16–18); that is, all properties, for example, having size, can be quantified as being greater or lesser (something can have the attribute of size to a greater or lesser degree). He also seems to think that all attributes besides extension (e.g., love, joyfulness) are just attributes of solidity (17). Pratt may have thought that properties themselves are composed of parts. This may be what he meant when he said that numbers themselves are composed of fractional parts (18), but I leave the matter open because it could be that Pratt thought of numbers as material substances and not as attributes.

Pratt on Spirit and Immaterial Substance

In his approach to characterizing matter and spirit, Pratt adopts a methodology according to which one starts with a definition of matter and spirit. On this point, Pratt was in agreement with his antagonist, the Reverend Taylder. According to Taylder, an immaterial substance/spirit is to be defined as something that exists that "is *not matter* and is evidently *distinct* from matter, which is *not dependent* on matter for its existence, and which possesses properties and qualities *entirely different* from those possessed by matter" (2).[15] Pratt thinks that something like this is what the immaterialist needs to defend the reality of an immaterial spirit, but he thinks that nothing could possibly exist that was *entirely different* from matter. As far as I can tell, his reasons for this are threefold. First, he thinks that if spirit is entirely different from matter, specifically, if it is unextended and without spatial location, then causal interaction between spirit and body—an interaction that Pratt claims requires both interacting entities to have spatial extension and location—becomes impossible, and this is absurd (15). Second, Pratt uses an epistemological test of imaginability to judge the intelligibility of some entity existing or not existing. If something cannot be pictured or imaged by way of sensation, then it does not exist, and, says Pratt, we simply cannot imagine an unextended, unlocated spirit with no parts (13). Finally, the most important reason Pratt rejects the reality of immaterial spirits is his view of existence noted above. If, indeed, existence itself requires extension, location, and solidity, then it follows trivially that a spirit, insofar as it lacks these, does not exist.

Rejecting Taylder's claim that material and immaterial substances must have no properties in common, Pratt adopts a different approach to defining these terms. He claims that all one needs to do to distinguish matter from spirit is to show that they have some differences, not that they need to be entirely different. But, Pratt argues, given that two substances have some different properties, it does not follow that one is material and the other is not. For example, iron, gold, and a host of other substances have some properties that differ from the others, but all this shows is that they are all different kinds of matter (2–3, 29). Similarly, from the fact that spirit has some properties that differ from other material substances, it only follows that spirit is a certain type of matter.

Perhaps following John Locke, Pratt thought that the notion of "thinking matter" is clearly coherent, possible, and, in fact, actual (3).[16] As already noted, just as the properties of stone and wood are different, yet each is still a material substance, so it is with gross and spirit matter. From the fact that mental properties—for example, the powers of thought, feeling, and free choice—characterize spirit and not unintelligent matter, it only follows that spirits are certain kinds of material substances, not that they are immaterial ones.

What is the difference between gross and spirit matter? Minimally, spirit matter is more refined and purer than gross matter. As Doctrine and Covenants 131:7 says, "There is no such thing as immaterial matter. All spirit is matter, but it is more fine or pure, and can only be discerned by purer eyes." In addition to this, Pratt claims that spirit matter is free, intelligent, and teleological; whereas gross matter is determined, unintelligent, and mechanistic and that spirit matter has other properties of consciousness, for example, powers of perception (3, 4, 6).

As will be clarified in more detail later, whenever a thinker allows for the possibility that there is such a thing as thinking matter and uses mental properties to characterize matter, if that thinker is not careful, he or she will have no way to give content to the notion of immaterial spirit and will come perilously close to using "spirit matter" or "thinking matter" as just another term for what dualists mean by "immaterial spirit." Indeed, in one place Pratt says that the only difference between Taylder's notion of an immaterial self or soul and his own conception of an atom of spirit matter is the name each uses (7). However, Pratt does not leave the issue there. He offers a further characterization of spirit matter that clearly distinguishes it from what dualists have traditionally meant by soul or spirit. According to Pratt, spirit matter qua matter has the essential features of matter: extension and location, solidity, and so forth. For Pratt, "mind is an extended material substance" (15). Finally, no two particles of spirit or gross matter may occupy the same place at the same time (16).

Pratt's Philosophical/Theological Depiction of the Human Person

Given all that has been presented, a certain picture of human persons emerges. Put briefly, a human person is a combination of a fleshly body composed of corpuscles of gross matter, and a spirit body composed of corpuscles of spirit matter. Personal identity is the result, not of sameness of changeable fleshly body, but of the unchangeable substance called "spirit" (i.e., spirit body), which thinks, feels, reasons, and so forth (8). The spirit, or spirit body, preexists its entrance in the fleshly body and departs that body at death. It can condense and has elastic properties, and—very much like particulate notions of the ether—it is in the body in a straightforwardly spatial sense: the various particles of spirit matter occupy the porous places between the various particles of a person's fleshly body (5, 12, 15, 23).

Given that the human person qua spirit is a composite aggregate of particles of spirit matter, what does Pratt make of the unity of the self at and through time? Put briefly, he says that the unity of persons is like the unity of the parts of an iron bar subject to magnetism (22). To expand, Pratt addresses an argument for an immaterial soul based on the unity of the self discovered in self-consciousness: in self-awareness, we are conscious of being one and not many, and therefore we must be without separable parts that, if true, would turn us into a many—an aggregate. If materialism were true, then the self would be extended, divisible, and composed of separable parts. But since we know otherwise in self-awareness, materialism is false; and, given that materialism and immaterialism are the two live options, immaterialism is correct.

Pratt responds by asserting that not only is unity consistent with a plurality of parts, but, more importantly, the very notion of unity *requires* a plurality of parts (18). Pratt illustrates this by claiming that a number, for example, the number three, is composed of a plurality of fractional parts. Without the notion of parts, he opines, we cannot even form the notion of unity. Pratt goes on to claim that the unity of the self is closely analogous with the unity of the solar system or of a bodily organism, each of which is composed, respectively, of a plurality of planets and molecules (18).

According to Pratt, a mental state (e.g., a specific thought) is a state of a single, individual substance with extension and parts with all the essential characteristics of matter—a spirit body. This spirit body can be divided; and indeed, the unity of the self amounts to an infinite number of parts of spirit matter all being in the same mental state at the same time. So the unity of a person's mental state—the fact that a unified person is having a single thought at a specific time—amounts to the fact that all the corpuscles of spirit matter are simultaneously in that mental state, all these parts are aware of each other, and all get into the same mental state (20). This is what the unity of the person is, and the whole mind thinking some thought consists in each part of the spirit body thinking that thought together with the others. In my view, there are tremendous problems with this view, but to his credit, Pratt insists that consciousness cannot be the result of the organization of gross physical parts (7, 18).

Finally, Pratt argues that what makes all the spirit particles constituents of the same individual is that they and only they communicate with each other:

> Were it possible for the different parts of the mind to feel and think without being able to communicate their respective feelings to each other, then

every part that thus thought and felt would be a distinct individual, as much so as if it were separated for miles from all the rest, or, as if it were a separate organization. In this case, the whole being or mind which we before termed *I* would cease its individual unity; and each part which thought and felt independently, could appropriate to itself the term *I,* and with the greatest propriety could apply the term *YOU* to every other part which thought and felt distinctly and differently from itself. It is, therefore, because all parts of the mind seem to be affected in the same way, and apparently at the same time, that it is felt to be a single individual mind. It is this, and this only, that constitutes the unity of a thinking being, and not, as the immaterialist asserts, a something "without parts." (21)

A Critique of Pratt's Materialism

It would be inappropriate to criticize Pratt for appropriating certain features of a Newtonian worldview (e.g., Newton's specific views of an atom as a corpuscle and absolute substantial views of space and time), since recent Mormon thinkers admit that these features may well be obsolete. But more importantly, since we all have to do our best to work out our ideas within the most reasonable set of beliefs available to us at the time, Pratt can hardly be faulted for doing his best in this regard. However, certain other features of Pratt's Newtonianism transcend Newtonianism per se—for example, a commitment to some form of atomism—and to the extent that these features are still relevant, they are fair game. With this in mind, I want to focus my critique on four areas of Pratt's thought.

Pratt's Theory of Existence

Plainly put, Pratt's theory of existence is question-begging and inadequate, and it employs the wrong epistemological test to decide existence claims. Pratt employs his theory of existence as a decisive rebuttal against a dualist construal of spirit, and in so doing, he begs the very question at issue. For example, when Pratt tries to show that immaterial substances *cannot* exist, he does so by arguing that since an immaterial spirit is unextended, has no spatial boundaries, and is indivisible, it turns out to be nothing at all, based on his theory of what it is to exist (10–11). But this simply begs the question against the dualist, and unless Pratt offers independent justification of his view of existence—which he fails to provide—his argument here must be judged inadequate.

More importantly, Pratt's employment of his theory of existence not only begs the question against dualists, but it is also an inadequate theory of existence. A theory of existence is an account of what existence itself is, and to be adequate, it should accomplish at least three things. First, it needs to be consistent with and explain what actually does and does not exist. Second, it needs to be consistent with and explain what could have existed but either does not exist or is not believed to exist (perhaps falsely) by the person advocating a given view of existence. For example, even though unicorns do not, in fact, exist, they could have existed. A theory of existence must be broad enough to allow for more than the reality of things that just happen to exist. Third, a theory of existence must allow for the fact that existence itself exists. To put the point differently, it must not be self-refuting. For example, if someone claims that to exist is the same thing as to be inside space and time (existence itself is being spatiotemporally located), then (on at least some views) space and time would not themselves exist, since they are not inside space and time. Whatever existence amounts to, one thing is clear—it makes a real difference in the world, and it must itself exist to make such a difference. If existence itself does not exist, then nothing else could exist in virtue of having existence.

Given these requirements, Pratt's theory of existence fails to be adequate. On Pratt's view solidity exists, but it is not itself solid; extension exists, but is not extended; being divisible is not itself divisible. It also seems bizarre to say that numbers—for example, the number two—are divisible into parts, are extended, have solidity, and are related to space and time. I cannot argue the point here, but it seems that various abstract objects exist (entities that are not located in space and time), for example, numbers and other universals, and yet they fail to satisfy Pratt's theory of existence.[17] For these reasons, Pratt's theory of existence runs amuck of criteria one and three above.

Moreover, a better theory of existence is available: existence is not a property that belongs but is the belonging of a property. Existence is the entering into the predication or exemplification relation, and in general, the following characterization of existence seems to fit the three criteria for a theory of existence: *existence is either the belonging of some property or the being belonged to by a property.* Three implications follow from this. First, if something exists, then there is at least one property that it actually has. My car exists, and it has at least one property, its being red. Moreover, if something could have existed but does not, then there would have been at least one property it would have had. If unicorns would have existed, then there would have been entities with the property of having a single horn. Finally, nothingness is the complete absence of properties. If something does not exist and is, therefore, nothing at all, then it actually has no properties.

Given this characterization of existence, there is clearly room for the existence of things that do not satisfy Pratt's theory of reality. Suppose the number two really exists. Then we can make sense of this by saying that it actually has the property of being even, even though it fails to have solidity, be divisible, and so forth. Below, the notion of an immaterial spirit will be clarified; but for now, I simply note that such a notion will be seen to fit with my theory of existence, and thus I can make clear what it means for an immaterial spirit to be real, despite Pratt's claims to the contrary.

There is a final way to see the inadequacy of Pratt's theory of existence. According to Pratt, the proper epistemological test for judging whether something exists is determining whether it can be imaged (13). Only if you can imagine something, in the sense of having a mental sense image of it, can the thing in question exist. Pratt's employment of this test would seem to imply that he believes everything, including existence itself, must be sense perceptible. This follows nicely from Pratt's theory of reality, since on that theory everything that exists should, at least in principle, be sense perceptible (given that it has extension, shape, and solidity).

But this is not a correct requirement for existence in general, though it may be useful in verifying the existence of sense perceptible things such as tables and chairs. To see this, consider the following: How is it that we know that nothing could exist and be a square circle? It is because we know something about the properties of being square and being round, and on this basis we cannot coherently conceive of something having both. Since nothing could jointly exemplify these properties, we judge that nothing of this sort could exist, and our ground is the inability to conceive coherently of the state of affairs in question. Similarly, if we were considering whether the number two exists, we would be wondering if there actually were something with the relevant properties. Since it is conceivable that something have the property of being even without being extended in space, and since the number two actually has this property, we judge that it exists and is not extended.

To conceive of something is to be able to contemplate or think about it, and as such, it includes but goes beyond imaging something. If one can image something (a red ball), then one can conceive of it, but not conversely. There are things one can conceive (being human, timelessness, the laws of logic) that one cannot sensuously image.

Coherent conceivability is not an infallible test for existence. At first glance, one may think there could be such a thing as a fastest runner or a largest rock because it seems to be coherently conceivable. But on further reflection, we can correct our previous conception of possibility with a more reflective conception of the situation. Once we understand the properties of being fastest and being a runner, it becomes clear that for any rate of speed, a runner could go a bit faster; similarly, with the notion of a largest rock, one could always add an ounce to any rock. In this case we see that (1) conceivability is not an infallible test for existence; and (2) correcting inaccurate uses of conceivability involves insights into the relevant properties and the things that (allegedly) have them and therefore implicitly employs *the having of a property* as a notion of existence itself.

I wish to note two applications of this view of existence. First, existence itself is not sense perceptible, though some things that have it—for example, ordinary perceptual objects such as chairs—are sense perceptible because they exist and have a certain set of attributes (shape, color, etc.). For Pratt, existence itself and all existing things are sense perceptible, and Pratt is wrong about this. Second, my theory of existence opens up a clear sense in which entities such as abstract objects and immaterial spirits could exist and yet fail to satisfy Pratt's notion of existence. The possible existence or reality of such entities may not be imaginable, but they are coherently conceivable.

Before moving to the next area of critique, I cannot resist one more point. Pratt's discussion of existence includes an affirmation of an inconsistent triad—three propositions that cannot all be true: (1) Everything that exists is material. (2) Matter is divisible. (3) There are ultimate, indivisible particles of matter. Taken together, propositions (1) and (2) imply that everything that exists is material and divisible, and (3) implies that there is something that exists, is material, and is not divisible. The most reasonable move for Pratt, and indeed the view most consistent with his general view of reality, is to deny (3). As we will see below, however, this means that the self qua material object is divisible, and there are reasons to think that this is not so.

Pratt's Inadequate Treatment of Immaterial Substance

Among other things, Pratt's approach to immaterial substances exhibits two serious flaws: he employs "immaterial" as an infimae species and not as a genus, and he gives an inadequate treatment of the notion of an immaterial spirit, failing to adequately distinguish it from spirit matter.

To understand the first charge, we need to get clear on the notion of a *genus* (plural: *genera*) and an *infimae species*. Things can be classified in increasingly lower or higher categories. For example, we may classify the color of a fire engine in this way: a sense perceptible property, a color property, redness, a very specific shade of redness. Similarly, we may classify a dog as an animal, a mammal, a canine, a dog. An *infimae species* is a terminus point in a hierarchy of classification, the lowest level of classification beyond which there is no other. In our examples, being a specific shade of red and being a dog are infimae species. For our purposes, all the higher levels may be called genera. Thus, being a mammal or being a color property are genera.

In his debate with Taylder, Pratt was correct in his claim that immaterial substances, if such there be, could not be entirely different from matter. Assuming, for the sake of argument, that immaterial and material substances exist, both would be self-identical, both would have the property of being dependent on God, both would be substances, both would have existence, and so forth. So there would be at least some things they would hold in common. But Pratt seems to misunderstand Taylder's point, and in any case he errs in applying this insight. When Taylder says that spirit "possesses properties entirely different from matter," I do not think he means that spiritual and material substances have no properties whatever in common. Rather, I think he means, or at least he should have meant, that "material" and "immaterial" characterize different genera for classifying substances, and thus they must have no properties in common relevant to the distinction in genera. This is not as difficult to understand as it sounds. A lizard and a dog may have some things in common—for example, each is a living thing—but the genera "being a reptile" and "being a mammal" are different, and as such, the properties that constitute each must be entirely different. The features of being a reptile and being a mammal must be different or else they would not amount to distinct, contrasting genera. From this it does not follow that individual reptiles and mammals have nothing in common (lizards and dogs are alive, gold is not).

Furthermore, given that being a reptile and being a mammal are genera, it follows that there are various kinds of reptiles and mammals, that is, various infimae species that fall under each. Similarly, if being immaterial and being material are genera, there would be various kinds of immaterial substances and material substances. Examples of the former may be being a number, a mathematical point, an angel, God, a human spirit, and various kinds of animal souls. Examples of the latter are being gold, sodium, or iron.

Unfortunately, whereas Taylder correctly uses "immaterial" as a genus, Pratt seems to attack a straw man by taking it to be an infimae species. Pratt claims that just because two substances have different properties, it does not follow that one is material and one is not. So far so good. From the fact that one animal has different properties from another, it does not follow that one is a mammal and the other is not. One could be a dog and the other a cat, though it still might be the case that one is a dog and the other is a lizard.

But when Pratt gives illustrations of his claim, he selects different infimae species under the genus "material substance." For example, he claims that just because the properties of stone and wood, or iron and gold are different, it does not follow that they are not all material. From this, it would seem that he likens "being immaterial" to "being gold" or "being iron," and the latter are infimae species. For Pratt, being material is the genus; and being spirit, being gold, being iron are all different kinds of material substances. In my view, Pratt fails to give adequate arguments for this move and largely rests his case on the analogies just mentioned. But it seems to me that they fail to address Taylder's point because his arguments employ "immaterial" as a genus, and Pratt simply assumes that it is an infimae species to rebut Taylder.

Who is correct here? Is "immaterial" a genus or an infimae species under the genus "material substance"? I shall address this question after I focus on Pratt's inadequate treatment of spirit, especially his failure to distinguish it from spirit matter.

Note first that Pratt thinks that thinking matter is possible. By this he means that the various mental properties of consciousness—sensation, other forms of awareness, thought, belief, desire, volitional choices done for the sake of ends—could characterize material substances. If this is so, then granting, for the sake of argument, the reality of immaterial spirits, one cannot use mental properties to characterize the nature of a spirit, since those properties are consistent with both a spirit and a material substance. To get at the nature of spirit, one must look elsewhere. But here is where the difficulty lies.

To see the problem, let us begin with an analysis of the notion of a substance.[18] In general, a substance is a primitive, underived unity of actual and potential properties or parts at a time; it sustains absolute sameness through accidental change; and it has an essence that answers the most fundamental question, What kind of thing is this? and that grounds its membership in its infimae species. For purposes of illustration, God, an angel, a human spirit, a dog, and an atom of gold are all substances. Being red is a property and not a substance; being larger than is a relation and not a substance; being a flash of lightning is an event and not a substance.

Note that the characterization just given is a formal one; that is, it merely states necessary conditions for any thing to count as a substance without giving material content necessary to distinguish one kind of substance from another. When it comes to characterizing specific kinds of substances, it seems that there are only two things one can do: state the formal criteria, and list a set of dispositions or potentialities as the material content for a specific kind of substance. For example, a characterization of an atom of gold as a substance might go something like this: It is a primitive, underived unity of actual and potential properties or parts at a time (having the power to melt at such and such degrees, dissolving in aqua regia, having atomic number seventy-nine, which, in turn, is the potential to attract a certain number of electrons, to resist inertial changes to degree thus and so); it sustains absolute sameness through accidental change; and it has an essence (being gold) that answers the most fundamental question, What kind of thing is this? and that grounds its membership in its infimae species (the natural kind *gold*).

Note that the formal aspects of the definition of gold are the same as those for a substance in general, and the material content is listed in parentheses. Note also that the various properties listed in parentheses that give material content to "being gold" so as to distinguish it from "being iron" are dispositions or potentialities: properties that are actualized by a gold atom if certain conditions obtain (e.g., gold will dissolve in aqua regia if placed in it). Substances are more than their potentialities; indeed, it seems reasonable to say that something can have potential properties only if it has actual properties: No potentiality without actuality! Unfortunately, it is very difficult to say what the essence of a substance is without making reference to its potentialities. Thus, we say that gold is *that which* has the potential to do x, y, and z; iron is *that which* has the potential to do f, g, and h; and so on.

By way of application, it is hard if not impossible to characterize adequately a specific kind of substance without reference to the various potentialities it has by its very nature and that distinguish its essence from the essence of other kinds of substances. But now a difficulty arises for Pratt—and, indeed, for all those who think that thinking matter is possible. By taking the various potentialities for thought, feeling, sensation, and so forth to be consistent with being a material and an immaterial substance, the very notion of being a spirit is rendered vacuous—and surely this is too strong. Even if there are no spiritual substances, surely the claim that there are is intelligible and filled with content. Yet the thinking matter thesis renders empty any attempt to give content to the notion of a spirit. During the days of John Locke (who first introduced the thesis that thinking matter is possible), those who accepted the possibility of thinking matter had a terrible time giving any content to the notion of a spirit. About all they could say was that it has bare being. But this is hardly informative; and in any case, it could be used to characterize the number two or any other "immaterial" entity. Even if there happen to be no spirits, it is surely wrong to say the very notion of a human spirit or of God as a spirit is vacuous and only capable of formal characterization.

Most dualists would characterize a spirit as an immaterial (i.e., at least unextended, without solidity, and incapable of division into separable parts) substance with the formal characteristics of a substance in general and with the ultimate potentialities of sensation, emotion, thought, free action for a purpose, belief, moral awareness, and so forth. Not only does Pratt's thesis of thinking matter render the notion of an immaterial spirit vacuous, it also seems to imply that his notion of spiritual matter is just an immaterial substance by another name. Note that Pratt clearly has a dualism of spirit and gross matter. His characterization of the difference comes perilously close to the dualist distinction between material and immaterial substances. Indeed, in one place Pratt admits that his notion of an atom of spirit matter is merely a verbal difference in the name he uses in comparison with the traditional notion of an immaterial spirit (7). Such is the dilemma facing all those who think that thinking matter is possible. They, like Pratt, must find some way to distinguish thinking matter from immaterial spirit or else they offer a distinction without a difference.

Interestingly, Pratt does, in fact, offer such a distinction, but it seems to imply falsehoods regarding human persons. An atom of spirit matter has extension and solidity and is divisible, yet none of these would be applicable to an immaterial substance. Is it really true that the self has extension and solidity? I believe the answer is no. Through "introspection," we are able to know about our own mental states—what our thoughts, sensations, feelings are—and we are able to be aware of our own selves. True, one cannot have a sense impression of one's own ego, but one is still able to be aware of one's self. Indeed, it is because one can be directly aware of one's self that one is able to identify which mental states and body are his—they are the ones "attached" to one's own self, and one knows one's own self directly in a way independent of one's knowledge of one's mental states and body.

There are a number of things about ourselves of which we are aware by attending to ourselves. One is aware that he or she is unextended (one is "fully present" at each location in one's body, as Augustine claimed), and this is why one does not think of oneself as literally four-fifths of a person when one's arm is amputated. One is also aware that one is not a complex aggregate of separable parts, nor is one the sort of thing that can be composed of physical parts. Rather, one is aware of being a basic unity of inseparable faculties that sustains absolute sameness through change (one is an entity per se), and that is not capable of gradation (one cannot become two-thirds of a person). It is true that in multiple personality and split brain cases, one can be divided in the sense of functioning in a fragmented way, but this is just a loss of integration of functioning, not a literal division of the person.

In near-death experiences, people report themselves to have been disembodied. Even if these reports are false, they are both clearly intelligible (e.g., they at least might be true) and they seem to express what people know about themselves through introspection such that this knowledge serves as a ground for what they judge could or could not happen to them. In these reports, people are not aware of having bodies in any sense. Rather, they are aware of themselves as unified egos that exemplify sensations, thoughts, and so forth.

Moreover, Christians who understand the biblical teaching that God and angels are bodiless spirits also understand by direct introspection that they are like God and angels in the sense that they are spirits with the same sorts of powers God and angels have, but that they also have bodies. Moreover, the New Testament teaching on the disembodied intermediate state is intelligible in light of what they know about themselves, and it implies that humans will, and therefore can, exist temporarily without our bodies.

In 2 Corinthians 12:1–4, Paul asserts that he may actually have been disembodied. He claims that he may have been absent from *the* body, not from one of his bodies (i.e., the fleshly body). Apparently Paul did not feel a need to specify one body (the fleshly one) from another (the spirit body), since he only knows of one body, which he temporarily left behind. This is clearly the most natural way to read this text, and the burden of proof is on those who wish to interpret Paul as claiming that he was merely out of one of his bodies.[19] Surely part of the grounds for Paul's willingness to consider his complete disembodiment a real possibility were his own awareness of his nature through introspection, his recognition of his similarity to God and angels in this respect, and his knowledge of biblical teaching about a completely disembodied intermediate state.

According to Pratt, since a human person is identical to a spirit body composed of atoms of spirit matter, a human has elastic properties and is literally capable of condensing or expanding (23). But this is highly counterintuitive, and indeed the vast majority of human beings around the world would find this ridiculous unless they were indoctrinated into a system that requires it to be so. The first-person knowledge cited above explains why people would almost universally reject the notion that a person, especially one without a fleshly body, has elastic properties. One may have an expanded ego, but not in Pratt's sense! Pratt's claim that we are aggregates of spirit matter is hard to sustain in light of the evidence of first-person introspection; and in the absence of strong, overriding counterarguments, which Pratt fails to provide, the first-person evidence provides good reasons for rejecting Pratt's assertion.

By way of application, it is false to employ "immaterial" as an infimae species to claim that a spirit is a *kind* of material substance. Rather, "immaterial" is a genus, and there are various kinds of spirits—human, angelic, divine.

Pratt Confuses Properties with Events

Properties are attributes that things can exemplify. Having shape is a physical property that a material object can exemplify. The proposition *pizza is good* is a mental property, called a kind of thought that a self can exemplify. Without being too technical, an event is the occurrence of a property at a time. An apple turning red in early June, a flash of lightning at midnight, an occasion where TenElshof thinks that pizza is good after church are all events. Properties are universals, and events are particulars—namely, specific occasions involving properties. Some events are extended through space; they are composed of smaller events, and they could be divided into subevents or expanded into larger ones.[20] An example would be a flash of lightning. Other events do not seem to have these traits. The event of thinking that pizza is good does not seem to be extended through space, it has no size or shape, and it is not composed of separable subevents.

With this background in mind, we are in a position to analyze an exchange between Taylder and Pratt. According to Taylder, if the mind and its various internal states were physical, then they would be extended through space, have shape and size, be composed of smaller units, and so forth. On this supposition, argued Taylder, it would be appropriate to talk about "the twentieth part of our belief, the half of a hope, the top of memory, the corner of a fear, the north side of a doubt" (4–5; cf. 19–20). Pratt offers the following rejoinder: It is, indeed, absurd to think of thoughts and so forth in the way Taylder claims. But Taylder's argument confuses a property with a substance. Thought, hope, fear, joy, and so forth are properties, not substances. If they were substances, then they would be divisible, have extension, and so forth. In this case, the absurdities to which Taylder points would follow. But these physical traits (having extension, being divisible, etc.) should be applied only to substances and not to properties. Since thought, hope, and so forth are properties, Taylder's argument is confused, and his conclusion does not go through.

Did Pratt sufficiently rebut Taylder's argument? He did not. And in fact, it was Pratt, not Taylder, who was confused. Note carefully that Taylder's language makes it clear that he is talking about individual mental events and not mental properties. He speaks of *a* hope, *a* fear, *a* doubt. Pratt changes the subject to properties and speaks of thought, hope, fear as properties. This is significant because in addition to substances, certain physical events, such as a flash of lightning, are extended through space and are composed of smaller events such that they are divisible. Consider a brain event that occurs while one is having a thought. The event itself occurs in a specific region of the brain; it is extended, has shape and size, and as a whole event is composed of numerous smaller electrical, biochemical events in the brain and nervous system. The physical features of the brain event can be seen on a computer screen, given the right instrumentation. Now the brain event is, indeed, capable of description in Taylder's terms—it has a twentieth part, a top side, a north side, and so forth. Yet it seems absurd, as both Taylder and Pratt admit, that the thought itself has these features. What follows from this is that mental events are not physical events. By focusing on properties and not events, Pratt's rejoinder misses the mark because both material substance and at least some physical events do have the troublesome features pointed out by Taylder.

Moreover, it is at least arguably the case that Pratt's materialism blinds him to the existence of nonquantitative properties. A quantitative property—for example, size, having mass—is one that can be numerically described to a greater or lesser extent. Some properties are nondegreed altogether: there is no sense in which they can be possessed by something to a greater or lesser degree. Something either has or fails to have a nondegreed property. Examples would be being human and being even, exemplified by Dan Yim and the number two, respectively. Other properties can be possessed to a greater or lesser extent in a nonquantitative way. For example, one can have more or less love for another, not in the sense that one has twice the amount of love, but in the sense that the intensity or purity of the love grows. Neither nondegreed (being even) nor nonquantitative degreed (being love) properties is a quantitative property (having size). Pratt's materialism drives him to describe love and joy as properties of solidity. Now just as being shaped is a property of the property of being circular such that both are quantitative properties, it may well be that characterizing love and joy as properties of the property of solidity turns them into quantitative properties. If so, this would seem to be a mistake.

The Problem with Pratt's Account of Personal Identity

Recall that on Pratt's view, the unity of a person's mental state amounts to the fact that all the corpuscles of spirit matter are simultaneously in that mental state; all these parts are aware of, and can communicate with, each other; and all get into the same mental state. This is what the unity of the person is, and the whole mind thinking some thought consists in each part of the spirit body thinking that thought together. What makes all the spirit particles constituents of the same individual is that they, and only they, communicate with each other. I cannot develop a detailed critique of Pratt's view here, but I offer a precis of three responses to his depiction of the self.

First, the unity of consciousness cannot be treated as a collective unity of separate entities. There are at least two ways one may try to depict the unity of consciousness in this way. To grasp the first strategy, consider one's awareness of a complex fact, say one's own visual field consisting of awareness of several objects at once, including a number of different surface areas of each object. Now one may claim that such a unified awareness of one's visual field consists in the fact that there are a number of different (gross or spiritual) physical parts, each of which is aware only of part of, and not the whole of, the complex fact. As William Hasker has argued, this will not work, because it cannot account for the fact that there is a single, unitary awareness of the entire visual field.[21] Only a single, uncomposed mental substance can account for the unity of one's visual field or, indeed, the unity of consciousness in general.

On the other hand, one may try to depict the unity of consciousness by analogy with a group of people. We may say that the crowd at Arrowhead

Stadium is thinking about football in the sense that each and every person in the crowd is thinking about the game simultaneously. But this will not work either, since in this case, there is no single activity of thinking of football that we can ascribe to the crowd itself, over and above the thoughts of each attendee. Moreover, if there were such a single activity of the crowd taken as a whole, in some way or another composed of each attendee's thoughts, the crowd itself, taken as a whole unit, should be aware of the plurality of individual thinkings that add up to its own thought. These notions seem absurd when applied to individual human persons, yet this is precisely Pratt's model of the self.

Second, according to Pratt, a human self is real if and only if there exists a set (infinite in number!) of spirit atoms such that all and only the members of this set are aware of, and in communication with, each other and get into the same mental state at once. But it seems obvious that his analysis is neither necessary nor sufficient for the existence of a real, unified human self. For one thing, it is not necessary. A person is the same self even if he/she is currently having several different mental states, for example, simultaneously feeling pain in the toe or hunger in the stomach, thinking about stocks, listening to music, and seeing a stop sign. A multiplicity of mental states does not entail more than one self. Or, put differently, a single self can have many mental states at once. Applied to Pratt's view, even if a subgroup of one's composing mental atoms decided to shut off communication with the rest and to get into a different mental state from the others, it would not follow that the self had divided into two different selves. Yet this absurd notion that the self could so divide is entailed by Pratt's position.

Furthermore, it is not sufficient. Just because there is a group of spirit atoms that fit Pratt's analysis, it does not follow that there is one and only one human self. Suppose that all of Smith's spirit atoms were in the same mental state, say, thinking about roses. Now suppose that these spirit atoms become aware of, and communicate with, the spirit atoms that compose Jones, such that they all get into the same mental state with each of Smith's. On Pratt's view, Jones has now merged with Smith to form one self, but this seems absurd. Unified selves are not the sorts of things that can literally merge into one new self in this way.

Third, Pratt has the relationship between unity and diversity reversed. Pratt claims that diversity is metaphysically prior to unity; that is, something cannot be a unified entity unless it is composed of a diversified plurality of parts. For him the very notion of unity requires a plurality of parts. But this is backward. To see this, the very notion of a part implies some sort of unity. If some unity, say a heap of salt, can be a unity only if it contains a diversity of parts, then we are considering the parts themselves to be units of some sort. Without units, there is nothing to play the role of part to compose higher unities. It may be that some of the parts are composed of smaller parts and so forth. A heap of salt is composed of granules of salt; these are composed of other parts, and so forth. But this cannot go on forever or it generates a vicious infinite regress.

To see this, consider philosopher D. M. Armstrong's description of a vicious infinite regress. Armstrong argues that when an analysis of something contains a covert appeal to the very thing being analyzed, it generates a vicious infinite regress because the analysis does not solve anything but merely postpones a solution.[22] No advance has been made. He says that this is like a man without funds who writes checks to cover his debts, and so on, forever. Now this is exactly the sort of regress involved in Pratt's view of unity and diversity. Pratt attempts to give an analysis of unity in terms of diversity of parts: to say of some object, x, that it is a unity means that x is a plurality of parts. But this analysis contains a covert appeal to unity in the notion of a part. This can be brought out by filling out Pratt's analysis: to say of some object, x, that it is a unity means that it is a plurality of unities. These further unities (parts) are further composed of a diversity of further unities, and at no stage in the analysis is the notion of a unity analyzed away. No advance has been made, and the regress is vicious. For this and other reasons, I believe Pratt's account of personal identity must be rejected.

Concluding Remarks

To Latter-day Saints

I wish to conclude the chapter with two brief remarks. The first one is directed to Mormons who think recent developments in physicalism can be of help to them. This does not seem to be true. For one thing, some forms of current physicalism set aside genuinely mental properties/events in favor of some physicalist alternative. This does not seem consistent with Mormon theology, which seems to be committed to genuinely mental properties. Otherwise, the distinction between gross and spirit matter would seem to collapse. For another, those forms of current physicalism that allow for property/event dualism still employ a view of gross and not spirit matter to depict the self. The real issue for Mormons is the metaphysics of immaterial substance vs. spirit/matter substance, not mental properties; and current physicalism is of little help regarding this issue. Moreover, many of the points I have raised against Pratt (e.g., about the unity of the self, the problem of the intelligibility of the notion of immaterial substance, etc.) would apply with equal force to alternative versions of Mormon materialism. The burden is on Mormons to develop their views in a way that avoids these problems or else to justify a dismissal of the problems themselves, and either alternative will be a hard sell.

Joseph Smith, like Orson Pratt, appears to have mistakenly identified substance in general with material substance, with the result that "immaterial" means "without substance" and thus "without existence." Interestingly, Smith said:

> In tracing the thing to the foundation, and looking at it philosophically, we shall find a very material difference between the body and the spirit; the body is supposed to be organized matter, and the spirit by many, is thought to be immaterial, without substance. With this latter statement we should beg leave to differ, and state that the spirit is a substance; that it is material, but that it is more pure, elastic and refined matter than the body; that it existed before the body, can exist in the body; and will exist separate from the body, when the body will be mouldering in the dust; and will in the resurrection, be again united with it.[23]

It is clear that Smith equates "immaterial" with "without substance" and thus misunderstood the traditional substance dualist position. In the early nineteenth century, many skeptical attacks on Christianity included the criticism that Christianity was unscientific and false in part because of its immaterialist ontology. It seems that Smith adopted his unique materialist viewpoint as an apologetic accommodation to the skeptics rather than try to defend a very defensible traditional view. It may well be that Smith was groping for a way to express some traditional form of substance dualism that would be immune to the skeptics' criticisms but was only able to formulate a fairly crude substitute.

Happily, for Latter-day Saints who find some of my objections against Mormon materialism persuasive, or at least plausible, Smith's statement may offer them a way out. He invites us to look at the mind/body problem *philosophically*, and that is what I have attempted to do here. Perhaps an acceptable Mormon response to these issues would be to develop Smith's crude dualism along the lines of a more traditional substance dualist position, rather than seeking to advocate some contemporary version of physicalist dualism between two sorts of matter.

To Christian Physicalists

My second remark is directed to orthodox Christians who are physicalists. In Christian theology, the doctrine of the image of God presents a tight parallel between human persons and God; moreover, on this view God is a spirit and in no way a corporeal object. To their credit, Mormons are consistent in claiming that if humans are material objects, then so is God, and conversely. Orthodox Christians need to be careful in their attempts to apply material composition views or topic neutral accounts of mental states to questions about the ontology of human persons because their claims can be used to argue that God himself is physical.[24] For example, some orthodox Christians use the problem of causal interaction between mind and matter to justify anthropological physicalism, but Pratt used the same argument to justify a corporeal God.

At the end of the day, the Christian religion is dualistic regarding both God and humanity, and Pratt's attempt to show the superiority of Mormon physicalism over the absurdities of immaterialism must be judged a failure. In the next decade or so, the existence and nature of immaterial substance will be a central intellectual issue for orthodox Christian thinkers, and they should seek to be modern-day Taylders, not Pratts, however much the discussion has moved to different ground.

PART III

Mormonism and Christianity

Introductory Essay

The question of whether Mormonism should be properly considered a Christian faith is a controversial one. Latter-day Saints insist that it should be, whereas evangelical Protestants and others have often claimed that it should not. The issue of Mormonism's relationship with Christianity is not just controversial, but also more complicated than people on either side of the divide usually acknowledge. The issue is complicated further by Mormonism's claim to be not simply a Christian denomination but a unique restoration of early Christianity. It is claimed that the doctrines of the Latter-day Saints are those of the earliest Christians and that Mormonism is the most pristine form of Christianity there is.

One important area in which LDS scholars claim that Mormonism restores lost ancient Christian teaching is on the nature and number of God. Whereas Catholics, Protestants, Orthodox, and Anabaptists all profess a monotheistic faith, LDS scholars argue that the earliest Christians did not. To the contrary, it has been argued that the earliest Christians and their ancient Jewish predecessors believed in a plurality of G/gods as the Latter-day Saints have historically affirmed. New Testament scholar Paul Owen tackles the issues related to this argument in chapter 8 and argues that the ancient Jews and earliest Christians were, indeed, monotheists.

Owen begins by discussing the Old Testament and intertestamental backgrounds of New Testament monotheism. He shows that in the Old Testament God is viewed as unique in his being, creator of all, and sovereign over all things. Some have objected that the ancient Jews were not interested in such "philosophical" issues as whether or not there is one unique God and have argued that passages that speak of the Angel of the Lord and the divine council prove that the ancient Jews were not strict monotheists. Owen answers each of these objections and then shows that Old Testament monotheism continued to be affirmed in the intertestamental period.

Owen then moves on to the New Testament data. There he argues that the earliest Christians reaffirmed the monotheism of the Old Testament, but they did so in a uniquely Trinitarian manner. The New Testament writers continued to view God as unique in his being, creator of all, and sovereign. However, in response to the incarnation of Jesus, they included Jesus and the Holy Spirit within that unique identity. Owen shows that Trinitarian theology is not a late development tacked on to the New Testament or something imposed by later church fathers unduly influenced by Greek philosophy. To the contrary, the New Testament authors themselves seem to presuppose a Trinitarian understanding of God's identity, not merely in individual proof texts but in the very foundations and structure of their theology.

Having thus argued for monotheism in the Old Testament, intertestamental period, and the New Testament, the third part of Owen's essay consists of responses to three scholars who have argued for conclusions opposite his own. Two of these scholars, Peter Hayman and Margaret Barker, are not Latter-day Saints, but their work is often appealed to by Mormons. Owen shows that Hayman and Barker's works are flawed in several respects and that their handling of texts is sometimes highly irresponsible. This is followed by a critique of a recent essay by LDS scholar Daniel C. Peterson.

If the monotheistic view of God as the absolute creator of the universe is at the heart of biblical Christian faith, as the authors of this book contend, then Mormonism's repudiation of that belief seriously calls into question its claim to be Christian. Other aspects of LDS doctrine also call this claim into question. Space did not permit discussion of the controversial question of Mormonism's relationship to Christianity in the landmark book *How Wide the Divide? A Mormon and an Evangelical in Conversation* (InterVarsity), which Craig Blomberg coauthored with LDS scholar Stephen E. Robinson. Some on both the LDS and evangelical side interpreted the book's silence on the subject to mean that Blomberg endorses the LDS claim. In chapter 9, Craig Blomberg addresses this question with great sensitivity and respect.

Blomberg states that he has "no desire to see the Latter-day Saints or any other professing Christian group as a whole or any individual within it remain outside the fold of true Christianity." He explains that from an evangelical or any other orthodox Christian perspective, the real difficulty is finding a *meaningful* way to include Mormonism within Christianity. He seeks to do this by asking whether Mormonism might be considered within the stream of historic Christianity, whether it might be considered a restoration of Christianity, and whether it might perhaps be thought of as a new form of Christianity. He concludes that as an institution or system of thought Mormonism cannot be meaningfully considered Christian in any of these senses. He then addresses the distinct question of whether individual Latter-day Saints might be considered Christians in the biblical sense of "being saved" or "converted." Here, he notes, a variety of factors must be taken into consideration. Depending on the circumstances, different answers may need to be given. In general, however, he does not feel that any individual should be considered a Christian based solely on his or her affirmation of the totality of Mormon doctrine. Blomberg concludes his chapter by stating that it is his fervent prayer that, through whatever means God should use, he will not always have to come to these conclusions. His prayer echoes our own.

8

MONOTHEISM, MORMONISM, AND THE NEW TESTAMENT WITNESS

PAUL OWEN

Paul Owen is Assistant Professor of Bible and Religion at Montreat College in North Carolina. He earned a B.A. in biblical languages from LIFE Bible College; an M.A. in New Testament from Talbot School of Theology; and a Ph.D. in New Testament language, literature, and theology from the University of Edinburgh, Scotland. Dr. Owen has published significant articles on Mormonism in *Trinity Journal, FARMS Review of Books* (an LDS publication), and *Element: An E-Journal of Mormon Philosophy and Theology*. His articles on other subjects have appeared in *Calvin Theological Journal* and *Journal for the Study of the New Testament*.

Any Christian who has engaged in religious discussions with members of the Church of Jesus Christ of Latter-day Saints knows that "monotheism" is a topic that (if discussed) is likely to reveal fundamental differences of opinion. To put it simply, Christians believe that God is one, whereas the Latter-day Saints believe that God is more than one.[1] It is not at all difficult to find quotes from LDS literature that make this point rather clearly. Joseph Smith is reported to have said in a sermon preached on June 16, 1844: "I will preach on the plurality of Gods. I have selected this text for that express purpose. I wish to declare I have always and in all congregations when I have preached on the subject of the Deity, it has been the plurality of Gods [that was preached]."[2]

That seems rather straightforward, and it is not difficult to find modern LDS writers saying pretty much the same thing. In this essay I would like to do the following. First, I will argue that the religion represented in the Old Testament is monotheistic. Second, I will show that this monotheistic religion was maintained in the period subsequent to the return from Babylonian exile. Third, I will demonstrate that this monotheistic outlook is shared by the New Testament writers, who nonetheless included Jesus Christ and the Holy Spirit alongside the Father in their doctrine and worship of God. Fourth, I will interact with two examples of non-LDS biblical scholars (Peter Hayman and Margaret Barker) whose research has been cited in support of LDS views regarding ancient Jewish monotheism (or lack thereof). Finally, I will interact with LDS scholar Daniel Peterson's attempt to argue that ancient Jews and Christians were something other than exclusive monotheists.

The Old Testament Background of New Testament Monotheism

I contend that the religion of the Old Testament was explicitly monotheistic and that this monotheistic outlook was inherited by Jesus and the apostles. In order to support this claim, it is necessary to define what I mean by "monotheistic" and to distinguish *monotheism* from the terms *polytheism* and *henotheism/monolatry*. My definition of Jewish monotheism is as follows: Jewish monotheism is the ancient belief that the finite order exists because of the creating and sustaining will of one unique and supremely powerful personal Being, who has revealed himself to the nation of Israel and demands universal worship and devotion.[3] Polytheism I take to be the belief in and worship of a plurality of gods, even if these gods are believed to be emanations of a supreme High God.[4] Henotheism/monolatry I take to be the acknowledgment that many ontologically comparable gods exist, although a decision has been made to worship only one God.[5]

The religion of the Old Testament is neither polytheistic nor henotheistic but is monotheistic. According to the definition set forth above, this involves at least three claims: (1) God is unique in his being; (2) God is the Creator of all things; (3) and God is sovereign over all that he has created.

Behold Your God—Unique in His Being

First of all, God is unique in his being. This means that—although God is not the only heavenly being—due to his unique identity he is the only being to whom worship is appropriately offered. Larry Hurtado notes that in ancient Jewish religion, "there is a concern to assert God's *uniqueness,* which is characteristically expressed by contrasting God with the other deities familiar to ancient Jews in the larger religious environment.... It is important to note that this concern for God's uniqueness also comes to expression in a contrast between God and his loyal heavenly retinue, the angels. For example, angels can be distinguished as created beings from God who is uncreated."[6]

Richard Bauckham expresses the point with admirable clarity:

> The typical Hellenistic view was that worship is a matter of degree because divinity is a matter of degree. Lesser divinities are worthy of appropriate degrees of worship. Philosophical monotheists, who held that all other divine beings ultimately derive from the One, nevertheless held the derived divinity of lesser divine beings to be appropriately acknowledged in cultic worship. The notion of a hierarchy or spectrum of divinity stretching from the one God down through the gods of the heavenly bodies, the daemons of the atmosphere and the earth, to those humans who were regarded as divine or deified, was pervasive in all non-Jewish religion and religious thought, and inseparable from the plurality of cultic practices in honor of a wide variety of divinities. Jews understood their practice of monolatry to be justified, indeed required, because the unique identity of YHWH was so understood as to place him, not merely at the summit of a hierarchy of divinity, but in an absolutely unique category, beyond comparison with anything else. Worship was the recognition of this unique incomparability of the one God.[7]

This relationship between God's incomparability and the demand of exclusive worship is illustrated in Deuteronomy 6:4–5: "Hear, O Israel: The LORD our God, the LORD is one. Love the LORD your God with all your heart and with all your soul and with all your strength." The Jewish Shema grounds Israel's exclusive devotion to Yahweh in a statement regarding God's unique identity. Hence, a concern is already evident to guard Yahweh's unique identity, not merely to warn against the practice of worshiping other gods. As Adela Yarbro Collins acknowledges: "The philosophical or theological issue *was* addressed by the authors and editors of the Deuteronomic literature. . . . The Deuteronomic reform was apparently not only a matter of where and how the God of Israel should be worshipped, but also a matter of *the divine nature*."[8]

Collins presumably takes the book of Deuteronomy to reflect the views of the monotheistic "reformation" alluded to in 2 Kings 22–23. Some biblical scholars have held that the books of Deuteronomy, Joshua, Judges, 1–2 Samuel, and 1–2 Kings are the work of an editor (or editors) working in the time of the exile.[9] Hence, the strong monotheism of the book of Deuteronomy could be explained as a novelty that was not dominant in Israelite religion before the time of the Babylonian exile. However, I am not persuaded by this hypothesis. It is, of course, possible that the book of Deuteronomy underwent editing by later scribes, but there are good reasons for maintaining that the substance of Deuteronomy goes back to the time of Moses himself (fifteenth or thirteenth century B.C.).[10] In any case, Mormons cannot consistently appeal to scholars who would explain the monotheism of Deuteronomy by appealing to a later exilic editor.[11] The Book of Mormon itself plainly indicates that Deuteronomy was written prior to the time of the exile (1 Nephi 5:11; 3 Nephi 20:23).[12]

But does Deuteronomy 6:4 actually support a monotheistic outlook? Some would argue that this verse only supports a henotheistic or monarchistic outlook, in which Israel is instructed to worship Yahweh alone without denying that other ontologically comparable gods exist.[13] Although this may be the politically correct position to take in the current scholarly climate, it substitutes hypothetical and speculative reconstructions of Israel's religious history for the words of the biblical text. As C. J. Labuschagne points out, the Hebrew word for "one" *(echad)* in Deuteronomy 6:4 refers to "somebody who has no family, and, applied to Yahweh, this means that He does not belong to any family of gods. This aspect distinguishes him from all other gods. Furthermore the confession that Yahweh is a Single One was directed against the concept of divine families common to many pagan religions."[14]

Other statements within the book of Deuteronomy also leave us in no doubt as to how 6:4 should be understood: "You were shown these things so that you might know that the LORD is God; besides him there is no other" (Deut 4:35). "Acknowledge and take to heart this day that the LORD is God in heaven above and on the earth below. There is no other" (4:39). "See now that I myself am He! There is no god besides me. I put to death and I bring to life, I have wounded and I will heal, and no one can deliver out of my hand" (32:39).[15] Such statements need not deny the existence of other heavenly beings (or "gods"), but such beings are not of the same exclusive category as the one true God: "They sacrificed to demons, which are not God—gods they had not known, gods that recently appeared, gods your fathers did not fear" (32:17).[16] As another Mosaic poem puts it: "Who among the gods is like you, O LORD? Who is like you—majestic in holiness, awesome in glory, working wonders?" (Exod 15:11).[17]

Behold Your God—Creator of All Things

A second concern that is central to ancient Jewish monotheism is the belief that God is the sole creator of all things.[18] The line between the Creator and creation is encountered in the first verse of the Bible: "In the beginning God created the heavens and the earth" (Gen 1:1). God acts alone in creation, as is stressed in Isaiah 44:24: "I am the LORD, who has made all things, who alone stretched out the heavens, who spread out the earth by myself." In Isaiah 40–55,[19] God's role as creator is fundamental to the Jewish understanding of monotheism: "'To whom will you compare me? Or who is my equal?' says the Holy One. Lift your eyes and look to the heavens: Who created all these? He who brings out the starry host one by one, and calls them each by name.... Do not know? Have you not heard? The LORD is the everlasting God, the Creator of the ends of the earth" (Isa 40:25–26, 28). "It is I who made the earth and created mankind upon it. My own hands stretched out the heavens; I marshaled their starry hosts.... [The Egyptians and Cushites will one day say] God is with you and there is no other; there is no other god" (Isa 45:12, 14). "For this is what the LORD says—he who created the heavens, he is God; he who fashioned and made the earth, he founded it; he did not create it to be empty, but formed it to be inhabited—he says: 'I am the LORD, and there is no other'" (Isa 45:18 cf. 42:5–8; 48:13–14).

It does not require the skills of a professional biblical scholar to see that such statements involve more than mere polemics against the worship of heathen gods.[20] Isaiah declared that Israel's God was the sole creator of heaven and earth—the one true God. The universe is divided neatly into two categories—eternal and created; God and not-God. There are no other options. The demand to offer worship to God alone is rooted in his unique identity as sole creator of the universe: "Blessed be your glorious name, and may it be exalted above all blessing and praise. You alone are the LORD. You made the heavens, even the highest heavens, and all their starry host, the earth and all that is on it, the seas and all that is in them. You give life to everything, and the multitudes of heaven worship you" (Neh 9:5–6). And, as Jeremiah confesses, "No one is like you, O LORD; you are great, and your name is mighty in power. Who should not revere you, O King of the nations? . . . But the LORD is the true God; he is the living God, the eternal King. . . . God made the earth by his power; he founded the world by his wisdom and stretched out the heavens by his understanding" (Jer 10:6–7, 10, 12).

Behold Your God—Sovereign Over All

A third feature highlighted in ancient Jewish monotheism is the absolute sovereignty of God as ruler of the universe. Larry Hurtado notes that ancient Jewish monotheism evidences "a concern to assert God's universal *sovereignty*. This is reflected with particular frequency in statements insisting that the one God created everything and rules over all, even nations that do not acknowledge this God. Even where spiritual powers of evil are pictured as opposing God, as is often the case in apocalyptic writings, their opposition is characteristically described as temporary, ultimately futile."[21]

This theme is highlighted especially in the book of Daniel:[22] "Then Daniel praised *the God of heaven* and said: 'Praise be to the name of God for ever and ever; wisdom and power are his. He changes times and seasons; he sets up kings and deposes them. He gives wisdom to the wise and knowledge to the discerning'" (Dan 2:19b–21). "The king said to Daniel, 'Surely your God is *the God of gods* and the Lord of kings and a revealer of mysteries, for you were able to reveal this mystery'" (2:47). "The decision is announced by messengers, the holy ones declare the verdict, so that the living may know that *the Most High* is sovereign over the kingdoms of men and gives them to anyone he wishes" (4:17). "Then I [Nebuchadnezzar] praised *the Most High;* I honored and glorified him who lives forever. His dominion is an eternal dominion; his kingdom endures from generation to generation. All the peoples of the earth are regarded as nothing. He does as he pleases with the powers of heaven and the peoples of earth" (4:34–35). "For he is *the living God* and he endures forever; his kingdom will not be destroyed, his dominion will never end" (6:26). "The king [of the last days] will do as he pleases. He will exalt and magnify himself above every god and will say unheard-of things against *the God of gods*. He will be successful until the time of wrath is completed, for what has been determined must take place" (11:36).

The book of Daniel—especially chapters 1 through 6—is full of polemics against the gods of the heathen, and it exhorts Jewish readers to avoid contamination with pagan religious practices. The message is not merely one of monolatry or henotheism, however. Religious devotion is to be reserved for the one God of Israel, *for he is the sole ruler over all things in heaven and on earth*. Again, this does not require the denial of the *existence* of other heavenly beings or gods, but such figures are radically and unmistakably subordinated to Yahweh, "the God of gods" (Dan 11:36).

Answers to Three Objections

Before continuing, it will be necessary to answer a few objections that could be raised against what has been written above. Due to space constraints, my replies will of necessity be brief.

Objection #1: Ancient Judaism was not interested in philosophical questions about God's uniqueness.

This objection can take a softer form and a harder form. In its harder form, it is sometimes contended that philosophical distinctions between God and other heavenly beings were not envisioned by ancient Jews prior to the Middle Ages.[23] In its softer form, it is argued that rigid monotheism (and hence the implication of ontological distinctions between God and other gods) did not arise prior to the exile. Simply put, preexilic Israelite religion was largely polytheistic until the seventh century B.C. During the Babylonian exile an increasingly hardened monarchism/henotheism developed, eventually leading to a fairly rigid monotheism in the postexilic period.[24]

An even softer form of this objection is raised by Gregory Boyd, an evangelical pastor and theologian.[25] Since I am going to address the views of Peter Hayman and Margaret Barker in more detail later in this essay, I would like to focus on Boyd's objection here. If I understand Boyd correctly, his contention is that the Augustinian tradition in Christian orthodoxy has had an undue influence on the way monotheism is understood. Whereas the gods of the biblical tradition are powerful beings who exercise considerable autonomy and hence are able to pose a real threat to the fulfillment of God's will in the earthly realm, Christian theology has transformed these gods into innocuous creatures (angels), who merely exist to carry out the unalterable decrees of an exhaustively sovereign God. Boyd believes that a return to the biblical viewpoint is philosophically and practically helpful, in that it recognizes that other independent heavenly agents exist—agents who are committed to causing pain and suffering in the created order. In other words, the problem of evil is solved by recognizing that God is not the only god who exists. It is these other gods who are in many cases responsible for the tragic events that unfold day by day in our world. These gods are not mere "angelic" agents who always carry out the will of the one God.

Boyd is, of course, careful to affirm that God is the only uncreated being, and the most powerful being in the universe, but he continually polemicizes against what he describes as "philosophical monotheism," by which he means the monotheism of the Augustinian tradition. While I appreciate Boyd's emotional and intellectual struggle with the reality of pain and evil, I do not believe he has provided the right answer by promoting a diluted form of monotheism. In my view, what Boyd disparagingly labels "philosophical monotheism" is merely a logical extension of the biblical doctrine of creation *ex nihilo*.[26] The same God who created the world exercises absolutely sovereign providence over it.[27] While Boyd pictures a universe involved in substantial cosmic warfare, the Bible places this warfare under the rubric of God's exhaustive control over all things.[28] Even the rebellious gods in some mysterious way do his bidding (cf. Judg 9:23; 1 Sam 16:14; 19:9; 1 Kgs 22:23).

The Bible never attempts to protect God from the charge of evil by placing subordinate gods between himself and human tragedy as Boyd attempts to do. The biblical gods/sons of God/angels are *not* viewed as fully autonomous agents with the genuine capacity to thwart God's plans and decrees. Many of the same passages that speak of subordinate gods/sons of God/angels serve the rhetorical function of highlighting the incomparable and unchallengeable sovereignty of the one true God.[29] M. L. West is correct to notice: "The difference between polytheism and monotheism, then, comes down to this: do we postulate different gods to account for different kinds of events, or do we adopt a reductionistic approach and postulate one highly versatile God, responsible for every kind of divine intervention?"[30] Although it is far from his intention, it seems to me that Boyd's solution points ultimately to a return to a polytheistic view of the universe, where different gods are invoked to explain different aspects of human experience.

The problem here is that Boyd—not Augustinian monotheism—has brought a foreign agenda to the biblical text in his attempt to rescue God from culpability for human tragedy by limiting God's exhaustive control over autonomous fallen agents. Far from being a return to the ancient Jewish and biblical worldview, Boyd has merely brought a pagan view of the heavenly world into the stream of Christian theology. As N. T. Wright correctly maintains:

> Creational monotheism obviously rules out *paganism,* the belief that the universe is populated by a fairly large number of divine beings who oversee different nations, different aspects of the created order . . . and/or different human activities. . . . Paganism can, obviously, avoid the problem of charging the supreme god with responsibility for the way things are, since the pagan lives in a confusing world where at any moment some deity may choose to act in a capricious or malevolent way.[31]

Biblical monotheism may cause a philosophical and practical dilemma for coming to grips with the reality of evil in the world, but it never postulates autonomous gods with the real capacity to thwart God's decrees as a way of creating a buffer between God and human tragedy. It is Boyd, not the classical Augustinian system of theology, who has set forth an unbiblical "philosophical monotheism."

***Objection #2:* The Angel of the LORD passages in the Old Testament prove that ancient Judaism was not rigidly monotheistic.**

This line of argument is especially highlighted by Margaret Barker.[32] However, a careful analysis of the Angel of the LORD passages reveals that it is quite possible to understand this enigmatic figure as an *earthly appearance* of the one God on specific occasions, rather than as a separate and ontologically subordinate God.[33] In Genesis 16:7–13, the Angel of the LORD who appears to Hagar is specifically identified with Yahweh, not as a second God: "She gave this name to the LORD who spoke to her: 'You are the God who sees me,' for she said, 'I have now seen the One who sees me'" (v. 13). Genesis 18:1 specifically says that the LORD was one of the "three men" (i.e., angels, cf. 19:1) who "*appeared* to Abraham." The appearance of the LORD to Jacob at Bethel in Genesis 28:13–17 is connected with the figure named the "angel of God" and "the God of Bethel" in 31:11–13. The "man" (i.e., angel) who wrestled with Jacob in Genesis 32:24–28 is identified with the *visible appearance* of God himself in 32:30 (cf. Hos 12:3–5). Jacob's blessing of Joseph in Genesis 48:15–16 identifies God with "the Angel."

Other preexilic traditions likewise seem to identify the Angel of the LORD with the earthly appearance of the LORD, rather than with a separate and ontologically subordinate God.[34] Exodus 3:2–6 equates the Angel of the LORD (v. 2) with the LORD (v. 7), which is to say—God himself (vv. 5–6). This is presumably the same Angel spoken of in Exodus 23:20–23. The Angel of the LORD (*melech YHWH*) is also naturally understood as a visible appearance of the LORD (rather than a separate God) in Judges 6:11–24 and 13:3–22. Although not all angelic appearances in the Old Testament can be explained as visible manifestations of God himself, many such passages can be understood along these lines. As Darrell Hannah correctly points out: "This [*melech YHWH*] significantly differs from later Jewish angelology. Here a separate being does not appear to be in view. The variation between the [*melech YHWH*] and [*YHWH*] in the texts appears to have originated from the theological paradox that sought to express both Yahweh's presence and the impossibility for humans of unmediated access to God. Thus, the [*melech YHWH*] appears to be in some sense an extension or manifestation of Yahweh."[35]

It only becomes necessary to identify the Angel of the LORD as a second God if one postulates (as Margaret Barker does) a linguistic and conceptual distinction between the Most High God (*El Elyon*) and the LORD (*YHWH*)—a distinction which itself rests on an entirely dubious reconstruction of Israel's religious history.[36]

Objection #3: **The Divine Council motif in the Old Testament shows that ancient Judaism was not monotheistic in an exclusive sense.**

Several scholars of religion have highlighted the divine council motif as constituting an important qualification of ancient Jewish monotheism.[37] Some evangelical scholars have likewise noted the importance of this imagery for illuminating the religious background of ancient Judaism. Larry Hurtado has written: "We may understand this ancient Jewish religious outlook as constituting a distinctive version of the commonly attested belief structure ... involving a 'high god' who presides over other deities."[38] The importance of the divine council motif has also been highlighted by Gregory Boyd, who insists: "It is important to note that the Old Testament certainly accepts that some such council exists, and that the members of this council have some say in how things are done. In sharp contrast to the Augustinian monopolizing view of divine sovereignty, the sovereign One in this concept invites and responds to input from both his divine and human subjects."[39]

Is such imagery inconsistent with a strictly monotheistic outlook? Has Augustinianism misleadingly downplayed the importance of this Old Testament motif?

There is no room here for an exhaustive study of the divine or heavenly council theme in the ancient world.[40] Here I simply want to make it clear from the beginning that I readily affirm *both* that heavenly council imagery is present in the Old Testament[41] and that it need *not* pose any threat to monotheism as it has been understood within the Judeo-Christian tradition. One key example of the divine council is in Psalm 82:1, 6: "God presides in the great assembly; he gives judgment among the 'gods' . . . I said, 'You are gods; you are all sons of the Most High.'" As LDS scholars have reminded us,[42] our understanding of monotheism needs to conform to the biblical materials, not the other way around. Therefore, "catholic," or creedal Christians ought to examine the divine council theme to see how it informs the framework of biblical monotheism rather than attempt to explain such imagery away.[43] All serious religious scholarship recognizes that the Bible was produced in a particular historical environment—it did not drop down out of heaven—and therefore it is to be expected that various ideas that are attested in the Old Testament will show points of contact with the broader world of the ancient Near East. The divine council motif is certainly one example of this reality.[44]

What role does the divine council play in the biblical literature produced by ancient Israel? It is important to note that there are distinctive features that highlight the contrasting religious perspective of the Israelites in comparison with their cultural neighbors. Mullen notes: "Within the biblical materials, the concept of an assembly of divine beings is found throughout the OT as an expression of Yahweh's power and authority. Yahweh is frequently depicted as enthroned over an assembly of divine beings who serve to dispense his decrees and messages."[45] This highlights an important distinctive of the divine council in Israelite religion. The Ugaritic texts make it clear that non-Israelite Canaanite religion held to a three-tiered structure: (1) the High God; (2) the major gods; and (3) the minor gods. As Mullen summarizes: "The Ugaritic materials reveal a concept of the council that may be summarized as follows: the major and minor deities of the pantheon met in assembly under the leadership of El to make those decisions concerning the cosmos that fell within the purview of the gods."[46]

What is significant is that in the Israelite assembly, the three-tiered structure has been supplanted by a two-tiered structure: (1) the High God

El/Yahweh; and (2) the gods/sons of God/angels.[47] S. F. Noll notes: "In the OT, the Canaanite pantheon is transformed into God's 'general assembly' with a guardian angel assigned to each Gentile nation."[48] Although some Latter-day Saints may want to argue that this is the result of Jewish scribal tampering with the biblical text, it is better understood in terms of Jewish reuse of older traditions from the wider Near Eastern environment. In other words, the transformation of the imagery is due to Israel's distinctive religious perspective in contrast with previous Canaanite and Mesopotamian cultures, rather than an intra-Jewish development in connection with the reforms of the Deuteronomistic school of thought. Korpel summarizes the evidence very nicely:

> The Hebrew tradition tends to eliminate the concept of a divine court with its complicated internal and external contacts. What remains is a vaguely described body of holy beings who have no other task but to serve God unconditionally. They are not allowed to do anything on their own initiative, as the prologue of the Book of Job shows. Because they still bear their Canaanite names in some of the earliest Hebrew traditions, it is certain that this council of "angels" constituted the remnants of the demolished Canaanite pantheon. Therefore it is understandable that the assembly of the gods is sometimes rebuked for its ineffectiveness. They are no longer real gods. It appears that the concept of Israel as the congregation of YHWH gradually eclipsed the idea of a divine congregation.[49]

We will consider the implications of the divine council motif later in this essay when we look more closely at the work of Daniel Peterson. For now, we simply note that the elimination of the "major" gods (as found in the Ugaritica) has the effect of creating a conceptual gulf between YHWH and the other members of the heavenly court. Within ancient Jewish religion, the one true God was utterly unique and ontologically incomparable to the other heavenly beings. The gods/sons of God/angels are radically subordinated to Yahweh and exist only as messengers and servants of the Great King.

The Second Temple Context
of New Testament Monotheism[50]

If it is true that the roots of Christian monotheism go back to the religion attested in the Old Testament, an even clearer case can be made for arguing that Judaism was firmly monotheistic in the Hellenistic and Roman periods (330 B.C. onwards).[51] As Richard Bauckham writes, "There is every reason to suppose that observant Jews of the late Second Temple period were highly self-conscious monotheists."[52] This is the historical context most relevant to the New Testament period (first century A.D.).

A few examples from the Apocrypha illustrate that Jews of this period were "self-consciously monotheistic,"[53] even if one were to argue that monotheism was not dominant in Israelite religion prior to the exile: "For *neither is there any god besides you*, whose care is for all people, to whom you should prove that you have not judged unjustly. . . . You are righteous and you rule all things righteously" (Wisdom 12:13, 15); "Then they [the Gentiles] will know, as we have known that *there is no God but you*, O Lord" (Sirach 36:5); "Please, please, God of my father, God of the heritage of Israel, Lord of heaven and earth, Creator of the waters, King of all your creation, hear my prayer! . . . Let your whole nation and every tribe know and understand that you are God, the God of all power and might, and that *there is no other* who protects the people of Israel but you alone" (Jdt 9:12, 14).

The Alexandrian Jewish philosopher Philo (30 B.C.–A.D. 50) was also a self-conscious monotheist.[54] Emil Schürer writes: "As a Jew, Philo emphasizes monotheism and the worship of God without images. Obviously this view stands in opposition to the pagan religions, but it can be harmonized quite closely with the conception of God found in Greek philosophic thought, without serious modification of the Jewish conception."[55] This standpoint comes through quite clearly in a number of places.[56] In Philo's work *On the Decalogue,* 65, he writes: "Let us, then, engrave deep in our hearts this as the first and most sacred of commandments, to acknowledge and honor one God Who is above all, and let the idea that gods are many never even reach the ears of the man whose rule of life is to seek for truth in purity and guilelessness." He also plainly confesses his monotheistic commitment when he writes in *On the Creation,* 172: "He that has begun by learning these things . . . that God is and is from eternity, and that He really is One, and that He has made the world and has made it one world, unique as himself is unique, and that He ever exercises forethought for His creation, will lead a life of bliss and blessedness."

A commitment to monotheism is also attested in Jewish prayers among the Dead Sea Scrolls.[57] We read in 4Q504 5:9: "For you are a living God, *you alone,* and *there is no other apart from you*." Likewise we read in 1Q35 1:5–6: "For you are an eternal God, and all your paths remain from eternity to eternity. And *there is no one apart from you*." In the Qumran hymns, we find that monotheistic rhetoric is used to *contrast* God with the other members of the heavenly court (i.e., the angels, cf. 4Q427 7 I, 13–15). In 1QH 15:28, 31–32 we find this profession of monotheistic faith: "Who is like you, Lord, among the gods? . . . For you are an eternal God and all your paths remain from eternity to eternity. And *there is no one apart from you."* And again in 1QH 18:8–10: "See, you are a prince of gods and king of the glorious ones, lord of every spirit, owner of every creature. Without your will nothing happens, and nothing is known without your wish. *There is no one besides you,* no one matches your strength, nothing, in contrast with your glory, there is no price on your might." Speaking of the acts of creation, we are told: "Besides him *there is no other, nor will there ever be another.* For the God of knowledge has established it and no one else with him" (1QH 20:10–11 cf. 4Q427 3 II, 10–11).

Likewise 4Q503 fragments 7–8 describe the God of Israel as "the God of all the armies of the gods" and as "God over all." This again shows that— just as in the Old Testament—the use of "divine" terminology to describe the members of the heavenly court was not necessarily a compromise of genuine monotheism,[58] for the other "gods" were acknowledged as ontologically subordinate to the one true God: "Who is like you, Lord, among the gods? Who (is) like your truth? Who is just before you when he is judged? No host could reply to your reproach, no one could endure before your anger" (1Q35 1:2–3). Heaven is the place where all the "angels" (cf. 4Q403 1:1) or "gods" (4Q403 1:2) offer worship to the Most High: "The chiefs of the praises of all the gods, praise the God of magnificent praises, for in the magnificence of the praises is the glory of his kingdom. . . . For he is the God of the gods of all the chiefs of the heights, and king of kings of all the eternal councils" (4Q403 1:32–34).

The above is only a brief sketch of the evidence, but it is sufficient to establish the fact that Jews of the late Second Temple period were giving clear testimony to the belief that the One God of Israel was in fact the only true and living God, Creator of heaven and earth. Hence, Adela Yarbro Collins is mistaken when she claims that "the strict monotheism of the Deuteronomic literature had already been 'stretched' or even ignored in much of the literature of Second Temple Judaism. Many Jews of that period evidently did not conceive of God as absolutely unique in a metaphysical sense."[59] Most Jews of this period certainly *did* conceive of God as absolutely unique, and it is within the context of this view of God that Judaism gave birth to a new religious movement in the first century A.D.

The Trinitarian Content of New Testament Monotheism

There is no question but that Christianity arose out of the matrix of Jewish monotheism. And yet, from a very early period, Christians were worshiping Jesus alongside God in their congregations without apparently sensing any theological or practical contradiction. Larry Hurtado has written: "Given that the religious attitudes of earliest Christians were shaped much by biblical/Jewish scruples about avoiding the cultic worship of other gods, humans, angels, and any figures other than the one true God of the biblical tradition, the explicit and programmatic inclusion of Christ in their devotional practice is quite interesting, even striking."[60] We have already attempted to demonstrate that the Jewish theological heritage of early Christianity was firmly committed to monotheism. What we will now sketch in this section are the ways in which monotheism was expanded to include Jesus and the Holy Spirit within God's unique identity in the religious faith of the earliest Christian church.[61]

A Reaffirmation and Expansion of the Shema

Deuteronomy 6:4–5 continued to exercise its influence in shaping the religious faith of the New Testament church: "Hear, O Israel: The LORD our God, the LORD is one. Love the LORD your God with all your heart and with all your soul and with all your strength." Jesus identified the Shema as the most important of all the commandments (Mark 12:29–30). It is likely that Jesus also alluded to Deuteronomy 6:4 when he declared to the Jews in John 10:30: "I and the Father *are one*"—hence, including himself alongside the Father in the Jewish affirmation of one Lord and God. The Jews certainly understood the import of his claim, for in 10:33 they accuse him of claiming to be God! The Jewish Shema is also echoed in other New Testament texts: "Now to the King eternal, immortal, invisible, *the only God*, be honor and glory for ever and ever. Amen" (1 Tim 1:17). "You believe that *there is one God*. Good! Even the demons believe that—and shudder" (Jas 2:19). "To *the only God* our Savior be glory, majesty, power and authority, through Jesus Christ our Lord, before all ages, now and evermore! Amen" (Jude 25).

One of the most theologically enlightening allusions to Deuteronomy 6:4 is found in 1 Corinthians 8:4–6: "We know that an idol is nothing at all in the world and that *there is no God but one*. For even if there are so-called gods, whether in heaven or on earth (as indeed there are many 'gods' and many 'lords'), yet for us there is but *one God*, the Father, from whom all things came and for whom we live; and there is but *one Lord*, Jesus Christ, through whom all things came and through whom we live" (emphasis added). What is interesting here is the way the Jewish Shema was reinterpreted by the early Christians in order to include both the Father (one God) and the Son (one Lord). On this passage N. T. Wright comments:

> Paul, in other words, has glossed "God" with "the Father," and "Lord" with "Jesus Christ," adding in each case an explanatory phrase: "God" is the Father, "from whom are all things and we to him," and the "Lord" is Jesus the Messiah, "through whom are all things and we through him.". . . Paul has placed Jesus *within* an explicit statement, drawn from the Old Testament's quarry of emphatically monotheistic texts, of the doctrine that Israel's God is the one and only God, the creator of the world. The Shema was already, at this stage of Judaism, in widespread use as *the* Jewish daily prayer. Paul has redefined it christologically, producing what we can only call a sort of christological monotheism.[62]

What this adaptation of Deuteronomy 6:4 shows is that in the early decades of the first century, Jewish Christians were including Jesus within the unique identity of Israel's "One God" without acknowledging any breach of biblical monotheism.[63]

A Christological Exegesis of the Old Testament

The above example from 1 Corinthians 8:4–6 offers evidence of a broader phenomenon that shows how the earliest Christians were including Jesus within the unique identity of God as he is found in Israel's scriptures— namely, the habit of applying to Jesus Old Testament texts that originally applied to Yahweh.[64] We can only mention a few examples here. Joel 2:32 is cited by Peter in Acts 2:21: "And everyone who calls on the name of the Lord will be saved." This Old Testament passage speaks of an eschatological day when Yahweh will save his people. Yet the allusions to this verse in Acts 2:36 and 38 make it appear that Joel 2:32 is understood so that it is Jesus' *name* that is to be called upon for salvation (cf. Acts 4:12).[65] This christological application of Joel 2:32 is even more explicit in Romans 10:9–13. There Paul writes that, "if you confess with your mouth, 'Jesus is Lord,' and believe in your heart that God raised him from the dead, you will be saved. . . . for, 'Everyone who calls on the name of the Lord will be saved.'" So Martin Hengel notes: "In the original text, Kyrios [Lord] refers to God himself, but for Paul the Kyrios is Jesus, in whom God makes a full disclosure of his salvation."[66]

Perhaps the most striking example of this phenomenon comes from Philippians 2:6–11, which is widely acknowledged as a Pauline citation of an early Christian hymn. This passage contains some striking statements regarding the divine status of Jesus: he possessed God's nature (2:6a), and he was equal with God (2:6b) prior to his incarnation (2:7–8). The divine one who became enfleshed was subsequently exalted by God to the highest possible heavenly status (2:9a). God made the name of Jesus equivalent to the divine name YHWH (2:9b).[67] What is perhaps most striking, however, is what is found in 2:10–11: "that at the name of Jesus every knee should bow, in heaven and on earth and under the earth, and every tongue confess that Jesus Christ is Lord, to the glory of God the Father." This is an astonishing adaptation of one of the clearest monotheistic texts in all the Old Testament—Isaiah 45:22–24: "Turn to me and be saved, all you ends of the earth; for I am God, and there is no other. By myself I have sworn, my mouth has uttered in all integrity a word that will not be revoked: Before me every knee will bow; by me every tongue will swear. They will say of me, 'In the LORD alone are righteousness and strength.' All who have raged against him will come to him and be put to shame."[68]

In an astonishing exegetical move, Isaiah 45:22–24 has been read to refer to the eschatological vindication of Jesus Christ, when God the Father compels all creation to acknowledge the lordship of the Son.[69] Whereas Isaiah depicted every knee as bowing to Yahweh and every tongue confessing *him* as LORD, Paul understands this prophecy in terms of the confession and acknowledgment of *Jesus'* universal lordship.[70] Every earthly and heavenly power will one day acknowledge that Jesus has been exalted to the highest place—which can only mean God's own heavenly throne—and that the divine name YHWH and Jesus' name are to be revered as one and the same (Phil 2:9). As Richard Bauckham writes: "The Philippians passage is therefore no unconsidered echo of an Old Testament text, but a claim that it is in the exaltation of Jesus, his identification as YHWH in YHWH's universal sovereignty, that the unique deity of the God of Israel comes to be acknowledged as such by all creation. Precisely Deutero-Isaianic *monotheism* is fulfilled in the revelation of Jesus' participation in the divine identity. Eschatological monotheism proves to be christological monotheism."[71]

Two Key Christological Motifs in the New Testament

Many books have been written that address the topic of the deity of Christ in the New Testament.[72] I have no intention of attempting to discuss here all the passages in the New Testament that indicate that the early Christian church was already including Jesus within the unique identity of Israel's One God long before the christological debates of the subsequent centuries.[73] Instead, I will briefly sketch two key motifs in the New Testament that clearly illustrate *how* Jesus was being included within God's unique identity by the earliest Christians.

Jesus—the Son of Man

First of all, I would highlight the identification of Jesus as the Son of Man, which is especially prominent in the gospels.[74] The background to this identification lies in Daniel 7:13–14: "In my vision at night I looked, and there before me was one like a son of man, coming with the clouds of heaven. He approached the Ancient of Days and was led into his presence. He was given authority, glory and sovereign power; all peoples, nations and men of every language worshiped him. His dominion is an everlasting dominion that will not pass away, and his kingdom is one that will never be destroyed." This prophetic vision speaks of a member of the human race who will be exalted in God's presence to such a degree that the whole world will worship him and submit to his regal authority. He will reign as the monarch of God's eternal kingdom (cf. 2:44; 7:27).

What is significant about the application of "Son of Man" to Jesus is that the figure in Daniel's vision appears to share God's dominion over the world in a special way that transcends what might be expected for any mortal being. There are other examples in Jewish literature of special human figures who are exalted to places of heavenly authority,[75] and there appears to be evidence of contemporary Jewish reusage of Daniel 7 around the New Testament period,[76] so the application of the text to Jesus (by himself and his followers) is not entirely unprecedented. Nonetheless, it appears likely that the influence of Daniel 7 played a role in helping the earliest Christians to articulate their belief in Jesus' divine status—that is, his inclusion within the unique identity of the One God.[77]

The title Son of Man is applied to Jesus in several contexts that attribute to him what can only be described as a "divine" status.[78] In Mark 2:10, Jesus, the Son of Man, claims to have authority to forgive sins. As his Jewish audience recognized, this involved a potentially blasphemous claim of unique divine authority (Mark 2:5–7). In Mark 2:28 Jesus, the Son of Man, claims to be Lord of the Sabbath, possibly alluding to Exodus 20:11: "Therefore the LORD blessed the Sabbath day and made it holy." This striking claim again attributes to Jesus a position of authority that observant Jews would recognize as belonging to God alone.

Another place where the title Son of Man is linked with a unique divine status is in Mark 14:62, where Jesus replies to the High Priest's question whether he is the messianic Son of God: "'I am,' said Jesus. 'And you will see the Son of Man sitting at the right hand of the Mighty One and coming on the clouds of heaven.'" The Jewish response to this statement is predictable—blasphemy! In Jesus' reply to the High Priest, Daniel 7:13 is conflated with Psalm 110:1 (cf. Mk. 12:35–37), which means that the Son of Man will, in fact, be seated on God's own *heavenly* throne (cf. 1 Chr 29:23).[79] Craig Evans notes that "When we remember that the throne of Daniel 7:9 had burning wheels, we should think that Jesus has claimed that he will sit with God on the Chariot Throne and will, as in the vivid imagery of Daniel 7, come with God in judgement."[80]

This linkage of the title Son of Man with the divine status of Jesus appears also in two texts outside the canonical gospels. In Acts 7:56 Stephen sees Jesus standing at God's right hand in a heavenly vision: "I see heaven open and the Son of Man standing at the right hand of God." The Jewish leaders recognize the echo of Jesus' own "blasphemous" claims and decide to execute Stephen. The implied divine status of Jesus is then affirmed by Stephen's subsequent action—he addresses a prayer to Jesus (7:59–60)![81] Observant Jews were well aware that prayers were to be addressed to God alone.

One final text that must be mentioned is Revelation 1:13, where John sees among the lampstands "someone like a son of man, dressed in a robe reaching down to his feet and with a golden sash round his chest." This of course alludes to Daniel 7:13; but, significantly, the text goes on to describe the exalted Son of Man in terms that recall the description of the Ancient of Days in Daniel 7:9–10 and the angelic "man dressed in linen" in Daniel 10:5–6,[82] as well as the "likeness of the glory of the LORD" in Ezekiel 1:26–28: "His head and hair were white like wool, as white as snow, and his eyes were like blazing fire. His feet were like bronze glowing in a furnace, and his voice was like the sound of rushing waters. . . . His face was like the sun shining in all its brilliance" (Rev 1:14–16).

The conflation of Son of Man and Ancient of Days imagery may reflect the LXX reading of Daniel 7:13, which depicts the Son of Man coming "as if [he were] the Ancient of Days"—rather than coming "unto the Ancient of Days" as in the traditional Hebrew text (and some ancient Greek versions of Daniel).[83] James D. G. Dunn notes that this vision in Revelation 1:13–16 appears to reflect a theological "blurring of distinction between Yahweh, the one like a son of man, a glorious angel and the glory of God."[84] Once again, the identification of Jesus as the Son of Man involves a claim that he shares in God's own unique divine status.

Jesus—the Wisdom/Word of God

A second body of texts that attest to Jesus' divine identity revolve around the theme of divine Wisdom. Several writers in the New Testament appear to have understood Jesus as the embodied Wisdom of God.[85] It is important to understand that when Jews of the period spoke of God's Wisdom, this was a way of speaking of God himself, acting in a particular manner toward his creation.[86] As James Dunn puts it: "The Wisdom and Word imagery is all of a piece with this—no more distinct beings than the Lord's 'arm,' no more intermediary beings than God's righteousness and God's glory, but simply vivid personifications, ways of speaking about God in his active involvement with his world and his people."[87]

Several Jewish texts illustrate the way Wisdom was viewed as a personified aspect of God's own unique identity—distinct from the temporal order: "The LORD brought me forth as the first of his works, before his deeds of old; I was appointed from eternity, from the beginning, before the world began. . . . I was there when he set the heavens in place, when he marked out the horizon on the face of the deep . . . and when he marked out the foundations of the earth. Then I was the craftsman at his side" (Prov 8:22–30). "In the assembly of the Most High she opens her mouth, and in the presence of his hosts she tells of her glory: 'I came forth from the mouth of the Most High, and covered the earth like a mist. I dwelt in the highest heavens, and my throne was in a pillar of cloud. . . . Before all ages, in the beginning, he created me, and for all the ages, I shall not cease to be'" (Sirach 24:2–4,9). "For wisdom is more mobile than any motion; because of her pureness she pervades and penetrates all things. For she is a breath of the power of God, and a pure emanation of the glory of the Almighty . . . For she is a reflection of eternal light, a spotless mirror of the working of God, and an image of his goodness" (Wisdom 7:24–26).

A closely related motif in Jewish literature is the Word of God, which appears to express the same idea as God's Wisdom. We read in the Wisdom of Solomon 9:1–2, 4: "O God of my ancestors and Lord of mercy, who have made all things by your *word,* and by your *wisdom* have formed humankind to have dominion over the creatures you have made . . . give me the wisdom that sits by your throne." The biblical psalms also associate both Word and Wisdom with God's act of creation (Pss 33:6; 104:24). In any case, it would appear that Jews of this period were familiar with biblical and nonbiblical traditions that personified God's Wisdom/Word in order to speak of God's relations with the temporal order. As Bauckham puts it: "The personifications have been developed precisely out of the ideas of God's own Wisdom and God's own Word, that is, aspects of God's own identity. In a variety of ways they *express* God, his mind and his will, in relation to the world."[88]

Understood against this backdrop, the linkage of Jesus with the divine Wisdom in the New Testament can be understood as a way of including Christ within God's own unique identity. Christ is none other than God himself, acting within the temporal order in creation and redemption (cf. Wis 7:27; 8:3–4, 13; 9:17–18). As we found to be the case with the Son of Man motif, the linkage of Jesus with the divine Wisdom also goes back to the teaching of Christ himself.[89] Jesus' exhortation addressed to the weary and burdened to come to him and receive *instruction* (cf. Matt 11:25–26) in Matthew 11:28–30, recalls Wisdom's exhortations in Proverbs 8:1–11 and Psalm 34:11–13. Sirach 51:23–26 appears to be in the background of the invitation to take Jesus' *yoke* (Matt 11:29): "Draw near to me, you who are uneducated, and lodge in the house of instruction. . . . I opened my mouth and said, Acquire wisdom for yourselves without money. Put your neck under her yoke, and let your souls receive instruction; it is to be found close by. See with your own eyes that I have labored but little and found for myself much serenity." Jesus' claim to offer exclusive knowledge of the Father in Matthew 11:27 may reflect Wisdom of Solomon 8:4: "For she [Wisdom] is an initiate in the knowledge of God."

It is also interesting to compare Luke 11:49 with Matthew 23:34.[90] Whereas in Luke 11:49 it is "the Wisdom of God" who sends the prophets, in Matthew 23:34 Jesus *himself* acts in the place of Wisdom. Scholars have asked many questions about the original wording of this saying of Jesus; but whatever view one takes on the matter, it would appear that Jesus and the Wisdom of God were linked by those who passed on the traditional sayings of the Lord. As Craig Evans notes: "In Jewish thinking of the first century, Jesus' speaking and acting as though he were God's Wisdom would have made a significant contribution to early christology."[91]

This linkage of Jesus and Wisdom was picked up by followers of Jesus such as Paul. In 1 Corinthians 1:30–31 he writes: "It is because of him that you are in Christ Jesus, who has become for us wisdom from God—that is, our righteousness, holiness and redemption. Therefore, as it is written: 'Let him who boasts boast in the Lord.'" Here not only is Jesus identified with God's Wisdom, but Paul makes it clear that *as such* Christ is included in the unique divine identity. He does this by alluding to Jeremiah 9:23–24 and applying to the Lord Jesus what originally was spoken of Yahweh. As God's Wisdom, Jesus is included within the very identity of the God of Israel, as God himself acting in the temporal order for the redemption of his people.

Another Pauline text that develops the Wisdom motif christologically is Colossians 1:15–20:

> He is the image of the invisible God, the firstborn over all creation. For by him all things were created: things in heaven and on earth, visible and invisible, whether thrones or powers or rulers or authorities; all things were created by him and for him. He is before all things, and in him all things hold together. And he is the head of the body, the church; he is the beginning and the firstborn from among the dead, so that in everything he might have the supremacy. For God was pleased to have all his fullness dwell in him, and through him to reconcile to himself all things, whether things on earth or things in heaven, by making peace through his blood, shed on the cross.

Many scholars believe that the above passage is a citation of an earlier Christian hymn, which attests to the primitive origin of its high Christology. Christ is here identified as the visible expression of God himself, the eternal ruler over the entire created order. Christ shares in the unique identity of God by participating in his exclusive actions of creation and universal lordship.[92] As many have pointed out, the lofty descriptions of Christ in this passage are partially dependent on the depictions of Wisdom in Sirach and the Wisdom of Solomon (cf. Sir 24:1–12; 43:26; Wis 1:7, 14; 6:21–22; 7:24–26).[93] Ben Witherington correctly notices, however, that the application of this imagery to Christ results in theological developments that go beyond what is explicitly attributed to Wisdom in earlier Jewish literature: "While there is an element of uniqueness involved in talking about the pre-existence and incarnation of a personal being who took on flesh and became Jesus the Messiah, the sapiential material with its exalted praise of Wisdom helped prepare the way for such an idea."[94]

Understood against its Wisdom background, we can see that Colossians 1:15–20 is essentially a Pauline expression of the same divine Christology articulated in the prologue of John's gospel: "In the beginning was the Word, and the Word was with God, and the Word was God. He was with God in the beginning. Through him all things were made; without him nothing was made that has been made. . . . The Word became flesh and made his dwelling among us. We have seen his glory, the glory of the One and Only, who came from the Father, full of grace and truth" (John 1:1–3, 14).[95]

The Triadic Portrait of God in the New Testament

Thus far we have examined a number of ways by which the New Testament writers included Jesus Christ within God's own unique identity without breaching their own monotheistic commitment inherited from Judaism.[96] But there is an important aspect that has thus far been left out of the equation—What about the Holy Spirit? Does the New Testament support the move from a *binitarian* view of God (including the Father and the Son) to a *trinitarian* view that includes the Holy Spirit alongside the other two divine persons? Yes, it does, and it is to this issue that we now direct our attention.[97]

Numerous passages in the New Testament include the Holy Spirit alongside the Father and the Son in such a way as to suggest a triadic understanding of God. One of the better-known passages is found at the end of Matthew's gospel: "Then Jesus came to them and said, 'All authority in heaven and on earth has been given to me. Therefore go and make disciples of all nations, baptizing them in the name of the Father and of the Son and of the Holy Spirit'" (Matt 28:18–19). Here we see that Jesus' possession of universal divine authority is linked with a triadic formula that identifies the singular "name" of God as Father, Son, and Holy Spirit. The worldwide Christian mission is founded on the Trinitarian revelation of God's true identity. Richard Bauckham's comments on this verse are well worth quoting:

> The scene is a Gospel equivalent to the last part of the christological passage in Philippians 2:5–11. But whereas in that passage it is the Old Testament divine name, YHWH, that the exalted Christ receives, here the disciples are to baptize "in the name of the Father and of the Son and of the Holy Spirit" (verse 19). The formula, as in the phrase "calling on the name of the Lord" which New Testament usage takes up from the Old with reference to baptism and profession of Christian faith, requires precisely a divine name. "The

Father, the Son and the Holy Spirit" names the newly disclosed identity of God, revealed in the story of Jesus the Gospel has told.[98]

This "triadic" pattern is especially well attested in the letters of Paul. In 1 Corinthians 12:4–6 we read: "There are different kinds of gifts, but *the same Spirit*. There are different kinds of service, but *the same Lord*. There are different kinds of working, but *the same God* works all of them in all men." The terms *Spirit, Lord,* and *God* appear to be three designations of the One whose rule was manifest in the context of the gifted congregation. These three Persons are set in contrast with the pagan idols (12:2) who used to be the object of their worship and the inspiration of their utterances. According to Paul, the worship of the Christian community now centers around these three divine Persons. As Gordon Fee writes: "He begins in vv. 4–6 by noting that diversity reflects the nature of God and is therefore the true evidence of the work of the one God in their midst. Thus, the Trinity is presuppositional to the entire argument, and these opening foundational words are the more telling precisely because they are so unstudied, so freely and unselfconsciously expressed."[99]

Another important passage is found in 2 Corinthians 13:14, where Paul writes: "May the grace of the Lord Jesus Christ, and the love of God, and the fellowship of the Holy Spirit be with you all." What is significant about this triadic formula is that it occurs within a prayer on behalf of the Corinthian congregation. Paul felt free to invoke Jesus Christ and the Holy Spirit alongside God the Father in prayer without apparently sensing any breach of his monotheistic religious commitment.[100] Fee notices that "this suggests that Paul was in fact trinitarian in any meaningful sense of that term—that the believer knows and experiences the one God as Father, Son, and Spirit, and that when dealing with Christ and the Spirit one is dealing with God every bit as much as when one is dealing with the Father."[101]

A third key passage is Ephesians 4:4–6: "There is one body and *one Spirit*—just as you were called to one hope when you were called—*one Lord*, one faith, one baptism; *one God* and Father of all, who is over all and through all and in all." But does this same passage not make it clear that the Lord Jesus and the Holy Spirit are only divine in some sort of derivative sense, ultimately subordinate to God the Father? Fee's observations are again helpful:

> If the last phrase in this passage re-emphasizes the unity of the one God, who is ultimately responsible for all things—past, present, and future—and subsumes the work of the Spirit and the Son under that of God, the

entire passage at the same time puts into creedal form the affirmation that God is *experienced* as a triune reality. Precisely on the basis of such experience and language the later church maintained its biblical integrity by expressing all of this in explicitly trinitarian language.[102]

It should be kept in mind that orthodox Trinitarianism has always been careful to maintain a *functional* subordination of the Son and the Spirit *to the Father*. The Son and the Spirit are included within God's own identity precisely *as* the Son and Spirit *of God*. The Son is God because he is all that the Father is (not the other way around). The Spirit is God because in him the presence of the Father and the Son is known within the Christian community. The Spirit is the Spirit of the Father and the Son, and he proceeds *from them* (not the other way around). The divine nature that the Son and the Spirit possess is precisely the divine nature of the Father—he remains the reference point.[103]

In any case, the above three references are by no means the only passages in the New Testament that seem to presuppose a Trinitarian understanding of God's identity,[104] but they should be sufficient to establish the point. When writers such as Paul spoke of God as an experienced reality among the Christian churches, they were drawn into a pattern of speech wherein the full identity of God could only be named by speaking of three divine persons—the Father, the Son, and the Holy Spirit.[105]

Critiques of Peter Hayman, Margaret Barker, and Daniel Peterson

Quite obviously, what has been written above represents my own views, although it is certainly the case that much of what I have argued reflects the opinion of a significant body of biblical and theological scholarship. However, several scholars have argued in recent years that ancient Judaism was something other than monotheistic, and this obviously has a direct bearing on how we understand the origins of Christianity.[106] Hence, the final section of this essay is devoted to a critical interaction with two non-LDS scholars (Peter Hayman and Margaret Barker),[107] whose research is often cited by Mormon apologists, and one prominent LDS scholar (Daniel Peterson).

A Critique of Peter Hayman

Peter Hayman has argued in a widely cited essay that Judaism was not monotheistic in any meaningful sense prior to the Middle Ages: "It will be my contention ... that it is hardly ever appropriate to use the term monotheism to describe the Jewish idea of God, that no progress beyond the simple formulas of the Book of Deuteronomy can be discerned in Judaism before the philosophers of the Middle Ages, and that Judaism never escapes from the legacy of the battles for supremacy between Yahweh, Ba'al and El from which it emerged."[108]

Hayman appeals to several lines of evidence in an attempt to make his case. In his first argument he cites documentary evidence—in Sepher Yetzirah, Genesis Rabbah, and the book Bahir from the Kabbalah—that the doctrine of creation *ex nihilo* was not held within ancient Judaism.[109] Hayman correctly notes that God's unique status is compromised if matter is eternal with him, and he is correct to ask: "But where does this leave Judaism's supposed monotheism? Is a doctrine of monotheism conceivable without a doctrine of *creatio ex nihilo?*"[110]

Unfortunately, Genesis Rabbah is cited out of context in the attempt to establish his point. Hayman cites the following statement from Genesis Rabbah 1.5 on Genesis 1:1: "R. Huna said, in the name of Bar Qappara: 'If it were not written explicitly in Scripture, it would not be possible to say it: *God created the heaven and the earth*. From what? From *the earth was chaos* [*tohu*], etc.'"[111] What Hayman leaves unquoted is the immediately previous sentence, which, in the Soncino edition, reads: "Thus, whoever comes to say that this world was created out of tohu and bohu and darkness, does he not indeed impair [God's glory]!" The translator notes: "Here, however, they [*tohu* and *bohu*] are regarded, together with darkness, as forms of matter which according to some who deny *creatio ex nihilo* was God's raw material in the creation of the world. *The object of the Midrash here is to refute that view.*"[112] Hayman also ignores Genesis Rabbah 1.9 on Genesis 1:1, wherein "a certain philosopher" is told in no uncertain terms by R. Gamaliel that God himself created all the materials from which the world was made, rather than merely being a great artist who was assisted by good materials.

Hayman's other two examples both come from the Kabbalah. However, these texts create as many problems as they solve and are hardly the best examples on which to try to establish what was widely believed within Judaism prior to the Middle Ages. First, it is far from clear that the esoteric views expressed in the documents of the Kabbalah accurately reflect what was widely held by Jews *of their own time,* not to mention those of earlier periods.[113] Second, even if one accepts such documents as testimony to mainstream Jewish views (which is a questionable assumption), it is not at all clear that Hayman's citations establish the eternality of matter. Sepher

Yetzirah does teach that the substance of creation was formed from chaos, but within the complicated cosmogony of the Kabbalah, chaos itself was formed out of God's pure Mind, or Wisdom.[114] The Bahir teaches, not the eternality of matter per se, but rather the strange doctrine that Evil has a metaphysical reality within God.[115]

In any case, a misquoted citation from Genesis Rabbah and two citations from the Kabbalah hardly constitute strong evidence that the doctrine of creation *ex nihilo* was not formulated within Judaism prior to the Middle Ages. Hence, Hayman's first argument that God was not viewed as metaphysically unique in status during this period is unconvincing.

Hayman's second argument is drawn from Moshe Idel's work on the Kabbalah:[116] "He [Idel] argues that the *unio mystica* can be found in Judaism even in its most extreme forms, and he quotes an impressive array of texts to support his argument. Many of these presuppose that humans can become divine and dispose of the powers of God."[117] Unfortunately, for those who would wish to follow his work in this area, Idel himself acknowledges that he is virtually the only specialist in the area of Jewish mysticism who interprets "mystical union" with God in the Kabbalah in such a radical fashion.[118] For Hayman to cite Idel's eccentric views on this matter without further substantial argumentation constitutes a fallacious appeal to authority that lacks persuasive power.

Hayman does attempt to support Idel's views by an appeal to the transformation of Enoch into Metatron in the pseudepigraphal work of 3 Enoch.[119] I would have to agree that Enoch's transformation in this document is unusual (3 En. 4:1–5; cf. 2 En. 22), and possibly *borders* on a break with monotheism.[120] Deification is probably not too strong a term for describing the transformation of a man into "the lesser YHWH" (3 En. 12:5) and "Prince of the Divine Presence" (12:1).[121] Enoch/Metatron is "greater than all the princes, more exalted than all the angels, more beloved than all the ministers, more honored than all the hosts, and elevated over all potentates in sovereignty, greatness, and glory" (4:1).[122]

However, even within the document itself, there are attempts to qualify Metatron's divine status in such a way as to protect the unique identity of the One God:[123] (1) Enoch is seated, not on God's own throne, but on "a throne *like* the throne of glory" (10:1).[124] (2) Enoch is said to be appointed, "as a prince and a ruler over all the denizens of the heights, *apart from the eight great, honored, and terrible princes* who are called YHWH by the name of their King" (10:3). This suggests that Enoch is *not* in fact exalted to the highest possible heavenly status, for there are eight other angelic "princes" above him. God himself is exalted even above these heavenly princes; hence the eight angels create a buffer between Enoch and the One God. (3) In 3 Enoch 16, Anapiel YHWH (presumably one of the eight heavenly princes) gives Metatron a lashing when Aher sees Metatron "seated upon a throne like a king" (16:2) and declares: "There are indeed two powers in heaven!" (16:3). Metatron is forced to stand up and vacate his throne when it is sensed that God's unique status has been threatened (16:5).[125]

Hayman also appeals to various texts in the Dead Sea Scrolls and the New Testament that assert that the destiny of the faithful is to enjoy an angelic status in heaven.[126] But it should be obvious that this falls short of making humans equal to God, since angels (unlike God) were recognized as created beings in Judaism.[127] Hence, although 3 Enoch does provide some evidence of a form of deification in sectarian Judaism that might *appear* to break with Jewish monotheism, this by no means reflects the general tendency of Jewish religious piety, which is to jealously preserve the unique identity of the One God. Philo's comments are surely more representative of mainstream Jewish opinion, when he comments on the pagan notion of deification: "But that displacement was of nothing petty, but of the greatest of all that exists, when the created and corruptible nature of man was made to appear uncreated and incorruptible by a deification which our nation judged to be the most grievous impiety, since sooner could God change into a man than a man into God" (*On the Embassy to Gaius*, 118).

This brings us to Hayman's third argument against characterizing ancient Judaism as monotheistic. Hayman argues that Jewish angelology shows that God was not an ontologically unique being: "Yahweh belongs to this class of beings, but is distinguished from them by his kingship over the heavenly host. However, he is not different from them in kind. This reflects the probable origin of Yahweh as one member of the heavenly host, namely the national god of the Israelite people, who became king of the gods when he was identified with El Elyon, the head of the Canaanite pantheon."[128] Hayman neglects to mention the fact that the angels (unlike God) were recognized as *created* beings in Jewish religious texts of the Second Temple period.[129] This *does* mean that Yahweh is different from them in kind. Carol Newsom correctly notes: "Although angels are spirits and may be called 'gods' [*elim, elohim*], they are created beings."[130]

Hayman appeals to Deuteronomy 32:8–9 in an attempt to find a remnant of the idea that Yahweh was originally distinct from the Most High and belonged to the angelic host.[131] These verses state: "When the Most High gave the nations their inheritance, when he divided all mankind, he set up boundaries for the peoples according to the number of the sons of Israel [or sons of God]. For the LORD's portion is his people, Jacob his allotted inheritance." While Hayman is surely correct in favoring the reading "the sons of God" (as in the DSS and some witnesses to the LXX) over "the sons of Israel" (as in the MT) in 32:8, this does not necessarily lead to a polytheistic understanding of the text.[132] His case really depends on his reading of verse 9, wherein he argues that the LXX presumes a Hebrew original that would have begun with "*and Yahweh's portion* (Heb: *vayehiy cheleq YHWH*) was his people" rather than "*for Yahweh's portion* (Heb: *kiy cheleq YHWH*) is his people." According to Hayman's reading of the text, Yahweh was one of the "sons of God" to whom a particular nation (Israel) was given by the Most High.[133] However, there is no Hebrew manuscript evidence directly supporting the LXX reading of 32:9. The fragmentary witness to 32:9 among the Dead Sea Scrolls favors the MT rather than the LXX.[134]

The broader literary context leaves us in no doubt as to how these verses should be understood: "And when you look up to the sky and see the sun, the moon and the stars—all the heavenly array—do not be enticed into bowing down to them and worshiping things the LORD your God has apportioned to all the nations under heaven. But as for you, the LORD took you and brought you out of the iron-smelting furnace, out of Egypt, to be the people of his inheritance, as you now are" (Deut 4:19–20). Subsequent Jewish interpretation also interpreted the passage in this manner: "He appointed a ruler for every nation, but Israel is the Lord's own portion" (Sir 17:17; cf. Jubilees 15:31–32).[135]

Hayman's final two arguments require only a brief mention. He cites three magical texts in which the divine name is invoked alongside various angelic figures. According to Hayman, "they show religious beliefs untouched by those of Deuteronomy and the rabbis. They, and the many others like them, can hardly be described as monotheistic. Indeed, they are scarcely even 'monarchistic,' to use Vriezen's term, since Yahweh is reduced to not much more than an efficacious magic name."[136] Of course, the fact that the divine name is invoked alongside the names of angels is no proof that Jews did not distinguish between God and the angels.[137] The best recent scholarship in this area is agreed that whatever was involved in Jewish magical invocations of YHWH and the angels, it did *not* constitute a break with the monotheistic religious commitment of Judaism.[138]

Finally, Hayman cites examples of a "dualistic pattern" in Jewish texts, wherein various chief agents of God are depicted as participating in his sovereign rule over the world.[139] Unfortunately, numerous cases of this religious pattern are listed without careful attention to the specific contexts in which they occur. Metatron, Michael, and Melchizedek (to name three of the most prominent figures) are all carefully subordinated to the One God in Jewish religious literature. We have already discussed Metatron above. In the Dead Sea Scrolls it is *the God of Israel* who will "exalt the authority of Michael above all the gods and the dominion of Israel over all flesh" (1QM 17:7–8).[140] Michael's dominion in heaven will be paralleled by Israel's dominion on earth. In both cases, the authority is bestowed by God himself, so how does this threaten his unique divine status?

The description of Melchizedek in 11QMelchizedek is potentially more striking.[141] There, Melchizedek is identified with the "god" (*elohim*) of Psalm 82:1a (11QMelch 2:10). This identification is not really a revolutionary development, however, since we have already seen that the designation of angels as "gods" is compatible with a monotheistic outlook. The same text identifies "Belial and the spirits of his lot" with the *elohim* ("gods") of Psalm 82:1b–2 (11QMelch 2:11–12). This again shows that the term *god* or *gods* is being used to refer to angelic beings, who are explicitly said to be created by God elsewhere in the Dead Sea Scrolls: "You created Belial for the pit, angel of enmity; his domain is in darkness, his counsel is for evil and wickedness. All the spirits of destruction walk in the laws of darkness" (1QM 13:11–12). Melchizedek should likewise be understood as a created angel, distinct from God.

The distinction between Melchizedek and God is maintained in this text in two ways: (1) Melchizedek is identified with the "god" (*elohim*) who will "stand in the assembly *of El*" (Ps 82:1a). *El* is thereby distinguished from the *elohim* (according to the reading of this psalm which was held at Qumran) in such a way that Melchizedek is included among the "gods" (*elohim*) of the heavenly court, yet distinguished from the One God. (2) 11QMelchizedek 2:13 clearly distinguishes Melchizedek from God and makes him the agent of *El's* judgments: "Melchizedek will carry out the vengeance of *God's* judgements." In these two ways, the subordination of Melchizedek to God is maintained, despite the Qumran text's curious interpretation of Psalm 82.

The above examples show that it is not sufficient to merely cite instances where divine agents are exalted to places of special heavenly authority. One must also take into account the ways in which such agents are distinguished from, and subordinated to, the One God.[142] When such examples are examined in their proper literary and religious contexts, it can be shown with a high degree of consistency that a monotheistic outlook is usually maintained. Hayman's attempt to overthrow the "older" consensus that ancient Judaism—at least by Second Temple times—was firmly monotheistic fails to convince. Latter-day Saint scholars and apologists should no longer appeal to Hayman's study on this matter unless they can demonstrate that the criticisms raised in this essay are in some way wide of the mark.

A Critique of Margaret Barker

Another scholar whose views are sometimes cited by LDS writers is Margaret Barker. In her book, *The Great Angel: A Study of Israel's Second God,* Barker attempts to defend the following thesis:

> What has become clear to me time and time again is that even over so wide an area, the evidence points consistently in one direction and indicates that pre-Christian Judaism was not monotheistic in the sense that we use that word. The roots of Christian trinitarian theology lie in pre-Christian Palestinian beliefs about the angels. There were many in first century Palestine who still retained a world-view derived from the more ancient religion of Israel in which there was a High God and several Sons of God, one of whom was Yahweh, the Holy One of Israel.[143]

Unlike Hayman, Barker writes from a position of religious commitment. Yet in many ways these two scholars arrive at similar conclusions. Both attempt to explain the worship of Jesus within early Jewish Christianity by arguing that at least many first-century Jews were not in fact monotheists after all. Barker's wide-ranging study is very ambitious, and there is not room here to offer a critique of her entire book, which covers a vast body of material from the Old Testament to the early church fathers. Instead, I will focus on Barker's use of the Old Testament, of Philo, and of the New Testament.

Barker's Use of the Old Testament

In contrast to the views expressed earlier in this essay, Barker believes that a significant body of evidence can be uncovered from the Old Testament, showing that preexilic Jewish religion was not monotheistic at all. Many of her arguments are open to serious question from both religious and historical standpoints, however. For instance, Barker argues that the Old

Testament designation of the angels as "sons of God" shows the polytheistic origins of Israelite religion.[144] Yet this is by no means the case, since, as Carol Newsom points out, in the biblical tradition grammatical constructions such as *bene ha elohim* (the sons of God) "identify generic categories (divine beings), not genealogical relationships."[145] Marjo Korpel also notes that, in contrast to the Ugaritic pantheon, "nowhere in the Old Testament is God explicitly called a Father of gods, even though sons of God [*bny 'l(hym)*] are attested. Probably the uniqueness of God, the *one* Father ['*b 'hd*], prevented this."[146] Barker overlooks the fact that "no sexual behavior of God has been described in the Old Testament. Therefore it has to be expected that also childbirth in a more literal sense, such as in the myths of Ugarit, will be non-existent."[147] Thus, the mere designation of the angels as "sons of God" is no proof of polytheism in preexilic Israel, even if the expression bore such a connotation in the wider Canaanite culture.

Barker places a great deal of emphasis on the role of the "Deuteronomists" in her reconstruction of Israel's religious development.[148] According to her theory, First Temple Jewish religion was very different from the religion that emerged from the ashes of the Babylonian exile. During and after the exile, the Deuteronomists instituted wide-ranging religious reforms that carried on the earlier program of King Josiah (cf. 2 Kgs 22–23; 2 Chr 34–35). These reforms involved the elevation of Law and demotion of Wisdom, the quenching of heavenly ascents and visions of God, and the enforcement of strict monotheism.[149] In Barker's words:

> The reform of Josiah/the Deuteronomists, then, reconstructed as best we can from both biblical and non-biblical sources, seems to have been a time when more than pagan accretions were removed from the Jerusalem cult. Wisdom was eliminated, even though her presence was never forgotten, the heavenly ascent and the vision of God were abandoned, the hosts of heaven, the angels, were declared to be unfit for the chosen people, the ark (and the presence of Yahweh which it represented) was removed, and the role of the high priest was altered in that he was no longer the anointed. All of these features of the older cult were to appear in Christianity.[150]

Barker's reconstruction could be questioned on numerous points of detail—nearly every paragraph contains assertions that require more argumentation than she provides. But in any case, the whole hypothesis of a Deuteronomistic "movement" that enforced sweeping and novel changes in Israelite religion and that engaged in extensive rewriting of Israel's scriptures is open to serious question on both methodological and historical grounds.[151]

But more fundamentally, it should be kept in mind—especially by Mormon apologists who wish to use the results of her study—just exactly what her hypothesis implies in terms of one's view of the Bible. If one wishes to follow Barker, it must be assumed that Josiah's reforms had a *negative* influence on the religion of Judah—which is precisely the opposite of what the Bible states: "Neither before nor after Josiah was there a king like him who turned to the LORD as he did—with all his heart and with all his soul and with all his strength, in accordance with all the Law of Moses" (2 Kgs 23:25). Furthermore, if one wishes to maintain with Barker that the Deuteronomistic movement had a negative impact on the religious faith of Israel, then one is compelled to reject the teaching of a large body of biblical literature. Deuteronomy, Joshua, Judges, 1–2 Samuel, 1–2 Kings, large chunks of Isaiah and Jeremiah, as well as other prophetic books were all written or heavily edited (according to this theory) by the Deuteronomists.[152] These writings all promoted the ideals of Second Temple religion, which Barker contrasts with the religion of the First Temple that emerged in a fresh way with the rise of Christianity.[153] It goes without saying that orthodox Christians will be unwilling to reject such a large portion of the Bible—I suspect many members of the LDS Church would likewise be uncomfortable in doing so. Yet it is inconsistent to cite the conclusions of Barker's study while paying no attention to the arguments and methods used in arriving at those views.[154]

Barker's handling of specific Old Testament texts is sometimes rather naive for a scholar of her reputation. For instance, we are told that Yahweh is an angel, since he is called "the Holy One of Israel," and the angels are also called "holy ones."[155] Likewise, we are asked to believe that Yahweh is one of the sons of God, because the Hebrew verb translated "present themselves," which occurs in Job 1:6, also appears in Psalm 2:2, where the scene depicts those who do not acknowledge the Lord's superiority: "Thus the prologue to Job depicts a heaven where Yahweh is one among many and is challenged to test the loyalty of his servant. . . . It is almost a pre-moral polytheism, and Yahweh, one of the sons of God, is a part of this world."[156] Both of these assertions involve basic word-study fallacies that ought to embarrass any first-year Bible college student.

Barker has an unfortunate habit of reading into texts ideas that simply are not there. For instance, she cites 1 Chronicles 29:20, 23 as evidence that "Yahweh was manifested in human form in the Davidic King."[157] First Chronicles 29:20 says that the people "bowed low and fell prostrate before the LORD and the king." Barker would have us believe that this means they worshiped the

LORD *and* the king.[158] But this reading is excluded by the previous lines, which Barker neglects to cite: "Then David said to the whole assembly, 'Praise the LORD your God.' So they all praised the LORD, the God of their fathers." Clearly, although they worshiped in David's *presence,* it was the LORD who was the *object* of their praises. Nor does 1 Chronicles 29:23 imply the deification of the Davidic king: "So Solomon sat on the throne of the LORD as king in place of his father David." This simply means that Solomon ruled as the LORD's representative, since his throne ultimately belonged to God.

Barker's Use of Philo

Barker also appeals to the Alexandrian Jewish philosopher Philo in the attempt to show that many Jews of the first-century A.D. were something other than monotheistic: "Philo was a contemporary of the first Christians, a Jewish philosopher living in Alexandria where he was a leader of the community. His voluminous writings should provide the best possible background to any understanding of the New Testament but they are rarely used for this purpose because Philo's Judaism is very unlike the Judaism we have always assumed to be the 'orthodoxy' of Palestine."[159]

Unfortunately, Barker continually cites isolated passages from Philo, without due regard for their contexts, in the attempt to prove her case. For instance, she claims that Philo supports the notion that the high priest was deified in ancient Jewish religion.[160] Yet Philo himself explicitly denies this very thing: "Who then [is the high priest], if he is not a man? A God? I will not say so, for this name is a prerogative, assigned to the chief prophet, Moses" (*On Dreams,* II.189). Philo does affirm that the high priest is raised above the level of fleshly mortality through mystical union with the Immortal (cf. *On Dreams,* II.230–32), but he denies that this is to be understood as a literal deification: "And if he [the high priest] then becomes no man, clearly neither is he God, but God's minister" (*On Dreams,* II.231).

Barker also repeatedly misunderstands Philo's comments that at first glance appear to deify Moses on the basis of Exodus 7:1:[161] "Then the LORD said to Moses, 'See, I have made you like God to Pharaoh.'" One passage she never gets around to quoting is from Philo, *The Worse Attacks the Better* (161–62):

> It follows as a consequence of this that, when Moses is appointed 'a god unto Pharaoh,' he did not become such in reality, but only by a convention is supposed to be such.... What then do we gather from these words? That the wise man is said to be a god to the foolish man, but that in reality he is not God, just as the counterfeit four-drachma piece is not a

tetradrachm. But when the wise man is compared with Him that IS, he will be found to be a man of God; but when with a foolish man, he will turn out to be one conceived of as a god, in men's ideas and imagination, not in view of truth and actuality.

But it is in the descriptions of the divine Logos, or Word, that Barker sees the ultimate proof that Philo was not a monotheist: "Philo is quite clear what he means by Logos; he was describing a second God: 'For nothing mortal can be made in the likeness of the Most High One and Father of the Universe but (only) in that of the second God, who is his Logos' (*Questions on Genesis,* II.62)."[162] Another example comes from *On Dreams,* I.228–30, where we find Philo commenting on Genesis 31:13 (LXX):

> And do not fail to mark the language used, but carefully enquire whether there are two Gods; for we read 'I am the God that appeared to thee' not 'in my place' but 'in the place of God' as though it were another's. What then are we to say? He that is truly God is One, but those that are improperly so called are more than one. Accordingly the holy word in the present instance has indicated Him who is truly God by means of the articles saying 'I am the God', while it omits the article when mentioning him who is improperly so called, saying 'Who appeared to thee in the place' not 'of the God' but simply 'of God'. Here it gives the title of 'God' to his chief Logos, not from any superstitious nicety in applying names, but with one aim before him, to use words to express facts.[163]

A closer look at both passages, however, shows that in neither instance does Philo actually intend to say that there are two ontologically distinct Gods.[164] In *Questions and Answers on Genesis* II.62, Philo, commenting on Genesis 9:6, asks: "Why does (Scripture) say, *as if* (speaking) of another God, 'in the image of God He made man' and not 'in His own image'?" Notice that Philo says "as if" (Gk: *hos*) the Scripture were speaking of *another* God. This shows that, despite appearances, Philo does not mean "another" God when he describes the Logos as "the second God" (*ton deuteron theon*). What does he mean then? Quite simply, *he is commenting on the wording of the text,* in which God refers to himself in the third person—"He (i.e., God) made man in the image of God." From this wording Philo derives two figures— God, and his Logos, the "second" God in whose image man was made. Philo speaks of a "second God" simply because the wording of the text implies a repetition of the word *God* (*theos*).

One might object that the word *theos* only occurs once in the LXX text of Genesis 9:6. So how is it that Philo reads the text as if the presence of a second *theos* could be assumed? Because Philo was well aware that behind Genesis 9:6 lay Genesis 1:27 (LXX): "And *God* made man, according to the image of *God* he made him." The word *theos* appears twice in the text, which is why Philo can speak of a "second" *theos* in whose image man was made: "For just as God is the pattern of the Image, to which the title of Shadow has just been given, even so the Image becomes the pattern of other beings, as the prophet made clear at the very outset of the Law-giving by saying, 'And God made man after the Image of God' (Gen. i. 27), implying that the Image had been made such as representing God, but that man was made after the Image" (*Allegorical Interpretation*, III.96).

The other passage appealed to by Barker is Philo, *On Dreams,* I.228–30. Once again, however, Philo's language *is dictated by the wording of the text*, not by some alleged belief in multiple Gods. The LXX of Genesis 31:13 reads: "I am *the God* who appeared to you in the place of *God*"—Philo then adds, "*as though* it were another's." As in Genesis 1:27, the word *theos* appears twice in the verse, in such a way as to suggest that two figures are involved. Yet again, Philo is careful to qualify what he is saying by using the Greek word *hos*—"as though" there were actually *another* God. Philo is well aware that according to verse 11, it is "the angel of God" who is speaking, and he is attempting to reconcile the wording of the text with his monotheistic assumptions. If it is true that "God is One," then how is this passage—which appears to speak of two Gods—to be understood?

Fortunately, Philo supplies his own interpretation, which makes it clear that he understands the Logos to be the visible manifestation of God himself. Philo is willing to speak (on rare occasions) of a *second* (*deuteros*) God when the wording of the biblical text requires it, but this "second" God is not to be understood as *another* (*heteros*) God. Mortal creatures are not capable of beholding God as he is in his own hidden being, so God appears to them in the form of the Logos:

> It was given in order that, since there are not in God things which man can comprehend, *man may recognize His subsistence.* To the souls which indeed are incorporeal and are occupied in His worship it is likely that He should reveal Himself as He is, conversing with them as friend with friends; but to souls which are still in a body, *giving Himself the likeness of angels,* not altering His own nature, for He is unchangeable, but conveying to those

which receive the impression of His presence a semblance *in a different form,* such that they take the image to be not a copy, but that original form itself. (*On Dreams,* I.231–32)

As the above passage makes clear, the angelic appearance of God to Jacob was a visible appearance of God himself in a different form. Note also the following statement:

Why, then, do we wonder any longer at His *assuming the likeness of angels,* seeing that for the succour of those that are in need He assumes that of men? Accordingly, when He says 'I am the God who was seen of thee in the place of God' (Gen. xxxi. 13), understand that *He occupied the place of an angel only so far as appeared,* without changing, with a view to the profit of him who was not yet capable of seeing the true God. (*On Dreams,* I.238)

Philo's complex understanding of the relationship between God and the Logos is laid out in another passage, which illustrates the fact that the Logos is at the same time identified with God and yet distinguished from him:

In the first place (there is) He Who is elder than the one and the monad and the beginning. Then (comes) the Logos of the Existent One, the truly seminal substance of existing things. And from the divine Logos, as from a spring, there divide and break forth two powers. One is the creative (power), through which the artificer placed and ordered all things; this is named "God." And (the other is) the royal (power), since through it the Creator rules over created things; this is called "Lord." (*Questions and Answers on Exodus,* II.68)[165]

This interpretation of the data is in keeping with most contemporary scholarship, which agrees that Philo understood the angelic Logos to be a visible manifestation of God himself in a different form.[166] As Alan F. Segal writes: "Philo takes the story to mean that the mystic can see a figure of God which is a 'second God,' but that figure does not compromise monotheism. . . . Philo allows for the existence of a second, principal, divine creature, whom he calls a 'second God,' who nevertheless is only the visible emanation of the High, ever-existing God."[167] Likewise, Emil Schürer notes: "Philo does not comment on the ambivalence of the Logos, in that it is neither personal nor impersonal. For him the Logos is both a person distinct from God and a designation of God in a particular relation—that of his activity."[168]

Barker's Use of the New Testament

We have seen that at least two areas of Barker's study are open to challenge on both religious and historical grounds. Her reading of the Old Testament is questionable on a number of fronts and involves a wholesale rejection of the authority of a large portion of the Bible. Likewise, her appeal to Philo is plagued by the tendency to cite isolated statements without due regard for their broader contexts. The religion of the Old Testament was indeed monotheistic, and educated first-century Jews such as Philo were likewise firmly committed to monotheism.[169] We shall now see that Barker's reading of the New Testament is also flawed.[170]

Barker contends that the earliest Christians identified Jesus as Yahweh, "the firstborn of the sons of God."[171] In other words, they recognized the Son of God as the Great Angel—Israel's second God (to borrow the wording of the book's title). As one examines Barker's handling of the New Testament data, it becomes clear that she repeatedly works from the assumption that if one can show that Jesus was identified with Yahweh (which can easily be done), this is proof that Jesus was Israel's *second* God. But as we have seen, the evidence that Yahweh was distinguished from the Most High God by the ancient Israelites is far from conclusive. Therefore, for Jews who were familiar with the Hebrew Bible, the identification of Jesus as Yahweh would have implied, not that he was a *second* God, but that he was somehow to be included within the identity of the *One* God (Deut 6:4). As Jesus said: "I and the Father are one" (John 10:30); and "Anyone who has seen me has seen the Father" (John 14:9); and "The Father is in me, and I in the Father" (John 10:38).

If Barker's reading of the New Testament is correct, then why is the Son never described as a "second" God? Why is he never designated as "another" God? Why does the plural "Gods" never occur in the New Testament with reference to the persons of the Godhead? And if Christ is, in fact, the Great Angel, the firstborn of the angelic sons of God, then why is the New Testament so careful to distinguish the Son *from* the angels?[172] These points raise significant doubts regarding both Barker's understanding of the relationship between Jesus and God in early Christianity and the portrayal of ancient Jewish religion on which her interpretation of the New Testament depends. Mormon apologists should think long and hard about whether it will prove profitable to cite Barker's work in support of their own understanding of the relationship between Christ and God.

A Critique of Daniel Peterson

The question of monotheism in ancient Judaism and Christianity has also been addressed in a recent essay by Daniel C. Peterson. Peterson sets out to explore Jesus' citation of Psalm 82:6 in John 10:34 against the backdrop of the divine council motif in the Hebrew Bible and other ancient texts: "Once we have divested ourselves of certain theological prejudices that are, apparently, foreign to ancient Hebrew and early Christian thought, the Latter-day Saint claim that God and humankind are akin seems a promising basis upon which to resolve the apparent disagreement between the reference of Psalm 82:6 to heavenly gods and the reference of John 10:34 to mortal human beings."[173] In essence, Peterson attempts to argue that the LDS belief in polytheism and the divine nature of humankind enables us to reconcile Jesus' application of this psalm to his human audience with its original meaning, which involved the gods of the heavenly council: "In all Christendom it is only the Latter-day Saints, to whom a doctrine of the antemortal existence of human beings and of their literal kinship with God has been revealed, who recognize that gods and men form a single class, differentiated along a spectrum of holiness, wisdom, and power."[174]

In contrast to Hayman, Peterson engages in a detailed discussion of a wide range of evidence and is usually careful to avoid selective citations of primary and secondary literature. On the other hand, his analysis is more focused than that of Barker, and in general he avoids the sort of sweeping and unsubstantiated assertions that frequently weaken her overly ambitious study. The combination of depth and breadth in Peterson's research raises it to a level beyond that of these other scholars and poses a more serious challenge to orthodox Christian theology. I do not have space here to offer a point-by-point response to Peterson's arguments, but I do feel that his essay can be questioned on a number of points.

Did Jesus Claim to Be "a god" or "God"?

Peterson claims that Jesus was only accused of making himself "a god," since the Greek word *theos* in John 10:33 lacks the definite article.[175] Although this translation is grammatically possible, it is weakened by the fact that this is a response to Jesus' claim: "I and the Father are one" (10:30). Why would the Jews conclude that by claiming to be "one" with the Father, he was actually claiming to be a second god?[176] On the other hand, Jesus' claim is naturally understood in terms of inclusion within the unique identity of the One God (Deut 6:4). Peterson is correct to insist that Jesus is not the Father, but he misses the fact that Jesus identifies the One God of the Shema as both the Father and the Son.

Can the Septuagint Be Trusted?

Peterson castigates the Septuagint (LXX) for "routinely" suppressing underlying polytheism in the Hebrew Bible.[177] Yet this can only weaken the idea that the earliest Christians were something other than strict monotheists, since, as Melvin Peters notes, the LXX "was the Bible of the early Christian Church. It was not secondary to any other scripture; it was Scripture. . . . The LXX also provides the context in which many of the lexical and theological concepts in the NT can best be explained."[178] Therefore, the "suppression" of polytheism was apparently part of the theological heritage of early Christianity. Does Peterson really want to pit this theological heritage against his own?

Was the Hebrew Conception of God the Same as Israel's Pagan Neighbors?

Peterson draws upon Canaanite parallels in order to illuminate the divine council motif in Psalm 82.[179] It is obvious, I think, that he attempts to highlight features of the Canaanite pantheon that are similar to aspects of LDS belief.[180] There can be no question but that the divine council in the Hebrew Bible shows connections with the broader religious environment.[181] However, Peterson implies that the difference between Israel's religion and her pagan neighbors was only a matter of worship *practice* (monolatry), rather than how God was conceptualized (monotheism).[182] But there were important differences between the Hebrew and Ugaritic *conceptions* of God, which deserve more treatment than Peterson offers. The divine council imagery in Psalm 82 must be set within the historical context of Israel's unique religious perspective.

Among the many differences pointed out by Marjo Korpel between the Ugaritic pantheon and the Hebrew conception of God are the following six features:

- "Whereas in the polytheistic pantheon of Ugarit there was naturally room for both male and female deities, it was a consequence of monotheism that in the Old Testament God is predominantly male."[183]
- "Whereas in Ugarit it was apparently the intention of the poets to ascribe a splendid and even superior love-life to the deities, the early turn to monotheism forced the Israelite tradition to restrict this

310

anthropomorphic imagery to the relation between God and his people."[184]

- "Whereas all Canaanites were fond of theophoric personal names containing the element *ìm* 'Mother' such names are entirely lacking not only in the Old Testament but also in epigraphic Hebrew sources. It must be concluded that there was a historically traceable reluctancy to compare God to a mother. No doubt this was less the result of patriarchal bias than the logical outcome of the early choice for monotheism."[185]

- "The family of the Ugaritic gods consists of fathers and mothers, sons and daughters, brothers and sisters. To the family of Ilu also belong the Canaanite kings who were considered to be sons of Ilu and who after their death were supposedly deified. In the Old Testament, however, no term for 'family' is ever used for the entourage of YHWH, nor is his people ever called his family or his race—not even in a metaphorical sense."[186]

- "In Ugarit the god Ilu, head of the pantheon, was primarily regarded as the physical father of the gods. Only secondarily was he considered to be the father of man in the sense that he was the creator of mankind. Thus the literal meaning of the epithet 'Father' prevailed in Ugarit. In the Old Testament the epithet 'Father' is used in its metaphorical meaning only, as the creator-father of man. There are no texts referring to YHWH as being the father of divine beings."[187]

- "Already in the earliest traditions of Israel the claim to an exclusive position of YHWH-El creates patent differences between the metaphorical language used in Ugarit and in the Old Testament. Its consequences were thought through on such a broad scale that it is impossible to imagine that all this was the work of a handful of scholars in the Exile."[188]

I am not convinced that Peterson's study takes adequate account of such differences in his discussion of Psalm 82 and other biblical texts. The Hebrew Bible does contain references to a divine council, but the relationship of God to the other members of the heavenly court in the biblical literature differs in important respects from the Canaanite pantheon.[189]

Who Are the "gods" of Psalm 82?

Peterson believes that LDS theology helps to reconcile Jesus' citation of Psalm 82:6 with its original context. He understands Psalm 82 in light of texts such as Abraham 3:22–23 in the Pearl of Great Price, where premortal spirits are gathered in a heavenly council and appointed as rulers. This connection is understandable from an LDS perspective, although I think it more likely that Abraham 3:22–23 has been influenced by Psalm 82.[190] In any case, nearly all of the references to "gods" of the divine council in the OT are best understood as *poetic depictions* of pagan gods as subservient members of Yahweh's heavenly court.[191] Psalm 82:8 shows that this is the case: "Rise up, O God, judge the earth, for all the nations are your inheritance." It is the gods of the nations who are the objects of God's judgment in this psalm.

This interpretation receives further support from: (1) the fact that Deuteronomy 32:8–9 appears to lie behind Psalm 82, where the "sons of God" are clearly the gods of the nations;[192] and (2) the fact that the conflation of heavenly "gods" and earthly pagan rulers in Psalm 82 is paralleled in Isaiah 14:12–17 and Ezekiel 28:1–19, where the kings of Babylon and Tyre are poetically depicted as members of the divine assembly who face judgment for their arrogance.[193] As Robert Chisholm writes of Psalm 82: "The rulers are actual human kings (cf. vv. 2–4) who, for rhetorical effect and in accord with their arrogant self-perception, are addressed as if they were members of the divine assembly known from Canaanite myth (vv. 1, 6–7)."[194] I do not claim that this *disproves* Peterson's reading of the text in light of his own religious viewpoint, but it does demonstrate that one need not turn to LDS theology in order to make sense of the original meaning of Psalm 82 and its application to rebellious humans by Jesus in John 10:34–36.

Were El and Yahweh Distinct Gods in Ancient Judaism?

In his discussion, Peterson assumes the conclusions of those who argue that El and Yahweh were originally two distinct gods: "In the earliest Israelite conception, according to this view, father El had a divine son named Jehovah or Yahweh. El, or Elyon ('the Highest' or 'the Most High'), and Yahweh were distinct."[195] Of course, the biblical text often appears to identify El *as* Yahweh, but this is explained as a late religious development: "By the tenth century B.C., however, El and Yahweh had come to be identified with one another.... Thus, after roughly the tenth century before Christ, no evidence of any distinct Israelite cult of El is extant, except in his guise as Yahweh."[196]

I must confess that I find it difficult to understand why Peterson would want to accept the destructive conclusions of historical-critical scholarship, particularly when the evidence does not at all demand it.[197] In a detailed study of the biblical traditions, Johannes C. de Moor has shown that theophoric personal names in the period up to David overwhelmingly favored Yahwistic and (especially) Elohistic names, in contrast to the many *pagan* theophoric toponyms (i.e., place names) attested in the same period.[198] The evidence supports the following two conclusions:

- "Contrary to what might be expected on the basis of the research of Tigay and Fowler theophoric biblical personal names from the time up to David show a preference not for Yahweh but for El. This trend is present in all the tribes of Israel. Yet, the number of Yahwistic names is so high that we must assume the popularity of Yahwism to have started long before David made Zion the national centre of worship for YHWH. Moreover, the correspondence in meaning between Yahwistic and Elohistic personal names is so high that El and YHWH may well have been names of the same God centuries before David."[199]

- "The remarkable divergency between the personal names and the toponyms speaks against the supposition that the religion of the early Israelites was in no way distinct from that of their neighbors. Even if a number of 'pagan' personal names was [sic] altered later on it cannot have been a major corrective operation because many of these names were transmitted faithfully. However, the circumstance that only a single personal name (*bn 'nt*) appears to contain the name of a goddess will require an explanation. Either such names were corrected systematically or even in the premonarchical period YHWH did not have an official consort."[200]

In other words, Peterson (and those scholars upon whom he depends) needs to explain why most Israelites prior to the time of David were naming their children after El/Yahweh if monotheism was a religious development that arose after the Exile. He also needs to explain the overlap in usage of the names El and Yahweh, if they were viewed as distinct Gods during this period.[201] If one is to argue that the biblical evidence is unreliable, then it will be necessary to explain why the biblical record still *preserves* some pagan theophoric personal names, and even more pagan theophoric toponyms.[202]

To sum up, while Peterson's study offers a major challenge to traditional views of Judeo-Christian monotheism, his interpretation of Psalm 82 and John 10 is by no means the only way the evidence can be read. His interpretation of John 10:30–33 overlooks an important allusion to Deuteronomy 6:4 and misses the nuance of Jesus' claim to be "one" with "the Father." He forgets the fact that the Septuagint played a major role in shaping the theology of the early church when he castigates it for suppressing polytheism. He overlooks important distinctions between Israelite monotheism and Canaanite conceptions of God and the heavenly world. His attempt to reconcile the original meaning of Psalm 82 with Jesus' application in John 10 assumes the correctness of the LDS view of the nature of humankind and is by no means the only way to avoid accusing Jesus of quoting the Bible out of context. Finally, Peterson overlooks important evidence that El and Yahweh were already identified as the same God in Israelite religion long before the tenth century B.C.

Conclusion

In conclusion, the religion of the Bible is monotheistic from start to finish. The New Testament writers included Jesus Christ and the Holy Spirit alongside God the Father in their worship and in their view of God's identity— but they did not abandon their monotheistic outlook inherited from Judaism. Recent attempts to argue that ancient Judaism was something less than monotheistic frequently depend on misleading citations and inadequate attention to the broader context of the documents and the writers to whom they appeal. Such arguments also depend on liberal approaches to biblical books such as Deuteronomy and Isaiah 40–55 that are inconsistent with the high view of scripture affirmed in the LDS Articles of Faith: "We believe the Bible to be the word of God as far as it is translated correctly."[203] The biblical evidence leads, not to a polytheistic religion, but to the Trinitarian religion that came to be formulated in the Nicene Creed. As Larry Hurtado writes: "This monotheistic concern is in fact what lies behind the central Christian doctrine of the Triune God. . . . The dominant (or at least ultimately the more viable) Christian concern was to develop an understanding of Jesus' divine significance *within the framework of faith in one God.*"[204]

It is my hope that—rather than understanding Christ's divine status within the polytheistic context of a pantheon—members of the Church of Jesus Christ of Latter-day Saints may come to embrace Christ as the incarnate revelation of the One God. May we all confess with the Apostle John: "We have seen his glory, the glory of the One and Only, who came from the Father, full of grace and truth. . . . No one has ever seen God, but God the One and Only, who is at the Father's side, has made him known" (John 1:14, 18).

9

IS MORMONISM CHRISTIAN?

CRAIG L. BLOMBERG

Craig L. Blomberg is Professor of New Testament at Denver Seminary. He earned a B.A. in religion from Augustana College, an M.A. in New Testament from Trinity Evangelical Divinity School, and a Ph.D. in New Testament from the University of Aberdeen, Scotland. Dr. Blomberg is a widely respected New Testament scholar and the author of such books as *The Historical Reliability of the Gospels* (InterVarsity), *Jesus and the Gospels* (Broadman), *Neither Poverty Nor Riches: A Biblical Theology of Possessions* (InterVarsity), and *1 Corinthians* in the *NIV Application Commentary* (Zondervan). He is the coauthor of *Introduction to Biblical Interpretation* (Word) and *How Wide The Divide? A Mormon and an Evangelical in Conversation* (InterVarsity). He has contributed essays to many reference works and edited volumes and has published in such journals as *Biblical Theology Bulletin, BYU Studies, Catholic Biblical Quarterly, Journal for the Study of the New Testament, Journal of the Evangelical Theological Society, Themelios,* and *Trinity Journal.*

With absolute incredulity Mormons often hear or read the charge that their faith is not Christian. How could it not be Christian? After all, isn't the very name of Jesus Christ in the name of their church—the Church of *Jesus Christ* of Latter-day Saints? Isn't their Book of Mormon subtitled "Another Testament of *Jesus Christ*"? Is not the apex of its story line a record of an appearance of the resurrected Christ to the peoples inhabiting the New World? And is not the purpose of the Book of Mormon as well as the LDS Church's extensive missionary program to encourage and provide opportunity for people everywhere to "come unto Christ" (Jacob 1:7)? Moreover, Latter-day Saints worship Christ as the divine Son of God, the Messiah of Israel, and the Savior of the world. They believe that he suffered as the atonement for sin, that he bodily rose from the dead, and that he will one day return, as the New Testament teaches, to set up his kingdom on earth.[1]

Given these and other doctrinal overlaps with historic Christianity, the average Mormon is mystified as to how any objective, rational person could cast doubt on Mormonism's Christian character. Besides, the Latter-day Saint thinks, if Mormonism is not Christian, then what is it? It is not Jewish, Islamic, Hindu, Buddhist, or the offshoot of any other world religion. Nothing is left besides "Christian." People who deny this obvious conclusion must be either hopelessly deceived or willfully dishonest.[2]

The average evangelical Christian's perception of the Latter-day Saints, by contrast, is quite different. They have usually been taught to consider Mormonism a "cult," lumped together with as wide-ranging religious phenomena as the Jehovah's Witnesses, Transcendental Meditation, and the Branch Davidians. The "cults," in turn, are often combined with the occult, so that many evangelicals have some vaguely defined fear that it could be personally harmful to associate with Latter-day Saints, even as friends, lest something overtly satanic befall them.[3] Not only are Mormons non-Christians in their minds, but for some, it seems that Mormons should not even receive the love and friendship Jesus commands his disciples to exhibit even to their enemies (e.g., Luke 6:27). Instead, they are shunned and at times even vilified. "Speaking the truth in love" (Eph 4:15) is thus often sacrificed by both sides in the debate.[4]

It is thus with considerable trepidation that I write this essay. In a previous work dialoguing with Mormonism, I explicitly wrote that the book did "not intend to address the question of whether Evangelicals and Mormons are both, in certain instances, bona fide Christians, however worthwhile that issue might be to discuss."[5] That did not stop people in both camps, however, from falsely claiming that I was indeed implying Mormonism to be Christian—some of them eventually admitting that they had not bothered to read the book in its entirety, including my disclaimer.[6] To tackle this question directly now runs the risk of alienating everyone I did not previously alienate! I fear that my LDS friends will now accuse me of anti-Mormonism, no matter how courteous and objective I try to be.[7] And many evangelicals may complain that I am too soft and gracious in my critique. But Ephesians 4:15 remains in my Bible, so I must proceed and hope for the best.

Uses of the Term *Christian* with Respect to a Religious Movement

Historic Christianity?

To address the question "Is Mormonism Christian?" obviously requires a New Testament definition of *Christian*. The Greek counterpart *Christianos* occurs only three times in the New Testament (Acts 11:26; 26:28; and 1 Pet 4:16), each time in a context of "outsiders" seeking a label for the fledgling Jesus movement. No formal definition of the term ever appears in the Bible. Probably the most common way the term is used in contemporary English is to denote a person who is a member of an Orthodox, Catholic, or Protestant church, the three historic divisions of the faith over the centuries of the church's existence. Thus the *World Book Encyclopedia* article on "Christianity" begins as follows: "Christianity is the religion based on the life and teachings of Jesus Christ. Most followers of Christianity, called Christians, are members of one of three major groups—Roman Catholic, Protestant, or Eastern Orthodox."[8] Based on this definition, Mormonism is clearly not Christian, nor has it ever claimed to be so.

Indeed, the uniquely Mormon scriptures declare that all of Christendom after the apostolic age prior to 1830 was "a church which is most abominable above all other churches," whose founder is the devil (1 Nephi 13:5–6).[9] In Doctrine and Covenants 29:21, that "great and abominable church" is called the "whore of all the earth." Joseph Smith, we are told, was commanded not to join any existing Christian denomination, "for they were all wrong," "all their creeds were an abomination in [God's] sight," their "professors were all corrupt," and their religious worship all a hypocritical pretense (Joseph Smith —History 2:19).

Restored Christianity?

Instead, the Latter-day Saints claim that their church is the restoration of the original Christianity of Jesus and the apostles. The *Encyclopedia of Mormonism* puts it this way:

> The Church of Jesus Christ of Latter-day Saints does not see itself as one Christian denomination among many, but rather as God's latter-day restoration of the fulness of Christian faith and practice. Thus, from its earliest days LDS Christians sought to distinguish themselves from Christians of other traditions. Other forms of Christianity, while bearing much truth and doing much good under the guidance of the Holy Spirit, are viewed as incomplete, lacking the authority of the priesthood of God, the temple ordinances, the comprehensive understanding of the plan of salvation, and the nonparadoxical understanding of the Godhead.[10]

In order to support this claim, Mormons argue that the original church underwent a great apostasy as Jesus' apostles died off, produced in large measure by the corrupting influences of Hellenistic philosophy as the gospel traveled increasingly into non-Jewish territory. Thus, the major doctrinal developments of the second through sixth centuries of Christianity, culminating in the various creeds and councils, cannot be seen as the logical outworking of New Testament Christianity but are aberrant deviations from the faith. Not until the revelation given to Joseph Smith was true Christianity ever again restored.[11]

There are several historical observations that make this reconstruction of early Christianity untenable, however. First, while it is undeniable that both Hellenistic culture in general and non-Christian philosophy in particular influenced the form of postapostolic Christianity, the amount and suddenness of transformation required to defend the Mormon view of apostasy simply cannot be elicited from the ancient sources available to us. A slow process of change over several centuries led to the emergence of the highly institutionalized Roman Catholic Church, quite different from the more informally organized churches of the New Testament, but no one event or period in early Christian history can be seen as determinative of this shift.[12] The earliest extant post-New Testament creed, known as the Old Roman Creed, which emerged in the late second and early third centuries, was already Trinitarian in its organization, and every line in it parallels numerous New Testament texts that use almost the identical wording.[13] The third-century Apostles' Creed, the earliest and most widely accepted of the ancient "ecumenical" creeds, differs only slightly from its Old Roman predecessor. And the fourth-century Nicene Creed simply expands on the Apostles' Creed, section by section, even as it introduces language reflective of larger debates within the Greco-Roman world.[14] Even that language, however, is more often a critique of Hellenistic "corruption" of Christianity than a product of it.[15]

Second, these observations are partly granted by certain recent LDS writings that, instead of trying to demonstrate how corrupt early postapostolic Christianity became, mine the preconciliar literature for supposed parallels to Mormon distinctives.[16] They regularly build on the classic modern-era claim by Protestant liberals of past generations of scholarship like Adolf von Harnack and Walter Bauer, who argued that what the various councils labeled heresy often predated the views that emerged as orthodoxy.[17] Thus, they point to numerous excerpts of intertestamental Jewish apocrypha and pseudepigrapha, the writings of the mostly orthodox church fathers of the second century, and the more eccentric gnostic and New Testament apocryphal literature that demonstrate that other Jews and Christians have at times believed in such doctrines as the preexistence of souls, the corporeality of God, the ontological subordination of the Son to the Father, and so on.

Unfortunately, these discussions contain numerous fallacies. The majority of these alleged parallels come from sources themselves implicitly or explicitly influenced by Hellenistic philosophy. The Latter-day Saints cannot have it both ways. If this philosophy was primarily a corrupting influence on authentic Christianity, then it is no argument in their favor that a majority of their ancient "parallels" come from exactly that Hellenistic philosophy.[18] Moreover, numerous studies have demonstrated that Hellenism had permeated deeply into Palestine well before the time of Christ; every portion of New Testament Christianity was a mix of ideas that shared common ground with Jewish and Greco-Roman thought and that also differed with both arenas of thought in varying ways.[19] Very few non-LDS scholars today, either liberal or conservative, believe that one can map out the first few centuries of Christian thought by tracing straight-line developments from orthodoxy to heresy or vice versa.

In addition, a fair number of the parallels cited by contemporary Mormons simply do not teach what it is alleged they do. For example, most of Stephen Robinson's references to early Christian belief in the corporeality of God are talking about the Incarnation—the Son taking upon himself human flesh, not the Father having a body as in the uniquely Mormon claim. So too, all of Robinson's references to divinization in the early church, mostly from *Greek* Orthodoxy, have to do with people taking on the moral characteristics of God, not his ontological distinctives.[20] Finally, even where there are genuine conceptual parallels, they come from disparate enough sources that they do not add up to evidence for the distinctively Mormon *system* of thought (or worldview) within any *one* ancient author or branch of the church. Thus, Bickmore can cite pre-Christian Jewish sources for a fascination with an exalted angel almost parallel to God the Father, gnostic sources for esoteric rites with some similarities to various secretive LDS ceremonies, and largely "orthodox" church fathers who debated the preexistence of the soul (though usually *not* the existence of the soul prior to the creation of the earth).[21] But one cannot find all of these beliefs in any one place, much less do they add up to any coherent doctrinal system as in modern-day Mormon thought.

Third, even if we granted the greater measure of apostasy in early postapostolic Christianity that Mormons have often claimed, with vestiges of distinctively LDS beliefs and practices scattered about, one would still have to demonstrate that these distinctives corresponded to *original* Christianity as defined by Jesus and the apostles. But such tenets are even more conspicuously absent from the New Testament than from the church fathers. Teachings about additional scriptures, the corporeality of God, deification, the premortal existence of souls, and the like find even less support (indeed, arguably, *no* support) in the New Testament than in postapostolic Christianity, and many Latter-day Saints recognize this. Hence, Joseph Smith's claim that the "abominable church" had taken away numerous "plain and precious parts of the gospel" (1 Nephi 13:34).

Now to defend this charge, Mormonism has two options. The first is to argue that the text of the New Testament itself is corrupt, substantially beyond the actual variations that textual criticism can demonstrate. This is seemingly one of the central reasons that Joseph Smith produced his own "Inspired Version" of the Bible.[22] Unfortunately, there is almost never any manuscript evidence from antiquity to support the most theologically significant changes Smith made to the Bible; virtually all of the these fall into the category of what textual critics would call the "easier readings"—changes that a scribe would introduce in copying that are designed to solve theological problems and smooth out awkward features of the text[23]—not variants that would commend themselves as the original readings of the text. And, contrary to certain LDS claims,[24] we have a relatively unbroken history of the transmission of the New Testament text that does not leave sizable enough gaps for sweeping changes to have been made in the copying of its documents. From the first decades of the second century, we find numerous quotes of the New Testament in the church fathers; by the late second century, we have sizable fragments of entire books preserved; and by the third and fourth centuries, hundreds of papyri and the great uncials begin to appear.[25]

The other option is for the Latter-day Saints to concede that we do have the New Testament documents very well intact but to argue that entirely separate books have been lost from the canon.[26] But again, there is not a shred of solid historical evidence to support this claim. Early Christian writers do occasionally quote from some lost apocryphal document, but these quotations do not contain distinctively Mormon doctrine. A large quantity of post-New Testament Christian literature, both orthodox and heterodox, still remains extant, and readers can consult this material for themselves to see how different it is from LDS theology.[27] In answering the question "Without records how do we know what happened?" Joseph F. McConkie candidly replies, "The restoration of the gospel is the most perfect evidence."[28] It is, in fact, the *only* evidence he cites; the circular reasoning of his argument should be obvious.

What is more, it is now widely acknowledged by biblical scholars, including not a few Roman Catholics, that the highly institutionalized forms of Christianity that created the Roman church developed *after* the apostolic age. Accounts of apostles having to appoint successors to themselves (cf. Acts 1:15–26) and to authorize the reception of the Holy Spirit (cf. Acts 8:14–17) appear only once each in the New Testament and did not become normative *patterns* of ecclesiastical practice until later centuries.[29] Peter receiving the "keys of the kingdom" (Matt 16:19) in its original context is considerably removed from the later concept of one infallible ruler of the church.[30] The "monarchical episcopacy" as a defining mark of "early Catholicism," so crucial to the LDS argument that the true church exists only where there are duly authorized leaders performing various sacred ceremonies, is itself a second-century corruption of pure New Testament Christianity, not its original form.[31] Finally, the entire argument that the distinctive beliefs and practices of Mormonism could have successfully been suppressed (or simply lost) on such a massive scale at some point in early Christian history, when we have relatively unbroken testimony of a representative cross section of early Christian belief throughout each generation of its first several centuries of existence, defies credibility.

A New Form of Christianity?

We have seen, then, that Mormonism does not fit any historic Christian option and that its claim to be a different, *restored* form of Christianity also fails. But is there, perhaps, a third way in which it might be considered Christian—not as the restoration of the original form, but as a newly revealed fourth branch of Christendom? In many respects, the LDS claims might prove more persuasive had Joseph Smith treated the Book of Mormon, not as the translation of a centuries-old work, but as brand new revelation from God, as he did with his subsequent Doctrine and Covenants.[32] After all, a large number of LDS doctrines and practices that do find prior Christian precedent most closely parallel the broader Restorationist movement in early nineteenth-century America.

Consider, for example, the following list:

- Belief in an apostasy in the early church, which the Reformation did not adequately correct, necessitating a further Restoration
- Belief in the necessity of believers' baptism by immersion for salvation
- Dependence on Acts 2:38 for the sequence of saving actions, which include faith, repentance, baptism, forgiveness of sins, the gift of the Holy Ghost, and appropriate good works to demonstrate persevering to the end, upon which eternal life can then be assured
- A rejection of all the historic creeds and confessions of faith of the church
- A desire to separate from all other existing forms of Christianity but to unite as the one true church of Jesus Christ
- Using a name for one's church that referred only to Christ and not to any human leaders
- Strong anti-Calvinism; against all five points of the "TULIP"—total depravity, unconditional election, limited atonement, irresistible grace, and the (guaranteed) perseverance of the saints
- Preaching against "faith only," especially in light of James 2:24

- Ambiguity as to whether or not the Holy Ghost is a person
- The necessity of weekly Communion, but avoidance of wine due to teetotalism
- Against paid clergy, clerical titles, and the factiousness caused by denominationalism
- A spirit of self-reliance, a stress on tithing, and a strong concern to care for the genuinely needy in Christian circles and elsewhere
- An emphasis on Sabbath-keeping and the restoration of morality to a church and culture widely perceived to have become antinomian
- The generation of a new translation of the Scriptures
- The ultimate harmony of science and religion
- A sharp distinction between the dispensations of the patriarchs, the law, and the gospel
- Belief in the establishment of God's kingdom in America in a more complete form than in any previous era of church history, described as "building Zion"
- A renewed missionary zeal
- A charismatic, iconoclastic founder[33]

One might be forgiven for thinking that this list described elements of religion newly revealed to Joseph Smith, but in fact every item was a central tenet of the preaching of Alexander Campbell, from which the Disciples of Christ movement was formed.[34] One of Campbell's brightest followers, with whom he discoursed extensively, was Sidney Rigdon, who later became Joseph Smith's "right hand man."[35] George Arbaugh, who chronicled in detail Smith's career-long doctrinal pilgrimage increasingly away from orthodox Christianity, was even able to say that at its inception, Mormonism was a "Campbellite sect."[36]

Of course, Campbell strictly limited his sources of authority to the Old and New Testaments. Joseph Smith had other influences for his more unparalleled "revelations." To be sure, a sizable amount of the Book of Mormon alludes to, and even explicitly quotes from, the King James Bible, including passages that subsequent textual criticism has demonstrated were not in the original manuscripts of Scripture.[37] But Smith also became a Mason, and there are numerous parallels between the Masonic Lodge ceremonies and LDS temple rituals.[38] He heard countless preachers from numerous denominations who passed through the Palmyra, New York, area and read voraciously from local libraries.[39] Whether or not we will ever be able to pin down one specific literary source for the general plot of the Book of Mormon is probably irrelevant; there was enough oral and written speculation in Smith's day about the settling of the Americas by the Indians, possibilities of ancient Jewish pilgrimage to the New World, concerns over the salvation of those who had died without ever hearing the gospel (both in ancient Israel and in the Western Hemisphere), debates about the Negro race as possibly cursed by God, and hopes for America becoming a Christian Utopia (a new Israel and the site of Christ's return) that it is completely understandable that all these elements should appear in the Book of Mormon and subsequent writings by Smith.[40] The standard LDS apologetic of how unlikely it is that the "poorly educated" (formally speaking) young Smith could have created his revelations without divine inspiration overlooks all of these clearly documented influences on his early life and thought.[41]

Now as we speculate as to whether Mormonism could be considered Christian in the sense of simply a new nineteenth-century denomination, we must stress that this is not what the Latter-day Saints themselves claim. Nevertheless, it seems that they would be overjoyed if orthodox Christians would at least grant them that much.[42] One obstacle to this acknowledgment, then, becomes the fact that, shorn of its Restorationist claims, Mormonism appears to relate to historic Christianity much as Christianity came to relate to Judaism: it changes enough elements to be classified better as a completely new religion.[43]

Perhaps an analogy will help here. Suppose suddenly a group of Caucasian Swedes announced that God had given them a new work of scripture that contained many of the teachings of the Qu'ran in it. A contemporary prophet had translated it into Swedish from ancient tablets purportedly written in an otherwise unknown language called reformed Persian, but those tablets are unavailable for anyone to examine. Despite Muslim convictions about the inerrancy of the Qu'ran, this new religious movement claims that Islamic scripture is corrupt, missing many fundamental doctrines that the prophet Mohammed had in fact promulgated, including an account of Sweden being settled by middle-eastern Arabs long before the Vikings. What is more, the cardinal tenets of Islam—the monotheism of Allah and Mohammed as the prophet who brought final, definitive revelation from God—have been disproved; in fact, the Qu'ran's original views more resembled the polytheism Muslims believe Mohammed rejected than the monotheism centrally proclaimed throughout their history. While Mohammed himself was a great spokesman for Allah, there is a Swedish prophet continuing to receive revelation from God today who can supersede anything in the Qu'ran that he wishes. Meanwhile, the standard summary of Islamic religion is to be rejected as "abominable," and most of Islam's holy men are viewed as corrupt.

The analogy could, of course, be extended. But could we seriously expect any faithful Muslim today to simultaneously reject this new sect's claims to have restored original Islam and yet accept it as a legitimate expression of the Muslim faith?[44] Presumably, the Latter-day Saints would similarly reject claims by a splinter group from within their own midst to be truly Mormon if they differed in this many fundamental ways from the larger parent organization.

There is, however, a possible way forward for Mormonism. Stephen Robinson himself draws parallels to how Roman Catholics and Protestants finally made substantial progress in interfaith dialogue in the last half-century.[45] This became possible largely due to the historic Vatican II Council in the mid–1960s. Among other things, Catholicism toned down its claims for papal authority (mildly) and for the impossibility of salvation outside the Catholic Church (dramatically).[46] Subsequent ecumenical gatherings of leading Catholic scholars and church authorities with both Lutherans and interdenominational groups of evangelicals have led to considerable agreement on the nature of justification by faith and Christian mission, respectively.[47] Significantly, in each of these developments the resulting agreements more closely resemble the theology of Luther than that of the Counter-Reformation.

Most evangelicals, I am convinced, would be thrilled to observe parallel developments within Mormonism.[48] Clearly, both the Vatican and Salt Lake City have an advantage not available to Protestants—a magisterium that can make authoritative pronouncements that supersede previous belief and practice. In both instances, this can take place very formally and suddenly, as when a pope speaks *ex cathedra* or an LDS president announces a new revelation from God. In Mormon history this has happened only twice: to cease practicing polygamy (1890), and to rescind the ban on blacks from the priesthood (1978). In each case, one by-product, whether or not intended, was to move Mormonism more in line with historic Christianity on the issue at hand.[49] Clearly, such revelations could again move the LDS Church in what evangelicals would consider more biblical directions.

A more common kind of shift is less formal. Just as there are many segments of Western Catholicism that almost entirely disregard the still-official pronouncements of past eras of the Catholic Church about worshipping

Mary or avoiding contraception (to use one theological and one moral illustration), so too the LDS authorities could simply decide not to stress those teachings that, from a historic Christian perspective, are most aberrant or offensive. If one is to believe the public persona of the LDS authorities today, this is already occurring, at least to some extent. Mormons widely perceive a movement over the last fifteen years or so, beginning with the presidency of Ezra Taft Benson, to call their church back to its roots, that is, to the Bible and the Book of Mormon.[50] Given the orthodoxy of the Bible and the smaller amount of heterodoxy in the Book of Mormon compared with Joseph Smith's later writings,[51] this development should be welcomed.

Similarly, the current LDS president, Gordon B. Hinckley, when asked in an interview for *Time* magazine whether the teaching of the Mormon Church today was that "God the Father was once a man like we are," replied, "I don't know that we teach it. I don't know that we emphasize it. I haven't heard it discussed for a long time in public discourse."[52] President Hinckley's latest book, *Stand for Something*,[53] speaks eloquently of ten cardinal virtues needed in American society today, and quotes liberally from the Old and New Testaments but not once by chapter and verse from any of the uniquely Mormon scriptures. Yet Hinckley makes his points compellingly and gives numerous illustrations from his life and that of other Mormons, including an occasional quotation from Brigham Young. Obviously this is a deliberately chosen strategy to have the greatest national impact—but if it can work so well, why not do it consistently, in-house as well as publicly? Just as renewal-movement Catholics today cite the Bible far more often than the Apocrypha or church tradition, so LDS spokespersons could substantially limit their teaching to clearly biblical texts and doctrines. (I am *not* claiming that this would be sufficient to make the LDS Church fully orthodox, merely that it would be a good first step in narrowing "the divide.")

The same could hold true for other areas that divide Mormonism from the historic Christian world. Writers like Stephen Robinson and Robert Millet are already demonstrating an acceptable diversity within LDS faith on central tenets such as the nature of God (absolutist not finite), the deification of believers (always subordinate to, and contingent on, God the Father), and salvation (by grace through faith), with frequent supporting quotations from orthodox Christian writers like C.S. Lewis and John MacArthur.[54] And there are signs that others are starting to follow in their wake.[55] Thus, I disagree with Francis Beckwith that changes in Mormonism must "go through" Joseph Smith and Brigham Young; that is, they must account for how those two church leaders said things that are seemingly contradicted by subsequent developments in LDS circles.[56] This was not the approach taken by Vatican II (or numerous other Catholic councils over the centuries) with respect to prior papal pronouncements. A church that believes in ongoing revelation or authoritative church tradition by definition looks to the most current form of that revelation or tradition to define its beliefs. It could actually prove counterproductive to try to stress to Catholics or Mormons (or anyone else!) that current beliefs seem to contradict former ones, if one approves of the current beliefs. Those groups might then be tempted to revert back to the older, less desirable beliefs!

I know that the scenarios I have sketched in the last five paragraphs seem far too radical to be conceivable by most current Mormons. But then Vatican II seemed impossible to Catholics even at the beginning of the 1960s. At the same time, it is important to stress that Roman Catholics already agreed with Protestants on fundamental doctrines such as the Trinity, the attributes of God, the relationship of the two natures of Christ, and so on.[57] On much smaller scales, who would have predicted the major (though not universally accepted) changes even more recently within Seventh-Day Adventism or the Worldwide Church of God, both of which now have sizable evangelical constituencies? The Reorganized Latter Day Saints have likewise changed dramatically, largely in the direction of liberal Protestantism, and have officially renamed themselves the "Community of Christ."

Shorn of its unorthodox theology, Mormonism would still have enormous contributions to make to the contemporary religious world: a strong commitment to win people to Christ; a biblical emphasis on numerous fundamental moral values, including putting family relationships as a central priority in life; generous financial giving; a good blend of self-reliance and helping others who genuinely cannot care for themselves; all the strengths of classic Arminianism with its emphasis on human free will and responsibility;[58] mechanisms for spiritual growth and accountability for every church member; educational institutions for all ages of people; elaborate church organization, accompanied by genuine community and warm interpersonal relationships; a desire to restore original Christianity and remove corrupting influences from it; social and political agendas often similar to evangelical counterparts; and so on. What a force for good in the world Christianity could be if historic, orthodox Christians could in good conscience link hands with a truly evangelical Mormonism! But we have not arrived at that stage yet.

Use of the Term *Christian* with Respect to an Individual

If none of the discussion thus far points to a way to label current Mormonism Christian *as an entire institution or system of thought,* what then of individual Mormons? Here LDS authors are, if anything, even more impassioned in their claims to merit the title "Christian." Peterson and Ricks, for example, return to the New Testament and conclude, "What made a person a Christian in the first century, and what makes a person a Christian today, is, simply, a commitment to Jesus Christ."[59] Later they put it this way, "If anyone claims to see in Jesus of Nazareth a personage of unique and preeminent authority, that individual should be considered Christian."[60] At first glance, such definitions seem eminently reasonable. But on further reflection, they are much broader than New Testament usage. The Indian Hindu Mohandas Gandhi would probably have qualified, given the sentiments he periodically expressed about Jesus as the greatest of religious teachers. More notably, these definitions would require all of the false teachers censored in the New Testament to be labeled Christian as well. Even the Judaizers in Galatia were *professing* Jewish Christians, zealously convinced that they were serving Christ as preeminent, even while requiring obedience to the Law to ensure salvation.[61] Yet Paul twice consigns to hell anyone who continually preaches their message (Gal 1:8–9)! And Jesus speaks equally curtly of those who name him as Lord but do not do his Father's will. On Judgment Day he "will tell them plainly, 'I never knew you. Away from me, you evildoers!'" (Matt 7:23). A meaningful definition of a word must make clear what it excludes as well as what it includes.

What all this points out is that Peterson and Ricks's definitions determine only who *claims* to have Christian faith, not who is genuinely *regenerate.* Or to put it another way, when evangelicals raise the question of whether or not an individual rather than an entire religious body is Christian, they are normally asking the question "Is such a person *saved?*" Thus, the very language that Peterson and Ricks find so "idiosyncratic"—someone declaring "I have been an active and committed Lutheran since my earliest youth; I became a Christian last July"[62]—is completely intelligible and widespread among evangelical Christians. In this kind of sentence, "Lutheran" simply means a member of a particular Lutheran church; whereas Christian means "converted." Sadly, in many liberal Protestant congregations and in even larger numbers of Catholic and Eastern Orthodox churches, it is possible to attend and be involved for years without ever hearing the message that one must personally accept Jesus as Lord and Savior and allow him to transform every area of one's life. It often requires some experience outside such congregations to lead to an individual's salvation.[63]

Can a Mormon, then, be a Christian in this narrower, more biblical sense of "being saved" or "converted"? To answer this question, we must consider several scenarios. First, *anyone* can become a Christian by sincerely trusting in the Jesus of the New Testament as personal Lord (God and Master) and Savior and by demonstrating the sincerity of that commitment by some perceivable measure of lifelong, biblical belief and behavior. But I cannot take for granted that any given member of the LDS Church is automatically saved by virtue of church membership any more than I assume that a member of my own Baptist church is automatically saved by such membership. Probably every religious group in the history of the world has had people join it through some formal, external membership process without a corresponding internal change of heart to justify the genuineness of their professed conversions. But can an LDS Church member *become* a true Christian through genuine heartfelt conversion? The answer is "of course," and there has never been any evangelical dissent on this point.

A second question is a little harder. Can such a genuinely converted person *remain* within the LDS Church? The question is partially parallel to the question evangelicals have debated concerning converted Roman Catholics,[64] to which today there would be a widespread (though not unanimous) consensus that again the answer is "yes," though the desirability of such a decision would be more hotly debated. Calvinist evangelicals, of course, would have to answer the question affirmatively, since they believe that the genuinely converted will necessarily persevere in their true faith. And Calvinists and Arminians alike would agree that a truly saved person does not subsequently forfeit that salvation simply because of an external matter such as church membership. But the vast majority of all evangelicals would surely also think that it would be wisest for "born-again" Mormons to change their church membership to an evangelical Protestant congregation where there would be a lesser likelihood of experiencing a mixture of true and false teaching.

Slightly different is the case of the evangelical Christian who seems to have had a genuine conversion experience and years of Christian involvement to authenticate it, and who then becomes a Mormon, a scenario that is becoming increasingly common in today's religious world. When once-active Christians simply give up all church involvement, most evangelicals refer to them as "backslidden," not as unsaved. Should evangelicals-turned-Mormon be viewed any differently?[65] Of course, one understandable response is to declare, by definition, that anyone who makes that radical a break from their past demonstrates in so doing that they were never really saved in the first place. I have no difficulty believing that this is true for some individuals, especially in light of the close New Testament parallel described in 1 John 2:19. But experience makes it difficult for me automatically to assume that this approach accounts for all such people.

George Barna, in a poll the findings of which were publicized in 1998, surveyed a broad cross section of Americans about their religious beliefs and determined, to the extent that polls can determine such things, that 26 percent of Mormons answered the relevant questions in a way that is compatible with historic Christian belief and professed to be "born again."[66] Barna's own explanation for how this was possible was to observe that Americans today join churches for a host of reasons other than doctrine—most notably because they have found a warm, caring fellowship of friends—and in many cases hold doctrinal beliefs inconsistent with the official teachings of the churches they join. Given that I have observed this phenomenon running rampant among evangelical churches with which I am familiar, it is hard to believe that the Latter-day Saints are exempt from similar behavior. Pursuing the analogy with evangelical churches even further, it is not difficult for me to imagine large numbers of Latter-day Saints, as in the traditional Christian world, not even knowing in detail everything their church officially teaches (especially if some of the more idiosyncratic items are seldom if ever mentioned), or not feeling any strong obligation to affirm peripheral doctrines.[67] In our highly syncretistic world, I can readily imagine that many of the Latter-day Saints who identified themselves as "born again" are among the evangelical converts to Mormonism who, rightly or wrongly, are convinced that they can keep all of their previous beliefs and commitments and simply add some more on top of them.[68]

A final question is the hardest to answer. Can a person who has had no religious influence on his or her life except the teaching and practice of the LDS come to true, saving faith *within* the LDS Church, if he or she is exposed to the full range of official Mormon doctrine and sincerely believe all of that teaching?[69] Regrettably, I cannot in good conscience answer affirmatively. For all the reasons discussed in the sections of *How Wide the Divide?* that I authored by myself, it seems to me that there still remain major contradictions of fundamental doctrinal issues between historic Christianity and official LDS teaching that make it impossible to *consistently* believe all of the Bible and simultaneously believe all official Mormon doctrine.[70]

But in addition to recognizing that persons can be inconsistent without realizing it, I also recognize that many of my Mormon friends disagree with my conclusions at this point.[71] I also want to stress that it is never appropriate for any believer to pontificate with utter certainty about the eternal state of another person's soul; mercifully, that role is reserved exclusively for God. Nevertheless, I feel compelled to reiterate the point that I have made repeatedly before, especially since it has so often been misquoted and misrepresented. I would love to discover at some time that a genuinely "evangelical Mormonism" existed. I have no desire to see the Latter-day Saints or any other professing Christian group as a whole or any individuals within it remain outside the fold of true Christianity. It is simply that, despite numerous encouraging signs, I do not believe we have yet reached that state of affairs.[72] Neither am I trying to define Mormonism out of Christianity. The real problem from an evangelical perspective—or any orthodox Christian perspective—is to find a *meaningful* way to include Mormonism within Christianity. I cannot, as of this writing, therefore, affirm with integrity that either Mormonism as a whole or any individual, based solely on his or her affirmation of the totality of LDS doctrine, deserves the label "Christian" in any standard or helpful sense of the word. But my fervent prayer is that, through whatever developments God may wish to use, I will not always have to come to that conclusion.[73]

A Final Comment

Latter-day Saint scholar Eugene England has claimed that "some Evangelicals' intolerance for Mormons has taken extreme forms, including the claim that Mormons are not Christians."[74] But is the conclusion that Mormonism is not Christian necessarily an extreme form of intolerance? For the reasons that have been discussed in this chapter, I do not believe it is. However, it is true that evangelicals have often made such claims in a very uncharitable manner. We do well to take to heart the following words that J. Gresham Machen penned many years ago about Protestant liberalism:

> In maintaining that liberalism in the modern Church represents a return to an un-Christian and sub-Christian form of the religious life, we are particularly anxious not to be misunderstood. 'Un-Christian' in such a

connection is sometimes taken as a term of opprobrium. We do not mean it at all as such. Socrates was not a Christian, neither was Goethe; yet we share to the full the respect with which their names are regarded. They tower immeasurably above the common run of men; if he that is least in the Kingdom of Heaven is greater than they, he is certainly greater not by any inherent superiority, but by virtue of an undeserved privilege which ought to make him humble rather than contemptuous.[75]

It is important to apply these same sentiments, *mutatis mutandis,* to the LDS faith. When they are so applied, the claim that Mormonism is not Christian is neither intolerant nor extreme nor uncharitable.

PART IV

The Book of Mormon

Introductory Essay

Mormonism's birth stems from Joseph Smith's claim to have been shown the location of gold plates, which he translated by the "gift and power of God." These plates contained the history and theology of ancient inhabitants of the New World and were revealed to him by the angel Moroni, the resurrected son of the general and prophet Mormon, who was the primary author/editor of the plates (and thus the name of the book). The primary narrative of the Book of Mormon begins with an account of the journey of a pious Israelite named Lehi and his family as they fled from Jerusalem shortly before the fall of the city to the Babylonians. Lehi's family traveled to the New World and there established themselves. The narrative continues with an historical-theological account of Lehi's descendants and the numerous wars and interactions between the (sometimes) righteous Nephites and the unrighteous Lamanites, up until the time that the Nephite culture came to an end with the death of its last prophets, Mormon and Moroni. According to Smith and the Latter-day Saints, the theological aspect of the record contains the "fullness of the gospel" that was lost when early Christianity suffered a "Great Apostasy."

Since it was published in 1830, the authenticity of the Book of Mormon has been at the center of controversy. Many theories have been put forward about how Joseph Smith had either authored or plagiarized the text, possibly with help from others. Criticism of the Book of Mormon has usually focused either on trying to prove one of these theories or on discrepancies in Smith's accounts of his finding and translating the book. Others have focused on things mentioned in the text that appear to be anachronistic or out of place in the New World during the time of events that the Book of Mormon purports to describe (e.g., certain plants, metals, technologies). Few non-Mormons, however, have given much attention to what are perhaps the two most important claims the Book of Mormon makes about itself. According to LDS scholar Kent P. Jackson, "The most fundamental claim made by the Book of Mormon is that it is an authentic ancient book."[1] To this should be added the claim that the Book of Mormon is an authentic translation and not a nineteenth-century composition.

Latter-day Saint scholars have expended much energy in efforts to show that the Book of Mormon does, indeed, evidence having been originally written in a Semitic language by ancient peoples of Israelite descent. According to them, the Book of Mormon parallels genuinely ancient Near Eastern characteristics in the names of its characters, its language, and the cultures it describes. Furthermore, LDS scholars argue that many of these features could not have been derived from the King James Version of the Bible or other works available to Joseph Smith. The best explanation for the presence of these parallels, we are told, is that the Book of Mormon is precisely what it claims to be, an ancient text written by peoples of a Near Eastern cultural background that was translated by Joseph Smith.

In chapter 10, Thomas J. Finley evaluates some of the evidence LDS scholars have cited in favor of an authentic ancient Near Eastern background for the Book of Mormon. He begins by discussing criteria by which one can determine whether parallels should be considered significant. He then discusses four aspects of the Book of Mormon that purportedly exhibit an ancient Near Eastern background. First, Finley looks at the Book of Mormon's recurring motif of writing sacred records on metal plates and compares this with Near Eastern examples of writings on metal. Second, Finley evaluates thirteen types of Hebraisms that LDS scholars have identified in the text. Hebraisms are grammatical constructions that are awkward in English because the English text is rigidly following the word order of an underlying Hebrew original. In the third section, Finley interacts with the work of LDS scholars who claim that several Book of Mormon names that are not found in the King James Version of the Bible have been verified as authentic Near Eastern names in various inscriptions and ancient documents that have been discovered by archeologists. Finally, in the last section of the essay Finley discusses the geography of 1 Nephi's account of the flight of Lehi and his family from Jerusalem and whether anything in the account shows first-hand knowledge of the area. Finley concludes that, on the basis of these four lines of evidence, there is no reason to conclude that the Book of Mormon is an authentic Near Eastern text. To the contrary, in his examination of these features, especially the linguistic features, Finley shows that the Book of Mormon is more likely to be a modern text.

In the last chapter of this book, David J. Shepherd tackles the second key claim that the Book of Mormon makes about itself: that it is an authentic translation. Shepherd begins by discussing the rise of Translation Studies as a distinct subdiscipline and the advances that scholars in this field have made in categorizing and understanding the different types of translation. The most common understanding of what a translation is has been labeled by Translation Studies scholars as interlingual translation, that is, translation of a text in one language directly into another language. In the first main section of his essay, Shepherd offers interesting discussions of the three other main types of translation that have been identified: indirect translation, intralingual translation, and pseudotranslation. Having identified the chief characteristics of each type of translation, in the second part of the essay Shepherd discusses the various ways in which a genuine interlingual translation can be distinguished from a pseudotranslation. Various types of external and internal evidence can be appealed to, and Shepherd illustrates each from past examples of disputed texts that have been shown to be either translations or pseudotranslations.

Having carefully laid the groundwork for properly distinguishing genuine translations from pseudotranslations, Shepherd applies this to the Book of Mormon's claim to be a genuine interlingual translation. He briefly describes some of the lines of evidence that have been appealed to by both the detractors and supporters of the Book of Mormon. He observes that much of this evidence deals with external or cultural issues, but the most important type of evidence in assessing the Book of Mormon's claim is linguistic. Shepherd points out that the Book of Mormon provides a ready means of linguistically testing whether it is, in fact, a translation.

It is well known that the Book of Mormon quotes large sections from the Old Testament book of Isaiah. Critics have charged that Joseph Smith simply copied this material from the King James Version of the Bible (KJV). Latter-day Saint scholars, however, have noted that in many places the Book of Mormon's Isaiah material differs from the KJV. Moreover, they have argued that the Book of Mormon's Isaiah material reflects ancient textual traditions and versions that are more accurate than those followed by the KJV translators. They have suggested that Smith followed the KJV rendering for the sake of familiarity where it was accurate, but diverged from it when the text on the gold plates differed from the KJV. Whether the Book of Mormon Isaiah material really does reflect an underlying Hebrew text that differs from the KJV, or whether Smith took his text from the KJV and simply changed it on occasion for some reason or other provides an ideal test for determining whether the Book of Mormon is a translation or pseudotranslation. Therefore, in his last section Shepherd examines the Book of Mormon's Isaiah material and the claims of LDS scholars.

10

DOES THE BOOK OF MORMON REFLECT AN ANCIENT NEAR EASTERN BACKGROUND?

THOMAS J. FINLEY

Thomas J. Finley is Professor and Chair of the Department of Old Testament and Semitics at Talbot School of Theology, Biola University. Finley earned a B.A. from Biola University, an M.Div. in Old Testament from Talbot School of Theology, and an M.A. and Ph.D. in Near Eastern languages from the University of California at Los Angeles, specializing in Semitics and Western Akkadian. Finley is the author of *A Commentary on Joel, Amos, and Obadiah* in the Wycliffe Exegetical Commentary (Moody Press) and *Joel, Obadiah, and Micah* in the Everyman's Bible Commentary (Moody Press). He served as editor of the three volumes on Ezekiel in *A Bilingual Concordance to the Targum of the Prophets* (E. J. Brill) and has published academic articles in *Bibliotheca Sacra, Grace Theological Journal, Journal of the Evangelical Theological Society, Journal of Translation and Textlinguistics, Vetus Testamentum,* and *Zeitschrift für Althebraistik*. He serves on the editorial board of *Journal for the Aramaic Bible*.

A number of Mormon writers have produced studies recently that claim that "evidence can be adduced—largely external and circumstantial—that commands respect for the claims of the Book of Mormon concerning its ancient Near Eastern Background."[1] If we set out to test the hypothesis that the Book of Mormon really represents the ancient culture of its reputed authors, what would we look for? A basic criterion would surely be that certain features that have parallels from the ancient Near East could not be explained on the basis of the culture of Joseph Smith himself. Such features, in order to have true evidential value, should have specific characteristics that would rule out the explanation that the book is simply a product of early-nineteenth-century America.

First, a parallel should be specific enough that it cannot be explained by general human experience. For example, Nephi describes how he secretly entered Jerusalem by night in order to recover the brass plates from Laban (1 Nephi 4). Hugh Nibley takes this as a parallel with the Lachish Letters: "Almost casual references to certain doings by night create the same atmosphere of tension and danger in both stories."[2] As I have argued elsewhere,[3] it is not possible to derive such a parallel from the Lachish Letters, but even if the parallel really existed, it would be too general to have any value. Carrying out missions of the sort depicted by Nephi under the cover of darkness is a universal experience.

Second, a parallel should be something beyond what Joseph Smith could have known from the KJV (including Apocrypha). It might be objected that this assumes that Joseph Smith simply copied his material from the KJV rather than accepting at face value his own account of how the Book of Mormon came into existence, especially in light of various eyewitness testimonies. It is not my purpose here to examine the validity either of Joseph Smith's testimony or of the witnesses.[4] However, I think the criterion I am suggesting is valid. The fact that the language of the Book of Mormon reflects the idiom of the KJV is admitted by all sides.[5] It is true that one would expect a translation of ancient material to occur in the idiom of the translator, but in this case the language of the KJV was already archaic even in the time of Joseph Smith. The expressions of the KJV greatly influenced the religious language of the time, but the idiom permeates all portions of the Book of Mormon, whether in overtly religious genres such as prayers and visions or in what are represented as historical narratives. It is at least a reasonable assumption for an outsider to Mormonism that the KJV might have influenced the Book of Mormon. That does not necessarily detract from its originality; it simply means that a parallel found in both the ancient Near East and in the KJV cannot have as much weight as a parallel that is known only from the ancient Near East.

Third, any parallel should be examined thoroughly to see how it functions in both contexts. It will not do to find something that immediately seems parallel but that on further reflection functions differently in the different contexts. It is often customary, for example, for a father to "give away" his daughter in marriage at a wedding ceremony. This could be considered a parallel to a culture like that of the Old Testament, where a father would have the authority to determine marriage issues for his daughter. However, the functional differences between the current practices in North America and the ancient customs are so great that the parallel is only superficial.

Fourth, one should always keep in mind the possibility of accidental parallels. For example, the English pronoun "she" has exactly the same phonological shape and meaning as the corresponding term in the ancient Akkadian (Assyrian and Babylonian) language. But this parallel is more easily explained as accidental than because of some relationship between the two languages. If a large number of parallels that meet the first three criteria begin to accumulate, then it becomes less and less likely that any true parallels are accidental.

Fifth, it should be noted that anachronisms are more significant than parallels for determining the historical setting of a written work. If a story purports to come from the early 1960s, but one of the characters mentions the Internet, then it would be reasonable to assume that the story was actually written in the 1990s or later.

The primary questions to be answered by this chapter are: Does the Book of Mormon evidence having been written by Semites in ancient times? How does it compare with known ancient Near Eastern literature? Do the societies and cultures described in the Book of Mormon appear to be genuinely ancient and Near Eastern (culturally) in ways that can not be derived from the English Bible (especially the KJV)? Have LDS scholars discovered any features of the text that are most plausibly explained by the hypothesis that Joseph Smith translated the book from ancient gold tablets? This chapter will focus on four areas: (1) the gold/brass plates mentioned in the Book of Mormon and from which Joseph Smith translated; (2) linguistic issues related to "Hebraisms" in the English text of the Book of Mormon; (3) Book of Mormon names that do not occur in the King James Version of the Bible but that are said to be attested in ancient inscriptions; and (4) the geography of the Old World journey of Lehi and his family after they escaped from Jerusalem as recorded in 1 Nephi.

Ancient Near Eastern Writing on Metal and the Gold/Brass Plates

The Book of Mormon mentions plates of brass or of gold that were used to preserve a wide variety of materials, from genealogies to history and prophecy.[6] Joseph Smith described records that were "engraven on plates which had the appearance of gold, each plate was six inches wide and eight inches long, and not quite so thick as common tin. They were filled with engravings, in Egyptian characters, and bound together in a volume as the leaves of a book, with three rings running through the whole. The volume was something near six inches in thickness, a part of which was sealed. The characters on the unsealed part were small, and beautifully engraved."[7]

There is no question that metal was sometimes used as writing material in the ancient world, including the Near East.[8] However, such examples do not seem to parallel the lengthy Book of Mormon, since they normally contain a small amount of material and imitate standard writing procedures for the time. For example, two silver scrolls discovered in a family tomb just outside Jerusalem date to the late seventh century B.C. (about the time that Nephi was supposed to have lived), but they are tiny scrolls that were rolled up in such a way that a string could be inserted through the center so they could be worn around the neck. They contained only excerpts from the priestly blessing of Numbers 6:24–26.[9]

At the palace of Darius I (Apadana), one gold and one silver plate containing the king's trilingual inscription was found "in a stone box beneath the northeast corner of the main hall of the Apadana."[10] Duplicate plates were found "in a stone box beneath the southeast corner of the main hall of the Apadana."[11] This inscription contains only eight lines of cuneiform writing repeated in three languages. The purpose of the inscription was to describe the extent of Darius's kingdom and to request the god Ahuramazda for protection for him and his "house." Cuneiform was normally written with a stylus on a clay tablet while it was still wet, but scribes also incised the wedge-shaped signs on stone and occasionally on metal. Even so, there is no parallel among materials in cuneiform writing for the many plates it would have taken to record even the book of 1 Nephi.

The copper scroll from cave three of Qumran rather uniquely has a longer text (though not nearly as long as the Book of Mormon). Two of three original pieces of thin (about 1 mm) pure copper were attached together and rolled up like a scroll. The third piece apparently became detached before the scroll was hidden in the cave. The two rolled-up pieces that were found were each about 2.6 feet long and a foot wide. After a complicated procedure at the University of Manchester in England, the "completely oxidized" scrolls were unrolled to reveal some twelve columns of text.[12] There are several theories about the contents of the scroll, which refers to valuable items and where they were hidden. The most likely explanation is that these items were owned by the Jerusalem Temple and that someone placed the scroll in the cave to hide it from the Romans around A.D. 70. Unlike the brass or gold plates discussed in the Book of Mormon, this work attempted to imitate a "standard parchment scroll." The text did not contain religious or literary matter but "appears to be an administrative document which simply enumerates, in a dry bookkeeping style" the inventory of items.[13]

Both the silver scrolls found in Jerusalem and the copper scroll at Qumran show that the normal form of writing for literary content was on *scrolls.* Even though the KJV mentions "a plate of pure gold" with the phrase "Holiness to the Lord" engraved on it (Exod 28:36; cf. 29:30), that was an item small enough to place on the "mitre" or turban of the high priest. The two "tables of stone" that Moses received from the Lord contained the Ten Commandments (Exod 34:4, 28; Deut 4:13). Otherwise, stone was used for monumental inscriptions. Wooden tablets for brief notes may be indicated at Isaiah 30:8 and Habakkuk 2:2. Excavations in Egypt and Mesopotamia show that these could be prepared for writing with a coat of plaster or wax.[14] It was also popular to write short texts on broken pieces of pottery. Otherwise, papyrus and leather were the material of choice for larger literary texts.[15] The only ancient items that remotely resembled a book form were "the common folded double boards, which scribes in the ancient Near East used for notebooks, which are very similar in appearance to a double door."[16] These "notebooks" were covered with wax, and the scribe would make impressions in it to be used as a model for those who would incise inscriptions on stone.

Turning back to the Book of Mormon, the emphasis on the "plates of brass" (1 Nephi 4:38, etc.), "plates of ore" (Mosiah 21:27), "plates of gold" (Mosiah 28:11), "plates of Nephi" (1 Nephi 9:1–4), and "plates of Jacob" (Jacob 3:14) is quite impressive.[17] It appears to be a motif or minor theme of the entire book. The entire Book of Mormon, according to the title page, is "An Account Written by the Hand of Mormon upon Plates Taken from the Plates of Nephi." These "plates of Nephi" were passed on from generation to generation, and additional records were added to them. Considering just the brass plates from the time of Nephi and his father Lehi, they contained "the record of the Jews and also a genealogy of my forefathers" (1 Nephi 3:3), "the law" (1 Nephi 4:16), "the doings of the Lord in other lands, among people of old" (1 Nephi 19:22), portions of the book of Isaiah (2 Nephi 6–8), and the prophecies of Nephi's father Lehi (2 Nephi 4:1–2). These recordings were quite extensive, and it would have been at least awkward to transport them from place to place.[18] In contrast, the extremely important materials of the Bible were passed on through scribal transmission on leather, papyrus, and parchment—materials much more easily transportable and convenient to use. While metal was used in the ancient Near East for writing material, the dissimilarities in usage with the Book of Mormon outweigh the similarity of material.[19]

Linguistic Issues

Some Mormon scholars have claimed that certain linguistic features in the Book of Mormon support Joseph Smith's assertion that "through the medium of the Urim and Thummim I translated the record by the gift and power of God."[20] John Tvedtnes, for example, refers to "Hebraisms" in the Book of Mormon that reflect "the language that the Nephites used in daily speech—Hebrew."[21] That is, Tvedtnes is claiming that Joseph Smith translated from his source in a fairly literal manner, so that sometimes certain idioms can be explained best by assuming an underlying Hebrew form. Since Joseph Smith didn't know Hebrew at the time he did the translation, such findings would give at least circumstantial evidence to support the claim of divine inspiration. That the Nephites spoke Hebrew appears certain to Tvedtnes because "not only did they come from Jerusalem, where Hebrew was commonly spoken at that time, but Moroni himself indicated that they knew Hebrew (see Mormon 9:32–34)."[22]

Tvedtnes lists a total of thirteen categories of features found in the Book of Mormon that indicate an idiom that would be "awkward or unexpected in English, even in Joseph Smith's time. Yet they make good sense when viewed as translations, perhaps as too literal translations, from an ancient text written in a Hebrew-like language."[23] These categories include: (1) construct state ("plates of brass" rather than "brass plates"); (2) adverbials ("with patience" rather than "patiently"); (3) cognates ("taxed with a tax"); (4) compound prepositions ("by the hand of" for "by"); (5) the conjunction ("and" used to connect each member of a list of items); (6) subordinate clauses (prepositions plus "that," as in "because that"); (7) the relative clause (the relative not immediately after its antecedent); (8) extrapositional nouns and pronouns ("I beheld the wrath of God, that it was upon ..."); (9) "interchangeable prepositions" ("faithful in" when speaking of God); (10) comparison ("choice above all other lands"); (11) naming conventions ("and they called the name of the city Moroni"); (12) possessive pronouns ("hear the words of me"); and (13) words used in unusual ways ("heads" to describe things that are chief or precious, or "to wife" instead of "for a wife").[24]

Most of the features Tvedtnes lists are also found commonly in the KJV, and it makes good sense that the KJV could have influenced the author's phrasing and style of writing even where he was writing creatively and imaginatively.[25] This is especially true in that the features examined are quite characteristic of the KJV, marking it as a relatively literal translation. For example, for the naming convention whereby the Hebrew idiom is "call the name X," Tvedtnes lists four passages from the Book of Mormon.[26] "We did call the name of the place Shazer" occurs at 1 Nephi 16:13 (also Alma 23:17; 50:13–14; and Mosiah 1:2). I was able to find twenty-seven places in the KJV where a similar expression occurs. Thus, for example, at Genesis 4:17, "[Cain] called the name of the city, after the name of his son, Enoch."[27]

One more example will have to suffice to illustrate how the use of cognate structures in the Book of Mormon could have been influenced by the KJV. Tvedtnes lists seven examples of expressions like "taxed with a tax" (Mosiah 7:15) or "work all manner of fine work" (Mosiah 11:10). Such expressions are also found in the KJV (in both Old and New Testaments), and in some cases they even have similar wording to the corresponding expression in the Book of Mormon, as the following table illustrates:

Book of Mormon	Reference	KJV	References
"work all manner of fine work"	Mosiah 11:10	"to work all manner of work" / "to work all works"	Exod 35:35; 36:1; 1 Kgs 7:14
"and he did judge righteous judgments"	Mosiah 29:43	"the judgment which the king had judged"	1 Kgs 3:28
		"with what judgment ye judge"	Matt 7:2
		cf. "they shall judge it according to my judgments"	Ezek 44:24; cf. 23:24; Num 35:24
"this was the desire which I desired of him"	Enos 1:13	"With desire I have desired to eat this Passover"	Luke 22:15
"I will work a great and a marvelous work"	1 Nephi 14:7	"I will work a work in your days"	Hab 1:5; Acts 13:41; cf. John 6:28; 9:4

While the majority of Tvedtnes's examples can be illustrated by multiple comparisons from the KJV, he has listed a few cases that seem more unique to the Book of Mormon.[28] Three examples, according to Tvedtnes, "give the impression of having been translated from" Hebrew sentences where "the word that marks the beginning of a relative clause . . . does not always closely follow the word it refers back to" as might be expected in a normal English construction.[29] Thus, "The Egyptians were drowned in the Red Sea, who were the armies of Pharaoh" (1 Nephi 17:27). In this case the relative pronoun *who* refers back to the Egyptians.

Actually, the relative pronoun (*which* or *who*) in Hebrew normally directly follows its antecedent noun or noun phrase, just as in English.[30] Sentences like the example he gives from 1 Nephi 17:27 would be rare, though perhaps possible in biblical Hebrew. There are cases where the main noun is first modified by a phrase and then further modified by a relative clause, as in the phrase: "the sins of Jeroboam son of Nebat, *which* he had caused Israel to commit" (2 Kgs 10:29 NIV; emphasis mine). In this case the NIV has followed the literal order of the Hebrew, with the relative *which* separated from its antecedent, "sins," by the phrase "of Jeroboam son of Nebat."

An example closer to 1 Nephi 17:27 occurs in Jeremiah 37:1: "And king Zedekiah the son of Josiah reigned instead of Coniah the son of Jehoiakim, *whom* Nebuchadrezzar king of Babylon made king in the land of Judah" (KJV; emphasis mine). Here the KJV gives the literal order, with the relative *whom* referring to "Zedekiah." First Nephi 16:37 does not seem to be what one would expect as a literal translation from Hebrew: "Our brother Nephi . . . has taken it upon him to be our ruler and our teacher, who are his elder brethren." In biblical Hebrew this would likely be expressed by a circumstantial clause with connecting "and" ("our brother Nephi . . . has taken it upon him to be our ruler and our teacher, *and* we are his elder brethren").

Finally, Tvedtnes's third example, if translated literally from a Hebrew text, should read, "then the-ones-living without God shall confess." Mosiah 27:31 has, "Then shall they confess, who live without God in the world," while the better English form suggested by Tvedtnes is "then shall they who live without God in the world confess." The degree to which Tvedtnes's suggested translation and the translation in the Book of Mormon reflect the literal Hebrew appears to be roughly the same.[31]

Otherwise, the only unique issues that Tvedtnes raises are that the Book of Mormon uses the expression "arrived to" rather than "arrived at" or "arrived in" in the 1830 edition at 1 Nephi 17:14 and that, according to Alma 13:18, Melchizedek "did reign under his father." As for "arrived to," in this instance it is true that the idiom is not found in the KJV. In fact, in that version a form of "arrive" occurs only with "arrived at" and only in two places in the New Testament (Luke 8:26; Acts 20:15). The single example of "arrived to" in the Book of Mormon was corrected later to "arrived in." Since a variety of prepositions are possible for the Hebrew that underlies "arrive at" or "come to,"[32] including no preposition at all (2 Kgs 11:16; Isa 30:4), this example is of limited value. Joseph Smith's peculiar expression was not impossible in English either. The *Oxford English Dictionary* lists "arrive into" or "arrive to" as obsolete expressions.[33]

What about the statement that Melchizedek "did reign under his father" (Alma 13:18)? The Hebrew preposition for "under" also has the sense of "instead of," so is this a case where Joseph Smith must have translated rather than composed the passage? Taking the preposition "under" at its face value, the statement would mean that Melchizedek derived his authority to reign from his father or that he reigned at the same time that his father reigned.

If the preposition "under" really means "instead of" here, then the alleged translation would be not just overly literal but defective; in English the two prepositions communicate entirely different ideas. Literal translations can accomplish their purpose only to the extent that it is still clear what they mean in the target language, but if a literal rendering causes miscommunication, that makes it a bad translation. Joseph Smith did not claim to be able to translate the Book of Mormon because he had studied Hebrew or Egyptian or any other language. He stated that he did his work "by the gift and power of God." It would seem unusual, then, that his translation would fail to communicate properly.

Several years after Tvedtnes published his study, Royal Skousen did an additional study that focuses on expressions in the Book of Mormon "that appear to be uncharacteristic of English in all of its dialects and historical stages. These structures support the notion that Joseph Smith's translation is a literal one and not simply a reflection of either his own dialect or King James English."[34] Skousen points out that in the original text of the Book of Mormon (1830) some conditional sentences occurred that were more like Hebrew than English. In one type of conditional sentence in Hebrew the result clause is joined to the conditional clause by a conjunction that is often translated "and." Fourteen clauses from the Book of Mormon similarly used "and" before they were later corrected.[35]

I will treat here the nine examples that Skousen lists (he does not mention what the others are). The first one, from 1 Nephi 17:50, reads as follows: "If he should command me that I should say unto this water be thou earth and it shall be earth;[36] and if I should say it, it would be done." Skousen takes "and it shall be earth" as the conclusion to the first "if" statement. That is how the current edition of the Book of Mormon reads it: "If he should command me that I should say unto this water, be thou earth, it should be earth; and if I should say it, it would be done." There is another way to read the original form, though. If "and it shall be earth" is part of the Lord's quotation, then there is a simple sequential idea: "Do this and it will happen." The whole sentence would have a form like this:

If he should command X and if I should say it, it would be done.

Here "X" stands for the Lord's statement: "Say unto this water, be thou earth and it shall be earth." To me, the original form is more logical. Two events have to happen before the result can take place: the Lord has to issue a command, and Nephi has to carry it out. The revised form obscures that.

Skousen's remaining examples all come from Helaman 12:13–21:

13 yea and if he sayeth unto the earth move *and* it is moved

14 yea if he sayeth unto the earth thou shalt go back that it lengthen out the day for many hours *and* it is done . . .

¹⁶ and behold also if he sayeth unto the waters of the great deep be thou dried up *and* it is done

¹⁷ behold if he sayeth unto this mountain be thou raised up and come over and fall upon that city that it be buried up *and* behold it is done . . .

¹⁹ and if the Lord shall say be thou accursed that no man shall find thee from this time henceforth and forever *and* behold no man getteth it henceforth and forever

²⁰ and behold if the Lord shall say unto a man because of thine iniquities thou shalt be accursed forever *and* it shall be done

²¹ and if the Lord shall say because of thine iniquities thou shalt be cut off from my presence *and* he will cause that it shall be so

These instances more clearly use *and* to introduce the result clause, although verses 13–14 might be viewed as support for verse 15: "And thus, according to his word the earth goeth back." That is, "If he says X and it happens, then it has happened according to his word."

When these verses were edited for the second edition of the Book of Mormon, the word *and* was not changed to *then;* rather, it was simply dropped. While Skousen's observation is interesting, I think it may still be the case that this construction was influenced by the KJV in its original form. The conjunction *and* occurs 51,714 times in the KJV. By comparison, the NIV reduces this by about 40 percent.[37] It is surely a prominent feature of the KJV, and that could have influenced Joseph Smith to use it even in some of his result clauses.[38]

Skousen's second illustration of a non-KJV feature concerns the usage of "and it came to pass." Actually, as I will show, this feature seems almost certainly to be from the influence of the KJV, but first I will lay out Skousen's argument. He points out that many of the occurrences of "and it came to pass" are found "in inappropriate contexts." In fact, in the 1837 edition, "Joseph Smith removed at least 47 of these apparently extraneous uses of this well-worked phrase. In most cases, there were two or more examples of 'it came to pass' in close proximity; in some cases, nothing new had 'come to pass.'" The Hebrew word in question is *wayehi,* and "the King James translators avoided translating [it] whenever it wouldn't make sense in English, especially when too many events were 'coming to pass' or when nothing had really 'come to pass'—in other words, in those very places that the original text of the Book of Mormon 'inappropriately' allows 'and it came to pass' to occur."[39]

I cannot agree with Skousen's reason for why the translators of the KJV sometimes did not render *wayehi* with "and it came to pass." In biblical Hebrew the term is used in two very different ways. In addition to "and it came to pass," *wayehi* can also mean "and he was" or "and it was" (Hebrew has no separate form for the neuter pronoun *it*). If a noun subject occurs in the same clause with *wayehi*, then the expression has this second meaning. For example, at the end of each day of creation in Genesis 1 we are told "*wayehi* evening *wayehi* morning, day X." This translates into literal English as "and there *was* evening and there *was* morning, the Xth day."[40] Or in Genesis 5:32 we are given Noah's age with the following statement: "*wayehi* Noah 500 years old." That is, "and Noah *was* 500 years old." It is not that the King James translators didn't translate it, as Skousen claims; they translated it a different way when the context called for it (shown above by "was" in italics).

When *wayehi* means "and it came to pass," the sentence is structured differently. The clause in which *wayehi* occurs does not have a proper subject, and it is *always* followed by an expression of time.[41] The first time that the KJV uses "and it came to pass" is at Genesis 4:8: "and it came to pass, *when they were in the field,* that Cain rose up against Abel his brother, and slew him." Notice the expression of time marked by italics. Cain slew Abel *when they were in the field.* With a computer concordance of the Bible, it is easy to check that the translators of the KJV clearly recognized this Hebrew idiom. All the occurrences of "and it came to pass" in the Old Testament have the expression of time in the clause.[42]

Turning to the Book of Mormon, we find that there are often examples where the idiom correctly follows that of the Hebrew: "And it came to pass that *when he had traveled three days in the wilderness,* he pitched his tent" (1 Nephi 2:6). As expected, a time expression occurs in the clause with "and it came to pass," and a main clause follows with the action that happened at that time. On many other occasions, though, the Book of Mormon deviates from the Hebrew idiom in various ways. Most commonly it attaches "and it came to pass" directly to the main verb with no intervening reference to time (or any other type of circumstance): "And it came to pass that he returned to his own house at Jerusalem" (1 Nephi 1:7).

The following sentence from 1 Nephi 3:13 illustrates another major departure from the Hebrew idiom: "And behold, it came to pass that Laban was angry." "Behold" is another characteristic KJV translation, this time for Hebrew *hinneh*. In Hebrew the word *and* is integrally connected to the part meaning "it came to pass," so it would not be possible to place "behold" between the two parts. Also, the expression "and behold" would have to occur at the beginning of a sentence. The only way it might be expressed in Hebrew would be to deviate from *wayehi* proper and have something like, *wehinneh* [and behold] *hayah* [it came to pass].

This could represent the underlying Hebrew, except for one additional characteristic of *hinneh* (behold). It shows the perspective of someone *other than* the narrator (either that of some character in the narrative or of the reader), while "it came to pass" marks the narrator's perspective. Consider the following examples from the KJV:

> And it came to pass, when he was come near to enter into Egypt, that he said unto Sarai his wife, Behold now, I know that thou art a fair woman to look upon. (Gen 12:11)
> And it came to pass after these things, that one told Joseph, Behold, thy father *is* sick. (Gen 48:1)
> And it came to pass, that in the morning, behold, it was Leah. (Gen 29:25)
> And it came to pass in the time of her travail, that, behold, twins were in her womb. (Gen 38:27)

"And it came to pass" always belongs to the narrator. "Behold," on the other hand, can be used either by a narrator (examples 3 and 4) or by someone who is being quoted (examples 1 and 2). When the quoted figure uses it, he or she draws the attention of another participant to some significant fact. It shifts the focus of attention from the speaker to the listener. The same thing happens when the narrator uses "behold." Attention shifts away from the narrated details to some particular point that the reader is invited to ponder or wonder at. That is why "behold it came to pass" never occurs in the KJV. The two introductory phrases operate on the basis of different, mutually exclusive perspectives.

As the following examples of "behold it came to pass" show, the way the Book of Mormon uses "behold" differs from how the KJV or the original Hebrew use it.

> For behold, it came to pass that the Lord spake unto my father, yea, even in a dream, and said unto him. . . . (1 Nephi 2:1)
> For behold, it came to pass that fifty and five years had passed away from the time that Lehi left Jerusalem. (Jacob 1:1)

> Behold, it came to pass that I, Nephi, did cry much unto the Lord my God, because of the anger of my brethren. (2 Nephi 5:1)
>
> Now behold, it came to pass that I, Jacob, having ministered much unto my people in word, (and I cannot write but a little of my words, because of the difficulty of engraving our words upon plates) and we know that the things which we write upon plates must remain. (Jacob 4:1)

The first two sentences appear to be strictly third person narration, yet they are introduced by "for behold." For the third sentence, the first person narrator is also the focus of attention in the main clause. Since Hebrew *hinneh* refocuses attention in the main clause to a different participant, a sentence like this would be impossible for Hebrew. The last sentence does not even have a focal point that the "behold" draws attention to. It trails off in a lengthy explanation about the plates with writing on them. It is thus expository in genre, whereas "it came to pass" would imply narration (which it normally does in the Book of Mormon).

What are we to make of the way that "and it came to pass" or "behold it came to pass" are used in the Book of Mormon? The way sentences can be put together with these phrases is quite unlike any Hebrew that I have ever seen.[43] One possibility is that Joseph Smith translated plates that were in some other language than Hebrew. Hugh Nibley suggests an Egyptian background for "and it came to pass":

> Nothing delighted the critics more than the monotonous repetition of "it came to pass" at the beginning of thousands of sentences in the Book of Mormon. Here again is something that Western tradition found completely unfamiliar. Instead of punctuation, the original manuscript of the Book of Mormon divides up its phrases by introducing each by an "and," "behold," "now," or "It came to pass . . . ." Simply outrageous—as English literature, but it is standard Egyptian practice. Egyptian historical texts, Grapow points out, "begin in monotonous fashion" always with the same stock words; at some periods every speech is introduced with the unnecessary "I opened my mouth." Dramatic texts are held together by the constant repetition of *Khpr-n,* "It happened that" or "It came to pass." In Egyptian these expressions were not merely adornments, as Grapow points out, they are a grammatical necessity and may not be omitted.[44]

Because of the KJV, "Western tradition" was not "completely unfamiliar" with "and it came to pass," and in the KJV the idiom holds narrative together by frequent repetition (as well as by a simple *and*). Nibley might find it more difficult to explain "behold, it came to pass." At the very least, the choice of "behold" as a connecting word when it has a function unfamiliar to the KJV or to biblical Hebrew seems out of place for what Mormon researchers are claiming.

Does it make sense, though, that Egyptian rather than Hebrew was the reputed original language of the early Nephites? According to Tvedtnes:

> We do not know exactly what language was used on the original plates of the Book of Mormon. Nephi described the writing system as a combination of "the learning of the Jews and the language of the Egyptians" (1 Nephi 1:2). Moroni, writing a thousand years later, called it "reformed Egyptian" (Mormon 9:32–34). This might mean that they used Egyptian symbols to represent Egyptian words, or that they used Egyptian symbols as a shorthand to represent Hebrew words, or even that they used both Egyptian and Hebrew symbols to represent Hebrew words.[45]

Since Lehi, Nephi's father, was descended from Joseph, son of Jacob (1 Nephi 5:14), and also lived "at Jerusalem in all his days" up to the first year of King Zedekiah (1 Nephi 1:4), it seems logical to expect that he and his family spoke Hebrew as their native language. While there were strong connections between Egypt and Judah around 600 B.C., and even examples of Hebrew written with Egyptian (hieratic) characters,[46] it would be odd that Nephi would record information to be handed down through his family in the Egyptian language itself. Moreover, the prophet Jeremiah warned the people against relying on Egypt for help against the Babylonians. Someone from those who supported Jeremiah would be expected to use Hebrew rather than Egyptian. The only reason I can think of for Nephi to use Egyptian writing for his records is that it would presumably take up less space than Hebrew writing, though even that is doubtful.[47]

Considering only "and it came to pass" in the Old Testament, the KJV renders *wayehi* this way 336 times. In the Book of Mormon "and it came to pass" occurs 1,123 times. "Behold" never occurs together with "it came to pass" in the KJV; "(and) behold it came to pass" occurs 28 times in the Book of Mormon. "Behold" itself occurs 1,104 times in the KJV and 1,651 times in the Book of Mormon.[48] It is more likely that the idiom of the KJV, rather than an underlying Hebrew or Egyptian, influenced Joseph Smith.

Another unusual usage in the Book of Mormon is the common word *amen*. In the KJV of the Old Testament, the term occurs 27 times, normally as a spoken response of one or more individuals to a statement made by someone else. For example, in Deuteronomy 27:16 we read, "Cursed *be* he that setteth light by his father or his mother. And all the people shall say, Amen." Only in the Psalms do we find *amen* added at the end of a statement of praise to the Lord (Pss 41:13; 72:19; 89:52).[49] In the New Testament *amen* occurs an additional 51 times and can be used for affirming a word of praise (Rom 1:25); but it is also used to close a book (Matt 28:20; Mark 16:20), to close a prayer (Matt 6:13; 1 Cor 14:16), to emphasize the truth of a previous statement (Rom 15:33; 2 Cor 13:14; 1 Pet 5:14; 1 John 5:21; Rev 1:7), and as a substitute for Christ himself (Rev 3:14). The usage in the Book of Mormon resembles that of the New Testament more closely than of the Old Testament. It closes a book (1 Nephi 22:31; 2 Nephi 33:15; Enos 27; Mormon 9:37; Ether 15:34; Moroni 10:34) or a prayer (Alma 31:18; 3 Nephi 13:13; Moroni 4:3), and it often emphasizes the truth of a previous statement (1 Nephi 9:6; 14:30; 2 Nephi 2:30). It is also added to a statement of praise (2 Nephi 10:25; 31:21), but it never occurs as a statement that the people are urged to say.

The way the author of the Book of Mormon used common wording from the KJV either in an unusual idiom or in ways more characteristic of the New Testament supports the thesis that the Book of Mormon does not have an ancient Near Eastern origin. Rather, the Book of Mormon falls in line with what normally happens when an author tries to imitate an archaic style (in this case KJV English). Some prominent features are copied but used in a manner inconsistent with the original usage. For example, a few years ago two scholars compared the old Hebrew script used on some of the Dead Sea Scrolls with the Siloam tunnel inscription, which is usually attributed to the time of Hezekiah of Jerusalem (late eighth century B.C.). Because of many similarities between the allegedly ancient script of the Siloam inscription and the script of the Dead Sea Scrolls that was known to be later, they concluded that the Siloam inscription is not so ancient.[50] This evoked an avalanche of negative response from other scholars, including some who are experts in paleography, the study of how written characters change over time.[51] It seems that there were subtle differences in the letters of the Siloam inscription that clearly marked it as more ancient than the Dead Sea Scrolls. Even though later scribes at Qumran used the earlier script, they wrote it in a way that betrayed its later origin. Similarly, the sometimes unusual way that Joseph Smith used common phrases from the KJV apparently shows that his language was not really ancient, whether dating from the time of the KJV or from an even more ancient language.

Book of Mormon Names

Recently there has been a fair amount of discussion among Mormon scholars about names found in the Book of Mormon that are also found in various ancient sources.[52] In one article on Book of Mormon names, John A. Tvedtnes, John Gee, and Matthew Roper claim:

> The names described in this article deal a serious blow to critics of the Book of Mormon. Found in both the Book of Mormon and ancient inscriptions, these names are Hebrew in origin, as one would expect for people who emigrated from ancient Jerusalem. Except where noted, these names are not known from the Bible. Of particular interest is the fact that most of these names are attested in inscriptions dating to the time of Lehi. Indeed, some are relatively common for that time period. We can only speculate about how they made their way to the New World—whether on the brass plates of Laban or on the large plates of Nephi (which we no longer have) or in the names of the sons of Ishmael or their children or Lehi's grandchildren.[53]

According to Tvedtnes, Gee, and Roper, "in addition to Alma and Sariah, a number of other Nephite names are attested in ancient Hebrew inscriptions. These include Aha, Ammonihah, Chemish, Hagoth, Himni, Isabel, Jarom, Josh, Luram, Mathoni, Mathonihah, Muloki, and Sam, none of which appear in English Bibles."[54] In this section I will evaluate the supposed Hebrew backgrounds that LDS scholars have assigned to these names and whether they constitute evidence for an ancient Near Eastern background for the Book of Mormon.

It should first be noted that some of the names may not be found directly in the KJV but can easily be derived from it, and they were attested as names used during the time of Joseph Smith. This applies to the names Sam and Josh, which quite plausibly come from Samuel and Joshua. Regardless of whether or not a Hebrew inscription contains one of these names,[55] the derivation from the KJV and a name current with Joseph Smith has to be considered a viable explanation.

The name *Isabel* occurs once in the Book of Mormon (Alma 39:3). She was a "harlot" who caused Coriantum, the son of Alma, to "forsake the ministry." While the Isabel mentioned here is not the same as Jezebel, the Phoenician princess who married Jeroboam the son of Nebat (1 Kgs 16:31), the context makes it clear that there is some thematic connection. There is also a Jezebel in the New Testament who beguiles the Lord's servants "to commit fornication and to eat things sacrificed unto idols" (Rev 2:20 KJV). Surely biblical Jezebel could be the inspiration for Isabel in the Book of Mormon.

However, the Hebrew (Masoretic) pronunciation of Jezebel is /'Izevel/,[56] while the KJV has "Jezebel." The KJV spelling appears to be based on the Greek *Iezabel* (pronounced Yezabel and found both in the Septuagint for the OT passages and in Rev 2:20). Many scholars think that the Hebrew form is based on a deliberate scribal alteration to make the name mean something derogatory about the Phoenician god Baal. A name with the consonants *b'l'zbl* is attested on a Phoenician inscription.[57] The part of the name after the Phoenician god "Baal" contains all the consonants of the Hebrew but not the letter *yod*, which stands for a vowel.

The question is, how did Joseph Smith know what the underlying Hebrew was? Or did he? It happens that Isabel, a name with several variant spellings and derived from the French for Elizabeth, first appeared in England in the twelfth century, and by the following two centuries, it was "one of the commonest female names in England."[58] It was used in America in the nineteenth century and is still in use today.[59] It even occurs in Shakespeare's *Henry V* as "that fair Queen [of France] Isabel."[60] In 1852 passengers on the steamboat *Isabel* on the Missouri River witnessed the explosion of the steamboat *Saluda,* and the *Isabel* offered assistance.[61] In sum, the name Isabel in the Book of Mormon was so readily available to Joseph Smith that it cannot prove much from an apologetic standpoint.

It is not possible to determine what Hebrew or Semitic form might theoretically lie behind many of the names in the Book of Mormon because they are attested only in their English form. When names are transliterated, they sometimes undergo certain changes due to the different sounds that are significant for different languages. Students of Hebrew are often surprised, for example, to discover that the name "Eve" has the sound /ḥawwa/ in Hebrew.[62] The Greek has /eua/ except where it translates the name as Zoe (life). The Latin Vulgate comes closer with Hava. Also the city of Tyre in Hebrew is /ṣur/. Characteristic of forms like these are sounds that are found in Hebrew but not in English (or Greek or Latin). This problem is recognized by Dana Pike as "one of the great challenges in working with the names in the Book of Mormon."[63] Another issue is that the pronunciation of Hebrew changed over the course of time. In all likelihood the name Joseph was probably more like /yosep/ or /yawsep/ at the time of Lehi; Ebed-melech, like /'abdimelek/ or /'abdimalk/.

The name *Chemish* in the Book of Mormon is a case in point (Omni 1:8–10).[64] Tvedtnes, Gee, and Roper connect it to the name of the Ammonite god Chemosh, "spelled *Kmš* in prevocalic Hebrew and Ammonite (related languages)."[65] Yet why do they decide that the *ch* in Chemish is the same as that found in the name Chemosh, unless they are assuming that the KJV had an influence on Joseph Smith at this point? If it stands for the Hebrew consonant *ḥet*, as it occasionally does (Ra*ch*el; Na*ch*or [Josh 24:2]; Senna*ch*erib; the place name A*ch*metha [Ezra 6:2]), then the name would be different from the cited inscription. Also there is the issue of the vowel /i/ as opposed to the /o/ of Chemosh, especially when the KJV has "Chemosh" eight times (cf. Num 21:29; Judg 11:24). It is clear that Chemosh does correspond to the name of the Ammonite god; it is not so clear that Chemish does.[66]

For the names *Alma, Abish, Aha,* and *Ammonihah,* there is no certain way to know whether the first consonant represents Hebrew *ayin* or *aleph*. Alma could be read as *'Alma* (with *ayin*) or as *'Alma* (with *aleph*), two entirely different words. It is the latter form that was discovered among the Bar-Kochba letters (about A.D. 132) as a masculine name and may possibly relate to the form *a-lum* found at Ebla (ca. 2400–2000 B.C.).[67] Modern potential sources for the name Alma could be, among others, the phrase *alma mater* or even the transliterated Hebrew word for "virgin" or "young woman." It is quite possible that the young Joseph Smith heard the term in a sermon on Isaiah 7:14 ("Behold, a virgin [*'alma*] shall conceive, and bear a son, and shall call his name Immanuel"). Of course, it was applied in the Bible to a woman, not a man, but it would have been no different from many other biblical names that end with -a or -ah (Sheba, Mesha, Micha, Noah, Methuselah, Micah, and Ahijah). It seems unlikely that Joseph Smith would have thought that a name ending like this was more appropriate for a woman than a man.

As for the name *Abish,* it bears a strong similarity with Abishai, found twenty-five times in the KJV (cf. 1 Sam 26:6). Tvedtnes, Gee, and Roper cite the "name *'bš*', found on a seal from pre-exilic times (prior to 587 B.C.)" and "as a Semitic name on a wall relief in the tomb of Khnum-hotep III at Beni Hasan, Egypt, dating to the nineteenth century B.C."[68] Their explanation fails to account for the final *aleph* in the name on the cited inscriptions. It would indicate that a vowel had to follow after the /sh/, probably an /a/ if the name is to be interpreted as hypocoristic.[69] There is no reason to think that Abish is actually attested in the Semitic inscriptions cited when it does not fully represent what is written in the inscription.

The element *Aha* (name in Alma 16:5; Ether 1:9, 10; 11:10, 11) occurs initially in the KJV names Ahaz (2 Kgs 15:38), Ahaziah (1 Kgs 22:40), Ahava (Ezra 8:15), and Ahasai (Neh 11:13). These biblical names occur a total of 83 times in the KJV. In addition, the expression "Aha!" appears 10 times (e.g., Ps 35:21). The name *ʾḥ* occurs among the Samaria ostraca from the early eighth century B.C., and the person is further identified as "the Judean."[70] The name later appears among the Hebrew bullae (impressions made in clay by a seal) published by Yigael Shiloh.[71] From the form in the Book of Mormon, it is impossible to tell if the /h/ in Aha should stand for the Hebrew letter /h/ or /ḥ/.[72]

It does not appear to me that the name *Ammonihah* (Alma 8:6–9, 14, 16) actually shows up on the Hebrew inscriptions listed by Tvedtnes, Gee, and Roper.[73] First, the ending -ihah is not the same as -iah. Tvedtnes thinks the form -ihah may be due to Joseph Smith's "transliteration," but forms with -iah also occur in the Book of Mormon (e.g., Sariah and Mosiah). It is difficult to understand why the Hebrew sound /ya/ would be represented b -ihah. Nibley ascribes the spelling to "a common metatheses" [sic],[74] but why would such a metathesis occur in the divine name? Besides, even -hiah would not be like the names on the inscriptions.

Second, the name *Ammon* occurs only as the name of a people called *bene-ʿAmmon* ("the children of Ammon") or, rarely, *ʿAmmon* by itself (Ps 83:7) or *ʿAmmoni* ("Ammonite"; Neh 13:23).[75] It is never found as a personal name.[76] The ancestor of the Ammonites is himself called Benammi (Gen 19:38), apparently meaning "the son of my people." For this reason it is unlikely that the name *ʿmnyhw*/*ʿmnyh* is to be read as Ammon plus the divine name Yahweh. In fact, other scholars read it as Imannuyah(u), meaning "Yahweh is with us" and corresponding to Immanuel, "God is with us."[77] The Mormon writers give no evidence for equating the name with Ammonihah rather than the accepted Immanuyah.

Where should we look for the source of the name *Ammonihah*? Since -ihah appears to represent an ending attached to some other names (Camenihah, BoM 6:14; Mathonihah, 3 Nephi 19:4; Moronihah, Alma 62:43; Nephihah, Alma 4:17–18; Onihah, 3 Nephi 9:7; and Zemnarihah, 3 Nephi 4:17), then Ammonihah should be compared with Ammon, which occurs 91 times in the KJV (all but two in the form "children of Ammon," that is, Ammonites).

The names *Hagoth* and *Himni* share the uncertainty about the identity of their first consonant. Tvedtnes, Roper, and Gee compare Hagoth with biblical Haggith (2 Sam 3:4; 1 Kgs 1:5, 11; 2:13; 1 Chr 3:2), claiming that it "may have been vocalized Hagoth anciently."[78] They give no evidence for this assertion. Moreover, they also compare Himni with "*Ḥmn* on two Israelite seals" from the eighth and seventh centuries B.C. and with the biblical Heman: "The vowel at the end of Himni suggests that it is a gentillic form, meaning 'Hemanite.'"[79] The inscription has the initial consonant *ḥet*, while the name Heman has the consonant *he*.

According to Tvedtnes, Gee, and Roper, "several Hebrew inscriptions bear the name *Yrm*," dating from the general time of Lehi. The authors follow the standard interpretation of the name as a hypocoristic of the name Jeremiah and equate it with the name Jarom from the Book of Mormon.[80] From the analogous examples they give in their note, however, the name should be Jarum.[81]

Mathonihah (3 Nephi 19:4) and *Mathoni* (3 Nephi 19:4) should be compared with Mattan (2 Kgs 11:18; 2 Chr 23:17; Jer 38:1), Mattanah (Num 21:18, 19), Mattaniah (e.g., 2 Kgs 24:17; Ezra 10:26), and especially Matthew (often in the NT). It is significant that the only spelling with a /th/ occurs in the New Testament. That reflects the Greek transcription of a name of the same general form as the Old Testament names. The Hebrew form, if indeed it were as early as the time of Nephi, would not have had the sound /th/ in it; the KJV forms with /tt/ are closer to what would be expected from an underlying Hebrew form. Some other names from the KJV also contain the sound /oni/, as in the Mormon names: Benoni (Gen 35:18), Gideoni (Num 1:11; 2:22; 7:60, 65; 10:24), Armoni (2 Sam 21:8), Hazelelponi (1 Chr 4:3), Hachmoni (1 Chr 27:32), and Shiloni (Neh 11:5).

The vowels on the name *Muloki* (Alma 20:2; 21:11) were almost certainly not part of the name *Mlky* found on a bulla from Jerusalem that dates to about 600 B.C.[82] That name was Malki (compare Melchizedek, which is *malki-ṣedeq* in Hebrew), the vowels in Muloki being virtually impossible in Hebrew of such an early date. In addition, the letter *k* in Muloki is supposed to represent the corresponding letter from the inscription, yet with Chemosh (see above) the same letter is represented by *ḥ*. The first part of the name Melchizedek corresponds in its Hebrew form to the name on the inscription, yet here the KJV has *ch* rather than *k*. In the part of Melchizedek that is "zedek," the *k* stands for an entirely different Hebrew letter that is also found in the names Kadesh and Kohath. Still, the /k/ sound would be close to the way a name such as Molech or Melchizedek was pronounced in the time of Joseph Smith, and he could have derived Muloki from one or both biblical names.

Sariah (the wife of Lehi and Nephi's mother), according to some Mormon writers, is the same as the woman named Seraiah or Saryah in an Elephantine papyri of the fifth century B.C.[83] This can be compared with the common masculine name Seraiah in the KJV, meaning either "Yah(weh) is Prince" or "Yah(weh) has shown himself to be ruler."[84] It must also be observed that the /s/ in Sariah could represent any of at least three different consonants in Hebrew.[85]

When the names Sara (KJV for the forms in the New Testament), Sarah, Sarai, and Seraiah occur a total of 80 times in the KJV, it is not hard to imagine that the name Sariah could have been invented, with the parallel from Elephantine papyri simply an accident of history. Another factor to consider is that from all of the preexilic evidence from the Hebrew inscriptions we would expect the name to be spelled with a long ending for the -iah part of it, yielding Sar-yahu instead of Sar-ya.[86]

The consonants for the name *Luram* (Moroni 9:2) are attested from the Aramaic name *'dn-lrm* on a seal and on graffiti on three bricks of the eighth century B.C. from Hamath in Syria.[87] This means, according to Avigad and Sass, who read it as Adan-Luram, "may the Lord be exalted" or "the Lord is very exalted."[88] The letter *l* stands for a particle on the front of the verb and marks the name as Aramaic rather than Hebrew. It seems unlikely that an Aramaic name would turn up among the Lamanites about a thousand years after the alleged migration to the New World. The name in the Book of Mormon, which could be compared to Huram of the KJV (1 Chr 8:5; etc.), probably has an accidental correspondence to the inscription.

Numerous biblical names contain the divine name Yahweh or Jehovah (e.g., Isa*iah,* with the underscored part representing the divine name), especially around the time of Jeremiah and the supposed time of Nephi. It seems notable, then, that relatively few such names are found in the Book of Mormon. Aside from names in the quotations from Isaiah in 1–2 Nephi, it would appear that only the name Sariah might be analyzed as having it: "Yah(weh) is Prince." Contrast this with the book of Jeremiah, for which I have counted 29 names that have a suffixed form of /-yah/ or /-yahu/.[89] Among the bullae (seal impressions in clay) found in Jerusalem from about 600 B.C., forty-one names or nearly half the corpus end with /-yahu/. An additional three names have the divine element for Yahweh prefixed to the name (compare Jehoiada, "Yahweh has cared" or "Yahweh has chosen," Jer 29:26).[90] Exclusive of names found in the KJV, I have seen only the following names from the Book of Mormon that possibly have the divine name

Yahweh: Amalickiah (Alma 46:3–7); Ammonihah (Alma 8:9–9);[91] Camenihah (BoM 6:14); Mathonihah (3 Nephi 19:4); Moronihah (Alma 62:43); Mosiah (Mosiah 1:1–18); Nephihah (Alma 4:17–18); Onihah (3 Nephi 9:7); Sariah (1 Nephi 2:5); and Zemnarihah (3 Nephi 4:17).

Since this section has necessitated some complicated linguistic discussion of names, I will summarize the major points that have been made. First, it is next to impossible to claim with any certainty that a name in an ancient inscription matches one found in a source where the names are transliterated into a different script and no originals are available for comparison. The variety of ways in which the KJV transliterates the ancient Semitic names can be traced through the Latin (Vulgate) and the Greek (New Testament and Septuagint), and the KJV translators also had a desire to standardize variant forms of the same name. In addition, the translators had access to the Hebrew of the Old Testament for rendering the names as well. The same cannot be said for the Book of Mormon, for which the only source we have is what comes from Joseph Smith. Even so, if the claims of the Mormon writers regarding names from the Book of Mormon attested in ancient inscriptions are accepted, then it appears that the same sort of inconsistencies found in the KJV are also found in the Book of Mormon. That seems difficult to accept if it is claimed that Joseph Smith received these names through divine revelation.

Second, the claim of the Mormon writers that the names are not found in the KJV has to be tempered with the fact that many of those names (Sam, Josh, etc.) can be derived rather easily from a name in the KJV. Moreover, it cannot be ruled out that some of the names were known to Joseph Smith through some other source (e.g., Alma, Isabel, Sam, Josh).

Finally, the alleged correspondence between names from the Book of Mormon and the ancient inscriptions often does not follow what would be expected from pronunciation principles that have been established by scholars in the field. For example, Ammonihah should be Immanuyah (or Immanuyahu), Abish should be Abisha, Hagoth should be Haggith, and Jarom should be Jarum. A few isolated instances of apparent correspondence (certainty is prevented by the lack of vowels for the inscriptional evidence) are most likely accidents of history.

The Geography of 1 Nephi

Lehi left Jerusalem with his family, according to 1 Nephi, and "departed into the wilderness" (2:4). In his journey "he came down by the borders near the shore of the Red Sea; and he traveled in the wilderness in the borders which are nearer the Red Sea" (2:5). After "he had traveled three days in the wilderness, he pitched his tent in a valley by the side of a river of water" (2:6), which he named Laman. This river "emptied into the Red Sea; and the valley was in the borders near the mouth thereof" (2:8). At this valley the family camped in tents for some time, giving the sons opportunity to go back to Jerusalem to fetch the records of Laban, which were "engraven upon plates of brass" (3:3).

Where was the general area of this valley? Using only the details found in the Book of Mormon, it is impossible to discern whether it was located in the western Sinai or in the northwestern part of the Arabian peninsula.[92] The Red Sea, of course, can refer either to the sea on the western side of the Sinai, presumably where the Israelites crossed, or to the eastern side, where the sea also borders the Arabian peninsula. Later Mormon writers became convinced it was what we now know as Arabia, but the very general statements in the Book of Mormon do not lead to such an easy conclusion.[93] Actually, a journey through the Sinai would have the advantage of making it parallel the journey of the Israelites after they crossed the Red Sea.[94] In both cases the final destination was the Promised Land, but it was the Americas in the case of the Nephites, who reached it via ship from a place called Bountiful at the end of the wilderness journey.

If one assumes that the journey was through modern Arabia, did Joseph Smith know details about the geography of Arabia that were not available to him at the time that he recorded Nephi's account of the journey from Jerusalem to Bountiful? Eugene England tries to reconstruct a plausible route for such a journey and to show that Joseph Smith could not possibly have made up such an account.[95]

Nephi makes no reference to any countries traversed on this journey, which presumably would have included Moab, Edom, and Sheba if the journey was actually made through Arabia. A general lack of specific details about the travel seems unusual for a narrative that is devoted to detailing the defining journey for the Nephites. Even the time references are somewhat vague. Only two are specific, the "three days" of 1 Nephi 2:6 and another place that speaks of "four days" at sea (1 Nephi 16:13; cf. 18:15). The entire journey, either from the initial departure of Lehi from Jerusalem or possibly the portion of the journey between Nahom and Bountiful, took eight years (1 Nephi 17:4).

What about the "three days in the wilderness" of 1 Nephi 2:6? Does this mean three days after they arrived at the Red Sea or three days since they left Jerusalem? The account is not entirely clear. Chapter 2:4 says "he departed into the wilderness," leaving everything except his family and necessary provisions, and 2:5 also speaks of travel in the wilderness and then enumerates the members of his family, "which consisted of my mother, Sariah, and my elder brothers, who were Laman, Lemuel, and Sam." If the reference is to the time since leaving Jerusalem, then it would be much too short for a journey by foot to the Red Sea. England assumes that Nephi means three days after the party arrived at the Red Sea. This is a possible reading of the passage, but it also means that Nephi did not mention how long the journey from Jerusalem to the Red Sea took.

The term *borders* in the book of Nephi is a bit puzzling. In the KJV the term can mean borders of a country (Gen 47:21), boundaries of an area (Gen 23:17), territory or region (Num 20:17; Josh 13:2), and extremities or remotest parts (2 Kgs 19:23). Presumably the reference in Nephi is to the boundary between the "wilderness" and the Red Sea, but then how should "by the borders near the shore of the Red Sea" be distinguished from "in the wilderness in the borders which are nearer the Red Sea"?

England apparently assumes that *borders* means a ravine or wadi in the phrase "by the borders near the shore," though he doesn't state it that way: "The ancient route then moves long the beach for eighteen miles but turns east in the face of impassable cliffs, up the Wadi Umm Jurfayn and then down the Wadi El Afal ('the borders *near* the Red Sea') to the coastal plain again ('the borders *nearer* the Red Sea')."[96] Yet the text says first that the travel was "*by* the borders *near* the shore of the Red Sea" and "*in* the wilderness *in the borders* which are nearer the Red Sea." England's discussion fails to account for the different prepositions *by* and *in,* and it also omits the eighteen miles by the beach before the turn to the east. Plus, if *borders* means "ravines," one wonders why Joseph Smith didn't choose a term like *valley* or something that would be more descriptive.

Be that as it may, England's goal is to get the party to the oasis at Al Beda, because that is part of the ancient "Frankincense Trail." That trail came up from the southern part of Arabia along the western side of the peninsula through Mecca and Medina and ultimately on to Petra and points north.[97] From Aqaba a road headed south and then east to join the Frankincense Trail. It is essential to England's thesis that the journey of three days start from the Red Sea, because that allows for a trip of about seventy-six miles or three days until meeting up with the spice route.

After some time spent near the river Laman, the party crossed the river and journeyed in "nearly a south-southeast direction" for four days, pitching their tents again at a place they called Shazer (1 Nephi 16:12–13).[98] Nibley compared "Shazer" with Arabic *shajer*, "trees or place of trees."[99] Since these Nephites should have spoken Hebrew, any Hebrew cognate of the Arabic term (and none is currently known) should have been pronounced /ʂager/, with a hard "g" sound. The /j/ for /g/ of the Arabic is a late development (cf. how the Semitic word /gamal/ has developed into Arabic /jamal/ and has also been borrowed into English as "camel"), and the /ʂ/ (sh) of Arabic corresponds to Hebrew /ʂ/, a sound whose ancient pronunciation is uncertain but later merged with /s/ in Hebrew and Aramaic.[100] In any case, the "z" of the KJV normally reflects another sibilant in Hebrew.[101] In another place Nibley makes connections with a variety of variant forms: "Shihor, Shaghur, Sajur, Saghir, Segor (even Zoar), Shajar, Sozura, Shisur, and Shisar, all connected somehow or other and denoting either seepage—a weak but reliable water supply—or a clump of trees. Whichever one prefers, Lehi's people could hardly have picked a better name for their first suitable stopping place than Shazer."[102] These forms are either unrelated to Shazer or else still are late developments in relation to Nephi.[103] The Book of Mormon makes no reference to trees or to water at this place (1 Nephi 16:13–14). Perhaps a more likely source for Shazer was the place name Jazer in the KJV (Num 32:1; Josh 13:25; 21:39; 2 Sam 24:5; 1 Chr 26:31; Isa 16:8, 9; Jer 48:32). Note especially Isaiah 16:8, "they are come even unto Jazer, they wandered through the wilderness."

The direction of travel would be compatible with a trip down the Sinai peninsula following the basic route of the Israelites after they crossed the Red Sea, or with Arabia if the group used the Frankincense trail. Another route in Arabia that stayed closer to the Gulf of Aqaba actually moved in a south-southwest direction until the coast forced it to turn east.

From Shazer, the party encamped again after "many days" in order to "rest ourselves and obtain food for our families" (1 Nephi 16:17). They determined the proper direction for travel by consulting "a round ball of curious workmanship; and it was of fine brass. And within the ball were two spindles; and the one pointed the way whither we should go into the wilderness" (1 Nephi 16:10, 16). Elsewhere this device was called a "compass" (1 Nephi 18:12). The principle behind the compass apparently was first discovered in the twelfth century.[104] Possibly the idea that these travelers used a compass was based on a misunderstanding of the idiom "to fetch a compass" in the KJV (esp. Acts 28:13, "circled round" in the NKJV). Also at this place, Nephi's bow of "fine steel" broke while he was hunting, and his brothers' bows "lost their springs" (1 Nephi 16:18, 21). There is no evidence I am aware of for bows made of steel in ancient times. The "bow of steel" mentioned several times in the KJV should actually be a "bow of bronze."[105]

Leaving the unnamed location, the group arrived at a place where "we did pitch our tents again," having traveled "many days" in "nearly the same course as in the beginning" (1 Nephi 16:33). The next event mentioned is the death of Ishmael, "who was buried in the place which was called Nahom" (1 Nephi 16:34). Since we have no way of knowing for sure what the "h" in Nahom stands for, it is difficult to establish what its alleged ancient form might have looked like. Nibley connects it with an Arabic root, *nhim,* which means "to sigh or moan,"[106] whereas Warren and Michaela Aston mention the additional possibility of *nhm,* which means to "roar," "complain," or "be hungry."[107] Nibley further speculates that the party carried the body a great distance to bury it at a "desert burial ground."[108] The text says nothing about a time lapse between Ishmael's death and his burial at Nahom. For Nahom one might compare instead "Nachon's threshing floor" (2 Sam 6:6; the standard spelling in the KJV) and Naham in 1 Chronicles 4:19.

The events at Nahom reflect in some ways what happened at Kadesh during Israel's wandering in the wilderness. There Miriam died and was buried, and afterward the people rebelled against Moses and Aaron for bringing them to that place (Num 20:1–5). This could be compared with a rebellion that took place at Nahom: "And thus they did murmur against my father, and also against me; and they were desirous to return again to Jerusalem" (1 Nephi 16:36).

From Nahom "we did again take our journey in the wilderness; and we did travel nearly eastward from that time forth" (1 Nephi 17:1). This time the journey involved "much affliction in the wilderness"; it was a time when the women bore children and the party ate "raw meat." At the end of the journey "we did come to the land which we called Bountiful, because of its much fruit and also wild honey" (1 Nephi 17:5).[109] From there they "beheld the sea, which we called Irreantum, which, being interpreted, is many waters."

"Irreantum" should have been Hebrew since it was given by the Nephite travelers. The combination /ea/ would indicate probably an *aleph* between the two vowels, so that *-antum* would be an ending. The initial letter would be either *ayin* or *aleph,* so the root would have to be *'r'* (*ayin-resh-aleph*) or *'r'* (*aleph-resh-aleph*). If the initial letter is considered a prefix, then the root might be *nr'.* Biblical Hebrew knows of no ending *-antum,* and none of the possible root forms (even considering other variants for the final *aleph*) has a meaning that remotely resembles "water" or "many." The term is decidedly non-Hebrew in form and certainly unknown from biblical Hebrew.[110]

The basic details of the journey involved a trip from Jerusalem to the Red Sea and then travel along either the western part of Arabia or the western part of the Sinai, not far from the Red Sea, with an eastward turn at some point that brought the party out to an area of plenty after "much affliction in the wilderness." A setting in Sinai has the advantage that it recapitulates the exodus experience of the Israelites. The Nephites left Jerusalem during perilous times and then retraced the exodus journey from the Red Sea. Also, if the story is not based on a real event (other than the exodus from Egypt), then it might make more sense that Joseph Smith, with his limited knowledge of the geography of the area, chose a better-known area. However, even if the Arabian view is adopted, it still seems possible that Joseph Smith could have composed the story based on details available to him at the time.

Even England notes that all the various sources that Joseph Smith could have known about prior to 1835 "subscribe to the ancient Romantic idea of an 'Arabia Felix' in the south," though a more specific location tended to vary from the entire southern area to a few "fertile spots" in the interior and to the southwestern part of the country toward the Red Sea.[111] A map published in a Bible in 1839 shows Sheba just south of the center of the southern coast.[112] While this is after 1835, "when more careful explorations began to have their effect" (England), it seems doubtful that the general conception of the location of Sheba would not have been representative of earlier thinking as well. A work from 1806 also contains a map of the world that shows Arabia in its general shape and identifies the site of Mecca on the west coast. It also contains the following statement: "*Arabia-Felix,* or happy, on the south of the two former [*Arabia-Petraea* and *Arabia-Deserta*]. The two last seem to have been called Kedem, or the East, by the Hebrews. Scarce any part of Arabia is well watered; but Arabia-Felix is famed for vast numbers of fine spices and fruits."[113] Using this type of information, possibly gleaned from preachers, Joseph Smith could have assumed that a south-southeast route followed by an eastern route would land the Nephites somewhere in Arabia Felix. Ignorance of what Arabia was really like could have been almost helpful; the details of the story are similar to passages in the Bible that mention hunting for food (Gen 27:1–5; 1 Sam 26:20; Prov 6:5) or travels in the wilderness (Gen 16:7; 21:14–21; the wilderness wanderings of the Israelites; etc.). While the analyses of England and the Astons are interesting, they assume details about the travels of the Nephites that the Book of Mormon does not mention.

Conclusion

It is difficult at best for Mormon scholars to verify their claims that the Book of Mormon is based on an ancient document. Not having the original text from which the translation was made is a huge barrier to overcome, especially since the language of the supposed translation is in a strong King James idiom. Even worse, the researchers are not in complete agreement among themselves about whether the original would have been Hebrew or Egyptian, though the predominant view seems to lean toward Hebrew. Those languages are related as part of what is now called Afro-Asiatic (formerly "Hamito-Semitic"), but they are also more distant from each other than, say, Hebrew and Arabic or Hebrew and Akkadian (Assyrian and Babylonian).[114] It is a definite drawback not to know for sure which language was the original.

Despite these difficulties, Mormon researchers have attempted to show that alleged translations that are overly literal might reflect a Hebrew or Egyptian idiom. I have focused here on elements of usage that would be very difficult to reproduce by someone who had no knowledge of Hebrew. Moreover, the phrase "and it came to pass" is so pervasive in both the KJV and the Book of Mormon that it would be highly unlikely that its usage in the latter work would reflect Egyptian grammar rather than Hebrew. Careful attention to the details of how "and it came to pass" is used in the Book of Mormon actually lead to the opposite conclusion from that of the Mormon writers. The large differences in how the author used the phrase make it highly likely that Joseph Smith was imitating the style of the KJV rather than translating an ancient Hebrew original. The problem is only compounded when the impossible phrase "behold, it came to pass" is considered. The telling feature here is that "behold" has a function within a story that is at cross purposes with the function of "and it came to pass." Even if one were to argue that Mormon, who made an "abridgement" of the "plates of Nephi" (title page to the Book of Mormon) wrote in a language that was a later development of Hebrew, it would be hard to justify such a linguistic change. Of course, the whole argument of the Mormon apologists rests on the abridgement's representing accurately features of the ancient language, be it Hebrew or Egyptian.

A different kind of problem is encountered with names from the Book of Mormon that do not occur in the KJV but that are allegedly found on ancient inscriptions. From a transliteration it is impossible to be sure that the letters of most such names really do correspond. If there is no real correspondence, then the inscription cannot be entered as valid evidence. Two or three such names where the consonants do apparently correspond could easily be accidents of history. It would take more examples to establish the case, especially when other explanations would be easily at hand.

Geographical details about the journey from Jerusalem to Bountiful are so sketchy that it is not possible to decide whether the main part of it occurred in Sinai or in Arabia. Some connections with a plausible route in Arabia are interesting but speculative, being based on a series of assumptions about things that the Book of Mormon does not make explicit.

The issue of the brass or gold plates appears to be one of general similarities that have different functions within the points of comparison: ancient writing on metal and the Book of Mormon. In ancient times metal was an incidental medium used for texts much briefer than the Book of Mormon. The metal plates occur as a specific motif throughout the Book of Mormon, and the ones Joseph Smith said he saw were bound together like a notebook rather than attached and rolled up like a scroll.

This study has focused mainly on 1 Nephi, because his family would have been expected to know and use Hebrew from around 600 B.C. Many additional issues have been raised by Mormon writers, but it is not possible to examine them here. These include, among others, numerous literary studies that try to show parallelism, chiasm, or stylistic differences between the different alleged authors of the Book of Mormon.[115] The strong imprint of the KJV on the Book of Mormon also leads to an expectation of stylistic features such as parallelism or chiasmus in the latter work as well, but certainly there is room for additional study on these issues. It would also be important to take a closer look at the geographical issues raised by writers such as Eugene England in light of a more detailed study of the Arabian peninsula.

To sum up, how should we answer the primary question of this chapter? There is no solid evidence that the Book of Mormon was written by Semites in ancient times. Contrary evidence makes it more likely that the book is a product of Joseph Smith's time, with the KJV strongly influencing it. Its linguistic features and supposed original form on brass or gold plates differentiate it from known ancient Near Eastern literature. The social, cultural, and geographic features within the Book of Mormon derive easily from the KJV. In fact, some features are anachronistic even for the KJV. We have not discovered any features of the Book of Mormon that would make plausible the hypothesis that Joseph Smith translated it from ancient gold plates.

11

RENDERING FICTION
Translation, Pseudotranslation,
and the Book of Mormon

DAVID J. SHEPHERD

David J. Shepherd is Associate Professor of Old Testament at Briercrest Biblical Seminary in Saskatchewan, Canada. Shepherd earned a B.A. in ancient Semitic languages from the University of Saskatchewan, was a postgraduate research fellow at the Theological University in Kampen, Netherlands, and received his Ph.D. in Hebrew and Old Testament studies from the University of Edinburgh. Dr. Shepherd is a specialist on the techniques and characteristics of ancient translations of the Hebrew Bible into other Semitic languages and on the phenomenon of pseudotranslation. His articles have appeared in *Biblica, Journal for the Study of the New Testament, Journal of the Aramaic Bible, Journal of Jewish Studies,* and *Vetus Testamentum.*

And if there be faults they be the faults of man. But behold we know no fault, . . . therefore, he that condemneth, let him be aware.

—*MORMON 8:17*

Given the exceptional nature of the revelation to which Joseph Smith laid claim, it is hardly surprising that he felt it necessary to secure the signed testimony of several witnesses as a guarantee of the Book of Mormon's authenticity. Neither is it surprising, given the skepticism of many observers then and now, that editions of the Book of Mormon, beginning with the *editio princeps* (1830), have included these statements as external evidence of its credibility.[1] If the substance of these testimonies has remained largely unchanged from then until now, one way in which the first printing and subsequent editions of the "testimony of eight witnesses" do differ is in their characterization of Joseph Smith's role with regard to the Book of Mormon's emergence as a published work. While in later editions of the Book of Mormon this testimony and the title page of the work refer to Smith as the "translator," the original edition preferred instead to bestow on him the titles of "author and proprietor." At face value this might seem a significant change; however, Fawn Brodie, one of Smith's more skeptical biographers, admitted long ago that the terms "author and proprietor" were used in compliance with the copyright form of the day.[2] Indeed, whatever the legal conventions of the time, the claims of Joseph Smith, the "witnesses," and contemporary supporters leave little doubt that the role being ascribed to Smith was that of translator, rather than author, in the traditional understanding of both terms.

If it is clear, then, that the terminological shift from "author" to "translator" in subsequent editions of the Book of Mormon did not reflect a genuine alteration in the perception of Smith's role, what did it reflect? It would appear to suggest that Smith and his followers, along with most critics then and since, saw the roles of "translator" and "author" as mutually exclusive (or at least functionally distinctive) and were keen to identify Smith with the latter and not the former. This distinction between "translator" and "author" was no less important for those wishing to denounce Smith as a charlatan.

Unlike his supporters, however, Smith's opponents were eager to press upon him the role of fraudulent author so as to avoid legitimating the revelation of which he claimed to be merely the inspired translator. Thus, from the beginning the battle lines were drawn regarding Joseph Smith and the Book of Mormon: to his doubters, Smith was nothing more than the *author* of an elaborate deception; but to those who believed his claim, he was nothing less than the *translator* of a divine revelation.

The author of a text, be it literary or otherwise, has long enjoyed the interest and examination of the academy. It is only comparatively recently that translators and their work have been recognized as deserving specialized scrutiny within their own interdiscipline.[3] Translation studies has blossomed into a small but vital field of inquiry with scholars in Britain, America, Europe, and Israel making substantial contributions.[4] This is neither the time nor the place for even a summary review of these contributions, but one important advance in this new field is worth noting in the present connection: the recognition that although the distinctions between, for instance, "author" and "translator," or "original composition" and "translation" are in some sense intelligible ones, they are also more complex than was previously recognized. One example of such complexity has been identified by Rita Copeland in the *Ovide Moralise,* medieval texts in which translation and commentary/original composition are freely interspersed without any demarcation or delineation between them to alert the reader.[5] Early Bible translation shows the same blurring of distinctions: Jewish Aramaic translations or "targums" often integrate supplementary material drawn from earlier traditions seamlessly into their usually quite literal renderings of the Hebrew Bible.[6]

Of course, part of the academic enterprise is not merely to identify but also to name such complexity, even if such labels are necessarily contingent and tentative. It is hardly surprising, therefore, that as work has progressed within the field of translation studies, the once monolithic term *translation* has been fragmented and qualified in a variety of ways, including (but not limited to) indirect/mediated translation, intralingual translation, and even pseudotranslation. The purpose of the following discussion is to scrutinize the Book of Mormon through the lens of translation studies in the hope of moving toward a clearer understanding of its status, function, and classification. For the sake of clarity, it seems wise to begin with a discussion of the various subspecies of translation mentioned above before taking up the specific case of the Book of Mormon.

Types of Translation and Pseudotranslation

Indirect Translation

Although some have employed the phrase "indirect translation" to refer to renderings that tend to expand upon and elucidate the source text so as to provide a dynamic equivalence in translation, the expression is here used with a somewhat different intention.[7] For the purposes of our discussion, *indirect translation refers to a situation (and a product) in which a source text for a subsequent translation is itself a translation of a prior source text.* This type of indirect or mediated translation therefore describes a distance between translation and original text that is not necessarily semantic—for serendipity or linguistic accident may conspire to make the "translation of the translation" more semantically proximate than the initial translation—but may rather be seen as a distance of kinship. That is, whereas the translation (T) is an immediate relation of the original (O), the translation of the translation, or indirect translation (IT) is one step removed from O in terms of the translation process. The phenomenon of indirect translation is, of course, nothing new. For instance, Bible translation in antiquity provides countless examples of so-called daughter translations in which the three most influential versions of the Hebrew Bible (Syriac, Greek, and Latin) in turn gave birth to numerous descendants. These include, from the Greek: Coptic, Ethiopic, Armenian, Georgian, etc.; from the Syriac: Persian, Sogdian, Arabic; and from the Vulgate many of the medieval vernacular versions, including the Wycliffe Bible.[8]

While it was the loss of biblical Hebrew as a vernacular language that gave rise to these translations and the indirect translations that followed, it was the birth of a modern Hebrew language, eager to develop its own literature by borrowing from well-established literary canons, that produced a mirror image of this paradigm.[9] For instance, according to Gideon Toury, given the origins of the eighteenth- to nineteenth-century Jewish *Haskala* (enlightenment) in German culture, it is not surprising that texts originally composed in English were often translated into Hebrew via existing German translations. On the other hand, the rise of Nazism and the growing prestige of English ensured that by the middle of the twentieth century it was the latter language that now served as the mediator for German texts (particularly children's books) selected for translation into Hebrew. Indirect translation, then, whether disclosed or undisclosed, is nothing more nor less than secondhand translation—a mediated translation at least "once removed" from the original from which it has been (indirectly) translated via an intervening language.[10]

Intralingual Translation

We have seen above that indirect translation involves not merely a source language and a target language, but also a mediating language—a middleman, so to speak. Removing this middleman allows us to speak again of a more traditional understanding of translation: the reformulation of a text composed in one language into a target text belonging to a second language. Whatever the success or failure of this reformulation, the goal—the intention of the translator—is to somehow bridge the gap between the two languages so as to transfer the text across the divide. However simplistic or inadequate this metaphor may be, it is surely this "going between languages" that prompted Roman Jakobson to attach the term "interlingual translation" to what we normally understand as translation proper.[11] The observation that indirect translation involves at least three languages and interlingual translation requires no less than two leads us directly, if perhaps rather unexpectedly, to consider a type of translation that involves only one language. Wishing to distinguish this rare creature from its more commonplace cousin, Jakobson christened this type of rendering as "intralingual translation." In fact, Jakobson's own concise definition of the phenomenon—"'intralingual translation' or rewording is an interpretation of verbal signs by means of other signs of the same language"—furnishes us with an example of what he was attempting to show, namely, that the intralingual translation of a word or expression proceeds by the use of synonyms ("rewording") or circumlocutions ("an interpretation of verbal signs by means of other signs of the same language").

Jakobson's semiotic approach helped him to see the ways in which the search for synonymy when rewording *within* a language was directly analogous to the quest for equivalence when rewording *between* languages. Whereas in the case of interlingual translation the initial and primary gap to be bridged is the one that lies between the lexicon, grammar, syntax, and so forth of the source and target languages, the need for the rephrasing or rewording of a text within the same language is often rooted in a desire for more contemporary language, a smaller lexicon, or perhaps simplified syntax. When classic literature is paraphrased for younger readers with less extensive vocabularies, for instance, the primary transformation may be effected through the conscious restriction of the lexicon used by the translator.[12] On the other hand, the fourteenth-century English in which Chaucer wrote requires more extensive rewording and updating for it to be comprehensible at anything more than a very basic level for even a competent adult reader of English at the beginning of the twenty-first century.[13] If, however, updated versions of Chaucer might commonly be included among examples of intralingual translation, the fact that modern versions of *Beowulf*, composed originally in Old English (pre–tenth century) are often understood as interlingual translations—that is, translation proper—serves to show that the boundary between intralingual and interlingual translation is not always easily discerned.[14]

While translation in the traditional interlingual sense has been the generally preferred mode of producing modern English versions of the Bible (e.g., KJV, New English Bible, Jerusalem Bible), one of the twentieth century's best selling English Bibles was, in fact, an intralingual translation, or in the words of its creator, Kenneth Taylor, a "paraphrase."[15] In the creation of the *Living Bible Paraphrased* (LBP 1971) we see a convergence of the aims mentioned above: not only is it designed to update the archaic English for contemporary readers, but it is also attempting to simplify a "classic" for a younger audience. Taylor's Bible, or at least the one from which he found himself reading to his children, was an American version (ASV 1901) of the first wholesale revision of the King James Version (RV 1881). Taylor was dissatisfied with the archaic and literalistic English of the ASV. Although lacking the expertise to translate from the original Hebrew, Aramaic, and Greek texts, he set about rewording this translation for his children according to his own idiomatic and theological sensitivities.[16] The "paraphrases" that resulted were first employed by Taylor himself in his role as *paterfamilias* and college campus speaker, then later published by Tyndale House, the company he established for this purpose.

The *Living Bible* is, like the rewordings of *Robinson Crusoe* or *Dr. Jekyll and Mr. Hyde*, an intralingual translation. But it must also be clear that Taylor's paraphrase differs from these in that it is also, at the same time, an indirect translation. Whereas most instances of indirect translation involve, as we have seen, the interlingual translation (e.g., Latin) of an original text (e.g., Hebrew), which is then itself translated into a third language (e.g., English), in the case of the Living Bible, the mediating translation (nineteenth-century English) of the original (Greek, Hebrew, Aramaic) has been intralingually translated into a more contemporary form of the same language. It is primarily this nonreliance on the "original" source texts that has led to critical rejection of the *Living Bible*.[17]

Initially at least, the publishers made no attempt to disguise the fact that Taylor's work was dependent on an English version rather than texts in the original languages. This may be seen from the preface of the 1967 publication of the *Living New Testament Paraphrased*, where it is admitted that "the basic text used for this paraphrase is the American Standard Version of 1901, generally accepted by Bible scholars everywhere as a masterful work."[18] By 1974, however, the preface of the Coverdale House Publishers' edition of the *Living Bible* no longer referred to the ASV as the source text. The term *paraphrase* was retained but was provided with the gloss "popular translation" in parentheses:

> A word should be said here about paraphrases. What are they? To paraphrase is to say something in different words than the author used. It is a restatement of an author's thoughts, using different words than he did. This book is a paraphrase (or popular translation) of the Old and New Testaments.... There are dangers in paraphrases, as well as values. For whenever the author's exact words are not translated from the original languages there is a possibility that the translator, however honest, may be giving the English reader something that the original writer did not mean to say.

What appears above to be an admission of the *Living Bible's* dependence on an English version rather than the Hebrew, Aramaic, and Greek, however, turns out to be little more than an invocation of the traditional challenges faced by "the translator":

> This is because a paraphrase is guided not only by the translator's skill in simplifying but also by the clarity of his understanding of what the author meant and by his theology. For when the Greek or Hebrew is not clear, then the theology of the translator is his guide, along with his sense of logic.

In fact, a careful reading of this latter preface shows a consistent and studied ambiguity with regard to its use of the term *paraphrase*. This term was used by Dryden in the seventeenth century with reference to a middle way between literal and free approaches to translation.[19] By the latter half of the twentieth century, however, "to paraphrase" a text was simply "to express the meaning of (a passage) in other words" with no explicit reference as to whether these "other words" are understood to be derived from a language different from the original (interlingual translation) or from the same language (intralingual).[20] It seems clear from the preface of the *Living Bible* that the ambiguity of the term *paraphrase* was exploited by the publishers in order to ensure that their intralingual translation might compete against bona fide (i.e., interlingual) translations in the highly lucrative business of Bible publishing.[21] Further evidence of this is furnished by the recent release of the first "revision" of the *Living Bible Paraphrased.*

Having exploited the ambiguity of *paraphrase* in packaging the LBP as a popular translation, it seems that the marketers eventually felt the term itself to be a liability, perhaps because of its connotations of looseness and inaccuracy, and they dispensed with it altogether in the title *New Living Translation.*[22] We see from the foregoing that while the creators of the *Living Bible* never explicitly state that the sources for their English version are the Hebrew, Aramaic, and Greek texts, the terminology adopted and the manner in which this version was eventually marketed served to gloss over and minimize its basic reliance on an earlier English version. Whatever the intention of the publishers, it is quite obvious that this ambiguity might create the potential for confusion regarding the source text from which the *Living Bible Paraphrased* was derived. It is precisely this hint of confusion, of readers being mislead or hoodwinked, that has given rise to the suggestion that the *Living Bible Paraphrased* should in fact be understood as a "pseudo-translation."[23] To evaluate this suggestion, however, it is of course important to unpack what is meant, or could be meant, by the concept of pseudotranslation.

Pseudotranslation

As was the case with indirect translation, the term *pseudotranslation* has been used by some scholars to refer to a translation, in the traditional sense of the word, that deviates from its source text. For Gyorgy Rado, a translation can be termed a pseudotranslation when its deviations from the source text are so marked that it can no longer be thought of as a legitimate translation.[24] According to Rado, reworkings that transpose a given source text into another genre (i.e., novel to stage version) provide us with examples of pseudotranslation.

As with indirect translation, the term pseudotranslation has found, within translation studies more broadly, a quite different application. For Rado, the falseness of a pseudotranslation lies in the infidelity of the adaptation. For others, such as Anton Popovic and Gideon Toury, the conceit of a pseudotranslation is related to the question of whether a given target text is in fact the result of a translation at all. This is made clear by Popovic's equation of pseudotranslation with "fictitious translation": "An author may publish his original work as a fictitious translation in order to win a wide public, thus making use of the readers' expectations. The author tries to utilize the 'translation' boom in order to realize his own literary program."[25]

Generally preferring the term pseudotranslation to fictitious translation, Gideon Toury took up a discussion and illustration of the concept in the early 1980s before exploring the issues in greater depth again a decade later.[26] Toury's favorite illustration of the phenomenon of pseudotranslation is one derived from German literature at the end of the nineteenth century. In Leipzig in 1889, three pieces of prose fiction were published in German in a single volume titled *Papa Hamlet*. In addition to discussing the difficulties encountered in rendering the original work into German, the "translator's preface" provided an extensive biography of the Norwegian author, one Bjarne Peter Holmsen. The volume was reviewed widely in the German press and treated without exception as a bona fide translation until evidence began to emerge that all was not as it appeared to be. After several months during which Norway yielded neither the original work nor the elusive Mr. Holmsen, it emerged that the prose pieces had not been composed in Norwegian at all, nor, for that matter, had they been translated into German or any other language. It had, in fact, been written originally in German by Arno Holz (1863–1929) and Johannes Schlaf (1862–1941). It is clear now that Holz, Schlaf, and other German writers were able to introduce innovations into the resistant German literary tradition of the nineteenth century by presenting their original German compositions as translations from other literary traditions (Scandinavian and French among others).[27]

Toury's discussion of the phenomenon of pseudotranslation is primarily limited to examples drawn from a variety of "secular" European literary traditions down through the ages. However, given the potentially crucial influence of canonical texts, it is not surprising that the genre of "scripture" provides numerous instances of pseudotranslation that sit quite comfortably alongside cases such as that of *Papa Hamlet*. Neither is it surprising, in light of the importance of Christianity in the European literary/religious tradition, that the gospels have been a lightning rod for those interested in composing new scripture under the guise of translation.

Fascination with these fraudulent "gospels" has extended beyond popular readers to include scholars concerned to analyze the texts and evaluate the associated claims. While the twentieth century's most thorough treatment of "modern" pseudogospels (authored by E. J. Goodspeed) is unfortunately also its most dated, a more recent treatment by Per Beskow now exists to supplement Goodspeed's work.[28] There is neither the need nor the space to replicate the catalog of texts collected and analyzed by these scholars here, but a distinction noted by Beskow in his introductory chapter is germane to our discussion.[29] Some of the purveyors of the texts he discusses claim to have been the recipients of unmediated revelation (e.g., *Oahspe, The Urantia Book, The Occult Life of Jesus of Nazareth*); others prefer to advance the more modest, and for our purposes, more interesting claim that the text they are delivering to the public is, in fact, a "translation" of an ancient original or version. Examples drawn from modern apocrypha include English pseudotranslations from Italian[30] and Aramaic,[31] German pseudotranslations from Latin[32] and Coptic,[33] a French pseudotranslation from Tibetan (or Pali),[34] and an Italian pseudotranslation from Hebrew.[35]

In the case of *Papa Hamlet* we saw that the label of "translation" was applied falsely as a means of justifying or legitimating a text that might not have been accepted by its intended readership had it been presented as a text originally composed in the target language. For the scriptural pseudotranslations listed above, the label of "translation" legitimates the nonnative elements of the text, enabling the author to exploit the literary features and pedigree of the supposedly "original" language text. Furthermore, the authors' claims of "translation from the original" serve to root their work in the Judeo-Christian scriptural tradition where vernacular versions of holy books (e.g., Hebrew Bible or New Testament) in European languages are derived from original texts composed/revealed in languages now considered archaic or exotic (biblical Hebrew, Koine Greek).

In the case of both secular and scriptural pseudotranslations, of course, the unavailability of the "original" texts for examination and comparison with the putative translations is presented as accidental or incidental—the typical rejoinder being that books may easily go missing. However, it quickly becomes clear that this unavailability of the source text is no accident of circumstance but is a necessary factor in allowing the pseudotranslation to pass for a translation. In fact, on closer examination we see that this "unavailability" of a source or original text brings us to a crucial methodological issue raised by Toury in his discussion of pseudotranslation. As Toury himself notes, the lack of a source text introduces an element of indeterminacy into the investigation of pseudotranslation; and it is not always easy, nor possible, to distinguish between genuine translations—whose sources are now, for whatever reason, unavailable—and pseudotranslations, whose sources are unavailable by reason of having never existed in the first place.[36] Although

Toury acknowledges the importance of the demystification and unmasking of an apparent translation as an actual pseudotranslation before it may be analyzed as such, he neither poses nor pursues the question of how one might go about this demystification. If this unmasking is as crucial to analysis as Toury suggests, then it seems reasonable to determine how one might differentiate instances of genuine translation from pseudotranslation.

Differentiating Genuine Translation from Pseudotranslation

External Evidence

Confession

In the case of *Papa Hamlet,* the fact that the publishers could produce neither the translator, nor the author, nor ultimately the original Norwegian work ultimately led Holz and Schlaf to come clean regarding its actual origins. In fact, we might suspect that the German authors saw the ultimate unmasking of their translation as a "pseudotranslation" as an inevitable and perhaps even desirable outcome.[37] But whatever the authors' expectations, it is clear that *Papa Hamlet's* indubitable admission into the genre of "pseudotranslation" was made possible by the authors' similarly unequivocal confession of its composition by their own hands in German.

As in the world of the judiciary, the emergence of a confession is one way of closing a case with regard to the reclassification of a translation as a pseudotranslation. When, for whatever reasons, an author or publisher comes forward and admits that his "translation" is no translation at all, but an original composition in the target language, it seems entirely reasonable to classify this text as a pseudotranslation.[38] More often, however, such a confession of "pseudotranslating" is not forthcoming, thereby leaving unresolved the question of whether or not a given text should be seen as translation or pseudotranslation. Lacking an admission or confession, what other evidence might be admissible as a means of differentiating between texts genuinely translated and those that merely appear to be?

Appearance of a Source Text

One strong piece of external evidence in the case for or against pseudotranslation is the appearance of a preexisting source for the text being presented as a "translation"—although, as we will see, this type of external evidence can cut both ways.

Appearance of a source text in another language. On one hand, we may take the example of the book of Tobit, which up until recently was most anciently attested in longer and shorter Greek recensions.[39] Despite St. Jerome's claim to have translated his Vulgate version of Tobit from an Aramaic original, no such text was known to modern scholars, some of whom therefore steadfastly maintained that, despite the obvious traces of Semitic influence, Tobit was originally composed in Greek. While in the minds of these scholars the scribe originally responsible for the Greek versions of Tobit was seen to be an author, others suspected him to be merely its translator. With the discovery of the Dead Sea Scrolls, external evidence in the form of Semitic (Hebrew and Aramaic) manuscripts appeared that effectively unmasked Greek Tobit as a translation of a text composed in a Semitic language.[40] In other words, the appearance of a text in another language that has clearly given rise to the "translation" naturally speaks in favor of its classification as a bona fide translation. If, however, the appearance of a preexisting text in the suspected source language (e.g., Aramaic and Hebrew Tobit) may be cited as external evidence that another text (Greek Tobit) is in fact a translation, it is also true that the appearance of another type of preexisting text may also be strong external evidence that would recommend precisely the opposite verdict.

Appearance of a source text in the same language. If it may be shown that a "translation" is demonstrably dependent on a text that was not only already extant in the target language but also available to the translator, this would seem to be strong evidence of pseudotranslation. In 1849, for example, Chr. Ernst Kollman of Leipzig printed a text that purported to be an eyewitness account of the crucifixion and resurrection of Jesus (*Wichtige Enthüllungen über die wirkliche Todesart Jesu,* referred to by Beskow as *The Essene Letter*).[41] It was claimed that the German "translation" was derived from a Latin parchment scroll found in an Alexandrian monastery library—the scroll had, of course, long since vanished from the scene. This story might well have stood the test of time had Johann Nepomuk Truelle, a theologian of the time, not shown that the actual source text behind the Leipzig "translation" had, in fact, already existed in the German language for nearly half a century. Truelle established point by point how the Leipzig text was dependent upon Karl Heinrich Venturini's *Natürliche Geschichte des Grossen Propheten von Nazareth,* a novelistic treatment of the story of Christ published at the beginning of the nineteenth century.

A case with many similarities to the above is that of *The Report of Pilate* published by W. D. Mahan, a Presbyterian minister from Boonville, Missouri.

According to Reverend Mahan, in 1859 he received an English translation of an original Latin manuscript housed in the Vatican Library, which was none other than Pilate's own account of his involvement in the trial of Jesus. Although no corresponding Latin manuscript has been found that would corroborate Mahan's story, Per Beskow has shown that Mahan's *Report of Pilate* is incontrovertibly dependent on the short story "Ponce Pilate à Vienne," published in French by Joseph Méry in Paris in 1837. It is likely, Beskow suggests, that Mahan used an English translation of this French work, which was published under the title *Pontius Pilate's Account of the Condemnation of Jesus Christ and his own Mental Sufferings.*[42]

In the first instance above, we saw that the German "translation" was unmasked as a "pseudotranslation" through the appearance of a German text that clearly served as its source. In the case of Mahan, while his English *Report of Pilate* seems indeed to be dependent on a translation (the English version of "Ponce Pilate à Vienne"), it is clearly a pseudotranslation in the sense that the *Report of Pilate* is probably not dependent on Méry's French original, and almost certainly not connected to a Latin manuscript whose existence has never been demonstrated in either Vienna or Rome. In neither case has translation, in the *inter*lingual sense of the word, taken place; for the German and English pseudotranslations are nothing more than rewordings of texts already existing in these languages. Had the respective "translators" of these texts been content to make clear that they were simply rewording texts already existing in their respective languages, the matter would be closed. Their attempting to pass off *intra*lingual translations as *inter*lingual translations, however, means that their work should be understood as pseudotranslations.

It is perhaps useful at this point to return to the case of the *Living Bible Paraphrased* and Robinson's suggestion that it is in fact a pseudotranslation. It is obvious that the LBP is not a pseudotranslation in the sense that it is (on analogy with *Papa Hamlet*) an original composition being passed off as a translation. On the contrary, as Kenneth Taylor originally admitted, it is an *intra*lingual rewording of the American Standard Version (1901) of the Bible and not an *inter*lingual translation of the Hebrew and Aramaic and Greek texts.[43] This admission and the existence of the LBP's source text in the same language (ASV 1901) provide the external evidence that confirms it as both intralingual translation and pseudotranslation, akin in some respects to the two texts discussed immediately above. While Taylor, unlike the authors of *The Report of Pilate* and *The Essene Letter,* never claimed the LBP to be an *inter*lingual translation, the subsequent marketing of it seems to have been ambiguous enough to give some the impression that the LBP was derived directly from the "original" languages. Like the two more fraudulent examples, the LBP might also therefore be understood as a false translation (pseudotranslation) to the extent that it was presented, accepted, and functioned as an *inter*lingual translation (i.e., derived directly from the "original" languages) when it was actually a paraphrase or *intra*lingual translation (and derived from the "original" languages only via a mediating text already existing in English).

While external evidence may be mustered to indict the above texts as pseudotranslations, in many cases, no such external proof is forthcoming. Confessions of pseudotranslation are not easily extracted, and often the so-called translator will steadfastly maintain, in the face of all manner of criticism, that he has translated the text. Nor is corroboration in the shape of a source text, in either the same or a different language, likely to be forthcoming in many situations. On the one hand, the pseudotranslator's provision of an existing source text in his own target language is hardly to be expected, it being tantamount to a confession of guilt. On the other hand, it seems safe to presume that a bona fide translator, in order to validate his claims to have translated the source text faithfully, will be keen from the outset either to include a copy of the original language text or to provide accurate information regarding its whereabouts.

Internal Evidence

Where external evidence of the sort discussed above is not available, the differentiation of translation and pseudotranslation is likely to proceed on the basis of internal evidence—clues that a given text itself provides as to its own likely origins. Some pseudotranslations are found to incriminate themselves through their inclusion of anachronistic ideas or concepts.[44] For instance, according to Beskow, *The Essene Letter*'s dismissal of miracles and angels as popular superstition gives it away as a product of the Enlightenment rather than as a document produced by an ancient Essene community.[45] Further evidence of *The Essene Letter*'s fraudulent claims to antiquity may be seen in its author's reference to Jews in the third person, when, according to all available knowledge, the Essenes considered themselves to be Jewish through and through.[46] *La vie inconnue de Jesus Christ,* Nicholas Notovitch's supposed French translation from ancient Tibetan texts, is revealed as a fraudulent composition by its references to "the God Djaine"—an unlikely character in such a work if only because Jains or Jainas do not believe in gods but in *jinas,* or enlightened spiritual leaders.[47] In *The Gospel of the Holy Twelve*, supposedly translated from a first-century Aramaic text, the Palestine inhabited by Jesus is one where horses (rather than donkeys) carry burdens, where men train dogs to hunt, and where the gospel ministry is focused on promoting vegetarianism and animal welfare. In short, it is a world that seems far removed from Palestine and far more recent than the first century A.D.—no great surprise, given that it seems to have originated in the mind of an eccentric Anglican clergyman living in nineteenth-century Britain.[48]

As convincing as much of the above material would seem to be, it should be pointed out that this type of internal evidence is fundamentally weakened by the frank realization that our knowledge of the ancient world is fragmentary and must always be open to revision in the light of new discoveries (which is precisely what these texts claim to be). Take, for instance, the vegetarianism and concern for animals evident in *The Gospel of the Holy Twelve*. While the vegetarian concerns evident in this text are certainly best explained by the renewal of interest in vegetarianism in the nineteenth century, its appearance there was hardly without ancient precedent—proponents in antiquity included Pythagoras, Plato, and, in particular, Plutarch.[49] It is therefore improbable but not impossible that an ancient text might include vegetarian concerns of a sort expressed in *The Gospel of the Holy Twelve*. Ancient precedent for a concern for animals might be located in a reading of the Old Testament itself, where legal injunctions seem to proscribe certain treatment of animals as cruel or unjust.[50] The cogency of the above arguments is not the point. Rather, the discussion is intended to illustrate that this type of evidence, whether for or against pseudotranslation, will always be susceptible to more or less plausible counterarguments if for no other reason than that our knowledge of ancient culture and literature is always provisional.

It is important to note that, even if a particular text is viewed suspiciously on account of anachronisms and/or unusual or unexpected content, this does not necessarily imply pseudotranslation. While these issues of content may be relevant in judging the antiquity of a document, distinguishing between translation and pseudotranslation is ultimately a matter of assessing whether or not a linguistic transfer has taken place and how this transaction (or lack thereof) has been represented. As those familiar with the Greek of the New Testament can attest, such an assessment is by no means an easy or uncomplicated task. Like Tobit, discussed above, the Koine Greek of the New Testament itself shows traces of Semitic influence. But unlike Tobit, no Hebrew or Aramaic "original" of the New Testament has thus far come to light. This leaves scholars to debate whether the clearly Semitic tone and flavor of various portions of the Greek New Testament—in terms of modes of speech, vocabulary, and grammatical interference—is the result of Semitic influence on NT Greek (through various channels) or reflects the wholesale translation of the NT Gospels from, for instance, Aramaic.[51] Investigations of this sort are complicated greatly by the possibility of stylistic influence between traditions that have a history of contact via translation (be they Greek and Aramaic, or Hebrew and English). In cases of extensive contact and a tradition of translation between two languages, this linguistic interference, which seems to point to a source in another language, may in fact reflect the cumulative result of prolonged interpenetration of one language by another.

To summarize: we have seen that pseudotranslation may take the form of an original composition in a given language that is falsely presented as a translation *into* that same language from another (e.g., *Papa Hamlet*). We have also seen that the term *pseudotranslation* can be meaningfully applied to a text that may well be a translation of a certain type (intralingual, indirect, i.e., English to English) but that is then misleadingly presented as a quite different type of translation (*inter*lingual, direct, i.e., Hebrew to English). The unmasking of a pseudotranslation may in some cases be facilitated by the author/translator's own confession as to the nature of his activity. Alternatively, the truth regarding a text's origins may be clarified by the appearance of a likely source text, whether in the same language as the "translation" (confirmation of *intra*lingual and perhaps pseudotranslation) or in another language (confirmation of *inter*lingual translation). Deprived of these types of external evidence, the differentiation between translation and pseudotranslation must proceed on the less certain path of internal evidence—exploring the text itself for clues that will suggest whether it has in fact been translated or not.

Having devoted considerable space to a definition and exploration of some important concepts arising from the development of translation studies, we can now turn to see how these concepts may shed light on our understanding of the Book of Mormon.

The Book of Mormon: Translation or Pseudotranslation?

From the moment that Joseph Smith unveiled the Book of Mormon to the world, his work was dogged by accusations of pseudotranslation and fraudulent composition.[52] Of course, these claims were disputed almost immediately by Smith and those within his circle of support; the battle lines were soon drawn between those who denounced the work as a fraudulent composition and those who embraced it as Smith's inspired translation of an ancient text.[53] Although claims of Smith's fraudulent authorship continued to issue from different quarters in the years that followed (for the Rigdon-Spaulding theory, see below), the publication of Fawn Brodie's biography of Joseph Smith in 1945 gave fresh impetus to these suggestions of pseudo-translation. Brodie advanced the claim of pseudotranslation by pointing not only to the apparently dubious circumstances surrounding the Book of Mormon's origins but also to the anachronistic flavor of its narrative: its debt to nineteenth-century America rather than to antiquity was obvious to her from the fact that "its matter is drawn directly from the American frontier, from the impassioned revivalist sermons, the popular fallacies about Indian origin, and the current political crusades."[54]

Shortly after it was published, Alexander Campbell had also pointed to what he felt was the Book of Mormon's clearly anachronistic flavor; and at the turn of the century, William Linn was noting particular discrepancies between the picture of ancient America presented in the Book of Mormon and that emerging from anthropological and archaeological investigation.[55] In more recent times Per Beskow—finding Smith's own theory of the Book of Mormon's origins dubious—cites Linn's observations of anachronism approvingly as supporting his conclusion that the Book of Mormon is a pseudotranslation.[56] Internal evidence such as the observation of anachronism seems also to have encouraged the translation studies scholar Gideon Toury to include the Book of Mormon as one of his textbook examples of pseudotranslation. In referring to the Book of Mormon, he cites Brodie's claim that "the book is one of the earliest examples of frontier fiction, the first long Yankee narrative that owes nothing to English literary fashions."[57]

For whatever reason, neither Beskow nor Toury seem to acknowledge that, as we have seen, such internal evidence for pseudotranslation might be, and indeed has been, vigorously contested. In fact, even a cursory survey of work on the Book of Mormon reveals an astonishing effort on the part of Mormon scholars to undermine this type of argument and to present internal evidence of their own that would support the traditional Mormon claim that the Book of Mormon is an English translation of an ancient document. It seems unlikely that early critics could have imagined the volume of research that Mormons have, for example, recently devoted to squaring the cultural picture portrayed in the Book of Mormon with that revealed by Mesoamerican archaeology and anthropology.

The question of whether the metallurgy apparently represented in the Book of Mormon is, for instance, compatible with the Mesoamerican archaeological record has prompted considerable research by scholars such as John Sorenson.[58] Although it seems that some other professional archaeologists have been reluctant to be drawn into such discussions,[59] the limited response suggests that the archaeological record simply does not support the presence of the type of metallurgy and metalworking in Mesoamerica *during the period relevant* to the ancient American setting of the Book of Mormon.[60] Sorenson's primary explanation for the lack of early evidence is to emphasize the incomplete and contingent nature of the archaeological record.[61] While it seems evident to the present author that this defense of the Book of Mormon's "antiquity" (and by implication, its status as translation) is tenuous at best, it is also clear that arguments based on internal evidence that suggest pseudotranslation on the basis of anachronism will always be susceptible to counterarguments that legitimately recognize our incomplete knowledge of the past.

As noted above in our discussion of different types of internal evidence, however, the classification of a text as translation or pseudotranslation is primarily a linguistic matter rather than an issue of content. In recognition of this fact, considerable efforts have been expended to demonstrate that the English text of the Book of Mormon is a translation of a text written in either Egyptian or, as is often suggested, in Hebrew (albeit in Egyptian script).[62] In the case of the latter, for instance, the English text is examined for Hebraisms, that is, deviations from idiomatic English that reflect linguistic interference from the Hebrew original that supposedly lies behind the English version of the Book of Mormon. For example, John Tvedtnes has uncovered numerous "Hebraisms," which he sees as clear evidence that the English Book of Mormon is a translation of a Hebrew source.[63] We have already seen, however, that this type of linguistic argument is undermined when the text in question belongs to an extensive preexisting tradition of translation from the posited source language into the target language. Given the long tradition of comparatively literal translation of the Hebrew Bible into English, therefore, it is hardly surprising that, as Tvedtnes frequently admits, these Hebraisms of the Book of Mormon appear in, for instance, the Authorized Version (AV) of the Old Testament, a text with which Joseph Smith would have been quite familiar.[64] Again, although the present author finds the case for Hebraisms in the Book of Mormon less than compelling, it is impossible to decide with complete certainty whether the Hebraized English undeniably present in the Book of Mormon reflects reliance on existing traditions of Hebraized English (e.g., AV) or an actual Hebrew text. The absence of external evidence and our corresponding reliance on internal evidence will not allow the case to be closed definitively.[65]

One question that might reasonably be asked at this point is whether our assessment of the Book of Mormon as pseudotranslation is entirely reliant on internal evidence of the type sampled above. Thinking back to our previous discussion of external evidence, we remember that possible sources of such evidence included the confession of the author/pseudo-translator and the appearance of a source text of one sort or another. When we turn to the first of these, we see that Joseph Smith steadfastly maintained to his death that he was not the author of the Book of Mormon but its inspired translator. Nor did those included in his immediate circle attempt to incriminate him by suggesting that he did anything other than translate the plates that the witnesses claimed to have seen and lifted.[66] Unlike the authors of *Papa Hamlet,* Holz and Schlaf, Joseph Smith felt no compunction to confess to authoring the text he proudly presented to the world as his translation.

Of course, the appearance of the original source text from which Smith claimed to have translated the Book of Mormon might well have provided the external evidence to confirm his claims. The source text was, according to his own testimony and that of others, contained on plates that the witnesses saw and hefted. Unfortunately, a comparison between the texts supposedly contained by these plates and that which appears in the English Book of Mormon is impossible due to the disappearance of the plates soon after the completion of Smith's translation. Unlike the source texts of other pseudotranslations whose inaccessibility is, as we have seen, explained as accidental, temporary, or explicable by natural causes, the disappearance of the Book of Mormon was attributed by Smith to supernatural intervention. According to Smith's testimony, the plates were returned by him to the heavenly messenger who had originally delivered them.[67] Everyone concerned seems resigned to the fact that no source text in "reformed Egyptian" will be forthcoming—the doubters, because of their belief that the source never existed, the believers because they believe it has been returned to heaven.

It is worth remembering, however, that an original text in a different language (whose appearance would confirm Smith's claim to having translated the Book of Mormon) is not the only kind of external evidence that may be afforded by a source text. As we have seen in the case of *The Essene Letter* and the *Report of Pilate,* the appearance of a source text already existing in the same language as that of the claimed "translation" is strong external evidence of pseudotranslation. In fact, not long after it was published, the claim was made that the actual source of the Book of Mormon was not Smith's ancient plates but a manuscript written in English years earlier by one Solomon Spaulding. This accusation, originally made by an excommunicated Mormon in 1833, was blunted considerably by the discovery of said manuscript and the revelation that its text, apart from some general similarities, bore little resemblance to the Book of Mormon. Although one of Smith's non-Mormon biographers, Fawn Brodie, acknowledged some similarities between the two, such as an ancient voyage from the Old World to the New and the attribution of earthen mounds in New York and Ohio to savage wars, it was her authoritative dismissal of the "Spaulding Theory" that dealt it its death blow.[68]

At the same time that she dismissed the idea that Smith had relied on the Spaulding manuscript, however, Fawn Brodie revived the suggestion first made by I. Woodbridge Riley that parallels between the Book of Mormon and Ethan Smith's *Views of the Hebrews,* published in 1823 and again in 1825 in the county next to the one in which Joseph Smith spent his early years, strongly suggested its use in the composition of the Book of Mormon. The list of parallels that she compiles seems striking indeed. These include opening references to the destruction of Jerusalem and accounts of inspired prophets amongst the ancient inhabitants of America, inhabitants who were portrayed in both texts as highly civilized. She notes that both texts saw the gathering of the remnants of the house of Israel and their proselytization to Christianity to be the mission of the American nation. And she mentions that the "stick of Joseph" and "stick of Ephraim," which appear in *View of the Hebrews* as symbols of the Jews and lost tribes (respectively), appear in Joseph Smith's first advertising circulars announcing the Book of Mormon as "the stick of Joseph taken from the hand of Ephraim."[69]

In response to the parallels noted by Brodie and, perhaps more significantly, those noted by the Mormon historian B. H. Roberts, John W. Welch has drawn attention to ways in which the Book of Mormon and *View of the Hebrews* do not agree (so-called unparallels).[70] However, it must be remembered that to show that texts are dissimilar at points in no way vitiates suggestions of dependence, for the latter is built on the demonstration of commonality and accessibility and need not involve identity of two texts.[71] While it is perfectly reasonable to suggest that Joseph Smith drew structural and narrative materials from Ethan Smith's book, which was readily available for public consumption not long before the appearance of the Book of Mormon, it is clear from the "unparallels" that *View of the Hebrews* was not the sole or even the primary source for the Book of Mormon. In light of this, it provides a suggestive but shaky piece of external evidence in the form of a source text in English that Joseph Smith might well have used in the composition (and therefore pseudotranslation) of the Book of Mormon.

One final parallel mentioned by Brodie, namely, the extensive quotation of the Old Testament prophet Isaiah in both *View of the Hebrews* and Book of Mormon, does seem to point toward an existing source in English that was more certainly available to Joseph Smith and whose use in the production of the Book of Mormon can be more surely demonstrated.[72] This source is, of course, the King James/Authorized Version of the Bible (AV), which was already revered as one of the dominant English versions long before the dawn of the nineteenth century.[73] Scholars such as Anthony Hutchinson and Stan Larson have attempted to demonstrate the dependency of the Book of Mormon on the English Authorized Version in a variety of areas.[74] Larson, for instance, shows quite conclusively that the Book of Mormon's version of the "Sermon on the Mount" is demonstrably dependent on the English version that appears in the AV Gospel of Matthew and that this in turn relies on an underlying Greek text that is by no means as ancient or reliable as the NT text that has emerged since the beginning of the seventeenth century.[75] However, it is in their texts of the book of Isaiah that the agreement between the Book of Mormon and the text of the Authorized Version is most apparent.[76]

While this undeniable and substantial agreement would strongly suggest dependence of the Book of Mormon on the English version of Isaiah found in the AV, some scholars have chosen to focus on the differences (or unparallels, to reuse Welch's terminology) displayed by the two texts. These differences, it is claimed, argue against the dependence of the Book of Mormon on the AV in Isaiah, for they reflect variants in the underlying Hebrew Isaiah from which Joseph Smith claimed to have translated the English text.[77] Of course, to the extent that it might be mustered, this evidence would hint at the Book of Mormon's Hebrew origin and the necessity of Smith's translation of it into English. As we shall see, however, the evidence that is mustered does not appear to be able to support claims of an underlying Hebrew, let alone a Hebrew text that is either more ancient or more "original" than the Masoretic Text (MT).[78]

David P. Wright has responded to the suggestion that the Isaiah texts in the Book of Mormon point to variants in an underlying Hebrew text.[79] Wright provides a considerable volume of evidence that would suggest that almost every "Hebrew variant" that has been seen to be implied by the English text of the Book of Mormon is explicable as a modification or secondary development of the AV. More specifically, Wright shows that the divergences are most easily and economically explained as Smith's response to italicized words in the AV, his desire for smoothing and harmonizing irregularities, and his willingness to include additional material (such as conjunctions).[80] That the variations thought by some to be implied by the BoM Isaiah texts are unlikely to represent bona fide variants in an underlying Hebrew text is also suggested by recent work on the ancient textual and versional witnesses to Isaiah, illustrated below by means of an example.

It has been noted that BoM Isaiah includes the conjunction *and* at various places in Isaiah, where it is neither included in the KJV nor found in the Hebrew MT.[81] It has been suggested that these additional conjunctions in BoM Isaiah represent an underlying Hebrew text that possessed the *vav* conjunction at these same locations. Support for this suggestion is then gleaned from ancient versions such as the Greek Septuagint (LXX) and the Syriac Peshitta, which also show conjunctions at these locations.[82] The case seems to be further strengthened by the fact that one of the Hebrew texts of Isaiah found at Qumran (1QIsa[a]) also shows conjunctions at some of these same locations. While on the face of it, this agreement would seem to point to a bona fide "variant Hebrew text" underlying the English BoM Isaiah, recent research suggests otherwise. It is clear that modern English versions such as the AV, RSV, and so forth are no less in need of the addition, substitution, or omission of conjunctions in order to transform biblical Hebrew into acceptable, idiomatic versions in their respective languages than are ancient Greek, Aramaic, and Syriac translations.[83] The fact that these parallels are found in 1QIsa[a] might be significant had E. Y. Kutscher not shown this text to be an inferior, late, and popular version of Isaiah, modified in light of a Hebrew-Aramaic hybrid.[84] From this we see that the addition of "and" in the English BoM Isaiah is not at all likely to reflect an ancient text such as 1QIsa[a], but rather that the parallels are simply a function of a partial but explicable overlap in the conjunctional concerns of Joseph Smith and an anonymous Hebrew scribe.[85] It is clear, then, that the invocation of these ancient parallels to the addition of "and" in the Book of Mormon only shows that Joseph Smith found the English of the Authorized Version wanting in terms of conjunctions at various points and accordingly supplied *and* as he saw fit.

While the above discussion seems to show that the disagreements between the Isaiah texts of the Book of Mormon and the AV do not reflect the Book of Mormon's dependence on a source text in another language (Hebrew), what may be said in favor of its dependence on a source text in the same language? Wright marshals several pieces of evidence suggesting that BoM Isaiah is reliant on the English text of Isaiah found in the AV. First, he finds the fact that the Isaiah text of the Book of Mormon agrees literally and precisely with that of the AV for long stretches highly suspicious and indicative of the Book of Mormon's dependence on the latter rather than on a Hebrew text.[86] More substantially, Wright provides further evidence of the Book of Mormon's dependence on the AV text of Isaiah by showing how Joseph Smith's suspicion of italicized words in the AV led him to diverge frequently from the AV when coming across these "suspect" words in his base text.[87] Wright supplements these two pieces of evidence with the observation that the Book of Mormon presents instances where polysemy in English, not dependence on a Hebrew text, has led Joseph Smith to diverge from his AV Isaiah base text (see for instance: Isa 5:4//2 Nephi 15:4, Isa 48:3//1 Nephi 20:3, Isa 51:4//2 Nephi 8:4).[88]

It should be noted at this point that some scholars, in an attempt to make sense of the clear evidence for Joseph Smith's use of AV Isaiah, suggest that he followed this text only to the extent that the AV translation conveyed the correct meaning of the Hebrew.[89] It is clear, however, that this argument implies that wherever the BoM Isaiah text agrees with the AV Isaiah, the latter has correctly understood the text it translates. Unfortunately, however, the Authorized Version, despite its enduring popularity, had already begun to show its age by the time Joseph Smith began working on the Book of Mormon.[90] This is not to imply that for its time the AV did not represent first-rate scholarship and monumental effort. Rather, it suggests that in the nearly four hundred years since its appearance equally erudite scholarship and an explosion of knowledge in biblical studies has led in some cases (although not perhaps in as many as some suppose) to the conclusion that those translating for King James got it wrong.[91]

Wright correctly recognizes that a succession of instances where erroneous AV translations were uncritically reproduced by Joseph Smith in BoM Isaiah constitutes one of the strongest arguments against an independent translation (and in favor of the latter's use of the AV). This recognition leads Wright to cite a selective list of these erroneous translations that also appear in the text of BoM Isaiah. As valuable a starting point as this is, Wright's discussion of each example is, by his own admission, quite limited; and some of the instances he presents are perhaps rather less than convincing. For this reason the present author's modest contribution to the discussion will take the form of a more thorough illustration of selected erroneous or ill-informed translations in AV Isaiah that appear to have been uncritically reproduced in BoM Isaiah. Instances in which Wright and I are in agreement will be noted as such in the course of the following discussion.

The text of BoM Isaiah (2 Nephi 12:4b) agrees with AV Isaiah (2:4b) in providing the following rendering: "And he shall judge among the nations and shall rebuke (hôkîah) many people." While this Hebrew root (ykh) does appear with the sense of rebuke, reprove, or chide elsewhere in the Hebrew Bible (e.g., Prov 9:7–8; 15:12; 19:25), modern commentators agree that the parallelism here and at Isaiah 11:3 confirms the erroneousness of this AV translation and the appropriateness of "to decide or judge."[92] Modern versions accordingly provide "settle disputes" (NIV), "render decisions" (NASB), or "arbitrate" (NRSV). If Joseph Smith's BoM Isaiah text is an inspired and independent translation from a text like the MT, it is hard to understand why he should have committed the very same error that was made by the translators of the AV.

In Isaiah 3:2 and 3:3 the Hebrew provides a list of "supports"—human authorities in which Israel places its trust instead of relying on Yahweh (the champion, the man of war, judge and prophet, qōsēm and elder, captain and dignitary, counselor, conjurer, and nebôn lāhaš). The English translations supplied for these two terms in AV Isaiah seem to have been unduly influenced by the assumption that the "supports" would be necessarily condoned or approved of.[93] So, for instance, in the case of qōsēm, the AV translators supplied the approving equivalent "the prudent." But modern commentators agree that the reference here must be to divination, and modern English translations reflect this widespread scholarly agreement ("soothsayer" [NIV], "diviner" [NASB], "diviner" [NRSV]).[94] Likewise, in the case of nebôn lāhaš, which the AV Isaiah translators represented glowingly as "eloquent orators" (with the support of Targum and Syriac), we see that scholarly endeavour and the use of ancient Near Eastern sources has altered our view considerably. While lhš, like Akkadian luhhušu, refers basically to a whisper, its use suggests that it soon took on the connotation of conjuring.[95] Young concludes that the AV's rendering "eloquent orator" is essentially without foundation, despite being advocated by luminaries such as Luther and Calvin; modern English translations support this conclusion ("clever enchanter" [NIV], "skilful enchanter" [NASB], "expert enchanter" [NRVS]). When we discover that these clearly mistaken translations found in AV Isaiah also appear in Joseph Smith's BoM Isaiah (2 Nephi 13:2, 3), it becomes hard to reconcile Smith's claims to have produced an independent and inspired translation of the Hebrew with what seems clearly to be a dependence on a preexistent, and in this case inferior, English text.

As a means of impressing on his hearers/readers the severity of the impending catastrophe, the writer of Isaiah employs a string of reversals that the well-heeled, finely dressed "daughters of Zion" will suffer. Thus, the NRSV's rendering of Isaiah 3:24: "Instead of perfume there will be a stench; and instead of a sash, *niqpāh*; and instead of well-set hair, baldness; and instead of a rich robe, a binding of sackcloth; instead of beauty, shame." While the general structure of negative oppositions is clear, the AV Isaiah translators appear to have struggled with the counterpart of the "sash," rendering *niqpāh* as "rent" (i.e. tear).[96] While the nominal *niqpāh* is a *hapax legomenon* in the Hebrew Bible, modern commentators see the form as being clearly related to II *nqp* "to go around."[97] Modern English translations too are unanimous in their support of this interpretation, preferring to render *niqpāh* as "a rope" rather than "a rent."[98] Given the unanimity of this scholarly conclusion, it is worth asking why the English text of BoM Isaiah should share with AV Isaiah this clearly erroneous (or at least ill-informed) translation of the Hebrew. It would seem that the most likely answer to this question is that Joseph Smith did not translate Hebrew *niqpāh* at all but instead lifted the English translation of this term from AV Isaiah. Because at the time of producing the Book of Mormon Smith was not in a position to assess the quality or accuracy of the AV's translation of the Hebrew, the error was incorporated unwittingly into his own text.

Faced with a difficult Hebrew text in Isaiah 6:13b, some modern scholars choose to emend or modify the MT (*ʾēlāh wekāʾallôn ʾăšer bešalleket maṣṣebet bām zeraʿ qōdeš maṣṣebetāh*). Watts, for instance, follows both Iwry's acceptance of Dead Sea Scrolls Isaiah material and his emendation, translating: "Like the Terebinth or like the oak of an Asherah (*ʾăšerāh*) cast down (*mešalleket*) [becomes] a monument of a high-place (*bāmāh*)—the seed of the holy [will be] its monument." The NEB likewise reads *bāmāh* for *bām* seeing *maṣṣebet* as "sacred pole/post" in the usual sense and rendering, "a sacred pole thrown out from its place in a hill-shrine."[99] Wildberger demurs, preferring to read the MT as it stands (citing Hertzberg, Steinmann, Fohrer, Eichrodt, etc.) and translating, "as the oaks, and terebinths, which if someone fells them, shoots are still there. The shoots upon it are holy seed."[100] In fact, modern English translations generally parallel this preference for the unemended text (e.g., NRSV: "like a terebinth or an oak whose stump remains standing when it is felled. The holy seed is its stump.")

While it is clear that modern commentators disagree on precisely what Isaiah 6:13b does mean, they do seem to agree that it could not mean what the AV translators of Isaiah make the Hebrew to say, namely, "as a teil tree, and as an oak, whose substance *is* in them, when they cast *their leaves: so* the holy seed *shall be* the substance thereof." As Young points out, in Palestine the leaves of the oak (*quercus*), of which *'lôn* is a species, are narrow and (unlike those of other "oaks") do not naturally fall from their branches.[101] Without this knowledge, AV Isaiah's rendering of 6:13 must have seemed to Smith as likely as any; therefore, it is hardly surprising that he unquestioningly incorporated the AV translators' misinformed rendering into his own text (2 Nephi 16:13).[102]

As in the case above, scholars disagree on the correct understanding of the final word/phrase of Isaiah 8:20b: "Surely, those who speak like this *'ăšer 'ên-lô šāḥar*." Both Wildberger and Watts are convinced by Driver's suggestion to read *šāḥar* as "magic" or "power to overcome" while Clements and Kissane seem also to favor a translation of similar derivation ("witchcraft").[103] However, not all commentators on Isaiah are convinced, and for whatever reason, the opinions cited above have failed to find a place in current English translations, where the straightforward understanding of *šāḥar* as "dawn" is retained.[104] But neither of the above options are taken by the AV translators of Isaiah, who instead prefer to provide "light" as their equivalent for *šāḥar*. Only here in the Hebrew Bible do the AV translators supply this rendering for *šāḥar*, preferring elsewhere to provide expected expressions such as "morning" (Gen 19:15), "breaking of the day" (Gen 32:24 [25], 26 [27]), "the dawning of the day" (Josh 6:15), and "springing of the day" (Judg 19:25). More often, as we see in Isaiah itself, the English term "light" is used by the AV translators as an equivalent to Hebrew *'ôr*.[105] Why then does this unexpected and frankly inaccurate rendering appear in the AV? The answer is not altogether clear. It may be that the Christian AV translators' rendering here ("if they speak not according to this word, *it is* because *there is* no light in them") has been influenced by the famous conjunction of "word" and "light" in the christological symbolism of John 1.[106] On the other hand, it may have been the appearance of the "great light" at the beginning of Isaiah chapter 9 that has led to this unexpected AV rendering. In any case, because neither the immediate context nor the semantic domain of *šāḥar* seem to warrant the AV's rendering of this term with "light," it is remarkable, to say the least, that the supposedly inspired and independent rendering of the Hebrew text produced by Joseph Smith (2 Nephi 18:20) arrives at precisely the same equivalence here as in AV Isaiah 8:20. It seems more reasonable to suggest that BoM Isaiah imported this inaccurate rendering into its text along with the many quite laudable renderings the AV translators produced.[107]

Since at least the early 1960s, the Hebrew term *ṣalmāwet* has been understood to be related to the triliteral root clm, "to be dark."[108] This recognition, originally extending only to commentaries, began to penetrate modern English translations of the term in passages such as Isaiah 9:2 [1].[109] So, for instance, the NASB renders: "The people who walk in darkness will see a great light; Those who live in a dark land (*ʾereṣ ṣalmāwet*), the light will shine on them." The consensus of modern scholars on the subject is matched by the unanimity of the ancient witnesses that *ṣalmāwet* was a compound form composed of *ṣl* and *mwt*.[110] This etymology is in turn reflected in English translations such as the AV, who render our passage here in Isaiah 9: "The people that walked in darkness have seen a great light: they that dwell in the land of the shadow of death (*ʾereṣ ṣalmāwet*), upon them hath the light shined." It is not surprising that the AV translators of Isaiah would produce a rendering such as this. But it is slightly surprising that a divinely inspired and enabled translator such as Joseph Smith would "independently" arrive at the same erroneous translation as the AV translators of Isaiah, rather than clearly see in the Hebrew what modern commentators have come to realize. We see here further evidence to suggest that Joseph Smith did not merely adopt the English text of AV Isaiah when it was correctly interpreting the Hebrew, but he also unwittingly included it even when the AV Isaiah translation was flawed.

At Isaiah 9:5 [4], we see the AV translators valiantly but speculatively attempting to make sense of a verse which begins (*kî kol-seʾôn sōʾēn beraʾaš*) and then concludes: ". . . and garments rolled in blood; but *this* shall be with burning *and* fuel of fire." It is clear from the translation of verse 5a arrived at by the AV translators ("For every battle of the warrior *is* with confused noise") that while the semantic relationship between the verb and noun in the clause is understood to be close (battle/warrior), the actual meaning of the root sʾn has eluded the translators, and a contextual rendering has resulted. Since the time of the AV translation, and particularly within the last one hundred and fifty years, the rapid increase in our knowledge of other ancient Near Eastern lexica has begun to pay some dividends. Modern commentators on the book of Isaiah note that Akkadian parallels suggest *sōʾēn* to be a denominative verb derived from the noun *seʾôn*, which refers to a foot covering worn by soldiers.[111] This interpretation finds full endorsement in modern English versions such as the NRSV: "For all the boots of the tramping warriors and all the garments rolled in blood shall be burned as fuel for the fire." Again, however, we see that the agreement of the BoM Isaiah (2 Nephi 19:5) with AV Isaiah points *not* to an independent corroboration of the correctness of the AV translators, but rather to Smith's dependence on the contextual guess of those responsible for the AV.

Although limitations of space preclude the presentation of further examples, the above discussion could quite easily be extended.[112] It would seem, however, that these examples are sufficient to illustrate Joseph Smith's dependence on the AV, not merely when the AV interpreted the underlying Hebrew correctly, but also when, for whatever reason, an erroneous translation was produced. When placed alongside the evidence assembled by Wright with regard to both modifications in the vicinity of italics, and Smith's rewordings based on polysemy in the English of AV Isaiah, the discussion above confirms, at least to the present author's satisfaction, the identification of AV Isaiah as one source for the Book of Mormon.

It is interesting to note in this connection that Smith was not alone in re-presenting biblical translations from the AV in the context of his own inspired literary work. Half a world away and more than half a century later, Reverend Jasper Ouseley revealed his *Gospel of the Holy Twelve* to readers in Britain.[113] This work too included material that agreed precisely with the AV English version, not of Isaiah, but of the Gospels. Given Ouseley's claims to have received the English text from mediating spirits who had first translated it from the original Aramaic, he clearly felt that it was incumbent upon him to explain his work's verbatim agreement with the AV. His explanation was that spirits had given him guidance as to where to insert the quotations from the Authorized Version.[114]

Conclusion

If nothing else, the present study bears witness to the incontrovertible fact that the Book of Mormon has functioned, and continues to function, as a "translation" for a sizeable community of people across America and around the world. What this chapter has attempted to do is to bring critical concepts from translation studies to bear on the Book of Mormon so as to advance our understanding of its nature and significance. Although it will be faint praise indeed for defenders of Smith's "translation" work, it seems clear to the present author that the Book of Mormon is the most complex, ambitious, and influential pseudotranslation that the world has ever seen or is, indeed, ever likely to see. The primary grounds for coming to this conclusion will by now be quite evident—it seems quite clear that in producing the Book of Mormon, Joseph Smith was demonstrably dependent on source texts that were already extant and available in English. While the evidence for Joseph Smith's use of *View of the Hebrews* may be debated, it is the Book of Mormon texts of Isaiah that constitute the strongest case for his dependence, not on a Hebrew text as is claimed, but on an English text in the form of the Authorized Version. Even here, however, where his dependence was greatest, Smith's modifications to the AV Isaiah in producing the BoM Isaiah texts demonstrate that his work was not merely that of the copyist, but also, at times, that of the reworder or paraphraser.

At least with respect to the Isaiah material, Smith's work parallels that other American success story of pseudotranslation, the *Living Bible Paraphrased*. Smith, like Kenneth Taylor, produced an *intra*lingual translation of biblical texts. More specifically, both men took existing English language Bible translations belonging to the AV tradition and modified them as they saw fit. Both worked with texts that were themselves translations of earlier texts, and in this sense both created "versions" that were in fact indirect or mediated translations. In both cases the paraphrasing the men undertook has left their work open to accusations of pseudotranslation to the extent that their *intra*lingual rewordings (English to English) are falsely presented, intentionally or otherwise, as *inter*lingual translations (Hebrew to English). Unlike Taylor, however, Joseph Smith was not content to lightly rework and paraphrase existing scripture. Instead, armed with the courage of his considerable convictions, Joseph Smith set out to fashion his own scripture, creating for himself in the Book of Mormon a monument to his work as paraphraser and prophet.

FINAL CONCLUSIONS

FRANCIS J. BECKWITH,
CARL MOSSER,
AND PAUL OWEN

We now come to the final conclusions of this book, which we hope has made a significant contribution both to religious dialogue and to Christian apologetics. However, as the editors, we readily confess that this book is far from being the last word on Mormonism. Indeed, there is much more that could have been said from our side of the divide. This book does not contain chapters on topics such as deification, the Hellenization of early Christianity, and the theological-philosophical framework of the patristic fathers. We are aware that LDS scholars have raised important issues in each of these areas, and cogent responses from an orthodox Christian perspective have thus far been lacking. This book contains no chapters on the Book of Abraham or the Book of Moses in the Pearl of Great Price, nor does it answer all of the arguments LDS scholars have raised in favor of seeing the Book of Mormon as an authentic ancient book. Many important theological issues call out for attention, especially in light of developments in contemporary LDS theology. These include such topics as Mormon soteriology, Christology, ecclesiology, and theology proper.

In sum, there remains much work to be done, and we hope that evangelical scholars who read this book will come to share our vision for continued God-honoring Christian interaction with the truth claims of the LDS Church. We plan to contribute further to the discussion ourselves, but it will require the future labors of other Christian scholars to adequately address such a broad range of issues.

It is our prayer that this book will open eyes within the Christian community to the challenges at hand. There is a mistaken notion that Mormonism has no plausible apologetic arguments to raise in support of its own truth claims. Eyes need to be opened to the fact that the Mormon religion has a sophisticated body of scholarly apologetic that appears persuasive to many intelligent people. Unfortunately, the challenge here has been exacerbated because some figures within the evangelical apologetics community have, for various reasons, insisted that LDS defensive scholarship should not be responded to in any kind of detailed manner. Others have displayed a hostile attitude toward scholarship in general, indicating a preference that evangelicals in the academy leave the subject of Mormonism alone. Evangelical scholars must also accept part of the blame for sometimes being more interested in their own myopic scholarly pursuits than in contending "for the faith that was once for all entrusted to the saints" (Jude 3).

If Christians are to effectively meet the new Mormon challenge, the apologetics community needs to use Christian scholarship of the highest caliber. Our brightest and best biblical scholars, theologians, historians, and philosophers must remember that they have an obligation to use their abilities to promote and defend the message of the orthodox Christian faith. One way in which Christian apologists and scholars can begin fostering working relationships is through the education process itself. Christians who are called to serve in apologetics ministries must be properly educated, and this means that graduate programs must increasingly be crafted to suit the needs of such ministries. Otherwise, apologetics and Christian scholarship will continue to work in isolation from one another. A need that must therefore be addressed is the lack of credible and affordable graduate programs in apologetics and related areas that give due attention to alternative religions. A few schools are pioneering in this area, but much more needs to be done.

With this book we hope to offer a model of the way Christian apologetics ought to be carried out. We have made every effort to avoid caricatures of the views of those with whom we disagree. We have chosen contributing authors who were committed to keeping their tone courteous and their attention focused on the issues themselves. We have not attempted to gratuitously score points or to beat our religious opponents into submission. What we have done is to raise important questions about Mormon truth claims while at the same time extending an invitation to our LDS friends to consider afresh for themselves the message of historic, orthodox Christianity. We have approached this project with the intention of talking *to* Latter-day Saints, not *at* them, and we anticipate that they will have much to say in reply. When they do reply, then it will again be our turn to sit and listen. We emphatically insist that polemical engagement and courteous interreligious dialogue are not mutually exclusive options. To adapt the wisdom of Ecclesiastes: There is a time and place for debate and rigorous questioning; there is also a time and place for wholesome conversation and mutually instructive dialogue.

How do we expect this volume will be received by the LDS community? Of course, we anticipate that it will receive a variety of responses, but we hope that our critiques will be received in the spirit in which they are intended. We want to challenge fundamental LDS views regarding God, humanity, and the universe in which we live. We do not expect Mormon intellectuals to throw up their hands and concede defeat—that would be naive. But we do hope that this volume will contribute in some way toward encouraging LDS readers to reflect on the plausibility of some of their distinctive ideas that depart from biblical orthodoxy. To some degree, the leaders of the LDS Church have already proven willing to do this in several areas: polygamy, the Adam-God doctrine, blacks and the priesthood, and aspects of the Temple endowment ceremony. In recent years there has been increasing evidence of discomfort among Mormons regarding God's finitude and the traditional form of the eternal progression doctrine (involving an infinite regress of gods). There is evidence that the LDS Church is willing to adjust its doctrinal framework when Scripture and reason provide adequate warrant. We believe there is precisely such warrant for further changes within Mormonism regarding the doctrines of God and creation especially.

What, precisely, are we asking the LDS community to consider afresh? Here we can only sketch some of the areas where we believe traditional Mormon theology needs to change in order to better conform to Scripture and reason: (1) We believe the doctrine of the eternality of matter is fundamentally incompatible with biblical religion. Ideally, we would like to see the LDS Church embrace the traditional doctrine of creation *ex nihilo*. At the very least, we would encourage the LDS Church to consider the possibility that the world was created out of preexisting but not eternal matter. (2) We believe that the doctrine of monotheism is essential for any true and religiously valid knowledge of God. We would encourage the LDS Church to reject the notion of an infinite regress of gods as it has been traditionally articulated and to reconsider doctrines that necessitate a form of theological finitism. The monarchotheistic Mormon view is a step in the right direction, but it must be combined with the belief in the contingent nature of the universe. God must be recognized as ontologically unique, not merely as superior in status over all other reality. (3) We believe that the doctrine of the literal eternality of human persons is inimical to Christian faith, for central to a biblical worldview is the idea that we are created beings whose existence is contingent on the creative and loving will of our God. If the preexistence of spirits cannot be given up entirely, then we would encourage the LDS Church to consider a weakened form of this notion, in which the human spirit is viewed as preexistent but not as ontologically eternal (except perhaps in the ideal sense of eternal existence in God's mind).

There are other areas where we would *like* to see Mormon theology change: the doctrine of the materiality of spirit, the doctrine of divine embodiment, and the LDS form of the doctrine of the Trinity. But the three issues outlined above are absolutely fundamental and nonnegotiable. We do not feel that the status of Mormonism in relation to Christianity can ever change unless there is a willingness within the structures of the LDS Church to reconsider those issues.

In short, we want our Mormon friends to reconsider the nonnegotiable beliefs of historic Christianity. Christians in general—not just evangelicals— confess that there is but one eternal God, who created all things in heaven and on earth, visible and invisible. This One God is revealed in the One Lord Jesus Christ, who became incarnate for our salvation and whose presence is shed abroad among the people of God in the person of the Holy Spirit. It is this Triune God who is the only fitting object of religious devotion. He alone is the Living God, and it is to the praise of his glorious grace that the humble efforts of this book are adoringly offered.

NOTES

Chapter 1: The Apologetic Impulse in Early Mormonism

1. For instance, reporter Alan Wolfe was recently surprised to "discover" a "new" and apparently noteworthy intellectual movement in evangelical Christianity that had in reality been there all along. See Alan Wolfe, "The Opening of the Evangelical Mind," *Atlantic Monthly*, October 2000, 55–76.

2. Jan Shipps, *Mormonism: The Story of a New Religious Tradition* (Urbana and Chicago: University of Illinois Press, 1985), 3–4.

3. Richard L. Bushman, *Joseph Smith and the Beginnings of Mormonism* (Urbana and Chicago: University of Illinois Press, 1984), 122.

4. For a "fascinating" study on this, see Gary L. Bunker and Davis Bitton, "Mesmerism and Mormonism," *BYU Studies* 15 (1975): 146–70.

5. Leonard J. Arrington and Jon Haupt, "Intolerable Zion: The Image of Mormonism in Nineteenth Century American Literature," *Western Humanities Review* 22 (Summer 1968): 243–60.

6. Perhaps the closest to an intellectual was the converted Baptist clergyman Orson Spencer, who graduated from Union College in 1824 and from Hamilton Literary and Theological College in 1829. See Leonard J. Arrington and Davis Bitton, *The Mormon Experience: A History of the Latter-day Saints*, 2d ed. (Urbana and Chicago: University of Illinois Press, 1992), 29. Indeed, the very first LDS general authority to have attended college was the controversial Nauvoo Saint John C. Bennett, who had attended McGill University for one year. Orson Pratt was the first to receive an honorary degree—in this case from the short-lived University of the City of Nauvoo in 1841. See D. Michael Quinn, *The Mormon Hierarchy: Origins of Power* (Salt Lake City: Signature Books, 1994), 632. Leonard J. Arrington noted that the three figures thought to be the top intellectuals in LDS church history, B. H. Roberts, Orson Pratt, and Joseph Smith, were essentially self-taught ("The Intellectual Tradition of the Latter-day Saints," *Dialogue* 4 [1969]: 24).

7. D. Michael Quinn, *Early Mormonism and the Magic World View*, rev. ed. (Salt Lake City: Signature Books, 1998), 13; Stanley Jeyaraja Tambiah, *Magic, Science, Religion, and the Scope of Rationality* (Cambridge: Cambridge University Press, 1990), 31.

8. I discuss the vitality of popular religious and Enlightenment ideas in the minds of rural Americans in my book *The Village Enlightenment in America: Popular Religion and Science in the Nineteenth Century* (Urbana and Chicago: University of Illinois Press, 2000).

9. Arrington, "The Intellectual Tradition of the Latter-day Saints," 16. For another breakdown of the stages of LDS intellectual history, see Richard F. Haglund Jr. and David J. Whittaker, "Intellectual History," in *Encyclopedia of Mormonism*, ed. Daniel H. Ludlow (New York: Macmillan, 1992), 2:685–91.

10. Thomas F. O'Dea, *The Mormons* (Chicago: University of Chicago Press, 1957), 30–31.

11. Davis Bitton, "Anti-Intellectualism in Mormon History," *Dialogue* 1 (1966): 112. For another comment on the historical ebb and flow of general Mormon interest in the intellectual foundations of the faith, see Douglas J. Davies, *The Mormon Culture of Salvation: Force, Grace and Glory* (Aldershot, England: Ashgate, 2000), 36.

12. From the LDS periodical *Times and Seasons* 4 (1843): 125, as quoted in Bitton, "Anti-Intellectualism," 116.

13. David Brion Davis, "The New England Origins of Mormonism," as reprinted in *Mormonism and American Culture*, ed. Marvin S. Hill and James B. Allen (New York: Harper & Row, 1972), 21, 20. A response to Davis's interpretation can be found in Grant Underwood, "The New England Origins of Mormonism Revisited," *Journal of Mormon History* 15 (1989): 15–35.

14. Steven C. Harper, "Infallible Proofs, Both Human and Divine: The Persuasiveness of Mormonism for Early Converts," *Religion and American Culture* 10 (2000): 101.

15. Itinerant Protestant preacher Peter Cartwright noticed this hyper-competitive edge when he met Joseph Smith in 1839. He wrote that he heard Smith say on that occasion he would "raise up a government and . . . raise up a new religion that will overturn every other form of religion in the country." W. P. Strickland, ed., *Autobiography of Peter Cartwright* (New York: Carlton & Porter, 1857), 345. Dan Vogel thought there was evidence that Smith sought an "edge over his competitors" in his business as a treasure seeker and that he excelled the others in reputation ("The Prophet Puzzle Revisited," in *The Prophet Puzzle: Interpretive Essays on Joseph Smith*, ed. Bryan Waterman [Salt Lake City: Signature Books, 1999], 53). Historian Malcolm R. Thorpe believed the success of the Latter-day Saints over the "sects" in England was due to the LDS making a better case for "sacerdotal authority" than their rivals ("Early Mormon Confrontations with Sectarianism, 1837–40," in *Mormons in Early Victorian Britain*, ed. Richard L. Jensen and Malcolm R. Thorp [Salt Lake City: University of Utah Press, 1989], 68–69).

16. For a more comprehensive look at the "appeal" of early Mormonism in the culture at large, see Arrington and Bitton, *The Mormon Experience*, chapter 2.

17. From Eli Gilbert's letter to the editor in the *Latter Day Saint's Messenger and Advocate* (Kirtland, Ohio), October 1834, 10. Quoted in Harper, "Infallible Proofs," 108.

18. Philip L. Barlow, *Mormons and the Bible: The Place of the Latter-day Saints in American Religion* (Oxford: Oxford University Press, 1991), 11.

19. See Barlow, *Mormons and the Bible*, 48.

20. Ibid., 220.

21. Arrington and Bitton, *The Mormon Experience*, 30. In a note to this observation (p. 361, n. 34), the authors remind us of how crucial this selective literalism is in the origin of almost all new religious movements in American history. A. Leland Jamison wrote that "what we may call *the principle of selective emphasis*" was one of the most important ingredients for the "extensive proliferation of American religious groups" (James Ward Smith and A. Leland Jamison, *Religion in American Life* [Princeton: New Jersey: Princeton University Press, 1961], 1:179–80; emphasis in the original).

22. Barlow, *Mormons and the Bible*, 33.

23. Ibid., 45. Barbara McFarlane Higdon also confirmed the value of selective biblical usage in her study of early LDS sermons and preaching, "The Role of Preaching in the Early Latter Day Saint Church, 1830–1846" (Ph.D. diss., University of Missouri, 1961).

24. See D. Michael Quinn, ed., "The First Months of Mormonism: A Contemporary View by Rev. Diedrich Willers," *New York History* 54 (1973): 331–33.

25. Christian primitivism in the early nineteenth century has been studied extensively. Some of the most important studies are Theodore Dwight Bozeman, *To Live Ancient Lives: The Primitivist Dimension in New England Puritanism* (Chapel Hill: University of North Carolina Press, 1988); Richard T. Hughes, ed., *The American Quest for the Primitive Church* (Urbana and Chicago: University of Illinois Press, 1988); Richard T. Hughes and C. Leonard Allen, *Illusions of Innocence: Protestant Primitivism in America, 1693–1875* (Chicago: Uni-

versity of Chicago Press, 1988); Richard T. Hughes, *The Primitivist Church in the Modern World* (Chicago and Urbana: University of Illinois Press, 1995); and Samuel S. Hill, "A Typology of American Restitutionism: From Frontier Revivalism and Mormonism to the Jesus Movement," *Journal of the American Academy of Religion* 44 (March 1976): 65–76. For an extensive study of primitivism specifically in the Mormon context, see Marvin S. Hill, "The Role of Christian Primitivism in the Origin and Development of the Mormon Kingdom, 1830–1844" (Ph.D. diss., University of Chicago, 1968).

26. Nathan O. Hatch, *The Democratization of American Christianity* (New Haven: Yale University Press, 1989), 167.

27. For the religious background of the Smith family and the religious climate of the Palmyra/Manchester area in which they lived, see H. Michael Marquardt and Wesley P. Walters, *Inventing Mormonism: Tradition and the Historical Record* (San Francisco: Smith Research Associates, 1994), 43–62; Robert N. Hullinger, *Joseph Smith's Response to Skepticism* (Salt Lake City: Signature Books, 1992), 19–47; and John L. Brooke, *The Refiner's Fire: The Making of Mormon Cosmology, 1644–1844* (New York: Cambridge University Press, 1994), 59–88. Though it is a bit less focused on the religious background, see also Bushman, *Joseph Smith and the Beginnings of Mormonism*, 3–42.

28. Lucy Mack Smith, *Biographical Sketches of Joseph Smith the Prophet and His Progenitors for Many Generations* (London and Liverpool: Published for Orson Pratt by S. W. Richards, 1853), 37.

29. Ibid., 53–54.

30. Joseph Smith—History 1:19 from the Pearl of Great Price; emphasis mine.

31. Joseph Smith was not the first to make such a sweeping claim about all Christian institutions. Prior to Smith, self-appointed preacher Theophilus Ransom Gates proclaimed in publications from 1809 to 1827 that "every sect or constituted body of people in Christendom" was mired in apostasy. See Hatch, *The Democratization of American Christianity*, 176–79.

32. Richard L. Bushman reached a similar conclusion. He wrote: "The opposing responses [from Campbellites and other primitivists] suggest that Mormonism, while resembling the primitive Gospel movement in some respects, went beyond it in others" (*Joseph Smith and the Beginnings of Mormonism*, 180). Some see Joseph Smith as trumping the primitivists in yet another way: by reaching back much further than the pristine time of Jesus and the apostles. Klaus J. Hansen, for example, sees Smith in his "Book of Moses" as looking back to the time of Adam and the undefiled Garden, or to the "holy city of Enoch" for the ultimate restoration of all things (*Mormonism and the American Experience* [Chicago: University of Chicago Press 1981], 27).

33. Orson Spencer, *Letters Exhibiting the Most Prominent Doctrines of the Church of Jesus Christ of Latter-day Saints* (Liverpool: R. James, 1848), 8–9. Quoted in Arrington and Bitton, *The Mormon Experience*, 29–30.

34. Barlow, *Mormons and the Bible*, 101.

35. Mormon 9:19. Two historians have pointed out that compared to the Bible, the Book of Mormon (hereafter BoM) itself seemed to be rather light on the actual inclusion of miracle accounts in its text, but it was certainly strong in supporting the concept of miracles as a continuing feature of the true church. See Hullinger, *Joseph Smith's Response to Skepticism*, 135, and Jon Butler, *Awash in a Sea of Faith: Christianizing the American People* (Cambridge: Harvard University Press, 1990), 245.

36. Butler, *Awash in a Sea of Faith*, 245. Butler quotes reminiscences of the Mormons and miracle reports from a Freewill Baptist itinerant named Nancy Towles in her 1832

memoir, *Vicissitudes Illustrated in the Experience of Nancy Towles in Europe and America*, 2d ed. (Portsmouth, N.H., 1833), 152.

37. Gregory A. Prince, *Power From on High: The Development of Mormon Priesthood* (Salt Lake City: Signature Books, 1995), 112–13. Also see Quinn, *Mormon Hierarchy*, 22–23 and Bushman, *Joseph Smith and the Beginnings of Mormonism*, 154.

38. Doctrine and Covenants 24:13–14 (hereafter, D&C).

39. From the *Painesville Telegraph*, 7 December 1830. Quoted in Prince, *Power From on High*, 100–101.

40. Prince, *Power From on High*, 101.

41. Harper, "Infallible Proofs," 104–5. Harper's account comes from Esaias Edwards, "Autobiography," typescript from the special collections of the Harold B. Lee Library, Brigham Young University, Provo, Utah. The Farr family was also reported to have joined the church when LDS apostle Orson Pratt healed the mother of Winslow Farr in May of 1832. See Breck England, *The Life and Thought of Orson Pratt* (Salt Lake City: University of Utah Press, 1985), 30–33.

42. *Painesville Telegraph*, 7 December 1830. As cited in Bushman, *Joseph Smith and the Beginnings of Mormonism*, 123; and Prince, *Power From on High*, 116. For a more official LDS stance on the place and value of miracles today, see "Miracles" in Bruce R. McConkie, *Mormon Doctrine*, 2d ed. (Salt Lake City: Bookcraft, 1979); and Paul C. Hedengren, "Miracles," in *Encyclopedia of Mormonism*, 2:908–10.

43. Steven C. Harper, "Missionaries in the American Religious Marketplace: Mormon Proselytizing in the 1830s," *Journal of Mormon History* 24 (Fall 1998): 14.

44. According to Joseph Smith himself, the first person to speak in tongues was new convert and future LDS president Brigham Young at Smith's parents' house in 1830. See Donna Hill, *Joseph Smith: The First Mormon* (New York: Doubleday, 1977; repr., Salt Lake City: Signature Books, 1999), 152. There were two fascinating episodes in early LDS history that helped to perpetuate the idea that supernatural manifestations were following the Saints. The first involved prophesying, speaking in tongues, and visions for two days at the dedication of the Kirtland Temple in March 1836, although William McLellin seemed to think it had more to do with the amount of wine consumed and David Whitmer called it the "grand fizzle" (see Prince, *Powers From on High*, 127–29). The second legendary "manifestation" took place in August 1844 after the death of Joseph Smith. While Brigham Young was making the speech that helped confirm him as the successor of Smith, several people recalled that they saw Young's appearance and voice transform into those of Joseph Smith himself (see Arrington and Bitton, *The Mormon Experience*, 84–85).

45. Joseph Smith, *Teachings of the Prophet Joseph Smith*, compiled by Joseph Fielding Smith (Salt Lake City: Deseret, 1976), 375. The same document can be found in its original rough form as taken directly from the manuscript by Thomas Bullock in "K[ings] & P[riests] unto God & His Fa[the]r," A Sermon Delivered on 16 June 1844, in *The Essential Joseph Smith* (Salt Lake City: Signature Books, 1995), 255.

46. Joel Johnson, Excerpts from Autobiography (1802–1868), Special Collections, Harold B. Lee Library, Brigham Young University Library, Provo, Utah, 3–4, as quoted in Harper, "Infallible Proofs," 105.

47. See for example, Ray Allen Billington, *The Protestant Crusade 1800–1860: A Study of the Origins of American Nativism* (New York: Rinehart and Co., 1952); John Tracy Ellis, *American Catholicism*, 2d ed. (Chicago: University of Chicago Press, 1969), esp. chapters 1–2; Barbara Welter, "From Maria Monk to Paul Blanshard: A Century of Protestant Anti-Catholicism," in *Uncivil Religion: Interreligious Hostility in America*, ed. Robert N. Bellah and Frederick E. Greenspahn (New York: Crossroad, 1987), 43–71.

48. *Priestcraft Exposed and Primitive Religion Defended*, 1 April 1834, as quoted in Billington, *The Protestant Crusade*, 57; emphasis in the original.

49. 1 Nephi 14:9. Brodie tried to make a connection between some nativist material in the *Rochester Album* of February 29, 1828, and passages in the Book of Mormon (1830), pages 28 and 32. I don't know if Brodie is right about the connection, but the idea that the passages parallel the anti-Catholic sentiments of the day is obvious. See Fawn M. Brodie, *No Man Knows My History: The Life of Joseph Smith the Mormon Prophet*, 2d ed. (New York: A. A. Knopf, 1971), 59–60. That the 1 Nephi passages "prophetically" address Roman Catholicism is confirmed as early as 1832 by the LDS periodical *The Evening and Morning Star* 1 (no. 1): 3.

50. For samples, see Parley P. Pratt, *A Voice of Warning and Instruction to All People; Or An Introduction to the Faith and Doctrine of the Church of Jesus Christ of Latter-Day Saints, Commonly Called Mormons* (New York: W. Sanford, 1837) in the "Preface to the First American Edition"; Orson Pratt, "Christian Polygamy in the Sixteenth Century," *The Seer* 1 (December 1853): 175; and Brigham Young's comments in "We Talk a Great Deal About Our Improvements and Increase in Knowledge," a sermon delivered on 4 August 1867, as reprinted in *The Essential Brigham Young* (Salt Lake City: Signature Books, 1992), 195–96.

51. Hatch, *Democratization of American Christianity*, 168. Young, "We Talk a Great Deal About Our Improvements," 196.

52. Shipps, *Mormonism*, 51.

53. Joseph Smith—History 1:9–10, from the Pearl of Great Price.

54. See Whitney R. Cross, *The Burned-over District: The Social and Intellectual History of Enthusiastic Religion in Western New York, 1800–1850* (Ithaca: Cornell University Press, 1950), 43.

55. Hatch, *Democratization of American Christianity*, 173.

56. Ibid., 174.

57. Elias Smith, "On Predestination," *Herald of Gospel Liberty*, 15 September 1809, 112. As quoted in Hatch, *Democratization of American Christianity*, 139.

58. See Harper's views on the marketplace and religious competition of the time in his "Missionaries in the American Religious Marketplace."

59. For more on the universalist leanings of Smith's father and grandfather, see Bushman, *Joseph Smith and the Beginnings of Mormonism*, chapter 1; Hullinger, *Joseph Smith's Response to Skepticism*, chapter 4; and Marquardt and Walters, *Inventing Mormonism*, 46–47. See also Richard Eddy, *Universalism in America: A History*, 2 vols. (Boston: Universalist Publishing House, 1884–86) for a broader picture of universalism in this region of the country.

60. Among the general categories in American universalism were "ultra-universalism," the stance that there would be no punishment after death; and "restorationism," the stance that although everyone will eventually be saved, some will need to go through a type of restorative punishment after death. I want to make it clear that I am continuing to use the term *restorationism* as a synonym for "primitivist" movements in Christianity and not as a type of universalism.

61. Hazen, *Village Enlightenment in America*, 5–7.

62. See Hatch, *Democratization of American Christianity*, 181–82, and Brooke, *The Refiner's Fire*, 204. One of the most influential books making the case for Universalism as well as Unitarianism in the early republic was Hosea Ballou's *A Treatise on Atonement* (Randolph, Vt.: Sereno Wright, 1805).

63. D&C 76:31, 43.

64. McConkie, *Mormon Doctrine,* 669; emphasis mine.

65. For a fine analysis of the anti-universalist rhetoric in the Book of Mormon, the early universalist milieu, and the early evolution of the idea, see Dan Vogel, "Anti-Universalist Rhetoric in the Book of Mormon," in *New Approaches to the Book of Mormon: Explorations in Critical Methodology,* ed. Brent Lee Metcalf (Salt Lake City: Signature Books, 1993), 21–52. Also see Vogel's essay "The Prophet Puzzle Revisited," 55–56.

66. Zerah Pulsipher, "Autobiography," typescript from the special collections of the Harold B. Lee Library, Brigham Young University, Provo, Utah, 5–6, as quoted in Harper, "Missionaries in the American Religious Marketplace," 27–8.

67. For more on the historical context of this revelation and reaction to it, see Richard S. Van Wagner, *Sidney Rigdon: A Portrait of Religious Excess* (Salt Lake City: Signature Books, 1994), 112–13, and Vogel, "Anti-Universalist Rhetoric in the Book of Mormon," 47.

68. I am not here addressing the LDS distinctions between the Celestial kingdom and the heavens therein. Nor am I addressing the distinctive meanings of the terms *salvation, immortality, eternal life,* or *exaltation* in Mormon thought. For brief discussions of these concepts in the modern church, consult the relevant entries in McConkie, *Mormon Doctrine* or the *Encyclopedia of Mormonism.*

69. The chance at eternity in the Celestial kingdom was not only a motivator to join the church, but it was a good reason to be loyal as well. Prolific journal writer William Clayton recorded that Joseph Smith reminded him that disloyalty to Smith could cause a saint to lose his place in the "celestial kingdom." Clayton also wrote that whether or not a person in the next life could transfer from a lower heaven (the Terrestrial or Telestial) to the highest was a topic of discussion by church leaders on several occasions. George D. Smith, ed., *An Intimate Chronicle: The Journals of William Clayton* (Salt Lake City: Signature Books, 1995), 108, 442–43.

70. To this day answers to these questions play an important role in demonstrating the LDS system as more reasonable. See current LDS apostle Jeffrey Holland's article on the "Atonement of Jesus Christ" in the *Encyclopedia of Mormonism,* in which he writes: "The Church is also emphatic about the salvation of little children, the mentally impaired, those who lived without ever hearing the gospel of Jesus Christ, and so forth: these are redeemed by the universal power of the atonement of Christ and will have the opportunity to receive the fullness of the gospel in the spirit world" (1:85).

71. The passing of little children must have touched Smith himself very deeply, because he covers it frequently in his sacred writings. In addition to Moroni 8, see, for example, Mosiah 3:18, 3:21, 15:25; Alma 30:25; D&C 18:42, 29:46–7, 74:7, 93:38, 137:10; and Moses 6:54. Making sure that children who died went directly to the highest state of the afterlife was a key tenet of almost every new religious movement in the antebellum period. For an example involving Spiritualism, see my *Village Enlightenment in America,* 96.

72. Smith, *Teachings of the Prophet Joseph Smith,* 107, and D&C 76:72–79.

73. Smith, *Teachings of the Prophet Joseph Smith,* 179–80; D&C 124: 28–36, and sections 127, 128. For more on the historical context of the origination of the ordinance, see Prince, *Power From on High,* 87–89.

74. Benjamin Brown, *Testimonies for the Truth* (Liverpool: S. W. Richards, 1853), as quoted in Harper, "Infallible Proofs," 100.

75. Pratt, *A Voice of Warning*; Peter Crawley and Chad Flake, *A Mormon Fifty* (Provo, Utah: Friends of the Brigham Young University Library, 1984), entry 7.

76. Harper, "Missionaries in the American Religious Marketplace," 3–4.

77. See Hansen, *Mormonism and the American Experience,* 40; and Harper, "Infallible Proofs," 108.

78. See, for example, William Lane Craig, *The Historical Argument for the Resurrection of Jesus During the Deist Controversy* (Lewiston, N.Y.: Edwin Mellen Press, 1985); and Avery Dulles, *A History of Apologetics* (New York: Corpus Instrumentorum, 1971), esp. chapter 4.

79. Hullinger, J*oseph Smith's Response to Skepticism*, 5.

80. One part of this that has received considerable attention in recent years is Joseph Smith's fascination with esoteric traditions and folk magic, and the influence of these on the development of early Mormon thought and practice. See Brooke, *The Refiner's Fire*; Lance S. Owens, "Joseph Smith and Kabbalah: The Occult Connection," *Dialogue* 27/3 (1994): 117–94; and Quinn, *Early Mormonism and the Magic Worldview*. For LDS responses, see the review of Brooke by William J. Hamblin, Daniel C. Peterson, and George L. Mitton, "Mormon in the Fiery Furnace: Or Loftes Tryk Goes to Cambridge," *Review of Books on the Book of Mormon* 6/2 (1994): 3–58; and William J. Hamblin's review of Owens, "'Everything is Everything': Was Joseph Smith Influenced by Kabbalah?" *FARMS Review of Books* 8/2 (1996): 251–325. Quinn, throughout the revised and enlarged edition of his work, responds in great detail to the criticisms more conservative LDS scholars leveled against the first edition of his book. No doubt rejoinders will be forthcoming. Because of the complexity of the issues involved, I will make no attempt to evaluate these debates here.

81. LDS leader Orson Hyde used exactly this kind of message in his own evangelistic preaching. Harper noticed that some of his regular preaching notes contained prompts such as "Compare the situation of *modern* witnesses of this day with the *ancients*" (cited in Harper, "Missionaries in the American Religious Marketplace," 11).

82. In the1830 edition, however, the testimony of the witnesses was not at the beginning of the book, but was bound in at the back.

83. This "Testimony of the Eight Witnesses," along with the "Testimony of the Three Witnesses," is, of course, still found today in all official copies of the Book of Mormon published by the LDS church.

84. Gilbert in the *Latter-Day Saint's Messenger and Advocate*, 10.

85. Arrington and Bitton, *The Mormon Experience*, 41, 31, 32; emphasis mine.

86. Ibid., 41.

87. Hansen, *Mormonism and the American Experience*, 43.

88. Brodie, *No Man Knows My History*, 69. Brodie here confirms an observation made by Smith contemporary and Disciples of Christ founder Alexander Campbell. Whether out of jealousy from a competitor or not, Campbell noticed that the Book of Mormon attempted to answer every controversial issue of the day, including "infant baptism, ordination, the trinity, regeneration, repentance, justification, the fall of man, the atonement, transsubstantiation [*sic*], fasting, penance, church government, religious experience, the call to the ministry, the general resurrection, eternal punishment, who may baptize, and even the question of freemasonary [*sic*], republican government and the rights of man"(*Delusions: An Analysis of the Book of Mormon; with an Examination of Its Internal and External Evidences, and a Refutation of Its Pretenses to Divine Authority* [Boston: B. H. Greene, 1832], 13). Although his analysis is a bit hyperbolic, it remains one of the most important and perceptive statements about Smith and the Book of Mormon. After all, Campbell had a particularly good vantage point. He was influenced by many of the same societal currents, lived in the same region and time, and had some parallel religious aspirations.

89. Gordon Wood, "Evangelical America and Early Mormonism," *New York History* 61 (October 1980): 359–86.

90. Shipps, *Mormonism*, 149.

91. For a complete bibliography of Parley P. Pratt's thirty-one published works, see Peter Crawley, "Parley P. Pratt: Father of Mormon Pamphleteering," *Dialogue* 15 (1982): 23–26; for Orson Pratt's twenty-four, see England, *The Life and Thought of Orson Pratt*, 339–40.

92. As quoted in David J. Whittaker, "Orson Pratt: Prolific Pamphleteer," *Dialogue* 15 (1982): 27.

93. E. Robert Paul, "Early Mormon Intellectuals: Parley P. and Orson Pratt, a Response," *Dialogue* 15 (1982): 43.

94. Of course the Pratts gleaned from Smith not only the revelational data but also Smith's overly optimistic assessment of his ability to solve the world's knotty intellectual problems. Smith is recorded as saying, "I combat the errors of the ages; I meet the violence of mobs; I cope with illegal proceedings from executive authority; I cut the Gordian knot of power; and I solve mathematical problems of universities, with truth—diamond truth; and God is my 'right hand man'" (B. H. Roberts, ed., *History of the Church of Jesus Christ of Latter-Day Saints* [Salt Lake City: Deseret, 1932], 6:78).

95. Parley P. Pratt, *Key to the Science of Theology* (Liverpool: F. D. Richards, 1855), xiii–iv. In order to get the full flavor of this popular nineteenth-century work, one should consult an original or a reprint of editions one (1855) through five (1891). Modern LDS publishing houses sometimes print versions that were altered (without notifying the reader) by Apostle Charles W. Penrose, who expunged some of the most interesting passages that show that Pratt was thinking along the same lines as the spiritualists, mesmerists, and mind-cure practitioners of his day. For instance, he called the Holy Spirit a physical "substance . . . composed of individual particles . . . the grand moving cause of all intelligences" (39) and wrote of "eternal, self-existing elements" that "possess intelligence" (43). See Hazen, *Village Enlightenment in America*, 56–57, 161 n. 133; and Thomas G. Alexander, *Mormons in Transition: A History of the Latter-day Saints, 1890–1930* (Urbana and Chicago: University of Illinois Press, 1986), 280–81. To compare the modern versions of the *Key* with the original, see Jerald and Sandra Tanner, *Changes in the Key to Theology* (Salt Lake City: Utah Lighthouse Ministry, 1965).

96. For more on Orson Pratt's thought and how it fits into the pattern of popular religious thinking of his day, see Hazen, *Village Enlightenment in America*, 15–64.

97. Orson Pratt, *Absurdities of Immaterialism; or, A Reply to T. W. P. Taylder's Pamphlet, Entitled, "The Materialism of the Mormons or Latter-day Saints, Examined and Exposed."* (Liverpool: R. James, 1949).

98. An 1843 revelation recorded in D&C 131:7.

99. Orson Pratt, *Great First Cause; or, The Self-Moving Forces of the Universe* (Liverpool: R. James, 1851), 9.

100. Orson Pratt, *Key to the Universe, or a New Theory of Its Mechanism* (Liverpool, 1879). By the time he published this work, Pratt had already conceptualized the Holy Spirit as an ocean of thinking particulate matter filling the universe. He had hoped that his *Key* would be taken seriously on scientific grounds alone; hence, he did not mention this religious aspect of the "universal ether." See Orson Pratt, *The Holy Spirit* (Liverpool: Latter-day Saints Book and Millennial Star Depot, 1856).

101. Indeed, Orson Pratt indicated that he saw himself as both the new Johannes Kepler and new Isaac Newton for the restoration age (*Key to the Universe*, 89–90).

102. Verse from an LDS hymn by Parley P. Pratt, "An Angel from on High," in *Hymns of the Church of Jesus Christ Latter-Day Saints*, 1st ed. (Salt Lake City: Church of Jesus Christ Latter-day Saints, 1985), no. 13.

103. One work by Widtsoe that is not much read today is his fascinating little book *Joseph Smith as Scientist*. Originally published as a series of articles for the church periodical *Improvement Era* (1903–4), this book was an apologetic work in the tradition of Orson Pratt showing that the utterances of the prophet concurred with and anticipated modern advances in science. Ironically, at the same period in time, Albert Einstein was busy overthrowing many of the Newtonian and nineteenth-century conceptualizations that seemed to make Smith a "seer of science." See John A. Widtsoe, *Joseph Smith as Scientist: A Contribution to Mormon Philosophy* (Salt Lake City: YMMIA, 1908); and Erich Robert Paul, *Science, Religion, and Mormon Cosmology* (Urbana and Chicago: University of Illinois Press, 1992), 158–60.

104. Arrington, "The Intellectual Tradition of the Latter-day Saints," 22; and Stan Larson, "Intellectuals in Mormon History: An Update," *Dialogue* 26 (Fall 1993): 187–89.

105. Sterling McMurrin, "Brigham H. Roberts: A Biographical Essay," in B. H. Roberts, *Studies of the Book of Mormon*, 2d ed. (Salt Lake City: Signature Books, 1992), xxvi; Davis Bitton, "B. H. Roberts as Historian," *Dialogue* 3 (Winter 1968): 26. For a brief introduction to Roberts's ability as a theological/philosophical apologist, see David L. Paulsen's forward to the reprint of B. H. Roberts, *The Mormon Doctrine of Deity: The Roberts-Van Der Donckt Discussion* (Salt Lake City: Signature Books, 1998), v–xxvii.

106. B. H. Roberts, *Studies of the Book of Mormon*. Despite his devastating criticisms, there is good reason to believe that Roberts was able to cling to his faith in the authenticity of the Book of Mormon until the end of his life. See McMurrin, "Brigham H. Roberts: A Biographical Essay," xvii–xviii. Mormon apologist Daniel C. Peterson is right in stating that even if it were true that Roberts lost his faith, "[e]xactly how this would constitute evidence against the Book of Mormon . . . is not entirely clear" (from Peterson, "Is the Book of Mormon True? Notes on the Debate," in Noel B. Reynolds, ed., *Book of Mormon Authorship Revisited: Evidence for Ancient Origins* [Provo, Utah: FARMS, 1997], 163–64). However, the real difficulty lies not in Roberts's faith, but in McMurrin's admonition to let Roberts's provocative work "speak for itself" (xvii). Roberts's analysis of Book of Mormon problems is still one of the greatest challenges facing today's LDS apologists.

107. McMurrin, "Brigham H. Roberts: A Biographical Essay," xxi.

108. I will not list the recurrent names and topics here. Many are discussed or cited in the subsequent chapters of this book. Also see the discussion and extensive bibliographical notes in Carl Mosser and Paul Owen, "Mormon Scholarship, Apologetics and Evangelical Neglect: Losing the Battle and Not Knowing It?" *Trinity Journal* n.s. 19, no. 2 (1998): 179–205. One should also consult the FARMS catalog or Web site for information: http://farms.byu.edu.

109. See, for instance, Hansen, *Mormonism and American Culture*, chapter 7; Shipps, *Mormonism*, chapter 7; Alexander, *Mormons in Transition*, 272–310; Gordon and Gary Shepherd, *A Kingdom Transformed: Themes in the Development of Mormonism* (Salt Lake City: University of Utah Press, 1984), 201–7; and Mark P. Leone, *Roots of Mormonism* (Cambridge: Harvard University Press, 1979), esp. chapter 7.

110. For example, see Orson Pratt, *Deseret News* 22 (1873): 586; and Brigham Young, "Remarks by President Brigham Young, Delivered in Salt Lake City, May 14, 1871," in *Journal of Discourses* (Liverpool: F. D. Richards, 1855–66), 14:115–17.

111. For LDS attempts to address this issue, see John A. Tvedtnes and Stephen D. Ricks, "Jewish and Other Semitic Texts Written in Egyptian Characters," *Journal of Book of Mormon Studies* 5/2 (1996): 156–63; William J. Hamblin, "Reformed Egyptian" (Provo, Utah: FARMS, 1995); Daniel C. Peterson, "Is the Book of Mormon True? Notes on the Debate," in *Book of Mormon Authorship Revisited*, 150–52; and John L. Sorenson, "The

Book of Mormon as a Mesoamerican Record," in *Book of Mormon Authorship Revisited,* 453–57.

112. An episode that occurred over thirty years ago offered a very rare opportunity to confirm Joseph Smith's God-given translating abilities. In 1967 some of the original papyrus pieces used by Smith to "translate" the Book of Abraham surfaced in a New York City museum. In what must have been a heartbreaking discovery to many Mormons at the time, modern Egyptologists' translation showed that the documents had nothing whatsoever to do with the biblical patriarch Abraham. The implications for Smith's "translating" of the Book of Mormon should be obvious. For LDS perspectives, see H. Donl Peterson, *The Story of the Book of Abraham: Mummies, Manuscripts, and Mormonism* (Salt Lake City: Deseret, 1995) and John Gee, *A Guide to the Joseph Smith Papyri* (Provo, Utah: FARMS, 2000). For one evangelical Christian view, see Charles M. Larson, *By His Own Hand Upon Papyrus: A New Look at the Joseph Smith Papyri,* rev. ed. (Grand Rapids: Institute for Religious Research, 1992). For LDS reviews of this work, cf. John Gee, "A Tragedy of Errors," *Review of Books on the Book of Mormon* 4 (1992): 93–119; Michael D. Rhodes, "The Book of Abraham: Divinely Inspired Scripture," *Review of Books on the Book of Mormon* 4 (1992): 120–26. Also see Edward H. Ashment, "Reducing Dissonance: The Book of Abraham as a Case Study," in Dan Vogel, ed., *The Word of God: Essays on Mormon Scripture* (Salt Lake City: Signature Books, 1990), 221–35; Stephen E. Thompson, "Egyptology and the Book of Abraham," *Dialogue* 28 (Spring 1995): 143–60; and esp. Stan Larson, *Quest for the Gold Plates* (Salt Lake City: Freethinker Press, 1996), 85–132. Today most Mormons deny that the Book of Abraham is a translation (in the word's normal sense) of the Egyptian papyri. The agnosticism of LDS scholar Kent P. Jackson is typical: "Though the connection between the papyri and the 'Book of Abraham' is unclear, it appears that Joseph Smith's possession of the Egyptian texts influenced his attraction to things Egyptian and led to his bringing forth of the document concerning Abraham" ("The Sacred Literature of the Latter-day Saints," in *The Bible and Bibles in America,* ed. Ernest S. Frerichs [Atlanta: Scholars Press, 1988], 183).

113. Noel B. Reynolds, "Introduction," in *Book of Mormon Authorship Revisited,* 16. The method of ultimately pointing to spiritual confirmation is a distinct feature of the essays by LDS scholars in Susan Easton Black, ed., *Expressions of Faith: Testimonies of Latter-day Saint Scholars* (Salt Lake City: Deseret; and Provo: FARMS, 1996).

114. See Hazen, *Village Enlightenment in America.*

115. To see the strong relationship between their thinking and that of the early Mormons, see Andrew Jackson Davis, *The Principles of Nature, Her Divine Revelations, and a Voice to Mankind* (New York: Lyon and Fishbough, 1947); Ervin Seale, ed., *Phineas Parkhurst Quimby: The Complete Writings,* 3 vols. (Marina Del Rey, Calif.: De Vorss, 1988); and Orson S. Fowler, *The Christian Phrenologist* (Cazenovia, N.Y.: n.p., 1843). Interestingly, like Joseph Smith, A. J. Davis produced his lengthy work in a very short time while dictating to scribes. Davis, however, was in a self-described trance state; while Smith apparently used a seer stone in a hat.

Chapter 2: And the Saints Go Marching On

1. Controversy rages about how to define the term *cult.* Some advocate purely sociological definitions, while others propose theological definitions. Many times movements classified as cults according to a purely theological definition, like Mormonism, would not be classified as such according to most sociological models. Another problem with the word *cult,* whether defined theologically or sociologically, is that it tends to be closely associated

in the minds of many with the occult and with dangerous apocalyptic doomsday predictions, which are not usually defining characteristics of cults according to either type of definition. Furthermore, in some popular discourse, *cult* is little more than a four-letter word—and not just in the literal sense. Some writers, though purportedly using the term in some technically defined manner, have a tendency (possibly subconscious) to use the word's "excess baggage" to rhetorical effect. Because of this semantic confusion and because of how easily it can be exploited, it seems to me that it would be best not to use the word but to develop alternative vocabularies, especially with respect to the word's use as a precise theological term. In much of the evangelical community, however, *cult* (defined theologically) is the only word used at present to refer to religious movements that claim to be Christian but deviate from Christian orthodoxy. In this chapter I will use the term *New Religious Movement,* though I am not sure that is an entirely satisfactory term either.

2. My wording here is deliberate. It is my conviction that evangelical responses to Mormonism should focus on the evangelization of the movement as much as evangelizing individual Latter-day Saints. To this end, the insights developed by missiologists over the last thirty years about reaching unreached people groups can and should be adapted for the evangelization of Mormonism and other New Religious Movements.

3. Jack W. Carlson, "Income and Membership Projections for the Church through the Year 2000," *Dialogue* 4/1 (1969): 131–36.

4. Rodney Stark, "The Rise of a New World Faith," *Review of Religious Research* 26/1 (1984): 18–19.

5. I recalculated Stark's projections and came up with the higher figure of 267,450,000—nearly two and a half million more members than Stark's widely quoted figure of 265 million. The error appears to have been his and has been corrected. Stark is cited in a recent issue of *Christianity Today* as projecting a figure of 267 million (John W. Kennedy, "Southern Baptists Take Up the Mormon Challenge," *Christianity Today,* 15 June 1998, 28).

6. "So Far, So Good: A Brief Assessment of Mormon Membership Projections," *Review of Religious Research* 38/2 (1996): 175–78.

7. Calculating an average growth rate of 50 percent per decade from the 1997 yearend membership of 10,070,524, it is predicted that the LDS Church will have 580,717,160 members worldwide at the end of 2097. An average growth rate of 50 percent per decade is slightly *lower* than the average of the last four decades. The three years of reported and estimated growth since 1997 indicate that LDS growth is slightly under-pace for a 50 percent per decade growth rate. However, this is not inconsistent with historic growth patterns in which some years growth is slightly under-pace and in others it is far above-pace. At the time of this writing, the last full 10-year period for which calculations can be made (1989–99) shows a 47 percent rate of growth. Calculations based on a significantly slower growth rate of 30 percent per decade predict that there will be 138,830,725 Latter-day Saints at the end of 2097, still an impressive figure. If one begins from more recent membership figures, even those of merely two years later, one can see that LDS growth is on an exponential curve. The LDS Church reports having had a 1999 yearend membership of 10,752,986. At 50 percent growth per decade, in 2099 there would be 620,071,357 members of the LDS Church; at 30 percent, there would be 148,239,343 members.

8. Rodney Stark, "Modernization and Mormon Growth: The Secularization Thesis Revisited," in *Contemporary Mormonism: Social Science Perspectives,* ed. Marie Cornwall, Tim B. Heaton, and Lawrence A. Young (Urbana and Chicago: University of Illinois Press, 1994), 13.

9. This and other of my figures below are derived from the data reported in the *1999–2000 Deseret News Church Almanac* (Salt Lake City: Deseret News, 1998). There were

roughly 75,000 eight-year-old children of adult members baptized as compared with close to 320,000 converts. The precise ratio of converts to baptized children of members varies from year to year but remains in the 4:1 range.

10. Stark, "Modernization and Mormon Growth," 14.

11. Ibid., 14–22.

12. Gordon Shepherd and Gary Shepherd, "Mormonism in Secular Society: Changing Patterns in Official Ecclesiastical Rhetoric," *Review of Religious Research* 26/1 (1984): 28–42.

13. Stan L. Albrecht and Tim B. Heaton, "Secularization, Higher Education, and Religiosity," *Review of Religious Research* 26/1 (1984): 43–58.

14. Rick Phillips, "The Secularization of Utah and Religious Competition," *Journal for the Scientific Study of Religion* 38/1 (1999): 72–82.

15. Stark, "So Far, So Good," 177.

16. Stark, "Modernization and Mormon Growth," 20.

17. Stark, "The Rise of a New World Faith," 22, 26.

18. Douglas J. Davies, *The Mormon Culture of Salvation* (Aldershot, U.K.: Ashgate, 2000), 5.

19. Davies, *Mormon Culture of Salvation,* 214.

20. Ibid., 238.

21. In Utah and parts of Idaho, Pioneer Day (July 24) is celebrated to commemorate the entrance of Mormon pioneers into the Salt Lake Valley and the subsequent settlement of Utah and southern Idaho. It is not, however, a religious holiday. Its celebration is marked by parades, concerts, and fireworks—very similar to the July 4th celebration of America's independence.

22. The Mormon Corridor is the area roughly surrounding the route of U.S. Interstate Highway 15. It includes southeastern Idaho in the north, all of Utah, and parts of western Colorado, northern Arizona, southern Nevada, and southeastern California.

23. One might quibble with the particular way I have distinguished the concepts of culture, subculture, and society in this section since each of these has been defined both more narrowly and more broadly than my usage presupposes. I do not claim that my usage is necessarily the best way to distinguish these concepts, nor do I deny that there is an appropriate sense in which one can refer to "Mormon culture." My argument can easily enough be adapted to either a narrower or broader group of categories to reach the same conclusion.

24. The most recent estimations of the LDS Church's financial resources can be found in Richard N. Ostling and Joan K. Ostling, *Mormon America: The Power and the Promise* (San Francisco: HarperSanFrancisco, 1999), 113–29, 395–400. Also see the now outdated but still informative discussions in Robert Gottlieb and Peter Wiley, *America's Saints: The Rise of Mormon Power* (San Diego: Harcourt Brace Jovanovich, 1986), 95–128; and John Heinerman and Anson D. Shupe, *The Mormon Corporate Empire* (Boston: Beacon, 1985).

25. With all of the world religions, including Christianity, there are contexts in which it is necessary to define the religion so as to include the mainstreams as well as the sects and cults that branch off from them. No theological judgment should be inferred about any of the streams or branches when Christianity is defined so broadly. There are factors that lead me to believe that in some instances Mormonism should be classified, in a broad cultural sense, as Christian. For example, in a book on the world's religions, I would make the discussion of Mormonism a subsection or appendix of the section on Christianity. For Mormonism is clearly related to the Christian tradition in many ways and clearly does not belong in the sections on Islam, Judaism, Hinduism, or Buddhism. Nor does Mormonism warrant

a section of its own, since it is neither a world religion nor unrelated to any of the world religions. But being classified as "Christian" in such a broad sense is of almost no significance, and there are many other factors that need to be considered when determining whether Mormonism should be considered Christian in any sense more narrow than this (see the next two notes for some of those factors).

26. This is not a conclusion that necessarily depends on accepting orthodox Christian beliefs about the nature of Christianity. In addition to the theological reasons an orthodox Christian may have, the conclusion also rests on sufficient nontheological grounds that a Muslim, Hindu, or atheist scholar of religion might also reach it. While I think I understand why Latter-day Saints feel offense, I also think they have generally failed to appreciate the reasons for which non-Mormons reach this conclusion about the relationship between Mormonism and Christianity—reasons that stem, ultimately, from an appreciation of Mormonism's distinctiveness. To better understand such reasons, the Latter-day Saints might do well to consider analogous situations in the context of other world religions. For example, the Druze and Nusayriyyah movements are usually classified in books on world religions as Islamic sects. But in spite of protests from adherents that each movement really is an expression of Islam, perhaps even the only true expression, many would agree that the beliefs of these movements diverge so far from the mainstreams of the Islamic tradition that they really cannot be considered expressions of Islam in any significant sense (on the beliefs of each, see *The Encyclopaedia of Islam*, New Edition, 10 vols. [Leiden: Brill, 1960–2000], s.v. "Durûz," 2:631–36; and "Nusayriyya," 8:145–48). There is, of course, a broad, cultural sense in which the movements can and should be classified as Islamic since they are clearly related to Islam in ways that they are not related to any of the other world religions. But being categorized as Islamic in this manner is fairly insignificant and in some contexts can be quite misleading. Saying that the teachings of Druze or Nusayriyyah place the movements outside of Islam is in no way an expression of bias but is a conclusion reached by comparative theological analysis, worldview analysis, and/or historical and sociological reasons. In my opinion, it is a legitimate conclusion whose denial would be difficult to maintain. It is a conclusion that stems, ultimately, from an appreciation of the distinctiveness of each movement. The same holds true with regard to Mormonism and Christianity. One has failed to appreciate Mormonism's distinctiveness if one can classify it as Christian without qualification.

27. In addition to the topics Blomberg discusses, some other factors that must be considered when determining whether Mormonism is properly considered Christian make the issue much more complicated than Latter-day Saints or their critics usually admit. For example, from the point of view of worldview analysis, I think it is clear that Mormonism represents a radically different worldview than Christianity, even when Christianity is defined broadly enough to include most heterodox movements that claim to be Christian. But factors can be cited in favor of the LDS claim as well, and evangelicals should thoughtfully consider them rather than dismiss them out of hand. Both sides must consider such theological factors as how the New Testament writings identify the people of God, the fact that Mormonism is in some important ways both similar to and different from the heterodox movements responded to by the New Testament writers, the normative status of the ecumenical creeds, the issue of sectarianism, and developments in LDS theology. I hope to address this issue in detail at some point in the future.

28. Letter to the editor, *Christianity Today,* 10 August 1998, 9. I have calculated Mormonism's average annual growth rate to be slightly over 4.1 percent. I have not attempted to verify the evangelical growth rate Montgomery lists, but it is consistent with the figures I have seen before.

29. Paul Carden, "The Threat of the Cults on the Mission Fields of the World," *International Journal of Frontier Missions* 15/3 (1998): 147. I highly recommend this article to those involved in missions and those who train missionaries.

30. At present there are more Catholic than LDS missionaries, but the Roman Catholic Church is not the monolith many assume, and its missionaries are divided among numerous organizations and orders. The MARC 1998–2000 *Mission Handbook* reports that only about 42,000 career and short-term missionaries of all kinds were fielded by 824 U.S. and Canadian Protestant agencies (see John A. Siewart and Edna G. Valdez, eds. *Mission Handbook 1998–2000* [Monrovia, Calif.: MARC Publications, 1997], 74, 84). Approximately 85,000 full-time Protestant missionaries serve worldwide (and many are not evangelical). Of these an estimated 20 percent are on furlough at any given time. Many others are not involved in evangelizing but function as staff in enabling humanitarian agencies. In contrast, all of the regular 60,000 LDS missionaries proselytize eight to ten hours a day, six to seven days a week, fifty-two weeks per year. The average LDS missionary baptizes between six and seven converts per year. These figures take on exponential significance when it is considered that roughly one third of all eligible LDS males will serve a two-year mission, including converts to the faith. For more on LDS missions, see Gary and Gordon Shepherd, "Mormon Growth and Mormon Missions in the Modern World," in Shepherd and Shepherd, *Mormon Passage: A Missionary Chronicle* (Urbana and Chicago: University of Illinois Press, 1998), 1–18; and Dallin H. Oaks and Lance B. Wickman, "The Missionary Work of the Church of Jesus Christ of Latter-day Saints," in *Sharing the Book: Religious Perspectives on the Rights and Wrongs of Proselytism,* ed. John Witte and Richard C. Martin (Maryknoll, N.Y.: Orbis, 1999), 247–75, 400–403.

31. By way of comparison, according to David Barrett, if one were to combine the efforts of the large number of religious orders within the Roman Catholic Church, its total missionary force would involve about 150,000 missionaries (cited in Carden, "Threat of the Cults on the Mission Fields," 153).

32. Shepherd and Shepherd, *Mormon Passage,* 10; and Carden, "Threat of the Cults on the Mission Fields," 148.

33. See Corrie Cutrer, "Grow with God," *Christianity Today,* 2 October 2000, (Online: www.christianitytoday.com/ct/2000/011/18.26.html).

34. In the year 2000 survey, the BYU main campus ranked 78th out of 228 universities in the "National Universities" category. BYU-Hawaii ranked 11th among "Western Liberal Arts Colleges." Ricks College was not ranked because it was still a two-year school.

35. Southern Virginia College is a four-year private LDS institution located in Buena Vista, Virginia. According to their Web site (www.southernvirginia.edu): "Southern Virginia College is a private, not-for-profit, independent institution of higher education that endeavors to serve all who seek truth and strive to live by it, in particular members of The Church of Jesus Christ of Latter-day Saints, by providing a comprehensive liberal arts education in a morally structured environment."

36. In some as yet unpublished work, I discuss the dearth of evangelical contributions to what is now known as "Mormon studies" and the importance of more evangelicals entering this field of scholarship, from both historical and sociological disciplines. A significant evangelical participation in this field could bear fruit with relevance far beyond the issue of Mormonism.

37. See the December 1995, December 1996, August 1998, and November 2000 issues of *Insights: A Window on the Ancient World,* the newsletter of the Foundation for Ancient Research and Mormon Studies at BYU (FARMS).

38. See *Insights* (July 2000): 1, 7–8.

39. For example, Philip L. Barlow (Th.D., Harvard) teaches in the department of theology at Hanover College (Presbyterian). Kathleen Flake (Ph.D., Chicago) is Assistant Professor of American Religious History at Vanderbilt Divinity School. Stephen E. Thompson has a Ph.D. in Egyptology (Brown University) and is adjunct Assistant Professor of Archaeology at Boston University. Also worth mentioning, John M. Lundquist (Ph.D., University of Michigan) is the Susan and Douglas Dillar Chief Librarian of the Oriental Division, New York Public Library and is a well-known expert on ancient Near Eastern temples (see, for example, his article, "Biblical Temple," in *The Oxford Encyclopedia of Archeology in the Near East*, ed. Eric M. Meyers [New York: Oxford University Press, 1997], 325–29 and the literature cited in his bibliography. Also note the listings for fellow Latter-day Saint Donald W. Parry).

40. For example, Richard L. Bushman, author of the important study *Joseph Smith and the Beginnings of Mormonism* (Urbana and Chicago: University of Illinois Press, 1984) holds the Gouverneur Morris chair of history at Columbia University. Recently Latter-day Saint Gordon Gee resigned from the presidency of Brown University; he is now chancellor of Vanderbilt University.

41. Stephen E. Robinson, *The Testament of Adam: An Examination of the Syriac and Greek Traditions* (SBLDS; Chico, Calif.: Scholars Press, 1982).

42. Kent P. Jackson, *The Ammonite Language of the Iron Age* (HSM; Chico, Calif.: Scholars Press, 1983). This book is considered to be the definitive study of the Ammonite language.

43. Stephen D. Ricks, *Lexicon of Inscriptional Qatabanian* (Rome: Editrice Pontificio Instituto Biblico, 1989).

44. LDS scrolls scholars Andrew Skinner and Dana M. Pike have been assigned the editorship of volume XXXIII.

45. This list is by no means exhaustive. For specific examples, see the literature cited in Carl Mosser and Paul Owen, "Mormon Scholarship, Apologetics and Evangelical Neglect: Losing the Battle and Not Knowing It?" *Trinity Journal* n.s. 19, no. 2 (Fall 1998): 179–205.

46. Donald W. Parry, Andrew Skinner, Dana M. Pike, and David Rolph Seely.

47. LDS contributors to one or more of these reference works include: Philip L. Barlow, S. Kent Brown, Daniel Graham, William J. Hamblin, John M. Lundquist, Dana M. Pike, Stephen D. Ricks, Stephen E. Robinson, David Rolph Seely, and Jo Ann H. Seely. A handful of specific entries are cited in Mosser and Owen, "Mormon Scholarship," esp. 202, n. 103. It should go without saying that LDS participation in these projects does not diminish their value or usefulness.

48. Examples of this are too numerous to list here. Again, a number are cited throughout Mosser and Owen, "Mormon Scholarship," 179–205.

49. Avraham Gileadi, ed., *Israel's Apostasy and Restoration: Essays in Honor of Roland K. Harrison* (Grand Rapids: Baker, 1988). It should not be overlooked that the title reflects the Mormon belief that human history consists of a series of apostasies from and restorations of true faith. The LDS contributions are: Avraham Gileadi, "The Davidic Covenant: A Theological Basis for Corporate Protection" (157–63); Stephen D. Ricks, "The Prophetic Literality of Tribal Reconstruction" (273–81); and John M. Lundquist, "Temple, Covenant, and Law in the Ancient Near East and in the Hebrew Bible" (293–305). The title of Ricks's essay is a clear verbal allusion to the tenth LDS Article of Faith, which states, in part, "We believe in the literal gathering of Israel and in the restoration of the Ten Tribes; that Zion will be built upon this [the American] continent." In light of the important role temples,

covenants, and "gospel laws" play in Mormon religious life, it should be apparent why Lundquist would focus his study on these topics. Gileadi's essay also ties in with his LDS theology with respect to salvation and proxy baptism (though the connections are subtle and not appreciated without familiarity with Gileadi's other writings).

50. See the contributions by these men and others in the two-volume festschrift *By Study and Also by Faith: Essays in Honor of Hugh W. Nibley,* ed. John M. Lundquist and Stephen D. Ricks (Salt Lake City: Deseret and FARMS, 1990).

51. Quoted in Philip L. Barlow, *Mormons and the Bible* (Oxford: Oxford University Press, 1991), 147, n. 105. For more on Nibley, see Mosser and Owen, "Mormon Scholarship," 183–84.

52. See John L. Sorenson, *An Ancient American Setting for the Book of Mormon* (Salt Lake City: Deseret Book and FARMS, 1985, 1996).

53. See the references listed in n. 112 of Craig Hazen's chapter in this volume.

54. Brian D. Stubbs, "Looking Over vs. Overlooking Native American languages: Let's Void the Void," *Journal of Book of Mormon Studies* 5/1 (1996): 1–48; cf. "Was There Hebrew Language in Ancient America? An Interview with Brian Stubbs," *Journal of Book of Mormon Studies* 9/2 (2000): 54–63, 83.

55. Of course, even if there is evidence for ancient Semitic contact with the Americas, that does not count as positive evidence in favor of the Book of Mormon since it could easily, and perhaps more plausibly, be explained by other means. The apologetic significance would be that arguments against Mormonism that presuppose absolutely *no* cultural contact would be shown unsound. If LDS scholars could show that there was a definite influx of Semitic peoples of the correct cultural backgrounds at *precisely* the time periods the Book of Mormon purports, that would count as nondecisive evidence in favor of the Book of Mormon.

56. C. Wilfred Griggs, "The Book of Mormon as an Ancient Book," in *Book of Mormon Authorship: New Light on Ancient Origins,* ed. Noel B. Reynolds (Provo, Utah: BYU Religious Studies Center, 1982), 77.

57. James H. Charlesworth, "Messianism in the Pseudepigrapha and the Book of Mormon," in *Reflections on Mormonism: Judeo-Christian Parallels,* ed. Truman G. Madsen (Provo, Utah: BYU Religious Studies Center, 1978), 99–137. It is worth mentioning that other prominent non-LDS biblical scholars—Jacob Milgrom, David Noel Freedman, W. D. Davies, and Krister Stendahl—also contributed to this volume. I too would say that the Book of Mormon evidences parallels with the Pseudepigrapha, parallels that show it to be a pseudepigraphal document not written during the times it purports to have been written. One of the hallmarks of many of the ancient pseudepigrapha is that they purport to have been written at a time in the still-more-distant past by notable characters or at the time of notable historical events.

58. LDS philosopher David L. Paulsen has argued for the general thesis that God could be corporeal in "Must God be Incorporeal?" *Faith and Philosophy* 6/1 (1989): 76–87. He responds to philosophical arguments advanced in favor of divine incorporeality in a different article by the same name, "Must God Be Incorporeal?" in *Mormon Identities in Transition,* ed. Douglas Davies (London: Cassell, 1996), 204–10. Paulsen has tried to show in his article, "Early Christian Belief in a Corporeal Deity: Origen and Augustine as Reluctant Witnesses," *Harvard Theological Review* 83/2 (1990): 105–16, and "Reply to Paffenroth's Comment," *Harvard Theological Review* 86/2 (1993): 235–39, that the earliest Christians believed God to be embodied. He has treated these philosophical and historical themes together with specific reference to his Mormon beliefs in his lengthy article, "The Doctrine

of Divine Embodiment: Restoration, Judeo-Christian, and Philosophical Perspectives," *BYU Studies* 35/4 (1995–96): 7–94, and is currently working on a book tentatively entitled *The Mormon Doctrine of Divine Embodiment* (see *Insights* [July 2000]: 8).

59. The following are examples. The titles of some, especially the "book reviews," belie their true significance. David Lamont Paulsen, "Comparative Coherency of Mormon (Finitisitic) and Classical Theism" (Ph.D. diss., University of Michigan, 1975); David L. Paulsen, "Joseph Smith and the Problem of Evil," *BYU Studies* 39/1 (2000): 53–65; *idem*, "The God of Abraham, Isaac, and (William) James," *Journal of Speculative Philosophy* 13/2 (1999): 114–46; *idem*, "The Logically Possible, the Ontologically Possible, and Ontological Proofs of God's Existence," *International Journal for the Philosophy of Religion* 15/1–2 (1984): 41–49; *idem*, "Divine Determinateness and the Free Will Defence," *Analysis* (1981): 150–53; David L. Paulsen and R. Dennis Potter, "How Deep the Chasm? A Reply to Owen and Mosser's Review," *FARMS Review of Books* 11/2 (1999): 235–36; Blake T. Ostler, "Revisioning the Mormon Concept of Deity," *Element: An E-Journal of Mormon Philosophy and Theology* 1/1 (Online: www.element-mormon.org); *idem*, review of Craig L. Blomberg and Stephen E. Robinson, *How Wide the Divide?* (Downers Grove, Ill.: InterVarsity Press, 1997) in *FARMS Review of Books* 11/2 (1999): 103–77; *idem*, "Worshipworthiness and the Mormon Concept of God," *Religious Studies* 33/3 (1997): 315–26; *idem*, review of Francis J. Beckwith and Stephen E. Parrish, *The Mormon Concept of God: A Philosophical Analysis* (Lewiston, N.Y.: Edwin Mellen, 1990) in *FARMS Review of Books* 8/2 (1996): 99–146; *idem*, "The Mormon Concept of God," *Dialogue* 17/2 (1984): 65–93; Kent E. Robson, "Time and Omniscience in Mormon Theology," *Sunstone* 5/3 (1980), 17–23; *idem*, "Omnis on the Horizon," *Sunstone* 8/4 (1983): 21–23.

60. It should be clear that there is a need for both classical theists and "Open View" theists to philosophically evaluate Mormonism's truth claims. Since LDS philosophers find much affinity between their views of God and the Open View of God, proponents of the Open View in particular need to carefully determine where their views and LDS views about God diverge and to offer criticisms from the Openness perspective. With regard to the Godhead, the same holds true for proponents of the social theory of the Trinity.

61. With respect to the journals that FARMS publishes, I have in mind the *Journal of Book of Mormon Studies* more than the *FARMS Review of Books (FRB)* (or its predecessor, the *Review of Books on the Book of Mormon*). The quality of articles in each journal is uneven, the latter much more so than the former. I do not consider most issues of the *FRB* to be representative of the kind of LDS apologetic scholarship I have made reference to in this essay. Occasionally, important reviews/responses are published in the *FRB* that should be taken seriously (and I am not simply referring to the review of *How Wide the Divide?* which Paul Owen and I published in it). All too regularly, however, it publishes polemical reviews by individuals who lack both the qualifications and professionalism that reputable journals would require. If left uncorrected, this will only serve to tarnish the credibility of FARMS as an academic organization.

62. O. Kendall White, *Mormon Neo-orthodoxy: A Crisis Theology* (Salt Lake City: Signature, 1987).

63. White does not comment on the important issue of the *sufficiency* of grace for salvation, an important and distinct issue from the mere necessity of grace.

64. White, *Mormon Neo-orthodoxy*, 139. LDS apologists sometimes attempt to disprove the idea that earliest Mormonism had a distinctively Protestant flavor when compared with the Mormonism of the Nauvoo period and later. In my opinion, a straightforward reading of the Book of Mormon, the earliest sections of the Doctrine and Covenants, and the

Lectures on Faith prove the thesis beyond all reasonable doubt. All the attempts to read later Mormon theology into these early texts that I have seen are unconvincing to the point of credulity. For more on the "essential Protestant flavor" of earliest Mormon theology, see Thomas G. Alexander, "The Reconstruction of Mormon Doctrine," *Sunstone* 22/3–4 (1999): 15–29. This is a reprint of an important 1980 article with a retrospective postscript in which Alexander responds to some of the criticisms and attempts to disprove his thesis.

65. White, *Mormon Neo-orthodoxy*, xi.

66. Ibid., xxi.

67. Ibid., 175–76.

68. "Joseph Smith and Modern Mormonism: Orthodoxy, Neo-orthodoxy, Tension, and Tradition," *BYU Studies* 29/3 (1989): 49–68. In a more polemical response to White, Louis Midgley likewise emphasizes the role of the Book of Mormon in any developments that might be detected in contemporary Mormon theology. See Midgely, "A Mormon Neo-Orthodoxy Challenges Cultural Mormon Neglect of the Book of Mormon: Some Reflections on 'The Impact of Modernity,'" *Review of Books on the Book of Mormon* 6/2 (1994): 299, 309–10, 322, 332.

69. Millet, "Joseph Smith and Modern Mormonism," 66.

70. Because of this "almost *sola scriptura*" approach, in some earlier unpublished papers I labeled this contemporary movement in LDS theology "Mormon minimalism." However, I am no longer sure that this is necessarily the chief characteristic of the movement. Some LDS theologians that I would categorize as a part of this movement are less "minimalistic" than others in their use of traditional LDS writings as theological guides. What I have in the past termed "Mormon minimalism" is more of a trend or tendency in LDS theology than a single definable position. The movement will have to develop its distinctive characteristics further before a fully adequate term can be found by which to refer to it.

71. Craig L. Blomberg and Stephen E. Robinson, *How Wide the Divide? A Mormon and an Evangelical in Conversation* (Downers Grove, Ill.: InterVarsity Press, 1997).

72. This has not been the perception of some LDS scholars. In personal conversation, one prominent LDS scholar of a traditionalist bent told me that he thought Robinson's brand of Mormonism was "a little bit too Protestant."

73. John Bishop, "Can There Be Alternative Concepts of God?" *Noûs* 32/2 (1998): 175.

74. Eugene England, "The Good News—and the Bad," *BYU Studies* 38/3 (1999): 191–201.

75. In this paragraph, ibid., 193, 195, 196, 200.

76. This was particularly noticeable in a sermon entitled "Have you been Saved?" by Elder Dallin H. Oaks of the Quorum of the Twelve, given at the Spring 1998 General Conference of the LDS Church (later published in *Ensign* 28 [May 1998]). Oaks's comments appeared to draw extensively from Stephen E. Robinson's books, especially *Following Christ* (Salt Lake City: Deseret, 1995). Oaks has, in the past, openly commended the work of LDS theologians like Robinson and Millet. See Dallin H. Oaks, "Another Testament of Jesus Christ" *Ensign* 24 (March 1994). This article is also important with respect to the emphasis on the Book of Mormon characteristic of the contemporary trend in LDS theology I have been describing as well as the increasing emphasis the LDS Church has placed on Jesus Christ in recent years, which critics sometimes dismiss as a public relations ploy. (Articles from *Ensign* can be accessed via the church's official Web site: www.lds.org)

77. The only detailed interactions with contemporary LDS theology that I know of are Craig Blomberg's contribution to *How Wide the Divide?* and the review-essay on this book

by Paul Owen and Carl Mosser in the *FARMS Review of Books* 11/2 (1999): 1–102. For further bibliographical data on contemporary LDS theology, one should consult the footnotes of that review. The same issue includes two reviews of *How Wide the Divide?* by LDS scholars and four LDS responses to our review. Some of the comments made in the LDS reviews and responses are very interesting and shed important light on the current state of LDS theology.

78. I acknowledge that some ministry styles labeled "seeker-sensitive" do a good job dealing with apologetic issues and grounding people in Christian theology. However, in my experience many more do not than do.

79. I do not say this to demean the accomplishments of LDS scholars or because I place my faith in the accomplishments of scholarship. However, some Mormons misinterpreted previous publications, as if I were saying that evangelical scholars are not as skilled as their LDS counterparts or, even, as if I were saying there are *no* evangelical scholars. I am simply putting things in proper perspective.

80. The term "ecumenical dialogue" has been spoiled by the doctrinal promiscuity of liberal Protestants and Catholics as well as by their uncritical application of the term to describe dialogue with groups that make no claim to be Christian whatever. Even if it were not spoiled, though, it would not apply to LDS-evangelical dialogue. I prefer to speak of *inter*-religious and *intra*-religious dialogue, keeping the two sharply distinguished. At this stage, any LDS-evangelical dialogues (whether formal or informal) would be cases of *inter*-religious dialogue. They would need to be conducted in that light, and the failures of ecumenical dialogues consciously avoided. For a fine discussion of interreligious dialogue in the context of New Religious Movements, see Jason Barker, "Christians and Interreligious Dialogue," *Watchman Expositor* 15/4 (1998): Online: http://watchman.org/reltop/christiandialogue.htm.

81. The evangelical position on this is well known. From the LDS side, Apostle Dallin H. Oaks and Lance B. Wickman write: "Because of the nature of its divine mandate, the church is not free to engage in ecumenical discourse aimed at amalgamating its doctrines with other denominations. At the levels of doctrine and ecclesiastical polity, the church understands itself as a restored church charged with maintaining its integrity and independence from all other religious organizations. For this reason, the church does not engage in ecumenical dialogue aimed at homogenizing or compromising doctrine" ("The Missionary Work of the Church of Jesus Christ of Latter-day Saints," 274).

82. This raises the issue of the compatibility of the later theology of Joseph Smith and his successors with the teachings of the Book of Mormon and claims that they are inspired prophets on par with the Old Testament prophets and New Testament apostles. During an earlier stage in Mormonism's development, the LDS Church moved away from, and even repudiated, certain elements of Brigham Young's teachings (e.g., the Adam-God doctrine), but it did so without giving much thought to the implications of this for the LDS understanding of their presidents' prophethood. For many years, in fact, not only were the implications of this shift neglected, but it was denied that Young ever taught the doctrines. As Latter-day Saints move away from the traditional theology of the King Follett Discourse, assuming that this move continues, it is incumbent on them to do so in light of a more developed understanding of the prophethood of Smith, Young, and others. Many evangelicals will, no doubt, continue to be suspicious of any developments in LDS theology, no matter how encouraging they appear, if they are not accompanied by explicit repudiations of certain traditional doctrines and a frank admission that LDS prophets have, in the past, been mistaken in some of their public teachings.

Part II: The Mormon Worldview—Introductory Essay

1. On worldviews and the importance they have for how one lives, see Arthur F. Holmes, *Contours of a Worldview* (Grand Rapids: Eerdmans, 1983); James W. Sire, *The Universe Next Door: A Basic Worldview Catalog,* 2d ed. (Downers Grove, Ill.: InterVarsity Press, 1988); and Brian J. Walsh and J. Richard Middleton, *The Transforming Vision: Shaping a Christian World View* (Downers Grove, Ill.: InterVarsity Press, 1984). Coming from a perspective somewhat hostile to Christianity but still with some helpful insights is John Kekes, *The Nature of Philosophy* (Oxford: Basil Blackwell, 1980). For a helpful discussion of how to adjudicate between conflicting worldviews, see Ronald H. Nash, *Worldviews in Conflict: Choosing Christianity in a World of Ideas* (Grand Rapids: Zondervan, 1992).

2. Thomas V. Morris, *Our Idea of God* (Downers Grove, Ill.: InterVarsity Press, 1991), 139.

3. See Daniel O'Connor and Francis Oakley, eds., *Creation: The Impact of an Idea* (New York: Charles Scribner's Sons, 1969); Eugene M. Klaaren, *Religious Origins of Modern Science: Belief in Creation in Seventeenth-Century Thought* (Grand Rapids: Eerdmans, 1977); R. G. Collingwood, *An Essay on Metaphysics* (Oxford: Clarendon Press, 1940), 191–227, 252–57; Thomas F. Torrance, *The Ground and Grammar of Theology* (Charlottesville: University Press of Virginia, 1980), 44–74; Colin A. Russell, *Cross-Currents: Interactions Between Science and Faith* (Grand Rapids: Eerdmans, 1985); Christopher Kaiser, *Creation and the History of Science* (Grand Rapids: Eerdmans, 1991); Stanley L. Jaki, *Cosmos and Creator* (Chicago: Regnery Gateway, 1980); *idem,* "Theological Aspects of Creative Science," in *Creation, Christ, Culture,* ed. Richard W. A. McKinney (Edinburgh: T & T Clark, 1976); and David C. Lindberg and Ronald L. Numbers, eds., *God and Nature: Historical Essays on the Encounter between Christianity and Science* (Berkley: University of California Press, 1986).

4. On the presuppositions of science, in addition to references in the previous note, see Kekes, *The Nature of Philosophy,* 156–57 (also his discussion of the nature of presuppositions on 53–55); and, especially, J. P. Moreland, *Christianity and the Nature of Science* (Grand Rapids: Baker, 1989), 108–33.

Chapter 3: Craftsman or Creator?

1. One problem in responding to Mormonism's view of creation is an admitted *fluidity* to Mormon doctrine, in which no fixed creeds exist. But, since "the idea of cosmology is one central organizing theme in Mormonism," according to Erich Robert Paul, *Science, Religion, and Mormon Cosmology* (Chicago: University of Illinois Press, 1992), 4, it is worth exploring—even if there has been no successful attempt to develop some systematic thought in this area.

2. B. H. Roberts, *The Truth, the Way, the Life,* ed. Stan Larson (San Francisco: Smith Research Associates, 1994), 224.

3. Cf. the comments by Stephen E. Robinson on LDS acceptance of the Bible without the "theological add-ons" of orthodox Christianity in Stephen E. Robinson and Craig L. Blomberg, *How Wide the Divide? A Mormon and an Evangelical in Conversation* (Downers Grove, Ill.: InterVarsity Press, 1997), 138.

4. Not all scholars of Mormonism see the LDS view as free from the influence of Greek philosophy. For instance, Erich Robert Paul begins his book *Science, Religion, and Mormon Cosmology:* "Since its founding in 1830, Mormonism has not only evolved a new canon that set the religious movement apart from mainline Protestantism but also fashioned an ethos that embraces a positive scientism in keeping with the roots of *Greek rationalism*" (1, emphasis ours). A few pages later Paul speaks of Mormonism's "roots embedded in Greek and Hebrew traditions" (5).

5. From Stephen Robinson, personal correspondence (20 April 1998), in the author's possession. This conviction that science and Mormonism are *noncombative* in nature is also asserted in Erich Paul's book (e.g., p. 9) as well as in Richard F. Haglund Jr., "Science and Religion: A Symbiosis," *Dialogue* 8/3–4 (1973): 23–40. On the other hand, F. Kent Nelson and Stephen D. Ricks assert: "The [LDS] understanding [of creation] differs from both scientific and traditional Christian accounts in that it affirms God's purpose and role, while recognizing creation as organization of preexisting materials, and not as an *ex nihilo* event (creation from nothing)" ("Creation, Creation Accounts," in *Encyclopedia of Mormonism*, ed. Daniel H. Ludlow [New York: Macmillan, 1992], 1:340).

6. The primary division of labor is as follows: Paul Copan was the principal author of Part I and Part II, William Lane Craig for Part III. Singular personal pronouns in the notes refer to the principal author of that part of the essay.

7. Another important creation text is D&C 88:4–13 and 36–45. For a discussion of the various Mormon creation narratives, see Anthony A. Hutchinson, "A Mormon Midrash? LDS Creation Narratives Reconsidered," *Dialogue* 21/4 (1988): 11–74.

8. Alternatively, some form of eternal personalism might continue to be affirmed (see n. 263 below).

9. *How Wide the Divide?* 73–74, 208. Robinson does, however, refer to Smith's funeral sermon, the "King Follett Discourse" as "quasi-official" (85, 87). By Robinson's own criteria, a work needs to be sustained in General Conference before it is scripture or binding. Since this has not happened with the King Follett Discourse, there is no reason why it should not be set on par with other nineteenth-century sermons by LDS leaders.

10. Max Nolan, "Materialism and the Mormon Faith," *Dialogue* 22/4 (1989): 63–64.

11. Joseph Smith, *History of the Church of Latter-day Saints,* 7 vols., intro. and notes by B. H. Roberts (Salt Lake City: Deseret, 1978), 6:308–9 (=*TPJS*, 350–52).

12. *JD* 13:248.

13. *JD* 14:116.

14. *JD* 11:122.

15. *JD* 8:115.

16. *JD* 2:91.

17. *JD* 5:127.

18. Parley E. Pratt, *The Essential Parley E. Pratt,* ed. Peter L. Crawley (Salt Lake City: Signature Books, 1990), 193.

19. From Pratt's discourse given in the Tabernacle in Salt Lake City, 12 November 1876. Cited in B. H. Roberts, *The Mormon Doctrine of Deity: The Roberts-Van Der Donckt Discussion,* repr. ed. (Salt Lake City: Signature Books, 1998), 278.

20. Pratt as cited in Roberts, *The Mormon Doctrine of Deity,* 279.

21. James E. Talmage, *A Study of the Articles of Faith,* 50th ed. (Salt Lake City: Church of Jesus Christ of Latter-day Saints, 1971), first printed in 1899.

22. Talmage, *Articles of Faith,* 30 (2.1).

23. Ibid., 34 (2.1).

24. Ibid., 34 (2.1).

25. Ibid., 43 (2.1).

26. B. H. Roberts, *Seventy's Course in Theology: Third and Fourth Year* (Salt Lake City: Caxton Press, 1910), 4:70.

27. Ibid., 4:70.

28. John A. Widtsoe, *A Rational Theology* (Salt Lake City: Deseret, 1915), 11.

29. Ibid., 13.

30. "Creation, Creation Accounts," *Encyclopedia of Mormonism,* 340.

31. Lowell Bennion, "A Mormon View of Life," *Dialogue* 24/3 (1991): 60.

32. Blake Ostler, "The Idea of Pre-Existence in the Development of Mormon Thought," *Dialogue* 15/1 (1982): 59.

33. Blake T. Ostler, "The Mormon Concept of God," *Dialogue* 17/2 (1984): 67.

34. Stephen Robinson, personal correspondence (20 April 1998). Here Robinson's Hobbesian metaphysic appears to be reflecting what is stated in D&C 131:7–8: "There is no such thing as immaterial matter. All spirit is matter, but it is more fine and pure, and can only be discerned by purer eyes. We cannot see it; but when our bodies are purified we shall see that it is all matter."

35. Robinson, personal correspondence (20 April 1998).

36. Ted Peters, "On Creating the Cosmos," in *Physics, Philosophy, and Theology: A Common Quest for Understanding,* ed. Robert Russell, William Stoeger, and George Coyne (Vatican City: Vatican Observatory, 1988), 273–74. To avoid a deistic flavor of *creatio ex nihilo,* the doctrine of *creatio continua,* God's continued creative and sustaining power in the universe, must be added to give a fuller, biblical picture of God's creation. See Thomas Aquinas' *Summa Theologica* I.q.45, art. 2.

37. O. Kendall White Jr., "The Transformation of Mormon Theology," *Dialogue* 5/2 (1970): 11.

38. For example, Langdon Gilkey, *Maker of Heaven and Earth: The Christian Doctrine of Creation in Light of Modern Knowledge* (Garden City, N.Y.: Doubleday, 1959), chap. 3.

39. Friedrich Schleiermacher was chiefly responsible for collapsing the ideas of Creation and Preservation. See his work, originally published in 1821–22, *The Christian Faith,* trans. Richard R. Niebuhr (New York: Harper & Row, 1963), 1:148–52.

40. Augustine, *Confessions* XI.5.7.

41. Robert John Russell, "Finite Creation Without a Beginning," in *Quantum Cosmology and the Laws of Nature,* ed. R. J. Russell, Nancy Murphy, and C. J. Isham (Vatican City: Vatican Observatory, 1993), 309.

42. Stephen Robinson, personal correspondence (20 April 1998). Robinson cites as evidence B. W. Anderson, "Creation" in the *Interpreter's Dictionary of the Bible* (New York: Abingdon, 1962), 1:728.

43. Stephen Robinson, personal correspondence (20 April 1998).

44. Roberts, *The Truth, the Way, the Life,* 224.

45. Ibid., 225.

46. Ibid., 224. The work cited is Emil G. Hirsch, "Creation," in *The Jewish Encyclopedia: A Descriptive Record of the History, Religion, Literature, and Customs of Jewish People from the Earliest Times to the Present Day,* ed. Isidore Singer (New York: Funk and Wagnalls, 1903), 4:336.

47. Roberts, *The Truth, The Way, The Life,* 224 (all brackets are Roberts's).

48. Ibid., 224.

49. Ibid., 228.

50. Anthony C. Thiselton, "Semantics and New Testament Interpretation," in *New Testament Interpretation: Essays on Principles and Methods,* ed. I. Howard Marshall (Grand Rapids: Eerdmans, 1977), 80.

51. That is, the way a word was used *at the time of writing* (as distinguished from the *diachronic*—how a word was used over periods of time, which is where the study of a word's etymology is quite useful). The etymological study is useful as a last-resort method—namely, when the occurrence of a particular word is extremely rare and there is little else to go on.

52. Moisés Silva, *Biblical Words and Their Meaning: An Introduction to Lexical Semantics* (Grand Rapids: Zondervan, 1983), 51. See also D. A. Carson, *Exegetical Fallacies* (Grand Rapids: Baker, 1984), 26–32. Peter Cotterell and Max Turner state that the etymological fallacy is "a sufficiently dead horse in educated theological circles" (*Linguistics and Biblical Interpretation* [Downers Grove, Ill.: InterVarsity Press, 1989], 114).

53. James Barr, *The Semantics of Biblical Language* (Oxford: Oxford University Press, 1961), 109.

54. For instance, Daniel C. Peterson footnotes May's work when he claims that *creatio ex nihilo* is a second- or third-century doctrine ("Editor's Introduction" in *FARMS Review of Books* 10/2 [1998]: xvi, n).

55. Gerhard May, *Creatio ex nihilo: The Doctrine of "Creation Out of Nothing" in Early Christian Thought*, trans. by A. S. Worall (Edinburgh: T & T Clark, 1994); originally published as *Schöpfung aus dem Nichts* (Berlin: Walter de Gruyter, 1978). I have critically examined May's work at length in my article, "Is *Creatio ex nihilo* a Post-biblical Invention? An Examination of Gerhard May's Proposal," *Trinity Journal* n.s. 17 (Spring 1996): 77–93. In what follows I have freely adapted some material from that article.

56. For example, Daniel C. Peterson and Stephen D. Ricks (*Offenders for a Word* [Provo, Utah: FARMS, 1992], 96) mention an article by Frances Young, "*Creatio ex nihilo:* A Context for the Emergence of the Christian Doctrine of Creation," *Scottish Journal of Theology* 44 (1991): 139–51, which relies heavily on May and bypasses biblical exegesis (although Young argues, contra typical Mormon claims, that the formulation of the Christian doctrine of creation "is a clear sign that Christian intellectuals were not 'captured' by Greek philosophy" (139). Peterson/Ricks (*Offenders for a Word*, 96) and Peterson ("Editor's Introduction," xvi) refer to Jonathan Goldstein's "The Origins of the Doctrine of *Creatio ex nihilo*" in the *Journal of Jewish Studies* 35 (1984): 127–35.

57. Incidentally, Mormon scholar Stephen Ricks misreads Gerhard May's analysis of the emergence of *creatio ex nihilo* in the second-century Gnostic thinker Basilides when he says, "At root, this orthodox Christian doctrine [of creation] may have been a Gnostic heresy" (Stephen D. Ricks, "*Fides Quaerens Intellectum:* The Scholar as Disciple," in *Expressions of Faith: Testimonies of Latter-day Saint Scholars,* ed. Susan Easton Black [Salt Lake City: Deseret and FARMS, 1996], 179). May affirms that Basilides' (rather un-Gnostic) formulation of this doctrine arose *independently* from later orthodox Christian theologians, his thought being "left without any broad effect" on them (May, *Creatio ex nihilo,* 180). See my comments in Copan, "Is *Creatio ex nihilo* a Post-biblical Invention?" 81–84.

58. Walther Eichrodt, "In the Beginning: A Contribution to the Interpretation of the First Word of the Bible," in *Creation in the Old Testament,* ed. Bernhard W. Anderson (Philadelphia: Fortress, 1984), 72.

59. Ibid., 67.

60. Ibid., 72.

61. Walther Eichrodt, *Theology of the Old Testament,* Trans. J. A. Baker (Philadelphia: Westminster, 1967), 2:101.

62. Ibid., 2:102.

63. Nahum M. Sarna, *Genesis,* JPS Torah Commentary (New York: Jewish Publication Society, 1989), 5. R. K. Harrison affirms that the phrase "the heavens and the earth" is a merism that indicates totality, not simply two antonymic elements. See R. K. Harrison, "Creation," in Merrill C. Tenney, ed., *The Zondervan Pictorial Encyclopedia of the Bible* (Grand Rapids: Zondervan, 1975), 1:1022; see also Paul K. Jewett, *God, Creation, and Revelation* (Grand Rapids: Eerdmans, 1991), 457.

64. C. F. Keil and F. Delitzsch, *Commentary on the Old Testament,* vol. 1, *The Pentateuch,* trans. James Martin, repr. ed. (Grand Rapids: Eerdmans, 1986), 47.

65. Claus Westermann, *Genesis: A Practical Commentary,* trans. David E. Green (Grand Rapids: Eerdmans, 1987), 7.

66. Harrison, "Creation," 1:1023.

67. Ibid.

68. Edwin Hatch, *The Influence of Greek Ideas and Usages upon the Christian Church* (London: Williams and Norgate, 1891), 197. Interestingly, though Mormon scholar Keith Norman cites Hatch (*"Ex nihilo,"* 299), he passes over this remark about creation. Overall, Hatch overplays the influence of Greek thought on biblical doctrine and overlooks the deep Hebraic/Old Testament influence on various New Testament texts and Christian doctrines.

69. *"Fides Quaerens Intellectum:* The Scholar as Disciple," 179.

70. "Creation and Cosmogony in the Bible," *Encyclopedia Judaica* (Jerusalem: Encyclopedia Judaica, 1972), 5:1059.

71. The term *create* renders the qal and niphal forms of *bara'.* Humans are sometimes the subject of the piel form, but the etymological connection between the piel and other forms are doubtful (the piel may come from a different root). Nevertheless, as any student of Hebrew knows, even if the piel originally derives from the same root, this has no bearing on the point being made here.

72. Brevard S. Childs, *Myth and Reality in the Old Testament* (Naperville, Ill.: Allenson, 1960), 40. Childs sees *creatio ex nihilo* implicit in the text. God's action in creation "could hardly be brought into a smooth harmony with the fact of a pre-existent chaos. World reality is a result of creation, not a reshaping of existing matter" (40).

73. John Sailhamer, *Genesis Unbound: A Provocative New Look at the Creation Account* (Sisters, Ore.: Multnomah, 1996), 247–49.

74. Francis Brown et al., *The New Brown-Driver-Briggs-Gesenius Hebrew and English Lexicon,* repr. (Oxford: Clarendon Press, 1962), 135.

75. Jürgen Moltmann, *God in Creation: A New Theology of Creation and the Spirit of God,* trans. Magaret Kohl (San Francisco: Harper & Row, 1985), 72–73. For commentary on the inconsistency between Moltmann's exegesis on Genesis 1 and his panentheism (i.e., the confusion between creation out of nothing [*ex nihilo*] and continual creation [*continua*], rendering any distinction meaningless), see Allan J. Torrance, *"Creatio ex nihilo* and the Spatio-Temporal Dimensions with Special Reference to Jürgen Moltmann and D. C. Williams," in *The Doctrine of Creation: Essays in Dogmatics, History and Philosophy,* ed. Colin E. Gunton (Edinburgh: T & T Clark, 1997), 83–103; and Wolfhart Pannenberg, *Systematic Theology,* trans. Geoffrey W. Bromiley (Grand Rapids: Eerdmans, 1994), 2:14–15.

76. See John Sailhamer's discussion in "Genesis" in *Expositor's Bible Commentary,* ed. Frank Gaebelein (Grand Rapids: Zondervan, 1990), 2:21–23n. See also U. Cassuto, *A Commentary on the Book of Genesis,* Part 1 (Jerusalem: Magnes Press, 1992 repr.), 20. Cassuto argues that beginning with verse 2, the focus changes from the cosmos to creation's relationship to humanity, stressing the themes of "land" and "blessing," which prevail throughout the Pentateuch.

77. Sailhamer, *Genesis Unbound,* 250.

78. Moltmann, *God in Creation,* 73.

78. Ibid.

80. Werner Foerster, *"ktizô,"* in *Theological Dictionary of the New Testament,* ed. Gerhard Kittel, trans. Geoffrey W. Bromiley (Grand Rapids: Eerdmans, 1965), 3:1010.

81. A similar translation is endorsed by B. H. Roberts: "In the beginning, when God created the heavens and the earth, the earth was without form and void" (*The Truth, the Way, the Life,* 227). Compare with E. A. Speiser, who takes Genesis 1:1 as a construct rather than an absolute: "When God set about to create heaven and earth . . ." (*Genesis,* AB 1 [Garden City, N.Y.: Doubleday, 1964], 3); so also Luis I. J. Stadelmann (*The Hebrew Conception of the World: A Philological and Literary Study* [Rome: Pontifical Biblical Institute, 1970], 11). However, if what we have just argued is true, this would mean that Ian Barbour's assertion that Genesis argues for "the creation of *order from chaos*" rather than from nothing is misguided (Barbour, *Religion in an Age of Science,* 130)—and the LDS viewpoint as well.

82. Bernhard W. Anderson, *Contours of Old Testament Theology* (Minneapolis: Fortress, 1999), 88–89. Kenneth A. Mathews's analysis concludes that "v. 1 is best taken as an absolute statement of God's creation" (*Genesis 1–11:26,* NAC [Nashville: Broadman & Holman, 1996], 139).

83. *En archê epoiêsen ho theos ton ouranon kai tên gên.* = "In the beginning God created heaven and earth."

84. Victor P. Hamilton, *The Book of Genesis Chapters 1-17,* NICOT (Grand Rapids: Eerdmans, 1990), 107. The Vulgate also translates the verse as an absolute and treats it as an independent clause: *In principio creavit Deus coelum et terram.* Bruce Waltke lists "all ancient versions"—"LXX, Vulgate, Aquila, Theodotion, Symmachus, Targum Onkelos"— as understanding Genesis 1:1 as an "independent clause." See his "The Initial Chaos Theory and the Precreation Chaos Theory," *Bibliotheca Sacra* 132 (July 1975): 223.

85. C. F. Keil and F. Delitzsch, *Commentary on the Old Testament,* vol. 1, *The Pentateuch,* 46.

86. Ibid. The same conclusion is drawn by Hamilton, *Genesis 1-17,* 106.

87. Keil and F. Delitzsch, 46. Cf. Foerster, who says that this merism "embraces the cosmos" (*TDNT* 3:1012).

88. "The Initial Chaos Theory," 225. See Waltke's entire essay, 217–28.

89. Thomas E. McComiskey, "*bârâ*," in *Theological Dictionary of the Old Testament,* ed. R. Laird Harris, Gleason J. Archer, and Bruce K. Waltke (Chicago: Moody Press, 1980), 1:127. McComiskey mentions that *yâtzar* primarily emphasizes the *shaping* of an object.

90. "Exegetical Notes on Genesis 1:1–2," *Catholic Biblical Quarterly* 10 (1948): 142; see also Foerster, "*ktizô,*" 3:1010: *bârâ'* is used in the Old Testament "only of a divine action."

91. Arbez and Weisengoff, "Notes on Genesis," 144.

92. Ibid. Arbez and Weisengoff point out that scholars such as König, Reuss, A. Heidel, and Wellhausen draw this conclusion as well (144–45n).

93. Mathews, *Genesis 1-11:26,* 141.

94. So Armin Schmitt: "*Aus dieser Sicht ist es gut möglich, daß [aoratos] in Gen 1.2 platonisch beeinflußt ist. Auch [akataskeuastos] tendiert in diese Richtung.* = From this view it is well likely that [aoratos = unseen/invisible] in Gen. 1:2 is influenced by Platonism. [*Akataskeuastos* = unformed] also tends in this direction" ("Interpretation der Genesis aus hellenistischem Geist," *ZAW* 86 (1974): 150. Schmitt points out these particular terms are "an essential component of the Greek and especially the Platonic doctrine of origins that the world was conveyed/transformed from an initially disordered status to a condition of harmony and beauty (*eine wesentliche Komponente der griechischen und speziell der platonishen Weltentstehungslehre, daß die Welt aus einem anfänglich ungeordneten Status in einen Zustand der Harmonie und Schönheit überführt wird*)" (151).

95. See discussion in Hamilton, *Genesis 1–17,* 108–9; echoing this is Kenneth Mathews's extensive discussion in *Genesis 1–11:26,* 130–44.

96. Sailhamer, *Genesis Unbound*, 214; for a fuller discussion, see 213–22.

97. Sailhamer, *The Pentateuch as Narrative*, 85n.

98. Ibid.

99. Keil and Delitzsch, 47–48.

100. Ibid., 47.

101. Foerster, *"ktizô,"* 3:1012.

102. Derek Kidner, *Proverbs*, TOTC (Downers Grove, Ill.: InterVarsity Press, 1964), 78.

103. Carl F. H. Henry, *God, Revelation, and Authority* (Waco, Tex.: Word, 1983), 22.

104. Pannenberg, *Systematic Theology*, 2:17.

105. God's creation by divine fiat is also reflected in 2 Esdras 6:38: "I said, O Lord, You have indeed spoken from the beginning of creation; on the first day You said: 'Let heaven and earth be made,' and Your word accomplished the work."

106. Foerster, *"ktizô,"* 3:1012; "God created everything (without precondition)": W. H. Schmidt, *"bârâ',"* in *Theological Lexicon of the Old Testament*, ed. Ernst Jenni and Claus Westermann, trans. Mark E. Biddle (Peabody, Mass.: Hendrickson, 1997), 1:256.

107. Bruce Waltke, *Genesis: A Commentary* (Grand Rapids: Zondervan, 2001), 78, 68.

108. McComiskey, *"Bârâ',"* 1:173. See also Jewett's helpful discussion in *God, Creation, and Revelation*, 455–67; and W. H Schmidt, *"bârâ',"* 1:253–56.

109. F. F. Bruce, *The Epistle to the Hebrews*, NICNT (Grand Rapids: Eerdmans, 1964), 280.

110. Jaroslav Pelikan, "Creation and Causality in the History of Christian Thought," in *Evolution After Darwin*, ed. Sol Tax and Charles Callender (Chicago: University of Chicago, 1960), 3:34.

111. Paul Ellingworth, *Commentary on Hebrews*, NIGNT (Grand Rapids: Eerdmans, 1993), 569.

112. Ibid., 571.

113. Ibid., 568.

114. Ibid., 569. (Also note the chiastic structure Ellingworth identifies here.)

115. C. F. D. Moule, *An Idiom Book of New Testament Greek*, repr. (Cambridge: University Press, 1968), 168. Moule adds, however, that the order of the negative *mê* before the preposition *ek*, "from" or "out of," is somewhat awkward grammatically.

116. William L. Lane, *Hebrews 9-13*, WBC (Dallas: Word, 1991), 332.

117. Ibid. Without giving any substantial evidence for his assertion, Harold Attridge asserts that "a Platonic cosmogonic model" lies behind the formulation of this verse (see his *Epistle to the Hebrews* Hermeneia [Philadelphia: Fortress, 1989], 316).

118. Craig Koester, *Hebrews*, AB 36 (New York: Doubleday, 2001), 474, 481.

119. Keith Norman, *"Ex nihilo:* The Development of the Doctrines of God and Creation in Early Christianity," *BYU Studies* 3 (Spring 1977): 301: "As Werner Foerster admits. . . ." He does nothing of the sort! In fact, Foerster refers once again to Romans 4:17 to show that "creation involves the beginning of the existence of the world, so that there is no pre-existent matter" (*"ktizô,"* 3:1029).

120. Foerster, *"ktizô,"* 3:1010.

121. Ibid.

122. Ibid., 3:1029.

123. James D. G. Dunn, *Romans 1–8*, WBC 38A (Dallas: Word, 1988), 237; emphasis added.

124. Although Raymond Brown wrongly asserts that John 1:1–18 "does not necessarily have the same theology as the Gospel," Brown makes plain that the word *egeneto* ("come

into being") is used consistently to describe creation in the Septuagint in Genesis 1 (*The Gospel According to John I-XII*, AB 29 [New York: Doubleday, 1966], 6). Cf. D. A. Carson's discussion on how the Gospel of John's prologue actually introduces its major themes in *The Gospel According to John* (Grand Rapids: Eerdmans, 1991), 111–12.

125. For a survey of the biblical data regarding creation, see Karl Hermann Schelkle, *Theology of the New Testament*, trans. William A. Jurgens (Collegeville, Minn.: Liturgical Press, 1971), 1:3–61.

126. Brown, *Gospel According to John I-XII*, 8.

127. Ibid., 26.

128. Eichrodt, *Theology of the Old Testament*, 2:102.

129. Corresponds, that is, in chiastic fashion.

130. P. T. O'Brien, *Colossians, Philemon*, WBC (Waco, Tex.: Word, 1982), 46.

131. N. T. Wright, *Colossians and Philemon*, TNTC (Downers Grove, Ill./Grand Rapids: InterVarsity Press/Eerdmans, 1986), 73.

132. In E. K. Simpson and F. F. Bruce, *The Epistles of Paul to the Ephesians and to the Colossians*, NICNT (Grand Rapids: Eerdmans, 1957), 200. O'Brien also points out Christ's "temporal priority to the universe" (*Colossians, Philemon*, 47) as does N. T. Wright, *Colossians and Philemon*, 71 ("priority in both time and rank"; "the continuing temporal sense of the word is clear").

133. O'Brien, *Colossians, Philemon*, 47.

134. Ibid.

135. Ibid.

136. Foerster, *"ktizô,"* 3:1029. This is utterly contrary to the LDS claim made by Keith Norman that "a closer examination of the text [i.e., various 'exploited' passages in the New Testament] belies this [*ex nihilo*] interpretation" (*"Ex nihilo,"* 301)—despite the fact that Norman cites Foerster. This conclusion also applies to 2 Peter 3:5, which speaks of God creating "from water" and "by water." In accordance with Ps. 104 and Prov. 8, as *part* of the creative process, God divides the waters—which he had previously brought into being and with which he then covered the foundations of the earth—into the waters below and above. Water is the *material* from which (*ex*) the sky is created and *instrument* (*dia*) to create the sky (Douglas J. Moo, *2 Peter, Jude*, NIVAC [Grand Rapids: Zondervan, 1996], 170). Nothing suggests that the water is itself uncreated. Again, Ps. 104 and Prov. 8 suggest a two-step creative process. 2 Peter 3 focuses on the second stage, highlighting the importance of water in light of its being the means of judgment in the Noachian deluge.

137. Moltmann, *God in Creation*, 74.

138. Ian Barbour, *Issues in Science and Religion* (New York: Harper & Row, 1971, repr.), 384. Philosopher of science Ernan McMullin states that the doctrine of creation out of nothing, "an act of absolute bringing to be," took "firm shape only in the first centuries of the Christian era, in part at least in response to the prevalent dualisms of the day that represented matter as evil, or at least, as resistant to God's action." McMullin is willing to concede that hints of *creatio ex nihilo* can be found in Scripture (2 Macc 7:28 and Rom 1:20). See McMullin, "Natural Science and Belief in a Creator," in Stoeger, Coyne and George, *Physics, Philosophy, and Theology*, 56. Anglican priest and physicist John Polkinghorne sees 2 Maccabees 7:28 as the "earliest unequivocal statement of the idea of creation out of nothing," although he believes Genesis 1 stresses at least "the dependence of all upon the sovereign will of God for its existence," which is "certainly consonant with the central significance of *creatio ex nihilo*" (*Reason and Reality* [Philadelphia: Trinity Press International, 1991], 72).

139. Barbour, *Issues in Science and Religion*, 384.

140. Ian G. Barbour, *Religion in an Age of Science,* The Gifford Lectures 1989–91 (San Francisco: Harper & Row, 1990), 1:144.

141. Ibid., 129.

142. May, *Creatio ex Nihilo,* 24.

143. Barbour, *Religion in an Age of Science,* 2.

144. Hugh Nibley, "Treasures in the Heavens: Some Early Christian Insights into the Organizing of Worlds," *Dialogue* 8/3–4 (1973): 77.

145. Ibid., 82.

146. Stephen Robinson, personal correspondence (20 April 1998).

147. Peterson and Ricks assert on the basis of Anderson's article that "it is highly doubtful that the doctrine of *ex nihilo* creation is to be found in Genesis or anywhere else in the Old Testament" (*Offenders for a Word,* 95).

148. Anderson, "Creation," *IBD* 1:728. Elsewhere, Anderson states that the view of *creatio ex nihilo* is "not supported explicitly by the biblical text" (*Contours of Old Testament Theology,* 87), but he apparently means the specific creation text of Genesis, as the context indicates. Such a reading is reinforced by the present *IBD* quotation by Anderson, which cites New Testament evidence (Rom 4:17; Heb 11:3) for creation *ex nihilo.*

149. Irenaeus, *Against Heresies* III:X.3; cf. II:10.4.

150. Augustine, *Confessions* 12.7.

151. With Philo and some of these church fathers, however, it is not as clear as some scholars imply that they affirmed the eternality of matter, and others dissent from this opinion. On Philo, see, for example, the recent discussion in Colin E. Gunton, *The Triune Creator: A Historical and Systematic Study* (Edinburgh: Edinburgh University Press, 1998), 44–47 (cf. Philo, *On Providence,* fg. 1; *On the Eternity of the World,* 1–20, 150; *On the Decalogue,* 58; *On the Special Laws,* IV.187; *On the Creation,* 7, 20, 24, 26, 29, 36). With regard to Clement of Alexandria, E. F. Osborn states: "Clement is the first person to state and give reasons for the doctrine of creation *ex nihilo*" (*The Philosophy of Clement of Alexandria* [Cambridge: Cambridge University Press, 1957], 33). In a recent article, N. Joseph Torchia cites passages that he feels "clearly challenge any claim that [Justin and Athenagoras] accepted the notion of a material substrate eternally coexisting with God." Torchia is well aware of texts in which Justin speaks of creation out of "unformed matter" but suggests, following other scholars, that a theory of the creation of matter can also be drawn from what Justin says. "From this standpoint, even a commitment to the idea of pre-existent matter does not rule out a doctrine of creation *ex nihilo.* Indeed, God could have created matter prior to its formation or ordering" ("Theories of Creation in the Second Century Apologists and their Middle Platonic Background," *Studia Patristica* 26 [1993]: 194). Such examples could easily be multiplied.

152. May, *Creatio ex nihilo,* 257–8.

153. Torchia, "Theories of Creation," 192.

154. F. F. Bruce, *Epistle to the Hebrews,* 281n.

155. Ibid., 66.

156. I am grateful to D. A. Carson on this point.

157. Bernhard W. Anderson, *Contours of Old Testament Theology,* 87.

158. Gerhard von Rad, *Old Testament Theology,* trans. D. M. G. Stalker (New York: Harper & Row, 1962), 1:142n.

159. Claus Westermann, *Creation,* trans. John J. Scullion (Philadelphia: Fortress Press, 1974), 36.

160. For a different perspective, see Jonathan A. Goldstein, *II Maccabees,* AB 41A (Garden City, N.Y.: Doubleday, 1983), 307–15; *idem,* "The Origins of the Doctrine of *Creation ex nihilo," Journal of Jewish Studies* 35 (1984): 127–35; so also LDS scholar Keith Norman, *"Ex nihilo,"* 299. However, Westermann, who sees 2 Maccabees 7:28 as affirming *creatio ex nihilo,* claims that it is "no accident" that this idea should arise in a Hellenistic setting in defense of a biblical worldview ("God created the heavens and the earth")—not to mention that Judaism would be influenced to think of formless matter before creation. Although Westermann believes Genesis 1:1–2 does not explicitly affirm creation out of nothing (though he comes close to affirming this), he makes clear that the idea of matter's preexisting creation was not in the thinking of the biblical writer (*Genesis 1–11* [Minneapolis: Augsburg, 1984], 110).

161. Craig Evans, email correspondence, 12 November 2001.

162. Cited from Florentino García Martínez, *The Dead Sea Scrolls Translated,* 2d ed. (Leiden/Grand Rapids: Brill/Eerdmans, 1996), 6. All other citations are taken from this translation.

163. For a brief discussion of the doctrine of creation in the Qumran texts, see Daniel J. Harrington, "Creation," in *Encyclopedia of the Dead Sea Scrolls,* ed. Lawrence H. Schiffman and James C. VanderKam (Oxford: Oxford University Press, 2000), 1:155–57.

164. This translation is rendered by Jonathan A. Goldstein in "Creation *ex nihilo:* Recantations and Restatements," *Journal of Jewish Studies* 38 (Autumn 1987): 189. Goldstein defends his reading of *creatio ex nihilo* in Gamaliel's statement, *contra* David Winston, "The Book of Wisdom's Theory of Cosmogony," *History of Religions* (1971): 185–202; and David Winston, "*Creation Ex nihilo* Revisited: A Reply to Jonathan Goldstein," *Journal of Jewish Studies* 37 [1986]: 88–92. Mormon writers such as Peterson and Ricks cite Winston but neglect Goldstein's 1987 article defending previously made statements in his essay "The Origins of the Doctrine of Creation *Ex nihilo*" (though recanting others). Despite Peter Hayman's siding with Winston and announcing Goldstein's "conceding the weakness of his position" ("Monotheism—A Misused Word in Jewish Studies," *JJS* 42 [1991]: 3), Hayman does not deal with the Gamaliel question, and Goldstein staunchly defends his position.

165. Unformed space/void was made by God (Isa 45:7) as were darkness (Isa 45:7), water (Ps 148:4–5), wind (Amos 4:13), and the depths (Prov 8:24). Taken from Jacob Neusner, *Confronting Creation* (Columbia: University of South Carolina Press, 1991), 41–42.

166. *Shepherd of Hermas* 1.6: *ktisas ek tou mē ontos ta onta*; 26.1: *poiēsas ek tou mē ontos eis to einai ta panta.*

167. Denis Carroll, "Creation," in *The New Dictionary of Theology,* ed. Joseph Komanchak et al. (Wilmington, Del.: Michael Glazier, 1987), 249.

168. James Charlesworth, "Odes of Solomon," in *The Old Testament Pseudepigrapha,* ed. James Charlesworth (Garden City, N.Y.: Doubleday, 1985), 2:726–27.

169. Frederick James Murphy, *The Structure and Meaning of Second Baruch,* SBLDS (Atlanta: Scholar's Press, 1985), 43.

170. *Ap. Const.* 8.12.6, 8. May (p. 22n) and others (such as W. Bousset) view this section (§12) of the *Constitutions* as being a later Christian interpolation, but James Charlesworth, among others, does not think so ("Hellenistic Synagogal Prayers" in *Old Testament Pseudepigrapha,* 1:690n). At least the lack of consensus should preclude us from hastily dismissing it.

171. Stephen Ricks, "*Fides Quaerens Intellectum,*" 178.

172. Goldstein, "The Origins of the Doctrine of Creation *Ex nihilo,*" 127. Norbert M. Samuelson, *Judaism and the Doctrine of Creation* (Cambridge: Cambridge University Press,

1994) takes this view, but fails to take into account the subtleties suggested by Sailhamer (below).

173. One can read Rashi's comments in "Genesis," in *The Pentateuch and Rashi's Commentary*, vol. 1 (Brooklyn: S.S. & R., 1949).

174. Sailhamer, "Genesis," 22. See Sailhamer's extensive note on 21–23 for further discussion. See, in addition, John H. Sailhamer, *The Pentateuch as Narrative* (Grand Rapids: Zondervan, 1992), not only for his discussion of Genesis 1:1ff., but for his comments on the intertextuality and integrity of the Pentateuch. I am grateful to John Sailhamer for his discussion on this subject.

175. Foerster, *"Ktizô,"* 1:1016.

176. Ibid., 1:1017.

177. Ramban (Nachmanides), *Commentary on the Torah: Genesis,* trans. Charles B. Chavel (New York: Shiloh, 1971), 17.

178. For instance, Max Nolan writes that the "most striking element in Mormon theology and process theology alike ... is the idea that Deity is subject to process" ("Materialism and the Mormon Faith," *Dialogue* 22/4 [1989]: 73). Moreover, in Mormon metaphysics we have "the material [or unorganized matter] constituents of the world, and the intelligences embodied in the world, are uncreated and co-eternal with Deity" (ibid.). Nolan declares that "the open texture of process theology seems therefore to offer a useful way to approach the question of the Mormon metaphysical commitment" (ibid.).

179. Norman, *"Ex nihilo,"* 306.

180. Plato, *Timaeus* 30a, in *Plato: The Collected Dialogues,* ed. Edith Hamilton and Huntington Cairns, Bollingen Series 71 (Princeton: Princeton University Press, 1989), 1162.

181. See Plato *Timaeus* 30; Aristotle *Physics* 8.1.251a10–252a1; 8.6.259a10–15.

182. For an exposition of the argument in its historical context, see William Lane Craig, *The Cosmological Argument from Plato to Leibniz* (London: Macmillan, 1980); Harry Austryn Wolfson, "Patristic Arguments Against the Eternity of the World," *Harvard Theological Review* 59 (1966): 354–67; idem, *The Philosophy of the* Kalam (Cambridge: Harvard University Press, 1976); H. A. Davidson, *Proofs for Eternity, Creation, and the Existence of God in Medieval Islamic and Jewish Philosophy* (New York: Oxford University Press, 1987); and Richard C. Dales, *Medieval Discussions of the Eternity of the World* (Leiden: Brill, 1990).

There is another tradition of argumentation for *creatio ex nihilo* in a nontemporal sense, initiated by such church fathers as Tatian and Tertullian, that appeals to divine omnipotence. If matter were not itself created *ex nihilo* by God, then there would be something over which he lacked power, which contradicts his omnipotence. This argument also strikes at the heart of Mormonism since, according to LDS doctrine, God, as a material being, could not be the Creator of matter. In his unpublished paper "Was the Doctrine of Creation *Ex nihilo* Created Out of Nothing?" Blake Ostler seeks to undercut this persuasive argument by maintaining that there are nonlogical limits on God's power, as shown by recent philosophical analyses, that permit us to craft a definition of omnipotence according to which a God unable to create matter still counts as omnipotent. Unfortunately, Ostler has not understood the analyses he cites (e.g., Thomas P. Flint and Alfred J. Freddoso, "Maximal Power," in *The Existence and Nature of God* [Notre Dame: University of Notre Dame Press, 1983], 81–113), for the authors explicitly state that their definition appeals to *no* nonlogical limits on God's power. Moreover, Ostler's own redefinition is clearly inadequate in stating either necessary or sufficient conditions of omnipotence, for his definition falls prey to the customary counterexamples like the infamous Mr. McEar. Ironically, his definition requires that God have the ability to annihilate all matter, which undercuts the Mormon concept of

God. Despite the power of this line of argument on behalf of *creatio ex nihilo,* we have chosen to focus on temporal *creatio ex nihilo,* not only because a biblically and philosophically robust doctrine of *creatio ex nihilo* requires a temporal origin of the universe but also because LDS theologians often simply reject God's omnipotence. The question would then become whether a nonomnipotent being is truly worthy of worship, and such a discussion would take us off topic.

183. Talmage, *A Study of the Articles of Faith,* 34 (2.1).

184. Ludwig Wittgenstein, *Lectures on the Foundations of Mathematics,* ed. Cora Diamond (Sussex: Harvester Press, 1976), 103.

185. The story of Hilbert's Hotel is related in George Gamow, *One, Two, Three, Infinity* (London: Macmillan, 1946), 17.

186. What is the logical structure of the argument here? The proponent of the argument has two options open to him. On the one hand, he could argue that if an actual infinite were to exist, then the Principle of Correspondence would be valid with respect to it, and that if an actual infinite were to exist and the Principle of Correspondence were to be valid with respect to it, then the various counterintuitive situations would result. Therefore, if an actual infinite were to exist, the various counterintuitive situations would result. But because these are absurd and so really impossible, it follows that the existence of an actual infinite is impossible.

On the other hand, the proponent of the argument might call into question the premise that if an actual infinite were to exist, then the Principle of Correspondence would be valid with respect to it. There is no reason to think that the principle is universally valid. It is merely a convention adopted in infinite set theory. Now, necessarily, if an actual infinite were to exist, then either the Principle of Correspondence or Euclid's maxim that "The whole is greater than its part" would apply to it. But since the application of either of these two principles to an actual infinite results in counterintuitive absurdities, it is plausible that if the existence of an actual infinite were possible, then if an actual infinite were to exist, neither of these two principles would be valid with respect to it. It therefore follows that the existence of an actual infinite is impossible, since the counterfactual that "If an actual infinite were to exist, then neither principle would be valid with respect to it" is necessarily false.

187. David Hilbert, "On the Infinite," in *Philosophy of Mathematics,* ed. Paul Benacerraf and Hilary Putnam (Englewood Cliffs, N.J.: Prentice-Hall, 1964), 151.

188. Blake T. Ostler, review-essay of Francis J. Beckwith and Stephen E. Parrish, *The Mormon Concept of God: A Philosophical Analysis* (Lewiston, N.Y.: Edwin Mellen, 1991) in *FARMS Review of Books* 8/2 (1996): 127.

189. Norman Kretzmann, *The Metaphysics of Creation: Aquinas' Natural Theology in 'Summa contra gentiles' II* (Oxford: Clarendon, 1999), 182.

190. See William Lane Craig, *The* Kalam *Cosmological Argument,* Library of Philosophy and Religion (London: Macmillan, 1979), App. 2.

191. See William Lane Craig, "Graham Oppy on the *Kalam* Cosmological Argument," *Sophia* 32 (1993): 1–11; "The Origin and Creation of the Universe: A Reply to Adolf Grünbaum," *British Journal for the Philosophy of Science* 43 (1992): 233–40; Kalam *Cosmological Argument,* 193–94, 199; review article of *Time, Creation and the Continuum,* by Richard Sorabji, *International Philosophical Quarterly* 25 (1985): 319–26; "Professor Mackie and the *Kalam* Cosmological Argument," *Religious Studies* 20 (1985): 367–75.

192. Ostler, review of *The Mormon Concept of God,* 130.

193. Ostler's mistake is especially painful since he gratuitously scores Beckwith and Parrish for their apparent failure to grasp "the intricacies of infinite set theory" (ibid., 129)!

194. Ibid. Or again, he simply errs when he asserts that Saturn and Jupiter orbiting the sun from eternity would not have completed the same number of revolutions (Ostler, "The Doctrine of *Creatio ex nihilo*," 13). I think his error arises partly from the misimpression that "there is no such number as infinity" (14). This is a mistake; there is a whole system of transfinite arithmetic employing the transfinite cardinal numbers. $\aleph_0$, $\aleph_1$, $\aleph_2$, . . . are just as much numbers as are 0, 1, 2,. . . .

195. Ostler, review of *The Mormon Concept of God*, 130.

196. Cantor himself held that the argument against the infinity of the past is sound. In a letter of 1887 he wrote: "When it is said that a mathematical proof for the beginning of the world cannot be given, the emphasis is on the word 'mathematical,' and to this extent my view agrees with that of St. Thomas. On the other hand, a mixed mathematical-philosophical proof of the proposition might well be produced just on the basis of the true theory of the transfinite, and to this extent I depart from St. Thomas, who defends the view: *Mundum non semper fuisse, sola fide tenetur, et demonstrative probari non potest* [(That) the world did not always exist is held by faith alone, and it cannot be proved demonstratively]" (Cantor, in H. Meschkowski, *Probleme des Unendlichen: Werk und Leben Georg Cantors* [Braunschweig: Freidrich Vieweg, 1967], 125–26). I am indebted to Robin Small for this reference.

197. Cf. Ostler's intriguing comment that if we have a time machine, "we cannot actually visit the infinite number of past times because no matter how long we spent going back to the past in the future, the number of times that we will have visited will be finite. . . . However, there is a way to visit each of the infinite number of past times—to have lived through all of them. And that is just what Mormonism claims we and God have done" ("Doctrine of *Creatio ex nihilo*," 17).

198. Bertrand Russell, *Our Knowledge of the External World*, 2d ed. (New York: W. W. Norton, 1929), 170.

199. Such reasoning in support of the finitude of the past and the beginning of the universe is not mere armchair cosmology. Paul C. W. Davies, for example, utilizes this reasoning in explaining two profound implications of the thermodynamic properties of the universe: "The first is that the universe will eventually die, wallowing, as it were, in its own entropy. This is known among physicists as the 'heat death' of the universe. The second is that the universe cannot have existed for ever, otherwise it would have reached its equilibrium end state an infinite time ago. Conclusion: the universe did not always exist" (*God and the New Physics* [New York: Simon & Schuster, 1983], 11). The second of these implications is a clear application of the reasoning that underlies the deeper absurdity explained above: even if the universe had infinite energy, it would in infinite time come to equilibrium; since at any point in the past infinite time has elapsed, a beginningless universe would have already reached equilibrium, or as Davies puts it, it would have reached equilibrium an infinite time ago.

200. Ostler, review of *The Mormon Concept of God*, 128.

201. Ibid., 129.

202. Ibid., 130. In his as yet unpublished "Doctrine of *Creatio ex nihilo*," he presents a similar argument but mistakenly concludes that the set of all times visitable in a time machine is actually infinite (p. 16). This is confused because it begs the question by assuming that the past is in fact infinite, whereas if the past is finite, then the set of visitable times is in fact finite. What Ostler means to say is that the set of visitable pasts is actually infinite. But that does not entail the possibility of an infinite past, i.e., that an infinite past is a member of the set.

203. Ibid., 129.

204. A. Einstein, "Cosmological Considerations on the General Theory of Relativity," in *The Principle of Relativity,* by A. Einstein et al., with Notes by A. Sommerfeld, trans. W. Perrett and J. B. Jefferey (rep. ed.: New York: Dover Publications, 1952), 177-88.

205. A. Friedman, "Über die Krümmung des Raumes," *Zeitschrift für Physik* 10 (1922): 377-86; G. Lemaître, "Un univers homogène de masse constante et de rayon croissant, rendant compte de la vitesse radiale des nébuleuses extragalactiques," *Annales de la Société scientifique de Bruxelles* 47 (1927): 49-59.

206. Gregory L. Naber, *Spacetime and Singularities: An Introduction* (Cambridge: Cambridge University Press, 1988), 126–27.

207. E. Hubble, "A Relation Between Distance and Radial Velocity Among Extragalactic Nebulae," *Proceedings of the National Academy of Sciences* 15 (1929): 168–73.

208. John A. Wheeler, "Beyond the Hole," in *Some Strangeness in the Proportion,* ed. Harry Woolf (Reading, Mass.: Addison-Wesley, 1980), 354.

209. This should not be taken to mean that the density of the universe takes on a value of $\aleph_0$, but rather that the density of the universe is expressed by a ratio of mass to volume in which the volume is zero; since division by zero is impermissible, the density is said to be infinite in this sense. See Milton K. Munitz, *Cosmic Understanding* (Princeton: Princeton University Press, 1986), 111.

210. P. C. W. Davies, "Spacetime Singularities in Cosmology," in *The Study of Time III,* ed. J. T. Fraser (New York: Springer Verlag, 1978), 78–79.

211. John Barrow and Frank Tipler, *The Anthropic Cosmological Principle* (Oxford: Clarendon, 1986), 442.

212. Quentin Smith, "The Uncaused Beginning of the Universe," in *Theism, Atheism, and Big Bang Cosmology,* by William Lane Craig and Quentin Smith (Oxford: Clarendon, 1993), 120.

213. Arthur Eddington, *The Expanding Universe* (New York: Macmillan, 1933), 124.

214. Ibid., 178.

215. Keith E. Norman, "Mormon Cosmology: Can It Survive the Big Bang?" *Sunstone* 10/9 (1985): 10.

216. Ibid., 21. The last phrase in single quotation marks is from Paul Davies.

217. Ibid., 22.

218. For a detailed account, see William Lane Craig, "Naturalism and Cosmology," in *Naturalism: A Critical Appraisal,* ed. William L. Craig and J. P. Moreland, Routledge Studies in Twentieth-Century Philosophy (London: Routledge, 2000), 215–52.

219. See I. D. Novikov and Ya. B. Zeldovich, "Physical Processes Near Cosmological Singularities," *Annual Review of Astronomy and Astrophysics* 11 (1973): 401–2; A. Borde and A. Vilenkin, "Eternal Inflation and the Initial Singularity," *Physical Review Letters* 72 (1994): 3305, 3307.

220. Christopher Isham, "Creation of the Universe as a Quantum Process," in Russell, Stoeger, and Coyne, *Physics, Philosophy and Theology,* 385–87.

221. See John D. Barrow, *Theories of Everything* (Oxford: Clarendon, 1991), 67–68.

222. Stephen Hawking and Roger Penrose, *The Nature of Space and Time,* The Isaac Newton Institute Series of Lectures (Princeton: Princeton University Press, 1996), 20.

223. Some recent efforts have been made to describe a pre-Big Bang universe in terms of super-string or M-theory (M. Gasperini, "Looking Back in Time Beyond the Big Bang," *Modern Physics Letters A* [forthcoming]; *idem,* "Inflation and Initial Conditions in the Pre-Big Bang Scenario," pre-print) on the assumption of a "duality-symmetry" that associates a

geometric mirror image with the familiar post-Big Bang expanding space-time geometry. Apart from the problems that there seems to be (1) no way to join the pre- and post-Big Bang eras together, nor (2) any way to smooth the transition to a matter-dominated universe, the scenario is based on a nonexistent theory and so cannot even begin to be a plausible alternative. See G. F. R. Ellis, "Before the Beginning: Emerging Questions and Uncertainties," *Astrophysics and Space Science* 269–70 (1999): 693–720.

224. Beatrice Tinsley, "From Big Bang to Eternity?" *Natural History Magazine* (October 1975): 103.

225. Duane Dicus et al., "The Future of the Universe," *Scientific American* (March 1983): 99.

226. Tinsley, "Big Bang," 105.

227. Richard Schlegel, "Time and Thermodynamics," in *The Voices of Time,* ed. J. T. Fraser (London: Penguin, 1948), 511.

228. Duane Dicus et al., "Effects of Proton Decay on the Cosmological Future," *Astrophysical Journal* 252 (1982): 1, 8.

229. Novikov and Zeldovich, "Physical Processes near Cosmological Singularities," 401–2.

230. Joseph Silk, *The Big Bang,* 2d ed. (San Francisco: W. H. Freeman, 1989), 311–12.

231. See D. Hochberg, C. Molina-Paris, and M. Visser, "Tolman Wormholes Violate the Strong Energy Condition," *Physical Review D* 5904 (1999): 4011–19.

232. Roger Penrose, "Some Remarks on Gravity and Quantum Mechanics," in *Quantum Structure of Space and Time,* ed. M. J. Duff and C. J. Isham (Cambridge: Cambridge University Press, 1982), 4.

233. Ibid., 5.

234. Weyl curvature is the curvature of space-time that is not due to the presence of matter and is described by the Weyl tensor. Space-time curvature due to matter is described by the Ricci tensor. Together they make up the Riemann tensor giving the metric for space-time.

235. Hawking and Penrose, *Nature of Space and Time,* 129.

236. Ibid., 130.

237. Penrose, "Remarks on Gravity," 5.

238. Ibid.

239. Roger Penrose, "Time-Asymmetry and Quantum Gravity," in *Quantum Gravity 2,* ed. C. J. Isham, R. Penrose, and D. W. Sciama (Oxford: Clarendon, 1981), 249; cf. Hawking and Penrose, *Nature of Space and Time,* 34–35.

240. Penrose, "Time-Asymmetry," 249.

241. P. C. W. Davies, *The Physics of Time Asymmetry* (London: Surrey University Press, 1974), 104.

242. David H. Bailey, "Scientific Foundations of Mormon Theology," in *The Search for Harmony: Essays on Science and Mormonism* (Salt Lake City: Signature Books, 1993), 4. Cf. the statement of BYU physicist B. Kent Harrison: "The Big Bang's postulation that the universe suddenly comes into being sounds suspiciously like creation *ex nihilo*" ("Truth, the Sum of Existence," in *Of Heaven and Earth,* ed. David L. Clark [Salt Lake City: Deseret, 1998], 160). Harrison would evade this implication by denying that the Big Bang represents an absolute beginning: "The usual view among cosmologists . . . is that space and time 'began' at the Big Bang—in other words that it makes no sense to speak of their existence 'before' the Big Bang. From the standpoint that we have absolutely no information about such a prior existence, that is a reasonable position. On the other hand, . . . because we have no such information, we cannot conclude that there was no existence then!" (ibid., 166; cf. 160).

This reasoning is very confused. It seems to assume that the inference to an absolute beginning is based on the absence of information prior to $t = 0$. But that is quite wrong. The inference is based upon information that is immanent within the universe, namely, the natural laws governing an object in a process of gravitational self-collapse. (No one would infer nonexistence merely from absence of information, for then it would be reasonable to believe that no galaxies exist beyond our event horizon!) Of course, if the universe had an absolute beginning, it follows necessarily that we shall have no information about a prior state because there *was* no prior state. Harrison's characterization of the Standard Model as holding that "there was no existence then" is incoherent, for on the Standard Model there was no "then," as he seems to assume. Of course, Harrison is at liberty to reject the Standard Model, but then he owes us an alternative model that explains the evidence as well as the standard Big Bang approach does.

243. Bailey, "Scientific Foundations of Mormon Theology," 8.

244. Ibid., 9–10. Cf. *idem,* "Science and Mormonism: Past, Present, and Future," *Dialogue* 29/1 (1996): 89.

245. Henry Eyring, "World of Evidence, World of Faith," in *Of Heaven and Earth,* 60.

246. Harrison, "Truth," 173. Harrison believes that God's persistence in an eternally expanding universe "seems to be an unsatisfactory, passive, ungodlike way of prolonging existence or progression" (ibid., 173).

247. Eyring, "World of Evidence," 66.

248. If Eyring means to endorse some nonstandard model of the universe, such as an oscillating model, then he will not have escaped the inevitable consequences of thermodynamics. Indeed, if God is a living, physical being, then the second law seems essential to his survival, for in the absence of the second law, chaos would ensue. Thus, in whatever space-time world God lives, the same thermodynamic problem arises.

249. Eyring, "World of Evidence," 61.

250. Paul, *Science, Religion, and Mormon Cosmology,* 31. This fact is not appreciated by Mormon physicist Russell T. Pack, "Quantum Cosmology," *Sunstone* 11/1 (1987): 2–4, who denounces the view that God is a physical object existing in the universe as "ridiculous." He erroneously claims that "the Mormon God is *not* part of our universe and He is apparently not limited by either space or time" (ibid., 4). Whether Pack's view can avoid falling into classical theism remains to be seen.

251. Bailey, "Scientific Foundations of Mormon Theology," 8.

252. Harrison, "Truth, the Sum of Existence," 166; cf. Pack, "Quantum Cosmology," 4.

253. Bailey, "Scientific Foundations of Mormon Theology," 9.

254. Ibid.

255. Norman, "Mormon Cosmology," 23.

256. For semi-popular treatments of string theory, see Brian Greene, *The Elegant Universe* (New York: W. W. Norton, 1999); and Michio Kaku, *Hyperspace* (Oxford: Oxford University Press, 1994).

257. Bart Kowallis, "Things of the Earth," in *Of Heaven and Earth,* 41.

258. Harrison, "Truth, the Sum of Existence," 160.

259. Norman, "Mormon Cosmology," 23.

260. Ibid.

261. In his later "Science and Mormonism" (95), he also holds that given LDS commitment to continuing revelation "current church teachings at any given point in time should never be considered final, absolute, complete, or infallible. Instead they should be

considered as representing the best present understanding and certainly subject to change as knowledge and understanding grow."

262. Bailey, "Scientific Foundations of Mormon Theology," 10. Similarly, we suggest that Mormons take Joseph Smith's affirmation that "Man was also in the beginning with God. Intelligence, or the light of truth, was not created or made, neither indeed can be" (D&C 93:29) to mean that the individual essences of all creatures existed eternally in the mind of God. See Alvin Plantinga, *The Nature of Necessity* (Oxford: Clarendon, 1974), chap. 5.

263. Bailey, "Scientific Foundations of Mormon Theology," 11.

264. Ibid., 9. Other Mormon thinkers will demur. For example, Bart Kowallis, a geology professor at BYU, noting that eternity is "one of the main characteristics of God and godhood," exclaims, "Compared to infinity, what are a few billion trillion?" ("Things of the Earth," 42).

265. Bailey, "Scientific Foundations of Mormon Theology," 9.

266. Ibid.

267. Ostler, "The Idea of Pre-Existence in the Development of Mormon Thought," 73.

268. Especially see O. Kendall White, *Mormon Neo-orthodoxy: A Crisis Theology* (Salt Lake City: Signature Books, 1988). Also see White, "The Transformation of Mormon Theology," 10–11. He emphasizes that it is on the basis of *creatio ex nihilo* that the distinction between God's necessity and creation's contingency is traditionally established.

269. One gets the impression that some Mormon thinkers believe that eternal personalism is somehow incompatible with absolutism. But this is a mistake. See William Lane Craig, "Divine Timelessness and Personhood," *International Journal for Philosophy of Religion* 43 (1998): 109–24 and the literature cited therein.

Chapter 4: The God of Abraham, Isaac, and Joseph Smith?

1. Islam has also historically affirmed this general understanding of God and likewise roots it in the patriarchal tradition of ancient Israel. Muslims, however, consider Abraham's son Ishmael and his descendants the recipients of the divine promise, not Isaac and his descendants as the biblical writers do.

2. Stephen E. Robinson, *Are Mormons Christian?* (Salt Lake City: Bookcraft, 1991), 82. Emphasis added.

3. General studies of ANE cosmogonies in relation to the Old Testament include: S. G. F. Brandon, *Creation Legends of the Ancient Near East* (London: Hodder and Stoughton, 1963); Richard J. Clifford, *Creation Accounts in the Ancient Near East and in the Bible* (CBQMS 26; Washington, D.C.: Catholic Biblical Association, 1994); John D. Currid, "Cosmologies of Myth," in *Building a Christian World View*, ed. W. Andrew Hoffecker (Phillipsburg: Presbyterian and Reformed, 1988), 2:9–20; idem, *Ancient Egypt and the Old Testament* (Grand Rapids: Baker, 1997), 23–49.

4. Some scholars claim that the Ugaritic texts, especially the Baal Cycle, contain true cosmogonies (e.g., Loren R. Fisher, "Creation at Ugarit and in the Old Testament," *VT* 15 [1965]: 313–24; J. C. L. Gibson, "The Theology of the Ugaritic Baal Cycle," *Or* 53 [1984]: 202–19). Those who disagree include: John Day, *God's Conflict with the Dragon and the Sea: Echoes of a Canaanite Myth in the Old Testament* (Cambridge: Cambridge University, 1985), cf. 17; idem, "Canaan, Religion of," *ABD* 1:831; Jakob H. Grønbæk, "Baal's Battle with Yam—A Canaanite Creation Fight," *JSOT* 33 (1985): 27-44; Arvid S. Kaperlrud, "Creation in the Ras Shamra Texts," *ST* 34 (1980): 1–11; Marvin H. Pope, *El in the Ugaritic Texts*

(Leiden: Brill, 1955), 49; B. Margalit, "The Ugaritic Creation Myth: Fact or Fiction?" *UF* 13 (1981): 137–45; M. S. Smith, "Interpreting the Baal Cycle," *UF* 18 (1986): 319–20. It is significant that R. J. Clifford in an earlier study asserted that "the Baal stories are true cosmogonies" ("Cosmogonies in the Ugaritic Texts and in the Bible," *Or* 53 [1984]: 184). However, in his more extensive work on ANE cosmogonies, Clifford readjusted his former position and concluded that "the evidence [that the Baal cycle is cosmogonic] is insufficient to draw such a firm conclusion" (*Creation Accounts*, 120 n15).

5. The literature on Egyptian cosmogony and cosmology is immense, but in particular see: James P. Allen, *Genesis in Egypt: The Philosophy of Ancient Egyptian Creation Accounts* (New Haven, Conn.: Yale Egyptological Seminar, 1988); Rudolf Anthes, "Egyptian Theology in the Third Mellennium B.C.," *JNES* 18 (1959): 169–212; John D. Currid, *Ancient Egypt*, 53–73; Etienne Drioton, "Egyptian Religion," in *Religions of the Ancient Near East*, ed. E. Drioton et al. (New York: Hawthorn, 1959), 16–59; Jack Finegan, "Egyptian Religion," in *Myth & Mystery: An Introduction to the Pagan Religions of the Biblical World* (Grand Rapids: Baker, 1989), 47–60; Henri Frankfort, *Kingship and the Gods: A Study of Ancient Near Eastern Religion as the Integration of Society and Nature* (Chicago: University of Chicago Press, 1978), 148–61; Leonard H. Lesko, "Ancient Egyptian Cosmogonies and Cosmology," in *Religion in Ancient Egypt: Gods, Myths, and Personal Practice*, ed. B. E. Shafer (Ithaca, N.Y. and London: Cornell University Press, 1991), 88–122; Siegfried Morenz, *Egyptian Religion*, trans. A. E. Keep (London: Methuen, 1973), 159–82; J. M. Plumley, "The Cosmology of Ancient Egypt," in *Ancient Cosmologies*, ed. Carmen Blacker and M. Loewe (London: George Allen & Unwin, 1975), 17–41; Vincent A. Tobin, "Myths: Creation Myths," in *The Oxford Encyclopedia of Ancient Egypt* [*OEAE*], ed. Donald B. Redford (Oxford: Oxford University Press, 2001), 2:469–72; John A. Wilson, "Egypt," in H. Frankfort et al., *The Intellectual Adventure of Ancient Man: An Essay on Speculative Thought in the Ancient Near East* (Chicago: University of Chicago Press, 1946), 31–61. Along with the above, the primary Egyptian texts in English translation to consult include: Thomas G. Allen, *The Book of the Dead or Going Forth by Day* (Chicago: University of Chicago Press, 1974); Raymond O. Faulkner, *The Ancient Egyptian Pyramid Texts* (Oxford: Clarendon, 1969); *idem, The Ancient Egyptian Coffin Tests* (Warminster, U.K.: Aris & Phillips, 1973–78); *idem, The Ancient Egyptian Book of the Dead*, ed. C. Andrews (Austin: University of Texas Press, 1972); John L. Foster, *Hymns, Prayers, and Songs: An Anthology of Ancient Egyptian Lyric Poetry* (SBLWAW 8; Atlanta: Scholars Press, 1995); Miriam Lichtheim, *Ancient Egyptian Literature* (Berkeley: University of California Press, 1975–80); John A. Wilson, "Egyptian Myths, Tales, and Mortuary Texts," in *ANET*, 3–36.

6. The literature on the cosmology and cosmogony of Mesopotamia is also vast, but see specifically: Georges Contenau, "The Ancient Religions of Western Asia," in E. Drioton et al., *Religions of the Ancient East*, 82–114; Jack Finegan, "Mesopotamian Religion," in *Myth & Mystery*, 31–36; Alexander Heidel, *The Babylonian Genesis* (Chicago: University of Chicago Press, 1951); Thorkild Jacobsen, "Mesopotamia," in H. Frankfort et al., *The Intellectual Adventure of Ancient Man*, 125–84; *idem*, "The Battle Between Marduk and Tiamat," *JAOS* 88 (1968): 104–8; *idem, Toward the Image of Tammuz and Other Essays on Mesopotamian History and Culture*, ed. W. L. Moran (HSS 21; Cambridge: Harvard University Press, 1970); *idem, The Treasures of Darkness: A History of Mesopotamian Religion* (New Haven: Yale University Press, 1976); *idem, The Harps that Once . . . : Sumerian Poetry in Translation* (New Haven: Yale University Press, 1987); Samuel N. Kramer, *The Sumerians: Their History, Culture, and Character* (Chicago: University of Chicago Press, 1963), 112–64; *idem, Sumerian Mythology: A Study of Spiritual and Literary Achievement in the*

Third Millennium B.C., rev. ed. (Westport, Conn.: Greenwood Press, 1972); *idem, From the Poetry of Sumer: Creation, Glorification, Adoration* (Berkeley: University of California, 1979); Wilfred G. Lambert, "The Cosmology of Sumer and Babylon," in Blacker and Loewe, eds., *Ancient Cosmologies,* 42–65. Along with the above, for English translations of Mesopotamian texts, see: Stephanie Dalley, *Myths from Mesopotamia: Creation, the Flood, Gilgamesh and Others* (Oxford: Oxford University Press, 1989); Samuel N. Kramer, "Sumerian Myths and Epic Tales," in *ANET,* 37–59; Ephraim A. Speiser, "Akkadian Myths and Epics," in *ANET,* 60–119; A. K. Grayson, "Akkadian Myths and Epics," in *ANETSupp,* 501–18.

7. Important for understanding the nature of pagan religion is Yehezkel Kaufmann's influential "Pagan Religion," in *The Religion of Israel: From Its Beginnings to the Babylonian Exile,* trans. and abr. by M. Greenberg (Chicago: University of Chicago Press, 1960), 21–59. At several points this essay is indebted to Kaufmann's perceptive analysis.

8. According to Henri Frankfort, Egyptian religion consisted of a "multiplicity of questions" and a "multiplicity of answers" (*Ancient Egyptian Religion: An Interpretation* [New York: Harper & Row, 1948], 14–22).

9. The Egyptians believed that creation had a beginning. See Morenz, *Egyptian Religion,* 160–71; Currid, *Ancient Egypt,* 64. *Ma'at* essentially means "truth," "right," and "justice," "righteousness," and "order." *Ma'at* conveys the idea of cosmic or universal order and is the opposite of chaos. See John A. Wilson, *The Culture of Ancient Egypt* (= *The Burden of Egypt*) (Chicago: University of Chicago Press, 1951), 48–49; Morenz, *Egyptian Religion,* 113–26.

10. For discussions on Egyptian cosmology, see Lesko "Egyptian Cosmogonies," 116–22; Wilson, "Egypt," 35–49; Plumley, "Cosmology," 17–41.

11. Each day the sun god traveled during the night through the underworld, leaving the earth in a state of darkness and death. In the morning the sun was born anew from the primeval waters of Nun bringing order and life as it journeyed across the sky. In a hymn the sun is addressed: "Rise, rise, emerge from Nun by being rejuvenated in the condition thou didst find thyself in yesterday" (Morenz, *Egyptian Religion,* 171). The Nile also experienced death and rebirth, but on an annual cycle. Following a season of shrinking waters came the inundation of the Nile, being fed from the primeval waters of Nun. As the waters began to recede, small mounds of mud began to emerge, and as the sun rose anew and shone upon these islands new life sprang forth. For the life-giving significance of the Nile, see the Hymn to the Nile in Wilson, *ANET,* 372–73. Concerning the significance of the sun and the Nile in Egypt, see Wilson, "Egypt," 35–37, 43-44; Frankfort, *Kingship,* 156–59.

12. These peoples and their myths are generally designated as "Sumerian." However, the so-called Sumerians were part of the larger Mesopotamian civilization, so a sharp distinction should not be made between a Sumerian and Akkadian culture. See Clifford, *Creation Accounts,* 14–15; Jerrold S. Cooper, "Sumerian and Akkadian in Sumer and Akkad," *Or* 42 (1973): 239–46; G. S. Kirk, *Myth: Its Meaning and Function in Ancient and Other Cultures* (Berkeley: University of California, 1970), 85–86.

13. Kramer, *Sumerian Mythology,* vii. Also see Kramer's examination of the "Myths of Origins" (30–75) and his summary of Sumerian cosmology and cosmogony (viii-xvii). See also, Kramer, *Poetry of Sumer,* 20–49; Thorkild Jacobsen, "Sumerian Mythology: A Review Article," *JNES* 5 (1946): 128–52 (and in *Image of Tammuz,* 104–31); *idem,* "Mesopotamia," 152–65; Clifford, *Creation Accounts,* 13–53.

14. Although Enûma Elish is concerned with cosmogony, the story is primarily devoted to legitimizing Marduk as the supreme god of the Babylonian pantheon (so Heidel, *Babylonian Genesis,* 11). Jacobsen summarizes the objectives of Enûma Elish by writing: "It is a mythopoeic adumbration of Babylon's and Marduk's rise to rulership over a united Babylo-

nia, but projected back to mythical times and made universal. It is also an account of how the universe is ruled; how monarchy evolved and gained acceptance as a unifier of the many divine wills in the universe. It is a story of world origins and world ordering" (*Treasures,* 191; see also Jacobsen, "Mesopotamia," 168–69).

15. According to W. Lambert this cosmological conception is the Sumerian view that "goes back in Mesopotamia to at least 3,000 B.C. It continued virtually unchanged until the end of Babylonian civilization" ("Cosmology," 48–49).

16. The following is based on Jacobsen, "Mesopotamia," 130–50.

17. On these four gods and the other gods who made up the assembly, see further Jacobsen, *Treasures,* 95–143.

18. According to Jacobsen, this worldview "took shape . . . in the Proto-literate period, around the middle of the fourth millennium B.C." ("Mesopotamia," 128). See further, Thorkild Jacobsen, "Primitive Democracy in Ancient Mesopotamia," *JNES* 2 (1943): 159–72 (and in *Image of Tammuz,* 157–72).

19. Kaufmann, *Religion,* 24.

20. See Erik Hornung's insightful analysis of the Egyptian understanding of "nonexistence" in *Conceptions of God in Ancient Egypt: The One and the Many,* trans. J. Baines (Ithaca: Cornell University Press, 1971), 166–96, cf. 172–85; also see the summary of Hornung's presentation in Clifford, *Creation Accounts,* 101–4.

21. Translation by Lichtheim, *AEL* 1:47. Similarly, Pyramid Text, Utterance 71 reads: "The King was fashioned by his father Atum [sun god of Heliopolis] before the sky existed, before earth existed, before men existed, before the gods were born, before death existed" (translation by Faulkner, *Pyramid Texts,* Utterance 571[§1466]).

22. The Ogdoad (group of eight) consisted of four couples, gods and goddesses, each representing a particular quality of chaos. The Ogdoad included: Nun and Naunet, "the primeval waters"; Huh and Hauhet, "formlessness"; Kuk and Kauket, "darkness"; and Amun/Amon and Amaunet, "hiddenness." For texts concerning the Ogdoad, see in particular Pyramid Text, Utterance 301, and Coffin Text, Spell 76. For discussions on the Ogdoad, see Frankfort, *Kingship,* 154–56; Lesko, "Egyptian Cosmogonies," 94–95; Morenz, *Egyptian Religion,* 174–77; Wilson, "Egypt," 51–52.

23. For Heidel, Mummu is a third deity representing "mist rising from the two bodies of water and hovering over them" (*Babylonian Genesis,* 3; see also Alexander Heidel, "The Meaning of *Mummu* in Akkadian Literature," *JNES* 7 [1948]: 98–105). In contrast, Speiser simply transliterates the term because the term is "perhaps an epithet in the sense of 'mother'" (*ANET,* 61 n2). Similarly, Jacobsen considers the term *mummu* as an epithet for Tiamat and translates: "and the *matrix,* Tiamat—she who gave birth to them all" (*Treasures,* 168). According to the editors of *CAD, mummu* should be taken as an epithet for Tiamat translated as "crafts[wo]man" or "creator" (*Assyrian Dictionary,* ed. Miguel Civil et al. [Chicago: Oriental Institute, 1977], 10:197).

24. Translation by Speiser, *ANET,* 61. Unless indicated, the following excerpts from Enûma Elish will be taken from Speiser's translation in *ANET,* 60–72. Concerning lines 1–9, see further M. Held, "Two Philological Notes on Enuma elis," *Kramer Anniversary Volume: Cuneiform Studies in Honor of Samuel N. Kramer,* ed. Barry L. Eichler (Verlag Butzon & Bercker Kevelaer, 1976), 23–29.

25. In a bilingual story known as the Chaldean Cosmogony and the Foundation of Eridu there are many similar ideas as that of Enûma Elish. According to this myth, precreation is depicted as a period before temples and cities had come into being and all the lands were sea. For translations of the story, see Heidel, *Babylonian Genesis,* 61–63; Clifford, *Creation Accounts,* 62–65.

26. According to the Sumerian texts, it is typically the primeval sea from which creation originated. According to Kramer, "The Sumerian sages looked upon the primeval sea as a kind of first cause and prime mover, never asking themselves what preceded it in time and space" (*Sumerian Mythology,* viii). According to Lambert, the primeval sea was personified by Nammu, "Mother who gave birth to Heaven and Earth" and the "mother of Enki/Ea"; and in Enûma Elish Nammu is replaced by the pair Apsu and Tiamat ("Cosmology," 53–55).

27. See Hornung, *Conceptions,* 150.

28. See Pyramid Text, Utterance 587 (§1587) and Coffin Text, Spell 714.

29. See Hornung, *Conceptions,* 176.

30. See Coffin Text, Spell 80 (II:32–34).

31. For further discussion on the significance of the primeval hill, see Frankfort, *Kingship,* 151–54; Wilson, "Egypt," 50–51.

32. Translation by Lesko, "Egyptian Cosmogonies," 92. This method of creating by "spitting out" can also be seen in Coffin Text, Spell 76 (II:3–4). It is quite possible that Atum was also identified as the primeval hill as his name is "High Ground" or "High Hill" in Pyramid Text, Utterance 587 (§1587); so R. T. Rundle Clark, *Myth and Symbol in Ancient Egypt* (London: Thames and Hudson, 1959), 37–38; Plumley, "Cosmology," 28.

33. For discussions on the Ennead, see Frankfort, *Kingship,* 182–83; Lesko, "Egyptian Cosmogonies," 92–94; Wilson, "Egypt," 52–54.

34. For a detailed discussion concerning ancient Egyptian theogony, see Hornung, *Conceptions,* 143–51, 217–23. Also see Frankfort, *Kingship,* 182–83; Lesko, "Egyptian Cosmogonies," 92–94; Morenz, *Egyptian Religion,* 162–63; Wilson, "Egypt," 52–54.

35. Utterance 527 of the Pyramid Texts reads: "Atum is he who (once) came into being, who masturbated in On [Heliopolis]. He took his phallus in his grasp that he might create orgasm by means of it, and so were born the twins Shu and Tefenet" (translation by Faulkner, *Pyramid Texts,* 198 [§1248]). Coffin Text, Spell 245 (III:335) presents the creator god creating by both his mouth and masturbation.

36. Shu states that "Atum spat me out in the spittle of his mouth together with my sister Tefenet" (translation by Faulkner, *Coffin Texts,* 77–78 [II:4]).

37. Jacobsen suggests that Lahmu and Lahamu represent the silt that had formed in the primeval ocean (*Treasures,* 168). In contrast, W. Lambert proposes that the two gods had a function like Atlas, since they were pillars holding up the universe ("The Pair Lahmu-Lahamu in Cosmology," *Or* 54 [1985]: 189–202).

38. A Late Babylonian theogony from the city of Dunnu ("Theogony of Dunnu") presents creation beginning with a primeval pair: the Plough and the Earth. This couple are identified as the originators of creation who create the city of Dunnu and also procreate the Sea. For translations, see Dalley, *Myths,* 278–81; Grayson, *ANET,* 517–18; Wilfred G. Lambert and P. Walcot, "A New Babylonian Theogony and Hesiod," *Kadmos* 4 (1965): 64–72.

39. See Hornung, *Conceptions,* 147–48, 163–64; Morenz, *Egyptian Religion,* 25–26, 147–48, 169; Wilson, "Egypt," 50.

40. See Hornung, *Conceptions,* 295–97.

41. See the Shabaka Stone as translated by Wilson, *ANET,* 5. For extended discussions of the Memphite theology, see Allen, *Genesis,* 43–46; Frankfort, *Kingship,* 24–35; Wilson, "Egypt," 55–59.

42. Much of the following is indebted to Jacobsen's analysis in *Treasures,* 167–91.

43. See Tablet II:120–29.

44. See Tablet III:133–39.

45. See Tablet IV:21–28.

46. On Marduk's forming of the heavens and earth, see Tablet IV:130–V:67 (for translations, see Speiser, *ANET,* 67–68; Grayson, *ANET,* 501–2; Dalley, *Myths,* 254–57).

47. Hornung comments that the term "magic" (*ḥk*) parallels the term "power" (*ʾt*) in certain texts (*Conceptions,* 208; see Pyramid Text, Utterance 474 [§941] and Coffin Text, Spell 316 [IV:98–99]). For a concise list of the multiple uses of Egyptian magic, see J. A. Scurlock, "Magic (ANE)," *ABD* 4:466; see further John Baines, "Society, Morality, and Religious Practice," in *Religion in Ancient Egypt: Gods, Myths, and Personal Practice,* ed. B. E. Shafer (Ithaca: Cornell University Press, 1991), 164–72; J. F. Borghouts, *Ancient Egyptian Magical Texts* (Leiden: Brill, 1978); *idem,* "Magie," in *Lexikon der Ägyptologie* 3:1137–51; E. A. Wallis Budge, *Amulets and Talismans* (New Hyde Park, N.Y.: University Books, 1961), 133–76; Hornung, *Conceptions,* 209–11; Robert K. Ritner, "Magic," *OEAE* 2:321–36; Wilson, *ANET,* 6–7, 12–14.

48. Raymond O. Faulkner, "The Teaching for Merikare," in *The Literature of Ancient Egypt: An Anthology of Stories, Instructions, and Poetry,* ed. William K. Simpson (New Haven: Yale University Press, 1972), 191.

49. See Coffin Text, Spell 261 (particularly see the translation in Clark, *Myth and Symbol,* 77–78). See further, Hornung, *Conceptions,* 208; Baines, "Society," 165.

50. See Coffin Text, Spell 714; and Hornung, *Conceptions,* 208.

51. Hornung, *Conceptions,* 208. Hornung further writes: "The creator god has at his disposal three special powers that help him to plan and execute his work of creation: Sia, 'percipience' in planning the work; Hu, creative 'utterance'; Hike, the 'magic' that brings the world into being out of the creative word" (*Conceptions,* 76).

52. Ibid., 76. Cf. Coffin Text, Spell 1130 (VII:465–66) (translation in Faulkner, *Coffin Texts,* III:167–68).

53. See Hornung, *Conceptions,* 209.

54. See J. A. Scurlock, "Magic (ANE)," *ABD* 4:465; Budge, *Amulets and Talismans,* 84–126; A. Sachs, *ANET,* 335–38; Tzvi Abusch and Karel van der Toorn, eds., *Mesopotamian Magic: Textual, Historical, and Interpretive Perspectives* (Groningen: STYX, 1999).

55. Concerning Egyptian mythology Brandon states: "The most remarkable omission from this cosmogonic pattern is the creation of mankind" (*Creation Legends,* 56).

56. Wilson, "Egypt," 65, 66.

57. Translation by Faulkner, *Coffin Texts,* III: 167 (VII: 465).

58. Translation by Foster, *Hymns,* 109.

59. Faulkner, "Merikare," 191.

60. The teacher Ani of the end of the Eighteenth Dynasty writes, "Men are the equals of god (because of) their custom of listening to a man who brings a plea. Not only the wise man is his equal, as if the rest (were) so many cattle." "Thus," according to Hornung, "all men may be god's children from birth (Merikare), or may prove by their actions that they are images of god; the man with knowledge is also said elsewhere to be a 'likeness of god' and sons 'images' of their fathers; in these cases what is meant is not a simple similarity but a fundamental kinship of action, nature, and rank" (*Conceptions,* 138; see also Wilson, "Egypt," 55).

61. See Tablet VI:1–39.

62. For translations, see Dalley, *Myths,* 15–16; Speiser, *ANET,* 99–100, and for a complete translation of the epic, see Wilfred G. Lambert and A. R. Millard, *Atra-Hasis: The Babylonian Story of the Flood* (Oxford: Clarendon Press, 1969). For commentary, see Jacobsen, *Treasures,* 116–21; William L. Moran, "The Creation of Man in Atrahsis I:192–248,"

BASOR 200 (1970): 48–56; *idem,* "Atrahasis: The Babylonian Story of the Flood," *Bib* 52 (1971): 51–61; *idem,* "Some Considerations of Form and Interpretation in Atra-Hasis," in *Language, Literature, and History: Philological and Historical Studies Presented to Erica Reiner,* ed. F. Rochberg-Halton (AOS Monograph 67; Winona Lake, Ind.: Eisenbrauns, 1987), 245–55; Anne D. Kilmer, "The Mesopotamian Concept of Overpopulation and its Solution as Reflected in the Mythology," *Or* 41 (1972): 160–77.

63. A brief anomaly in Egyptian polytheism occurred during the middle of the fourteenth century B.C.E. Pharaoh Amenophis/Amenhotep IV, who changed his name to Akhenaten, step by step strategically replaced Amun with a different sun god, Aten. Akhenaten initially attempted to establish his sun god as the head of the pantheon, but subsequently tried to eliminate all the other Egyptian gods by instituting Aten as the one "sole god, beside whom there is no other" (Hymn to Aten). However, it is not conclusive whether the traditional gods were no longer thought to exist or if they were simply not mentioned (Hornung, *Conceptions,* 248–50; Baines, "Society," 188). Furthermore, the goddess Ma'at was tolerated throughout Akhenaten's reign (David P. Silverman, "Divinity and Deities in Ancient Egypt," in *Religion in Ancient Egypt: Gods, Myths, and Personal Practice,* ed. B. E. Shafer [Ithaca: Cornell University Press, 1991], 82). Additionally, amulets and other objects bearing images of the traditional pantheon from the period suggest that even followers of Akhenaten did not fully abandon their traditional beliefs (Silverman, "Divinity," 87). Despite his extensive efforts, Akhenaten's program did not endure beyond his reign. In fact, following the death of Akhenaten, the first step taken was the restoration of the traditional gods to their original positions. For further discussion on Akhenaten and Aten, see Hornung, *Conceptions,* 244–50; *idem, Akhenaten and the Religion of Light,* trans. D. Lorton (Ithaca: Cornell University Press, 1999); William J. Murnane, *Texts from the Amarna Period in Egypt* (SBLWAW 5; Atlanta: Scholars Press, 1995); Donald B. Redford, *Akhenaten: The Heretic King* (Princeton: Princeton University Press, 1984); Silverman, "Divinity," 75–87. For the creative work of Aten, see Akhenton's Hymn to Aten in Foster, *Hymns,* §45; Lichtheim, *Literature,* 2:96–100; and Wilson, *ANET,* 369–71.

64. Amun was originally the god of Thebes and "the hidden one" of the Ogdoad. Coalesced with the sun god Rê, Amun-Rê is elevated to the creator god and the "king of the gods" of the Egyptian pantheon during the Middle Kingdom and throughout most of the rest of ancient Egyptian history. For hymns concerning Amun-Rê, see Allen, *Genesis,* 48–55; Foster, *Hymns,* 55–79.

65. Regarding this phenomenon in Egypt, see Hornung, *Conceptions,* 217–50 (cf. 230–37), and Morenz, *Egyptian Religion,* 149–50. Concerning Mesopotamia, see in particular Thorkild Jacobsen, "Mesopotamian Gods and Pantheons" and "Ancient Mesopotamian Religion: The Central Concerns," in *Image of Tammuz,* 16–38, 39–47; Wilfred G. Lambert, "The Historical Development of the Mesopotamian Pantheon: A Study in Sophisticated Polytheism," in *Unity and Diversity: Essays in the History, Literature, and Religion of the Ancient Near East,* ed. H. Goedicke and J. J. M. Roberts (Baltimore: John Hopkins University Press, 1975), 191–99. This is also true of the Canaanite religion wherein El is considered the high god of the pantheon and as with the Mesopotamian and Egyptian religions "Canaanite religion in all its manifestations was always polytheistic" (J. Day, "Canaan, Religion of," *ABD* 1:831).

66. This is also true of the Canaanite pantheon. According to Frank M. Cross, in the myths concerning the Canaanite religion, El is identified as the creator, and creation is perceived as theogony (*Canaanite Myth and Hebrew Epic: Essays in the History of the Religion of Israel* [Cambridge: Harvard University Press], 43; so also Pope, *El,* 49–50). Hence, El is often identified as

the "father of the gods." However, El is not without origin. In discussing the Canaanite pantheon, Michael D. Coogan writes: "The head of the pantheon was El, as his epithets 'the King' and 'the Father of the Gods' indicate. In the lists of deities and of the offerings made to them, El generally precedes the other major gods, although he himself can be preceded by 'the older gods,' the generation of predecessors he had presumably supplanted before the period of Ugarit's zenith" (*Stories from Ancient Canaan* [Louisville: Westminster, 1978], 12; see also F. M. Cross, "'The Olden Gods' and Ancient Near Eastern Creation Myths," in *Magnalia Dei: The Mighty Acts of God: Essays on the Bible and Archeology in Memory of G. Ernest Wright*, ed. Frank M. Cross et al. [Garden City, N.Y.: Doubleday, 1976], 329–38).

67. Kaufmann, *Religion*, 21–22.

68. Kaufmann, "The Biblical Age," in *Great Ages and Ideas of the Jewish People*, ed. Leo W. Schwartz (New York: Random House, 1956), 9; see further Kaufmann, *Religion*, 40–42.

69. Kaufmann, *Religion*, 36. The notion of deification or *theôsis* found in the writings of the early church fathers and many Christian theologians since is predicated on precisely the opposite belief. Axiomatic to these writers is the idea that God and humanity are two different kinds of being—eternal and uncreated versus finite and created. Thus, the notion found within Christianity is at a fundamental level radically different from the pagan notion. This is clearly seen in that the Christian notion is focused on becoming like God through union with God (or Christ, the God-man). It is only through such a union that a human can possess any of the divine qualities such as immortality, glory, and incorruptibility. The pagan notion is not a union with a unique creator God but the exaltation or lifting up of a human to the level and status of the gods. I owe this point to Carl Mosser.

70. However, until recently Old Testament scholarship assumed creation theology in the Old Testament to be secondary at best. This was primarily derived from Gerhard von Rad's influential article wherein he concluded that "in genuinely Yahwistic belief the doctrine of creation never attained to the stature of a relevant independent doctrine. We found it invariably related, and indeed subordinated, to soteriological considerations" ("The Theological Problem of the Old Testament Doctrine of Creation," in *The Problem of the Hexateuch*, trans. E. W. T. Dicken [Edinburgh: Oliver & Boyd, 1965], 142). Such an understanding, however, can no longer be sustained as the following studies demonstrate: Walter Brueggemann, "The Loss and Recovery of Creation in Old Testament Theology," *ThTo* 53 (1996): 177–90; H. H. Schmid, "Creation, Righteousness, and Salvation: 'Creation Theology' as the Broad Horizon of Biblical Theology," in *Creation in the Old Testament*, ed. Bernhard W. Anderson (Philadelphia: Fortress, 1984), 102–117; Rolf P. Knierim, "Cosmos and History in Israel's Theology," *HBT* 3 (1981): 59–123 [repr. in *The Task of Old Testament Theology: Substance, Method, and Cases* [Grand Rapids: Eerdmans, 1995], 171–224); Claus Westermann, *Creation* (Philadelphia: Fortress, 1974); *idem, Elements of Old Testament Theology,* trans. D. W. Stott (Atlanta: John Knox, 1978).

71. The quotations from Scripture in this chapter are the author's own translation.

72. Scholars have recognized for a long time that creation *ex nihilo* is clearly implied in these texts. See, for example, Walther Eichrodt, *Theology of the Old Testament*, trans. J. A. Baker (OTL; Philadelphia: Westminster, 1961, 1967), 2:101–6; John E. Hartley, *Genesis* (NIBCOT 1; Peabody, Mass.: Hendrickson, 2000), 42; N. H. Ridderbos, "Genesis I 1 and 2," in *Studies in the Book of Genesis* (OTS 12; Leiden: Brill, 1958), 257; Gordon J. Wenham, *Genesis 1–15* (WBC 1; Waco: Word, 1987), 14.

73. See also Patrick D. Miller, "The Poetry of Creation: Psalm 104," in *God Who Creates: Essays in Honor of W. Sibley Towner*, ed. William P. Brown and S. D. McBride (Grand Rapids: Eerdmans, 2000), 90–91.

74. On the translation here, see Cleon Z. Rogers III, "The Meaning and Significance of the Hebrew Word אָמוֹן in Proverbs 8,30," *ZAW* 109 (1997): 208–21; Roland E. Murphy, *Proverbs* (WBC 22; Nashville: Thomas Nelson, 1998), 48 n30a.

75. See Gerhard F. Hasel, "The Significance of the Cosmology in Genesis 1 in Relation to Ancient Near Eastern Parallels," *AUSS* 10 (1972): 1–20; *idem,* "The Polemic Nature of the Genesis Cosmology," *EvQ* 46 (1974): 81–102; Currid, *Ancient Egypt,* 27–32; Wenham, *Genesis 1–15,* 1–40.

76. Some have thought that Genesis 1:1–2:4a is dependent on Enûma Elish (e.g., Hermann Gunkel, "The Influence of Babylonian Mythology Upon the Biblical Creation Story," in Anderson, *Creation in the Old Testament,* 25–52; Heidel, *Babylonian Genesis,* 128–40; E. A. Speiser, *Genesis* [AB 1; Garden City, N.Y.: Doubleday, 1964], 9–10). However, other scholars have shown that this is highly unlikely (see Wilfred G. Lambert, "A New Look at the Babylonian Background of Genesis," *JTS* 16 [1965]: 287–300; Clifford, *Creation Accounts,* 138–44). It cannot be denied that there are parallel thoughts between the two cosmogonies, but there are also parallels with Egyptian cosmogonies (see Currid, *Ancient Egypt,* 53–73; James K. Hoffmeier, "Some Thoughts on Genesis 1 and 2 and Egyptian Cosmology," *JANES* 15 [1983]: 39–49).

77. Hartley *Genesis,* 42.

78. Claus Westermann, *Genesis 1–11: A Continental Commentary,* trans. J. J. Scullion (Minneapolis: Fortress, 1984), 94, 97; Hartley, *Genesis,* 49. Concerning the various syntactical difficulties of Genesis 1:1–2 and exegetically substantiating the translation of verse 1 as "In *the* beginning God created the heavens and earth," see Walther Eichrodt, "In the Beginning: A Contribution to the Interpretation of the First Word of the Bible," in *Israel's Prophetic Heritage: Essays in Honor of J. Muilenburg,* ed. Bernhard W. Anderson and W. Harrelson (New York: Harper & Row, 1962), 1–10 [repr. in Anderson, *Creation in the Old Testament,* 65–73]; Hartley, *Genesis,* 40–42; Bruce K. Waltke, "The Creation Account in Gen 1:1–3 [In Five Parts]," *BSac* 132 (1975): 25–36, 136–44, 216–28, 327–42; vol. 133 (1976): 28–41; Wenham, *Genesis 1–15,* 11–13; Westermann, *Genesis 1–11,* 93–97.

79. Westermann, *Genesis 1–11,* 108–9; see also Gerhard von Rad, *Genesis,* rev. ed. (OTL; Philadelphia: Westminster, 1972), 49, 51.

80. Discussing Proverbs 8, John Goldingay writes, "Proverbs 8 takes us back to the time when there were no depths and no springs abounding with water issuing from the depths. There is no indication in Genesis 1 that God started from scratch in creating the world. Genesis presupposes the existence of the raw material for creation. It is not concerned with the question of the origin of this raw material. But Proverbs 8 does go behind that. Its concern, of course, no more corresponds to ours than Genesis's concern does. It wants to glorify wisdom. But its concern to do that happens to generate an assertion that satisfies the modern interest in where the raw material came from. Unlike the Babylonian creation story *When On High* (=Enûma Elish), it thinks back to a time when there was no matter, no raw material out of which the world might be created, and it then declares that God's being antedates that—rather than postdating it, like the Babylonian gods" ("Writing an Old Testament Theology," paper presented to the Old Testament Colloquium at Fuller Theological Seminary, Pasadena, Calif., 8 November 2000, 9).

81. In examining this phrase in the Psalms, James L. Mays writes, "The contexts in which the phrase appears show that its purpose is to identify Yahweh as the deity who *can* help and bless the people of the Lord because of Yahweh's power as creator of all that is" ("'Maker of Heaven and Earth': Creation in the Psalms," in *God Who Creates,* 76).

82. So Wenham, *Genesis 1–15, 19*; Westermann, *Genesis 1–11,* 114–15.

83. The two large luminaries are not mentioned by name and are obviously the "sun" and the "moon." This is most likely due to the overall polemical nature of the narrative. The sun and the moon, along with the stars, are not gods as Israel's neighbors would claim; they are created matter. See Hasel, "Polemical Nature," 88–89; *idem,* "Significance of the Cosmology," 12–15; Wenham, *Genesis 1–15,* 21–22.

84. The phrase "you are the God, you alone" is also found in 2 Kings 19:15 (also see v. 19).

85. See Ben C. Ollenburger, "Isaiah's Creation Theology," *Ex Auditu* 3 (1987): 56–63; *idem, Zion, the City of the Great King* (JSOTSup 41; Sheffield: Sheffield Academic Press, 1987).

86. The biblical text assumes that the plagues were divine interventions by God and not due to natural disasters (cf. Ex 8:19). For discussions on the issues, see Currid, *Ancient Egypt,* 108–20; James K. Hoffmeier, "Egypt, Plagues in," *ABD* 2:374–76; *idem, Israel in Egypt: The Evidence for the Authenticity of the Exodus Tradition* (New York: Oxford University Press, 1996), 144–55.

87. See Hornung, *Conceptions,* 139–40.

88. Egyptologists debate the divinity of the king. For an excellent discussion of the issues with a balanced assessment concluding that the king should be considered divine, see D. Silverman, "Divinity," 58–87. Concerning the concept of Egyptian kingship, see John Baines, "Ancient Egyptian Kingship: Officials, Forms, Rhetoric, Context," in *King and Messiah in Israel and the Ancient Near East,* ed. John Day (JSOTSup 270; Sheffield: Sheffield Academic Press, 1998), 16–53; Marie-Ange Bonhême, "Kingship," in *OEAE* 2:238–45; Frankfort, *Kingship,* 36–47; Hornung, *Conceptions,* 135–42; D. O'Connor and D. P. Silverman, eds., *Ancient Egyptian Kingship* (Probleme der Ägyptologie 9; Leiden: Brill, 1995).

89. In the event of the death of a pharaoh and until the installment of a new king, the land was thought to be in chaos. For instance, in the Prophecy of Neferti, there is no king in Egypt, so the land is in chaos; but with the installation of a new king there is the hopeful promise of *ma'at:* "Re should begin to recreate. The land is quite perished, no remnant is left, not the black of a nail is spared from its fate. (Yet) while the land suffers, none care for it, none speak, none shed tears: 'How fares this land!' The sundisk, covered, shines not for the people to see, one cannot live when clouds conceal, all are numb from lack of it. . . . The land is bowed down in distress, owing to those feeders, Asiatics who roam the land. Foes have arisen in the East, Asiatics have come down to Egypt. . . . Re will withdraw from mankind: though he will rise at his hour, one will not know when noon has come; no one will discern his shadow, no face will be dazzled by seeing [him], no eyes will moisten with water. He will be in the sky like the moon, his nightly course unchanged, his rays on the face as before. . . . Then a king will come from the South, Ameny, the justified, by name. . . . Then Order (*ma'at*) will return to its seat, while Chaos is driven away" (trans. by Lichtheim, *AEL,* 1:141–44; for other translations, see Wilson, *ANET,* 444–46; Raymond O. Faulkner, "The Prophecies of Neferti," in *The Literature of Ancient Egypt: An Anthology of Stories, Instructions, and Poetry,* ed. W. K. Simpson [New Haven: Yale University Press, 1972], 234–40). Concerning the king and *ma'at,* see Currid, *Ancient Egypt,* 118–20; Frankfort, *Kingship,* 51–60, 105–9, 148–51; Hoffmeier, *Israel in Egypt,* 149–55; Wilson, "Egypt," 71–86.

90. At his coronation during the Sed Festival, the Pharaoh was crowned with a Red Crown, representing Lower Egypt, and a White Crown, representing Upper Egypt. Immanent within these two crowns were two tutelary goddesses of the respective shrines of Lower and Upper Egypt, Wadjet the cobra and Nekhbet the vulture. In the Pyramid Texts,

Utterances 220 and 221 a presentation of the coronation is depicted but only involving the Red Crown of Lower Egypt. The crown is addressed as a goddess identified as the "Magician" and is subsequently placed on the king, endowing him with the power of the throne of Egypt. See Frankfort, *Kingship*, 107–9; Hornung, *Conceptions*, 209; Wilson, "Egypt," 71–74.

91. For discussions on the plagues as a direct challenge of the Egyptian king, see James K. Hoffmeier, "The Arm of God Versus the Arm of Pharaoh in the Exodus Narratives," *Bib* 67 (1986): 378–87; *idem*, "Egypt, Plagues in," 376–77; *idem*, *Israel in Egypt*, 149–55; R. Stieglitz, "Ancient Records and the Plagues of Egypt," *BAR* 13 (1987): 46–49.

92. The first two plagues were duplicated by Pharaoh's magicians. However, they could not reverse the plagues, and ironically, they actually made the conditions in Egypt worse.

93. See Terence E. Fretheim, "The Plagues as Ecological Signs of Historical Disaster," *JBL* 110 (1991): 392–94; *idem*, *Exodus* (Interpretation; Louisville: John Knox Press, 1991), 105–112. Cf. Currid, *Ancient Egypt*, 113–20.

94. There has been some debate among scholars about whether *ruah* ("spirit," "wind," "breath") in Genesis 1:2 should be translated "wind" and thereby thought of as material in nature. If so, the term *'elohim* is a superlative, and taken together, the phrase would be translated "mighty wind" or "great wind." However, it seems inconceivable to conclude that the term *'elohim* is used as a superlative in verse 2, while in verse 1 and the other thirty or so subsequent occurrences, it refers to the Creator-God (so Wenham, *Genesis 1-15*, 17). In addition, anywhere else that *ruah* is coupled with *'elohim* or *yhwh*, the phrase always refers to the Spirit or Wind of God and not the "Great wind." Wenham does translate *ruah 'elohim* as "Wind of God" because the verb *rhp* ("hovering") aptly describes the motion of the wind, and "Wind of God" is "a concrete and vivid image of the Spirit of God. The phrase does really express the powerful presence of God moving mysteriously over the face of the waters" (*Genesis 1–15*, 17). It is clear that the phrase *ruah 'elohim* here is conveying a manifestation of God even if one chose to translate the phrase as Spirit, wind, or breath of God. See further Brevard S. Childs, *Myth and Reality in the Old Testament* (SBT 27; London: SCM Press, 1962), 34–35; M. DeRoche, "The *ruah 'elohim* in Gen 1:2c: Creation or Chaos?" in *Ascribe to the Lord: Biblical and Other Studies in Memory of Peter C. Craigie*, ed. L. Eslinger and G. Taylor (JSOTSup 67; Sheffield: Sheffield Academic Press, 1988), 303–18; R. Luyster, "Wind and Water: Cosmogonic Symbolism in the Old Testament," *ZAW* 93 (1981): 1–10; H. M. Orlinsky, "The Plain Meaning of *Ruah* in Gen 1:2," *JQR* 48 (1957/58): 174–82; Ridderbos, "Genesis I 1 and 2," 241–46.

95. Hartley, *Genesis*, 43.

96. Some scholars claim that the original God of Israel was El and that Deuteronomy 32:6–8 identifies Yahweh as a son of El (here Elyon) and a member of the Canaanite pantheon (e.g., Mark S. Smith, *The Early History of God: Yahweh and the Other Deities in Ancient Israel* [New York: Harper & Row, 1990], 7; Peter Hayman, "Monotheism—A Misused Word in Jewish Studies?" *JJS* [1991]: 6). Several things render this hypothesis implausible. Not the least of the reasons is that the entire song refers to Yahweh (32:1–43) and that the immediate context directly speaks of Yahweh (v. 6). Thus, it is simply impossible to make a definitive distinction in this passage between Yahweh and Elyon. As Christopher Wright correctly states: "Yahweh, of course, is synonymous with Elyon here. There is no possibility that Yahweh is simply one of the 'sons of the gods' to whom nations are allocated. The point is that the one and only God, known to Israel as Yahweh, is the same Most High God ["Elyon"] who is sovereign among the nations of humanity" (*Deuteronomy* [NIBCOT 4; Peabody, Mass.: Hendrickson, 1996], 300). Furthermore, in the Old Testament the name

Elyon is a typical epithet used for Yahweh. As Frank M. Cross concludes, "El [and its own epithets, including Elyon] is rarely if ever used in the Bible as the proper name of a non-Israelite, Canaanite deity in the full consciousness of a distinction between El and Yahweh, god of Israel" (*Canaanite Myth and Hebrew Epic,* 44). See further 44–60; and *idem,* "אֵל *ʾēl*" *TDOT* 1:242–61.

97. Much scholarly attention has been given to the biblical references to the "asherah" (e.g., Ex 34:13; Deut 7:5–6; 12:3; 16:21–22; Judg 3:7; 6:25–26, 28, 30; 1 Kgs 14:15–16, 23; 15:12–13; 16:32–33; 18:19; 2 Kgs 13:6; 17:10, 16; 18:4; 21:3, 7; 23:4, 6, 7, 15; 2 Chr 24:18; Isa 17:8; 27:9; Jer 17:2; Mic 5:13) and the Hebrew inscriptions found in Kuntillet ʾAjrud and Khirbet el-Qom containing the phrase "Yahweh and his asherah" (see John Day, "Asherah in the Hebrew Bible and Northwest Semitic Literature," *JBL* 105 [1986]: 385–408). Some scholars claim that such references indicate that Yahweh had a consort, the goddess Asherah, who is identified as the consort of El in the Ugaritic texts (e.g., William G. Dever, "Asherah, Consort of Yahweh? New Evidence from Kuntillet ʾAjrud," *BASOR* 255 [1984]: 21–37; David N. Freedman, "Yahweh of Samaria and His Asherah," *BA* 50 [1987]: 241–49; Ruth Hestrin, "Understanding Asherah: Exploring Semitic Iconography," *BAR* 17 [Sept/Oct 1991]: 50–59; Saul Olyan, *Asherah and the Cult of Yahweh in Israel* [SBLMS 34; Atlanta: Scholars Press, 1988]). However, there is no evidence in the biblical texts or in the inscriptions that reference is being made to the goddess herself. Furthermore, where the worship of any other god apart from Yahweh is acknowledged, the Old Testament consistently condemns such activity, the asherah being no exception (see esp. Othmar Keel and Christoph Uehlinger, *Gods, Goddesses, and Images of God in Ancient Israel,* trans. T. H. Trapp [Minneapolis: Fortress, 1998], 177–281; Bernhard Lang, *Monotheism and the Prophetic Minority: An Essay in Biblical History and Sociology* [Sheffield: Almond, 1983], 39–40; André Lemaire, "Who or What was Yahweh's Asherah?" *BAR* 10 [1984]: 42–51; Patrick D. Miller, "The Absence of the Goddess in Israelite Religion," *HAR* 10 [1986]: 239–48; *idem, The Religion of Ancient Israel* [Louisville: Westminster John Knox, 2000], 29–45, 51–52; M. Smith, *The Early History of God,* 80–114; Jeffrey H. Tigay, "Israelite Religion: The Onomastic and Epigraphic Evidence," in *Ancient Israelite Religion: Essays in Honor of Frank Moore Cross,* ed. Patrick D. Miller et al. [Philadelphia: Fortress Press, 1987], 172–76; *idem, You Shall Have No Other Gods: Israelite Religion in Light of Hebrew Inscriptions* [HSS 31; Atlanta: Scholars Press, 1986], 26–30).

98. Kaufmann, *Religion,* 68.

99. See F. M. Cross, "The Council of Yahweh in Second Isaiah," *JNES* 12 (1953): 274–77; *idem, Canaanite Myth,* 186–90; E. G. Kingsbury, "The Prophets and the Council of Yahweh," *JBL* 83 (1964): 279–86; P. D. Miller, "The Prophets and the Council of Yahweh," *JBL* 83 (1964): 279–86; *idem,* "Cosmology and World Order in the Old Testament: The Divine Council as Cosmic-Political Symbol" *HBT* 9 (1987): 53–78; H. W. Robinson, "The Council of Yahweh," *JTS* 45 (1944): 151–57; C. R. Seitz, "The Divine Council: Temporal Transition and New Prophecy in the Book of Isaiah," *JBL* 109 (1990): 229–47.

100. See Miller, *Religion of Ancient Israel,* 27.

101. Those explicitly identified as members of Yahweh's council are referred to as "sons of God" (Job 1:6; 2:1; Ps. 89:6b); "holy ones" (Ps 89:5b, 7a); "host of the heavens" (1 Kgs 22:19–21, in which a member is identified as a "spirit" [v. 21]); or simply "the ones standing before him [Yahweh]" (Zech 3:4, 7). The only clear reference to Yahweh's council being identified as "gods" is Psalm 82; however, this psalm is being used as a polemic against the gods of Israel's neighbors (see below).

102. The plural "Let us," could be a reference to the council of God, the plurality of God himself, or simply a plural of deliberation (see Wenham, *Genesis 1–15,* 27–28; Westermann, *Genesis 1–11,* 144–45).

103. There is an obvious wordplay between "the man" and "the ground," emphasizing the human being's relationship to the earth (so Wenham, *Genesis 1–15,* 59). There are a number of texts that speak of humanity being made of matter (e.g., Gen 3:23; 18:27; Job 10:9; Ps 103:14).

104. For a historical overview of the various interpretations of the "image of God," see David J. A. Clines, "Humanity as the Image of God," in Clines, *On the Way to the Postmodern: Old Testament Essays, 1967–1998.* (JSOTSup 292, 293; Sheffield: JSOT, 1998), 2:448–56 (repr. of "The Image of God in Man," *TB* 19 [1968]: 53–103); and Westermann, *Genesis 1–11,* 147–55.

105. So Westermann, *Genesis 1–11,* 146. The term *tselem* occurs seventeen times in the Old Testament, and its predominant uses includes cast figures representing body parts and animals (1 Sam 6:5 [2 x], 11), formed idols or images that represented foreign gods (Num 33:52; 2 Kgs 11:18; 2 Chr 23:17; Ezek 7:20; Amos 5:26), and portraits of male human beings made or drawn to represent abominable cult images (Ezek 16:17) and Babylonian officials (Ezek 23:14).

106. Clines, "Humanity," 475.

107. Clines observes that Numbers 12:8 and Psalm 17:15 speak of a "form" of God, but if these passages are set alongside Isaiah 40:18, one would have to say that the "form" is strictly incomparable and so indescribable ("Humanity," 466). For a brief discussion of the anthropomorphic passages Ezekiel 1:25–28, Daniel 7:9–10, and Exodus 24:10, see Paul Owen and Carl Mosser, review of Craig L. Blomberg and Stephen E. Robinson, *How Wide the Divide? A Mormon and an Evangelical in Conversation* (Downers Grove, Ill.: InterVarsity Press, 1997) in *FARMS Review of Books* 11/2 (1999): 33-36.

108. Clines, "Humanity," 467. See also James Barr, "Theophany and Anthropomorphism," in *Congress Volume Oxford, 1959* (VTSup 7; Leiden: Brill, 1960), 31–38.

109. Clines, "Humanity," 480 (cf. 475–80); Edward M. Curtis, "Image of God (Old Testament)," in *ABD* 3:390–91.

110. See Clines, "Humanity," 480–95. Most scholars agree that humanity in the image of God includes the fact that human beings are God's representatives (e.g., Curtis, "Image of God," 390; Eichrodt, *Theology* 2:127; Hartley, *Genesis,* 47; von Rad, *Genesis,* 59–60; Wenham, *Genesis 1–15,* 31–32; pace Westermann, *Genesis 1–11,* 156–58).

111. On Clines' reading, according to Genesis 1 humanity does not have the image of God, nor is it *in* the image of God, but is itself the image of God ("Humanity," 475). Clines proposes that the phrase "in the image" should be translated "as our image" or "to be our image," taking the preposition *beth* in the sense of a *beth essentiae* meaning "as, in the capacity of" (cf. Ex 6:3) (pp. 470–71). However, Wenham demonstrates that this grammatical proposal is untenable because of the interchangeable use of the prepositions *beth* and *kaf* in Genesis 5:1 and 3, especially in connection with "image" and "likeness." According to Wenham, the *beth* in Genesis 1:26 and 27 means "according to, after the pattern of" (cf. Ex 25:9, 40). The phrase "according to our likeness" therefore appears to be an explanatory gloss indicating the precise sense of "in our image" (Wenham, *Genesis 1–15,* 29). Thus, human beings are made "in the image of God" and thereby bear a similarity to God. Due to this, human beings are God's representatives, God's vice-regents on earth. Yet this merely describes the function or the consequences of the divine image; it does not pinpoint what the image is in itself (p. 32). One must conclude that the most accurate way to translate the phrase is in its

classical and most natural sense of "in the image of God." (Clines also admits that this is the most natural meaning of the phrase, see "Humanity," 465.) Wenham's grammatical correction, however, does not discount Cline's proposals about the use of *tselem,* the ancient cultural understanding of "image," the fact that God has no form, and that humankind is God's representative on earth.

112. Wenham, *Genesis 1–15,* 32. See also Curtis, "Image of God (Old Testament)," 389–90; and John F. A. Sawyer, "The Meaning of בְּצֶלֶים אֱלֹהִים ('In the Image of God') in Genesis I-XI," *JTS* 25 (1974): 418–26.

113. Sawyer notes that the exclusive use of the term *bara'* ("create") reserved for God "together with immortality, which is denied to man in iii. 22, provides hard proof that, whatever else the divine image in man refers to, it does not imply identity" (i.e., humans and God are not the same kind of being) ("Image of God," 424).

114. See C. J. Labuschange, *The Incomparability of Yahweh in the Old Testament* (Leiden: Brill, 1966).

115. In attempting to attain a more exact definition of the idea of "God," Helmer Ringgren examines passages wherein "God" stands in antithesis to something else and notes that "'man' especially appears in antithesis to 'God'" (*TDOT* 1:273–75).

116. See Walther Zimmerli's discussion concerning this passage contrasting Yahweh the creator and the king of Tyre in his *Ezekiel 2: A Commentary on the Book of the Prophet Ezekiel Chapters 25–48,* trans. James D. Martin (Hermenia; Philadelphia: Fortress, 1983), 76–79.

117. John. E. Hartley, *Leviticus* (WBC 4; Dallas: Word, 1992), lvi. Also see Eichrodt, *Theology* 1:273–74.

118. The Hebrew term *qadosh* generally identifies something as "different," "uncommon," "divine," "transcendent," but does not necessarily designate that something is intrinsically moral or ethical. On this point, see Eichrodt, *Theology* 1:270–82; J. Muilenburg, "Holiness," *IDB* 2:616–23; Jackie A. Naudé, "קדשׁ (#7727)," *NIDOTTE* 3:877–87 (cf. 881–83); Th. C. Vriezen, *An Outline of Old Testament Theology,* 2d ed. (Oxford: Blackwell, 1970), 297–311; Gerhard von Rad, *Old Testament Theology,* trans. D. M. G. Stalker (New York: Harper & Row, 1962, 65), 1:204–8. For a classic treatment on holiness, see Rudolf Otto, *The Idea of the Holy,* trans. J. W. Harvey (New York: Oxford University Press, 1958).

119. Hartley, *Leviticus,* lvii. Cf. Eichrodt, *Theology,* 1:270–71.

120. Vriezen, *Outline,* 299.

121. John G. Gammie applies Rudolph Otto's work *The Idea of the Holy* to the great theophany at Sinai recorded in Exodus 19:16-25 and finds in it Otto's five elements of the holy: (1) *awefulness, dread, and wrath:* "And the whole mountain quaked greatly" (v. 18c); "God answered him in the thunder" (v. 19b); "Go down and warn the people . . . lest the LORD break out upon them (vv. 21–22); (2) *majesty and unapproachability:* "Take heed that you do not go up into the mountain or touch the border of it" (v. 12), "lest they break through to the LORD" (v. 21); "The people cannot come up to Mount Sinai" (v. 23); (3) *energy, vitality, and movement:* "The LORD descended upon it in fire; and the smoke went up like the smoke of a kiln" (v. 18ab); (4) *mystery:* "Lo, I am coming to you in a thick cloud" (v. 9a); (5) *fascination:* "Do not let the priests and people break through to come up to the LORD" (v. 24b)" (Gammie, *Holiness in Israel* [OBT; Minneapolis: Fortress, 1989], 5–7).

122. Ringgren, *TDOT* 1:283.

123. On the intricacies of this proof, see Rolf Knierim, "Revelation in the Old Testament," in *Old Testament Theology,* 157–58.

124. Much has been written on Psalm 82. In particular, see Hans-J. Kraus, *Psalms 60–150: A Continental Commentary,* trans. H. C. Oswald (Minneapolis: Fortress, 1989), 153–58; P. D. Miller, *Interpreting the Psalms* (Philadelphia: Fortress, 1989), 120–24; C. H. Gordon, "History of Religion in Psalm 82," in *Biblical and Near Eastern Studies: Essays in Honor of William S. LaSor,* ed. Gary A. Tuttle (Grand Rapids: Eerdmans, 1978), 129–31; James L. Mays, *Psalms* (Interpretation; Louisville: John Knox, 1994), 268–71; J. Morgenstern, "The Mythological Background of Psalm 82," *HUCA* 14 (1939): 29–126; R. T. O'Callaghan, "A Note on the Canaanite Background of Psalm 82," *CBQ* 15 (1953): 311–14; Marvin E. Tate, *Psalms 51–100* (WBC 20; Dallas: Word, 1990), 328–42; M. Tsevat, "Gods and the Gods in the Assembly: An Interpretation of Psalm 82," *HUCA* 40 (1969): 123–37.

125. See Thorkild Jacobsen, "Primitive Democracy in Ancient Mesopotamia," *JNES* 2 (1943): 159–72; idem, *Image of Tammuz,* 157–70; idem, *Treasures,* 86–91; E. Theodore Mullen, *The Assembly of the Gods: The Divine Council in Canaanite and Early Hebrew Literature* (HSM 24; Chico, Calif.: Scholars Press, 1980); idem, "Divine Assembly," *ABD* 2:214–17; D. Neiman, "Council, Heavenly," *IDBSup,* 187–88.

126. Although the psalm uses the epithets El (v. 1) and Elyon (v. 6b), terms that usually designate Yahweh in the Old Testament, there is strong evidence that this psalm is not referring to Yahweh's council. First, as noted above, outside this psalm the explicit members of Yahweh's council are never identified as *'elohim* "gods." In addition, the phrase "sons of Elyon" in verse 6b never refers to the members of Yahweh's council elsewhere in the Old Testament (although Deut 32:8–9 comes close if we are reading the LXX and Qumran texts with the addition of v. 43, but these ideas are not present in the MT), while Elyon is attested as a common epithet applied to various gods in the West Semitic region and is closely linked to the Canaanite god El (see E. E. Elnes and P. D. Miller, "Elyon," *DDD*: 293–99). Second, the term used in verse 1 for "assembly" is *'edah,* which is nowhere else in the Old Testament used to designate Yahweh's council (however, the corresponding Ugaritic term *'dt* is used for the council in Ugaritic texts, e.g., Epic of Kirta, *CAT* 1.15.II.7, 11, see Mullen, *Assembly,* 118–19; idem, "Divine Assembly," *ABD* 2:215). When *'edah* is used in construct with the divine name Yahweh, the phrase is solely reserved to indicate the nation Israel as the congregation of Yahweh (e.g., Num 27:17; 31:16; Josh 22:16–17; Ps 74:2). In the various texts that speak of a council of Yahweh, the terms that are used are *sod* (Ps 89:7a; Jer 23:18, 22) or *qahal* (Ps 89:5b). Further, as Mullen notes, "neither qahal nor sod is attested in Ugaritic as a term designating the assembly of the gods" ("Divine Assembly," 215).

127. This psalm is presented as a polemic against all other gods and perhaps specifically against the Canaanite pantheon. In contrast to texts that speak of Yahweh's council, there is no discussion here about a future action to be taken (e.g., Job 1:6–12; 2:1–6; 1 Kgs 22:19–23). Furthermore, Yahweh invites no discussion and solely makes a decision to condemn the gods. Several features of the assembly in Psalm 82 markedly distinguish it from the divine assemblies of Ugaritic and Mesopotamian literature: The gods are not gathered together, and there is no deliberation going on in this assembly. The gods do not confer authority upon God, nor do they defend themselves or devise a counterattack. There is no conflict over power. In fact, the gods here are represented as powerless and completely subject to the sole decree of God. Writing about Israel's religion and the concept of Yahweh in contrast with the gods of Israel's neighbors, Patrick D. Miller concurs when he states: "Psalm 82 is an explicit and possibly early manifestation of this opposition. While the gods who are gathered in the 'council of El' or 'divine council' (v. 1) are unnamed and do not speak, Yahweh stands up in their midst and condemns them all to death, in effect taking over all power, indeed all claim to deity, in the divine realm" (*Religion of Ancient Israel,* 28).

128. Miller remarks that the description of the powerlessness or incompetence of the gods in v. 5 is presented "in language reminiscent of the description in Isaiah 40–55 of the nothingness of the idols that have no capacity to see or know or discern anything" (*Interpreting*, 121).

129. Mullen, *Assembly,* 237. Also see Tsevat, "Gods in Assembly," 128.

130. There are ANE parallels to gods putting other gods to death for various reasons, as shown above with Kingu in Enûma Elish. However, there is no parallel found where one god announces a group or assembly of gods to death (so Miller, *Interpreting*, 122–23; Tate, *Psalms 51–100,* 338).

131. J. Mays states that: "This portrayal of the assembly of the gods is unlike any other because it announces the permanent adjournment of the assembly and the execution of its constituency: the psalm announces the death of the gods. It is a way of saying in the face of a polytheistic worldview, 'I believe in God the Father Almighty.' The notion of the council is used to dramatize a profound shift in understanding reality. The context for human life is not the careers of the gods of the nations but the reign of the Lord" (*Psalms,* 269–70).

132. Miller summarizes this psalm: "The whole divine world is rendered or asserted to be impotent. The psalm is the story of the death of the gods. The immortals are condemned to the fate of mortality and merit comparison with human beings and not God. In this sense the gods are clearly and permanently negated.... Only God, Elohim, has any power in the divine realm. There is, therefore, a sense in which one can say that while the reader of this psalm enters the world of the gods at the beginning of the psalm, he or she has left it forever at the end of the psalm.... The life of the gods is at an end" (*Interpreting*, 123). Also see Tsevat, "Gods in Assembly," 129–31.

133. Peter C. Craigie, *The Book of Deuteronomy* (NICOT; Grand Rapids: Eerdmans, 1976), 169.

134. The above translation is a literal rendition of the Hebrew phrase *shema' yisere'l yhwh 'eloheynu yhwh 'ehad.* The phrase can be translated in various ways. On its translation, see R. W. L. Moberly, "'Yahweh Is One': The Translation of the Shema," in *Studies in the Pentateuch,* ed. J. A. Emerton (VTSup 41; Leiden: Brill, 1990), 209–15.

135. Jeffrey H. Tigay, *Deuteronomy* (JPSTC; Philadelphia: Jewish Publication Society, 1996), 76; Moshe Weinfeld, *Deuteronomy 1–11* (AB 5; New York: Doubleday, 1991), 350.

136. Scholars tend to interpret the phrase as either speaking of Yahweh's uniqueness due to the overall message of Deuteronomy or speaking of the oneness of Yahweh due to the semantic character of *'ehad.* The text appears to contain a purposeful ambiguity, allowing both understandings as legitimate interpretations (so Duane L. Christensen, *Deuteronomy 1–11* [WBC 6A; Dallas: Word, 1991], 145; Craigie, *Deuteronomy,* 168–69; Patrick D. Miller, *Deuteronomy* [Interpretation; Louisville: John Knox Press, 1990], 97–104; Vriezen, *Outline,* 323–26; Weinfeld, *Deuteronomy 1–11,* 349–51; Wright, *Deuteronomy,* 95–97). This conclusion is supported by Mark 12:29, which also conveys both meanings, and both understandings are accepted here.

137. J. G. Janzen demonstrates that the Old Testament was concerned with the integrity of the nature of Yahweh and the unity of his purpose ("On the Most Important Word in the Shema," *VT* [1987]: 280–300; cf. Miller, *Deuteronomy,* 99–101).

138. Wright, *Deuteronomy,* 96.

139. Miller, *Deuteronomy,* 101; Wright, *Deuteronomy,* 96–97.

140. Ibid., 103.

141. So Ralph L. Smith, *Micah-Malachi* (WBC 32; Waco: Word, 1984), 289; cf. Weinfeld, *Deuteronomy 1–11,* 350–51.

142. For recent discussions on the issue of monotheism and polytheism in ancient Israel, see Susan Ackerman, *Under Every Green Tree: Popular Religion in Sixth-Century Judah* (HSM 46; Atlanta: Scholars Press, 1992); Diana V. Edelman, ed., *The Triumph of Elohim: From Yahwisms to Judaisms* (Kampen: Pharos, 1995); Robert Gnuse, *No Other Gods: Emergent Monotheism in Israel* (JSOTSup 241; Sheffield: Sheffield Academic Press, 1997); Johannes C. De Moor, *The Rise of Monotheism: The Roots of Israelite Monotheism*, rev. and enl. (Leuven: Leuven University Press, 1997); Hershel Shanks and Jack Meinhardt, eds., *Aspects of Monotheism: How God is One* (Washington, D.C.: Biblical Archeology Society, 1997); M. Smith, *The Early History of God*; Jeffrey H. Tigay, "Israelite Religion: The Onomastic and Epigraphic Evidence," 157–94; *idem, You Shall Have No Other Gods*. Also see Paul Owen's contribution in this volume.

143. For P. Hayman, "it is hardly ever appropriate to use the term monotheism to describe the Jewish idea of God" ("Monotheism," 2).

144. See Miller, *Ancient Israelite Religion*, 46–105.

145. It is important to note that Jeffrey H. Tigay's analyses of the hypocoristic names in the epigraphic and biblical texts during the monarchical period and following shows a despairingly low percentage of non-Yahwistic names (see, *passim*, "Israelite Religion"; *No Other Gods*). See further Jeaneane D. Fowler, *Theophoric Personal Names in Ancient Hebrew: A Comparative Study* (JSOTSup 49; Sheffield: Sheffield Academic Press, 1988); Miller, *Ancient Israelite Religion*, 40-43.

146. Regarding Moses as giver of the Torah, Walter Brueggemann states this well: "The mediation of Yahweh by Moses in the Torah of Sinai is monotheistic. James Sanders's notion of 'monotheizing tendency' may be pertinent, but so far as the utterance of Moses is concerned, this is not a tendency but a premise of all that follows. The relationship will be singular and exclusive. There will be no other gods, no images, no idols, no alternatives, no rivals, no competitors. Israel is allowed no 'wiggle room' in this relationship. Yahweh, the single voice of authority, mediated through the voice of Moses, the single authorized mediator, will speak, and Israel will answer. The horizon of this testimony includes none of the categories that surface in a history-of-religions approach: no henotheism, no practical monotheism, no residue of polytheism, no developmentalism. It is all Yahweh and only Yahweh. The singularity comes to be expressed ... in the jealousy of Yahweh, a jealousy like that of a scorned husband (Ezek 16:38-43)" (*Theology of the Old Testament: Testimony, Dispute, Advocacy* [Minneapolis: Fortress Press, 1997], 5580–81). For James A. Sanders's conception on "monotheizing tendency" referred to by Brueggemann, see Sanders, "Adaptable for Life: The Nature and Function of the Canon," in Cross et al., *Magnalia Dei*, 531–60.

147. I would like to thank Carl Mosser for his work revising and supplementing this section; several of the points are his.

148. Stephen E. Robinson asserts that, although the King Follett Discourse is uncanonized, it is considered "quasi-official" and has become, in effect, normative among the official teachings of the LDS church. See Blomberg and Robinson, *How Wide the Divide?* 85, 87.

149. Joseph Smith, *Teachings of the Prophet Joseph Smith* (comp. Joseph Fielding Smith; Salt Lake City: Deseret, 1976), 351–52. Hereafter abbreviated *TPJS*.

150. *EOM*, 1:341.

151. *TPJS*, 352, 353, 354.

152. *TPJS*, 208.

153. *TPJS*, 181.

154. *TPJS*, 208.

155. *TPJS*, 181.

156. Truman Madsen, *Eternal Man* (Salt Lake City: Deseret, 1966), 56.

157. David Lamont Paulsen, "Comparative Coherency of Mormon (Finitistic) and Classical Theism" (Ph.D. diss., University of Michigan, 1975), 74. A few pages later he writes, "In accord with classical theism, Mormon theism affirms that God perfectly exemplifies every moral value. That is, He is perfectly just, loving, kind, compassionate, veracious, no respecter of persons, etc. But His perfections are not eternal, but were acquired by means of developmental process. God, then, according to Mormon theology, is not unconditioned or unlimited. He is limited at least by other co-eternal existences: primal elements (mass-energy), space, time, primal intelligences (selves) and primal laws and principles. Nor has he always been 'God'" (79).

158. David L. Paulsen, "Joseph Smith and the Problem of Evil," *BYU Studies* 39/1 (2000): 58.

159. Sterling McMurrin qualifies this by writing, "Yet even though Mormon doctrine describes God as subject to space and time, it also holds that in certain ways he transcends the limitations imposed by them. His presence, for instance, is everywhere by virtue of his spiritual influence, or of the power of his creative word, while his divine knowledge anticipates the future even though the future is yet unexperienced, unique, and undetermined" (*The Philosophical Foundations of Mormon Theology* [Salt Lake City: University of Utah Press, 1959], 14). However, since the LDS God is wholly within the material universe and a component of it, *transcendence* is not really the correct word to refer to what McMurrin describes.

160. Parley P. Pratt, *Key to the Science of Theology,* 5th ed. (Salt Lake City: George Q. Cannon & Sons, 1891), 37.

161. Ibid., 38.

162. Joseph Fielding Smith, *Doctrines of Salvation* (Salt Lake City: Bookcraft, 1954, 1955, 1956), 2:27.

163. Bruce R. McConkie, *Mormon Doctrine,* 2d ed. (Salt Lake City: Bookcraft, 1966), 432.

164. Paulsen, "Comparative Coherency," 74; emphasis added.

165. See Carl S. Hawkins and Douglas H. Parker, "Law: Divine and Eternal Law," *EOM* 2:809.

166. For example, Rodney Turner writes: "Law did not create God; God created law. The Almighty did not begin his career as a cosmic Columbus who stumbled upon supposedly self-existing natural laws. If there was 'a great first cause' of all things, he was it. He is, as President Spencer W. Kimball said: 'The Creator who originated every law' (5). The Prophet Joseph Smith is quoted as saying that God, 'finding he was in the midst of spirits and glory, because he was more intelligent, saw proper to *institute laws* whereby the rest could have a privilege to advance like himself' (*TPJS* 354)" (Rodney Turner, "The Imperative and Unchanging Nature of God" *Lectures on Faith in Historical Perspective,* ed. Larry E. Dahl and Charles D. Tate Dahl (Provo, Utah: BYU Religious Studies Center, 1990), 214–15.

167. Paulsen, "Comparative Coherency," 73.

168. James E. Talmage, *The Articles of Faith* (Salt Lake City: Church of Jesus Christ of Latter-day Saints, 1957), 220–23, as cited in Paulsen, "Comparative Coherency," 73.

169. *TPJS*, 345–46; emphasis in the original.

170. Robinson, *How Wide the Divide?* 18; emphasis added.

171. The significance of this vision for Mormonism is found in the statement by Stephen E. Robinson: "We believe this not because it is the clear teaching of the Bible but because it was the personal experience of the prophet Joseph Smith in his first vision" (*How Wide the Divide?* 78).

172. Ibid., 80.
173. *EOM*, 4:1474.
174. *EOM*, 4:1474.
175. *Mormon Doctrine*, 789-90.
176. Paulsen, "Comparative Coherency," 79.
177. Ibid., 79.
178. *TPJS*, 354; emphasis added.
179. *How Wide the Divide?* 82.
180. In his article attempting to denounce any idea of monotheism in Judaism, Peter Hayman asks the question "Is a doctrine of monotheism conceivable without a doctrine of *creatio ex nihilo?*" ("Monotheism," 3). According to Hayman, there is no notion of *creatio ex nihilo* in the Hebrew Bible (Old Testament), and it is weakly rooted in Judaism even into the Middle Ages, so "we can only conclude that Judaism never escaped from the Canaanite mythological background which all scholars now see behind biblical teaching on creation. The potentially evil *tohu* and *bohu* has always been there, limiting God's power and frustrating his purposes. However often he defeats it, it always comes back because ultimately it is as primordial as he is himself" (p. 4). Despite Hayman's flawed understanding of the Canaanite background of the Old Testament depiction of creation, his argument turned on its head actually further substantiates monotheism in the Old Testament since God did, in fact, create *ex nihilo,* as this chapter and the previous one demonstrate.
181. Daniel C. Peterson, "'Ye are Gods': Psalm 82 and John 10 as Witnesses to the Divine Nature of Humankind," in *The Disciple as Scholar: Essays on Scripture and the Ancient World in Honor of Richard Lloyd Anderson,* ed. S. D. Ricks et al. (Provo, Utah: FARMS, 2000), 471–594; cf. 541, 555.
182. The main thrust of his extensive essay attempts to prove that those who are the members of God's council are premortal human beings (p. 553). Peterson's general argument as related to Psalm 82 is as follows. First, the Old Testament definitively speaks of a council of Yahweh. Second, the head of the Canaanite pantheon was El, who is the creator-god and father of the gods. Third, the members of the divine council are designated as "the sons of El," and one of his sons is Yahweh. Gradually El faded into the background while his preeminent son Yahweh among the rest came to the fore. Fourth, the divine council in the Old Testament is made up of gods, with Yahweh as the high god but functionally equivalent. The members of the assembly were delegated certain responsibilities and primarily served as heralds or messengers of the decrees of the council. In the Ugaritic texts the messengers of the council were gods, while the heralds of Yahweh's council were human prophets. Furthermore, Hebrew prophets stood in Yahweh's assembly. Consequently, "in the biblical and other references to the council of El, a blurring of the distinction between mortal human beings and angels, between mortal human beings and gods" (p. 509). Finally, Psalm 82 is clearly speaking of gods that make up the members of the council of God (see pp. 475–84 and 535–41). Supposedly, these premortal human beings obtain a body, later die as human beings, and then are deified (Peterson is not clear on how his section on the "Deified Dead" is related to Psalm 82; see pp. 509–16). These gods must be premortal human beings, because Jesus quotes Psalm 82:6 in reference to the mortal Jews he is addressing (John 10:34). Thus, the divine council of God consists of premortal human beings (pp. 541, 555).
In response, it is true, as shown above, that Yahweh has a council, but I am not convinced that Psalm 82 is speaking of Yahweh's council. Secondly, Yahweh is never spoken of in the Old Testament as a "son of El" or the son of any other being. Peterson is correct that Israel's prophets were messengers of Yahweh, but the prophet is never considered divine or

described as becoming divinized (see below). Finally, Jesus' quote of Psalm 82:6 is most likely his implementing the contemporary interpretation of Psalm 82 which understood it as referring to Israel receiving the Torah at Sinai, as has been argued by scholars such as James S. Ackerman, in "The Rabbinic Interpretation of Psalm 82 and the Gospel of John," *HTR* 59 (1966): 186–91, cf. 188; see also Jerome H. Neyrey, "'I Said: You Are Gods': Psalm 82:6 and John 10," *JBL* 108 (1989): 647–63; Raymond E. Brown, *The Gospel According to John 1–12* (Garden City, N.Y.: Doubleday, 1966), 410. Peterson makes reference to some of these works (most notably Neyrey), but he fails to show why the interpretation they offer is wrong. In fact, one can hardly tell what their position is based upon the quotations Peterson offers.

183. Peterson, "'Ye are Gods'," 509.

184. G. Cooke, "The Sons of (the) God(s)," *ZAW* 76 (1974): 47. This conclusion is confirmed by E. T. Mullen's highly respected analysis of the ancient Near Eastern concept of the "divine assembly." Mullen writes: "The Israelite traditions of the council, while paralleling those of Canaan and Phoenicia, introduce a new element—the prophet as herald/courier of the council. In the Ugaritic myths, the messages of the council ('El) were carried by *divine* beings; in Hebrew prophecy, the decree of Yahweh was delivered by the *human* prophet. The similarity between the divine messenger and the *human* prophet is remarkable. Both carried the absolute authority of the deity who dispatched them. They, in effect, *represented* the presence of the deity in the decree" (*Divine Assembly*, 279; emphasis mine). Ironically, Peterson quotes this very paragraph, but tries to use it to support his claim that the prophets as participants and heralds of the council demonstrates a blurring of distinction between mortal and divine ("Ye are Gods," 554, 504–8). Unfortunately, Peterson seems to have quite missed the point of Mullen's conclusion. The remarkable thing is that *human* prophets and *not* divine beings are those who participate in the council and deliver Yahweh's message. Thus, it is not the similarity in nature between the messengers that is remarkable, but the similarity in function! It should also be observed that there is a real problem with Peterson's claim that Psalm 82 is evidence for premortal human beings as members of Yahweh's council. Although Peterson acknowledges that Psalm 82 contains a portrayal of judgment that can be understood either as factual or fictional (see pp. 536-37), he fails to discuss the implications of this significant feature and explain how premortal human beings are once again part of a divine council that God has condemned to death (v 7).

185. *How Wide the Divide?* 17.

Chapter 5: A Tale of Two Theisms

1. Gordon H. Clark, *Thales to Dewey* (Grand Rapids: Baker, 1980; orig. 1957), 183; emphasis added.

2. James E. Faulconer, review of Francis J. Beckwith and Stephen E. Parrish, *The Mormon Concept of God: A Philosophical Analysis* (Lewiston, N.Y.: Edwin Mellen, 1991), in *BYU Studies* 32/4 (1992): 187. It should be noted that it is not the belief in continuing revelation per se that prevents Mormon theology from being systematized as much as it is Mormonism's particular view of continuing revelation. Old revelations can not only be added to, elaborated, or clarified but can also be openly contradicted and even discarded as no longer true. Joseph Smith himself seemed to hold a different view. On one occasion he determined that a bad angel had appeared to a woman rather than a true angel of light because it gave her a revelation that contradicted a former revelation (See *TPJS*, 214–15).

3. Faulconer, "Review," 187.

4. The term "monarchotheism" is found in P. E. Kretzmann, *The God of the Bible and Other "Gods"* (St. Louis: Concordia, 1943), 61.

5. I have written more on this conception in my book *God and Necessity: A Defense of Classical Theism* (Lanham, Md.: University Press of America, 1997), 81–119. Other works with material on what is often called Perfect Being Theology include: Thomas V. Morris, *Anselmian Explorations* (Notre Dame, Ind.: Notre Dame University Press, 1987); *idem, The Concept of God* (Oxford: Oxford University Press, 1987); *idem, Our Idea of God* (Downers Grove, Ill.: InterVarsity Press, 1991); Ronald H. Nash, *The Concept of God* (Grand Rapids: Zondervan, 1983); Edward R. Wierenga, *The Nature of God* (Ithaca: Cornell University Press, 1989); Richard Swinburne, *The Christian God* (Oxford: Oxford University Press, 1994); and *idem, The Coherence of Theism,* rev. ed. (Oxford: Clarendon, 1995). For a critique of Perfect Being Theology, see Barry Miller, *A Most Unlikely God* (Notre Dame, Ind.: Notre Dame University Press, 1996).

6. E.g., Clark Pinnock et al., *The Openness of God* (Downers Grove, Ill.: InterVarsity Press, 1994). For critiques of this position, see Norman L. Geisler, *Creating God in the Image of Man?* (Minneapolis: Bethany House, 1997); Francis J. Beckwith, "Limited Omniscience and the Test for a Prophet: A Brief Philosophical Analysis," *Journal of the Evangelical Theological Society* 36/3 (September 1993): 357–62; William Lane Craig, *The Only Wise God* (Grand Rapids: Baker, 1987).

7. William Lane Craig, "In Defense of Rational Theism," in J. P. Moreland and Kai Nielsen, *Does God Exist?* (Nashville: Thomas Nelson, 1990), 154.

8. See Parrish, *God and Necessity,* 23–119.

9. For a comparison of LDS and classical Christian views on the Godhead, see Paul Owen, "The Doctrine of the Trinity in LDS and 'Catholic' Contexts," *Element: An E-Journal of Mormon Philosophy and Theology* 1/1 (Online: www.element-mormon.org).

10. Lecture 2:2 in Larry E. Dahl and Charles D. Tate Dahl, eds., *The Lectures on Faith in Historical Perspective* (Provo, Utah: BYU Religious Studies Center, 1990), 39.

11. This is not the observation of someone who is an expert on the evolution of Mormon theism or the LDS scriptures, but seems prima facie a very defensible reading of both.

12. For works on the Mormon concept of God, see Gary James Bergera, ed., *Line Upon Line: Essays on Mormon Doctrine* (Salt Lake City: Signature, 1989); Craig L. Blomberg and Stephen E. Robinson, *How Wide the Divide?* (Downers Grove, Ill.: InterVarsity Press, 1997); Eugene England, "Perfection and Progression: Two Ways to Talk about God," in his *Making Peace* (Salt Lake City: Signature, 1995), 43–63; Truman Madsen, *Eternal Man* (Salt Lake City: Deseret, 1966); Sterling M. McMurrin, *The Philosophical Foundations of Mormon Theology* (Salt Lake City: University of Utah Press, 1959); *idem, The Theological Foundations of the Mormon Religion* (Salt Lake City: University of Utah Press, 1965); Blake T. Ostler, "The Mormon Concept of God," *Dialogue* 17/2 (1984): 57–84; *idem,* "Revision-ing the Mormon Concept of Deity," *Element: An E-Journal of Mormon Philosophy and Theology* 1/1 (Online: www.element-mormon.org); David Lamont Paulsen, "Comparative Coherency of Mormon (Finitistic) and Classical Theism" (Ph.D. diss., University of Michigan, 1975); B. H. Roberts, *The Mormon Doctrine of Deity: The Roberts-Van Der Donckt Discussion* (Salt Lake City: Signature Books, 1998; orig. 1903); *idem, The Truth, The Way, The Life: An Elementary Treatise on Theology,* ed. Stan Larson (San Francisco: Smith Research Associates, 1994); the essays in *FARMS Review of Books* 11/2 (1999); and, generally, *The Encyclopedia of Mormonism.* For a critique of Mormon theism, see Francis J. Beckwith and Stephen E. Parrish, *The Mormon Concept of God: A Philosophical Analysis* (Lewiston, N.Y.: Edwin Mellen, 1991). For Mormon responses, see James E. Falconer's review in *BYU Studies* (Fall 1992): 185–95; David L. Paulsen and Blake T. Ostler's review in *International Journal for Philosophy of Religion* 35 (1994): 118–20; and the long review

by Blake T. Ostler in *FARMS Review of Books* 8/2 (1996): 99–146. For a partial response to these reviews, see Francis J. Beckwith and Stephen E. Parrish, *See the Gods Fall* (Joplin, Mo.: College Press, 1997). For a review by a former Mormon, see Merlin B. Brinkerhoff, *North American Religion* 2 (1993): 262–64.

13. For discussion, see Beckwith and Parrish, *See the Gods Fall*, 95–134.

14. *TPJS*, 181.

15. For an extensive discussion of the nature of contingency and necessity, see Parrish, *God and Necessity*, 1–80; and Alvin Plantinga, *The Nature of Necessity* (Oxford: Clarendon Press, 1974).

16. See the discussion of intelligences in Paulsen, "Comparative Coherency," 67–70.

17. See *TPJS*, 345. This quotation comes from Smith's famous "King Follett Discourse" (*TPJS*, 342–60). This funeral oration has been reprinted in many places, e.g., B.H. Roberts, ed., *The King Follett Discourse* (Salt Lake City: Magazine Printing, 1963) and (excerpts) Richard N. Ostling and Joan K. Ostling, *Mormon America* (San Francisco: HarperSan-Francisco, 1999), 387–94.

18. For an example of this view, see Paulsen, "Comparative Coherency," 70–72. Paulsen's work is perhaps the most comprehensive and clearest exposition and defense of Mormon doctrine. Again, though, not all Mormons would agree with the way he develops Mormon doctrine.

19. See Beckwith and Parrish, *See the Gods Fall*, 98–109.

20. Blomberg and Robinson, *How Wide the Divide?* 92.

21. Mormon philosophers have often described their God as finite (e.g., McMurrin, *Theological Foundations;* Paulsen, "Comparative Coherency," *passim;* and Ostler, "Mormon Concept of God," *passim*). More recently, LDS philosophers have tried to back away from this term because it carries connotations they do not believe are religiously appropriate (see especially, David L. Paulsen and R. Dennis Potter, "How Deep the Chasm? A Reply to Owen and Mosser's Review," *FARMS Review of Books* 11/2 [1999]: 235–41).

22. For a comparison of the classical transcendent God with the process concept of God, wherein God is not transcendent in his being, and the problems entailed by the latter view, see Royce Gordon Gruenler, *The Inexhaustible God* (Grand Rapids: Baker, 1983). Many of the problems Gruenler raises for process theism also apply to Mormonism.

23. See, for example, D. M. Armstrong, *What Is a Law of Nature?* (New York: Cambridge University Press, 1986). For a short exposition of what laws mean, see Beckwith and Parrish, *See the Gods Fall*, 152.

24. For a good exposition of the point that nothing can be the cause of itself, see Norman Geisler and Winfried Corduan, *Philosophy of Religion*, 2d ed. (Grand Rapids: Baker, 1983), 183. Cf. Joseph Smith, "God himself could not create himself" (*TPJS*, 354).

25. *TPJS*, 373.

26. Orson Pratt, "The Pre-Existence of Man," *The Seer* 1 (September 1853): 132.

27. For an exposition of problems with an infinite number of gods, or of an actually infinite amount of anything existing, see Beckwith and Parrish, *The Mormon Concept of God*, 53–80; and Beckwith and Parrish, *See the Gods Fall*, 111–16. Also see the chapter by Paul Copan and William Lane Craig in this volume where these problems are discussed with respect to the universe being infinitely old. Copan and Craig also address the criticisms Latter-day Saints have raised against the line of reasoning Beckwith and I used in the above two books.

28. *TPJS*, 345–46.

29. Parrish, *God and Necessity*, 175–84.

30. Many of the points in this section are discussed in greater detail in my *God and Necessity,* 217–50. A simpler and shorter explanation can be found in Beckwith and Parrish, *See the Gods Fall,* 152–53 and 159–63.

31. Parrish, *God and Necessity,* 1–21 and 217–50.

32. *God and Necessity,* 185–215; Beckwith and Parrish, *See the Gods Fall,* 152, 154–58.

33. *God and Necessity,* 185–215, and Beckwith and Parrish, *See the Gods Fall,* 152, 154–158.

34. Parrish, *God and Necessity,* 185–215; Beckwith and Parrish, *See the Gods Fall,* 152, 154–58.

35. Parrish, *God and Necessity,* 23–48.

36. On the Anthropic Principle, see P. W. C. Davies, *The Accidental Universe* (Cambridge: Cambridge University Press, 1987); John D. Barrow and Frank Tippler, *The Anthropic Cosmological Principle* (Oxford: Oxford University Press, 1988); M. A. Corey, *God and the New Cosmology* (Lanham, Md.: Rowman and Littlefield, 1993); Richard Swinburne, *The Existence of God,* rev. ed. (Oxford, Oxford University Press, 1991), 300–22; Hugh Ross, *The Creator and the Cosmos* (Colorado Springs, Colo.: NavPress, 1993), 105–21; and William Lane Craig, "The Teleological Argument and the Anthropic Principle," in William Lane Craig and Mark S. McLeod, *The Logic of Rational Theism* (Lewiston, N.Y.: Edwin Mellen, 1990).

37. For a defense of the view that ethics depends upon God, see J. P. Moreland, "Ethics Depends Upon God," in Moreland and Nielsen, *Does God Exist?* 111–26; Cornelius Van Til, *Christian Theistic Ethics* (Phillipsburg, N.J.: Presbyterian and Reformed, 1980); Carl F. H. Henry, *Christian Personal Ethics* (Grand Rapids: Baker, 1977), 21–142; Robert M. Adams, *The Virtue of Faith* (Oxford: Oxford University Press, 1987), 97–192; and Gordon H. Clark, *A Christian View of Men and Things* (Grand Rapids: Eerdmans, 1952), 151–93.

38. Kim McCall, "What Is Moral Obligation Within Mormon Theology?," *Sunstone* 6/6 (November 1981): 27–31.

39. For an introduction to Kant's ethical theory, see Frederick Copleston, *A History of Philosophy* (Garden City, N.Y.: Image Books, 1964), 6:101–40.

40. Editors' Note: This question and answer are provided by Carl Mosser. We extend our thanks to Stephen Parrish for allowing us to insert it. Any weaknesses of this section are Mosser's, not Parrish's.

41. Actually, there are several distinct but similar problems of evil collectively referred to as "the problem of evil." Furthermore, as John S. Feinberg rightly notes, each theological system (or atheological system for that matter) has its own problem(s) of evil to solve peculiar to its truth claims (see his *The Many Faces of Evil: Theological Systems and the Problem of Evil* [Grand Rapids: Zondervan, 1994]). In my opinion, Feinberg takes his valuable observation a bit too far; it seems to me that there is still a significant sense in which we can speak of *the* problem of evil as something that transcends theological systems. There is a wealth of literature on the problem of evil. One can begin by consulting the essays and bibliographies found in R. Douglas Geivett and Brendan Sweetman, eds., *Contemporary Perspectives on Religious Epistemology* (New York: Oxford University Press, 1992); Marilyn McCord Adams and Robert Merrihew Adams, eds., *The Problem of Evil* (Oxford: Oxford University Press, 1990); Michael L. Peterson, ed., *The Problem of Evil: Selected Readings* (Notre Dame, Ind.: University of Notre Dame Press, 1992). Consideration of the problem of evil necessarily involves many other issues in philosophical theology and the philosophy of religion. Good introductions, readings, and bibliographies on these issues can be found in Louis P. Pojman, ed., *Philosophy of Religion: An Anthology,* 3d ed. (Belmont, Ca.:

Wadsworth, 1998) and Philip L. Quinn and Charles Taliaferro, eds., *A Companion to Philosophy of Religion* (Oxford: Blackwell, 1997).

42. A few have argued that Mormon theism better accounts for the design we perceive in the universe than does classical theism. For reasons related to the earlier discussions of this chapter I believe these claims fail. But even if they were right, the design in the universe is not a problem for classical theism. The LDS arguments are largely adaptations of the eighteenth-century Scottish philosopher David Hume's criticisms of traditional design arguments for God's existence. Unsurprisingly, the majority of criticisms raised over the years against Hume's critique also serve to undermine the Mormon argument. For a response to LDS design arguments, see Beckwith and Parrish, *The Mormon Concept of God,* 90–105 and, more briefly, *See the Gods Fall,* 118–24. LDS reviewers have failed to adequately address the arguments Beckwith and Parrish raise on this issue. Contemporary arguments to the design of the universe as a whole, not just by *a* God or gods, but by a *transcendent* Creator also count against Mormon design argument. See the works Parrish cited earlier on the design of the universe and the Anthropic Principle, and J. P. Moreland, *Scaling the Secular City: A Defense of Christianity* (Grand Rapids: Baker, 1987), 43–75 (pp. 65–66 are particularly relevant to Mormon arguments).

43. McMurrin, *Theological Foundations,* 91.

44. David L. Paulsen, "Joseph Smith and the Problem of Evil," *BYU Studies* 39/1 (2000): 53–65.

45. For example, the prominent atheistic philosopher William Rowe states: "Some philosophers have contended that the existence of evil is *logically inconsistent* with the existence of the theistic God. No one, I think, has succeeded in establishing such an extravagant claim. Indeed, granted incompatibilism, there is a fairly compelling argument for the view that the existence of evil is logically consistent with the existence of the theistic God" ("The Problem of Evil and Some Varieties of Atheism," *American Philosophical Quarterly* 16 [1979]; reprinted in Geivett and Sweetman, *Contemporary Perspectives,* 41.

46. For several of the most important essays (pro and con) evaluating the evidential argument, see Daniel Howard-Snyder, ed., *The Evidential Argument from Evil* (Bloomington: Indiana University Press, 1996).

47. A more readable version of Plantinga's famous "free-will defense" appears in his *God, Freedom and Evil* (Grand Rapids: Eerdmans, 1977).

48. Alvin Plantinga, *Warranted Christian Belief* (New York: Oxford University Press, 2000), 464.

49. Ibid., 481.

50. Ibid., 482.

51. There are, of course, many more details to LDS theodicies and variety between them than this summary will be able to mention. The primary LDS discussions of the problem of evil are Peter Appleby, "Finitist Theology and the Problem of Evil," in Bergera, ed., *Line Upon Line,* 83–88; John Cobb and Truman G. Madsen, "Theodicy" in *Encyclopedia of Mormonism,* 4:1473; Kathleen Flake, "Evil's Origins and Evil's End in the Joseph Smith Translation of Genesis," *Sunstone* 21/3 (Aug. 1998): 24–29; Madsen, *Eternal Man,* 53–61; McMurrin, *Theological Foundations,* 91–109; Ostler, "The Mormon Concept of God," 80–89; Paulsen, "Comparative Coherency," 91–154; *idem,* "Joseph Smith and the Problem of Evil;" and Roberts, *The Truth, The Way, The Life,* 373–83.

52. Paulsen, "Joseph Smith and the Problem of Evil," 54–55.

53. One of the great weaknesses of arguments against God's existence from the problem of evil is the fact that they assume notions of objective moral value that have no metaphysical

basis in the naturalist worldview. Their arguments assume a notion of moral value that is viable only if the God they are trying to disprove actually exists. Thus, a more promising way to argue is from the very fact of evil to the existence of God.

54. John Kekes, "Evil" in *Routledge Encyclopedia of Philosophy,* ed. Edward Craig (London: Routledge, 1998), 3:465. The general point that it is absurd to think that there must be evil in order for there to be good (as some LDS writers have stated) does not deny that certain goods may be possible only if certain evils are realized (e.g., compassion, courage, forgiveness).

55. Though space constraints prevent any kind of response here, it is worth noting that in his unpublished paper, "Finitism and the Problem of Evil," LDS philosopher R. Dennis Potter tries to make the advantages of finitism more definite with what he terms a "divine triage" strategy. In a triage hospital or emergency room, it is sometimes the case that more wounded will be in need of treatment than can be effectively treated by the medical staff on hand. In particularly bad instances, a doctor may be faced with a situation in which several patients come in with life-threatening wounds, but it is not possible to treat them all, even though all may be potentially treatable. The doctor, therefore, decides that she must allow certain patients to die while she treats others, somehow prioritizing which patients she will save. Analogously, Potter believes that God, as a finite being, is sometimes faced with such situations. Certain preventable evils occur because God has decided to prevent or work at curing greater evils. This seems to me a highly problematic solution to the problem of evil and one that would completely undermine all eschatological confidence.

56. See, throughout, Henri Blocher, *Evil and the Cross,* trans. David G. Preston (Downers Grove, Ill.: InterVarsity Press, 1994).

57. Similarities between Plato's view of creation, evil, and God and that of traditional Mormonism are most generally seen in Plato's (and his followers') repeated attributions of imperfection and evil to the recalcitrance of matter to the creator's will. For other parallels (including the idea of "opposition in all things"), see such passages as *Theaetetus,* 176b–177a; *Timaeus,* 30a-b; and *Republic,* II 379c.

58. David R. Griffin has presented a process theodicy based on the rejection of creation *ex nihilo* similar to Mormon theodicies. The following comments by Frederick Sontag in response to Griffin apply to the Mormon view as well. They are especially ironic in light of the common LDS accusation that orthodox Christian theology is the product of Greek philosophy:

> Griffin is clear that he is returning to an ancient notion of a limited God, and I think he is right in seeing that Plato excuses God from evil by making him not responsible for all but only for the good in the world. God does the best he can with materials that were given to him and not created by him. This point is important because much heat has been generated over the supposed borrowing of Greek notions by early Christian theologians. Griffin makes clear that, at least in this crucial point regarding God, Christian theology departed radically from Greek concepts. The early church fathers held to the omnipotence of God and rejected Plato's more limited deity. (Frederick Sontag in *Encountering Evil: Live Options in Theodicy,* ed. Stephen T. Davis [Atlanta: John Knox, 1981], 123).

59. *Encountering Evil,* 124.

60. Richard Bauckham, *The Theology of the Book of Revelation* (Cambridge: Cambridge University Press, 1993), 48, 51, 164.

61. Faulconer, review of *The Mormon Concept of God,* 192. The one notable attempt of which I am aware is David Paulsen's doctoral dissertation, "Comparative Coherency of

Mormon (Finitistic) and Classical Theism." Even this work does not cover many problems that the Mormons need to solve.

Chapter 6: Moral Law, the Mormon Universe, and the Nature of the Right We Ought to Choose

1. Stephen E. Robinson in *How Wide the Divide? A Mormon and an Evangelical in Conversation,* by Craig L. Blomberg and Stephen E. Robinson (Downers Grove, Ill.: InterVarsity Press, 1997), 10. For my critical assessment of this book, particularly Robinson's contribution, see Francis J. Beckwith, "With a Grain of Salt: Assessing a Mormon-Evangelical dialogue," *Christianity Today,* 17 November 1997, 57–59.

2. Joseph F. Smith, *Gospel Doctrine,* Vol. 2: *Selections From the Sermons and Writings of Joseph F. Smith* (Salt Lake City: The First Presidency of the Church of Jesus Christ of Latter-day Saints, 1971), 51.

3. For example, the work of Lynn Wardle, a law professor at Brigham Young University, has been especially important in responding to the challenge of same-sex marriage. See Lynn Wardle, "A Critical Analysis of Constitutional Claims for Same-Sex Marriage," *BYU Law Review* (1996): 1–96. I found his work defending the prolife position on abortion (Lynn Wardle and Mary Q. Wood, *A Lawyer Looks at Abortion* [Provo, Utah: Brigham Young University Press, 1982]) very helpful while working on my monograph, *Politically Correct Death: Answering the Arguments for Abortion Rights* (Grand Rapids: Baker, 1993).

4. See the first five chapters of C.S. Lewis, *Mere Christianity* (New York: Macmillan, 1948) where he presented a moral argument for the existence of God (classically conceived). Here I am arguing that classical Christian theism can ground moral law, whereas Mormon theism cannot. This is related to what Lewis was doing but not quite the same thing.

5. *TPJS,* 181.

6. *Encyclopedia of Mormonism,* s.v. "Time and Eternity," by Kent E. Robson.

7. Sterling M. McMurrin, *The Philosophical Foundations of Mormon Theology* (Salt Lake City: University of Utah Press, 1959), 24, 25.

8. See, for example, Susan Dimock, "The Natural Law Theory of St. Thomas Aquinas," in *Do the Right Thing: Readings in Applied Ethics and Social Philosophy,* 2d ed., ed. Francis J. Beckwith (Belmont, Calif.: Wadsworth, 2002).

9. For a more detailed presentation of the Mormon worldview and the place of the deity in it, see Francis J. Beckwith and Stephen Parrish, *The Mormon Concept of God: A Philosophical Analysis,* Studies in American Religion, vol. 55 (Lewiston, N.Y.: Edwin Mellen, 1991); and Francis J. Beckwith and Stephen Parrish, *See the Gods Fall: Four Rivals to Christianity* (Joplin, Mo.: College Press, 1997), chapter 3. In the latter work, Parrish and I point out that one can find in contemporary Mormonism at least two distinct identifiable views of deity: (1) plurality of finite gods theology, and (2) monarchotheism, a view that holds that there is one eternally existing though finite God, who is above all the other gods. Although the latter view is gaining ground among some Mormon intellectuals, the plurality of gods tradition seems to me to be the most dominant. For this reason, the focus in this chapter is on the former. However, even if the latter view becomes the dominant one in Mormonism, it is not clear that this God could serve as the ground of morality, for there is too much in Mormon writings that maintains that the moral law is something above God, e.g., see Joseph Smith Jr.'s comments in *History of the Church of Jesus Christ of Latter-day Saints,* introduction and notes, B.H. Roberts, 2d rev. ed. (Salt Lake City: Deseret Book, 1978), 6:303–13. (Hereafter *HC*)

10. The late Mormon apostle Bruce McConkie writes: "*Elohim,* plural word though it is, is used as the exalted name-title of God the Eternal Father." (*Mormon Doctrine,* 2nd ed. [Salt Lake City: Bookcraft, 1979], 224).

11. *HC,* 6:305–6 (=*TPJS,* 345–47); emphasis added.

12. *The Teachings of Lorenzo Snow,* comp. Clyde J. Williams (Salt Lake City: Bookcraft, 1984), 2.

13. Joseph Fielding Smith, *Doctrines of Salvation,* ed. Bruce R. McConkie, 3 vols. (Salt Lake City: Bookcraft, 1954–56), 1:10, 12; emphasis added.

14. Milton R. Hunter, *The Gospel Through the Ages* (Salt Lake City: Deseret, 1958), 104.

15. Hyrum L. Andrus, *God, Man and the Universe* (Salt Lake City: Bookcraft, 1968), 175.

16. D&C 93:29.

17. *Gospel Principles* (Salt Lake City: Church of Jesus Christ of Latter-day Saints, 1997), 14.

18. David Lamont Paulsen, "Comparative Coherency of Mormon (Finitistic) and Classical Theism" (Ph.D. diss., University of Michigan, 1975), 79.

19. McConkie, *Mormon Doctrine,* 386–87, 516–17, 750–51.

20. See *HC,* 6:305–12.

21. *HC,* 6:474 (=*TPJS,* 370).

22. Blake Ostler, "The Mormon Concept of God," *Dialogue* 17/2 (1984): 67.

23. B. H. Roberts, *Seventy's Course in Theology: Third Year and Fourth Year* (Salt Lake City: Caxton Press, 1910), 4:70.

24. Sterling M. McMurrin, *The Theological Foundations of the Mormon Religion* (Salt Lake City: University of Utah Press, 1965), 2. This quote may seem inconsistent with an earlier quote from McMurrin in which he states that the LDS worldview affirms, "in the matter of values, particularly moral values . . . an absolutistic character" (McMurrin, *Philosophical Foundations,* 24). I do not believe, however, that they are inconsistent. In one case, McMurrin is saying that Mormonism denies absolutism when it comes to the nature of God, but in the other case, McMurrin is saying that Mormonism affirms absolutism when it comes to moral values.

25. See, for example, McMurrin, *Philosophical Foundations; idem, Theological Foundations;* Paulsen, "Comparative Coherency"; Floyd Ross, "Process Philosophy and Mormon Thought," *Sunstone* 7/1 (1982): 17–25; and Garland E. Tickemyer, "Joseph Smith and Process Theology," *Dialogue* 17 (Autumn 1984): 75–85.

26. Paulsen, "Comparative Coherency," 72.

27. Ibid., 72.

28. D&C 131:7–8. It is interesting to note that Robinson maintains that the Mormon God can be physical as well as omnipresent: "One such assumption I hear a lot is that if God were to possess a physical body, this would make divine omnipresence impossible; such a God would be 'limited' or rendered 'finite' by that body. Therefore, the argument continues, God as perceived by the LDS could not be omnipresent. But the Latter-day Saints affirm only that the Father has a body, not that his body has him. The Father is corporeal and infinitely more, and if a spirit can be omnipresent without being *physically* present, then so can a God who possesses a body and a spirit" (*How Wide the Divide?* 88). But if the Prophet Joseph Smith is correct that even "spirits" are physical, then God cannot be omnipresent spiritually, since that would entail that God physically take up every bit of space in the universe. It seems, then, that Robinson's solution, though philosophically coherent,

is inconsistent with the LDS definition of "spirit." For a detailed critique along these lines, see David L. Paulsen and R. Dennis Potter, "How Deep the Chasm? A Reply to Owen and Mosser's Review," *FARMS Review of Books* 11/2 (1999): 238–39, n. 35.

29. "Materiality," originally published in the editorial columns of *The Prophet*, 24 May 1845. It is republished as an "authoritative Mormon utterance" in B. H. Roberts, *The Mormon Doctrine of Deity: The Roberts-Van der Donckt Discussion, to which is added a discourse, Jesus Christ: The Revelation of God, also a collection of authoritative Mormon utterances on the being and nature of God*, with a forward by David L. Paulsen (Salt Lake City: Signature Books, 1998), 255.

30. *HC*, 6:312 (= *TPJS*, 354).

31. Gregory P. Koukl in *Relativism: Feet Firmly Planted in Mid-Air* by Francis J. Beckwith and Gregory P. Koukl (Grand Rapids: Baker, 1998), 166.

32. J. L. Mackie, *The Miracle of Theism* (Oxford: Clarendon, 1982), 115. Mackie makes clear in chapter 1 of this book that he specifically has in mind the kind of God one finds in classical Christianity. He would not have said this about any concept of God.

33. In order to help the reader to better understand this problem, consider the examples provided by Richard Purtill, *Reason to Believe* (Grand Rapids: Eerdmans, 1974), 83–84:

It seems to be logically possible for A to be caused by B, for B to be caused by C, and so on, backward ad infinitum. There is, however, a very serious objection to this sort of "infinite regress," as it is called. . . .

For example, if A tries to borrow a lawnmower from B, and B replies, "I don't have one, but I'll borrow one from friend C," and C says, "I don't have one but, I'll borrow one from friend D," and so on, this is a case of the kind we are concerned with. Or if A asks B, his supervisor, for permission to take the afternoon off, and B says, "I can't give you permission without asking my supervisor, C," and C says, "I can't give you permission to give A permission unless I ask my supervisor, D," and so on, we have a case of this sort.

Now in these ordinary cases two things are clear:

1. If the series of things that don't have the property in question goes on to infinity, the first individual never gets that property. If everyone asked says, "I don't have a lawnmower, but I'll ask," A never gets the lawnmower. If every supervisor asked says, "I can't give you permission, but I'll ask," then A never gets the afternoon off.

2. If the first thing *does* get the property in question, then the series comes to an end, and does not go on to infinity. If A gets the lawnmower, someone along the line had a lawnmower without having to borrow one. If A gets his afternoon off, some supervisor could give permission without having to ask someone else.

34. McMurrin, *Philosophical Foundations*, 24–25. For an analysis of McMurrin's view, see Truman G. Madsen, review of Sterling McMurrin, *The Philosophical Foundations of Mormon Theology, BYU Studies* 1/2 (1959–60): 103.

35. Paul Copan, *True For You But Not True For Me* (Minneapolis: Bethany House), 60–61.

36. Kim McCall is one Mormon scholar who attempts to ground the moral law. He does so, however, by suggesting a quasi-Kantian approach that seems to presuppose the very moral laws that are in need of justification and explanation: "So, if in moral theory we are seeking a standard by which to judge actions, this standard will evaluate not the action itself but rather the reason it is being performed. Now the reason or subjective ground from which

we are acting can always be expressed in the form of a rule, e.g., 'if you're going to be embarrassed by some situation, avoid that situation' or 'always seek to make others happy.' So it is these subjective rules by which we act which are the proper objects of moral evaluation. They have the form of laws and our actions are morally worthy if those subjective rules out of which they are performed accord with universal moral laws. But since this standard is being proposed as the *fundamental* criterion of the morality of actions, logically prior to the existence of any substantive moral laws, conformity of the rules behind our actions with moral laws can only mean that those rules are worthy to be made into moral laws themselves. So the agent, to act rightly, must examine the reasons for his actions and ask whether he can in full rationality and honesty will that they should be universal laws" ("What is Moral Obligation with Mormon Theology? What Makes Right Acts Right and Wrong Acts Wrong?" *Sunstone* 6/6 [1981]: 31).

37. See, for example, Bertrand Russell, *Why I Am Not a Christian* (New York: Simon & Schuster, 1957), 590.

38. Socrates formulates it a bit differently: "Is the pious loved by the gods because it is pious, or is it pious because it is loved by the gods?" (Plato, *Euthyphro*, 10a. *The Collected Dialogues of Plato*, eds. Edith Hamilton and Huntington Cairns [Princeton: Princeton University Press, 1961]).

39. Robert Adams, "A Modified Divine Command Theory of Ethical Wrongness," in *Philosophy of Religion*, 2d ed., ed. Louis P. Pojman (Belmont, CA: Wadsworth, 1987), 528.

40. See Robert Adams, *Finite and Infinite Goods: A Framework for Ethics* (New York: Oxford University Press, 1999), 97–122; Paul Helm, ed., *Divine Commands and Morality* (Oxford: Oxford University Press, 1981); Janine Marie Idziak, "Divine Command Ethics," in *A Companion to Philosophy of Religion*, ed. Philip L. Quinn and Charles Taliaferro (Oxford: Blackwell, 1997), 453–59; Richard J. Mouw, *The God Who Commands* (Notre Dame, Ind.: University of Notre Dame Press, 1990); Philip L. Quinn, *Divine Commands and Moral Requirements* (Oxford: Clarendon, 1978); and *idem*, "Divine Command Theory" in *The Blackwell Guide to Ethical Theory*, ed. Hugh La Follette (Oxford: Blackwell, 2000), 53–73.

41. Hadley Arkes, *First Things: An Inquiry into the First Principles of Morals and Justice* (Princeton: Princeton University Press, 1986), 33.

42. See, for example, J. P. Moreland's remarks in his debate with Kai Nielsen, *Does God Exist? The Debate Between Theists and Atheists* (Amherst, N.Y.: Prometheus, 1993), 111–35.

43. Blake T. Ostler, review of *The Mormon Concept of God: A Philosophical Analysis* by Francis J. Beckwith and Stephen E. Parrish, *FARMS Review of Books* 8/2 (1996), 125.

44. Ibid., 126.

45. Ibid., 125, 126.

46. For an extended treatment of the issue that responds in detail to many of the kinds of objections Ostler and others have raised to God's necessary goodness, see Thomas V. Morris, "Duty and Divine Goodness" *American Philosophical Quarterly* 21/3 (1984): 261–68; reprinted in Thomas V. Morris, ed., *The Concept of God* (Oxford: Oxford University Press, 1987), 107–21. Jesus is God incarnate, and thus also necessarily good. Some have wondered how Jesus' necessary goodness is compatible with such facts about his life such as his being tempted in the wilderness by Satan (Matt 4:1–11; Mark 1:12–13; Luke 4:1–13; cf. Heb 4:15). Morris discusses God's necessary goodness and addresses such issues as Jesus' being tempted in *The Logic of God Incarnate* (Ithaca: Cornell University Press, 1986), 108–61.

47. Katherin A. Rogers, *Perfect Being Theology* (Edinburgh: Edinburgh University Press, 2000), 123.

48. Thomas V. Morris, *Our Idea of God: An Introduction to Philosophical Theology* (Downers Grove, Ill.: InterVarsity Press, 1991), 60–61.

49. Ibid., 64.

50. John Rawls, *Political Liberalism* (New York: Columbia University Press, 1993), 22–28. Rawls's two principles of justice are: (1) Each person has an equal claim to a fully adequate scheme of basic rights and liberties, which scheme is compatible with the same scheme for all; and in this scheme the equal political liberties, and only those liberties, are to be guaranteed their fair value. (2) Social and economic inequalities are to satisfy two conditions: first, they are to be attached to positions and offices open to all under conditions of fair equality of opportunity; and second, they are to be to the greatest benefit of the least advantaged members of society (pp. 5–6).

51. Rawls probably would not agree with my depiction of his view, for he considers his theory of justice to be deontological and not utilitarian or egoistic. He writes in one place that his principles of justice, like Immanuel Kant's, are categorical imperatives (*A Theory of Justice* [Cambridge: Harvard University Press, 1971], 253). However, some scholars, such as Michael Sandel (*Liberalism and the Limits of Justice* [New York: Cambridge University Press, 1983]); J. P. Moreland ("Rawls and the Kantian Interpretation," in *Simon Greenleaf Review of Law and Religion* 8 [1988–89]); and Keith Pavlischek, *John Courtney Murray and the Dilemma of Religious Toleration* [Kirksville, Mo.: Thomas Jefferson University Press, 1994], 208–12) have made assessments of Rawls's theory that are similar to mine.

52. See Sandel, *Liberalism*, 105–12.

53. Interestingly, a new movement in philosophy of science, Intelligent Design, makes the argument that the specified, and sometimes irreducible, complexity of biological organisms is evidence that they were designed by an intelligence. That is, once one understands how to identify products of intelligence, then one can reasonably infer an intelligent cause when one comes across such things in the natural world. See, for example, William A. Dembski, *Intelligent Design: The Bridge Between Science and Theology* (Downers Grove, Ill.: InterVarsity Press, 1999).

54. See Etienne Gilson's commentary on this matter in *The Christian Philosophy of St. Thomas Aquinas* (Notre Dame, Ind.: University of Notre Dame Press, 1956), 75–95.

55. Mackie, *The Miracle of Theism*, 118; emphasis added. It is worth noting that Mormon thinkers like James Talmage, B. H. Roberts, and John Widtsoe have explicitly taught that miracles are not intrusions into the natural order by a transcendent Being but the use of natural laws and principles by a God whose knowledge of these laws is more advanced than ours.

56. The work of philosopher Michael Ruse is illuminating in this regard. Defending an ethical system based on naturalistic evolution, Ruse writes that morality, in order to work, must *seem* real, "functioning as a collective illusion of the human race, fashioned and maintained by natural selection in order to promote individual reproduction." That is, "we think that we have obligations to others because it is in our biological interests to have these thoughts." ("The New Evolutionary Ethics," in *Evolutionary Ethics*, ed. M. H. Nitecki and D. V. Nitecki [Albany: State University of New York Press, 1993], 148). Ruse writes elsewhere: "Considered as a rationally justifiable set of claims about an objective something, it is illusory. I appreciate that when somebody says, 'Love thy neighbor as thyself,' they think they are referring above and beyond themselves. . . . Nevertheless, to a Darwinian evolutionist it can be seen that such reference is truly without foundation. Morality is just an aid to survival and reproduction, and has no being beyond or without this. . . . [A]ny deeper meaning is illusory" (*The Darwinian Paradigm: Essay on Its History, Philosophy and Religious Implications* [New York: Routledge, 1989], 268–69; citations omitted).

57. *How Wide the Divide?* 9.

58. In 1990 I volunteered to work with several LDS attorneys to develop and author arguments for briefs in a case brought before the Nevada Supreme Court (*Choose Life v. Del Papa* 801 P. 2d 1384 [Nev., Nov. 28, 1990] [No. 21325]). The case involved a suit by pro-life citizens of the state against Frankie Sue Del Papa, the secretary of state. The citizens argued that the ballot language Ms. Del Papa authored (ballot question no. 9) was biased. The court ruled partly for Del Papa and partly for the citizens, requiring Del Papa to modify the ballot language.

59. Special thanks to Carl Mosser for his comments on an earlier draft of this essay.

Chapter 7: The Absurdities of Mormon Materialism

1. See John Cooper, *Body, Soul, and Life Everlasting,* rev. ed. (Grand Rapids: Eerdmans, 2000); J. P. Moreland and Scott Rae, *Body and Soul: Human Nature and the Crisis in Ethics* (Downers Grove, Ill.: InterVarsity Press, 2000), chapter 1.

2. H. D. Lewis, *Christian Theism* (Edinburgh: T & T Clark, 1984), 125.

3. Sterling M. McMurrin, *The Theological Foundations of the Mormon Religion* (Salt Lake City: University of Utah Press, 1965), 1.

4. Ibid., 3.

5. Mormon philosopher David L. Paulsen notes that the term "matter" in this text should be interpreted to mean "substance," otherwise the assertion would be trivially true ("immaterial matter" is a contradiction). See his "Comparative Coherence of Mormon (Finitistic) and Classical Theism" (Ph.D. diss., University of Michigan, 1975), 72–73.

6. See the forward by David J. Whittaker in *The Essential Orson Pratt* (Salt Lake City: Signature Books, 1991), xv–xxxii.

7. McMurrin, Theological Foundations, 45.

8. Max Nolen, "Materialism and Mormon Faith," *Dialogue* 22 (1989): 70.

9. Ibid., 72–73.

10. T. W. P. Taylder, *The Materialism of the Mormons, or Latter Day Saints, Examined and Exposed* (Woolwich: R. Jones, 1849).

11. David J. Whittaker, *The Essential Orson Pratt,* xxiv.

12. John Wesley, "An Address to the Clergy," in *The Works of John Wesley,* 3d ed. (Grand Rapids: Baker, 1979), 10:481.

13. All page citations make reference to "Absurdities of Immaterialism," in *Orson Pratt's Works,* vol. 2 of *Important Works in Mormon History* (Orem, Utah: Grandin Books, 1990), 1–32.

14. For the distinction between essence and property that seems to be used by Pratt, see M. R. Ayers, "Mechanism, Superaddition, and the Proof of God's Existence in Locke's Essays," *Philosophical Review* 90 (April 1981): 225–29.

15. Ibid., 14.

16. See John Locke, *An Essay Concerning Human Understanding* (Dover, 1959), book IV, chap. III, sec. 6, p. 195. Cf. John W. Yolton, *Thinking Matter: Materialism in Eighteenth-Century Britain* (Minneapolis: University of Minnesota Press, 1983).

17. For a defense of the existence of universals construed as abstract objects, see J. P. Moreland, *Universals: A Study in Ontology* (London: Acumen Press; Montreal: McGill-Queen's University Press, 2001).

18. My analysis of substance is the classic one that stands in the grand tradition of Aristotle and Aquinas. Pratt's notion of substance is Newtonian (i.e., a solid corpuscle with at least primary qualities).

19. Latter-day Saints may respond to some of the biblical data regarding the intermediate state by appealing to scholars, such as Murray Harris, who have defended a "two-bodies" position and, thus, an embodied intermediate state. According to Harris, texts such as 2 Corinthians 5:1–10 are consistent with the view that at death a person is immediately given a resurrection body, thus eliminating a disembodied intermediate state. Unfortunately, several things are wrong with this suggestion. First, Harris's "two-bodies" view does not entail the falsity of a substantial, immaterial self as he himself admits: "The link between the Christian's successive forms of embodiment—the physical and the spiritual—lies in the same identifiable ego.... There are two dwellings but only one occupant. There is an identity of occupant but not of dwelling" (*Raised Immortal* [Grand Rapids: Eerdmans, 1983], 126). Second, intertestamental Judaism, with the possible exception of the Sadducees, held to a disembodied intermediate state; and New Testament teaching ought to be interpreted in light of that background with a burden of proof on those who opt for a bodily intermediate state. Exegetically, that burden has not been met. For more on this, see the sources in note 1 above. Third, in 2 Corinthians 5:1–10 Paul explicitly makes reference to his earthly body ("earthly tent" in v. 1), his future resurrection body (a "building from God" in vv. 1–3), and a period of nakedness without either. This period of nakedness seems clearly to be without a body, a fact made more evident when compared to other Pauline texts such as 2 Corinthians 12:1–4.

20. I leave open whether an event with a larger or smaller extension would be identical to a relevant event prior to extension. Nothing about my argument turns on this.

21. William Hasker, *The Emergent Self* (Ithaca: Cornell University Press, 1999), 122–46.

22. D. M. Armstrong, *Universals and Scientific Realism,* vol. 1, *Nominalism and Realism* (Cambridge: Cambridge University Press, 1978), 19–21.

23. *TPJS,* 207.

24. For a dialogue/debate on the thinking matter thesis and topic neutral definitions of the mental, see Clifford Williams, "Christian Materialism and the Parity Thesis," *International Journal for Philosophy of Religion* 39 (February 1996): 1–14; J. P. Moreland, "Locke's Parity Thesis About Thinking Matter: A Response to Williams," *Religious Studies* 34 (September 1998); 253–59; Clifford Williams, "Topic Neutrality and the Mind-Body Problem," *Religious Studies* 36 (June 2000): 203–7; J. P. Moreland, "Christian Materialism and the Parity Thesis Revisited," *International Philosophical Quarterly* 40 (December 2000): 423–40; and *idem,* "Topic Neutrality and the Parity Thesis: A Surrejoinder to Williams," *Religious Studies* 37 (March 2001): 93–101.

Chapter 8: Monotheism, Mormonism, and the New Testament Witness

1. I am well aware that the above statement is oversimplified. Christians also believe that the three *persons* of the Trinity share God's eternal divine Being, whereas Mormons acknowledge that God is "one" in the sense of there being one *Godhead* that rules over this earth. Some Mormons believe that God is one in an even stronger ontological sense and deny that there are other Gods beyond the God of this earth. Nevertheless, I think it a safe generalization to say that Christians largely emphasize God's oneness in conversations with Latter-day Saints, whereas Latter-day Saints *tend* to emphasize the doctrine of a plurality of Gods for apologetic purposes.

2. *Scriptural Teachings of the Prophet Joseph Smith* (hereafter *STPJS*), ed. Joseph Fielding Smith (Salt Lake: Deseret, 1993), 417. It is not within the scope of this essay to engage in a detailed analysis of LDS theism (aspects of which I have addressed in other places). For

the record, however, I personally believe that Joseph Smith's doctrine of a plurality of Gods has been largely misunderstood, and that a more subtle understanding of the Deity lies behind his statements on a plurality of Gods. In Smith's view, there is only one ineffable Divine Nature (D&C 88:41; 121:32), though there are many emanations of God, which are embodied in individual personages (D&C 88:12–20; 132:20–24). I believe this is brought out in Smith's comments on 1 Corinthians 8:5–6, where he proposes that the God appointed over this world is but one incarnation of the High God, whom the heavens cannot contain and who is in all and through all (*STPJS*, 348–49, 418–19). Apart from B. H. Roberts and Orson Pratt, however, few interpreters have captured the true intent of Smith's language, instead interpreting with wooden literalism statements that could be understood differently—hence leading to an imaginative polytheism. Smith himself was not a consistent polytheist, but rather a religious mystic whose understanding of the Deity was indebted to the esoteric speculations of Jewish Kabbalah. I recognize, however, that not all students of Mormonism will agree with my assessment, and hence I will not make a major issue of the "Kabbalistic background" to Joseph Smith's thought in this essay. On Joseph Smith and the Kabbalah, see Lance S. Owens, "Joseph Smith and Kabbalah: The Occult Connection," *Dialogue* 27/3 (1994): 117–94; and D. Michael Quinn, *Early Mormonism and the Magic World View*, rev. and enl. (Salt Lake: Signature, 1998), 296–306. For a dissenting opinion, see William J. Hamblin, "'Everything Is Everything': Was Joseph Smith Influenced by Kabbalah?" *FARMS Review of Books* 8/2 (1996): 251–321.

3. Compare this with the description of monotheism offered in *The Oxford Dictionary of the Jewish Religion,* ed. R. J. Zwi Werblowsky and Geoffrey Wigoder (New York: Oxford University Press, 1997), 477–78.

4. It is true that a monotheistic impulse can be discerned in the writings of many pagan philosophers and mystics, as is argued in the provocative essays collected in *Pagan Monotheism in Late Antiquity*, eds. P. Athanassiadi and Michael Frede (Oxford: Clarendon, 1999). However, as Larry Hurtado is correct to point out: "[I]n pagan religious *practice,* these [one/only god] formulae were fully compatible with the recognition and worship of all the gods, either as all valid manifestations of one common divine essence or as valid second-order gods under a high (often unknowable) god" ("First-Century Jewish Monotheism," *Journal for the Study of the New Testament* 71 [1998]: 12 n. 23; emphasis added).

5. In its ancient setting, monolatrous religious devotion is generally perceived as forming boundaries along nationalistic lines (i.e., each nation has its own god). N. T. Wright notes that "creational monotheism rules out *henotheism,* the belief that there are indeed other gods, but that Israel will worship only her own god. It is a matter of debate whether, and if so for how long, the ancestors of first-century Jews had held some such belief. Rejection of henotheism means, in practical terms, that Israel was committed to seeing her god as ontologically (and not merely practically) superior to the gods of the nations" (*The New Testament and the People of God* [London: SPCK, 1992], 249).

6. Hurtado, "First-Century Jewish Monotheism," 13.

7. Richard Bauckham, *God Crucified: Monotheism and Christology in the New Testament* (Carlisle: Paternoster, 1998), 15.

8. By Deuteronomic literature, Collins means the books of Deuteronomy, Joshua, Judges, 1–2 Samuel, and 1–2 Kings. See A. Y. Collins, "The Worship of Jesus and the Imperial Cult," in *The Jewish Roots of Christological Monotheism,* eds. C. C. Newman, J. R. Davila, and G. S. Lewis (Leiden: Brill, 1999), 235; emphasis added. For an introductory discussion, see Steven L. McKenzie, "Deuteronomistic History," in *The Anchor Bible Dictionary,* ed. David Noel Freedman (New York: Doubleday, 1992), 2:160–68.

9. For a balanced and helpful discussion of the issues, see J. Gordon McConville, *Grace in the End: A Study in Deuteronomic Theology* (Grand Rapids: Zondervan, 1993). Cf. *idem, Law and Theology in Deuteronomy* (Sheffield: Sheffield Academic Press, 1984).

10. See Andrew E. Hill and John H. Walton, *A Survey of the Old Testament* (Grand Rapids: Zondervan, 1991), 142–43; and (in greater detail) Gleason L. Archer, *A Survey of Old Testament Introduction: Revised and Expanded* (Chicago: Moody, 1994), 108–12, 274–83. "If one removes apparently late glosses and possibly some material in the final chapters, nothing remains in Deuteronomy that could not have come from the time of Moses" (W. S. LaSor, D. A. Hubbard, and F. W. Bush, *Old Testament Survey: The Message, Form and Background of the Old Testament* [Grand Rapids: Eerdmans, 1982], 180). Cf. Johannes C. de Moor, *The Rise of Yahwism: The Roots of Israelite Monotheism* (Leuven: Leuven University Press, 1990), 172, who suggests that Deuteronomy 6:4 fits the religious spirit of the time of Moses (Late Bronze Age). For an extended discussion of current scholarly views of Pentateuchal source criticism, see Gordon J. Wenham, "Pondering the Pentateuch: The Search for a New Paradigm," in *The Face of Old Testament Studies: A Survey of Contemporary Approaches,* eds. David W. Baker and Bill T. Arnold (Grand Rapids: Baker, 1999), 116–44.

11. LDS scholar Daniel C. Peterson continually (and inconsistently) assumes the critical conclusions of scholars who deny that preexilic Israelite religion was monotheistic, even though the Book of Mormon supports an early date for Deuteronomy and Isaiah 40–55—both of which are commonly taken as prime examples of the hardening monotheistic stance which the Deuteronomistic school promoted in the context of the Babylonian exile. See Daniel C. Peterson, "'Ye are Gods': Psalm 82 and John 10 as Witnesses to the Divine Nature of Humankind," in *The Disciple as Scholar: Essays on Scripture and the Ancient World in Honor of Richard Lloyd Anderson,* eds. Stephen D. Ricks, Donald W. Parry, and Andrew H. Hedges (Provo, Utah: FARMS, 2000), 487, 560 n. 34, 562 n. 49, 564 n. 68, 565 n. 85, 566 n. 92, 585 n. 267, 585 n. 268.

12. William J. Hamblin, a professor of history at Brigham Young University, has tried to argue in a private communication that 1 Nephi 5:11 need not include the traditional book of Deuteronomy as found in the Pentateuch, since it simply mentions five unidentified "books of Moses." Not only is this a contorted and obviously evasive argument, but it also fails to explain the rather clear allusion to Deuteronomy 18:15 in 3 Nephi 20:23. For a summary of Deuteronomic teachings in the Book of Mormon, see *EOM* s.v. "Deuteronomy" by Ellis T. Rasmussen (reprinted in *Scriptures of the Church: Selections from the Encyclopedia of Mormonism,* ed. Daniel H. Ludlow [Salt Lake: Deseret, 1992], 239–40); and Noel B. Reynolds, "Lehi as Moses," *Journal of Book of Mormon Studies* 9/2 (2000): 27–35, 81–82. The influence of Deuteronomy is too clearly attested in the Book of Mormon to allow for Hamblin's hypothesis.

13. Paul Sanders reflects this opinion when he asks: "The word 'monotheism' can be used to describe a religion which denies the existence of gods beside its own god. However, can such a strict form of monotheism be found in the Hebrew Bible?" (*The Provenance of Deuteronomy 32* [Leiden: Brill, 1996], 72). Sanders's statement serves a polemical purpose, since he wants to water down a hard definition of monotheism in order to lend greater plausibility to an early date for the materials in Deuteronomy 32 (pp. 426–27). While I believe he makes a strong case for a preexilic date for Deuteronomy 32, I do not believe it is necessary to retreat to a henotheistic definition of "monotheism" in order to do so. Sanders's study offers no analysis of Deuteronomy 6:4.

14. C. J. Labuschagne, *The Incomparability of Yahweh in the Old Testament* (Leiden: Brill, 1966), 137. Labuschagne goes on to note: "It is clear, then, that this is also a confession of Yahweh's incomparability. Being a single One, He is not only without family, but He is also unique in His kind, to the exclusion of all others; He is not merely a God amongst the host of gods, but, to say the least, One *over against* those many" (137; italics in original).

15. Paul Sanders attempts to argue that the rhetoric in Deuteronomy 32:39 does not contain any ontological claims about the uniqueness of God (*Provenance of Deuteronomy 32*, 419–20). But his line of argument is clearly driven by a perceived need to weaken the "strict" monotheism of the text in order to lend greater plausibility to a preexilic dating. I see no reason why the logic should not be read in the opposite direction: The early date of Deuteronomy 32:39 shows that scholarly assumptions about the gradual evolution of exclusive monotheism in Israelite religion ought to be scrapped in keeping with the biblical data.

16. The absolute distinction between God and the other heavenly beings is also brought out in Deuteronomy 32:43a as attested in the Dead Sea Scrolls and the LXX, both of which include a doublet calling upon the "sons of God" to "bow" in worship before the one true God.

17. For other examples of Yahweh's ontological uniqueness in the Old Testament, see 1 Sam 2:2; Ps 18:31; 86:8–10; 2 Sam 7:22; 1 Kgs 8:23; Isa 40:12–26; 43:10; 44:6–7; 46:5, 9; Jer 10:10.

18. See Bauckham, *God Crucified*, 10–13; *idem,* "The Throne of God and the Worship of Jesus," in *Jewish Roots of Christological Monotheism,* 45–47.

19. Many scholars date Isaiah 40–55 in the exilic period, and would argue that these chapters reflect the innovative reforms of the Deuteronomists. Hence, they would not offer testimony to monotheistic faith in Israel prior to the exilic period. However, there are good reasons for maintaining that the substance of the oracles in Isaiah 40–55 goes back to the testimony of Isaiah himself (740–681 B.C.). See LaSor, Hubbard, and Bush, *Old Testament Survey,* 371–78; Archer, *Old Testament Introduction,* 365–90; Hill and Walton, *Survey of the Old Testament,* 319–20; and L. La Mar Adams, "A Scientific Analysis of Isaiah Authorship," in *Isaiah and the Prophets,* ed. M. S. Nyman (Provo, Utah: BYU Religious Studies Center, 1984), 151–63. For further discussion with a wealth of secondary literature, see David W. Baker, "Israelite Prophets and Prophecy," in *The Face of Old Testament Studies,* 288–90. In any case, Latter-day Saints cannot consistently appeal to the views of scholars who would explain the monotheism of "Second Isaiah" in such a manner, for the Book of Mormon cites extended passages from Isaiah 40–55 (allegedly prior to the exile). See *EOM,* s.v. "Isaiah: Authorship" by Victor L. Ludlow (=*Scriptures of the Church,* 329–30).

20. Cf. Richard Bauckham: "It is important to notice that this conforms to the way Jewish literature regularly speaks of the worship due to God alone as different in kind, not merely in degree, from whatever kind of honor may appropriately be given by inferior to superior creatures. In these many Jewish texts worship is understood precisely as the acknowledgement of YHWH's qualitative uniqueness, his unique identity as only Creator and only Sovereign" ("The Throne of God and the Worship of Jesus," 46).

21. Hurtado, "First-Century Jewish Monotheism," 12–13; italics in original.

22. The date of the book of Daniel is contested by scholars, but I would maintain that there are solid reasons for accepting the substance of the stories, visions, and prophecies of this work as going back to Daniel himself (605–530 B.C.), even if the literary form of the book underwent some later editing. See Archer, *Old Testament Introduction,* 423–47; and LaSor, Hubbard, and Bush, *Old Testament Survey,* 665–67.

23. As is argued at length by Peter Hayman, "Monotheism—A Misused Word in Jewish Studies?" *Journal of Jewish Studies* 42 (1991): 1–15.

24. This is roughly the position of Margaret Barker, *The Great Angel: A Study of Israel's Second God* (London: SPCK, 1992), 4–27.

25. Gregory A. Boyd, *God at War: The Bible and Spiritual Conflict* (Downers Grove, Ill.: InterVarsity Press, 1997), 114–42.

26. See the contribution of Paul Copan and William Lane Craig in this volume for a rigorous defense of the biblical and orthodox doctrine of *creatio ex nihilo*.

27. Boyd (*God at War*, 120) approvingly cites N. T. Wright's label "creational monotheism," but he ignores Wright's following discussion of "providential monotheism": "The facts of recent history were then explained in terms of divine punishment for evil, or the strange outworking of long-term divine purposes whose future end remained for the moment obscure. . . . Belief in the existence of angelic and other mediators says more about the attempt of some Jewish writers to speak meaningfully about their god's *involvement with*, not detachment from, his creation" (Wright, *The New Testament and the People of God*, 250–51; italics original). This obviously runs against the grain of Boyd's use of biblical angelology to protect God from personal culpability for pain and tragedy.

28. A warfare worldview need not negate a strong view of divine determinism. The same Essene community at Qumran that produced the War Scroll (1QM)—which reflects a cosmic warfare view if there ever was one—also was capable of producing statements like: "From the God of knowledge stems all there is and all there shall be. Before they existed he made all their plans and when they came into being they will execute all their works in compliance with his instructions, according to his glorious design without altering anything" (1QS 3:15–16). Translations of the DSS are by Florentino García Martínez, *The Dead Sea Scrolls Translated: The Qumran Texts in English* (Grand Rapids: Eerdmans, 1996), 6.

29. See Pss 77:13–14; 96:4–10; 97:1–9; 82:1–8; 148:1–6; and Deut 10:14–17.

30. M. L. West, "Towards Monotheism," in *Pagan Monotheism in Late Antiquity*, 21.

31. Wright, *The New Testament and the People of God*, 250.

32. Barker, *The Great Angel*, 31–36.

33. See the helpful study of Darrell D. Hannah, *Michael and Christ: Michael Traditions and Angel Christology in Early Christianity* (Tübingen: Mohr, 1999), 19–24.

34. Note that Yahweh is never identified as an angel in the setting of the heavenly court. In the context of heaven, biblical writers are always careful to distinguish God from the angelic "sons of God."

35. Hannah, *Michael and Christ*, 20.

36. For an excellent discussion of this matter, see de Moor, *The Rise of Yahwism*, 234–47.

37. See Peterson, "Ye are Gods," 475–508; Barker, *The Great Angel*, 5–7; and Hayman, "Monotheism," 5–9.

38. Hurtado, "First-Century Jewish Monotheism," 22.

39. Boyd, *God at War*, 130.

40. For a helpful introduction to the topic, see E. T. Mullen, "Divine Assembly," in *Anchor Bible Dictionary*, ed. David Noel Freedman (New York: Doubleday, 1992), 2:214–17. Major studies include: E. T. Mullen, *The Divine Assembly: The Divine Council in Canaanite and Early Hebrew Literature* (Chico: Scholars Press, 1980); L. K. Handy, *Among the Host of Heaven: The Syro-Palestinian Pantheon as Bureaucracy* (Winona Lake: Eisenbrauns, 1994); and C. L'Heureux, *Rank Among the Canaanite Gods* (Missoula: Scholars Press, 1979).

41. The key Old Testament references include: Gen 6:2,4; Job 1:6; 2:1; 38:7; Pss 29:1; 82:6b; 89:6; Exod 15:11; Deut 10:17; Pss 77:13; 82:1, 6a; 86:8; 95:3; 96:4; 97:9; 135:5; 136:2; Dan 11:36.

42. See especially Stephen E. Robinson, *Are Mormons Christians?* (Salt Lake: Bookcraft, 1991), 65–69.

43. See Michael S. Heiser, "Deuteronomy 32:8 and the Sons of God," *Bibliotheca Sacra* 158 (2001): 52–74. Heiser's study is very helpful, though at some points he fails to sufficiently highlight important differences between the Israelite and Canaanite versions of the divine council (although cf. 72–74).

44. Richard Bauckham nuances the realities of the evidence very carefully. See his essay, "The Throne of God and the Worship of Jesus," 48.

45. Mullen, "Divine Assembly," 214.

46. Ibid., 215. Cf. Marjo Christina Annette Korpel, *A Rift in the Clouds: Ugaritic and Hebrew Descriptions of the Divine* (Münster: Ugarit-Verlag, 1990), 269–71, 273–77.

47. See Korpel, *A Rift in the Clouds*, 295–99.

48. S. F. Noll, "elim," in the *New International Dictionary of Old Testament Theology and Exegesis,* ed. Willem A. VanGemeren (Carlisle: Paternoster, 1996), 1:402.

49. Korpel, *A Rift in the Clouds*, 314.

50. The expression "Second Temple" is used to refer to the centuries subsequent to the rebuilding of the Jerusalem temple under Zerubbabel after the return of the exiles from Babylon (536–16 B.C.). Herod's expanded temple was later built on the same site (20 B.C.–A.D. 70).

51. See Hurtado, "First-Century Jewish Monotheism," 9–14; and Bauckham, *God Crucified,* 6–13.

52. Bauckham, *God Crucified,* 6.

53. All translations of the Apocrypha are from the New Revised Standard Version. Useful introductions to this body of literature include: Bruce M. Metzger, *An Introduction to the Apocrypha* (New York: Oxford University Press, 1957); and Daniel J. Harrington, *Invitation to the Apocrypha* (Grand Rapids: Eerdmans, 1999).

54. For helpful introductions to Philo, see Everett Ferguson, *Backgrounds of Early Christianity* (Grand Rapids: Eerdmans, 1993), 450–54; and Craig A. Evans, *Noncanonical Writings and New Testament Interpretation* (Peabody: Hendrickson, 1992), 81–86.

55. Emil Schürer, *The History of the Jewish People in the Age of Jesus Christ: Volume III. Part 2,* eds. G. Vermes, F. Millar, and M. Goodman (Edinburgh: T & T Clark, 1987), 880–81.

56. All translations of Philo are from the Loeb Classical Library edition.

57. For a helpful introduction to the Dead Sea Scrolls that highlights their significance for New Testament interpretation, see Evans, *Noncanonical Writings and NT Interpretation,* 49–68. On the theology of the DSS, see especially Helmer Ringgren, *The Faith of Qumran: Theology of the Dead Sea Scrolls,* expanded edition with a New Introduction by James H. Charlesworth (New York: Crossroad, 1995).

58. Contra the misleading claims of John J. Collins, "Powers in Heaven: God, Gods, and Angels in the Dead Sea Scrolls," in *Religion in the Dead Sea Scrolls,* ed. J. J. Collins and R. A. Kugler (Grand Rapids: Eerdmans, 2000), 9–28. Collins fails to highlight the many ways in which angels and exalted human figures are radically distinguished from and subordinated to the one God in the DSS. Collins emphasizes terminology instead of precise functions and status—which is a methodological error. For a more balanced sketch of God's unique ontological status in the Qumran literature, see Ringgren, *The Faith of Qumran,* 47–67.

59. A.Y. Collins, "The Worship of Jesus and the Imperial Cult," 236.

60. Larry W. Hurtado, "The Binitarian Shape of Early Christian Worship," in *The Jewish Roots of Christological Monotheism,* 191. For more detail, see *idem, One God, One Lord: Early Christian Devotion and Ancient Jewish Monotheism* (Edinburgh: T & T Clark, 1998).

61. As Kevin J. Vanhoozer notes, the term "identity" is "susceptible of several meanings: numeric oneness, ontological sameness or permanence in time, and the personal identity of self-continuity" ("Does the Trinity Belong in a Theology of Religions? On Angling in the Rubicon and the 'Identity' of God," in *The Trinity in a Pluralistic Age: Theological Essays on Culture and Religion,* ed. Kevin J. Vanhoozer [Grand Rapids: Eerdmans, 1997], 47). While I would not exclude any of these nuances from the definition of "identity" employed in this essay, I am most concerned here with the question of *personal* identity. The question of "numeric oneness" was more directly in focus in our discussion of the Old Testament materials, although this truth is certainly carried into the New Testament, as the immediately following section demonstrates.

62. N. T. Wright, "Monotheism, Christology and Ethics: 1 Corinthians 8," in *The Climax of the Covenant* (Edinburgh: T&T Clark, 1991), 120–36 (quote from p. 129; italics original). Further see Ben Witherington, *Jesus the Sage: The Pilgrimage of Wisdom* (Edinburgh: T&T Clark, 1994), 314–16; and Bauckham, *God Crucified,* 36–40.

63. Greg Stafford focuses on the fact that the Father is called "God," whereas Jesus Christ is called "Lord" in 1 Corinthians 8:4–6, as if this were evidence that Paul viewed the Son as somehow less "divine" than the Father. Yet this overlooks the connections with Deuteronomy 6:4, from which the terms "God" and "Lord" are both drawn. See Greg Stafford, *Jehovah's Witnesses Defended: An Answer to Scholars and Critics,* 2d ed. (Huntington Beach, Calif.: Elihu Books, 2000), 200–205.

64. For a thorough study, see David B. Capes, *Old Testament Yahweh Texts in Paul's Christology* (Tübingen: Mohr, 1992).

65. See Richard N. Longenecker, *The Christology of Early Jewish Christianity* (London: SCM, 1970), 44.

66. Martin Hengel, *The Son of God: The Origin of Christology and the History of Jewish-Hellenistic Religion* (London: SCM, 1976), 77.

67. See Longenecker, *The Christology of Early Jewish Christianity,* 128.

68. Greg Stafford is too quick to dismiss the connections between Philippians 2:10–11 and Isaiah 45:22–24, hence missing the astonishing assertion of Christ's divine status that the text contains. He also makes too much of the fact that God is said to exalt Jesus to his place of heavenly authority (2:9), overlooking: (1) the fact that this is *in contrast* to Jesus' humbled state during his mortality (2:7–8); and (2) the fact that Philippians 2:6 asserts that Jesus possessed God's nature and was equal to God prior to his incarnation (*Jehovah's Witnesses Defended,* 124).

69. It is not possible to retrace in a precise manner the exegetical steps from the original meaning of Isaiah 45:22–24 to its New Testament application. The LXX version of 45:23 does, however, read differently than the MT. There, the Greek reads: "*to me* shall bow every knee, and every tongue shall confess *to God,* saying. . . ." Perhaps Christian readers such as Paul felt this implied a distinction of figures in the verse (me and God) that allowed room for the Son and the Father.

70. See Hurtado, *One God, One Lord,* 96–97.

71. Bauckham, *God Crucified,* 53; italics original.

72. Two of the best studies (in my opinion) are: Raymond E. Brown, *An Introduction to New Testament Christology* (New York: Paulist, 1994); and Murray J. Harris, *Jesus as God: The New Testament Use of Theos in Reference to Jesus* (Grand Rapids: Baker, 1992). Also cf. Hengel, *The Son of God* (esp. 66–83, 89–93). For a different approach, which emphasizes early Christian devotional *practice* rather than divine titles, see Hurtado, *One God, One Lord,* 93–124.

73. The question as to whether subsequent christological reflection was faithful to the biblical witness or was largely a capitulation to Hellenistic philosophy is an interesting one, which unfortunately lies outside the scope of this essay. For further reading I would highly recommend Eric Osborn, *The Beginning of Christian Philosophy* (Cambridge: Cambridge University Press, 1981); *idem, The Emergence of Christian Theology* (Cambridge: Cambridge University Press, 1993); and Gerald Bray, *Creeds, Councils and Christ: Did the Early Christians Misrepresent Jesus?* (Fearn, Tain, Great Britain: Mentor, 1997).

74. See Matt 9:6; 12:8; 19:28; Mark 10:45; 14:62; Luke 12:8; 17:30; John 3:13–14; Acts 7:56; Rev 1:13. Many scholars deny that Jesus spoke of himself as "the Son of Man" with reference to Daniel 7; however, I am not convinced by their arguments. For cogent defenses of the historical reality of this claim on Jesus' part, see N. T. Wright, *Jesus and the Victory of God* (Minneapolis: Fortress, 1996), 512–19; and Marinus de Jonge, *God's Final Envoy: Early Christology and Jesus' Own View of His Mission* (Grand Rapids: Eerdmans, 1998), 86–94. David Shepherd and I have addressed the linguistic problems relating to Jesus' Aramaic idiom in the use of this expression in "Speaking Up for Qumran, Dalman and the Son of Man: Was *Bar Enasha* a Common Term for 'Man' in the Time of Jesus?" *Journal for the Study of the New Testament* 81 (2001): 81–122.

75. See the studies of Hurtado, *One God, One Lord,* 51–69; and James D. G. Dunn, "Was Christianity a Monotheistic Faith From the Beginning?" *Scottish Journal of Theology* 35 (1981): 307–10.

76. See Wright, *The New Testament and the People of God,* 312–20; *idem, Jesus and the Victory of God,* 514; and Dunn, "Was Christianity a Monotheistic Faith from the Beginning?" 314–17.

77. See Barker, *The Great Angel,* 225–28, although I would differ with some of the details of her reading of the evidence.

78. See Craig A. Evans, "Jesus' Self-Designation 'The Son of Man' and the Recognition of His Divinity," in *The Trinity: An Interdisciplinary Symposium on the Trinity,* ed. Stephen T. Davis, D. Kendall, and G. O'Collins (Oxford: Oxford University Press, 1999), 29–47.

79. This claim goes beyond what is attributed to Solomon in 1 Chronicles 29:23, for Solomon merely sat on God's *earthly* throne, whereas the heavenly context of the Son of Man vision in Daniel 7 makes it clear that Jesus was claiming to be the one who will be seated on God's *heavenly* throne—a prerogative reserved for God alone in Jewish thought.

80. Evans, "Jesus' Self-Designation," 45.

81. See Hurtado, *One God, One Lord,* 104.

82. It is interesting that this figure is not identified explicitly with either Gabriel (cf. 8:16; 9:21) or Michael (cf. 10:13, 21; 12:1). His identity remains obscure, leaving open at least the possibility of a connection with the Angel of the LORD encountered in preexilic biblical traditions.

83. See the close textual analysis of Loren T. Stuckenbruck, *Angel Veneration and Christology* (Tübingen: Mohr, 1995), 211–21.

84. Dunn, "Was Christianity a Monotheistic Faith from the Beginning?" 326. It may be left open for debate to what extent this "blurring" was already present in certain strands of first-century Judaism. I agree with Dunn that if it is attested at all, it is only found within "a thin strand of esoteric mysticism within Judaism which [may have] touched the Qumran community, but so far as we can tell only became more widely influential from the late first century AD on" (313).

85. See James D. G. Dunn, *The Theology of Paul the Apostle* (Grand Rapids: Eerdmans, 1998), 267–81. This claim has recently been challenged by Karen H. Jobes and Gordon D.

Fee in their contributions to *The Way of Wisdom: Essays in Honor of Bruce K. Waltke*, ed. J. I. Packer and Sven K. Soderlund (Grand Rapids: Zondervan, 2000): Jobes, "Sophia Christology: The Way of Wisdom?" (226–50); and Fee, "Wisdom Christology in Paul: A Dissenting View" (251–79). Jobes's essay offers many insightful criticisms of the way the figure of Wisdom-Sophia has been used in feminist theology. She is correct to insist that Wisdom was not conceived as a literal goddess in the biblical tradition, which maintains a monotheistic outlook. However, she goes too far, in my opinion, when she attempts to distance the conception of Wisdom in Hellenistic Judaism (e.g., Wisdom of Solomon) from John's view of the Logos in the prologue to his gospel: (1) Wisdom of Solomon 7:24 (cf. 1:7; 12:1) need not point to Stoic pantheism any more than Psalm 139:7–10; Ephesians 1:23; or Colossians 1:17 do. (2) Jobes's proposal that the parallels with Wisdom in John 1 may be intended to *contrast* the Logos with Wisdom is question-begging in the extreme. Why would John want to pit the Logos against Wisdom, especially since the roots of Jewish Wisdom theology go back to biblical traditions such as Proverbs 8? Furthermore, Jesus described himself in terms that recalled Jewish Wisdom traditions (cf. Matt 11:27–30), as Jobes appears to recognize (238). (3) Jobes's point that the term "wisdom" does not occur in John 1 is a desperate argument from silence that fails to account for the parallelism between God's word and wisdom in Wisdom of Solomon 9:1–2 (250 n. 50).

Fee's provocative essay is also unconvincing on several grounds: (1) Fee's analysis of Colossians 1:15–20 exaggerates the discontinuity with Jewish Wisdom traditions. For example, is there really a vast difference between being "the image of the invisible God" (Col 1:15), and being "an image of his goodness" (Wisdom of Solomon 7:26)? (2) Fee's denial that Proverbs 8:24–25 lies in the background of Paul's description of Christ as the "firstborn of all creation" will probably not convince many readers. Despite the lexical differences, it still speaks of Wisdom as being born prior to the creation of the world (cf. Col 1:15–16). Nor is Fee convincing in his attempt to deny that Wisdom is personified as God's agent in creation in Sirach 24:3 and Wisdom of Solomon 7:22; 9:1–2 (cf. v. 4). (3) Fee's claim that wisdom is literally created by God (unlike Christ) ignores the fact that different words are used to depict the origination of Wisdom and the created order in Proverbs 8:23–26. It furthermore neglects the question any ancient reader of Proverbs 8 would intuitively ask: Was there ever a time when God lacked the attribute of wisdom? The answer is obviously no, which is why we are told that Wisdom was appointed "from eternity" (Prov 8:23). (4) A general weakness of Fee's essay is that he fails to allow for the fact that the shape of Wisdom theology necessarily took on new features when applied to a real living person—the incarnate Son of God. Hence, some elements of discontinuity are natural and to be expected.

86. "Among other things, this way of speaking and conceptualizing enabled the pious to affirm the transcendence of God, on the one hand, and the immanence of God, on the other" (Evans, "Jesus' Self-Designation," 42).

87. Dunn, "Was Christianity a Monotheistic Faith from the Beginning?" 320. Cf. Bauckham, *God Crucified*, 20–22; and Hurtado, *One God, One Lord*, 41–50. For a different perspective, cf. Barker, *The Great Angel*, 48–67.

88. Bauckham, *God Crucified*, 21.

89. See Evans, "Jesus' Self-Designation," 40–43; Witherington, *Jesus the Sage*, 201–8.

90. It is clear that Matthew and Luke are recording the same saying of Jesus, although they have transmitted it in slightly different wording. Many scholars believe that behind Matthew's and Luke's versions of the saying lies an older source, which is commonly given the label of "Q" (short for the German *Quelle*—meaning "source").

91. Evans, "Jesus' Self-Designation," 42.

92. For a very different assessment and a well-argued discussion of this passage (focusing on Col 1:15–17), see Stafford, *Jehovah's Witnesses Defended*, 212–28. There is not room here to give Stafford's discussion the extended treatment it deserves, but I can only say: (1) I am not satisfied that he has fully appreciated the implications of calling the Son "the image of the invisible God," especially in the context of the other statements in this hymn; (2) I am not convinced by Stafford's attempt to distinguish between "all *creation*" (*pases ktiseos*) and "all things" (*ta panta*), especially since the full statement is that "all things were *created*" (*ektisthe ta panta*), hence excluding Christ from the realm of "all created things"; and (3) Stafford does not give adequate attention to the Wisdom background of the hymn, which helps us understand that Jesus is to be both distinguished from God and included within God's own unique identity—since Wisdom-language was a Jewish way of speaking of God himself acting in the temporal world.

93. See Witherington, *Jesus the Sage*, 266–72; and (reaching slightly different theological conclusions) James D. G. Dunn, *Christology in the Making: An Inquiry into the Origins of the Doctrine of the Atonement* (London: SCM, 1989), 187–94.

94. Witherington, *Jesus the Sage*, 270.

95. On the Wisdom background to John's prologue, see Witherington, *Jesus the Sage*, 282–89. Greg Stafford acknowledges this background in his study of the prologue but fails to recognize that Wisdom-language was a Jewish means of speaking of God himself acting in the temporal world, while at the same time protecting God's transcendence. See Stafford, *Jehovah's Witnesses Defended*, 311–15.

96. Nowhere in the New Testament are the persons of the Godhead described as "gods" in the plural, despite the fact that the Son (as well as the Spirit) is clearly described in divine terms. This militates against the view put forth by Greg Stafford (*Jehovah's Witnesses Defended*, 96–128, 348–55), that Jesus can be described in divine terms without breaching biblical monotheism, simply because Jews were already used to describing angelic members of the heavenly court as "gods." But none of the references to Jesus as God in the New Testament, or descriptions of him in divine terms, employ the poetic imagery of the heavenly council. Nowhere is Jesus included among the "gods" in that widely attested sense. This conforms to the fact that nowhere in Jewish literature (biblical or nonbiblical) does one find the plural term "gods" used in such a way as to include both God and the angels at once. (Yahweh is instead the "God of gods.") In John 10:30–38, Jesus clearly distinguishes between the lower sense in which angels and men can be called gods and his own *unique* divine status, which he shares with the Father (cf. 10:30,38). Furthermore, Hebrews 1:6–13 clearly draws a line between the angels of heaven and the Son, who is worshiped as God the Creator. Only the Son is "the radiance of God's glory and the exact representation of his being" (Heb 1:3), which radically distinguishes him from all the angels (1:4).

97. For more extensive theological discussions, see Gordon D. Fee, "Paul and the Trinity: The Experience of Christ and the Spirit for Paul's Understanding of God," in *The Trinity*, ed. Davis et al., 49–72; *idem*, "Christology and Pneumatology in Romans 8:9–11—and Elsewhere: Some Reflections on Paul as a Trinitarian," in *Jesus of Nazareth: Lord and Christ*, ed. Joel B. Green and Max Turner (Grand Rapids: Eerdmans, 1994), 312–31; Max Turner, *The Holy Spirit and Spiritual Gifts—Then and Now* (Carlisle: Paternoster, 1996), 169–80; *idem*, "The Spirit of Christ and 'Divine' Christology," in *Jesus of Nazareth*, 413–36; and Christoph Schwöbel, "Radical Monotheism and the Trinity," *Neue Zeitschrift für systematische Theologie und Religionsphilosophie* 43 (2001): 54–74.

98. Bauckham, *God Crucified*, 76.

99. Fee, "Paul and the Trinity," 54.

100. See Hurtado, *One God, One Lord,* 105.

101. Fee, "Paul and the Trinity," 53–54.

102. Ibid., 55.

103. As Larry Hurtado notes: "In short, in the proclamation and the religious practice reflected in the New Testament and characteristic of 'mainstream' Christian tradition down through the centuries, the significance of Jesus' redemptive and revealing work is seen and celebrated as deriving from his status as the unique agent of God's will. That is, the meaning of Christ is always expressed in terms of his relationship to God" (*At the Origins of Christian Worship* [Carlisle: Paternoster, 1999], 104).

104. See, for example: Rom 5:1–5; 8:9–11; 1 Cor 6:11; 2 Cor 1:21–22; 3:16–18; 4:5–6; Gal 3:1–5; 4:4–6; Eph 1:13–14, 17; 2:17–18; 3:16–19; 5:18–20; Col 3:16–17; 1 Thess 1:4–6; 2 Thess 2:13–14; Titus 3:4–7. Outside the Pauline corpus: Matt 3:16–17; John 14–16; 1 Pet 1:2; Jude 20–21.

105. I acknowledge that alternative understandings of these triadic passages are possible. One might prefer to maintain the view that the Holy Spirit is *only* a means of speaking of God's own activity in the world—much as we suggested above regarding the language of God's Wisdom/Word in Judaism. Or, alternatively, one might argue that the Holy Spirit should be regarded as a sort of exalted angelic agent of God. While I do not regard either of these explanations as exegetically or theologically adequate, they would be alternative ways of speaking of the Holy Spirit in highly exalted terms without breaching biblical monotheism. For an insightful critique of these two options, see Turner, *The Holy Spirit and Spiritual Gifts,* 176–78. It would seem that the biblical and Jewish background pushes us to recognize the Holy Spirit as *God's own presence* among his people (hence rendering the angelic agent view unlikely), whereas the inclusion of the Spirit alongside the Father and the Son forces us to recognize him as *a distinct person* within God's identity (hence weakening the analogy with Wisdom/Word). See further, Gordon D. Fee, *God's Empowering Presence: The Holy Spirit in the Letters of Paul* (Peabody: Hendrickson, 1994), 827–45, 905–10.

106. See Hayman, "Monotheism," 14–15; Barker, *The Great Angel,* 190–231; and Peterson, "Ye are Gods," 472–75, 542–53, 557–58 n. 7.

107. For citations of **Peter Hayman:** Daniel C. Peterson and Stephen D. Ricks, *Offenders for a Word* (Provo, Utah: FARMS, 1992), 71–72, 78; Peterson, "Ye are Gods," 493; Michael T. Griffith, *Refuting the Critics: Evidences of the Book of Mormon's Authenticity* (Bountiful, Utah: Horizon, 1993), 116; and Barry Robert Bickmore, *Restoring the Ancient Church: Joseph Smith and Early Christianity* (Ben Lomond, Calif.: Foundation for Apologetic Information and Research, 1999), 101. **Margaret Barker:** Peterson, "Ye are Gods," 566 n. 92; Barry R. Bickmore, "Not Completely Worthless," *FARMS Review of Books* 12/1 (2000): 290 n. 38, 291; *idem, Restoring the Ancient Church,* 106, 107, 108, 109, 111; and Martin S. Tanner, "Review of Melodie Moench Charles," *Review of Books on the Book of Mormon* 7/2 (1995): 20 n. 27, 29–30, 35–36.

108. Hayman, "Monotheism," 2.

109. Ibid., 2–4.

110. Ibid., 3.

111. Ibid., 2.

112. H. Freedman, trans., *Midrash Rabbah: Genesis I* (London: Soncino, 1939), 2 n. 5; emphasis added.

113. As one standard source states: "'Kabbalah' is the traditional and most commonly used term for the esoteric teachings of Judaism and for Jewish mysticism, especially the forms

which it assumed in the Middle Ages from the 12th century onward" (G. Scholem, "Kabbalah," in *Encyclopaedia Judaica,* eds. C. Roth and G. Wigoder [Jerusalem: Keter, 1971], 10:489). Gershom Scholem and others have argued that the *roots* of Kabbalah can be traced back through earlier forms of Jewish mysticism—which focused on the mysteries concerning creation (*Ma'aseh Bereshit*) and God's heavenly throne (*Ma'aseh Merkabah*)—to mainstream Jewish circles as early as the New Testament period. See Gershom Scholem, *Major Trends in Jewish Mysticism* (New York: Schocken, 1941); *idem, Origins of the Kabbalah* (Princeton: Princeton University Press/Jewish Publication Society, 1987). However, Peter Schäfer (another specialist in the Jewish mystical literature) has argued that the authors of such texts "cannot be the same rabbis who wrote the Mishnah, Talmud and Midrash. The worldview of the Merkavah mystics, as far as we can fathom it, is too different from that of the rabbis" ("The Aim and Purpose of Early Jewish Mysticism," in *Hekhalot-Studien* [Tübingen: Mohr, 1988], 293). Schäfer's view (if followed) calls into question Hayman's appeal to documents of the Kabbalah as witnesses to mainstream Jewish views.

114. There are also complications regarding the textual history of Sepher Yetzirah, which Hayman is intimately familiar with, yet chooses not to mention. Aryeh Kaplan notes: "No other Judaic text exists in so many versions" (*Sepher Yetzirah: the Book of Creation* [Northvale, N.J.: Jason Aronson, 1995], xxiv). Concerning its doctrine of creation, Kaplan notes: "Chakhmah [Wisdom], however, is on the level of Nothingness. It is from this Nothingness, however, that all things were created" (132). On the concept of Nothingness in the Kabbalah, see Scholem, "Kabbalah," 10:562–63.

115. Not all of the Kabbalists held this bizarre view. See Scholem, "Kabbalah," 10:583–88 for discussion. The Bahir's statement that Evil lies in the north of God "for the *tohu* is in the north, and *tohu* means precisely the evil that confuses men until they sin," may be based upon an esoteric reading of Jeremiah 4:6, 22–23.

116. See Moshe Idel, *Kabbalah: New Perspectives* (New Haven: Yale University Press, 1988), 59–73.

117. Hayman, "Monotheism," 4.

118. See Idel, *Kabbalah,* 59–60.

119. Enoch's transformation into Metatron is especially in focus in chapters 3–15.

120. See Dunn, "Was Christianity a Monotheistic Faith from the Beginning?" 312–14.

121. The angels themselves are depicted complaining that there was something inappropriate about a mortal receiving such an exalted heavenly status: "Lord of the Universe, what right has this one to ascend to the height of heights? Is he not descended from those who perished in the waters of the flood? What right has he to be in heaven?" (3 En. 4:7).

122. Translations of 3 Enoch are taken from P. Alexander, "3 (Hebrew Apocalypse of) Enoch," in *The Old Testament Pseudepigrapha,* ed. James H. Charlesworth (New York: Doubleday, 1983), 1:223–315.

123. Even if these qualifications are later glosses, they still show a Jewish concern to protect God's unique divine identity when it is sensed that the heavenly status of a human or angelic figure has become too exalted.

124. As noted by Darrell L. Bock, *Blasphemy and Exaltation in Judaism* (Grand Rapids: Baker, 2000), 127.

125. See on this, Bock, *Blasphemy and Exaltation,* 178–79.

126. See Hayman, "Monotheism," 5.

127. See Psalm 148:2–5; Jubilees 2:2; 10:8; Pseudo-Philo 60:2; 2 Enoch 29:3; 33:7; 2 Baruch 21:6; 1QS 3:15,25; 1QH 9:8–11.

128. Hayman, "Monotheism," 5.

129. See references listed above.

130. C. A. Newsom, "Angels," in *Anchor Bible Dictionary,* ed. David Noel Freedman (New York: Doubleday, 1992), 1:252.

131. See Hayman, "Monotheism," 6.

132. See on this Michael Heiser, "Deuteronomy 32:8 and the Sons of God," 52–74.

133. For cogent defenses of the view that "the Most High" and YHWH are identical here, see Mullen, *Assembly of the Gods,* 204; and Sanders, *The Provenance of Deuteronomy 32,* 371–74. Contra Peterson, "Ye are Gods," 501.

134. See Eugene Ulrich et al., *Qumran Cave 4: Deuteronomy, Joshua, Judges, Kings* (DJD 9; Oxford: Clarendon, 1995), 139. Paul Sanders points out: "Present-day scholars, however, commonly prefer retaining the MT [of Deut. 32:9] and regard the rendering in the LXX as a free one" (*The Provenance of Deuteronomy 32,* 160).

135. Admittedly, Deuteronomy 32:8–9 comes close to a monarchistic/henotheistic outlook, since YHWH is depicted as the national God of Israel alone. However, the affirmation that it is YHWH/the Most High who *delivered the nations over* to these other "sons of God" pushes in the direction of monotheism, since Israel's God is still ultimately in authority over all the nations.

136. Hayman, "Monotheism," 11.

137. Hayman claims that on a magic bowl, "Yahweh is even called an angel" (ibid., 10). Of course, what the bowl actually attests is "*yod-yod-yod* the Great, the angel." If anything, the implication is that an angel has been given the divine name (cf. Exod. 23:21; 3 En. 10:3; 12:5; 16:5), not that Yahweh is himself an angel.

138. See Stuckenbruck, *Angel Veneration and Christology,* 188–203; Hurtado, *One God, One Lord,* 28–30; and Clinton E. Arnold, *The Colossian Syncretism: The Interface Between Christianity and Folk Belief at Colossae* (Tübingen: Mohr, 1995), 32–60.

139. See Hayman, "Monotheism," 11–15.

140. On the role of Michael in Jewish religious texts, see Hurtado, *One God, One Lord,* 76–78; Hannah, *Michael and Christ,* 25–75; and Bock, *Blasphemy and Exaltation,* 165–69.

141. Many scholars believe Michael and Melchizedek represent the same figure in the Dead Sea Scrolls. See Paul J. Kobelski, *Melchizedek and Melchireša* (Washington, D.C.: Catholic Biblical Association of America, 1981), 71–74. Cf. Hannah, *Michael and Christ,* 70–74; Hurtado, *One God, One Lord,* 78–79; and Bock, *Blasphemy and Exaltation,* 169–73.

142. Compare the careful study of Hurtado, *One God, One Lord,* 71–92.

143. Barker, *The Great Angel,* 3.

144. Barker, *The Great Angel,* 4–7.

145. Newsom, "Angels," 1:248.

146. Korpel, *A Rift in the Clouds,* 239. Korpel points out, regarding the designation "sons of God" in the Old Testament, that in contrast with the older Canaanite myths, "in these texts the existence of the sons of God is not denied but they are totally subservient to YHWH, their origin is deliberately obscured, and any mythical feature has been carefully removed" (256).

147. Korpel, *A Rift in the Clouds,* 246.

148. Barker, *The Great Angel,* 12–27.

149. See ibid., 13–15.

150. Ibid., 15.

151. See especially, in *Those Elusive Deuteronomists: The Phenomenon of Pan-Deuteronomism,* ed. Linda S. Schearing and Stephen L. McKenzie (Sheffield: Sheffield Academic Press, 1999), Norbert F. Lohfink, "Was There a Deuteronomist Movement?" 36–66; and Robert R. Wilson, "Who Was the Deuteronomist? (Who Was Not the Deuteronomist?): Reflections on Pan-Deuteronomism," 67–82.

152. See Richard Coggins, "What Does 'Deuteronomistic' Mean?" in *Those Elusive Deuteronomists*, 22–35.

153. Barker believes that the religion of the First Temple was maintained prior to Christianity within the apocalyptic circles that produced 1 Enoch. See Barker, *The Great Angel*, 14.

154. It must be kept in mind that Barker's reconstruction does not merely involve the hypothesis of a Deuteronomistic history or a Deuteronomistic editing of certain biblical books—she goes beyond this to make *value* judgments. Some biblical scholars who might entertain aspects of the Deuteronomistic hypothesis would not share Barker's judgment that what has *come to be* recognized as "orthodox" Jewish monotheism, really represents the enforced religious agenda of a vocal minority within ancient Judaism. So Richard Coggins has recently asked regarding her work: "Is the orthodoxy of ancient Israelite religion really laid down along Deuteronomistic lines, as has recently been claimed?" ("What Does 'Deuteronomistic' Mean?," 23). Barker's view of the way Israel's history has been rewritten in the Deuteronomistic literature can only be described as a *conspiracy theory*.

155. See Barker, *The Great Angel*, 29–30.

156. Ibid., 6.

157. Ibid., 36. Cf. John Day, "The Canaanite Inheritance of the Israelite Monarchy," in *King and Messiah in Israel and the Ancient Near East*, ed. John Day (Sheffield: Sheffield Academic Press, 1998), 81–86.

158. Barker translates 1 Chronicles 29:20 as, "the people *worshiped* Yahweh and the king" (*The Great Angel*, 36). But the Hebrew verb *shachah* does not need to be translated "worship," unless the context demands it. The basic meaning is "to bow down," and that translation is perfectly appropriate here.

159. Barker, *The Great Angel*, 114.

160. See ibid., 122–25 (cf. 43–46). Barker expounds this thesis at length in her essay, "The High Priest and the Worship of Jesus," in *The Jewish Roots of Christological Monotheism*, 93–111.

161. See Barker, *The Great Angel*, 43, 81, 99. Slightly more puzzling is the description of Moses in the pseudepigraphal Ezekiel the Tragedian, 68–82. In a dream, Moses is invited by God to sit on the divine throne, to wear God's crown, and to exercise God's regal authority (represented by his scepter). The dream uses imagery from Genesis 37:9 and Daniel 7:13–14. For discussions of this unusual text, see Hurtado, *One God, One Lord*, 57–59; Bock, *Blasphemy and Exaltation*, 141–44; and Bauckham, *God Crucified*, 20 n. 34. Cf. Barker, *The Great Angel*, 42, 79.

162. Barker, *The Great Angel*, 116.

163. See ibid., 119.

164. Philo's descriptions of the Logos are varied and provide important background for early Christology. The Logos is the **Divine Representative** (*Who is the Heir*, 205); **Chief Angel** (*On the Confusion of Tongues*, 146; *Questions and Answers on Exodus*, II.13); **Instrument in Creation** (*Allegorical Interpretation*, III.96; *On the Sacrifices of Abel and Cain*, 8); **High Priest** (*On Flight and Finding*, 108; *On the Migration of Abraham*, 102; *Moses*, II.131–34; *On the Giants*, 52); and **Image of God** (*On the Confusion of Tongues*, 147).

165. Cf. Philo, *On the Cherubim*, 27–28; and *On Flight and Finding*, 95–97. Cf. Barker, *The Great Angel*, 154–55. In Barker's discussion, she completely misses the fact that Philo is not thinking of ontologically distinct Gods. Barker interprets with wooden literalness what Philo is attempting to imaginatively depict through philosophical contemplation. Cf. *Questions and Answers on Exodus*, II.68: "And this *the mind conceives* somewhat as follows. . . ."

166. See Hurtado, *One God, One Lord,* 44–48: "It is doubtful that Logos and other divine powers amount to anything more than ways of describing God and his activities. Thus, when Philo calls the Logos 'god' or 'second god,' he seems to mean only that the Logos is God as apprehended in his works of creation and redemption by means of human reason" (48). Cf. Hannah, *Michael and Christ,* 77–83; and Erwin R. Goodenough, *An Introduction to Philo Judaeus* (New Haven: Yale University Press, 1940), 130–44: "That is, the One God gives forth a stream from himself, the first representation of which is the Logos, most like God because it is the primal emanation. . . . Since the Logos is a projection of divine reality and being, it can be called God, and all the workings of the Logos can be called the acts or works of God" (131).

167. Alan F. Segal, *Two Powers in Heaven: Early Rabbinic Reports About Christianity and Gnosticism* (Leiden: Brill, 1977), 161, 164.

168. Schürer, *History of the Jewish People,* 884.

169. Cf. Philo, *On the Decalogue,* 64–65; and *On the Creation,* 170–172. See further, Goodenough, *Introduction to Philo,* 103–13. I would not deny that Philo's Middle Platonic views—which presumed God could have no direct contact with the material world—posed certain problems for his monotheistic outlook. Philo described the Logos as if it existed on a level *in between* Creator and creation (e.g., *Who Is the Heir,* 205). Nevertheless, because the Logos never attained an independent identity in Philo's thought (remaining an emanation from God's own being), his commitment to Jewish principles kept him within the bounds of monotheism. Middle Platonic assumptions caused similar problems for early Christian apologists such as Justin Martyr and Origen, whose understanding of the Son's identity was similar to Philo's Logos. The tensions remained unresolved until the Nicene fathers clearly identified the Son as a distinguishable relation within God's own substance rather than an emanation from God (so Justin, Origen), or worse, a creature (so Arius). Hence, Nicene theology marked a decisive break with all Platonic and subordinationist views that presumed that the true God could have no direct contact with the physical world. On Philo and the early church fathers, see David T. Runia, *Philo in Early Christian Literature* (Leiden: Brill, 1993); and Robert M. Berchman, *From Philo to Origen: Middle Platonism in Transition* (Chico: Scholars Press, 1984).

170. See Barker, *The Great Angel,* 213–31.

171. Ibid., 215.

172. See Hebrews 1:1–2:9. For further discussion, see Hannah, *Michael and Christ,* 122–62; Richard Bauckham, "Jesus, Worship of," in *Anchor Bible Dictionary,* 3:812–19; idem, *The Climax of Prophecy: Studies in the Book of Revelation* (Edinburgh: T & T Clark, 1993), 118–49; and Stuckenbruck, *Angel Veneration and Christology,* 257–65, 269–73. It is important to distinguish "angel Christology," which literally identifies Christ as an angel (so Barker), from "angelomorphic Christology," which refers to the fact that Christ is sometimes portrayed *visually* in the "form" of an angel (so Hannah, Stuckenbruck). Hannah also coins the term "theophanic angel Christology," which identifies Christ with the Angel of the LORD spoken of in the Old Testament. For the terminology, see Hannah, *Michael and Christ,* 12–13.

173. Peterson, "Ye are Gods," 553.

174. Ibid., 555.

175. Ibid., 472.

176. Peterson follows Jerome H. Neyrey in understanding "one" in terms of *equality* with God ("Ye are Gods," 473). Although this is true, it misses the nuance of the usage here. Jesus does not just claim to be one *with God,* and hence only equal to God; rather, he claims

to be one with *the Father*, and hence to *be* God! This is a development of what is found in John 5:18, where Jesus' claim to have God as his own Father (meaning they share the same nature), is understood in terms of "equality" (*ison*) with God. In biblical and Nicene terms, *the Son is all that the Father is*, though he is not the Father. For further discussion, see Jerome H. Neyrey, "'My Lord and My God': The Divinity of Jesus in John's Gospel," in *SBL 1986 Seminar Papers*, ed. Kent H. Richards (Atlanta: Scholars Press, 1986), 152–71.

177. Peterson, "Ye are Gods," 483, 564 n. 68.

178. Melvin K. H. Peters, "Septuagint," in *Anchor Bible Dictionary*, 5:1102.

179. See Peterson, "Ye are Gods," 484–501.

180. The parallels are usually obvious enough so as not to require explicit comment: e.g., El is the literal "father of the gods," and the "father of Man"; El has a divine consort; El was apparently the son of earlier generations of gods (see Peterson, "Ye are Gods," 487–89). On several occasions however, Peterson does highlight what he thinks are meaningful parallels (489, 494, 495, 498–99).

181. So Mullen, *Assembly of the Gods*, 113–284.

182. See Peterson, "Ye are Gods," 538–39.

183. Korpel, *A Rift in the Clouds*, 133.

184. Ibid., 231.

185. Ibid., 241.

186. Ibid., 263.

187. Ibid., 263.

188. Ibid., 628.

189. Comparisons between the Hebrew Bible and the Ugaritica must also keep in mind the chronological and geographical distance between the two bodies of literature. See on this, John Day, "Ugarit and the Bible: Do They Presuppose the Same Canaanite Mythology and Religion?" in *Ugarit and the Bible*, ed. G. J. Brooke, A. H. W. Curtis and J. F. Healey (Münster: Ugarit-Verlag, 1994), 35–52.

190. In particular, Abraham 3:26–28 may reflect the judgment motif in Psalm 82:1, 6.

191. Exod 15:11, cf. 15:14–15; Pss 77:13, cf. 77:14–15; 86:8, cf. 86:9–10; 96:4, cf. 96:5; 97:9, cf. 97:7; 135:5, cf. 135:8–12; 136:2, cf. 136:10–22.

192. See on this, Heiser, "Deuteronomy 32:8 and the Sons of God," 70–72; Mullen, *Assembly of the Gods*, 238; Sanders, *The Provenance of Deuteronomy 32*, 370–71; and Peterson, "Ye are Gods," 500–501.

193. See Heiser, "Deuteronomy 32:8 and the Sons of God," 62 n. 37; Mullen, *Assembly of the Gods*, 238–44; and Peterson, "Ye are Gods," 533–34. On the conflation between earthly rulers and heavenly beings in Psalm 82, cf. Mullen, *Assembly of the Gods*, 228 n. 195; Peterson, "Ye are Gods," 540; and Robert Chisholm, "A Theology of the Psalms," in *A Biblical Theology of the Old Testament*, ed. Roy B. Zuck (Chicago: Moody, 1991), 275–76.

194. Chisholm, "A Theology of the Psalms," 276.

195. Peterson, "Ye are Gods," 492.

196. Ibid., 494, 495.

197. For an example of how far some Mormons are willing to go, see Eugene Seaich, *Mormonism, the Dead Sea Scrolls, and the Nag Hammadi Texts* (Midvale, Utah: Sounds of Zion, 1980), 50–62. Seaich's book hits rock bottom when, rather than accept Jesus' affirmation of the Shema in Mark 12:29, he assumes that either a later Jewish convert put these words into his mouth or it "reflected Jesus' own belief at an early stage of his development" (61). There is, of course, no point in attempting to engage such fanciful circular reasoning.

198. See de Moor, *The Rise of Yahwism*, 10–41. The epigraphic and iconographic evidence points in the same direction. See Bill T. Arnold, "Religion in Ancient Israel," in *The Face of Old Testament Studies*, 397–99, for further discussion.

199. See de Moor, *The Rise of Yahwism*, 40.

200. See ibid., 41. Despite the assertions of some scholars (cf. Peterson, "Ye are Gods," 567 n. 92), there is no clear evidence that Yahweh ever had a consort in official Israelite religion. Cf. Korpel, *A Rift in the Clouds*, 217–19; and Arnold, "Religion in Ancient Israel," 411–13: "In sum, with regard to the Kuntillet 'Ajrud inscriptions in particular, one should not accept aberrations of classical Yahwism from the fringes of Israelite culture as normative expressions of preexilic religion" (413).

201. See de Moor, *The Rise of Yahwism*, 33, for conclusions based on the overlap in meaning of Elohistic and Yahwistic personal names.

202. Ibid., 33, 39.

203. The expression "as far as it is translated correctly" might be read so as to allow room for the denial of biblical inerrancy, but it surely stretches Joseph Smith's intention to use this as a loophole to discount the testimony of large blocks of the biblical record.

204. Hurtado, *At the Origins of Christian Worship*, 105, 106; italics original.

Chapter 9: Is Mormonism Christian?

1. For recent, widely distributed expositions of current Mormon belief, see Robert L. Millet, *The Mormon Faith: A New Look at Christianity* (Salt Lake City: Deseret, 1998); and Robert L. Millet and Noel B. Reynolds, eds., *Latter-day Christianity: 10 Basic Issues* (Provo, Utah: FARMS, 1998). For more detail, one has to turn to the writings of the late Bruce R. McConkie, which culminated in his *A New Witness for the Articles of Faith* (Salt Lake City: Deseret, 1985), while also recognizing that he was the most conservative of the LDS Twelve Apostles at that time.

2. For a detailed presentation of the evidence that often leads the Latter-day Saints to these kinds of conclusions, see Daniel C. Peterson and Stephen D. Ricks, *Offenders for a Word: How Anti-Mormons Play Word Games to Attack the Latter-day Saints* (Provo, Utah: FARMS, 1992).

3. The most recent example of such a treatment of so disparate a collection of groups is John Ankerberg and John Weldon, *Encyclopedia of Cults and New Religions* (Eugene, Ore.: Harvest House, 1999).

4. Stephen E. Robinson, a BYU professor of New Testament, and I tried to model a way of avoiding both of these extremes in our *How Wide the Divide? A Mormon and an Evangelical in Conversation* (Downers Grove, Ill.: InterVarsity Press, 1997). Reactions to the book were remarkably varied. Among fellow scholars it was widely praised, and it was voted by *Christianity Today* one of the fifteen best Christian books for 1997 (27 April 1998). Many Latter-day Saints were grateful for the courteous tone and attempts at objectivity but disappointed that I stopped short of labeling Mormonism Christian. Many evangelical countercult ministries criticized it, misrepresented it, and imputed erroneous motives to its authors. For a detailed summary of responses to the book, see Matthew R. Connelly and BYU Studies Staff, "Sizing Up the Divide: Reviews and Replies," *BYU Studies* 38 (1999): 163–72, with replies by Robinson (172–76) and myself (176–83) and endnotes to all three sections (183–90). The most egregious and inflammatory published misquotation of my views of which I am aware appears, ironically, in a newsletter from an organization entitled "Truth-in-Love Ministries" from Milwaukie, Oregon, which demonstrated neither truthfulness nor love on this occasion (see 180–81 and 190 n. 69 for details).

5. Blomberg and Robinson, *How Wide the Divide?* 199 n. 6.

6. In addition to scattered remarks in the literature surveyed by Connelly, "Sizing Up," and Robinson's and my responses, I have a thick file of correspondence with numerous such allegations.

7. The term *anti-Mormonism* seems to be used in LDS apologetic literature at times to dismiss anyone critical of Mormonism in any way as simply prejudiced, but if the term is to have any meaning it must be reserved for critique that is impolite, inaccurate, exaggerated, or filled with overgeneralizations. Otherwise "anti-Mormon" becomes merely a synonym for any non-Mormon who criticizes any aspect of Mormonism.

8. Henry W. Bowden, "Christianity," in *The World Book Encyclopedia* (Chicago and London: World Book, 1993), 3:524.

9. For a contrary interpretation, see Stephen E. Robinson, "Early Christianity and 1 Nephi 13–14," in *The Book of Mormon: First Nephi, The Doctrinal Foundation,* ed. Monte S. Nyman and Charles D. Tate (Provo, Utah: BYU Religious Studies Center, 1988), 177–91. Robinson argues that 1 Nephi 13 is a historical reference to the Hellenization of the Christian Church in the second century and thereafter, whereas 1 Nephi 14 uses apocalyptic symbolism to describe in dualistic fashion the conflict between those who follow Christ (whatever their denomination) and those who follow the devil.

10. Roger R. Keller, "Christians and Christianity," in *Encyclopedia of Mormonism,* ed. Daniel H. Ludlow (New York: Macmillan, 1992), 1:270.

11. For a good recent overview of these claims, see Kent P. Jackson, *From Apostasy to Restoration* (Salt Lake City, Deseret, 1996).

12. See esp. Jaroslav Pelikan, *The Emergence of the Catholic Tradition* (Chicago: University of Chicago Press, 1971).

13. For all the evidence, see J. N. D. Kelly, *Early Christian Creeds,* 3d ed. (London: Longman, 1972), 131–66.

14. For a fuller discussion, see Philip Schaff, *The Creeds of Christendom,* 3d ed., vol. 1 (New York: Harper and Bros., 1919), esp. 3–42, which discuss developments up through Athanasius. Bruce Demarest, "Creeds," in *New Dictionary of Theology,* ed. Sinclair B. Ferguson and David F. Wright (Downers Grove, Ill.: InterVarsity Press, 1988), 180, observes that "the main branches of Protestantism value the four creeds discussed above [Apostles', Nicene, Chalcedonian, and Athanasian] as faithfully embodying the teachings of Scripture." Speaking of the early creeds, Cyril of Jerusalem in about A.D. 350 put it memorably: "And just as a mustard seed contains a great number of branches in its tiny grain, so also this summary of faith brings together in a few words the entire knowledge of the true religion which is contained in the Old and New Testaments" (*Catechesis* V.12). More generally, see Gerald Bray, *Creeds, Councils and Christ* (Downers Grove, Ill.: InterVarsity Press, 1984).

15. R. P. C. Hanson, *The Continuity of Christian Doctrine* (New York: Seabury, 1981), 51–63.

16. The most detailed, recent example is Barry R. Bickmore, *Restoring the Ancient Church: Joseph Smith and Early Christianity* (Ben Lomond, Calif.: FAIR, 1999).

17. See esp. Adolf von Harnack, *History of Dogma,* 7 vols. (London: Williams & Norgate, 1896–99); and Walter Bauer, *Orthodoxy and Heresy in Earliest Christianity* (Philadelphia: Fortress, 1971; German orig. 1934).

18. The majority of texts adduced by Stephen E. Robinson throughout his *Are Mormons Christians?* (Salt Lake City: Bookcraft, 1991) fall into this category. Cf. further, Paul L. Owen and Carl A. Mosser, review of Blomberg and Robinson, *How Wide the Divide?* in *FARMS Review of Books* 11/2 (1999): 82–102.

19. The classic and fullest study is Martin Hengel, *Judaism and Hellenism*, 2 vols. (London: SCM; Philadelphia: Fortress, 1974).

20. Robinson, *Are Mormons Christians?* 60–65, 81–82. The same is true of the texts cited in Millet and Reynolds, ed., *Latter-day Christianity*, 25–29. For an excellent evangelical introduction to the topic of Eastern Orthodox belief in *theosis* (becoming deified), see Daniel B. Clendenin, ed., *Eastern Orthodox Christianity: A Western Perspective* (Grand Rapids: Baker, 1994) 117–37. For primary sources that agree, see *idem, Eastern Orthodox Theology: A Contemporary Reader* (Grand Rapids: Baker, 1995), 183–92 (esp. 184).

21. Bickmore, *Restoring the Ancient Church*, 138–48, 160–62, 318–23.

22. In 1843 Smith declared, "There are many things in the Bible which do not, as they now stand, accord with the revelations of the Holy Ghost to me" (quoted in Robert J. Matthews, "The Role of the Joseph Smith Translation in the Restoration," in Robert L. Millet and Robert J. Matthews, eds., *Plain and Precious Truths Restored: The Doctrinal and Historical Significance of the Joseph Smith Translation* (Salt Lake City: Bookcraft, 1995), 40.

23. For a helpful survey of the most important changes, see Monte S. Nyman, "The Joseph Smith Translation's Doctrinal Contributions to the Old Testament," in *Plain and Precious Truths*, 55–71; and Andrew C. Skinner, "Doctrinal Contributions of the Joseph Smith Translation of the New Testament," in *Plain and Precious Truths*, 72–103.

24. E.g., Joseph F. McConkie, "Restoring Plain and Precious Truths," in *Plain and Precious Truths*, 32–33.

25. The fullest survey of the state of the art in New Testament textual criticism is Kurt Aland and Barbara Aland, *The Text of the New Testament*, rev. ed. (Leiden: Brill; Grand Rapids: Eerdmans, 1989).

26. E.g., Robinson, in Blomberg and Robinson, *How Wide the Divide?* 63.

27. The standard collection of New Testament apocrypha translated into English, with introductions to each book and references to documents known only via quotations from the church fathers, is Edgar Hennecke, *New Testament Apocrypha*, 2 vols., ed. Wilhelm Schneemelcher (Cambridge: James Clarke; Louisville: Westminster/John Knox, 1992). For the gnostic literature, see James M. Robinson, *The Nag Hammadi Library in English*, rev. ed. (Leiden: Brill, 1988); for the more orthodox earliest church fathers, Michael W. Holmes, ed. and rev., *The Apostolic Fathers* (Grand Rapids: Baker, 1992).

28. McConkie, "Plain and Precious," 33.

29. Cf., e.g., the Roman Catholic commentaries by Joseph A. Fitzmyer, *The Acts of the Apostles* (New York and London: Doubleday, 1997), 221; Luke T. Johnson, *The Acts of the Apostles* (Collegeville, Minn.: Liturgical Press, 1992), 57; and Rudolf Schnackenburg, *Ephesians: A Commentary* (Edinburgh: T & T Clark, 1991), 327–28.

30. Cf. the Roman Catholic, Raymond E. Brown, *An Introduction to the New Testament* (New York and London: Doubleday, 1997), 221. Interestingly, prior to the 1560s, even Catholic tradition was as likely to see Christ (or Peter's confession) as the "rock" on which the church would be built as to argue that it was any authority invested in Peter and his successors themselves! See J. E. Bigane III, *Faith, Christ or Peter: Matthew 16:18 in Sixteenth Century Roman Catholic Exegesis* (Washington, D.C.: University Press of America, 1981).

31. See, e.g., Donald Guthrie, *New Testament Theology* (Downers Grove, Ill.: InterVarsity Press, 1981), 701–89, who concludes, "There was certainly no hierarchical system" in New Testament church organization (789).

32. Cf. the testimony of David P. Wright, "Statement," *Sunstone* 12/3 (1988): 43, to the effect that "more and more Mormon scholars are recognizing that if the book [of

Mormon] does not entirely derive from a nineteenth century provenance, it has been largely colored by concerns of that era."

33. LDS author Richard L. Bushman (*Joseph Smith and the Beginnings of Mormonism* [Urbana: University of Illinois Press, 1984], 179–88) notes some but not all of these parallels and understandably focuses rather on the differences between Campbell and Mormonism.

34. For a convenient introduction, see Lester G. McAllister, ed., *An Alexander Campbell Reader* (St. Louis: CBP Press, 1988). For extensive primary source material, cf. Alexander Campbell, *The Christian System, in Reference to the Union of Christians, and a Restoration of Primitive Christianity, as Plead in the Current Reformation* (Nashville: Gospel Advocate, 1956, repr. ed.). Also see the early Campbellite work by Walter Scott, *The Gospel Restored: A Discourse* (Cincinnati: O. H. Donogh, 1836; repr. Kansas City, Mo.: Old Paths, 1949).

35. From a Campbellite perspective, see Leroy Garrett, *The Stone-Campbell Movement* (Joplin, Mo.: College Press, 1981), 379–87. It is also interesting that Campbell demonstrates an extensive knowledge of the early church fathers, of whom LDS apologists regularly argue Joseph Smith would have had little knowledge. It is possible that Smith could have gained some knowledge of the church fathers second hand through conversations with Sidney Rigdon. Smith could have also learned of the church fathers through Bible encyclopedias, church histories, and other reference works as he apparently did with regard to John Chrysostom on the Marcionite practice of baptism for the dead. See *TPJS*, 222.

36. George B. Arbaugh, *Revelation in Mormonism* (Chicago: University of Chicago Press, 1932), 217.

37. See Blomberg, in Blomberg and Robinson, *How Wide the Divide?* 49–50 for a sampling of many that I have observed.

38. See Richard N. Ostling and Joan K. Ostling, *Mormon America: The Power and the Promise* (San Francisco: HarperSanFrancisco, 1999), 193–96, and the literature there cited.

39. On reading materials available to Smith in the Palmyra area, including works known to have been owned or read by Smith, see D. Michael Quinn, *Early Mormonism and the Magic World View*, rev. ed. (Salt Lake City: Signature, 1998), 178–236.

40. Ostling and Ostling, *Mormon America*, 21–29, 275–76, and the literature there cited. For more detail, cf. the Mormon author writing under the pseudonym, Robert C. Webb, in *The Real Mormonism* (New York: Sturgis and Walton, 1916), 400–26. Bushman (Joseph Smith, 128–40) notes that this "environmental" explanation of the Book of Mormon is the most common non-LDS account of its genesis. Again, he stresses the unique features of Joseph Smith's thought, and these must be given proper emphasis. But the question may still be raised whether or not Mormon scholars have adequately accounted for the environmental parallels they admit are present if this book were really the product of the first millennia before and after Christ.

41. By way of contrast, historic Christianity readily acknowledges that each portion of the Bible emerged in a specific time, place, and culture, tailor-made by God to address issues of concern to his people in that milieu. One can trace clear historical development and progressive revelation from one biblical period to the next in a fashion that is absent from the Book of Mormon, which reads more like a compendium of theological propositions frequently repeated and awkwardly inserted into a putative historical framework.

42. E.g., Robinson, in Blomberg and Robinson, *How Wide the Divide?* 141. This also seems to be the brunt of Millet and Reynolds, eds., *Latter-day Christianity*, 1–5.

43. See esp. Jan Shipps, *Mormonism: The Story of a New Religious Tradition* (Urbana: University of Illinois Press, 1985). Subsequently, Shipps discusses Mormonism's status as a Christian church, leaving the question somewhat open, though clearly more willing to grant

the label (see "'Is Mormonism Christian?': Reflections on a Complicated Question," *BYU Studies* 33 [1993]: 439–65). This is most centrally due to her conviction that to construct the kind of opponent that fundamentalists create of the LDS Church, one must employ "an other" with properties and attributes "very close to, but not exactly the same as" oneself. Thus, the opponents "cannot be truly foreign" (461). This may well be the case. Mormonism is by no means completely foreign to evangelicals, but that does not necessarily make it Christian.

44. Even the uniquely American "Nation of Islam," with certain striking parallels to LDS theology and practice as over against the parent religion from which it broke, is normally rejected as heretical by mainstream (Sunni and Shi'ite) Islam.

45. E.g., Robinson, *Are Mormons Christians?* viii.

46. For an excellent evangelical overview, see David F. Wells, *Revolution in Rome* (Downers Grove, Ill.: InterVarsity Press; London: Tyndale, 1973). For a more detailed Catholic summary, cf. Christopher Butler, *The Theology of Vatican II* (London: Darton, Longman & Todd, 1967).

47. Most recently, see, respectively, the 1999 joint declaration of the Vatican and the Lutheran World Federation, cited in part in Ostling and Ostling, *Mormon America,* 329–30; and "Evangelicals and Catholics Together: The Christian Mission in the Third Millennium," *First Things* 43 (May 1994): 15–22, with subsequent clarifications.

48. Inevitably there are some who only complain that such discussions do not go far enough and who do not appreciate the gains that are made, as demonstrated by certain evangelical reactions to the changes in Catholicism. But it is scarcely as controversial in most American circles today for evangelicals to speak of at least a segment of Catholicism as genuinely Christian as it was a generation ago. In many other parts of the world, the changes have been less sweeping (at times even nonexistent) and traditional animosity understandably remains.

49. Of course, a fair amount of early-nineteenth-century American Christianity was also proslavery. But this was not the dominant perspective throughout church history. For the role Christianity played in earlier emancipation movements, see esp. David B. Davis, *Slavery and Human Progress* (Oxford: Oxford University Press, 1984).

50. Cf. esp. Ezra T. Benson, *Come Unto Christ* (Salt Lake City: Deseret, 1983); *idem, A Witness and a Warning: A Modern-day Prophet Testifies of the Book of Mormon* (Salt Lake City: Deseret, 1988).

51. See, e.g., the numerous texts in the Book of Mormon that, shorn from Smith's later interpretive grid, seem clearly to teach classic Trinitarian doctrine and salvation by grace through faith alone. I have cited a number of these in Blomberg and Robinson, *How Wide the Divide?* 124, 176–77.

52. Ostling and Ostling, *Mormon America,* 422. Richard Ostling was himself the interviewer and quotes Hinckley here verbatim from his transcript of that interview.

53. Subtitled *10 Neglected Virtues That Will Heal Our Hearts and Homes* (New York: Random House, 2000).

54. See, e.g., Stephen E. Robinson, *Believing Christ* (Salt Lake City: Deseret, 1992); *idem, Following Christ* (Salt Lake City: Deseret, 1995); Robert L. Millet, *Jesus Christ: The Only Sure Foundation* (Salt Lake City: Bookcraft, 1999). Even more recently, Robert L. Millet's exposition of the prodigal son (*Lost and Found: Reflections on the Prodigal Son* [Salt Lake City: Deseret, 2001)] is almost entirely in keeping with historic Christian understandings and ranges widely among standard evangelical scholarship in his numerous lengthy quotations.

55. Cf. the numerous LDS reviews of Blomberg and Robinson, *How Wide the Divide?* and the response to Mosser's and Owen's evangelical review in *FARMS Review of Books* 11/2 (1999):

103–264, in which certain prominent LDS writers are revising their language on some of these doctrines. (These reviews also demonstrate the hesitancy of other LDS scholars to go as far.) Similarly encouraging was Apostle Dallin Oaks's landmark address to the LDS General Conference in April 1998, "Have You Been Saved?" These encouraging trends bear some resemblance to what LDS author O. Kendall White called "Mormon neo-orthodoxy," in *Mormon Neo-Orthodoxy: A Crisis Theology* (Salt Lake City: Signature Books, 1987).

56. Francis J. Beckwith, review of Blomberg and Robinson, *How Wide the Divide?* in *Christianity Today* 41 (November 1997): 59.

57. For recent discussion of the similarities and differences among Protestants, Catholics, and Orthodox, see James S. Cutsinger, ed., *Reclaiming the Great Tradition* (Downers Grove, Ill.: InterVarsity Press, 1997).

58. Obviously, some staunch Calvinists will not agree in admitting that Arminianism has strengths!

59. Peterson and Ricks, *Offenders for a Word*, 27.

60. Ibid., 185.

61. For the fullest reconstruction of what we can know or infer about these Judaizers, see throughout, J. Louis Martyn, *Galatians* (New York and London: Doubleday, 1997).

62. Peterson and Ricks, *Offenders for a Word*, 177.

63. Without knowing it, Peterson and Ricks actually chose an example that I have personally used (except for the date), precisely because I was raised in one of the most liberal wings of contemporary Lutheranism, baptized as an infant, and even confirmed in the church, and yet did not personally own my faith until I heard the historic gospel message through a Youth for Christ club in my high school and saw it visibly transforming my peers in a way I had never witnessed in my church!

64. Especially when one recognizes that official Catholic doctrine has never repudiated major medieval "stumbling blocks" such as the Council of Trent. Actual Catholic practice in any given parish, of course, varies widely throughout the world, from churches at one end of a spectrum heavily influenced by the charismatic renewal movement (esp. in the Western World) to those at the opposite end that have created a syncretistic mixture of traditional Catholicism and indigenous spiritism, paganism, and superstition (esp. in the Two-Thirds World).

65. Interestingly, compared to the entire American Christian population, a disproportionately large percentage of "countercult ministries" explicitly affirm Calvinist theology (for which there are a variety of historical causes). But it is not clear that they have always addressed these kinds of questions in ways consistent with their professed Calvinism.

66. See www.barna.org/cgi-bin/PageCategory.asp?CategoryID=16 and www.barna.org/cgi-bin/PageCategory.asp?CategoryID=8. Barna's poll identified persons as "born again," not on the basis of self-identification, but on the answers they gave to two questions. First, respondents were asked: "Have you ever made a personal commitment to Jesus Christ that is still important in your life today?" Those who answered in the affirmative were asked a question about life after death. Those who selected, out of seven possible answers, "When I die, I will go to Heaven because I have confessed my sins and have accepted Jesus Christ as my savior" were then categorized as "born again."

67. Indeed, Ostling and Ostling, throughout their work *Mormon America*, cite numerous examples of Latter-day Saints who do not believe everything their church officially teaches, often describing people who wish to remain anonymous. And it only stands to reason that for every person who is willing to talk to a journalist, even on the promise of anonymity, there are several others who believe similarly but would never admit it in so "risky" an environment.

68. Indeed, I have met such people. Given the current stress in LDS proselytizing that basically says exactly this, such developments ought not to surprise. Cf. President Hinckley's remarks on the "Larry King Live" Christmas 1999 television special, the gist of which was to appeal to non-Mormons to join the LDS Church and "bring all the good you have with you and let us see if we can't add to it."

69. What exactly counts as "official Mormon doctrine" is of course disputed. What I have in mind includes at least the Book of Mormon, Pearl of Great Price, Doctrine and Covenants, and what the Latter-day Saints themselves refer to as the "official declarations" of the living prophets—i.e., the successive presidents of the LDS Church. Arguably, the five most objectionable common Mormon doctrines, admittedly not all held by all Latter-day Saints, are: (1) a finite theism in which God at some point in eternity past was merely a man and not divine; (2) a view of the universe as not eternally contingent on the will or being of God; (3) the denial of the necessity of prevenient grace to overcome humanity's sinful disposition in the process of conversion or regeneration; (4) the denial of Trinitarian monotheism; and (5) the denial of the classic Christian understanding of the relationship of the two natures of Christ.

70. See especially Blomberg, in Blomberg and Robinson, *How Wide the Divide?* 45–52, 104–8, 121–26, 175–85.

71. Most notably Robinson, throughout his singly authored portions of Blomberg and Robinson, *How Wide the Divide?*

72. For similar, quite recent conclusions, cf. Richard J. Neuhaus, "Is Mormonism Christian?" *First Things* 101 (2000): 97–115. For empirical data of church members' relatively recent beliefs that support those conclusions, see Martin Johnson and Phil Mullins, "Mormonism: Catholic, Protestant, Different?" *Review of Religious Research* 34 (1992): 51–62.

73. A modest and seemingly achievable next step, as I pointed out in my "Response" to Connelly, "Sizing Up," 182, would be to organize one or more formal or informal conferences among leading evangelical and LDS scholars and church authorities to continue the quest for mutual understanding. Then no one individual or institution would bear the brunt of the inevitable criticism from the self-appointed watchdogs of our respective constituencies, which at times can be quite debilitating in its effect.

74. Eugene England, "The Good News—and the Bad," Review of Craig L. Blomberg and Stephen E. Robinson, *How Wide the Divide?* (Downers Grove, Ill.: InterVarsity Press, 1997) in *BYU Studies* 38/3 (1999): 192.

75. J. Gresham Machen, *Christianity and Liberalism* (New York: Macmillan, 1923), 8.

Part IV: The Book of Mormon—Introductory Essay

1. Kent P. Jackson, "The Sacred Literature of the Latter-day Saints," in *The Bible and Bibles in America,* ed. Ernest S. Frerichs (Atlanta: Scholars Press, 1988), 170.

Chapter 10: Does the Book of Mormon Reflect an Ancient Near Eastern Background?

1. *EOM,* s.v. "Book of Mormon Near Eastern Background," by Hugh W. Nibley (reprinted in Daniel H. Ludlow, ed., *Scriptures of the Church: Selections from the Encyclopedia of Mormonism* [Salt Lake City: Deseret, 1992], 163).

2. Hugh W. Nibley, "Two Shots in the Dark," in *Book of Mormon Authorship: New Light on Ancient Origins,* ed. Noel B. Reynolds (Provo, Utah: FARMS, 1996 [repr. of 1982 ed.]), 121.

3. Thomas Finley, "A Review of Hugh Nibley's Comparisons between the Book of Mormon and the Lachish Letters," paper presented at the national meeting of the Evangelical Theological Society, Orlando, Florida, 19 November 1998. Online: http://www.irr.org/mit/nibley.html.

4. See Royal Skousen, "Criticial Methodology and the Text of the Book of Mormon," *Review of Books on the Book of Mormon* 6/1 (1994): 129–32 for the argument that Joseph Smith was not familiar with the KJV when the Book of Mormon was produced. A different picture is painted by Philip Barlow: "Young Joseph probably knew the Bible better than [Orson] Pratt and others have thought" ("Before Mormonism: Joseph Smith's Use of the Bible, 1820–1829," *Journal of the American Academy of Religion* 57/4 [1989]: 746). Also see Philip L. Barlow, *Mormon and the Bible: The Place of the Latter-day Saints in American Religion* (New York: Oxford University Press, 1991), 3–42.

5. See, e.g., Barlow, "Before Mormonism." He notes that "Joseph Smith grew up in a Bible-drenched society—and he showed it" (741).

6. See *EOM*, s.v. "Book of Mormon Plates and Records" (=*Scriptures of the Church*, 178–87).

7. "The Wentworth Letter," 1 March 1842. *LDS Collectors Library for Windows*, CD ROM, 1995 Edition.

8. For LDS studies of this issue, see C. Wilfred Griggs, "The Book of Mormon as an Ancient Book," in *Book of Mormon Authorship*, 79–87; Paul R. Cheesman, "External Evidences of the Book of Mormon," in *By Study and Also by Faith*, ed. John M. Lundquist and Stephen D. Ricks (Provo, Utah: FARMS, 1990), 2:78–84; and H. Curtis Wright, "Ancient Burials of Metal Documents in Stone Boxes," in *By Study and Also by Faith*, 2:273–334.

9. See Gabriel Barkay, "The Divine Name Found in Jerusalem," *Biblical Archaeology Review* 9/2 (March/April 1983): 14–19. "Both plaques were rolled five or six times, probably in the same way documents written on flexible material were rolled up" (Gabriel Barkay, "The Priestly Benediction on Silver Plaques from Ketef Hinnom in Jerusalem," *Tel Aviv* 19 [1992]: 176). See *idem*, 139–94 (including an appendix by Marina Rasovsky, David Bigelajzen, and Dodo Shenhav, "Cleaning and Unrolling the Silver Plaques").

10. University of Chicago, "Texts from Achaemenid Times," n.p. [cited 5 August 2000]. Online: http://www-oi.uchicago.edu/cgi-bin/aritextbrowse.pl?text=dph&language=ak&banner=yes&translation=yes. See the "Catalogue Entry" for "DPhAk." A photograph of the inscription is printed in Roland G. Kent, *Old Persian*, 2d ed. (American Oriental Series 33; New Haven, Conn.: American Oriental Society, 1982), plate II.

11. University of Chicago, "Texts from Achaemenid Times."

12. Al Wolters, *The Copper Scroll: Overview, Text and Translation* (Sheffield: Sheffield Academic Press, 1996), 9–10. His figures are "roughly 30 by 80 cm. each."

13. Ibid., 10–11.

14. Ibid., 6, n. 12.

15. The earliest known Hebrew papyrus is apparently a letter written in the eighth or seventh century B.C. and found as part of the Dead Sea Scrolls in the cave at Murabbaat (Ernst Würthwein, *The Text of the Old Testament* [Grand Rapids: Eerdmans, 1979], 7–8).

16. *TDOT* 3:231. See also Kurt Galling, *Biblisches Reallexikon* (HAT 1; Tübingen: J.C.B. Mohr [Paul Siebeck], 1937), 464. This has been compared with the term *delet* (door) in one of the Lachish Letters, but it is a disputed meaning (cf. Finley, "Review of Hugh Nibley's Comparisons," 2).

17. What the KJV calls "brass" was more correctly bronze, an alloy of tin and copper. Nearly all the references to metal plates in the Book of Mormon are to "plates of brass." One

passage mentions "plates of gold" (Mosiah 28:11), and they consisted only of those plates "found by the people of Limhi" and delivered to Mosiah. The same plates appear to be also the "plates of ore" of Mosiah 21:27 (cf. Alma 37:21–31; Helaman 6:26; Ether 1:1–5; 15:33). The Book of Ether was said to be excerpted from these plates (Ether 1:1–5).

18. J. M. Sjodahl attempts to deal with some of the logistical problems that might have been caused by the plates (*An Introduction to the Study of the Book of Mormon* [*LDS Collectors Library*], 35–46). He assumes the plates that Joseph Smith worked from were not pure gold but "ore," as described in 1 Nephi 19:1; Mormon 8:5. Using an illustration of Hebrew written without vowels, he calculates that 45 plates could have contained the "unsealed one-third" of the book, and that this portion from which Joseph Smith worked could have been under 50 pounds.

19. Contrast with John Tvedtnes: "Although perceived as an anomaly and a fabrication by scholars of his day, recent discoveries have vindicated Joseph Smith's account of a record written on gold plates and buried in the earth in a stone box. Indeed, the practice now appears to have been common among the cultures from which the Book of Mormon peoples derived" (*The Most Correct Book: Insights from a Book of Mormon Scholar* [Salt Lake City: Cornerstone, 1999], 28 [based on discussion in 25–28]).

20. From "The Wentworth Letter."

21. John Tvedtnes, "The Hebrew Background of the Book of Mormon," in *Rediscovering the Book of Mormon,* ed. John L. Sorenson and Melvin J. Thorne (Salt Lake City: Deseret, 1991), 77–78; cf. Sidney Sperry, "Hebrew Idioms in the Book of Mormon," *Journal of Book of Mormon Studies* 4/1 [Spring 1995]: 218–25).

22. Tvedtnes, "Hebrew Background," 77.

23. Ibid., 91.

24. Ibid., 79–91. "To wife" appears to be a genuine English expression, though it is labeled archaic by the *Oxford English Dictionary,* which lists the idioms "to take to wife," "to give to wife," "to have to wife," and "to will to wife." It occurs 46 times in the KJV, including Mark 12:23 and Luke 20:30, 33 where the Greek does not use a preposition. Moreover, there are passages from the OT where the underlying Hebrew does not use a preposition: Gen 26:34; Exod 2:1; Lev 21:14; 1 Kgs 7:8; 11:19; 16:31; 1 Chr 7:15; 2 Chr 11:18; 21:6; Neh 7:63.

25. Some of Tvedtnes's features are also described by William Rosenau in *Hebraisms in the Authorized Version of the Bible* (Baltimore: Friedenwald, 1903), esp. 111–28. Overlapping categories include "cognate accusatives," "construct state" [Rosenau's terms are "genitive of material" and "genitive of attribute"], "adverbials" [Rosenau, "preposition with noun for adverb"], "compound prepositions," and the conjunction *and.*

26. Tvedtnes, "Hebrew Background," 89.

27. See also Gen 16:13; 21:3; 22:14; 26:20, 21, 22; 28:19; 32:2, 30; 35:15; 41:51; Exod 17:7, 15; Num 11:3, 34; 21:3; Judg 2:5; 18:29; 1 Sam 7:12; 2 Sam 5:20; 6:8; 1 Kgs 16:24; 2 Kgs 14:7; 1 Chr 14:11; 2 Chr 3:17; Job 42:14.

28. Only after I did my study did I notice another study by Edward H. Ashment ("'A Record in the Language of My Father': Evidence of Ancient Egyptian and Hebrew in the Book of Mormon," in *New Approaches to the Book of Mormon,* ed. Brent Lee Metcalfe [Salt Lake City: Signature Books, 1993], 329–93), which demonstrates that Tvedtnes's examples are "not confined to the Book of Mormon" but also appear in other writings authored by Joseph Smith (359; see further, "Appendix A: Hebraisms in the 1833 Book of Commandments," 375–80).

29. Tvedtnes, "Hebrew Background," 87.

30. The construction in Genesis 1:11 ("fruit trees making fruit after their kind which its seed is in it") is so rare that the editors of the standard edition Hebrew text (*Biblia Hebraica Stuttgartensia*) propose deleting the word translated "after their kind" on the basis of verse 12 ("trees producing fruit which its seed is in it").

31. Ashment lists ten examples from the 1833 Book of Commandments, including this one which seems very similar to Tvedtnes's examples: "that the promises of the Lord might be fulfilled, *which* he made to his people" ("'A Record in the Language of My Father,'" 378–79). Only three of his examples appear to be pertinent to the discussion (two in II:6; VII:1).

32. It may be *'ad* (Deut 9:7), *'el* (2 Chr 23:15), *l* (Judg 20:10; Ezra 2:68), and *b* (Judg 7:17).

33. Second edition, 1989. It lists Cromwell in 1539 ("Yesterday arrived to me hither Your Majesties servants"), Tonstall in 1539 ("Into what howse or place so euer ye shall arriue") and Barrow in 1661 ("He shall in good time arriue to his designed journey's end").

34. "The Original Language of the Book of Mormon: Upstate New York Dialect, King James English, or Hebrew?" *Journal of Book of Mormon Studies* 3/1 (1994): 34.

35. According to Skousen, 1 Nephi 17:50 was "accidentally removed" when Oliver Cowdery was producing the printer's manuscript (P) by copying from the original manuscript (O)," while Joseph Smith himself corrected the other thirteen in the second edition of the Book of Mormon ("Original Language," 34).

36. To this point as given by Skousen. The remainder of the verse is taken from a 1981 edition of The Book of Mormon.

37. 29,600 times in the NIV. These figures were calculated with Bible Works for Windows™, version 4.0.

38. Again, after my own study, I saw Ashment's critique of Skousen, where he concludes: "The evidence from the Book of Mormon and the D&C illustrates that both works originated from the same author" ("'A Record in the Language of My Father,'" 363; see further, "Appendix B: Conditional Clauses in the 1830 Edition of the Book of Mormon, the Book of Commandments, and Jeremiah," 380–88). His example of the KJV of Jeremiah 5:1 for "and" in the result clause is interesting in that the NKJV and the NAB both retain "and."

39. Skousen, "Original Language," 35.

40. The KJV combined these two to give a more unified sense to each day: "And the evening and the morning were the Xth day." The NASB, NIV, and NRSV give the more literal translation in this case.

41. There are a few cases of "and it came to pass" without the time expression in the New Testament. These may be partly due to a looser use of the idiom (as a Hebraism) in the New Testament and partly to the failure of the translators of the KJV to handle the Greek expression properly.

42. To make comparison with the Book of Mormon simpler, I have excluded minor variants on the KJV "and it came to pass," such as "so it came to pass" (Deut 2:16; 1 Sam 13:22) or "but it came to pass" (Judg 15:1; 1 Sam 18:19). In these cases the clause still makes a reference to a time. Once (2 Kings 15:12) the KJV has "and so it came to pass" for *wayehi ken,* a clause that refers to the fulfillment of a word of the Lord. In Genesis 1:7, 9, 11, 15, 24, and 30 the KJV renders this idiom with "and it was so." Occasionally the KJV inserts the time reference into the middle of the "and it came to pass" idiom: "And in process of time it came to pass" (Gen 4:3; cf. Josh 1:1; Judg 1:1; 2 Sam 8:1; 1 Chr 18:1; 2 Chr 13:15). Finally, in three places "it came to pass" (but not "and it came to pass") translates something other than *wayehi* (2 Kgs 24:20; Isa 48:5; and Jer 52:3).

43. Robert Smith rightly points out that the distribution of "and it came to pass" in the KJV depends on the genre ("'It Came to Pass' in the Bible and the Book of Mormon," FARMS preliminary report, 1984). Thus the phrase is absent from any of the poetic books. A more thorough study of the Book of Mormon in this light could prove helpful. Smith does not distinguish between "and it came to pass" and "and it will come to pass," and that probably skews the results. The latter phrase occurs in the Bible most frequently in prophetic statements rather than narrative. Evidently "and it came to pass" strictly for narration was easy enough to imitate in the Book of Mormon, though I have seen some places where it is used for explanatory information rather than narrative in a strict sense (cf. Alma 57:7, 13; 58:1).

44. Hugh Nibley, "Strange Things Strangely Told," in *Since Cumorah*, CWHN 7, ed. John W. Welch, 2d ed. (Salt Lake City: Deseret and FARMS, 1988), 150. Nibley makes several references in this quotation to Grapow, *Das Hieroglyphensystem*, 23–30. I have not been able to locate this work by Grapow, though there are other works on Egyptian that he has written.

45. Tvedtnes, "Hebrew Background," 77.

46. An inscription from ancient Arad (late 7th to early 6th centuries B.C.) in the Negev area has two columns of hieratic signs that give a list of various commodities (probably grains and wine) and their amounts. The scribe may have been an Egyptian who was part of an occupation force during the reign of Jehoiakim (see 2 Kgs 23:34–35; Yohanan Aharoni, *Arad Inscriptions* [Jerusalem: Israel Exploration Society, 1981], 55–64). At Arad and elsewhere, the hieratic Egyptian numerals were also used on some inscriptions. John Tvedtnes thinks the Arad inscription and another inscription from the northern part of Sinai in Egyptian hieratic with a few Hebrew numbers are significant with relation to his contention that an original Hebrew of the Book of Mormon could have been transcribed into Egyptian (*Review of Books on the Book of Mormon*, 38 [from *LDS Collectors Library*]). It makes sense for economic texts that were involved with commerce between Egypt and Judah to have a combination of Egyptian and Hebrew writing, especially where numerals and commodities are concerned. This still seems a long way from the type of material recorded in the Book of Mormon. The *Papyrus Amherst* 63 of the second century B.C. contains "a paganized version of Psalms 20:2–6," but it is rather late in relation to the alleged time of Nephi. For the text from Sinai, see Rudolph Cohen, "Did I Excavate Kadesh-Barnea?" *Biblical Archaeology Review* 7:3 (May/June 1981): 28–30.

47. See Ashment, "A Record in the Language of My Father," 351–54.

48. The influence of "behold" as a verb rather than an interjection is negligible for these statistics, which were determined by using Hermeneutika Bible Research Software's *Bible Works for Windows* 4.0™ (1999) for the KJV and an online search engine for the Book of Mormon (http://www.hti.umich.edu/m/mormon/index.html).

49. At Psalm 106:48 there is a summons to the people: "And let all the people say, Amen. Praise ye the Lord."

50. John Rogerson and Philip R. Davies, "Was the Siloam Tunnel Built by Hezekiah?" *Biblical Archaeologist* 59/3 (1996): 138–49.

51. The following brief articles, all of which react negatively to the article by Rogerson and Davies, appeared in *Biblical Archaeology Review* 23/2 (1997): Jo Ann Hackett, "Spelling Differences and Letter Shapes Are Telltale Signs," 42–44; Frank Moore Cross, "Because They Can't See a Difference, They Assert No One Can," 44; P. Kyle McCarter Jr., "No Trained Epigraphist Would Confuse the Two," 45–46; Ada Yardeni, "They Would Change the Dates of Clearly Stratified Inscriptions—Impossible!" 47; André Lemaire, "Are We

Prepared to Raze the Edifice?" 47–48; Esther Eshel, "Some Paleographic Success Stories," 48–49; Avi Hurvitz, "Philology Recapitulates Paleography," 49–50.

52. See "Seeking Agreement on the Meaning of Book of Mormon Names," *Journal of Mormon Studies* 9/1 (2000): 28–39, 77–78 [Paul Y. Hoskisson, "Lehi and Sariah," 30–31; Jeffrey R. Chadwick, "The Names Lehi and Sariah—Language and Meaning," 32–34; Dana M. Pike, "Response to Paul Hoskisson's 'Lehi and Sariah,'" 35–36; John A. Tvedtnes, "Lehi and Sariah Comments," 37; Paul Y. Hoskisson, "Response to the Comments," 38–39]; and John A. Tvedtnes, John Gee, and Matthew Roper, "Book of Mormon Names Attested in Ancient Hebrew Inscriptions," *Journal of Mormon Studies* 9/1 (2000): 42–51, 78–79. The last article mentioned lists a number of additional Mormon scholars who have written on the issue.

53. Tvedtnes, Gee, and Roper, "Book of Mormon Names," 45.

54. Ibid., 43.

55. "Sam" on a seal from the seventh century B.C., as the authors admit, is read by some as "Shem." See Tvedtnes, Gee, and Roper, "Book of Mormon Names," 51, with full references on 79 n. 60. "Josh" is represented by the Hebrew consonants *yš* or *y'wš* (where *š* stands for the sound /sh/ in English and the *w* stands for either the vowel /u/ or /o/) in a number of inscriptions cited in the article (Lachish letters, Elephantine Papyri of the fifth century B.C., and some Hebrew bullae from about 600 B.C.), and they are the initial consonants in the name Josiah. The three letters by themselves are normally read as Ja'ush (for Ya'ush), for which see Bezalel Porten, *Archives from Elephantine: The Life of an Ancient Jewish Military Colony* (Berkeley: University of California, 1968), 143; Nahman Avigad, *Hebrew Bullae from the Time of Jeremiah: Remnants of a Burnt Archive* (Jerusalem: Israel Exploration Society, 1986), nos. 30, 66, 67; John C. L. Gibson, *Textbook of Syrian Semitic Inscriptions,* vol. I, *Hebrew and Moabite Inscriptions* (Oxford: Clarendon, 1971), 37. There is no direct evidence for the pronunciation "Josh." Possibly the name Josiah contracted the sequence /a'u/ into /o/ when the divine name was included, but such a contraction would have been later than the sixth or fifth century B.C. Gibson states that "the only possible vocalization [for the name in the Lachish Letters] is [ū]" (ibid., 37 n. 1).

56. The issue of /b/ versus /v/ is irrelevant to the present discussion.

57. See BDB, 33 (Strong's Number 348). The inscription cited may be found in *Corpus Inscriptionum Semiticarum: Pt. 1. Inscriptiones Phoeniciae* (Paris: Academie des inscriptions & belles-lettres, 1881), 158. See also D. Harvey, "Jezebel," *IDB,* 2:905–6. N. Avigad noted a Phoenician seal with the spelling *yzbl,* which according to him "explains the Greek spelling of the Septuagint" ("The Seal of Jezebel," *Israel Exploration Journal* 14:4 [1964]: 274–76).

58. E. G. Withycombe, *The Oxford Dictionary of English Christian Names,* 3d ed. (Oxford: Clarendon, 1977), 164.

59. George Stewart, *American Given Names: Their Origin and History in the Context of the English Language* (New York: Oxford University Press, 1978), 147.

60. *Henry V* (I, ii, 81).

61. B. H. Roberts, *Comprehensive History of the Church,* 4:78–79. From *LDS Collectors Library.*

62. The transliteration symbol *ḥ* has a sound similar to the *ch* in the Scottish word *loch.* The symbol *ṣ* has a sound similar to *ts,* s in *hits.* The symbol *š* has the sound *sh,* as in *show.*

63. "Response to Paul Hoskisson's 'Lehi and Sariah,'" 36.

64. Similar problems to those discussed here pertain to Hagoth and Himni.

65. Tvedtnes, Gee, and Roper, "Book of Mormon Names," 46.

66. Mormon scholar Kent Jackson published a comprehensive list of all Ammonite personal names known at the time, none of which are claimed by any Mormon, as far as I can determine, to be found in the Book of Mormon ("Ammonite Personal Names in the Context of the West Semitic Onomasticon," in *The Word of the Lord Shall Go Forth: Essays in Honor of David Noel Freedman in Celebration of His Sixtieth Birthday,* edited by Carol L. Meyers and M. O'Conner [Winona Lake, Ind.: Eisenbrauns, 1983]), 507–21. Jackson also authored *The Ammonite Language of the Iron Age* (HSM 27; Chico, Calif.: Scholars Press, 1980).

67. Yigael Yadin, *Bar-Kokhba,* 176; Giovanni Pettinato, *The Archives of Ebla: An Empire Inscribed in Clay* (Garden City, N.Y.: Doubleday, 1981), 139.

68. "Book of Mormon Names," 46, citing Nahman Avigad and Benjamin Sass, *Corpus of West Semitic Stamp Seals* (Jerusalem: Israel Academy of Sciences and Humanities, 1997), 66–67; and James B. Pritchard, *The Ancient Near East in Pictures Relating to the Old Testament,* 2d ed. (Princeton: Princeton University, 1969), 2–3, 249.

69. A hypocoristic name is from a name otherwise compounded with a divine name, but with the divine name dropped out. Thus, the name Micah (*myk*) is a shorter form of either Michael (with the divine element El) or Micaiah (with the divine element from Yahweh). Compare Mormon scholar Dana Pike's two articles in the *Anchor Bible Dictionary*: "Names, Hypocoristic" (4:1017–18); and "Names, Theophoric" (4:1018–19). He makes no claim there regarding the Book of Mormon.

70. Gibson, *Textbook . . . Volume 1,* 10 (li:3). Presumably the name was pronounced /'aḥa/ and was possibly a hypocoristic of Ahijah.

71. Yigael Shiloh, "A Group of Hebrew Bullae from the City of David," *Israel Exploration Journal* 36 (1986): 29, no. 34.

72. See above. Tvedtnes, Gee, and Roper also cite *'aḥiyāh(û),* but that is simply the name Ahijah of the KJV ("Book of Mormon Names," 46).

73. "Book of Mormon Names," note 31 cites Nahman Avigad, "Hebrew seals and sealings and their significance for biblical research," in Supplements to *Vetus Testamentum* 40 (1988): 14; and Nahman Avigad, "Two Seals of Women and Other Hebrew Seals" (in Hebrew), *Eretz-Israel* 20 (1989a): 90.

74. Hugh Nibley, *An Approach to the Book of Mormon,* CWHN 6, ed. John W. Welch, 3d ed. (Salt Lake City: Deseret and FARMS, 1988), 289.

75. Actually, the form in the text of Nehemiah 13:23 is *'Ammoniyyot,* since as an adjective it needs to have a feminine plural form to modify the Hebrew term for "women."

76. The name *Amon,* which occurs eighteen times in the Old Testament and was borne by King Hezekiah's grandson, cannot be considered in relation to the name on the inscription. In addition to lacking the doubling of the /m/, *Amon* begins with the letter aleph rather than with ayin, which is the initial letter on the inscriptional name.

77. Avigad, "Hebrew Seals and Sealings," 14; Walter Kornfeld, *Onomastica Aramaica aus Ägypten* (Vienna: Verlag der Österreichischen Akademie der Wissenschaften, 1978), 67; *The New Koehler-Baumgartner in English,* 2:846.

78. Tvedtnes, Roper, and Gee, "Book of Mormon Names," 47. The Ammonite seal which contains the name *Hgt* was not included in Kent Jackson's work ("Ammonite Personal Names") but can be found, as Tvedtnes et al. note, in Walter E. Aufrecht, *A Corpus of Ammonite Inscriptions* (Ancient Near Eastern Texts and Studies 4; Lewiston, N.Y.: Mellen, 1989), 34–35.

79. Tvedtnes, Roper, and Gee, "Book of Mormon Names," 47. They cite W. E. Staples, "An Inscribed Scaraboid from Megiddo," in *New Light from Armageddon: Second Provisional Report (1927–29) on the Excavations at Megiddo in Palestine,* ed. P. L. O. Guy (Chicago: University of Chicago, 1931), 49–68, figs. 33–34; Avigad and Sass, *West Semitic Stamp*

Seals, 99; Nahman Avigad, "Some Unpublished Ancient Seals" (in Hebrew), *Bulletin of the Israel Exploration Society* 25 (1961): 242, plate 5:4.

80. Tvedtnes, Roper, and Gee, "Book of Mormon Names," 49.

81. Ibid., 78 n. 41 lists the examples of Baruch from Berechiah, Nahum from Nehemiah, Shallum from Shelemiah, and Zaccur from Zechariah.

82. Shiloh, "Hebrew Bullae," 29–30.

83. A. E. Cowley, ed., *Aramaic Papyri of the Fifth Century B.C.* (Oxford: Clarendon Press, 1923), no. 22. The name occurs in a broken context, and Paul Hoskisson notes that "restorations cannot provide absolute proof but rather at best a suggestion" ("Response to the Comments," 38). The restoration seems reasonable.

84. Ludwig Koehler and Walter Baumgartner, *The Hebrew and Aramaic Lexicon of the Old Testament,* trans. and edited M. E. J. Richardson (New York: E. J. Brill, 1996) 3:1357; Martin Noth, *Die israelitischen Personennamen im Rahmen der gemeinsemitischen Namengebung* (New York: Georg Olms, 1980), entry 1292.

85. The emphasized /s/ in each of the following is a different letter: Jeru*s*alem; I*s*rael; *S*odom. A fourth and less common possibility is represented by *S*idon, which is also a river in the Book of Mormon (Alma 2:15; 3:3).

86. The ending that represented the divine name about 600 B.C. was /yahu/. A short ending /ya/ developed after the Babylonian exile and is found among the Elephantine papyri and late inscriptional material. In the Hebrew Bible, names with /ya/ and with /yahu/ are attested in both early and late texts, but there is a trend for the later texts to move to the names with /ya/. The KJV normally represents either the short or the longer form with–iah or ija, not bothering to distinguish forms with the longer ending even for the same name. For example, the names Hezekiah, Seraiah, Isaiah, and Elijah all have both spellings in the Hebrew but only one spelling in the KJV.

87. Nahman Avigad and Benjamin Sass, *Corpus of West Semitic Stamp Seals* (Jerusalem: Israel Academy of Sciences and Humanities, 1997), 285 n. 760.

88. Ibid., 476.

89. The Hebrew Bible has forms with /-ya/ and /-yahu/ as variant forms. In Jeremiah, seventeen names are spelled both ways. In the inscriptions from the area of Judah that pre-date the Babylonian exile, the only spelling that occurs is /-yahu/. The KJV spells these names only with–iah or with–ijah (cf. note number 83).

90. Shiloh, "Hebrew bullae," 31.

91. If one accepts the doubtful proposition that the–ihah ending represents the divine name.

92. The reference to the "south-southeast" direction of their travel occurs only at 1 Nephi 16:12–13, after the party had crossed the river Laman.

93. Contrast with Warren and Michaela Aston: "The record kept by Lehi and Sariah's younger son Nephi makes it clear that the group ... traveled in the desert wilderness in 'nearly a south-southeast direction' (1 Nephi 16:13) along the eastern coast of the Red Sea. This very specific direction seems to have been followed throughout the first phase of their journey, as verses 14 and 33 go on to indicate" (*In the Footsteps of Lehi: New Evidence for Lehi's Journey across Arabia to Bountiful* [Salt Lake City: Deseret, 1994], 4). I fail to see how 16:14 and 33 can be taken to refer all the way back to the initial trip from Jerusalem. The language of v. 33 could easily refer back simply to 16:13. Besides, the trip from Jerusalem even to the eastern branch of the Red Sea would have been in a south-southwest direction anyway. There is nothing specific in the Book of Mormon that has to indicate that the trip was "along the eastern coast of the Red Sea," if by the Red Sea is meant the part that separates Sinai from modern Arabia. The KJV

clearly indicates that the Israelites crossed the Red Sea (even if the Hebrew more accurately means "Reed Sea"; Exod 13:18; 15:4), and traditionally it has been held that this portion of the Red Sea was on the western side of the Sinai peninsula (cf. "Red Sea" in *The Universal Bible Dictionary,* ed. John MacPherson [London: Hodder and Stoughton, 1842]; and the map inserted between the pages of Exod 13 in *The Holy Bible According to the Authorized Version,* prepared and arranged by George D'Oyly and Richard Mant [London: Society for Promoting Christian Knowledge, 1839]). It cannot be excluded that the account in 1 Nephi envisions a south-southeastern trip down the eastern coast of the Sinai (western) branch of the Red Sea.

94. Terrence L. Szink demonstrates a number of parallels between the Nephite journey and the exodus from Egypt, though he does accept that the journey of the Nephites was through Arabia ("Nephi and the Exodus," in *Rediscovering the Book of Mormon,* ed. John L. Sorenson and Melvin J. Thorne [Salt Lake City: Deseret, 1991], 38–51).

95. Eugene England, "Through the Arabian Desert to a Bountiful Land: Could Joseph Smith Have Known the Way?" *Book of Mormon Authorship,* 143–56. "Arabia" in the New Testament included the Sinai peninsula (Gal 4:25), in agreement with Roman sources (see Robert Houston Smith, "Arabia," in *Anchor Bible Dictionary,* 1:325; G. W. Bowersock, *Roman Arabia* [Cambridge: Harvard University Press, 1983], 1–2).

96. England, "Through the Arabian Desert," 151.

97. For a map of the entire trail, see Thomas J. Abercrombie, "Arabia's Frankincense Trail," *National Geographic* 168/4 (October 1985): 485.

98. According to England, Shazer was about a hundred miles south of Al Beda or about four days travel, corresponding to "the prominent ancient oasis now called Wadi Al Azlan" ("Through the Arabian Desert," 151).

99. Nibley, "Book of Mormon Near Eastern Background" (*Scriptures of the Church,* 164).

100. Sabatino Moscati et al., *An Introduction to the Comparative Grammar of the Semitic Languages: Phonology and Morphology* (Wiesbaden: Otto Harrassowitz, 1969), 44.

101. It is /ṣ/ pronounced /ts/ in Modern Hebrew but a velarized sibilant in more ancient Hebrew.

102. Hugh W. Nibley, *Lehi in the Desert, The World of the Jaredites, There Were Jaredites,* CWHN 5 (Provo, Utah: FARMS, 1988), 78–79.

103. Shihor (Josh 13:3; 1 Chr 13:5; Isa 23:3; Jer 2:18) is probably an eastern branch of the Nile or one of the lakes in the eastern delta. It probably means "the pond of Horus" (see Koehler-Baumgartner in English).

104. *Encyclopedia Britannica.* Online: ⟨http://www.britannica.com/bcom/eb/article/0/0,5716,25420+1+25014,00.html⟩. Hugh Nibley argues that "it would be an obtuse reader indeed who needed someone to spell out for him the *resemblance* between ancient arrow-divination and the Liahone: two 'spindles or pointers' bearing written instructions provide superhuman guidance for travelers in the desert" (in *Since Cumorah,* "Some Fairly Foolproof Tests," 259). Arrows drawn out of a bag to answer questions about whether to take a journey or how fast to go still seems to me remote from a device with "two spindles" inside a "round ball" of "fine brass," one of which "pointed the way whither we should go into the wilderness." That sounds more like a modern compass than like ancient "arrow divination." Nibley's sources for how the arrow divination was used in travel do not prove that this method was as ancient as 600 B.C.

105. The Hebrew is *nechusha,* which always means "bronze" or "copper" (2 Sam 22:35; Job 20:24; Ps 18:34; Jer 15:12). Neither steel nor bronze seems a very practical construction for a serviceable bow (as opposed to an ornamental one). Peter C. Craige thinks Psalm 18:34

may refer to either "a wooden bow with bronze decoration, or the bronze tipped arrows shot from large bows, or it may merely be a poetic way of describing the great strength of the warrior's bow" (*Psalms 1–50*, WBC 19 [Waco, Tex.: Word, 1983], 176. Perhaps the translators of the KJV chose "steel" as a better metaphor for strength than "brass," but Nephi's bow of "fine steel" is contrasted in the same chapter with a bow he made himself out of wood (1 Nephi 16:18, 23).

106. *Lehi in the Desert*, 78–79. Mourning by the women can be derived as easily from the KJV as from the custom of "desert Arabs" (see 2 Sam 14:2; Jer 9:17, 20; Ezek 8:14; Luke 23:27). An unrelated Hebrew root would be *n-ḥ-m*, "to comfort," but in this case it is not stated that the Nephites assigned the name, so it would not have to be derived from the Hebrew (H. Simian-Yofre, *Theological Dictionary of the Old Testament* 9:341: "Most experts no longer accept an original semantic identification of Heb. *nhm* with Arab. *nhm*, 'breathe heavily,' both because of critical objections to deriving the meaning of a word from its etymology and because the concrete semantic field associated with *nhm* in the OT clearly differs from that associated with Arab. *nhm*").

107. *In the Footsteps of Lehi*, 12. The root *nhm* is the one listed by G. Lankester Harding (*An Index and Concordance of Pre-Islamic Arabian Names and Inscriptions* [Toronto: University of Toronto, 1971], 602), and that root does not occur in any Hebrew names. The *Dictionary of Modern Written Arabic* by Hans Wehr, 3d ed. (Ithaca, N.Y.: Spoken Language Services, 1971) lists the meanings as "to have a ravenous appetite, be insatiable; to be greedy, covetous" (1005). The /o/ vowel in Nahom is a problem that no one has dealt with. The Astons give a number of variant spellings, none of which contains either /o/ or /u/ in the second syllable.

108. *Lehi in the Desert*, 78–79. Warren and Michaela Aston (*In the Footsteps of Lehi*, 14–25) present evidence that the name is connected with an ancient burial area and a tribe located northeast of Sana'a. Further research is needed, but preliminarily I would say that they have not offered convincing evidence that the name would be as old as the time of Nephi's reference. The geographical evidence is impressive only if one assumes a trip through Arabia rather than Sinai.

109. Warren and Michaela Aston think they have probably found the site of Bountiful at the outlet of the Wadi Sayq in Oman at the border with Yemen (*In the Footsteps of Lehi*, 27–59).

110. Nibley speculates about various possible Egyptian derivations but does not actually decide on one: "It is enough to know that in Lehi's day the ocean was designated by epithets, and that the sea to the east was called 'many waters' by the Egyptians" (*Lehi in the Desert*, 78).

111. "Through the Arabian Desert," 154, n. 2.

112. D'oyly and Mant, *The Holy Bible According to the Authorized Version*, vol. 1.

113. *Bibliotheca Sacra, or Dictionary of the Holy Scriptures*, ed. James Morison (Edinburgh: Abernethy and Walker, 1806), 1:105; map between 508 and 509. It appeared in Scotland, but such works were undoubtedly often transported across the Atlantic.

114. See James P. Allen, "Egyptian Language and Writing," under "Languages" in *Anchor Bible Dictionary*, ed. David Noel Freedman (New York: Doubleday, 1992), 4:188–93; E. Lipiński, *Semitic Languages: Outline of a Comparative Grammar* (Leuven: Peeters, 1997), 23–27.

115. See Noel B. Reynolds, ed., *Book of Mormon Authorship Revised: The Evidence for Ancient Origins* (Provo, Utah: FARMS, 1997), esp. John W. Welch, "What Does Chiasmus in the Book of Mormon Prove?" (199–224); John L. Hilton, "On Verifying Wordprint

Studies: Book of Mormon Authorship" (225–53); Donald W. Parry, "Power Through Repetition: The Dynamics of Book of Mormon Parallelism" (295–309). Also see Roger R. Keller, *Book of Mormon Authors: Their Words and Messages* (Provo, Utah: BYU Religious Studies Center, 1996).

Chapter 11: Rendering Fiction

1. While in modern editions, the respective testimonies of "The Three" and "The Eight" witnesses often appear before the text of the Book of Mormon itself, in the case of the first edition, these statements were apparently printed at the end of the work.

2. F. M. Brodie, *No Man Knows My History: The Life of Joseph Smith*, 2d ed. (New York: Vintage, 1995), 79. See also M. A. Smith and J. W. Welch, "Joseph Smith: Author and Proprietor," in *Reexploring the Book of Mormon*, ed. J. W. Welch (Salt Lake City: Deseret, 1992), 154–57.

3. Although much important work had already taken place in the 1960s (see, for instance, E. A. Nida, *Toward a Science of Translating* [Leiden: Brill, 1964]), it was in 1972 that James S. Holmes issued his programmatic essay, "The Name and Nature of Translation Studies" (Amsterdam: Translation Studies section [repr. in *idem, Translated! Papers on Literary Translation and Translation Studies* [Amsterdam: Rodopi, 1988], 67–80).

4. S. Bassnett-McGuire, *Translation Studies*, rev. ed. (London and New York: Routledge, 1991).

5. R. Copeland, *Rhetoric, Hermeneutics and Translation in the Middle Ages: Academic Traditions and Vernacular Texts* (Cambridge: Cambridge University Press, 1991).

6. See, for instance, D. Shepherd "Translating and Supplementing: A(nother) look at the Targumic Versions of Genesis 4:3–16," *Journal of the Aramaic Bible* 1/1 (1999): 125–46.

7. This first understanding of "indirect translation" is found in E. Gutt, *Translation and Relevance* (Oxford: Basil Blackwell, 1991), who suggests that the approach is frequently adopted in Bible translation when the sociocultural world encoded in a given target language differs radically from that of the source text.

8. For a brief but comprehensive summary of Bible translation throughout the ages, see E. A. Nida, "Translations," in *The Oxford Companion to the Bible,* ed. B. M. Metzger and M. D. Coogan (Oxford: Oxford University Press, 1993), 749–78.

9. G. Toury, *Descriptive Translation Studies and Beyond* (Amsterdam and Philadelphia: Benjamins, 1995), 129–146.

10. While M. Shuttleworth and M. Cowrie, s.v. "indirect translation," in *Dictionary of Translation Studies* (Manchester: St. Jerome, 1997) highlight that indirect translation may arise as a result of the prestige of a mediating language or of the translator's ignorance of a source language, they suggest that it is a procedure that is generally not approved of. However, this disapproval must be qualified, not only by Shuttleworth and Cowrie's own admission of the current widespread practice of indirect translation in various areas of the literary world, but also, as we have seen, by its abundant use in ancient translation. These qualifications suggest that the disapproval of indirect translation is culturally and/or temporally specific and is the function of an orientation toward, and privileging of, source text or language.

11. R. Jakobson, "On Linguistic Aspects of Translation," in *On Translation,* ed. R. Brower (New York: Oxford University Press, 1966), 232–39. "Interlingual translation or translation proper is an interpretation of verbal signs by means of some other language" (233).

12. See for instance John Grant's retelling of Robert Louis Stephenson's *Dr. Jekyll and Mr. Hyde* (London: Usborne, 1995). In some longer works, rewording and simplification of

difficult or archaic words is often accompanied by some type of abridgment, as in James Dunbar's retelling of Daniel Defoe's *Robinson Crusoe* (London: Dorling Kindersley, 1998), or Tony Ross's reworking of Lewis Carroll's *Through the Looking Glass* (London: Random House, 1992).

13. See amongst many possible examples of such rewordings, Brian Stone's "translation" of selected Chaucer tales in *Love Visions* (London: Penguin, 1983). As an alternative to full-blown "translation," the same publisher also offers the original text of Chaucer in their Critical Studies/Master Studies series, where the archaic English is, however, accompanied by extensive commentary and numerous lexical entries.

14. *Beowulf* has been translated most recently and most famously by the celebrated Irish poet Seamus Heaney (London: Faber, 1999).

15. For the ambiguity of the term *paraphrase*, see below.

16. Criticism of the LBP from scholarly quarters has been as resounding as it has been enduring. For a relatively recent discussion and select bibliography of reviews, see H. M. Orlinsky and R. G. Bratcher, *A History of Bible Translation and the North American Contribution* (Atlanta: Scholars Press, 1991), 236–44.

17. "Lacking the competence to control the Bible in the original, it [LBP] constitutes the paraphraser's variation on the theme of the American Standard Version rather than of the original authors' words" (*History of Bible Translation*, 237). Interestingly, the widespread critical rejection did not prevent the LBP from becoming a Bible "best-seller."

18. *The Living New Testament, Paraphrased* (Wheaton, Ill.: Tyndale House, 1967) incorporated *Living Letters* and *Living Gospels*, which had up until then been published separately (the former as early as 1962).

19. In Dryden's terminology literal translation was represented by "imitation," whereas free translation was understood as "metaphrase." See M. Shuttleworth and M. Cowrie, *Dictionary of Translation Studies*, s.v., "Paraphrase," 121. Dryden, "Preface to Ovid's epistles, translated by several hands" [1680], in George Watson, ed., *Of Dramatic Poesy and Other Critical Essays* (London: Dent, 1962), 1:262–73.

20. See, for instance, *Oxford Pocket Dictionary* (Oxford: Oxford University Press, 1969), s.v. "Paraphrase."

21. LBP preface: "This book, though arriving late on the *current translation scene* [author's emphasis], has been under way for many years."

22. Those responsible for the NLT attempt to justify this name and buttress the NLT's claims to (interlingual) "translation" status by outlining a process of revision that has apparently had reference to the Greek, Hebrew, and Aramaic texts.

23. D. Robinson, s.v. "Pseudotranslation," *Encyclopedia of Translation Studies*, Mona Baker et al., eds. (London: Routledge, 1998).

24. G. Rado, "Outline of a Systematic Translatology," *Babel* 25/4 (1979): 187–96.

25. A. Popovic, "Fictitious Translation," in *Dictionary for the Analysis of Literary Translation* (Edmonton: University of Alberta, 1979).

26. G. Toury, "Translation, Literary Translation and Pseudotranslation," in *Comparative Criticism* 6, ed. E. S. Shaffer (Cambridge: Cambridge University Press, 1984), 73–85, includes a précis of his "Pseudotranslation as a Literary Fact: The Case of *Papa Hamlet,*" *Hasifrut/Literature* 32 (1982): 63–68 (Modern Hebrew, with English summary). See also *idem, Descriptive Translation Studies and Beyond* (Amsterdam and Philadelphia: John Benjamins, 1995), 40–52. While it is clear that Toury's understanding of pseudotranslation (1995) agrees in substance with that of Popovic, the former's definition is formulated slightly differently. For Toury, it is texts that have been presented as translations with no corresponding source texts

in other languages ever having existed—hence no factual "transfer operations" and translation relationships—that go under the name of pseudotranslations, or fictitious translations.

27. See G. Toury, *Descriptive Translation Studies*, 47 for the particularly interesting case of Carl Bleibtreu's pseudotranslation (supposedly from the French): *Dies Irae: Erinnerungen eines franzoesischen Offiziers an die Tage von Sedan* (Stuttgart: Carl Krabbe, 1882). Toury discusses examples of French, Russian, and Modern Hebrew pseudotranslations from English.

28. E. J. Goodspeed, *Famous "Biblical" Hoaxes* (Boston: Beacon Press, 1956); Per Beskow, *Strange Tales about Jesus: A Survey of Unfamiliar Gospels* (Philadelphia: Fortress Press, 1983).

29. Per Beskow, *Strange Tales*, 9.

30. *The Report of Pilate* (*Strange Tales*, 52).

31. *The Gospel of the Holy Twelve* (*Strange Tales*, 67); *The Essene Gospel of Peace* (*Strange Tales*, 82–83).

32. *The Crucifixion and the Resurrection of Jesus by an Eyewitness* (*Strange Tales*, 42).

33. The "Letter of Benan" is mentioned by both Goodspeed (*Hoaxes*, 50–57) and R. L. Anderson, "Imitation Gospels and Christ's Book of Mormon Ministry" (Provo, Utah: FARMS, 1986), 62–3.

34. *The Unknown Life of Christ* (*Strange Tales*, 58–59).

35. *The Death Warrant of Jesus* (*Strange Tales*, 24).

36. G. Toury, *Descriptive Translation Studies*, 40.

37. Although as Toury discovered (*Descriptive Translation Studies*, 50, n. 9) when he located a volume of *Papa Hamlet* in one library, news of Holz and Schlaf's authorship may not have been published as widely as the work itself was under the name of Holmsen.

38. In addition to Holz, Schlaf, and some of the other pseudotranslators mentioned by Toury, one thinks of Nicholas Notovitch, who many years after the publication of *The Unknown Life of Christ* seems to have admitted what had already been demonstrated by others, namely, that no "translation" had ever taken place (*Strange Tales*, 61).

39. For review of recent scholarship on the book of Tobit, see C. A. Moore, "Tobit" in D. N. Freedman, ed., *Anchor Bible Dictionary* (New York: Doubleday, 1992), 5:585–94.

40. It is perhaps worth mentioning that the debate as to whether Greek Tobit is reliant on a Hebrew or Aramaic version currently leans toward the latter but is by no means settled. See, for instance, G.W. E. Nickelsburg, "Tobit," in *Jewish Writings of the Second Temple Period*, ed. M. Stone (Philadelphia: 1984), 40–46.

41. The discussion of this example and the ones that follow rely heavily on the analysis undertaken by Beskow, *Strange Tales*, 42–50, 51–56.

42. In Mahan's defense, this English translation seems to have been ascribed by the publishers to a Latin work, a distortion of Méry's original claim to have been "inspired" to write the story after having read Latin manuscripts. In any case, as Beskow makes clear, Mahan was soon unmasked as a forger of the first rank.

43. "The Story of the *Living Bible*," *Eternity* 34 (1973): 64–65, 74–75.

44. Beskow, *Strange Tales*, 8.

45. Ibid., 45.

46. Ibid.

47. Ibid., 59.

48. Reverend Gideon Jasper Richard Ouseley (see *Strange Tales*, 71).

49. See K. Akers, *The Vegetarian Source Book*, 2nd ed. (Arlington, Va.: Vegetarian Press, 1989). One reading of Genesis might draw certain implications from the vegetarian character of the diet prescribed to mankind before the Fall (Gen. 1:29–30).

50. Deut. 22:6–7: "If you happen to come across a bird's nest, in any tree or on the ground, with young ones or eggs, and the mother sitting upon the ground or upon the eggs, you shall not take the mother with the young." For an example of the use of such a passage toward eco-theological ends see, J. Barton, *Ethics and the Old Testament* (London: SCM, 1998), 40–44.

51. For an extensive treatment of the major issues see J. A. Fitzmyer, *The Semitic Background of the New Testament* (Grand Rapids: Eerdmans, 1997).

52. See Louis C. Midgely "Who Really Wrote the Book of Mormon?" in *Book of Mormon Authorship Revisited: The Evidence for Ancient Origins*, ed. N. B. Reynolds (Provo, Utah: FARMS, 1997), 106–11, for a recent critical discussion of these early accusations. He notes that they had begun to be made even before the official publication of the BoM.

53. Prior to the publication of the Book of Mormon the suggestions of pseudotranslation seem to have focused on the circumstances surrounding its discovery and the unreliable character of Joseph Smith. The more extensive criticism of Alexander Campbell, however, was leveled not only at Smith but at the character and contents of the work. See L. C. Midgely, "Who Really Wrote the Book of Mormon?" 109.

54. F. Brodie, *No Man Knows My History,* 69.

55. These include unknown and unprecedented animal species and the existence of steel in the New World prior to Columbus. See W. A. Linn, *The Story of the Mormons* (New York: n.p., 1902), 97. Alexander Campbell's critique of the Book of Mormon appeared in 1831 in his paper, *Millennial Harbinger,* and included the following, oft-quoted summary dismissal: "This prophet Smith, through his stone spectacles, wrote on the plates of Nephi, in his Book of Mormon, every error and almost every truth discussed in New York for the last ten years."

56. Beskow, *Strange Tales,* 33–34.

57. G. Toury, *Descriptive Translation Studies,* 42.

58. J. L. Sorenson, "Metals and Metallurgy Relating to the Book of Mormon Text," (Provo, Utah: FARMS 1992); *idem, An Ancient American Setting for the Book of Mormon* (Salt Lake City: Deseret and FARMS, 1985).

59. J. L. Sorenson, "Viva Zapato! Hurray for the Shoe," *Review of Books on the Book of Mormon* 6/1 (1994): 297–361, esp. 297.

60. D. G. Matheny, "Does the Shoe Fit? A Critique of the Limited Tehuantepec Geography," in *New Approaches to the Book of Mormon: Explorations in Critical Methodology,* ed. B. L. Metcalfe (Salt Lake City: Signature, 1993), 269–328. "The majority of the specimens date to late Classic times falling outside of the Book of Mormon period. The few that are genuinely Early Classic or slightly earlier seem to be trade pieces not produced in the area. We are still left with virtually the entire span of time covered by Book of Mormon events with no metallurgy in the area chosen by Sorenson" (291).

61. J. L. Sorenson, "Viva Zapato!" 327, 328, 329–330. "Be a little more patient. Recognize the selectivity of the 'archaeological record.' Only a fraction of the total record has been, or likely ever will be, dug up" (330).

62. E. H. Ashment, "'A Record in the Language of My Father': Evidence of Ancient Egyptian and Hebrew in the Book of Mormon," in Metcalfe, *New Approaches,* 337–38, characterizes theories focusing on ideographic, conceptual source languages as being "more conservative" to the extent that they attempt to "accommodate evidence about Joseph Smith's actual translation methodology." Alternatively, more liberal theories concentrate on reconstructing a linguistically realistic system that has given rise to the English text.

63. J. A. Tvedtnes, "The Hebrew Background of the Book of Mormon," in *Rediscovering the Book of Mormon,* ed. J. L. Sorenson and M. J. Thorne (Salt Lake City: Deseret and FARMS, 1991), 77–91. Phenomena identified by Tvedtnes as suggesting Hebrew interference include an overrepresentation of the construct state, prepositional adverbials, cognate accusatives, compound prepositions, extrapositional nouns and pronouns, interchangeable prepositions, possessive pronouns, conjunctions, unusual subordinate clauses, the "late" appearance of the relative pronoun, unusual words, and Hebraized forms of comparison and conventions of naming. For an evaluation of some of these claims, see chapter 10 by Thomas J. Finley in this volume.

64. Tvedtnes, "Hebrew Background," 80, 84, 87. In an attempt to buttress the argument that the anomalies in the English of the Book of Mormon should be attributed to a Hebrew *Vorlage* rather than an existing translation tradition of Hebraized English Bibles, some scholars attempt to show that these Hebraisms do not appear in Joseph Smith's other writings and were edited out of later editions of the BoM. With regard to the first issue, see the exchange between Ashment ("A Record in the Language of My Father") and R. Skousen ("Critical Methodology and the Text of the Book of Mormon," *Review of Books on the Book of Mormon* 6/1 [1994]: 132–35) where the latter does not seem to take account of a possible appearance of the "if. . .and" construction in the KJV of Jeremiah 5:1. The "editing out" of these "Hebraisms" in later editions of the BoM would seem only to suggest that subsequent editors/readers of the BoM did not share Smith's affection for the AV's tolerance of Hebrew linguistic interference.

65. Although Ashment, "A Record in the Language of My Father," 364–66, also points to instances where alleged Hebraisms in the BoM are not only absent from idiomatic English but also are not to be expected in Hebrew itself.

66. S. D. Ricks, "Joseph Smith's Translation of the Book of Mormon" (Provo, Utah: FARMS, 1986); J. W. Welch and T. Rathbone "The Translation of the Book of Mormon: Preliminary Report on the Basic Historical Information" (Provo, Utah: FARMS, 1986); R. L. Anderson, *Investigating the Book of Mormon Witnesses* (Salt Lake City: Deseret, 1981).

67. The following testimony from *Joseph Smith—History* 1:60 is reprinted in the introduction of most editions of the Book of Mormon: "When, according to arrangements, the messenger called for them [i.e., the plates], I delivered them up to him; and he has them in his charge until this day."

68. Brodie, *No Man Knows My History,* Appendix A; *EOM,* s.v. "Spaulding Manuscript" by L. D. Chase (reprinted in D. H. Ludlow, ed., *Scriptures of the Church: Selections from the Encyclopedia of Mormonism* [Salt Lake City: Deseret, 1995], 602–4).

69. See Brodie, *No Man Knows My History,* 47, for other parallels. As Brodie notes, a substantial list of parallels was composed by the Mormon historian B. H. Roberts in 1922 (although not published until 1985). For parallels between the two Smiths' [Joseph and Ethan] interpretation of Isaiah, see D. P. Wright, "Joseph Smith's Interpretation of Isaiah in the Book of Mormon," *Dialogue: A Journal of Mormon Thought* 31/4 (1998): 192–96.

70. J. W. Welch, "View of the Hebrews: 'An Unparallel,'" in Welch, *Reexploring the Book of Mormon,* 83–87.

71. The assumption of those who would deny any dependence of the Book of Mormon on Ethan Smith's *View of the Hebrews* seems to be that an inconsistent use of the latter by Joseph Smith would be somehow unusual or unexpected. (See, for example, Welch, "View of the Hebrews," 83: "Since the alleged points of contact are scattered throughout *View of the Hebrews,* and in some cases are claimed to be quite specific, this assertion becomes plausible only if we assume that Joseph knew *View of the Hebrews* quite well and implicitly

accepted it as accurate. If he did so, then he should have followed it—or at least not contradicted it—on its major points.") It seems, however, that if he did indeed make use of *View of the Hebrews,* Joseph Smith might well have chosen not to follow it on various "major" points, whether out of a fear of incurring charges of plagiarism by agreeing too much with it or perhaps out of a genuine disagreement with Ethan Smith's account on any number of different grounds, including theological, literary, or historical.

72. Brodie, *No Man Knows My History,* 47; Welch, "View of the Hebrews," 84, while acknowledging that both the works of Joseph and Ethan Smith quote prophetic texts, notes that *View of the Hebrews* includes Old Testament prophecies not found in the Book of Mormon.

73. For a digestible history of the English Bible and the place of the Authorized Version in it, see G. Hammond, *The Making of the English Bible* (New York: Philosophical Library, 1983). In his brief treatment of the Book of Mormon, Philip L. Barlow, *Mormons and the Bible: The Place of the Latter-day Saints in American Religion* (Oxford: Oxford University Press, 1991) gives special attention to parallels between BoM and AV (26–32) before concluding that "despite scholarly progress on several fronts, considerable mystery yet shrouds the Book of Mormon" (32).

74. A. Hutchinson, "A Mormon Midrash: LDS Creation Narratives Reconsidered," *Dialogue* 21 (1988): 11–74. See also the two examples (Isa 9:3//2 Nephi 19:3; Matt 5:6//3 Nephi 12:6) provided in *idem,* "The Word of God Is Enough," in Metcalfe, *New Approaches,* 13–14; Stan Larson, "The Historicity of the Matthean Sermon on the Mount in 3 Nephi," in *New Approaches,* 115–64.

75. Larson, "Sermon on the Mount in 3 Nephi," 115–64. The present author does not find the critique of R. Skousen ("Critical Methodology and the Text of the Book of Mormon," 121–29) sufficiently convincing to vitiate Larson's thesis.

76. J. A. Tvedtnes, "Isaiah Variants in the Book of Mormon," in *Isaiah and the Prophets,* ed. M. S. Nyman (Provo, Utah: BYU Religious Studies Center, 1984), 165, suggests that of the 478 verses of Isaiah that appear in the BoM, 201 agree with the Authorized Version. For a list of Isaiah texts in the BoM, see *EOM,* s.v. "Isaiah: Texts in the Book of Mormon" (=*Scriptures of the Church,* 331–33).

77. Tvedtnes, "Isaiah Variants," 165–77.

78. It is these two latter criteria that Tvedtnes ("Isaiah Variants," 165–77) seems to feel the need to fulfil.

79. See the summary treatment of the subject in D. P. Wright, "Joseph Smith's Interpretation of Isaiah in the Book of Mormon," 182–85.

80. The reader is referred to the extensive discussion of the topic provided in D. P. Wright, "Isaiah in the Book of Mormon. . .and Joseph Smith in Isaiah," online: http://members.aol.com/jazzdd/IsaBoM1.html (1998; updated, March 2000).

81. The frequent appearance of the *vav* conjunction (often translated "and") in narrative passages in the Hebrew Bible gives many native speakers of Indo-European languages the impression that biblical Hebrew is rather "too coordinated" (and X. . . .and Y. . .and Z, etc.).

82. Tvedtnes, "Isaiah Variants," 169.

83. For more specific discussion, see D. Shepherd, "Will the Real Targum Please Stand Up? Translation and Co-ordination in the Aramaic Versions of Job," *Journal of Jewish Studies* 51/1 (2000): 88–116.

84. E. Y. Kutscher, *The Language and Linguistic Background of the Isaiah Scroll* (Leiden: Brill, 1974), 1–95.

85. Even if BoM Isaiah could somehow be shown to depend on the text-type reflected in 1QIsaᵃ (rather than simply parallel the Qumran text), the latter's variations from the MT

have for the most part been shown to be inferior and derivative vis-à-vis the MT. See Kutscher, *Background of the Isaiah Scroll;* and D. Shepherd, "11QAramaicJob: The Qumran Targum as an Ancient Aramaic Version of Job" (Ph.D. diss., University of Edinburgh, 2000), 298–337, 346.

86. D. P. Wright, "Isaiah in the Book of Mormon. . .and Joseph Smith in Isaiah," Part 1: King James Version Language, online: http://members.aol.com/jazzdd/IsaBoM1.html. Wright suggests that were the BoM to be an independent translation, it would not show literal agreement but a "KJV flavour."

87. D. P. Wright, "Isaiah in the Book of Mormon. . .and Joseph Smith in Isaiah," Part 2: KJV Italics and the BoM Isaiah, online: http://members.aol.com/jazzdd/IsaBoM2.html.

88. D. P. Wright, "Isaiah in the Book of Mormon. . .and Joseph Smith in Isaiah," Part 4: Disparities with Hebrew Language, Text and Style, online: http://members.aol.com/jazzdd/IsaBoM4.html. Of course, it is natural and essential for an independent, idiomatic English translation to show "disparities with Hebrew language, text, and style," and some discrepancies highlighted by Wright (i.e., distortion of parallelism) might legitimately be explained away as such. It is neither natural nor essential, however, that deviations from the Hebrew clearly point to a dependence on polysemy in English. As Wright understands, this clearly suggests the phenomenon of indirect translation discussed in the first section of this paper.

89. H. Nibley, *Since Cumorah* (CWHN 7; Provo, Utah: FARMS, 1988), 113: "To the world to which the English translation of the Book of Mormon was addressed there was only one acceptable Bible, the King James translation. And so the Book of Mormon follows that. But no edition or translation is perfect, and the Book of Mormon does not follow the King James version slavishly by any means—that is a thing which the critics overlook. As long as the King James version conveys the correct meaning, it is naturally the text to follow." See also Larson, "Sermon on the Mount in 3 Nephi," 116–117, for discussion of others holding this view.

90. This aging may be seen both in terms of the source text it relied upon (Larson, "Sermon on the Mount in 3 Nephi," 117), and, as we shall see below, in the way in which it interpreted/translated this text. The ASV 1901, the first major American revision of the AV, on which we saw the LBP to be dependent, bears witness to this same awareness.

91. For an illustration of the resilience of the translation tradition stemming from the King James Version, see D. Shepherd, "Violence in the Fields? Translating, Reading and Revising in Ruth 2," *Catholic Biblical Quarterly,* forthcoming.

92. *BDB,* 406–7; John D. Watts, *Isaiah 1–33* (WBC; Waco: Word, 1985), 27; E. J. Kissane, *The Book of Isaiah* (Dublin: Browne and Nolan, 1943), 1:27; H. Wildberger, *Isaiah 1–12,* trans. T. H. Trapp (Minneapolis: Fortress Press, 1991), 92.

93. R. E. Clements, *Isaiah 1–39* (London: Marshall, Morgan & Scott, 1980), 48: "His purpose was not to comment or reflect upon the capabilities of such people, but rather to insist that they would simply cease to be available, whatever people thought about their services."

94. See, for instance Wildberger, *Isaiah 1–12,* 129–130; Clements, *Isaiah 1–39,* 47; Watts, *Isaiah 1–33,* 38; E. J. Young, *The Book of Isaiah* (NICOT; Grand Rapids: Eerdmans, 1965) 1:139 n. 5; and Kissane, *Book of Isaiah,* 37.

95. See Wildberger, *Isaiah 1–12,* 131, for discussion and citation of relevant Near Eastern sources. Also see Clements, *Isaiah 1–39,* 48; and *BDB,* 538.

96. *Oxford English Dictionary:* "1. The result of rending or tearing apart; a separation of parts produced by tearing or similar violence; esp. a large tear in a garment or piece of woven stuff. 1535 COVERDALE Matt. ix. 16 Then taketh he awaye the pece agayne from

the garment, & the rent ys made greater. 1601 SHAKES. Jul. C. III. ii. 179 See what a rent the enuious Casca made."

97. *BDB*, 669; Young, *Book of Isaiah*, 169; Watts, *Isaiah 1–33*, 44; Kissane, *Book of Isaiah*, 47; and Wildberger, *Isaiah 1–12*, 146.

98. See for example, ASV, NIV, NAB, RSV, NRSV, etc.

99. Clements, *Isaiah 1–39*, 78 notes Driver's suggestion to read *maṣṣebet* as *min + ṣebet* but does not endorse it wholeheartedly.

100. Wildberger, *Isaiah 1–12*, 248.

101. Young, *Book of Isaiah*, 265 n. 53.

102. D. P. Wright, "Isaiah in the Book of Mormon. . .and Joseph Smith in Isaiah," Part 3: KJV Translation Errors in the BoM Isaiah, online: http://members.aol.com/jazzdd/IsaBoM3.html.

103. Wildberger, *Isaiah 1–12*, 364; Watts, *Isaiah 1–33*, 125; Kissane, *Book of Isaiah*, 106; Clements, *Isaiah 1–39*, 102, notes Akkad. *sāhiru* ('spell, counter-spell") in this connection.

104. See NIV, NASB⁹⁵, NRSV, RSV, NJB, etc; cf. Young, *Book of Isaiah*, 319 n. 42.

105. Of the 27 occurrences of *ʾôr* in Isaiah, only once (18:4) is it not rendered by the AV with "light."

106. Of course these two concepts are already conjoined in Ps 119:105, which antedates John considerably.

107. D. P. Wright, "Isaiah in the Book of Mormon. . .and Joseph Smith in Isaiah," Part 3: KJV Translation Errors in the BoM Isaiah, online: http://members.aol.com/jazzdd/IsaBoM3.html.

108. D. W. Thomas, "*ṣalmāwet* in the OT," *Journal of Semitic Studies* 7 (1962): 191–200. The corrected vocalization will be either *ṣalmôt* or *ṣalmût*.

109. Watts, *Isaiah 1–33*, 130–31; Young, *Book of Isaiah*, 324 n. 55; and Wildberger, *Isaiah 1–12*, 386.

110. e.g., Vulgate: *umbra mortis;* Targum: *ṭûlê môtāʾ*; Syriac: *telālê mawtâ*.

111. For discussion of the Akkadian parallels (*ṣēnu*), see *NIDOTTE* 3:218, and L. Koehler and W. Baumgartner, *The Hebrew and Aramaic Lexicon of the Old Testament* (Leiden: Brill, 1995), 2:738.

112. Isa 10:4//2 Nephi 20:4; Isa 10:15//2 Nephi 20:15; Isa 10:27//2 Nephi 20:27; Isa 13:15//2 Nephi 23:15; Isa 13:22//2 Nephi 23:22; Isa 29:16//2 Nephi 27:27; Isa 53:3//Mosiah 14:3.

113. The full title is *The Gospel of the Holy Twelve: Known also as the Gospel of the Perfect Life, translated from the Aramaic and edited by a disciple of the Master, and with former editions compared and revised*, 2d ed. (n.p., n.d.) [Brighton, 1903].

114. Beskow, *Strange Tales*, 73.

GLOSSARY

Apostasy Abandonment of the faith, falling away. Latter-day Saints believe that in the early centuries of the Christian era there was a "Great Apostasy" in which the Christian church fell away from the true faith. This necessitated the restoration of a pristine Christianity by Joseph Smith in 1830.

Book of Mormon One of the Standard Works (i.e., Scriptures) of the LDS Church. Joseph Smith claimed to have received inscribed metal plates from an angel named Moroni from which the Book of Mormon was translated by the gift and power of God. The work describes the religious and military history of peoples who migrated to the New World in ancient times as well as a post-resurrection appearance of Christ to some of their descendants.

Christology The study of the person, nature, and status of Christ in relation to God and humanity.

Cosmology The study of the origin and nature of the universe.

Creation ex nihilo The orthodox Christian view that God created the world "out of nothing" (Latin, *ex nihilo*).

Creation ex materia The view that God created the world out of eternally existing chaotic matter. This view was widely affirmed in the religions of antiquity and in the Greek philosophical tradition.

Creed A concise statement of faith. The three most important creeds for orthodox Christianity are the Apostles' Creed, the Nicene Creed, and the Definition of Chalcedon. Although not called a creed by Latter-day Saints, the Articles of Faith printed in the Pearl of Great Price functions much like a creed for the LDS Church.

Doctrine and Covenants (D&C) One of the Standard Works (i.e., Scriptures) of the LDS Church, comprised mostly of the revelations of Joseph Smith and a few from his successors.

Evangelicalism A term referring to the transdenominational movement of orthodox Christians, primarily Protestants, who emphasize the need for world evangelization and personal conversion to Christ, and who maintain a high view of the Bible as the unique inspired and authoritative written revelation of God.

General Authority A leader within the LDS Church higher than a bishop or stake president, usually a Seventy, Apostle, or member of the First Presidency.

Hapax Legomenon A Hebrew, Aramaic, or Greek word that occurs in the Bible only once.

Hebrew Bible A synonym for the Old Testament.

Hellenistic An adjective meaning "Greek." Usually used to describe Greek language, religion, or philosophy of the period after the conquests of Alexander the Great.

Intertestamental An adjective referring to the period or writings produced between the close of the Old Testament and the beginning of the New Testament.

King Follett Discourse An important sermon preached by Joseph Smith near the end of his life at the funeral of a Mormon named King Follett. The *KFD* is not considered one of the Standard Works of the LDS Church but is widely viewed as quasi-canonical and authoritative. It is an important statement because it teaches several doctrines that are important to traditional Mormon thought but are not found in the Standard Works.

Materialism The philosophical view that all which exists is material in nature. Cf. *Physicalism*.

Merism A literary device emphasizing the entirety or totality of something by referring to it by two or more of its constituent parts.

Metaphysics Most generally, the philosophical investigation of the nature, constitution, and structure of reality with focus on those aspects of reality that are partially or entirely beyond the purview of the physical sciences.

Missiology The study of world missions.

Mormon A member of the Church of Jesus Christ of Latter-day Saints, headquartered in Salt Lake City, Utah. An adjective referring to the teachings or practices particular to the LDS Church. This term should not be used to refer to the members of the Reorganized Church of Jesus Christ of Latter Day Saints, headquartered in Independence, Missouri.

Mormonism The religion of the Church of Jesus Christ of Latter-day Saints.

Mutatis mutandis A Latin phrase used to indicate that, with necessary alterations, an argument or point applies in one case just as it does in another.

Nicene An adjective pertaining to the Council of Nicaea (A.D. 325) and the creed it produced (revised at the Council of Constantinople in A.D. 381).

Ontology A term derived from the Greek word for *being*. Sometimes ontology is used as a synonym for the entire discipline of metaphysics. More precisely, ontology is the branch of metaphysics concerned with the study of what exists, what does not exist, and the nature of existence itself.

Patristic A term pertaining to the age and writings of the Church Fathers (Latin, *patres*) of the first eight centuries.

Pearl of Great Price One of the Standard Works (i.e., Scriptures) of the LDS Church, composed of sections from Joseph Smith's revision of the Bible, an alleged translation of ancient Egyptian papyri known as the Book of Abraham, Joseph Smith's autobiographical account of the translation of the Book of Mormon and the founding of Mormonism, and the Articles of Faith of the LDS Church.

Philo of Alexandria A Jewish philosopher who was a contemporary of Jesus and Paul.

Physicalism Generally, the philosophical view that all that exists is physical in nature. With respect to the nature of human persons, it is the view that humans are entirely physical beings and are not composed of an immaterial soul or spirit in addition to their body. Cf. *Substance Dualism*.

Pseudepigrapha Ancient Jewish and Christian writings explicitly claiming to have been written by notable figures from Israel's past but which are recognized to have been written by someone other than the person mentioned in the text. Although "falsely attributed," these works often provide valuable insight into ancient Judaism and Christianity.

Sans French for "without" or "apart from."

Second Temple Judaism Judaism of the period after the return from the Exile until shortly after the Jewish Revolt of A.D. 70.

Standard Works A term referring to the four canonical scriptures of the LDS church: the Bible (KJV), Book of Mormon, Doctrine and Covenants, and the Pearl of Great Price.

Substance dualism The view that the body and soul are distinct entities composed of different kinds of substances, one material and one immaterial. Cf. *Physicalism.*

Theodicy An attempt to account for why evil exists despite the existence of a good and almighty God.

Transliteration A word from one language written in the letters of another (e.g., writing a Hebrew or Chinese word with Roman letters).

Trinity The normative Christian doctrine which teaches that the Father, Son, and Holy Spirit are three distinct and co-equal persons who are one being, God.

Umwelt A German word roughly meaning "environment."

Urstoff A German word referring to primary or original matter.

SUBJECT INDEX

INDEX OF AUTHORS

INDEX OF BIBLICAL
AND ANCIENT LITERATURE

The New Mormon Challenge

New Testament

Dead Sea Scrolls

Other Ancient Writings

INDEX OF LDS STANDARD WORKS

Doctrine and Covenants

Pearl of Great Price

Moses

Abraham

Joseph Smith — History

We want to hear from you. Please send your comments about this book to us in care of the address below. Thank you.

GRAND RAPIDS, MICHIGAN 49530

WWW.ZONDERVAN.COM